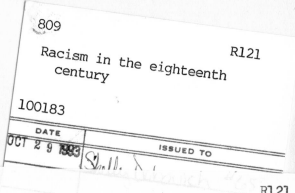

STUDIES IN
EIGHTEENTH-CENTURY CULTURE

Proceedings
THE AMERICAN SOCIETY FOR
EIGHTEENTH-CENTURY STUDIES
VOLUME 3

STUDIES IN EIGHTEENTH-CENTURY CULTURE

STUDIES IN EIGHTEENTH-CENTURY CULTURE

RACISM IN THE EIGHTEENTH CENTURY

edited by HAROLD E. PAGLIARO
Swarthmore College

THE PRESS OF
CASE WESTERN RESERVE UNIVERSITY
CLEVELAND & LONDON
1973

Contents

100/83

Preface

ALL BUT ONE of the following essays—Robert Darnton's "The
High Enlightenment and the Low-Life of Literature in Pre-Revolutionary France"—were presented at the third annual meeting of
the American Society for Eighteenth-Century Studies, held in Los
Angeles at the University of California, in March, 1972. The Society owes a debt of gratitude to G. S. Rousseau, who was chairman of the program committee for the annual meeting; he com-
missioned a wide-ranging set of papers from many disciplines,
including French, German, Spanish, Russian, and English literature, as well as from history, philosophy, musicology, cultural geography, and history of science. Professor Darnton's article, which
earlier appeared in *Past and Present* for May 1971, was awarded
the first annual ASECS prize for a scholarly article in eighteenth-
century studies; it is here reprinted, as will be future prize-winning
articles, to bring it to the special attention of members of the Society. Though only about a third of the papers in the present volume fall within the limits of the meeting's one symposium—its
subject was racism in the eighteenth century—the Publication Committee of the Society has decided to continue the practice of adopting the subject of the symposium as the title of the Proceedings so
that the annual meeting and its printed record may be linked together, despite the partial inaccuracy that results from so doing.

With the possible exception of A. Owen Aldridge's article on
Feijoo, the essays on racism in the present volume indicate clearly
that in the eighteenth century groups of whites—and individual
whites as well—whenever they were faced with the social necessity
for regarding persons of color en masse, found ways of denying
them equality with whites and found theoretical support for such
denial. Like the ways, the theories now seem unacceptable: they

reveal more the need of the whites to rationalize a preestablished policy than they do objectivity. Whether these formulations couple white skin and Christianity, black skin and non-Christian religions; or white skin and intelligence, black skin and dullness; or white skin and energy, black skin and torpor, they all turn on the need to justify and thus help perpetuate sets of mind or social practices already in existence.

In certain circumstances, the "white" European imagination might both sponsor and receive persons of color. The "noble savage," Chinese and other eastern sages, Crusoe's clear-headed and loyal Friday, Johnson's Francis Barber, and Blake's Little Black Boy all enjoyed a special beneficence from the minds that begot them —I believe that in one obvious sense, at least, Johnson fathered the Francis Barber we know—and all were met in a kindly way by the world that first received them, though time saw variations in this initial response, at least in some cases. But it is nevertheless true that the "white mind" of the eighteenth century, very much like our own in this regard, executed such maneuvers of the psyche as would allow it to prove to its own satisfaction its superiority to "minds of color" and to justify whatever social advantages it might have gained over those minds as entirely natural.

In a discussion following the presentation of papers during the symposium on racism—part of the discussion is recorded below— Richard H. Popkin, Herbert Marcuse, Magnes Mörner, and Winthrop B. Jordan attempted to cope with a fundamental problem in the objective treatment of racism: that of defining racism itself. I believe their remarks will suggest several conclusions about the task they set themselves and about the subject of racism. Most obvious among these conclusions is that a definition is hard to reach. Closely related is the fact that the experts are cautious in what they say, less because they are unwilling to risk a tentative generalization than because they know the subject too well to be satisfied with formulations that come readily to mind. Perhaps the most important thing to be noted in their speculations, however, is that they are drawn inevitably to *expressions* of racism—to *acts* that may be thought of as racist—as they attempt to frame a definition. At the same time they seem to hesitate as they point to external evidence alone, probably because such evidence—acts or expressions—amounts to no more than symptoms of an interior set of psychic energies that eludes the definer's probing eye. Though I understand the reticence of the experts and the very good reasons for it, I shall over the next few pages presume on the reader's indulgence with a handful of speculations about racism, not because I believe that they will survive a scientific investigation of the subject —they will not, I am sure—but because they may stimulate the reader to conclusions of his own, as he rejects or modifies my suggestions, which I regard much more as means to set the theme of this volume than as theories useful in themselves.

Surely it is true of any human expression or act that it is the symptom or culmination merely of an interior set of energies, which are themselves hidden from observation. What then is the special value of distinguishing between the symptoms and their interior origins in the matter of racism? What is the value of trying to infer that which by definition cannot be observed? My answer would be that there exists no special value, not absolutely, at least. But the distinction may be important here, as it might be elsewhere, depending on the quality or level of understanding of the subject hoped for. For the purposes of defining racism legally, say, it might remain expedient or necessary to treat it simply in terms of the actions it begets. For the purposes of defining it socially, it may be enough to treat it in terms of the urban ills it produces (though here questions abound as to what ills one may lay at the door of racism). But for the purpose of defining its psychological effects on the exploited, one surely would want to know as much as possible about its psychic origins in the racist mind.

As I have intimated, Professor Popkin and his panel of distinguished experts are under no illusion that they have yet struck close to the heart of the matter. Nevertheless, their comments and one or two of the points adduced in the papers on racism presented here may be taken to indicate something about the nature of the interior process that begets racist expressions or actions. For one thing, the actions seem to be psychologically self-defending, and the self-defender's comments on those actions are often rationalizations; as I have earlier suggested, they generally seek to justify and thus perpetuate sets of mind or social practices already in existence. If the relationship between the hidden process I have posited and the gesture, in the form of conduct or rationalization, were constant, there would be little basis for speculating about the problem beyond its external symptoms. But such, I believe, is not the case. Rationalizations and preconceptions appear in a thousand disguises. For example, Professor Aldridge's essay makes it quite clear that Feijoo, for all his broad-mindedness and humanity, argues out of an enlightened but nonetheless fixed religious position, that he is more concerned to preserve the word of God as he conceives it than he is to learn the truth about the origins of black peoples, his nominal concern. And yet despite such unintentional indirections, which may put one on the *qui vive* to find preconceptions and rationalizations —racial prejudice, if you will—everywhere, occasional exceptions occur. They seem to me less notable for humanitarian reasons— less notable, that is, because they promise humankind's ultimate deliverance from the confining need for racial prejudice and all that this need implies—than they do for the fleeting glimpse they provide of the psychic mechanism beneath the surface of things.

David Lowenthal's article "Free Colored West Indians: A Racial Dilemma" makes the point that the white fathers of children of color almost uniformly sought ways of circumventing the laws and practices that might have disadvantaged their offspring, even though these very fathers upheld racist institutions as they operated against other persons of color. One might explain the inconsistency by saying that parental love is stronger than racial prejudice. But it seems more useful here to point out that in certain circumstances, probably not unique, the awareness by a white, when the white had the initiative, of another as a person of color did not simply preclude a constructive and abiding relationship between them. Such relationships probably had their destructive sides, but most relationships, however close, are to a considerable extent destructive. Finally, it seems to me important that something in the way of a human relationship beyond prejudice, if not without it, was possible, and possible not only in isolated instances, say through the special sensitivity and power of rare whites to identify themselves with persons of color, but generally, in a culture of considerable magnitude.

The perception by a white of a person of color as different—even overwhelmingly different, to judge from the general response—ordinarily produces defensive reactions and rationalizations. Such a process argues initial fear in the white perceiver, and the reaction or expression that follows the perception seems to be a means of coping with it. It may be that this initial response is ineradicable, but the evidence suggests that it is at least subject to modification, even though for most such modification something as nearly absolute as parenthood may be required. But occasionally even someone not so obviously related as a parent may accept the idea that someone "clearly other" than himself is somehow related to him. It seems to me, as I shall try to show soon, that Samuel Johnson and William Blake were such persons.

I should like to offer one or two more suggestions about the perhaps ineradicable initial response. As I have said, the response likely includes a very strong sense of the object as *alien*: it must appear to be entirely other, inadmissible as an extension of the observer. To some extent such responses, I suggest, mark the appraisal of every person by another, and are not peculiar to racial encounters. (Profound personal needs common to almost all men and women have given shape to conventions or social structures that attenuate this reaction, which makes itself fully felt only when the supportive structures are in danger; generally we "like" or "love" or "accept" or "respect" each other despite our fright, because these conventional attitudes—natural or not—allay primary fear, or make it possible to get the world's work done despite it.) Of course, we need not regard others as alien and dangerous, but such appraisals seem likely to have a prominent place in our view of the world. Thus, the interior process that accounts for racist expressions or attitudes may result from the primary appraisal of others, uncorrected; or, if some modification of the initial appraisal occurs—as generally it must, I would imagine—the result would be a conventional attitude, some form of racial prejudice, an expression or attitude we recognize as "racist."

If such a reaction to the alien object is indeed the root cause of racism, the problem may never be effectively dealt with. Not only may the reactive process itself be inaccessible, but it may be the root cause of other problems as well. Perhaps our proneness to adopt roles or identities that predetermine, as it were, our way of coping with the world is a function of a process that sees the enemy—alien others—all around. Do we not after all unconsciously structure and maintain such identities as will guarantee our survival socially, economically, domestically, amorously? It may even be that the intellectual structures we allow to enter consciousness as "meaning" are also a function of the process that sees a ubiquitous enemy, so that we understand only to the degree that we can either escape fright or accept fear. Moreover, it may be that we allow only such meaning as will reinforce the elements of our prestructured identities, with the result that we are bound in the endless mills of our doubtfully wrought selves, with only occasional intimations that we are so bound. If it is true that the ineradicable process I have postulated is the cause not only of racial prejudice, but of our way of appraising, behaving, and understanding generally, then it is likely that any serious effort to cope with the one difficulty would involve us in the other related matters, and thus it seems reasonable to suggest that only the spiritual renovation of every man and woman would eliminate racism. I make the point not to prescribe the cure, but to indicate what I take to be the scope of the illness.

A less radical solution to the problem would be the shaping of constructive conventions of acceptance, which might be made so available to the generality of whites as to be unself-consciously adopted by them. About such a solution one may feel a momentary confidence. It seems easier to change a sculpture with a hammer and chisel than with telepathy or prayer. But the analogy is false. A moment's thought brings the realization that for the reform of such an institution as racism, except momentarily and superficially, fundamental changes in human attitudes would still be essential. So one awaits the permeation of society by the benign fair-mindedness of theoreticians of the subject. Or one looks to one's own feelings and thoughts in the matter, ever more closely. Or one considers the example of the persons one has known in whom the forces of racial prejudice were allayed, if not eradicated.

Our own century has made several large efforts to overcome the problem, efforts that have been given shape as laws, and less formally, as points of view more or less expected or required in certain social contexts. Beyond these surface changes, little seems to have been accomplished. Certainly the problem is beyond question monumental still, though it may be that in some individual minds there has begun to emerge a more flexible address to the matter than has obtained generally in the past.

On the other hand, I think of Samuel Johnson and William Blake each as representing a different facet of the white imagination, as it honestly confronts the problem and takes it so seriously as to incorporate it into consciousness for more than a brief time. Both men had reservations about the intellectual equality of blacks and whites, and yet both of them, in quite different ways, saw beyond this fundamental skepticism and in consequence accorded blacks an order of equality. It is possible, of course, that their behavior was simply expiatory, but it seems likelier that it was compensatory—a rather different matter. Each gave to a black what had been in a special sense withheld by a white society. Johnson made his servant Francis Barber financially independent, and Blake gave his Little Black Boy a mind no more or less prone to love and rationalization than the mind of any little English boy.

No one could argue that Samuel Johnson was free of racial prejudice, and it is easy to think of him as paternalistic in his treatment of Francis Barber. First of all, Johnson apparently thought some races naturally inferior to others. Then, he always sided with Frank (as he called Barber) in domestic squabbles, as if to offer special protection. Further, he required Barber to pray with him, and as various entries in *Diaries, Prayers, and Annals* make clear, he instructed his servant in religion. Even the unusually large annuity he left Barber, seventy pounds, at a time when noblemen were thought generous if they left their servants of long standing fifty pounds a year, may be regarded as a paternalistic gesture.

But the fact remains that Johnson's exaggeratedly fair treatment of Barber extended over a period of more than thirty years, from the very beginning of their relationship in 1752. It was hardly the kind of behavior summoned forth at the last moment to make up for earlier thoughtlessness, much less for overt mistreatment. My aim is not to praise Johnson, though by any usual standards praise is in order, but to stress a consistency of attitude that argues a considered repudiation of white society's way of doing things and very likely repudiation of his own basic prejudice as well. Johnson's knowledge of himself and his sense for humanity moved him to behave towards Barber not quite in the way that he behaved towards every one else—to what two persons did he behave in just the same way, after all?—but in the way appropriate to Barber's predicament, given Johnson's ethic. I suggest that in this relationship Johnson showed a consistent sensitivity to another that alone can mitigate the otherwise destructive elements in human confrontations.

Blake's Song of Innocence "The Little Black Boy" clearly assumes racial prejudice in England, presumably at the date of composition of the poem sometime before 1789. Indeed, there had been during the decade of the 1780's a good deal of antislavery agitation, which doubtless contributed to Blake's feeling on the subject. But it hardly needs observing that, like Johnson, Blake had from his early years been passionately opposed to slavery. As every reader knows, the poem itself does not oppose slavery, at least not directly. What it does is to present the attitude of the Little Black Boy —both what he takes it to be and what despite himself he reveals it as being—as he considers his predicament in English society.

> My mother bore me in the southern wild,
> And I am black, but O! my soul is white;
> White as an angel is the English child
> But I am black as if bereav'd of light.
>
> My mother taught me underneath a tree,
> And sitting down before the heat of day,
> She took me on her lap and kisséd me,
> And pointing to the east, began to say:
>
> "Look on the rising sun; there God does live,
> And gives his light, and gives his heat away;
> And flowers and trees and beasts and men receive
> Comfort in morning, joy in the noon day.

"And we are put on earth a little space,
That we may learn to bear the beams of love;
And these black bodies and this sun-burnt face
Is but a cloud, and like a shady grove.

"For when our souls have learn'd the heat to bear,
The cloud will vanish; we shall hear his voice,
Saying: 'Come out from the grove, my love & care,
And round my golden tent like lambs rejoice.' "

Thus did my mother say, and kisséd me;
And thus I say to little English boy:
When I from black and he from white cloud free,
And round the tent of God like lambs we joy,

I'll shade him from the heat till he can bear
To lean in joy upon our father's knee;
And then I'll stand and stroke his silver hair,
And be like him, and he will then love me.

Having received and repeated his mother's lesson verbatim, a fact that in itself suggests his naïveté, a lack of self-awareness really, the Little Black Boy expresses confidence in the notion that he has endured more in the way of the world's experience than has the white. Accordingly, he expects that when they get to heaven, he will be in a position to help the white boy to cover the spiritual ground the Black Boy has traveled while still on earth. This conscious view of the matter is displaced, however, first by means of uncertain clues, and then by means of the last line the Black Boy speaks, the last line of the poem. Early indications that the Little Black Boy is uncertain of his feelings about his social predicament despite his mother's clear lesson are his uses of the terms "black" and "white" so that both mean both "good" and "bad." But the evidence that absolutely undercuts his declared opinion that he is spiritually better off than the white boy is his unconscious revelation that he does not expect the white boy to come up to his standard—though that effect will be achieved—so much as he anticipates their *being alike*, with the crucial consequence for the Little

Black Boy that the English boy *will love him*: "And be like him and he will then love me."

Blake's identification with the Black Boy is different from Johnson's with Francis Barber. Yet both eighteenth-century authors responded profoundly to the needs of a fellow human—a black fellow human. Like Johnson, Blake had a prejudice as to the intelligence of blacks: "O African! black African! (go winged thought widen his forehead)." But instead of building some irrelevant self-serving construction on that prejudice, Blake moved beyond it with abiding sympathy, and wrote a poem that simultaneously reveals the Black Boy's cruel plight and defines him as a fellow human, emotionally indistinguishable from whites. Though in my opinion whites accord whites no greater respect, examples of such respect between blacks and whites are infrequent, to say the least. Nor do they seem to be more frequent now than they were in the eighteenth century. Then and now generosity between the races has required a knowledge of oneself and a stamina for acting sympathetically out of that knowledge. Perhaps a change will be brought about by institutional means, from the outside of men and women to the inside, instead of the other way around. So far the signs that it may be so seem few indeed.

I wish to thank the colleagues who have read and commented on many of the essays in this volume. They did a large share of the editor's work, and I am grateful to them: Professors Thompson Bradley, David Cowden, James D. Freeman, Hugh M. Lacey, Jean A. Perkins, Hoyt Trowbridge, and P. Linwood Urban. I also owe thanks to Mrs. Thelma Miller, secretary of the Department of English Literature, Swarthmore College, for typing and keeping track of the rather large correspondence connected with the gathering of these essays for publication, and for her help in typing sections of the manuscript as well. Her patience and care were enormously helpful to me.

No effort has been made to normalize either the style of the essays presented here or the form of documentation. It seemed more reasonable, given the varied practices among the many disciplines represented in these Proceedings, to leave such matters to the discretion of individual scholars.

RACISM
IN THE EIGHTEENTH CENTURY

In Praise of Conversation:

Communication Between Disciplines*

James L. Clifford

W HEN I WAS ASKED to say a few words this evening, I won-
dered why. What could a confirmed Johnson scholar have to say to
an interdisciplinary group such as this? Dr. Johnson is hardly remembered by most people for his interest in the other arts; indeed,
there are numerous stories proving just the opposite. He showed
little interest in music. There are many amusing anecdotes, how
authentic I cannot tell, which show him completely insensitive.
He is reputed once to have asked "And pray, sir, who is Bach? Is he
a piper?"[1] and when he once found a violin hanging on the wall at
the home of young Francis Newbery, in whose future Johnson was
much involved, he berated him sternly: "Young man, give the fid-
dle to the first beggar man you meet, or you will never be a scholar."[2] Johnson refused to be impressed by skillful performances of
baroque music. Once when taken to hear a famous violinist, whose
pyrotechnics were universally admired, Johnson was inattentive
and obviously bored. When his host tried to point out how difficult
the piece was, Johnson burst forth "Difficult do you call it, Sir? I
wish it were impossible."[3]

Apparently because of his very bad eyesight, he was scarcely
more interested in the visual arts. As Boswell admitted, Johnson
"had no taste for painting," and Sir Joshua Reynolds recalled that,
when he and his friend would come into another friend's house,
Johnson would rush to examine the backs of the books on the
shelves, while Sir Joshua observed the paintings.[4] At times Johnson

* Presidential address delivered at the annual dinner in Los Angeles, 24
March 1972.

3

showed his disinclination to talk about other disciplines, such as politics or history. He once complained to Mrs. Thrale that at a Club meeting he had sat next to Charles James Fox, who insisted on talking at length about Catiline's conspiracy. When Mrs. Thrale asked him what he had done, Johnson replied: "I withdrew my attention, and thought about Tom Thumb."[5] Johnson was, first and foremost, an insular literary man. Proverbially he had little curiosity about Continental customs; he is reputed to have once agreed with a remark of an old friend who said, "For any thing I see, foreigners are fools."[6]

But this is the folk image of Dr. Johnson—the eccentric character whom most people like to remember. It is only one side of the man. As Donald Greene and others have convincingly shown, there are other sides to Johnson which tend to be forgotten.[7] Although the amusing individual anecdotes may well be true, the parochial Johnson they suggest is false. Roy Wiles has recently shown that he had inherently a strong response to beauty.[8] While Johnson disliked supercilious foreign visitors, one of his closest friends was an Italian, Giuseppe Baretti, who taught him a great deal about Continental literature. If Johnson was not a willing concertgoer, or a great enthusiast for Bach or Handel, one should remember that the two leading musicologists of his day, Sir John Hawkins and Dr. Charles Burney who wrote the first extensive histories of music, were among his most intimate friends. If his nearsightedness made it impossible for him to look at pictures on a wall, some of the greatest painters and architects were his closest associates, and we now know that he served as a willing ghostwriter for groups of artists in their attempts to arrange exhibitions of their works. Indeed, he supported the aspirations of the artists in many ways. If Johnson could be bored by interminable talk about Catiline's conspiracy, he was vitally interested in historical theory and did not scorn the past. The breadth of his interests—science, psychology, ancient literatures, language—was enormous.

Moreover, what is sometimes forgotten is the fact that what we usually think of as Johnson's Club was essentially an interdisciplinary group.[9] Although the members may not have been specifically chosen with this in mind, and some rarely attended meetings, they did represent a wide spectrum of professions. Remember Johnson and Boswell's amusing conversation in Scotland, when they projected the Club as taking over the various departments of a college.[10] Just think for a moment about the makeup of that famous Club, which met at the Turk's Head Tavern in Gerrard Street, London. Who were some of the original members? There was Sir Joshua Reynolds, one of the leading painters of his day, and a writer on art, whose idea it was in the first place. Later there was Sir William Chambers, a well-known architect. There were Edmund Burke and other important politicians. One tends to forget that the man we regard as the leading historian of the age, Edward Gibbon, was a member, if reputedly a silent one. As I have already pointed out, Sir John Hawkins was a musicologist and a legal expert. The Club also included Joseph Banks, an eminent scientist, Sir William Jones, an oriental linguist, Anthony Chamier, a stockbroker, Robert Chambers, a law professor, Oliver Goldsmith, not very knowledgeable in any field but a great writer; and there were dramatists, several physicians, bishops and churchmen—representatives of almost any profession you might mention.

One could say that The Club, at least in official makeup, was a model of interdisciplinary variety. It was quite clear to the members that consorting with other experts in different fields was the best possible way to widen and enrich their own understanding of life. Relaxed talk after a meal, around a table with brilliant people in all professions, was something to be cherished. I have used Johnson's Club as my example merely because I know something about it. I might have cited examples of other groups on the Continent having different ways of getting together—the salons and social gatherings of the Enlightenment—where this same wide coverage was achieved.

Indeed, one of the most important aspects of the Enlightenment, or if you prefer the eighteenth-century approach to life, was the attempt to see life as a whole, in all its ramifications. An intelligent man of that time would have been shocked by any suggestion that it was a waste of time for him to enquire into the activities of brilliant people in other fields. The appearance of the various encyclopedias and biographical dictionaries during that period shows clearly this universal curiosity.

In our day, with the triumph of specialization, we tend more and more to be pushed into narrow prisons. In large universities a scholar probably sees regularly only those who have offices in his own building. An expert in baroque art may never meet a colleague interested in biological theories of the eighteenth century, or a specialist in Alexander Pope. Our large national societies tend to stratify this alienation. If you teach languages you go to the Modern Language Association, if history to the American Historical Association, if music, to the American Musicological Society, if art, to the College Art Association. They meet at different times in different places. And even at the MLA convention, those in English Literature may never see those with similar interests in French or German.

Of course, what I am saying has been obvious for a long time. All I am doing is making the same old complaints. But, happily, there appears at last to be some movement in the other direction. Now our society, meeting nationally for the third time, stands out as one of the best examples of this new trend. The obvious success of the annual meetings, and the enthusiasm aroused around the country in smaller regional gatherings, is surely evidence that we are on the right track. But it is still something of a struggle to break down the walls of the insulated professions. We very much need to enlist the cooperation of more art historians and musicologists, of more historians of science, economists, and church historians. This is not easy. Despite the enormous efforts of those responsible for making our association come alive, still more missionary work is needed. Thus my subject is the need for more concentrated effort to interest representatives of other disciplines.

As one possible way, I should like to cite a specific example— how some of us at Columbia University have attempted to organize a truly interdisciplinary, though much smaller, group to meet once a month for talk about the eighteenth century. Although we did not consciously imitate Johnson's Club, what finally has materialized bears a striking resemblance to it. In the first place, we decided to keep our group small—never more than twenty members—and to allow no more than two or three representatives from any department. (Not that we kept rigidly to this rule, for occasionally by resorting to one strategem or another, we got around this restriction.) From the start our group was thought of as a gathering of experts, and to the horror of many of our colleagues students were excluded, except for one who acted as secretary. Another requirement was that the person chosen must like to talk, but must not be a compulsive talker. We tolerated no long speeches. Very carefully we started enlisting members, not limiting ourselves to Columbia but looking generally to the New York metropolitan area. I must say that when we were through we had put together an impressive group. Merely to mention a few names will show you what I mean. There were Peter Gay and Robert Webb from History, Rudolf Wittkower from Fine Arts, Paul Henry Lang from Music, Otis Fellows from French, Robert Halsband from English, Joseph Bauke from German, Allen Hazen from Bibliography, and Jean Hecht from Social History. The group also included an eminent legal historian, a philosopher and aesthetician, and a sociologist. Somehow we never were able to round up a gregarious historian of science who lived near New York or anyone who specialized in eighteenth-century church history.

As the years progressed, the membership inevitably changed. Arthur Wilson was with us for only a few years; Bob Webb and Albert Hofstadter moved away. We enlisted various others whose names you will recognize—Leo Gershoy, Orest Ranum, John Middendorf, Robert Loy, John Pappas, Aram Vartanian, Russian experts Marc Raeff and Harold Segel, and a modern printer who has a tremendous knowledge of eighteenth-century paper and printing methods.

From the start it was a great success—that is, if attendance figures can be used as proof. There were seldom any absentees. Most of us would have missed any other engagement rather than our eighteenth-century seminar. Our practice has been to have dinner, then a short paper or statement by one of the members or by a visiting scholar, and then hours of exciting talk. Peter Gay admits in the Preface to his great work on the Enlightenment that many of the ideas in his two volumes were thrashed about from every angle at meetings of our small interdisciplinary group. Such exchanges were and continue to be an exciting process.

If our list of members does not strike you as quite as impressive as that of Johnson's Club, in some ways it comes close. And with what I hope is forgivable egotism, I shall claim that some of our talk was just as brilliant as theirs. The one rule we had which would have horrified the Great Cham is that we fixed and rigidly held to an hour of adjournment. In this effete age, with all our transportation problems, we decided to avoid very long arguments extending into the wee hours of the morning.

I realize that being in a big city gave our seminar an immediate advantage. Still, there are other large cities, and clusters of smaller ones. In many places it would be possible to find numbers of experts in varied fields who might also like to argue with others in different disciplines.

If it were possible to organize other small units of this sort, they would not only be a delight to their members; they would be a source of power to your national Society. What could make them really successful would be breadth of coverage and the insistence on talk as the major requirement. Merely to schedule scholarly lectures and the reading of papers will not work. What we need is more discussion among philosophers and biologists, legal experts and sociologists, literary critics and musicologists, art historians and physicists, all having some interest in a single large period of history such as the eighteenth century.

Now I am perfectly aware of certain major objections that may be raised against my plan. It leaves out students altogether, and perhaps young faculty members as well. In our day, when all the emphasis is on student participation, my view may sound hopelessly outdated and aristocratic, since the members of the groups, as I conceive of them, would all be experts—in other words, the elite! But students and young faculty members should be encouraged to form their own interdisciplinary groups; and in the end the students would gain from each other and from the enriched and revitalized teaching they would receive. At least that is what one hopes.

Another objection is that in the twentieth century it is becoming increasingly difficult to communicate between various disciplines. The technical language in specialized fields is sometimes incomprehensible to those not accustomed to its use. Our experience at Columbia has not shown this to be a crippling problem. Even in the mid-twentieth century, major eighteenth-century areas of study can be argued about in ordinary English.

There is, too, another kind of objection: that my plan appears to put the seal of approval on modern specialization. Would it not be better to forget all about individual specialties, and particularly in educational institutions, strive for the rounded man? Should we not be exerting all our energy to breaking down the existence of the exclusive disciplines? Merely by using the term "interdisciplinary" we accept the multifarious divisions. Should we not instead explain it all as "the ecology of eighteenth-century thought" or use such terms as "ecosystems"? Frankly, this seems to me to be hopelessly unrealistic. If we did so we would produce a race of dilettantes who would have nothing important to say to their colleagues. If every one of us had superficial knowledge of all the different approaches to life there would be little of value to talk about. It is precisely the fact that there is a wide diversity among specialists that gives point to such organizations as ours.

The important rules—at least from our experience—are these. The group must be kept small—never over twenty—and there should be representatives from a wide spectrum of disciplines, perhaps as many as ten, some of them fields not normally covered by one's everyday reading. And members should be chosen carefully, in order to be certain that each candidate could talk with pleasure and argue without rancor, and never at length. No one should be accepted if he is like the poet Coleridge, who could never be stopped. A prospective member should be observed as a guest speaker at a meeting before he is asked to join. Much depends on the kinds of people who do the talking.

What is so marvelously stimulating are the quick interchanges, the flashes back and forth, the sudden widening of some topic or theme from a literary or historical source to take in parallels in art and music, in aesthetic theory and economic practice, or to suggest

9

possible sources in psychology or social history, or inevitable results in other fields. The quick insights or broadening vision can be most exhilarating. Indeed, they can be the most rewarding part of scholarly life. I know that for me the experiences in our brilliant little group are what I have cherished most during the past ten years.

If I end like a radical preacher, with an exhortation that you go out and change the world, at least I mean well. Even if you do not take me seriously about forming clubs like Dr. Johnson's—though I firmly believe you should—do keep supporting Don Greene, Lester Crocker, Louis Gottschalk, Peter Stanlis, and the other promoters of our American Society for Eighteenth-Century Studies.

NOTES

1. Madame d'Arblay, *Memoirs of Dr. Burney* (1832), II, 94.
2. Charles Welsh, *A Bookseller of the Last Century* (1885), pp. 127, 145.
3. *Johnsonian Miscellanies*, ed. G. B. Hill (1897), II, 308.
4. Boswell's *Life of Johnson*, ed. Hill and Powell (1934), IV, 320; II, 364–65.
5. *Johnsonian Miscellanies*, I, 202–3.
6. *The Correspondence of James Boswell Relating to the Making of the Life of Johnson*, ed. Marshall Waingrow (1969), p. 366.
7. See in particular Donald Greene's *Samuel Johnson* (Twayne, 1970).
8. Roy M. Wiles, "Samuel Johnson's Response to Beauty," *Studies in Burke and His Time*, XIII (Winter 1971–72), 2067–82.
9. James M. Osborn of Yale is completing a history of The Club, using surviving early records.
10. *Life of Johnson*, V, 108–9. A slightly fuller version may be found in Boswell's *Journal of a Tour to the Hebrides* (original version), ed. F. A. Pottle and Charles H. Bennett (1936), pp. 78–79.

Pope's Eloisa *and the* Heroides *of Ovid*

Hoyt Trowbridge

I

THERE IS A REMARKABLE discrepancy in critical judgments of Pope's *Eloisa to Abelard* between his own period and later times. For almost a century, Émile Audra says, the poem was generally considered in both France and England to be "la plus belle et la plus émouvante des épîtres amoureuses."[1] If anything, he understates the enthusiastic admiration felt for the poem by readers and critics from its publication in 1717 to the end of the eighteenth century. In 1756, *Eloisa* was "in the Hands of all, and in the Memories of most readers."[2] Joseph Warton, who thought that it would outlive all but two or three other poems by Pope, described it as "one of the most highly finished, and certainly the most interesting, of the pieces of our author."[3] Critics of the 1780's praise it in even more superlative terms; Dr. Johnson calls it "one of the most happy productions of human wit," excelling every composition of the same kind. Gilbert Wakefield says that Gray's *Elegy* is more finished and pathetic than any other poem in the world—"Pope's *Eloisa* alone excepted"—and William Mason regards Pope's epistle as "such a *chef d'oeuvre*, that nothing of the kind can be relished after it."[4]

As Audra's remark implies, this consensus of admiration did not outlast Pope's century. Some nineteenth-century readers, including Byron,[5] continued to believe that *Eloisa* was a beautiful and moving poem, but for the most part its reputation was buried, along with almost everything Pope wrote, in the revolution of taste ini-

11

tiated by Wordsworth's epoch-making *Preface.* In our own century, in spite of the sweeping revaluation of Pope which has been in progress for some forty years, the poem has by no means recovered the critical esteem in which it was held during his age. According to Geoffrey Tillotson, Mason "spoke the enthusiasm of a past century. The modern reader is inclined to overlook or disparage *Eloisa to Abelard*." Tillotson does his best to make the poem sound worth reading, but his remarks about its "rhetoric," "geometrizing," and "operatic flights" seem more likely to discourage any reading at all than to open the way toward a fair and unprejudiced appraisal.[6] A more perceptive and sophisticated reader, Reuben Brower, leaves the poem in little better case. His chapter on *Eloisa* in *The Poetry of Allusion* presents a systematic comparison with Pope's formal model, the *Heroides* of Ovid. Brower knows these poems, in the original, as well as most professed classical scholars, and he reads them as living poetry. Yet his subtle analyses of the language of particular passages in Ovid and in Pope do not add up to any convincing account or defense of the poem as a whole. There are "moments we remember and treasure in *Eloisa to Abelard*," Brower says, but he finds no overall design or formal structure except a succession of *coups*, *tirades*, and remembered scenes, following Ovidian patterns of wit and rhythm. If this is all the poem has to offer, Brower is quite right in concluding that *Eloisa to Abelard* may strike us as "remarkable" or "fine," but that in reading it we are not likely to feel "how moving" or "how convincing."[7]

Where a contrast between contemporary opinion and later judgment is so sharp, there is surely some reason to surmise that the fault may lie not in the poem but in us, in our way of reading it. The readers and critics of a poet's own time may, of course, be mistaken in their judgments of his works; as Dr. Johnson says, contemporary opinion is often distorted by local and temporary prejudices, by biases of interest or passion. But biases of another kind may distort the judgment of later ages even more drastically—blindnesses and deafnesses of perception, prejudices of taste, aesthetic principle, or critical method. Wordsworth and his successors put many such blinders on the minds of men, and, though scholars try to remove them, we too often continue to think and read

12

through those distorting glasses. The readers of a poet's own time, who are likely to share his philosophical, artistic, and critical perspectives, are surely in a better position to understand what he is doing and how his poems should be read than those bred in a different intellectual and aesthetic milieu. Critics of a later age, recognizing such a divergence of taste and judgment, should at least ask themselves whether they may not be failing to read the work "with the same spirit that its author writ."[8]

The aim of this paper is to attempt to recover that spirit and to present a reading of *Eloisa to Abelard* which is guided by it. The argument will be in two parts, historical and critical. In the first, after reconstructing from editions and criticisms of Ovid the way of interpreting and judging the *Heroides* which was shared by most competent readers during the Restoration and the early eighteenth century, I shall propose an hypothesis as to the artistic intention controlling Pope's poem. The second part will analyze and appraise the poem in the light of that intention, but it will make use of interpretive and critical principles of my own choosing. I hope that Pope's epistle, seen in this perspective, will seem a much better poem than has usually been thought since the time of Warton, Johnson, Wakefield, and Mason.

II

In summarizing the conception of Ovid which prevailed generally in both France and England before and during Pope's lifetime, I shall follow for the most part an outline provided by Dryden in his preface to Ovid's *Epistles* and in eight other essays in which he discusses Ovid's poetry, which together comprise much the fullest and most systematic statement of a view which he shared with many other critics.[9] A few of the latter will be quoted for further illustration of particular points, and additional references will be cited in footnotes.

For Dryden and other readers and critics of that age, the most important of Ovid's poems were the *Metamorphoses* and the *Heroides*, especially the latter. These epistles, he says, are "generally granted to be the most perfect pieces of Ovid,"[10] and he based his general conception of Ovid as a poet on those poems. They were for him the definitive example of Ovid's poetry, and the other writings, including even the *Metamorphoses*, were interpreted as approximations to the same type.

Dryden's criticism of the *Heroides* looks in two directions, taking the poems first as the standard examples of their kind, the heroic epistle, then as works to be judged, like any others, by the extent to which they realize the ideal possibilities of that form. The definition and laws of the heroic epistle must be inferred from Ovid's practice, since he was the inventor of the genre; but his own poems are to be judged by their conformity to the definition and the rules inferable from it. According to Dryden, the *Heroides* have some defects, which a perfect example of their kind would avoid.

The heroic epistle, as adumbrated though never fully achieved by Ovid, is a kind of poem closely related to the drama. Of all the Romans, Dryden says, Ovid "had a genius most proper for the stage."[11] In his epistles, the poet does not speak in his own person; the words of the poem are those of "feigned persons," dramatic characters.[12] The poet pictures human nature in disorder, "the movements and affections of the mind, either combating between two contrary passions, or extremely discomposed by one."[13] Ovid is described in very similar terms by Joseph Trapp just six years before *Eloisa to Abelard* first appeared in print. Of all the ancient poets, he says, "none understood nature more than he, or expressed her various conflicts better." In the story of Medea and Jason in *Metamorphoses* VII, for example, "the poet wonderfully describes the dubious strife between love and shame, reason and affection, as he does in many other places."[14] In the age of Dryden and Pope, Ovid was read as a dramatist of the emotions, depicting disordered or conflicting passions through the speeches and actions of feigned persons in moments of intense feeling.

In the critical theory of that period, the definition of a genre includes both its subject matter, the particular aspect of nature with which it is concerned, and also its mode of treatment—whether mimetic or non-mimetic, effected through narration or by direct dramatic representation, and the like. To be complete, however, the definition must also distinguish the poetic effect peculiar to the form—its proper pleasure and instruction, and the specific emotional impact it has upon the reader or audience. To achieve these effects is the governing purpose of all works belonging to the given genre, and therefore also the poetic intention of the writer of such a work.

Trapp arrives at a rather vague description of the effect and purpose of the Ovidian epistle through a contrast between poems of the sublime and the marvellous, which impress on the mind something great, unusual, and portentous, and other kinds which excite "grief, pity, terror, and work upon other passions." Asserting that the "great art of Poetry" is to move the passions, he cites "Phyllis to Demophoön" in the *Heroides* as particularly affecting, "wonderfully adapted to move compassion."[15] Dryden had previously expressed the same notions more clearly and forcefully. Ovid, he writes in the *Essay of Dramatic Poesy*, "had a way of writing so fit to stir up a pleasing admiration and concernment, which are the objects of a tragedy, . . . that, had he lived in our age, . . . no man but must have yielded to him."[16] The poet's dramatic representation of a soul in conflict moves the soul of the reader through imaginative identification and sympathy to a parallel emotional response. "I will appeal to any man, who has read this poet," Dryden says in the preface to *Ovid's Epistles*, "whether he finds not the natural emotion of the same passion in himself, which the poet describes in his feigned persons?"[17] This tragic or quasi-tragic effect is the proper pleasure of an heroic epistle, its poetic purpose and intent.

In most ways, Dryden and others in that age believed, Ovid's epistles were admirably adapted to the aims of their kind. The Roman poet understood the passions, felt them within himself, and represented them truly and vividly, through just and lively images. His poems are also beautifully ordered and unified: "our Poet has always the goal in his eye, which directs him in his race; some beautiful design, which he first establishes, and then contrives the means, which will naturally conduct it to his end."[18]

But there is an "allay"[19] in the gold of Ovid's poems. As Quintilian and Seneca had observed long before,[20] he did not always know when to give over, when a thought or feeling had been sufficiently

15

expressed, and he was also too often led astray by his over-ingenious fancy into "unseasonable and absurd conceits," inappropriate to a poem of true and intense feeling. But his worst fault, deplored by dozens of seventeenth- and eighteenth-century critics, is what Dryden calls Ovid's "darling sin"—the love of wit.[21] In an essay on "The Character of Tragedies," St.-Evremond writes:

> The soul when it is sensibly touched does not afford the mind an opportunity to think intensely, much less to ramble and divert itself in the variety of its conceptions. It is upon this account that I can hardly bear with Ovid's luxurious fancy. He is witty in his grief, and gives himself a world of trouble to show his wit when we expect nothing but natural thoughts from him.[22]

Ovid was Addison's favorite classical example of false or mixed wit, and Dryden repeatedly speaks of his "boyisms" and "puerilities," his verbal turns and puns. Even in the *Heroides*, the most perfect of his poems, "he often writ too pointedly for his subject, and made his persons speak more eloquently than the violence of their passion would admit: so that he is frequently witty out of season."[23] In a poem of tragic emotional quality, wit is out of place; it breaks the reader's pity and thus destroys the very thing the poet is building.[24]

This way of reading the epistles is probably far off the mark, if the standard for validity in interpretation is the "real" or "Roman" Ovid, the *Heroides* of Ovid's own intention. In the *Amores* he himself contrasts majestic and haughty tragedy with his own more delicate elegiac muse:

> sum levis, et mecum levis est, mea cura, Cupido;
> non sum materia fortior ipsa mea.[25]

Modern scholars, especially in the last thirty years or so, have tended to consider Ovid's wit not as an accidental defect, at odds with the poet's artistic purpose, but as essential to his poetic aim.[26] There have been many Ovids in the two millennia since his death, and the Ovid of the seventeenth century may have been just as chimerical as the medieval *Ovide Moralisé*.

Our concern, however, is not with Ovid himself but with the *Heroides* as conceived and read by Pope. The hypothesis I want to propose is that he interpreted and judged them very much as his predecessors and contemporaries did—as dramatic poems of tragic quality and effect—and that in the letters of Abélard and Héloïse, as transmitted to him through the intermediaries so meticulously described by Audra, he saw materials which might be shaped into an epistle more beautiful and moving than any of Ovid's own. It would avoid the errors of the Roman poet, his repetitions, conceits, and unseasonable wit, but in other respects would conform to the idea of the kind which Ovid founded. Such a poem, following Dryden's principles, would represent nature in disorder, the mind of a feigned person combating between contrary passions. Its effect would be to stir pity, and it would have a beautiful unity of design, driving always to one end—a resolution of the speaker's conflict and a catharsis of the reader's feeling. If *Eloisa to Abelard* is to be read "with the same spirit that its author writ," I believe it should be judged in the light of these aims.

III

Before turning to the poem itself, we should recognize that both the *Heroides* and *Eloisa to Abelard* can be called either dramatic or tragic only in a qualified sense. Such poems are dramatic, in a literal definition, because none of the words are the poet's. All must be understood as spoken by an imagined person; the subject of the poem is the thoughts and feelings of that person, as arising from his or her character and situation. But these poems are not meant to be acted, and the epistolary device removes them one degree from direct representation. They are not plays, for there is only one speaker, the poem is a single, self-contained speech, and there is no external action. Their effect, too, cannot be fully tragic. Pity may certainly be aroused, if the speaker suffers, but since she is not in danger our fear for her must be much less intense than that produced by a fully tragic dramatic action; it would be, at most, a kind of moral concern, lest the speaker's mind break down or think and feel in self-destructive ways. Granting these reservations, I should like to take Pope's poem seriously both as drama and as tragedy, in the limited senses indicated.

17

In a poem of this kind, we may distinguish four essential elements: a dramatic situation, a speaker with a distinct individual character, a sequence of thoughts and feelings arising from the reaction of the speaker to the situation, and finally the style or artistic medium through which all these are expressed. In reading the poem, we may not be conscious of them as separate aspects; the poem, if successful, has a single massive effect. But for purposes of analysis and criticism, we may differentiate these elements, taking them in turn and testing each to determine its value in relation to the poet's intention, as postulated above; the organizing principle which binds them together should emerge in the course of the analysis. As a whole and in all its parts, the poem should be informed and animated by the pervasive influence of its poetic purpose.

For twentieth-century readers, the greatest barrier to appreciation of Pope's poem is its style. To ears trained to a different music, its diction and syntax may well seem artificial and cold, the chime of its couplets monotonous and jingly. To Root and Tillotson, both defenders of the poem, its manner seems "rhetorical," by which they apparently mean something like "artificial" or "ornamental" —suited perhaps to analysis and aphoristic statement, but poorly adapted to the expression of feeling.[27] These prejudices die slowly; thirty years after those critics, Murray Krieger is still asking whether any style could be less suited to convey the immediacy of Eloisa's passionate struggle than "Pope's most polished version of that most finished verse-form, the heroic couplet."[28] One wonders what he would say of the alexandrines of Corneille and Racine as a vehicle for tragic expression.

For some years, however, several scholars have been helping us to see that the couplet, as Pope used it, is capable of a wide range of effects, and to discriminate those effects more subtly and perceptively. The general thesis of John A. Jones' book, *Pope's Couplet Art*, is that the styles of Pope's major poems tend in each case toward a dominant pattern, the "couplet norm," which is different for each poem and appropriate to its particular subject and genre. "For his passionate nun," Jones says in his chapter on *Eloisa*, "Pope created a distinctive stylistic decorum; and artist that he was, he used it in this poem alone." Sharply differentiating the styles of *Eloisa*, the *Rape of the Lock,* and the *Essay on Criticism,* Jones analyzes nine long passages in Pope's epistle in minute detail; of one pair of verses, for example, he says that it is "not like Pope's typical balanced couplet: it has no pivotal caesura, it lacks chiastic syntax, or meaning, and the negating climax overwhelms and canals all three preceding statements" in the twenty-line verse paragraph of which it is a part. Granting that Eloisa sometimes "makes points and creates a kind of emotional symmetry based on the oppositions of nature and grace," Jones argues that this occurs in passages which express the intellectual aspect of her deeper emotional conflict; the antithetical statements, only one element in the poem's style, "release powerful emotions, which . . . engulf and transcend antithesis and debate."[29] The concept of the couplet norm may be open to question, and some of Jones' descriptions are perhaps too rhapsodical, but he does a good deal to lessen those blindnesses and deafnesses which are still too much with us.

Although Jones' chapter assumes that *Eloisa* is a poem of inward conflict, told and experienced from the first-person point of view and moving throughout toward a final resolution, his argument is not explicitly or systematically guided by a generic definition such as I am proposing here. In a more theoretical approach, deriving the qualities of style appropriate to an heroic epistle from the definition of that form, I believe we could assert that the essential requirement for any tragic style is simply the power to express thought, feeling, and character.[30] Since drama is not life but art, since tragedy is serious and intense, since its characters have moral stature and human importance, and since their fates concern us deeply, its language not only may but should depart quite widely from the norms of colloquial speech as used in ordinary life, so long as it remains clear, expressive, flexible, and actual. In applying such criteria to Pope's poem, we should remember that it is a letter, not literally a speech, and also that both the writer and its recipient are "two of the most distinguished persons of their age in Learning and Beauty," as Pope notes in his "Argument" to the poem. One sign that the style of *Eloisa* does vividly communicate thought, feeling, and character is that we really forget, after the first few lines, that we are reading a letter; our awareness of ink and paper magically dissolves, and even voice is almost forgotten, so that we think we are within the very mind of Eloisa, as her soul reaches out to her absent lover.

Without attempting to emulate Jones' detailed analyses, I may comment briefly on three representative passages. The first expresses Eloisa's resignation to her lot and looks forward, unconsciously, to the vision of her death at the end of the poem. The language is simple and direct, an intensified and elevated, yet natural way of writing:

> Yet here for ever, ever must I stay;
> Sad proof how well a lover can obey!
> Death, only death, can break the lasting chain;
> And here ev'n then, shall my cold dust remain,
> Here all its frailties, all its flames resign,
> And wait, till 'tis no sin to mix with thine.
>
> [171–76]

In this there is nothing epigrammatic; it is neither stiff nor pointed, but fluid, supple, and intense.

In another passage, the manner is different:

> Oh happy state! when souls each other draw,
> When love is liberty, and nature, law:
> All then is full, possessing and possest,
> No craving Void left aking in the breast:
> Ev'n thought meets thought ere from the lips it part,
> And each warm wish springs mutual from the heart.
> This sure is bliss (if bliss on earth there be)
> And once the lot of Abelard and me.
>
> [91–98]

These words are not "rhetoric," in the pejorative sense of that much-abused word, so often applied to the style of *Eloisa* by old-fashioned critics. If the second and third verses have a strongly marked caesura and a balance of subject-predicate against subject-predicate and of active against passive participle, the reason is that Eloisa's mind is sufficiently keen and clear to think in such terms naturally. The passage as a whole is alive with feeling and with character; the words are those of a thoughtful and intelligent woman, generalizing in a brief moment of fond remembrance about the great experience of her life.

Still different, though not more suited to the changing moods of a tragic monologue, is Eloisa's account of her dreams:

> I wake—no more I hear, no more I view,
> The phantom flies me, as unkind as you.
> I call aloud; it hears not what I say;
> I stretch my empty arms; it glides away:
> To dream once more I close my willing eyes;
> Ye soft illusions, dear deceits, arise!
> Alas no more!—methinks we wandring go
> Thro' dreary wastes, and weep each other's woe;
> Where round some mould'ring tow'r pale ivy creeps,
> And low-brow'd rocks hang nodding o'er the deeps.
> Sudden you mount! you becken from the skies;
> Clouds interpose, waves roar, and winds arise.
> I shriek, start up, the same sad prospect find,
> And wake to all the griefs I left behind.
>
> [235–48]

The contrast in style between these dramatic lines and any passage in the *Essay on Criticism,* the Horatian imitations, or the *Dunciad* should be evident to the most tone-deaf ear; the shifting tones and speeds of the language express vividly the fluctuating moods of Eloisa's waking and dreaming, the sharpness of her frustrated longing, the sadness of her loneliness and grief. In these passages and many others, with their varying tones and tempos, we find a style which preserves a tragic dignity and elevation, is entirely in character for the speaker, and yet is capable of expressing a wide range of tragic emotions. The style is not Shakespearean, but it is a style worthy of tragedy and adapted to its needs.

Of the "situation," as I have called it, much less needs to be said. Like all the great love stories of the world, the loves of Abélard and Héloïse are essentially tragic. The obstacle to the lovers' happiness, more final and complete than in the other great love stories, makes the suffering of Héloïse more terrible than Isolde's or Juliet's. At the same time, it makes impossible any resolution in action. This fact, which for the novelist or playwright constitutes a fatal defect in the story, is an advantage to Pope, since in a tragic epistle there is no external action; what is needed is a static situation and an internal resolution.

Eloisa's immediate situation, as Pope represents it in the poem, is that of a woman still deeply in love but absent from her lover, living in a cloister, and cut off from him both by his emasculated condition and by her own religious vows. Pope pictures her at the most poignant moment, as she tries to answer the letter which has rewakened all her old passions. This situation, as it interacts with her character, creates the conflict which the poem must finally resolve: that struggle of "grace and nature, virtue and passion" of which Pope speaks in "The Argument."

Some readers have felt that the conflict is one-sided—that the pull of religion on Eloisa is far weaker than the pull of her sexual desire. Brower finds that "the Christian experience expressed in *Eloisa to Abelard* is curiously external, and curiously generalized." Eloisa has little of the mystic about her, he thinks: "Indeed her chief religious emotion is guilt, the pang of conscience, rather than positive love of God or any vivid experience of salvation."[31] The question is important, because the poem collapses as drama if Brower is right.

It may be readily conceded, since Pope is very explicit about it, that Eloisa's original motives for taking vows were not religious: "Not grace, or zeal, love only was my call" (117). The length of time since her separation from Abelard and her entrance into monastic life is not specified, but is clearly very long; through all those years, she has lived as her sisters live, trying sincerely not only to do penance for her sin but to obey and love her God. Yet even at the moment of writing, she cannot give herself wholly to religion:

> All is not Heav'n's while *Abelard* has part,
> Still rebel nature holds out half my heart;

Nor pray'rs nor fasts its stubborn pulse restrain,
Nor tears, for ages, taught to flow in vain.
[25–28]

She is, as Brower says, fully conscious of the sinfulness of her love, both past and present, and the prevailing impression of her life as a nun is one of penitence, renunciation, and "voluntary pains" (18).

But a basic purpose of that life, part of its daily rhythm, is contemplation—"heav'nly-pensive" contemplation, Eloisa calls it in the second line of the poem. She practices it, too: "No more these scenes my meditation aid,/ Or lull to rest the visionary maid" (161–62). Though she contrasts her own divided heart with the serenity of the blameless Vestal, she recognizes the joy which flows from that kind of commitment, and there are times when her own heart fully responds:

But let heav'n seize it, all at once 'tis fir'd,
Not touch'd, but rapt; not waken'd, but inspir'd!
[201–2]

Her vision of the whispering Angels and winged Seraphs, the white virgins, and the Spouse himself who welcome the vestal to heaven (216–22) expresses her religious feelings eloquently, as does her own acceptance, near the close, of grace, hope, and faith (297–300). If rebel nature holds out half her heart until the end of the poem, the other half not only knows the joy and peace of heavenly love but is powerfully drawn to it. This side of her nature seems to me fully realized in dramatic terms.

Eloisa's character, though foreshadowed in the sources, is largely Pope's own creation. Many of the details can be paralleled in the writers analyzed by Audra, but in Bayle, Bussy, and Hughes, as in the original Latin letters, these details lie scattered, mixed with much that is alien and irrelevant.[32] Pope has shaped this material to his own idea, selecting those elements which contribute to his aim. Some of the finest touches have no parallel in the sources, and all are transformed by his art.

23

In the interpretation of drama, character must be inferred by the reader or audience from signs—from what each person seeks and avoids, approves and disapproves, from the way they think and the emotions they express. Only a few salient traits of Eloisa's character, those most basic to our sense of her as tragic, can be mentioned here, and even these can be illustrated by only a small sampling of the signs from which we infer them.

Eloisa is "good" in the Aristotelian sense; that is, we feel her to be far superior ethically to ourselves, to average humanity. This is true not only in the sense that she fully accepts the moral values which condemn her past and present passion, judging herself more severely than any of us would wish to judge her. It is also shown in a certain magnanimity and generosity of spirit. The pain she has suffered for so long has not made her self-centered, blind to the feelings of others, resentful of those who are free from such suffering; she shows this in her attitudes toward "the wedded dame," toward her sisters, the blameless vestals, toward Abelard himself. She states, as a fact well known to him, that he was the seducer: "Thou know'st how guiltless first I met thy flame" (59). But she does not use this fact to blame him, nor to excuse herself; it is simply the truth, though it has its effect on our opinion of both lovers. The penalties have fallen more heavily on herself than on him, since passion is still alive in her; but if she could, she would take the whole punishment upon herself: "Ah more than share it! give me all thy grief" (50). This goodness is the basis of our pity for her, since her suffering so far exceeds her fault, and it also makes clear from the beginning the impossibility for her of any action which would be injurious to him.

A quality in Eloisa which has been overlooked or unmentioned by critics is her high intelligence. This might be taken for granted from known history, and Pope himself draws attention to it in his "Argument," but it is also manifested dramatically throughout the poem. Pope has eliminated all the theological argument that takes up so much space in the Latin letters, but at a purely human level his Eloisa is the most clear-sighted of women. Unlike most of Ovid's heroines, she is never befuddled, never deceived by her feelings. When she feels most intensely, she continues to see everything

24

as it is and in its true proportions. An aspect of this quality of mind is her honesty with herself. When she calls on heaven for help, she immediately asks herself: "but whence arose that pray'r?/ Sprung it from piety, or from despair?" (179–80). And she knows that her tears are sometimes "too soft," arising not from sincere repentance but from grief for her lost love (270; cf. 194). It is this clarity of mind that defines her dilemma so sharply—for herself and for us —and it is an essential psychological cause, along with her goodness, of her final decision to give up all hope for even the most minimal realization of her love in this life.

But perhaps the most basic of all her extraordinary qualities, for the tragic effect of Pope's small internal drama, is Eloisa's wholeheartedness, her complete lack of any self-protective reservations or qualifications: she has given herself totally, once and for all. It was for this love that she had become a nun, "When, warm in youth, I bade the world farewell" (110). Pope is following the sources when Eloisa says that, though often pressed to marriage by Abelard, her desire was to follow no laws but those which love has made (73–90); as Tillotson observes, however, Pope purifies the issue by omitting the practical argument (present in Hughes) that marriage would have injured Abelard's career and by basing her refusal wholly on the nature of a "true passion," undiluted by human ties, legalisms, and worldly considerations.[33] The depth, intensity, and unexpungeable quality of her love is manifested by the whole texture of her impassioned letter—by her longing for his presence, by the almost inextricable mixing within her mind of the idea of God and the image of Abelard, by her dreams and the painful wakening from them, by her faith that her love was and still is returned, "mutual from the heart" (96). When she hopes near the close that saints will embrace Abelard "with a love like mine" (342), the wish does not seem to us blasphemous or bombastic; we feel that she has earned the right to make such a comparison.

The last and most important of the four elements in Pope's poem is the sequence of thoughts and feelings through which Eloisa passes. Here we should recognize, I believe, that there is one sense in which the poem may truly be called "rhetorical"; it is the sense in which all of Ovid's *Heroides* are rhetorical, and for that matter

25

many speeches in almost all plays—that is, they are attempts to persuade, addressed by one fictitious person to another. Although Eloisa is certainly expressing herself throughout her letter, she is also pleading with him (as most of Ovid's heroines do) first to write to her, then to come to her. These pleas, eight times repeated, are the structural backbone of the drama.

Eloisa's pleas are entirely different from the rhetoric of Ovid's deserted women, because her own character and her relation to her lover are fundamentally different. Though Ovid's heroines differ from each other in character, most of them are self-centered, self-pitying, morally weak, hurt and angry, and much afraid that they have been betrayed. But Eloisa shows none of these traits, and she is completely confident that she is still loved; she assumes that there is truth, honesty, and unselfish concern for the other on both sides. It is characteristic of her personality, of the nature of her love, and of the tone of her appeals to Abelard that when she slips, just once, into an argument that is not quite candid:

> Ah, think at least thy flock deserves thy care,
> Plants of thy hand, and children of thy pray'r,
> [129–30]

she quickly recognizes that this is unfair to him and unworthy of herself:

> See how the force of others' pray'rs I try
> (O pious fraud of am'rous charity!)
> But why should I on others' pray'rs depend?
> Come thou, my father, brother, husband, friend!
> [149–52]

Hers is a rhetoric which Plato himself might approve, since it is based on truth and understanding.

In this plotless kind of poem, the action is a movement of the soul from one state to another—from reawakened desire, through pleas for his coming, to a renunciation of all desire for reunion with him on this earth, and a final acceptance of death and a hope for spiritual union in heaven. This sequence is that goal, which directs

26

the poet in his race: that "beautiful design, which he first establishes, and then contrives the means, which will naturally conduct it to his end." As plot, according to Aristotle, is the "soul" of a play, its organizing and individuating principle, so this movement of the soul, unfolding in time, is the principle which unifies and binds together all the elements of Pope's plotless inner drama.

Following the broad sequence outlined above, we may divide the poem into four main sections. The first 58 lines are expository; they establish the immediate situation (the convent setting, her receipt of Abelard's letter), and indicate the conflicting elements in her feeling: love and religion, Abelard and God. In lines 59–118, with admirable economy and dramatic propriety, Pope reveals through Eloisa's own thought the main outline of the preceding events, giving us everything we need to know about the past: their clandestine happiness, the terrible vengeance of her family, and her entrance into the religious life.

The central section of the poem (119–288), continuing her pleas for Abelard's return, reaches its climax, and the crisis of the drama, in her despairing cry:

> Come, if thou dar'st, all charming as thou art!
> Oppose thy self to heav'n; dispute my heart;
> Come, with one glance of those deluding eyes,
> Blot out each bright Idea of the skies.
> Take back that grace, those sorrows, and those tears,
> Take back my fruitless penitence and pray'rs,
> Snatch me, just mounting, from the blest abode,
> Assist the fiends and tear me from my God!
> [281–88]

But this wish reveals to her, even as she speaks, the full destructiveness of her plea: the impossibility for her of this solution, and above all the spiritual ruin it would bring to him. Abruptly, then, in a revulsion of feeling which Pope has solidly grounded in her character, she completely reverses her plea:

> No, fly me, fly me! far as Pole from Pole;
> Rise *Alps* between us! and whole oceans roll!

Ah come not, write not, think not once of me,
Nor share one pang of all I felt for thee.
Thy oaths I quit, thy memory resign,
Forget, renounce me, hate whate'er was mine.
[289–94]

The last 77 lines of the poem, beginning with the passage just quoted, present the gradual resolution of her conflict and the dying away of her tragic passion. She renounces all rights to his presence or even to his memory, bids adieu to all her "long lov'd, ador'd ideas" of him, welcomes heavenly grace, foresees her death, imagines that she is called to eternal rest and peace by the spirit of a sainted sister, hopes that Abelard will perform the last rites, envisions his later ascent into heaven, welcomed by angels and saints, and prays that they may at last be laid together in "one kind grave" —reunited without sin, conflict, or penalty. She has one last spasm of desire, hoping that when he returns as she is dying Abelard will "Suck my last breath, and catch my flying soul!" But she immediately rejects the thought; he must come in "sacred vestments," holding the cross, not as lover but as priest (324–28). Three additional consoling thoughts close the poem: that lovers in future ages will visit their common grave and be moved to "mutual pity," that a devoted worshipper may sometime drop "one human tear" for them, and be forgiven, and that "our sad, our tender story" may some day be told by a future bard (343–66). For the reader as well as for Eloisa, these final thoughts complete the tragic catharsis. Her grief will end in the grave, and her love, sanctified by penitence and sacrifice, will be reconciled with her piety. The poem ends, as a tragedy should, not in pain but in peace.[34]

IV

For almost a century and a half, from the beginning of the nineteenth century until well into the twentieth, it was difficult for anyone to do justice to the literature of the eighteenth century, and most conspicuously to its poetry. The radical changes begun both in the writing of poetry and in poetic theory and criticism by Blake, Wordsworth, and Coleridge—a by-product of the even more profound and sweeping revolution in philosophy initiated by Kant —brought a flood of poems, wonderfully beautiful in themselves, but organized on new formal principles and employing new conventions, wholly unknown to their eighteenth-century predecessors. They also introduced alien standards of critical judgment and a different habit in reading, so that the poetic assumptions, techniques, intentions, and effects of Pope and others were misunderstood or condemned, the ability to perceive and appreciate his poems on their own terms almost wholly lost.

In the last four decades, literary scholarship has done much to correct these misunderstandings. Partly through a process of historical reconstruction, as in Audra's seminal study, partly through fresh critical readings guided by twentieth- rather than nineteenth-century aesthetic principles and methods of interpretation, as in Brower's sensitive and illuminating book, scholars and critics have reopened the case for Pope as a poet, producing many valuable new insights and judgments. In his preface to *Essential Articles for the Study of Alexander Pope*, in fact, Maynard Mack is bold enough to say that the process of critical revaluation, begun in the 1930's, was virtually complete by the early '60's.[35]

Whatever may be the case with Pope's other poems, I do not believe that any canonical interpretation and evaluation is attained either in the two articles on *Eloisa to Abelard* which Mack included in his anthology or in more recent essays by other critics, though all of them illuminate the text in varying aspects and degrees.

Here I have tried to recover Pope's own intention. Since Audra, everyone has recognized the fact that the epistle is a poem *"traitant à la manière d'Ovide une matière nouvelle"*[36]—the new matter, of course, being the story of Héloïse and Abélard, as reinterpreted by French and English translators and adaptors in the latter part of the seventeenth century. I have followed the same clue, but have raised several questions not previously asked. How did Pope and his contemporaries read the *Heroides*? If Pope took Ovid as his formal model, what kind of a poem did he suppose himself to be writing? If *Eloisa* is a poem of that kind, what are the parts of which it is composed, by what organizing principle are the parts bound together in a unified poetic whole, and what kind of emotional effect is the poem designed to produce? If it is governed by such aesthetic intentions, how did Pope select and shape the *matière nouvelle* to those ends? And finally, how well does the poem realize concretely the formal and affective potentialities inherent in its kind?

It would be absurd to claim that the reading presented here is final and definitive. The whole argument is hypothetical, resting on the series of "if" clauses stated above, and any or all of these hypotheses might be challenged. The "if" clauses, in turn, depend upon theoretical assumptions as to interpretive method and evaluative criteria which have not been explicitly formulated in this essay, much less examined and defended philosophically, and which many present-day critics do not accept. Such an argument will surely not be convincing to a critic like Krieger, who finds in the poem almost the same dramatic movement that I have described, including the "all-passion-spent acceptance that Eloisa has achieved" at the end, but who regards all that as merely the "official rhetoric" of the poem; Pope's language has a life of its own, anarchic or chaotic, which subverts his rational design and makes the poem a partial failure, though an attractive one to post-Freudian taste.[37] We are arguing from different premises, as Sydney Smith said in a famous joke, and I fear we could never reach agreement.

But there is some comfort in the knowledge that Warton and Johnson, Wakefield and Mason, intelligent critics of Pope's own century, believed *Eloisa to Abelard* to be a most beautiful and touching poem, a unique masterpiece in its own kind. I like to think they would approve if I conclude by saying, "Yes, I do feel, when I read this poem, 'how moving' and 'how convincing.' "

NOTES

1. Emile Audra, *L'Influence française dans l'oeuvre de Pope* (Paris: Champion, 1931), p. 443.
2. Advertisement to *An Elegy Written in an Empty Assembly-Room* (1756), quoted by Geoffrey Tillotson, ed., *The Rape of the Lock and Other Poems*, Twickenham ed., II (London: Methuen, 1940), 399.

All citations of *Eloisa to Abelard* will refer to this edition, giving line numbers within parentheses in the text.

3. Joseph Warton, *An Essay on the Writings and Genius of Pope* (London, 1756), I, 333–34.

4. Johnson, *Lives of the English Poets*, ed. Hill (Oxford, 1905), III, 235–36; Gilbert Wakefield, *The Poems of Mr. Gray* (London, 1786), p. 167; William Mason, Preface to *Poems by William Whitehead* (London, 1788), III, 35.

5. Byron, *Letters and Journals*, ed. R. E. Prothero (London: John Murray, 1900), IV, 489.

6. Tillotson, pp. 288–91.

7. Reuben A. Brower, *Alexander Pope: The Poetry of Allusion* (Oxford: Clarendon Press, 1959), pp. 83–84. For other discussions of the poem, see Henry Pettit, "Pope's *Eloisa to Abelard*: An Interpretation," *University of Colorado Studies*, No. 4 (1953), pp. 67–74; Brendan P. O'Hehir, "Virtue and Passion: The Dialectic of *Eloisa to Abelard*," *Texas Studies in Literature and Language*, II (1960), 219–32; Robert P. Kalmey, "Pope's *Eloisa to Abelard* and 'Those Celebrated Letters,'" *PQ*, XLVII (1968), 164–78; Rebecca Price Parkin, *The Poetic Workmanship of Alexander Pope* (Minneapolis: University of Minnesota Press, 1955), esp. pp. 12–16, 145–46, and her "Alexander Pope's Use of Biblical and Ecclesiastical Allusions," *Studies on Voltaire and the Eighteenth Century*, LVII (1967), 1183–1216, esp. pp. 1193–1200; also the works referred to in notes 27, 28, and 29 below.

8. Pope, *Essay on Criticism*, II, 34. Pope applies this principle in his postscript to the *Odyssey*, where he defends the poem against Longinus: "Whoever reads the Odyssey with an eye to the Iliad, expecting to find it of the same character, or of the same sort of spirit, will be grievously deceived, and err against the first principle of Criticism, which is to consider the nature of the piece, and the intent of his author." He goes on to argue that if Homer has "accomplished his own design, and done all that the nature of his Poem demanded or allowed, it still remains perfect in its kind, and as much a master-piece as the Iliad" (*Poems*, Twickenham ed., X [London: Methuen, 1967], 382, 384).

9. See especially the prefaces to *Annus Mirabilis*, *Ovid's Epistles*, and the *Fables*, and the dedication of *Examen Poeticum*. Briefer comments occur in the *Essay of Dramatic Poesy*, the prefaces to *Troilus and Cressida* and to *Sylvae*, the *Discourse on Satire*, and the *Parallel of Poetry and Painting*.

10. Preface to *Ovid's Epistles*, in *Essays*, ed. W. P. Ker (Oxford: Clarendon Press, 1926), I, 236. Cf. *Les XXI Epîtres d'Ovide* (Lyon, 1556), pp. 9–10; Henry Peacham, *The Compleat Gentleman* (1622), in J. E. Spingarn, ed., *Critical Essays of the Seventeenth Century* (Oxford: Clarendon Press, 1908), I, 125–26; and Gaspar Bachet, Sr. de Méziriac, *Commentaires sur les Epistres d'Ovid* (La Haye, 1716; originally published 1626), I, 73.

11. *Essay of Dramatic Poesy*, Ker, I, 53. Bachet says: "Entre tous les ou-

vrages de ce grand poëte, le livre de ses epistres est celui qui est la plus remply de belles conceptions, le mieux limé, et le plus poly" (*Commentaires*, I, 73).

12. Preface to *Ovid's Epistles*, Ker, I, 233. Warton says that Ovid deserves much credit for inventing "this beautiful species of writing epistles under feigned characters. It is a high improvement on the Greek elegy; to which its dramatic nature renders it greatly superior. It is indeed no other than a passionate soliloquy; in which, the mind gives vent to the distresses and emotions under which it labours: but by being directed and addressed to a particular person, it gains a degree of propriety, that the best-conducted soliloquy, in a tragedy, must ever want" (*Essay on Pope*, I, 286).

13. Preface to *Annus Mirabilis*, Ker, I, 15; cf. 53, 233–34. According to Audra, Pope "eut alors écrit quelque chose comme la miniature d'une tragedie française, où les incidents ne sont rien, et où la marche de l'action est faite de ces alternances dans le coeur des personnages" (*op. cit.*, p. 432).

14. Joseph Trapp, *Lectures on Poetry* (Latin version 1711; English trans. 1742), Lect. VIII, in Scott Elledge, ed., *Eighteenth-Century Critical Essays* (Ithaca: Cornell University Press, 1961), I, 242–43.

15. Trapp, *ibid.*

16. Ker, I, 53.

17. Preface to *Ovid's Epistles*, Ker, I, 233. Cf. Ovid, *Epistolarum Heroidum Liber* (London, 1702), A2 verso; Samuel Garth, *Ovid's Metamorphoses, in Fifteen Books*, 2nd ed. (London: J. Tonson, 1720), I, xxiii.

18. Preface to *Ovid's Epistles*, Ker, I, 235. Cf. Garth, I, xix; René Rapin, *Reflections on Aristotle's Treatise of Poesy in General* (1674), in Scott Elledge and Donald Schier, eds., *The Continental Model* (Minneapolis: Carleton College and the University of Minnesota Press, 1960), p. 282.

19. Ker, I, 234.

20. Seneca, *Controv.* ix. 5, 17; Quintilian, *Instit.* X. i. 88, 98.

21. Ker, I, 233–35. Cf. Garth, I, xxvii–ix; Rapin in Elledge and Schier, p. 275; Trapp in Elledge, I, 231–32.

22. Charles de Saint-Evremond, "On the Character of Tragedies" (1672), in Elledge and Schier, p. 150.

23. Ker, I, 233–35; cf. II, 9, 193–94, 255–57. See also Addison, *Spectator*, Nos. 62, 279, and *Miscellaneous Works*, ed. A. C. Guthkelch (London: G. Bell, 1914), I, 145. Garth and Trapp raise the same objection.

24. In the preface to the *Fables*, Dryden says: "On these occasions the poet should endeavour to raise pity; but, instead of this, Ovid is tickling you to laugh. Virgil never made use of such machines when he was moving you to commiserate the death of Dido; he would not destroy what he was building" (Ker, II, 257). Cf. Addison, *Miscellaneous Works*, I, 145–46.

25. Ovid, *Amores* III. i. 41–42.

26. E. K. Rand says that the *Heroides* should be regarded "not as unsuccessful attempts at tragic monologue, but as thoroughly competent studies of women's moods" (*Ovid and His Influence* [New York: Longmans, Green, 1928], p. 22). L. P. Wilkinson calls Ovid a "baroque spirit before his time" and says that "The *Heroides* were probably not intended to move; they are a display of virtuosity designed to entertain" (*Ovid Recalled* [Cambridge: the University Press, 1955], pp. 97–99). See also T. F. Higham, "Ovid: Some Aspects of His Character and Aims," *Classical Review*, XLVIII (1934), 105–16, and Hermann Fränkel, *Ovid: A Poet Between Two Worlds* (Berkeley and Los Angeles: University of California Press, 1945), pp. 36–46.

27. R. K. Root, *The Poetical Career of Alexander Pope* (Princeton, 1938), pp. 94–102; Tillotson, pp. 288–91.

28. Murray Krieger, " 'Eloisa to Abelard': The Escape from Body or the Embrace of Body," *ECS*, III (1969), 28–47.

29. John A. Jones, *Pope's Couplet Art* (Athens: Ohio University Press, 1969), chap. 6. William Bowman Piper, *The Heroic Couplet* (Cleveland: The Press of Case Western Reserve University, 1969), also contributes greatly to appreciation of the wide range of effects possible to the couplet form, though he concentrates on the style of Pope's discursive and satirical poems, from the *Essay on Criticism* to Dialogue II of the *Epilogue to the Satires*; he does not discuss *Eloisa to Abelard*.

30. For fuller development of this conception of a tragic style, see Moody E. Prior, *The Language of Tragedy* (Bloomington: Indiana University Press, 1966), chap. 1, and Elder Olson, *Tragedy and the Theory of Drama* (Detroit: Wayne State University Press, 1961), pp. 88–89, 112–25.

31. Brower, p. 82. Dr. Johnson does not seem to find any lack of religious feeling in Eloisa: "The mixture of religious hope and resignation gives an elevation and dignity to disappointed love, which images merely natural cannot bestow" (*Lives*, III, 236). Speaking of the historical Héloïse, Etienne Gilson says in his remarkable series of lectures that her problem is "to find in the passion this man inspires the strength required for a life of sacrifice which is both meaningless and impossible save on the level of the love of God." He suggests that Héloïse was perhaps "far closer to divine charity than many others who dethrone God for a great deal less than Abelard" (*Héloïse and Abélard*, tr. L. K. Shook [Ann Arbor: University of Michigan Press, 1960], p. 96). For Gilson's comment on Pope's poem, see pp. ix–x.

32. Nothing could be further from Pope's treatment than the ironic and cynical, even comic account given by Bayle in his articles on Abélard and on Héloïse. Pope's selective use of his sources is recognized by Root (p. 96), and Tillotson (p. 280), but since they do not define the aims which guide his choice and shaping of details, they give only a vague sense of his independence and originality. A better, though very brief, comment on his use of his sources is that of George Sherburn, ed., *The Best of Pope* (New York: T. Nelson & Sons, 1929), pp. 403–4.

33. Tillotson, pp. 404–5 n.

34. Warton's comment is perceptive: "ELOISA, at the conclusion of the EPISTLE . . . is judiciously represented as gradually settling into a tranquillity of mind, and seemingly reconciled to her fate" (*Essay on Pope*, I, 332).
35. Maynard Mack, *Essential Articles for the Study of Alexander Pope*, rev. ed. (Hamden, Conn.: Archon Books, 1964).
36. Audra, p. 402.
37. Krieger, pp. 45–47.

Freedom, Libertinism, and the Picaresque

Maximillian E. Novak

A BIBLIOGRAPHY OF WORKS on the picaresque compiled in 1966 listed over six hundred titles suggesting surprisingly diverse theories about the genre,[1] yet most critics probably feel they have some notion of what the word means. Frank Chandler, one of the earliest writers on the picaresque, dealt with it as the "literature of roguery," a body of subject matter which could encompass *Guzmán de Alfarache, Moll Flanders*, the *Roman Comique*, and *Vanity Fair*, while Dunlap, in his *History of Fiction* published in 1814, saw fit to group picaresque fiction with *Gargantua and Pantagruel* as a species of comic romance. However much one might envy the simplicity of Chandler's approach, few modern critics would accept *Vanity Fair* or *Gargantua* as picaresque works, yet the need to classify them remains. E. D. Hirsch has demonstrated that as readers we are forced to think in terms of an "intrinsic genre" and as scholars, we inevitably think in terms of historical genre.[2] Plainly those who read *Moll Flanders*, not as an example of the novel or the picaresque, but rather as a member of the same literary species as the *Confessions* of Saint Augustine, will experience it differently from those who read it as a member of the same species as Castillo Solórzano's *La Garduña de Sevilla*, which though told in the third person has, in Rufina, a female rogue very much like Moll.[3]

What I intend to do in this paper is, first, to examine three recent prescriptive theories of picaresque fiction which have tended to drop the fiction of Lesage, Defoe, and Smollett as either unpicaresque or trivial (as I see it, these theories misunderstand the ways in which the eighteenth century modified the picaresque to suit its

35

own sensibility). And secondly, to argue that the picaresque is not so much a narrow genre as, like satire, a universal mode which, while it shares with the novel of manners a concern with the real world, represents the very opposite of that form in its organizing principles: its free movement, its free form, and its view of middle and upper-class social and political conventions through a character who, as a result of circumstance or choice, has been partially or fully liberated from those conventions. What I am offering, I should add, is less a general theory of the picaresque than an interpretation of the English response to it during the Restoration and eighteenth century, when translations from the Spanish and the French made picaresque fiction the chief rival to romances and novellas.

The clearest statement of problems involved in defining the picaresque appears in several essays by Claudio Guillén, now collected in a volume called *Literature as System*.[4] At times, Guillén is willing to speak of the picaresque "in the wider sense of the term," and then to ask the key question "How wide is that?" In the essay "Genre and Counter-genre," Guillén takes a sensible attitude toward genre as completely separate from universal models. In this broad sense genres are seen as shifting in different eras and occasionally becoming obsolete. Since he accepts Croce's argument that "genres" have little or nothing to do with external form, one could assume that he might accept the idea that the picaresque might be found in poetry as well as prose, though from the definition he advances in this essay, it would seem impossible to have a picaresque drama. He writes:

> Let us say—hastily—that the picaresque model can be described in the following way: it is the fictional confession of a liar. Besides the writer knows that the picaresque tale begins not *in medias res* but with the narrator's birth, that it recounts in chronological order the orphaned hero's peregrination from city to city, and that it usually ends—that is, it can end—with either the defeat or the conversion of the inner man who both narrates and experiences the events.[5]

There seems to be nothing very hasty about this definition, but under careful scrutiny its credibility appears to slip away. Does the hero have to be an orphan in the literal sense? Estebanillo González has all kinds of problems with his family, including disputes over property. And while it may seem easy to throw out Espinel's *Marcos de Obregón* (as Guillén in fact does) on the grounds that the hero is not an "outsider," we may well ask, "How far outside must he be?" Is it not enough that Marcos serves many masters, and wanders far from the place of his birth—the only place in which he feels truly at home?

As a solution to this problem of the *degree* of picaresqueness, Guillén refers to Robert C. Elliot's application of Wittgenstein's observations on the problems involved in defining games. What one must do is decide on works which are incontrovertibly picaresque and ask whether another work can belong to the same category. This involves what Guillén calls a decision question, and such a decision exists for both the critic and the artist. Thus writers like Lesage and Smollett may have thought they were writing picaresque fiction while actually writing something very different. Granted! But do we have accord on a satisfactory model even for the Spanish picaresque? A. A. Parker, for example, tends to make *Lazarillo de Tormes* into a "precursor" of the picaresque, a work not truly of the same genre as *Guzmán de Alfarache*, whereas Guillén accepts the idea that *Lazarillo* represents "a crucial moment in the rise of the European novel"—a definite point in time at which a new genre came into existence. Plainly no agreement can be reached on the nature of the picaresque until there is some accord on the model which will fit most of the works in the genre and from which works will be seen to diverge.

In the essay "Toward a Definition of the Picaresque," Guillén attempts to lay down some specific guidelines for defining "picaresque in the strict sense." This represents a more serious attempt to come to terms with a definition based on "the original Spanish tradition" than the brief definition above, but the process of inclusion and exclusion, once specific works are named, seems very questionable. For example, he classifies Defoe's fiction among works which do not follow the picaresque pattern of focusing on "the interaction between a growing individual and his environment."[6] Now interestingly enough, in the past, following Ian Watt, I argued in my *Economics and the Fiction of Daniel Defoe* that "by empha-sizing the particular character and his social problems,"[7] Defoe had departed from the picaresque tradition. If Guillén's general princi-ple is correct, then there can be no question that *Moll Flanders* de-serves to be treated as a modified form of picaresque fiction, since Defoe held with Locke that the social environment shapes the in-dividual from earliest childhood. Though I am now willing to modify my position, I am not at all certain that Guillén would mod-ify his. Evidently, agreement on what works will satisfy what gen-eral criteria will not come easily.

But Guillén's categories are extremely useful as a starting point. Summarized, his eight defining qualities for the picaresque are: (1) a dynamic psycho-sociological situation; (2) a pseudo-autobio-graphical form; (3) a partial and prejudiced point of view; (4) a critical reflective attitude on the part of the narrator; (5) a stress on the material level of existence; (6) a wide spectrum of social classes observed; (7) a hero moving horizontally through space and vertically through society"; and (8) a loosely episodic form. Insofar as some of these categories are related to form, they seem to counter the Crocean attitude in the essay on genre, but other problems are even more crucial. Take numbers six and seven. Could one write a picaresque novel about a hero who travels up an elevator from one apartment to another in an expensive high rise apartment house or hotel? Such a hero would be moving vertically in space and socially not at all. This may seem facetious, but, in fact, at one point Thomas Mann's Felix Krull seems very close to this possibility. Do we insist on a dynamic social interaction or is movement of any kind sufficient? Do we insist on a "stress on the material level of existence" or do we merely want a degree of real-istic detail of the kind that was once the exclusive preserve of pica-resque fiction but which Richardson introduced into the novel of manners? The separation of styles, as Auerbach demonstrated, is a fact of literary history. This is not to say that such separation should be raised to the level of a governing or defining principle.

I could make some of the same objections to the principles laid down in categories two to four on the question of point of view. That an autobiographical effect is an important part of picaresque

38

fiction is unquestionably true, but it is not at all certain that third person narrative is incapable of providing such an effect. The confessional aspect of the picaresque has never struck me as central. What we *can* say is that an intrusive narrative of the type found in Fielding's *Tom Jones* creates a sense of control which is antithetical to the feeling of freedom that the picaresque provides.

I will mention two other critics who, I feel, set up definitions of picaresque fiction which tend to be overly limiting, A. A. Parker and Stuart Miller. I am in complete agreement with Parker when he writes that the "picaresque novel . . . arises as an exposition of the theme of freedom, including the concept of moral freedom."[8] But instead of exploiting this central question of freedom, Parker locates the seriousness of the picaresque in its advocacy of a life of moral control and Christian repentance. In Parker's view, the world, as the picaro experiences it, presents a vivid example of the effects of original sin, and the sooner the picaro comes to the understanding that he must turn toward the life to come, the sooner he will understand himself and the human condition.

There is no quarrelling with Parker's contention that such a theme makes an admirable basis for great fiction, but it hardly fits the pattern of picaresque fiction as we know it, and would create a complete break between modern picaresque fiction and picaresque fiction of the past—a break which seems to belie what appears to be a strong connection. Given Parker's view, every work after *Guzmán de Alfarache*, with the possible exception of Grimmelshausen's *Simplicissmus* must appear as a decline. Defoe is classified among the morally unaware, Lesage is dismissed as trivial, and Smollett's *Roderick Random* is thrown out as "in no sense an exploration of human delinquency."[9]

To make "delinquency" in this sense the central quality of the picaresque is surely an error—an error even for *Guzmán de Alfarache*. Guzmán moralizes a great deal, but there are passages that suggest that he enjoys his freedom without reservation, and his account of his conversion to the picaro's life is told with considerable gusto. That there is some irony behind an image of a life without spinning or sowing is very likely, but there is also an undeniable amount of creative energy in such passages. Alemán's work ends with the promise of a third part. Are we to suppose that it was to depict his life in Christian retirement? Hardly! No doubt Parker teaches us to accept Alemán's serious moral commitment; on the other hand, we should always be aware that, for the most part, his book was read for its roguish adventures and romantic novellas. The English translation of de Luna's continuation of *Lazarillo de Tormes*, which was always reprinted with the original in the Restoration and eighteenth century, has a dedicatory poem at the end by a T. P., who praises the publisher for the service he has rendered the public in printing the work and concludes:

> No length with LAZARO prevails
> Till th' Readers eyes grow dim,
> GUZMAN & his long-winded tales
> Are SPANISH ROGUES to him.

As Guillén argues, the history of a book is larger than the intent of its author. In its original form, Alemán's work is very different from a Christian sermon, and the excisions of translators and editors producing versions "purged of superfluous moralizing," as Lesage's was advertised, suggests that its place in the history of picaresque fiction owes more to Alemán's ability to create vivid fiction than to his concern with sin and delinquency. In fact, Brémond's version, the translation of which probably influenced Defoe, made Guzmán's sermons an integral part of his character and highlighted the personality of the rogue as never before. Even Alemán, in his second part, complained that although he had written a work with the title of "the Watch-Tower of mans life, they have put the nickname of *Picaro* thereupon, and now it is knowne by no other name."[10] Like Chandler, one early English commentator simply lumped "Gusmanick, Busconick, [and] Scarronick" writers together as writers of rogue fiction.[11]

If Parker overstates the importance of specific moral content, Stuart Miller is overly prescriptive about the form of the picaresque.[12] In stressing the sense of chaos engendered by the adventures of the picaro, he fails to see any order. His model picaresque fiction would have to be *Estebanillo Gonzáles*, who rushes through five adventures and three countries in a single page and soon loses the reader's interest. Miller's approach makes the doubtful assertion that the picaresque hero is incapable of love, observes that Roderick Random falls in love with Narcissa, and then proves that *Roderick Random* is not a work of picaresque fiction. Now, such an argument fails to examine the nature of Roderick's passion, which in spite of his rhetoric, is almost entirely physical, or the way in which Roderick pursues marriage to a wealthy woman long after he has vowed eternal love to Narcissa. *Gil Blas* suffers the same fate as *Roderick Random*; among the modern novels Ellison's *Invisible Man* makes it, while *Felix Krull* somehow does not.

Such diversity of emphasis might engender despair, but there is at least one point on which all appear to agree, and that is on the notion that the picaresque is somehow involved with a sense of freedom. Guillén speaks of movement and changing roles, Parker of moral freedom, and Miller of chaos, but they all mean roughly the same thing—in both form and content the picaresque involves an examination of freedom and randomness. Events occur in an apparently random fashion, characters appear and disappear without any necessary pattern, the hero is free from social conventions, free even from the burden of a single personality, for he assumes many roles. As a late eighteenth-century poem on Lazarillo put it:

He took what Shape he pleas'd to take, was often Up and Down
Cou'd either be a Saint or Rake, a Courtier or a Clown—[13]

He is sexually liberated, or at the very least, he observes the sexual liberation of others. He moves freely in space, and his narrative will usually move freely in time. Much, perhaps all, of his freedom is illusory, but for a large part of his narrative we are allowed to believe freedom exists. The very nature of first person narrative or its equivalent effect suggests a sense of immortality that conquers death itself. The picaro, like Tennyson's Ulysses, is always capable of another voyage, particularly if the bookseller will buy another part.

Since the picaro often takes the role of a servant, he is continually swinging between the poles of freedom and servitude, always opting for freedom. It is the freedom of the beggar's life that makes

100/ 83

it attractive to de Luna's Lazarillo. And when Saul Bellow's Augie March confesses that he is "varietistic" at heart, he aligns himself with the traditional picaro in his willingness to turn his back on comfort and the customary social forms of success to pursue his destiny in the flux of life. And in what amounts to a picaresque formula, which Defoe was later to exploit for *Colonel Jack*, Estebanillo Gonzáles extolls the life of a "Rake" as superior to the life of "Honour":

> What I got by these Vailes together with my Allowance, and Wages, maintain'd me Comfortably, and I slept undisturb'd. Jealousie did not keep me waking; I had no Creditors to Dunn me; no Children to cry for Bread; nor Servants to put me into Passion; so that I car'd not a Straw whether the *Turk* had the better or the *Persian* the worst, or what became of the World. I liv'd at my ease, and my Debts were paid; I valu'd not Punctillo's of Honour; and made a Jest of the Notions of Reputations; for in my Opinion there is no Life like that of a Rake.[14]

Of course this freedom does not include freedom from starvation. Hence the picaro's continual preoccupation with survival and his adherence to a materialistic philosophy in which interest and money appear to be the chief motivating forces of life. But this element is subordinate to that of freedom, for as Lazarillo points out, "I have always chosen rather to eat Cabbage and Garlick without working; then to work, and feed upon Henns and Capons."[15]

Even Guillén's definition of the picaro as a liar falls under the general category of liberty. Alemán's Guzmán is somewhat apologetic about the necessity for lying to "great men," but in John Savage's 1708 translation of Brémond's version, Guzmán revels in the freedom of being able to play with the truth:

> Lying was my predominant quality, a Talent Nature has bestow'd upon me, which I had practis'd from my Childhood, and I cou'd not give it over if I was to have been hang'd. I often told Lies out of mere Wantonness, and without any manner of Occasion. I us'd to say I wonder'd why any man wou'd give himself so much Trouble to tell Truth? 'Twas the Vice of Blockheads, that had not Wit enough to tell a lie. 'Tis never good to speak Truth in any thing. . . . Nay, this method of Pro-

ceeding is not only necessary to the Great, but to our Equals, if we wou'd be thought sociable Creatures, and not Misanthropes or Manhaters.[16]

Alemán's Guzmán belongs to the schlemiel branch of the picaro family. He is a great liar, but he has a terrible memory and forgets what he said. Brémond's Guzmán is more of a rogue. But both explore the freedom from fact and truth, that wide road so much more pleasing to the imagination of the picaro than the straight and narrow path of "Honour." Well might we marvel at a recent study which attempted to find justification for Moll Flanders' lies in contemporary treatises on casuistry.[17] In lying imaginatively and at a prodigious rate Moll is not only being herself, she is also revealing her literary ancestry.

The genuine pleasure that the picaro takes in his freedom has been captured successfully in cinematic terms by Robert Bresson in *Pickpocket* (1959), where the hero revels in his dexterity, removing billfold after billfold and often returning it to the victim's pocket in order to enjoy his skill more completely. That the hero ends up in prison and that he discovers his true self only in confinement is a lesson of both *Pickpocket* and, in part, of *Guzmán de Alfarache*. But even where freedom is viewed ultimately in a negative light, it remains the thematic center of the picaresque.

In 1707 a collection of translations, mostly picaresque fiction, appeared under the title, *The Spanish Libertines*. As might have been expected, the translator, John Stevens, argued that the works he included were intended to expose vice. But he also praised them for their "Variety and surprizing Accidents." The word "Libertines" in the title might have had the relatively neutral meaning of "one who goes his own way," but it could hardly have failed to conjure up the belief in moral freedom which found its best intellectual expression among writers like Theophile de Viau, Sorel, and Cyrano de Bergerac in France. In England, libertinism had become strongly rooted in the masculine love ethic of Steven's time. It also had been the central code of Restoration Comedy. Libertinism argued not merely for sexual freedom and for a life of sensations rather than of thoughts; it also argued for a life free from the conventions of society. Though it was the code of wits and gentlemen, in an odd way the picaro shared many attitudes with the libertine. And aside from Osborne's *Advice to A Son*, *The English Rogue* of Richard Head and Francis Kirkman is probably the best expression of libertine thought produced in England.

I do not want to press this point too hard, but there is surely some analogy between the scene of libertine debauchery in the second part of *Lazarillo de Tormes* and the sexual banquet in Sorel's *Comical History*. Unlike heroes and heroines of romance, the picaro or picara is not noted for chastity. In the case of Roderick Random, there is the direct statement that he regarded himself as a "libertine." Narcissa may represent a superior passion for him, but he is always willing to accept any woman fortune happens to drop in his lap. (Defoe's Roxana argues the part of the female libertine at several points.) The picaro is not always successful in his amours, but in the picaresque sex is included among the varieties of experience encountered by the hero.

I am not arguing that the picaresque hero is equivalent to the libertine hero.[18] What I am suggesting is that a heroine like Fanny Hill is not incompatible with the picaresque and that rather than speaking of the material level of existence as a mark of the picaresque, we should speak of its philosophic materialism. Such a viewpoint may be completely discredited in the telling of the tale, but the discrediting is usually the work of the repentant narrator or the result of irony, neither of which cancels the deeds of the liberated hero. *The English Rogue*, for example, depicts various kinds of sexual freedom, idealizing the woman who feels she can take her pleasure in sex as freely as the male, and showing a number of adventures in which two or more women are involved with one man. Included in the book is a poem by the heroic rogue, illustrating most of the double entendres on sex of which the English language was capable at the time, and a feminist libertine song of which the following stanzas are typical:

> 'Tis liberty which we adore,
> It is our wealth and only store;
> Having her we all are free,

44

Who so merry then as we?
'Tis she that makes us now to sing,
And only she can pleasure bring.

As I am free, so will be still,
For no man shall abridge my will:
I'll pass my life in choicest pleasure,
On various objects spend my treasure:
That woman sure no joy can find,
Who to one man is only join'd.[19]

The English Rogue has songs celebrating the pleasures of wine as well as women, and those who live within the conventions of society—conventions absurd to rogue and libertine alike—are treated as fair game for the liberated rogue.

Now this sense of freedom should be accompanied by a form which provides a proper sense of randomness in the adventures of the picaro. Characters may play an important part in one section of the work and then disappear completely, or they may reappear in strange places and at surprising moments. (Miller calls this a "dance" of characters.) The total effect is a feeling of flux and variety. That the narrator may remind the reader of an overall design in the universe throughout the novel or make such a pronouncement at the end is not very important in considering the picaresque as a mode, for the sense of freedom experienced by the reader as event follows event is not to be removed by professions of strict design in human destiny. Even if, in the end, human freedom is revealed as an illusion, picaresque fiction frequently reminds us of the variety of the world as God's creation.

I want to emphasize this relationship between form and subject matter because what Alan Friedman says of the "stream of events" and the "open form" of modern fiction in *The Turn of the Novel* was always true of the picaresque.[20] Friedman suggests that the picaresque went on and on without any significance in its form. But Roderick Random's name suggests the obvious randomness of his life, and the English translation of a work closely resembling the picaresque, Sorel's *Comical History*, has the hero deciding at the

45

end to live "no more at random."[21] That the picaresque attempted to capture the chance appearance of life is beyond question. The stunning comeback of picaresque form may have something to do with Friedman's points about modern concepts of the cosmos, but in fact many modern works resemble their early models in asserting some meaning, whether human or divine, in the flux of events.

In arguing the importance of freedom in the picaresque, I have neglected some formal questions because they lay aside from my main purpose. Guillén, for example, tries to distinguish between the picaresque hero on the one hand and the fool and jester on the other. But if we consider freedom the central idea of the picaresque, the distinction seems unimportant. In fact, the picaresque hero seems to alternate roles, sometimes becoming the victim, sometimes the victimizer, sometimes rogue, sometimes fool. And given this pattern, the birth and deserved rank of the hero seem relatively unimportant. Roderick Random may be born to be a man of rank and wealth, but if he has to suffer the fate of the picaro, have chamber pots dumped on his head, be tricked by sharpers in London and starved as a soldier in the French army, his rank is of little functional importance. I also feel that a genuinely roguish figure like Gil Blas' servant or Colonel Jack's tutor is often sufficient to sustain a picaresque movement in a work even after the protagonist may have found a comfortable niche in society. Of course, at this point we tend to lose interest in the original hero. He can no longer say, with Felix Krull, "I am only able to live in conditions that leave my spirit and imagination completely free."[22]

The novel of manners, as it developed from Richardson through Austen, depicted a closed world of social forms.[23] Its opposite, the picaresque, presented the appearance of an open world through an open form. Some of the changes that Defoe, Lesage, and Smollett made in the picaresque paralleled developments in the novel of manners, but in *Moll Flanders, Roderick Random,* and *Gil Blas* none of them departs from the basic structure or the realistic treatment of "low themes of the picaresque." We know, or think we know, all about the rise and development of the novel; it is about time for a thorough work on the continuity of the picaresque and other fictional forms.

NOTES

1. See Joseph Ricapito, "Toward a Definition of the Picaresque," unpub. diss., Univ. of California, Los Angeles, 1966.
2. *Validity in Interpretation* (New Haven: Yale Univ. Press, 1967), pp. 78–89.
3. See Peter N. Dunn, *Castillo Solórzano and the Decline of the Spanish Novel* (Oxford: Basil Blackwell, 1952), pp. 116, 120, for an occasional comparison. One incident involving the theme of "the trepanner trepann'd" is very much like Defoe.
4. (Princeton: Princeton University Press, 1971). Some of my remarks on this work as well as on the works of A. A. Parker and Stuart Miller will appear in a forthcoming review in *Studies in the Novel*.
5. *Literature as System*, p. 120.
6. *Ibid.*, p. 77.
7. Maximillian E. Novak, *Economics and the Fiction of Daniel Defoe* (Berkeley: Univ. of California Press, 1962), p. 67. See also Ian Watt, *The Rise of the Novel* (Berkeley: Univ. of California Press, 1959), pp. 94–96.
8. *Literature and the Delinquent* (Edinburgh: Edinburgh Univ. Press, 1967), p. 19.
9. *Ibid.*, p. 127.
10. *The Rogue*, trans. James Mabbe [1623] (London: Constable, 1924), III, 127.
11. *The Life and Death of Young Lazarillo, Son and Heir of Old Lazarillo De Tormes* (London: J. Leake, 1688), p. 172.
12. *The Picaresque Novel* (Cleveland: Press of Case Western Reserve Univ., 1967).
13. This appears under the frontispiece of an edition published in Edinburgh without publisher or date.
14. *The Life of Estevanillo Gonzales*, in *The Spanish Libertines*, trans. John Stevens (London: Samuel Bunchley, 1707), p. 344.
15. At the A.S.E.C.S. conference, a member of the audience asked me whether I thought that the main character in Diderot's *Le Neveu de Rameau* could be classed as a picaro. I said that I did not think so, though on reconsideration I find fascinating the notion that the materialistic picaro might have evolved in this direction.
16. *Lazarillo, or the Excellent History of Lazarillo de Tormes*, trans. David Rowland (London: William Leake, 1653), sig. T2.
17. See George Starr, *Defoe and Casuistry* (Princeton: Princeton Univ. Press, 1971).
18. Antoine Adam argues convincingly that the libertine ethic was essentially aristocratic, but insofar as the libertine was an outsider who regarded his own freedom in matters of sex and sensual pleasures as beyond the usual rules of society, he had his counterpart in the rogue who also sang of his freedom and criticized society as a cheat. The resemblance is obvious enough in Samuel Richardson's *Clarissa Harlowe*,

where Lovelace can appeal to the vicious Joseph Leman on common grounds of self-interest and a realism toward notions of virtue. Thus the rogue and libertine join in a war against the middle class. See Antoine, *Les Libertines au XVIIᵉ siècle* (Paris: Buchet/Chastel, 1964), pp. 7–18; and Richardson, *Clarissa Harlowe* (London: Everyman Library, 1932), II, 147–53 (Letter XLI).

19. *The English Rogue*, (London: George Routledge, 1928), p. 164. The shift in libertine thought from a static contemplation of God to the joys of motion appears in one of the earliest libertine writers, Ferrante Pallovicino, who in one work has a cloistered nun tell a disguised angel, "Oh, how gladly would we exchange the imaginary Paradice for the Liberty you have to travel! How can you blame so unparallelled a Blessing? Motion is even the Life of Life: It is the Property of the most sublime Beings, and is therefore most coveted by the greatest Minds. Behold the Sun, the unwearied Sun; consider the Moon, the Stars and Planets: they never stop, or take any Rest; but delight in their continual Motion." The Angel makes the appropriate response about God as the unmoving mover but sympathizes with the nun's desires for motion and her hatred of sexual repression. See *The Celestial Divorce* (London: William Boreham, 1718), pp. 116–17.

20. (New York: Oxford Univ. Press, 1966), pp. xvi–xviii, 35–37.

21. Charles Sorel, *The Comical History of Francion* (London: Francis Leach, 1655), Bk. XII, p. 40. This is an accurate translation of the original "*au hassard*."

22. Thomas Mann, *Confessions of Felix Krull: Confidence Man,* trans. Denver Lindley (New York: Knopf, 1955), p. 31.

23. The moral crisis of Jane Austen's *Mansfield Park* occurs when Sir Thomas Bertram returns to his house to discover his children and their companions indulging in a performance of Kotzbue's *Lover's Vows*. Sir Thomas orders an end to the performance at once, because he finds the possible effect of assuming the roles of Kotzbue's characters upon the personalities of the young actors terrifying in its moral implications. Whereas the evil effects of masquerades on the social fabric was one of the standard subjects of the novel of manners, the freedom to change personalities, costumes, and names was always one of the distinguishing marks of the picaresque.

Pinpoint of Eternity:

The Sufficient Moment in Literature

Peter Salm

ARISTOTLE HELD in the seventh chapter of the *Poetics* that tragedy must have a beginning, middle, and end, that a beginning is that which does not follow anything by necessity, and that an end is that which does follow something else, but itself is followed by nothing. There is no need to assume that Aristotle's remarks should be applied to tragedy alone. They were meant to apply to all the genres of literature then practiced. He had after all subsumed Homer's epics under his definition of tragedy and used the words poetry and tragedy interchangeably.

Each fresh attempt at understanding Aristotle's passage leaves one with a sense of frustration. What is it that, in Butcher's translation, "does not follow anything else by cause or necessity"? It is the "beginning" of a literary work. The definition of "middle" and "end" follows naturally from the first assumption. But from the vantage point of our age, such a way of bracketing reality into discrete units is not possible, except as a convenient means of anchoring our awareness.

There are no beginnings, middles, and ends in the stream of human events; what one person experiences as an end, the other will consider a beginning. Causes and necessities are endless and without beginnings. Only the imaginative faculty can give form to events, and having done this, select those events which will conform.

Aristotle praises Homer for centering his epic poems around an action that "in our sense of the word is one," and we must wonder how Homer came to such a unified vision. It is not the same as the

49

unity of a single character such as Ulysses, as Aristotle assures us in the eighth chapter of the *Poetics*; nor is such unity properly represented by a theme like "the wrath of Achilles." Neither of these would serve adequately to explain the selection of materials included in the epic. What the poet creates—if he is successful—is the complete fusion of a given sequence of events with a vital idea or concept which to him arises from that sequence. This is not to say by any means that either the fable or the concept exists as a separate entity before the creation of the work. The events of the plot are selected and shaped according to an idea—and the idea and plot can no longer be isolated in terms of either an ethical or philosophical concept on the one hand, or a chronological series of events on the other. The successful fusion of the two results in a category of human endeavor which is neither philosophy nor history, but art.

We ought not to quibble with the circularity of a process in the course of which data are gathered according to an idea which in turn is determined by the data. It is a creative circularity, the hermeneutic circle par excellence, in which the mind flits back and forth between idea and fact.[1] Concepts are shaped and modified by experience, which in turn is selected and arranged according to the concept. In works of literature, neither the conceptual nor the factual aspects are stabilized, until the process of artistic creation, and indeed of the reader's empathic re-creation, is complete; and when it is, the idea inherent in the work is so enmeshed in its texture that it will be impossible to isolate it from its poetic realization. By the same token, the concrete facts structured in accordance with their poetic "idea" are imbued with a flavor and significance which irretrievably set them off from their neutral and empirical ground. The meaning of a poem is not to be located in an abstraction derived from it nor in a generalization, but in a specific aesthetic quality which is its essence. Idea and factuality are fused into a new alloy, as it were, different from the addition of its component parts and not reducible to them. It should not be difficult to evolve a general topology of literature according to whether the stress is on the particular or on the universal. W. K. Wimsatt takes an impressive initiative toward such a goal for English literature in his article "The

Concrete Universal," first published in 1947.[2] Clearly a literature dealing with types rather than realistically drawn characters, as well as literature exemplifying lucid and well-known concepts of virtue, love, or patriotism, puts its stress on universality. Seventeenth-century France would preeminently belong to that movement and so would the Augustan period in England. We find its theoretical echo in the *Discourses* of Joshua Reynolds; it is succinctly stated in the famous passage from Chapter X of *Rasselas*, where Dr. Johnson writes: "The business of a poet . . . is to examine, not the individual, but the species . . . he does not number the streaks of the tulip. . . ." It is also among the propositions in Pope's *Essay on Criticism*.

The opposite position is clearly an important tendency in romanticism, not in Shelley but in Keats, not in Hölderlin but in Heine. In his marginalia to a text by Joshua Reynolds, William Blake writes: "To generalize is to be an idiot. To particularize is above all the distinction of merit."

An account of this preference for detail or generalization might well deepen an understanding of literary sensibilities in varying periods. Realism and naturalism will emphasize the concrete detail —but the ideational content of Flaubert's *Madame Bovary* need therefore not be less clear than that of Richardson's *Pamela: or Virtue Rewarded*. The question is rather how the detail is pressed into the service of its correlated idea and how one is affected by the other. Such a history may well be worth pursuing.

However, I should like the concrete-universal in this study to appear as a central aesthetic phenomenon rather than as an historical point of reference. The illustrative examples chosen here merely indicate that an historical account would add to the understanding of certain developments. The aesthetic fusion of the concrete-universal is that which in Hegel's *Aesthetik* appears as *das sinnliche Scheinen der Idee* (the sensuous radiance of the idea) and in Coleridge, in his comment on the excellence of Shakespeare, as the "union and interpenetration of the universal and particular." Wordsworth, in the *Essay Supplementary to the Preface to Lyrical Ballads*, sees it as "ethereal and transcendent poetry, yet incapable to sustain her existence without sensuous incarnation." In Camus'

Rebel, poetry is the "reconciliation, without apparent effort, of the unique with the universal."

In pointing to an imperious human need for organizing experience into patterned entities, I do not mean to explain the phenomenon of poetry or literary creativity. The poetic act does, however, exemplify a basic need to relate discrete and disparate data to each other and to express them as new and significant wholes. This in itself has nothing to do with Aristotelian imitation or romantic expression. It is a process which imaginatively reiterates the norms and communal insights of language itself. A view of language enunciated by Benjamin Lee Whorf in his book *Language, Thought and Reality* makes the analogy plausible: "And every language is a vast pattern-system, different from others, in which are culturally ordained the forms and categories by which the personality not only communicates, but also analyzes nature, notices or neglects types of relationships and phenomena, channels his reasoning and builds the house of his consciousness."[3]

Clearly, this shaping or patterning impulse is not confined to the artist; it is indispensable to a creative consciousness. Shelley has often been criticized for blurring the distinctions between what is and is not poetry in his *Defence of Poetry* by calling the poets the "unacknowledged legislators of the world." I believe that this criticism is mistaken. Clearly Shelley made the distinction between poetry and non-poetry not on the basis of a specific calling or profession but rather on the basis of poetry as a principle of expression pervading to a greater or lesser extent all human endeavor. A poet more than others embodies this principle, though he by no means holds exclusive rights to it. Such a conception need be no less precise than the one usually associated with neoclassicism and New Criticism, which sternly derive their definition from acknowledged poetic artifacts. I believe that poetry, in renovating speech and sensibility, is deeply implicated in a creative process which is not the exclusive province of any group or profession. For this reason Shelley was not vague or imprecise, but profoundly perceptive when he said:

> In the infancy of society every author is necessarily a poet, because language itself is poetry. . . . Every original language near

to its source is in itself the chaos of a cyclic poem: the copiousness of lexicography and the distinctions of grammar are the works of a later age, and are merely the catalogue and the form of the creations of poetry.

Before Shelley, Vico in the early eighteenth century and Herder in its closing decades had seen a common impulse behind language and poetry, and in our time we may well find links between the structuralist critics' concern with language systems and the predominant romantic views concerning the origin of poetry. Geoffrey Hartman, for example, in an article on structuralism boldly speculates that "Grammar, language, and poetry might . . . be looked at . . . as a second power and second mode of naming. We could think of literature as a hoard of sacred or magical words that the poet, as secular priest, makes available."[4]

My own awareness of the importance to literature of the concrete-universal first came to me through a preoccupation with Goethe's *Faust* and subsequently with Goethe's natural science.[5] The perceptions of the poet Goethe and those of the natural scientist Goethe are closely related and can be subsumed under a single creative activity which accounts for both. The poetic vision in Goethe's plant morphology and color theory is never at odds with what is meant to be its scientific or philosophic truth.

Goethe may have been the last of the great unfragmented minds. His natural science gave body and strength to his poetry, and his poetic faculty gave his writings in natural philosophy a quality of controlled sensuous involvement not usually associated with scientific writings. His sensibility was militantly undivided, and to preserve its wholeness, Goethe fought a lonely and futile battle against the application of mathematics to natural phenomena. "What is correct in mathematics, except its own exactitude?" is recorded as one of his maxims. Mathematical theories and hypotheses were "cradle songs to lull the students." On the other hand, a highly advanced sensibility favored by circumstances could advance upon and participate in an "archetypal form," which would reveal its concrete presence as well as its "theory." The most celebrated instance is Goethe's *Urpflanze*, the archetypal plant, which he had envisioned while observing specimens in the botanical garden of

Palermo. The excitement produced in him by such a vision can be felt in a letter to his beloved friend, Frau von Stein:

> The archetypal plant will be the strangest creature in the world; nature herself shall be envious of it. With this model and the key to it one is in a position to invent an infinity of plants which will have to be consistent with each other, that is to say, even if they do not exist, they yet could exist, not at all as picturesque or poetic shadows but containing an inner truth and necessity. [June 9, 1787][6]

It should be understood that Goethe's vision of a leafy configuration was not a Platonic idea, because it was not static and immutable, nor were its concrete manifestations faded copies. This configuration contained *actu et potentia* all other forms of dicotyledonous plant life and extended in time as well as in space. It is perhaps tempting to dismiss such visions as mystical and cabbalistic quackery, yet Goethe's place in the establishment of plant and animal morphology as a science is fairly secure.

Both the *Urpflanze* in biology and the "circle" in Goethe's theory of color are "visible ideas" to which Goethe liked to refer as *offenbare Geheimnisse* (self-revealing mysteries). Remarkably enough he also used this expression for his poetry, especially his *Faust*. The fulfilled moment which Faust seeks can be interpreted as the final metamorphosis of a crude instance of such a "moment" at the beginning of the play, just as the leaves of the plant undergo progressive transformations until the "cruder juices" are refined to become the proper food for the calix, stamen, and pistils of the blossom.

The remarkable aspect of the blossom is its spatial compression and the simultaneity of its development. The spaces between the nodes of the plant's stem are reduced almost to a point, and what had been successive development in the growing plant is now a simultaneous presence in the flower. This "highest moment" is also the moment of sexual union whose result, the seed, contains "actually and potentially" the entire cycle of its metamorphosis.

I should like to call attention to a single *Augenblick*, the most highly developed instant in the *Faust* poem, describe its characteristics and perhaps use it as a model for other such moments in liter-

54

ature; for it seems to me that Goethe's *Augenblick* in *Faust* had an objective presence in the substance of the wager. But rather than merely erecting its luminous presence before the mind's eye, Goethe attempted, successfully, I believe, to search for a culminating human experience by probing the limits of poetry.

The third act of the second part of *Faust* contains the phantasmagoric encounter between Faust, lord of a medieval castle, and Helen of Troy, who is conjured up from Homer's past. She is not a ghostly figure but a concrete and wholly rendered poetic character. Before the actual encounter with Faust, she is seen in Menelaus' palace; Troy has been sacked and Helena restored to her shores. The nordic Mephisto is uncomfortable and out of place in Greek antiquity, but his presence is felt behind the disguise of a lady-in-waiting. He proceeds to reproach Helena for her past escapades, including not only those known from Homer or Virgil, but those from subsequent medieval legends as well. There is history as well as legendary reality (if, for the purpose of our consideration, we regard Homer's Helena as "historical"). Mephisto accuses Helena of having consorted with Theseus, Patroclus, and Achilles, as well as with Paris. And Helena appears to be aware of her place in human consciousness and of the precarious play of forces upon which her poetic actuality depends. Mephisto mercilessly exploits her apparent weakness until he gains a momentary victory. Helena faints and her reality disintegrates before our eyes:

> *Verwirre wüsten Sinnes Aberwitz nicht gar.*
> *Selbst jetzo, welche denn ich sei, ich weiss es nicht.*
> [8875–76]

> Do not derange completely my distracted wit.
> Even now, whoever I may be, I cannot tell.

And then as Mephisto presses on, her concreteness recedes into the night from which she sprang:

> *Ich als Idol, ihm dem Idol verband ich mich.*
> *Es war ein Traum, so segen die Worte selbst.*
> *Ich schwinde hin und werde selbst mir ein Idol.*
> [8879–81]

I, as an idol, joined an idol;
it was a dream, the Gods themselves declare it.
I fade away and now become an idol to myself.[7]

This regression, however, is a remarkable poetic process which in one instant unfolds layer upon layer of a phantasmagorical moment. History is about to be telescoped in the moment of the encounter between Faust and Helena. Helena herself has become an amalgam of poetic concreteness and legendary idea, but the fusion in a moment of self-awareness yields with clarity its original components. The seams are laid bare when Helena, the heroine, steps out of her emblematic nature and becomes "an idol to myself." The self-conscious separation of the temporal self from its timeless meaning makes clear the ephemeral quality of their momentary union, a point of poetic ignition which is gone by the time one's attention is drawn to it.

With respect to this centrally poetic phenomenon, the analogies between Goethe's science and poetry are particularly instructive. In that sense, Helena in the context of the medieval scenario of the episode is the *nunc stans*, the eternal present, bridging three millennia of history. It is a poetic unity in the strictest and most paradoxical sense, where time and space are condensed into a point of pure meaning.

Goethe's "archetypal plant" is poetic science as well as scientific poetry. The abstract concept is completely fused with its visual form. One has no existence without the other. They have been irreversibly fused by "action" (*handeln*), a creative dynamism which in Goethe's case is above all the making of poetry, and it seems reasonable to interpret the word *handeln*, which occurs frequently in his maxims and in his other writings, as *poetic* activity: "Theory and practice are in steady conflict with one another—whatever union between them can be effected by reflection is illusory; only action can unite them" (*Jubiläumsaugsabe* XXXIX, 115). The poet accomplishes something which is rationally impossible; he has not abstracted from experience but given it full particularity; nor has he merely exemplified an underlying philosophical idea. Rather, he has fused the two poles of human possibilities. The impossibility and paradoxical quality of the concrete-universal is at the heart of poetry. To wish to be at the same time completely concrete and completely universal is to aspire to be divine. This is an important meaning of the impossible yet imperious Faustian wish: to live the moment of eternity.

> *Werd'ich zum Augenblicke sagen:*
> *Verweile doch! du bist so schön!*
> *Dann magst du mich in Fesseln schlagen,*
> *Dann will ich gern zugrunde gehn!*

> If ever I should tell the moment:
> Oh stay! You are so beautiful!
> Then you may cast me into chains,
> Then I wish to be annihilated![8]

For this ultimate concrete-universal, Faust is willing to go to hell. Yet he is prepared to wager his soul on his conviction that even Satan cannot give him this greatest of all gifts. If he could, perdition would not be too high a price. Perhaps Faust remembers that in the fourth chapter of the Gospel of St. Luke, it was Satan who had tempted Christ with a similar moment:

> 5 And the devil, taking him up into an high mountain, showed unto him all the kingdoms of the world in a moment of time.
> 6 And the devil said unto him, All this power will I give thee, and the glory of them: for that is delivered unto me; and to whomsoever I will give it.
> 7 If thou therefore will worship me, all shall be thine.[9]

"All the kingdoms of the world in a moment of time"—this moment, a mere pinprick, from the Greek *stigme chronou*, is the most irresistible gift offered to man. In both Luke and Goethe's *Faust*, it is offered by the devil. It is illicit because it usurps the prerogative of divinity; yet Faust's ambition is both sinful and sacred. He is saved despite his guilt, or rather because of it.

Faust's impossible ambition to experience the supreme moment is in fact Goethe's poetic articulation of an ancient and persistent

57

dream. In the second century A.D., Luke represented it as a tempta-tion. At the beginning of the fourteenth century, Dante saw it as an Empyrean vision of the divine in the thirty-third and last canto of the *Divine Comedy*:

O abbondante grazia ond'io presunsi
ficcar lo viso per la luce etterna,
tanto che la veduta vi consunsi!

Nel suo profondo vidi che s'interna,
legato con amore in un volume,
ciò che per l'universo si squaderna:

sustanze e accidenti e lor costume,
quasi conflati insieme, per tal modo
che cio ch'i' dico è un semplice lume.

La forma universal di questo nodo
credo ch'i' vidi, perche piu di largo,
dicendo questo, mi sento ch'i' godo.

Un punto solo m'e maggior letargo
che venticinque secoli alla 'impresa,
che fè Nettuno ammirar l'ombra d'Argo.

O abounding grace by which I dared
to fix my look on the Eternal Light
so long that my sight was spent!

In its depth I saw that it contained,
bound by love in one volume,
that which is scattered in leaves through the universe,

substances and accidents and their relations
as it were fused together in such a way
and what I tell of is one simple light.

I believe that I saw the universal form
of that node, because in telling of it
I feel my joy expand.

A single point makes for me deeper oblivion
than twenty centuries upon the enterprise
that made Neptune wonder at the shadow of the Argo.[10]

And at the beginning of the nineteenth century William Blake
wrote in the "Auguries of Innocence":

To see the world in a Grain of Sand
And a Heaven in a Wild Flower.
Hold Infinity in the Palm of your Hand
And Eternity in an Hour.

And in our time we come upon a similar notion in Jorge Luis
Borges, realized most epigrammatically in the two-page *Parable of
the Palace*, and in a more broadly narrative fashion in *The Aleph*.

The Yellow Emperor, in the *Parable*, shows the poet his palace
and goes with him through his vast, labyrinthine domain spread
over terraces "like gradins of an almost boundless amphitheater"
traversed by many rivers and streams. "At the foot of the penulti-
mate tower" the poet recites his immortal poem, of which the text
has been lost. Near the end of the *Parable* we read:

> There are those who believe that [the composition] consisted of
> a line of verse; others, of a single word. What is certain, and
> incredible, is that all the enormous palace was, in its most mi-
> nute details, there in the poem, with each illustrious porcelain
> and each design on each porcelain and the penumbrae and the
> light of each dawn and twilight, and each unfortunate or happy
> instant in the glorious dynasties of mortals, of gods and dragons
> that had inhabited it from the unfathomable past.[11]

The narrator in *The Aleph* finds himself at the "ineffable center"
of his story while standing uncomfortably, somewhat against his
better judgment, on a stairway leading up from the dark and clut-
tered basement of a house in Buenos Aires. There the Aleph hov-
ered before him: a luminous apparition two or three centimeters
in diameter:

In that single, gigantic instant I saw millions of acts both delightful and awful; not one of them amazed me more than the fact that all of them occupied the same point in space, without overlapping or transparency. What my eyes beheld was simultaneous, but what I shall now write down will be successive, because language is successive. . . . On the dark part of the step, toward the right, I saw a small iridescent sphere of almost unbearable brilliance.[12]

It remains to be established that the "point" in literary time and space is the concrete-universal in its most radical and paradoxical sense. Experience, infinitely condensed until it is devoid of the dimensions of time and space, reaches the universality of a mathematical concept outside time and space. On the other hand, the "concreteness" of such a moment is vouchsafed by the inherent experiences which are not illustrations of an abstract principle but integral aspects of its mode of being. To a greater or lesser extent, the condensation of experience into the *Augenblick* or the "grain of sand" or the "node of light" is also the manner in which literary expression culminates in images, metaphors, and symbols or "objective correlatives," for these are the points of ignition where successive events are fused into simultaneity.

The continuing vitality of this *topos* can be felt by passages such as the following from *Krapp's Last Tape*:

> *Krapp*: Just been listening to that stupid bastard I took myself for thirty years ago, hard to believe I was ever as bad as that. Thank God that's all done with anyway. [*Pause*] The eyes she had! [*Broods, realizes he is recording silence, switches off, broods, finally.*] Everything there, everything, all the—[*Realizes this is not being recorded, switches on.*] Everything there, everything on this old muckball, all the light and dark and famine and feasting of . . . [*hesitates*] . . . the ages! [*In a shout.*] Yes![13]

What are these moments of intensity? As Goethe knew very well, the fusion of experience and theory is rationally impossible and can be grasped only during brief moments of poetic consummation. It cannot be maintained over great stretches of discourse. The ultimate goal of such a moment is the lyrical outcry which contains the world, or, as in Borges' *Parable*, a single word for a kingdom.

In lyric poetry as well as in a novel, a vision of the whole must go along with every detail and narrative excursion. Such an overall vision is never logical but has the specific aesthetic coherence to which it belongs. A longer work can on occasion compress, as if by magic, the successiveness of a long plot into simultaneity and a greatly intensified present tense. Part of the fascination of such an exquisite moment is its paradoxical nature: the pinpoint of "now" should stand for a life and the "here" should stand for spatial infinity.

The irreconcilable oppositions seldom appear as simple paradoxes of time and space. Goethe's organic outlook on life and literature was based on a dialectic of an endless series of polarities, including male and female, light and darkness, good and evil. Polar opposites seem to infect one another and one pair can symbolize another, but the prototypal opposition in literature is successiveness and simultaneity. While Goethe explicitly made the all-encompassing "moment" the center of his greatest drama, it has been the concern of many subsequent writers.

The title of the short story by E. M. Forster "The Eternal Moment" (1905) is also the title of a successful novel written by its protagonist, Miss Raby. As a wrinkled and famous woman, she returns to the town of Vorter in the Dolomites, the site of a youthful encounter with a young mountaineer:

> . . . the incident upon the mountain had been one of the great moments of her life . . . perhaps the greatest, certainly the most enduring. . . . There was more reality in it than in all the years of success and varied achievement which had followed, and which had rendered it possible. A presumptuous boy had taken her to the gates of heaven; and, though she would not enter with him, the eternal remembrance of the vision had made life seem endurable and good.[14]

The return to Vorter has a catalytic effect on the heroine, the hardened and sophisticated authoress. Miss Raby's "moment" is as charged with contradiction as the *Augenblick* had been in Goethe's

Faust. The sophisticated lady had been overtly outraged and secretly enchanted by the clumsy advances of a peasant boy. As a remembrance, the incident was both ludicrous and of profound significance for Miss Raby; but, above all, it was a pinpoint of time and space, a *stigme* which both symbolized and contained eternity.

With so superbly conscious an artist as Thomas Mann, the nature and function of time was almost an obsession. It is close to the heart of the matter in *The Magic Mountain* (1924). For Hans Castorp, time devoid of vital experience appears foreshortened in retrospect, while even one intensely lived moment may appear both significant and long. Mann concentrates the polar possibilities of the experience of time into the chapter entitled "Snow." Against the doctor's orders, Hans Castorp has ventured forth to ski on the slopes above the Swiss sanatorium, high above Davos. He is surprised by a sudden blinding blizzard and loses his way. Inadvertently, he walks in a circle, and instead of returning to the safety of the sanatorium he finds that he has merely reached his original footprints in the snow. Exhausted, he discerns the outlines of an alpine hay shelter through the whirling snow and finds makeshift protection by leaning against one of its sides. Castorp gently drifts into dreamy unconsciousness, and in the grip of the icy blasts, envisions a Mediterranean civilization, a serene and idyllic social scene. Yet, hidden in a recess of a temple, Castorp witnesses the enactment of a bloody sacrifice. The childlike happiness of the society he beholds is obtained at a gruesome price.

When Castorp's exhaustion subsides and he returns to full consciousness, he is convinced that much time has passed, for what he has seen with so much beautiful detail might have taken weeks to absorb. So when he looks at his watch, the old reliable pocket watch inherited from his father, he is startled: "Preposterous! Could it be he had lain here in the snow only ten minutes or so, while all these scenes of horror and delight and those presumptuous thoughts had spun themselves in his brain, and the hexagonal hurly vanished as it came?"[15] The snowstorm had come and gone. The bright sun had returned before he lost consciousness. Castorp's senses had been exceptionally keen. Here is a modern and transparent example of an image of historical time and ample geographical space which is concentrated and telescoped into a single vision. Hans Castorp is startled by this trick of his imagination, so that one can see the justice of Mann's statement in the essay "The Making of the Magic Mountain," appended to the American translation:

> [The book] depicts the hermetic enchantment of its young hero within the timeless, and thus seeks to abrogate time itself by means of the technical device that attempts to give complete presentness at any given moment to the entire world of ideas that it comprises. It tries, in other words, to establish a magical *nunc stans*, to use a formula of the scholastics.[16]

And the eminent Germanist, Hermann Weigand, confirms the success of Mann's undertaking:

> Here, in the affirmation of life, worked out as a principle transcending the dualism and dialectics of the two pedagogical fencers we have without question the spiritual climax of the whole novel. Hovering there, between life and death, Hans Castorp is for a moment elevated to a position of clarity, the acme of his capacity to span the poles of cosmic experience. The vision fades almost at once, but it leaves a residual effect on his personality that time cannot obliterate.[17]

It is one thing poetically to achieve the "eternal moment" and quite another to make the moment the subject of a fable. Forster's "Eternal Moment" tends toward the latter, though the entire short story is a multiple projection of the title. The young heroine's erotic experience on the mountain, its sublimation in her successful novel, and the ludicrously painful attempt to recapture the essence of the "eternal moment" by returning to the scene where it had all happened so many years earlier—all these envelop each other in concentric links through time. The "moment" itself, however, is not seen from the inside. It is recounted by Miss Raby as an event preceding the story proper. We learn of the "eternal moment" by exposition and are witnesses to its effects on all who come under its influence.

Writers like Goethe and Thomas Mann, whose essential mode is irony, are by necessity involved with polarities. The need for psychic elbow room between commitments calls for a loosening-up of the connection between word and reference, not by any means in order to create obscurity, but rather to create multiple references where precision is essential to maintain the effect of irony. The ironic mode is based on polarities, almost by definition. While it holds the contraries apart and keeps them from fusing, it still relates them to each other.

It is different in the "eternal moment." The compression into a single center leaves neither room nor time for movement between opposing poles. And therefore there is no room for irony within the context of reconciled paradoxes.

Kierkegaard castigated the romantics because their "romantic longing for infinity hollows out actuality." Infinity, Kierkegaard believed, must be sought within reality and not beyond it. "As man shall not put asunder what God has joined together, so neither shall man join together what God has put asunder, for such a sickly longing is simply a longing to have the perfect before its time."[18] Kierkegaard therefore believed in the necessity of irony in literature, though he conceded that irony is not truth but a *way* to truth. The moment of truth itself is a chiliastic vision, direct, unmetaphorical, and cleansed of irony.

NOTES

1. See Heidegger, *Sein und Zeit* (Halle a.d.S., 1929), p. 153; Wellek and Warren, *Theory of Literature*, 2nd ed. (New York, 1956), p. 247.
2. PMLA, LXII (March, 1947), 262–80; also in *The Verbal Icon* (New York, 1958), pp. 69–83.
3. (Cambridge, Mass., 1956), p. 252.
4. "Structuralism: The Anglo-American Adventure," *Yale French Studies* (October, 1966), p. 149.
5. See my *Poem as Plant: A Biological View of Goethe's* Faust (Cleveland, 1971).
6. Translation mine.
7. This and the preceding translation are mine.
8. Translation mine.
9. This passage was pointed out to me by Herbert S. Long, Professor of Classics at Case Western Reserve University, and I gratefully acknowledge my debt to him.
10. *The Divine Comedy*, tr. John D. Sinclair (New York, 1958) III, 482–83.

11. *A Personal Anthology*, tr. Carmen Feldman Alvarez del Olmo (London, 1968), p. 88.
12. *The Aleph and Other Stories*, tr. Norman Thomas di Giovanni in collaboration with the author (New York, 1971), p. 13.
13. Samuel Beckett, *Krapp's Last Tape* (London, 1965), pp. 17–18.
14. E. M. Forster, *The Eternal Moment and Other Stories* (London, 1928), p. 179.
15. *The Magic Mountain*, tr. H. T. Lowe-Porter (New York, 1958), p. 497.
16. *Ibid.*, p. 725.
17. Hermann Weigand, *Thomas Mann's Novel* Der Zauberberg (New York, 1933), p. 23.
18. Soren Kierkegaard, *The Concept of Irony, with constant reference to Socrates*, tr. Lee Capel (New York, 1964), p. 341.

Benjamin Constant and the Enlightenment

Beatrice C. Fink

THE BASIC FACTS of Benjamin Constant's cosmopolitan life have long been in the public domain: his Swiss birth in 1767 and Protestant upbringing; his brief periods of formal training in Germany and Scotland; the crucial stay in Weimar in 1804, during which he became acquainted with Goethe and Schiller; his sojourns at Coppet in Mme de Staël's entourage; his role as legislator and statesman during the Consulate, the Hundred Days, the Second Restoration, and the July Monarchy.

Additional light was thrown on Constantian biography by Alfred Roulin's publication in 1952 of the *Journaux intimes*, the only version of Constant's diaries considered authoritative today.[1] The *Journaux* testify to the voluminous reading and meditating that took place during the 1804 visit to Germany. They also contain references to an "ouvrage de politique" he was writing in 1806. The full significance of these notations, however, was not felt until the seven-volume *Oeuvres manuscrites de 1810* was put at the disposal of scholars by the Bibliothèque Nationale less than a decade ago.[2] These manuscripts contain nearly all of Constant's pre-1810 writings which had remained unpublished. They reveal the existence of several heretofore unknown works such as histories of Frederick the Great and Ferdinand of Brunswick. They contain the first French translation of Godwin's *Enquiry Concerning Political Justice*, followed by a commentary on that work. They also establish within reasonable limits the dates of composition of certain items that were published at a much later time, in particular a number of essays in the 1829 *Mélanges de littérature et de politique*.

Most importantly, they totally discredit Elizabeth Schermerhorn's image of Constant writing his best-known political treatises "at a white heat," in response to events of the day.[3] On the contrary, the *O.m.* demonstrate conclusively that these treatises derive from two earlier works, the *Principes de politique applicables à tous les gouvernements* and the *Fragments d'un ouvrage abandonné sur la possibilité d'une constitution républicaine dans un grand pays.* These works, whose very titles have an eighteenth-century ring, make up more than half of the manuscripts' seven volumes. They constitute a stockpile, so to speak, from which the author drew for chapters of *De l'esprit de conquête et de l'usurpation*, the published or 1815 version of the *Principes de politique*, the *Réflexions sur les constitutions*, etc.

Benefiting from these and other newly available manuscripts, a number of recent publications alter the traditional *Adolphe*-enshrouded image of Constant.[4] Scholarly studies of the non-fictional works naturally take into consideration the author's eighteenth-century cultural and intellectual heritage.[5] The task of systematically assessing the full impact of eighteenth-century thinkers on Constant, however, remains unfinished. While the scope of this paper can hardly encompass an undertaking of such magnitude, its objective is to serve as a prolegomenon by centering analysis on certain links between Constant and selected writers. Among the various thought currents instrumental in formulating Constantian philosophy, that of teleological historicism appears to be vital and relatively unexplored. I have, accordingly, emphasized its importance in the body of my arguments.

Apart from their textual revelations, the *O.m.* indicate that Constant formulated the essence of his philosophical and political system at an earlier date than has been supposed, namely in the eighteenth century proper or in the initial years of the nineteenth, at a time when he was discovering Montesquieu and the great German minds of the day. The diary entry for January 28, 1804, for example, reads in part: "Continué les extraits d'Herder. . . . Lu Montesquieu. Quel coup d'oeil rapide et profond. . . . Conversation avec Robinson, disciple de Schelling. . . . Passé la soirée avec Schiller" (*Oeuvres*, p. 261).

Consider first his links with Montesquieu. Constant's political treatises repeatedly refer to *L'Esprit des lois*, which they resemble not only in form but also in the institutional framework they deploy and in the implication that liberty may result from a correct organization of the state. For Constant as for Montesquieu, the essential question is not so much where the locus of power resides as how power can be controlled. Constant's *bête noire* was *l'arbitraire*, i.e., unchecked authority. This expression appears frequently in his theoretical writings and reflects fears generated by the revolution of 1789 and by the Napoleonic experience. Constant shares with Montesquieu, as do all eighteenth-century philosophers of Lockean extraction, a fundamental reverence for individual rights, thus subscribing to what Isaiah Berlin calls negative liberty or liberty from outside interference.[6] In fact, Constant's fight for individual liberty was waged, above and beyond his theoretical writings, as orator, pamphleteer, and defender of persecuted Protestants, much as Voltaire's before him. Constant does not, however, share Montesquieu's faith in legislation as social panacea, a faith Montesquieu held in common with a number of Encyclopaedists. Nor, on the other hand, does he go so far as Godwin, who would gradually dispense with all governmental control mechanisms. He does retain Montesquieu's concept of laws, positive and organic, as tools for guaranteeing rights and decentralizing power. In the realm of economic policy he takes a similar stand by adhering to the laissez-faire doctrines of Adam Smith, also a subject of his intellectual admiration.

One could at this point dismiss Constant as merely another early nineteenth-century liberal. Ample precedent exists for so doing. Behind the individualistic libertarian, however, lies an *alter ego*, less pragmatic, sensitized by a different current of ideas, in fact a genuine resident of Becker's "Heavenly City." This is where one begins to think of Herder, Rousseau, Condorcet, Godwin, and others who endowed history with meaning and purpose, steadfastly believing in the perfectibility of man, a march from darkness to light.

The concept of the meaningfulness of history, of the great march forward in which mankind advances from one stage of psychological and social development to the next, runs through all of Constant's theoretical writings. The five-volume *De la religion* and the posthumous *Du polythéisme romain* are richly illustrated elaborations of this theme, as are a number of shorter works, including an unpublished essay on equality.[7] The *O.m.* contain a two-part disquisition on the perfectibility of the human race.[8] A diary entry for January, 1805, informs us that it was meant to be an introduction to selections from Herder's *Ideen zur Philosophie der Geschichte der Menschheit*, which Constant refers to elsewhere as "un superbe ouvrage" (*Oeuvres*, p. 444).

Constant's thesis in *Perfectibilité* is that individual and society alike are governed by the force of ideas in a progressive march where nothing is left to chance, where everything participates in a "compulsion générale." He divides the history of civilization into a series of epochs in which individual authority gives way to that of the class and eventually to that of the nation as a whole. The progression begins with theocratic slavery and reaches the so-called contemporary era of legal conventions via civil or lay slavery, feudalism and hereditary nobility. Each stage contains elements of the next and is a stepping stone towards the ultimate goal of mankind. On a factual plane, the end of the process is social equality, reminiscent of Rousseau's ideal "état civil."

Constant's interpretation of history is basically non-empirical, despite his assertions to the contrary and his efforts at historiography.[9] Perfectibility denotes a norm, one which the author identifies with a tendency towards equality. The norm is an ethical one, given that Constant variously identifies equality with truth, justice, liberty, happiness, and enlightenment.

A number of similarities with Herder's historical idealism emerge, Constant's claim that "c'est aux idées seules que l'empire du monde a été donné" being more than mere oratory.[10] It is the idea of perfectibility and therefore of equality, truth, justice, etc., that motivates men to contribute to the advancement of mankind. Historical events such as natural cataclysms and revolutions are merely catalysts, not causal agents. The momentum towards perfection, or what Herder terms the advance from "Menschheit" to "Humanität," is endogenous to the historical process, deriving from an inner law of its own. It alone, according to both authors, endows man's existence with meaning and dignity.

70

In *Perfectibilité* and elsewhere, Constant condemns Godwin and Condorcet for being visionaries (*O.m.*, n.a.f. 14,362, folio 83). He blames their elaboration of Utopian constructs for failure to discover the true nature of the purposive law governing human conduct. He unduly stresses their acts of faith in the future they depict, while himself remaining unaware of the strong similarity between his teleology and theirs. The works he has in mind are Condorcet's *Esquisse d'un tableau historique des progrès de l'esprit humain* and Godwin's *Political Justice*.[11]

At the turn of the century, Constant was an habitué of Mme de Condorcet's salon at Meulan, a favorite gathering spot for ideologues such as Cabanis and Fauriel. Ideologues, of course, were far from being idealists, their thinking representing a transitional phase between eighteenth-century philosophy à la Condillac and nineteenth-century Comtian positivism. Constant shared with them his political convictions and sensationalist epistemology but saw the world in less mechanistic terms. By a curious coincidence, he was being guided by the defunct Marquis' historicism, while frequenting his far less prophetically inclined widow. Constant was thoroughly familiar with Condorcet's writings and cites him nearly as often as he does Montesquieu and Smith, especially when dealing with educational policies. He is strangely silent in Condorcet's respect, however, when he launches into historical progressivism. Yet there are some basic similarities, as in the case of Herder.

The epochs constituting a chronological chain of being both in the *Esquisse* and in *Perfectibilité* are at once factual and normative, representing an attempt to capsulize empirical history while setting an ethical goal for mankind. Since ideas are the dynamic factors in human development in both cases, progress is immanent in the growth of reason. The process is secular in that divine Providence has been replaced by human will and creativeness.

A further resemblance centers on the dialectical character of both systems, for it is the inner contradictions of one epoch which cause it to give way to the next. With Condorcet, history is a conflict between the forces of good and evil, with the latter sowing the seeds of their own destruction. A case in point is the medieval period, during which superstition generated a new learning which ultimately undermined its foundations. For Constant, change is likewise the result of conflict, partial truths, called "opinions érronées," giving way in the end to absolute truth after a series of "luttes passagères" (*Mélanges*, p. 408). In either case, therefore, the familiar eighteenth-century idea of progress generated by technological innovation and increasing knowledge takes on the appearance of a philosophy of history understood in terms of logical causation and heralding the Romantic concept of national destiny. Finally, and most significantly, both historical schemes are egalitarian on a prescriptive as well as descriptive level, equality being a moral goal to be pursued independently for its own sake as well as the proclaimed end of the historical process. Condorcet depicts his brave new world in the tenth epoch of the *Esquisse*. Constant's optimistic historicism is deployed in *Egalité* as well as *Perfectibilité*.[12] Both Condorcet and Constant widen the base of progress, the former by centering on his theories of education, the latter by systematically attacking "privilèges" and characterizing them as historical anachronisms. Equality, in fact, is another designation for social harmony. It can be approached in different ways and at differing speeds depending on particular circumstances. At times an automatic regulator, not unlike Adam Smith's "Unseen Hand," functions smoothly. At others, cataclysms or violent revolutions, spurred on by ideas, operate as the inescapable motors of progress. To what extent such revolutions are truly endogenous to the historical process or are exogenous inputs of man calculated to accelerate humanity's forward march is never made entirely clear. Quite apart from the dualist (factual/normative) character of their philosophies of history, Condorcet and Constant run into a difficulty encountered by all historical prophets: there is no way to distinguish between what was meant to be and what simply happened.

Constant's ties with Godwinian thought are less apparent.[13] The author of *Political Justice* is repeatedly criticized by Constant for philosophical anarchism. Indeed, one wonders at times why Constant went to the effort of translating Godwin unless it was simply the better to refute him. His main bone of contention is, as it is with Condorcet, Godwin's visualization of the historical process. Since Constant did not himself formulate his *telos* in any but the most abstract terms, his position as critic is comfortably sound. He is particularly emphatic in condemning what he considered to be Godwin's simplistic belief that in time society would settle its differences without resort to any form of political organization. Government, writes Constant in "De Godwin, et de son ouvrage sur la justice politique," is not an intrinsic evil, but must be perpetuated in order to guarantee individual freedom. "Il n'en faut point hors de sa sphère; mais dans cette sphère il ne saurait en exister trop" (*Mélanges*, p. 218). Godwin's basic concern was with determining how the state can be dispensed with; Constant's, with how its prerogatives can be kept in check.

Yet upon closer inspection, one finds that Godwin's anarchism is related to Constantian liberalism.[14] Both have strong laissez-faire overtones. Ideally, an existing government should function as a non-interfering body which intervenes only when the rights of individuals are impaired or threatened. For Godwin, all control mechanisms are slated to disappear. Yet does not Constant's historicism imply that the negative state is equally a short or medium-term proposition? After all, his so-called epoch of legal conventions, which corresponds to the contemporary period, is itself but a passing stage. Constant describes laws as "factices, susceptibles de changements, créées pour remplacer des vérités encore peu connues" (*Mélanges*, p. 413).

Even though the paths of Godwinian and Constantian historical marches may not coincide, they do occasionally converge. Both thinkers, for example, place heavy emphasis on an automatic regulator, hence their mutual gradualism: insofar as possible, one should work with existing institutions. How compatible this is with Godwin's anarchism or Constant's defensive legalism is not immediately apparent, but this is a matter for discussion elsewhere. The two systems also resemble one another along ethical lines. A reading of *Political Justice* reveals a concern for inequality, specifically in the economic domain. Its presence, according to Godwin, leads men astray in their desires, perverts the integrity of judg-

73

ments, discourages intellectual attainment, and multiplies vice.[15] By inference equality, or an equality-oriented movement, has the same enlightening effect as for Constant.

The author of *Perfectibilité* was familiar with a number of other writers of historical bent, among them Turgot, Priestley, Price, Müller, Fichte, and Schelling. The name of Hegel, however, is strangely absent, even though such concepts as the cunning of reason and the *Zeitgeist* could very well be applied to Constant's scheme. He never mentions Hegel nor is the great dialectician's work included in available catalogs of Constant's library.

At this point, the psychological and ethical components of Constantian teleological historicism warrant examination. When Herder, Condorcet, Godwin, or Constant write about the meaningfulness of history and the perfectibility of man, they assume that human nature is capable of undergoing fundamental evolution and change. The psychological hedonism—behaviorism, if one prefers —of the Encyclopaedists and the Utilitarian school is mechanistic in nature. Man is conditioned by his environment and acts rationally in order to maximize pleasure or utility. While he can be molded by exterior forces (hence the significance of the legal apparatus), his urges and responses are predictably invariable.[16] The psychology of perfectible man, on the other hand, is developmental. It reflects the evolution from mechanical to biological or organic modes of thought that took place in the course of the eighteenth century.

Within the Montesquieu-like constitutionalism of the *Principes* and the *Fragments, homo utilitaris* is kept in check by institutional means. Radically different from this sybaritic individual is Constant's abstract man participating in the historical process. For *homo perfectibilis*, individual and social responsibility does not have to be superimposed; it develops during the general process of mind realizing itself. The former model is abandoned in favor of the latter when Constant resorts to psychological dualism and dialectical reasoning.

A comparison with Rousseau's idea of latent *perfectibilité* is in order. Constant evaluates the citizen of Geneva much as he does Godwin, albeit in more vituperative terms, since he connects his speculations with the less attractive aspects of the French Revolution. His heart is in the right place, Constant observes, but his system is defective. The first book of the manuscript *Principes* is mostly a critique of Rousseau's concept of general will and what is considered to be its totalitarian implications. The stricture runs through Constant's works. So do certain important resemblances.

There is nothing in Constant's writings quite like Rousseau's second *Discours* or *Contrat social*. Yet the latter's presence is strongly felt in various attempts at establishing what borders on an anthropological history of mankind. A yawning gap divides Constant's pre-social from his social man. The latter lives in a kinetic world, whereas the amoral "sauvages" cannot change since the world they live in is "stationnaire" (*O.m.*, n.a.f. 14,362, folio 90). Rousseau says: ". . . ce passage de l'état de nature à l'état civil produit dans l'homme un changement très remarquable en . . . donnant à ses actions la moralité qui leur manquait auparavant."[17]

At some point in time, declares Constant in *Perfectibilité*, mankind is thrust into group living by a natural catastrophe. Common dangers create new feelings and bonds among men: the vision of suffering evokes pity, that of unhappiness, sympathy (*O.m.*, n.a.f. 14,362, folio 91). Society, as in Rousseau's discourse on inequality, produces a totally different man, one capable of goodness and endowed with reason. By engendering an ethically-conscious and reasoning man, society provides the driving force which converts a static world into a universe of motion. Eventually, changes take place on a group level as well, as an atomistic conglomeration gives way to an organic society. Group dynamics, in Constant's view, creates a common will differing from all "intérêts particuliers," and he declares that

> chacun est libre individuellement parce qu'il n'a, individuellement, à faire qu'à lui-même ou à des forces égales aux siennes. Mais dès qu'il entre dans l'ensemble il cesse d'être libre, parce que le mouvement de l'ensemble s'empare de lui, et non seulement le subjugue mais le modifie. [*O.m.*, n.a.f., 14, 362, folio 110.]

The freedom Constant refers to is clearly equivalent to Rousseau's *liberté naturelle*. In a well-known passage of the *Contrat social*, Rousseau distinguishes between *liberté naturelle*—free-

75

dom in the state of nature—and *liberté civile*—social freedom. The former is based on force and is equated with "l'impulsion du seul appétit"; the latter is defined and delimited by the general will. It encompasses moral freedom, "la liberté morale, qui seule rend l'homme vraiment maître de lui" (*Oeuvres complètes*, III, 365). The basic differences between the two theoreticians are along institutional lines and reside in their attitudes towards contemporary society—pessimism and retreat on Rousseau's part, mild optimism and participation on that of Constant. They hold in common, however, an image of man capable of perfecting himself by becoming increasingly reasonable, enlightened and just, given the proper social context. They likewise envision perfection as equality. In fact, Constant's *Egalité* is notably evocative of Rousseau's second *Discours.*

Sensing the pitfalls of conjecture, hence less assured and open in his rationalistic stand than is Rousseau, Constant is emphatic in his reliance on experience supplemented by logic. However, from the outset of *Egalité*, it is apparent that his "empirical" law of historical causation is more likely a personal quest for Paradise Lost. Prior to a society-producing calamity, there existed a golden age during which perfect or natural equality prevailed. Inequality came in the wake of society. Were it not for group living, it would soon disappear, for men are born equal, and their psycho-physical differences would be insignificant were not the consequences thereof intensified and stabilized by the institutional edifices of those who happen to be stronger at a moment in time. Equality is characterized as an ubiquitous human need and the most natural of all desires. It is, as with Rousseau, primarily an ethical concept: "Equité est synonyme de justice, or équité dérive d'égalité" (*Egalité,* p. 11).

Although social existence and its attendant conflicts of interest carry the seeds of inequality, they also engender the wherewithal of salvation. The process of inequalization will eventually be reversed as man proceeds from one historical epoch to the next: "Ces quatre révolutions, la destruction de l'esclavage théocratique, de l'esclavage civil, de la féodalité, de la noblesse privilégiée sont autant de pas vers le rétablissment de l'égalité naturelle" (*Mélanges,*

p. 407). Constant draws his own conclusions, but the premises are those of Rousseau.

For both Constant and Rousseau, therefore, psychological factors are vital to the structure and logic of their systems. In Constant's case, this obliged him to transcend the mechanistic psychological model which prevailed in eighteenth-century thought by formulating a developmental one. He does much the same in the domain of ethics, finding a morality of enlightened self-interest insufficient for his needs. The greatest good for the greatest number is simply not good enough.

Repeatedly, Constant declares that utility cannot serve as a standard of right and wrong. His rejection of relativistic ethics does not stem from an allegiance to Kant, as his diary makes clear. Rather, it derives from a desire to differentiate his position from that of the strict Utilitarians. This he does for several reasons. His historical system requires an absolutist ethical goal. One cannot tend towards what is more or less pleasurable, or useful, depending on time and circumstance. Furthermore, the ethics of enlightened self-interest, as viewed by Constant, assumes a permanently self-centered individual, one incapable of increasing perfection. Finally, and most significantly, the negation of an intrinsic moral absolute and the rejection of inalienable natural rights are incompatible with his attitude towards religion. This is the real reason behind his repeated denunciations of Helvétius, Bentham, and thinkers of similar persuasion.

While denouncing organized religion in the best eighteenth-century fashion, Constant consistently emphasizes the importance of religious feeling. This feeling designates an emotionalism with religious overtones (a romantic notion) and also nature's guiding light. In the preface of *De la religion*, the author analyzes in detail the reasons for which enlightened self-interest is ethically unacceptable, not the least of which is its use as a substitute for "émotions religieuses" by the *philosophes*. It deflects man from his higher self, diverting him from his "destination véritable." Its tendency to encourage expediency (e.g., to condone legalized murder) can, in fact, lead to a "dépravation de notre nature." It is thus not only deficient but actually counter-productive as an ethical system. It is, in essence, a glorification of the profit motive.[18]

The specific target is usually Helvétius, but Constant vents his ire on Bentham as well. In an essay entitled "De M. Dunoyer et de ses ouvrages" he accuses Bentham of reducing the notion of right to that of profit via his utility principle. "Le principe de l'utilité . . . réveille dans l'esprit de l'homme l'espoir d'un profit et non le sentiment d'un devoir. Or, l'évaluation d'un profit est arbitraire." Actions cannot be more or less just, whereas they can be more or less utile. He adds with a flourish "vouloir soumettre le droit à l'utilité, c'est vouloir soumettre les règles éternelles de l'Arithmétique à nos intérêts de chaque jour" (Mélanges, pp. 144–45).

Rejecting enlightened hedonism, Constant opts for a system which guides man towards perfection via "la sentiment intime, l'abnégation de nous-mêmes et la faculté du sacrifice" (De la religion, I, xxxiv). Self-realization replaces pleasure-derived happiness as a goal. The word bonheur, be it noted, is used sparingly by the author.

Constant's ethic of inner perfection tinged with religious feeling has obvious Rousseauistic overtones. So does a notion of freedom which Constant distinguishes from its "formes extérieures" (O.m., n.a.f. 14,362, folio 44). In reality, there are two types of freedom for him, as for Rousseau. In his Fragments d'un essai sur la littérature dans ses rapports avec la liberté, he establishes a scale of values between two types of freedom, one more superficial than the other. He explicitly characterizes the inner moral one as an intrinsic component of man. It is also dynamic, a developing instinct, hence a vital mechanism of the historical march. It resembles Rousseau's liberté morale in that it is ethically autonomous; it is self-directed and controlled. For Constant, it represents "l'instinct plus ou moins développé de l'égalité" (O.m., n.a.f. 14,362, folio 32). For Rousseau, equality is likewise contingent upon moral freedom. Even though Constant does not try to work out the stochastics of ethical freedom on a social scale, he does, like Rousseau, attempt to resolve the conflict between obligation and freedom by fusing these seemingly warring concepts.

Analysis of Constantian historicism and its psychological and ethical components thus reveals a more complex philosophy than past critics have recognized. Constant, it appears, thought of history as the product of social change generated over time by the ceaseless efforts of man to bring social reality into compatibility with his need for equality. Although the issue is not discussed overtly, there is the implication that progress, in the inexorable march toward equality, accelerates over time because man becomes more perfect, and therefore more demanding of equality, as he grows and learns. Temporary setbacks and periods of apparent inertia are to be anticipated but will not persist indefinitely, because permanent stability in the social system requires that the bulk of mankind be content with the situation. Given his assumptions, this can occur in Constant's system only when universal equality has been achieved. Such a view of history obviously brings to mind Condorcet, Herder, Godwin, Rousseau, and others who thought in terms of the meaningfulness of history, the perfectibility of man, and absolutist rather than relativistic morality.

And yet, as we have seen, there is another Constant, a statesman who grappled with the problems of practical politics. This Constant frequently wrote like an early nineteenth-century liberal drawing inspiration from Montesquieu and the Utilitarians. This is hardly surprising since historicist systems of thought rarely provide much guidance in coping with concrete policy problems. There is also something to be said for the view that responsibility and active participation in worldly affairs tend to make even the best of philosophers somewhat eclectic. The issue of compatibility between these diverse philosophical inheritances in Constant's work thus merits study, but it is unlikely to prove strategic in any overall assessment of Constant's performance as a thinker. Indeed, one can guess that such a study would show that philosophers, no less than mechanics, must adapt their tools to the nature of the specific problems they confront.

NOTES

1. Benjamin Constant, *Journaux intimes*, ed. Alfred Roulin and Charles Roth (Paris: Gallimard, 1952); reprinted in Benjamin Constant, *Oeuvres* (Paris: Gallimard, 1957). See also Pierre Deguise, "Inédits de Benjamin Constant," *Revue de Paris*, August 1963, pp. 91–106.

2. Nouvelles acquisitions françaises, 14,358 to 14,364. These manuscripts hereafter cited as *O.m.*
3. Elizabeth Schermerhorn, *Benjamin Constant* (London: Heineman, 1924), p. 257.
4. The most extensive Constant manuscript collection is housed in the Bibliothèque cantonale et universitaire de Lausanne. Most significant among new publications are Pierre Deguise, *Benjamin Constant méconnu* (Geneva: Droz, 1966), and Paul Bastid, *Benjamin Constant et sa doctrine*, 2 vols. (Paris: Armand Colin, 1966). The former concentrates on the five-volume *De la religion* and reminds us that religion, its history and philosophy, was Constant's overriding preoccupation. Bastid's voluminous intellectual biography includes an extensive investigation of Constant's political ideas. A Constant bicentennial in 1967 generated a series of articles contained in Pierre Cordey and Jean-Luc Seylaz (editors), *Benjamin Constant: Actes du congrès de Lausanne, October, 1967* (Geneva: Droz, 1968). Two recent critical editions are worthy of mention as well: Benjamin Constant, *Ecrits et discours politiques*, 2 vols., ed. Oliver Pozzo di Borgo (Paris: Pauvert, 1964), and Benjamin Constant, *De la perfectibilité de l'espèce humaine*, ed. Pierre Deguise (Lausanne: L'Age d'homme, 1967). See also Béatrice W. Jasinski, *L'Engagement de Benjamin Constant* (Paris: Minard, 1971), for the period 1794–96.
5. In his *Clartés et ombres du siècle des lumières* (Geneva: Droz, 1969) Roland Mortier includes a chapter on "Constant et les 'Lumières'," pp. 144–56. The text originally appeared in *Europe*, No. 467 (March, 1968), pp. 5–21. Mortier includes Constant's heretofore unpublished "Esquisse d'un essai sur la littérature du XVIIIᵉ siècle" as an appendix to his chapter. Constant's essay is contained in *O.m.*, n.a.f. 14,362, folios 109–11.
6. Isaiah Berlin, *Four Essays on Liberty* (London: Oxford University Press, 1969), pp. 122–31.
7. *Du moment actuel et de la destinée de l'espèce humaine, ou histoire abrégée de l'égalité* (Lausanne, Bibliothèque cantonale et universitaire de Lausanne, CO 3292); hereafter cited as *Egalité*.
8. In n.a.f. 14,362, folios 66 to 94, entitled "De la perfectibilité de l'espèce humaine" and "Fragments d'un essai sur la perfectibilité de l'espèce humaine" respectively. The first part, modified to incorporate some elements of the second, was published in Constant's *Mélanges de littérature et de politique* (Paris: Pichon et Didier, 1829), pp. 387–415. The *Mélanges* text also appears in Deguise, *supra* note 4. Both manuscript essays will hereafter be cited as *Perfectibilité*.
9. *Démontrer par les faits* are the words he uses to describe his method *(O.m.*, n.a.f. 14,362, folio 89).
10. *Ibid.* See J. Gottfried von Herder, *Idées pour la philosophie de l'histoire de l'humanité*, ed. Max Rouché (Paris: Aubier, 1962), Book XV.
11. Jean-Antoine-Nicolas Caritat de Condorcet, *Oeuvres*, Vol. VI, ed. Condorcet O'Connor and M. F. Arago (Paris: Firmin Didot, 1847–49);

William Godwin, *Enquiry Concerning Political Justice and Its Influence on Morals and Happiness*, ed. F. E. L. Priestley, 3 vols. (Toronto: University of Toronto Press, 1946).

12. For additional details see Beatrice C. Fink, "Benjamin Constant on Equality," *J.H.I.*, XXXIII, no. 2 (1972), 307–14.

13. See Benjamin Constant, *De la Justice politique*. Translation of William Goodwin's *Enquiry Concerning Political Justice*, ed. Burton R. Pollin (Québec: Les Presses de l'Université Laval, and Albany: State University of New York Press, 1972). Constant's "Fragments d'un essai sur la perfectibilité de l'espèce humaine" is included in an appendix.

14. Constant implicitly confirms this in the opening remarks of his essay by qualifying *Political Justice* as "un ouvrage qui réunit les principes de liberté les plus purs" (*O.m.*, n.a.f. 14,362, folio 24).

15. *Political Justice*, I, 453.

16. There are, of course, divergences among the Encyclopaedists with respect to this general psychological model. Diderot for example, in keeping with ideas expressed in the *Rêve de d'Alembert* and the *Réfutation suivie de l'ouvrage d'Helvétius intitulé L'Homme*, leans towards an evolutionary or organic concept of human nature.

17. Jean-Jacques Rousseau, *Oeuvres complètes*, III (Paris: Gallimard, 1964), 364.

18. Benjamin Constant, *De la Religion considérée dans sa source, ses formes et ses développements*, I (Paris: Leroux, 1824), xxiii–xxxii.

The High Enlightenment and the Low-Life of Literature in Pre-Revolutionary France*

Robert Darnton

Where does so much mad agitation come from? From a crowd of minor clerks and lawyers, from unknown writers, starving scribblers, who go about rabble-rousing in clubs and cafés. These are the hotbeds that have forged the weapons with which the masses are armed today.

P. J. B. Gerbier, June 1789

The nation's rewards must be meted out to those who are worthy of them; and after having repulsed despotism's vile courtiers, we must look for merit dwelling in basements and in seventh-storey garrets. . . . True genius is almost always *sans-culotte*.

Henri Grégoire, August 1793

THIS ESSAY IS INTENDED to examine the late Enlightenment as historians have recently studied the Revolution—from below. The summit view of eighteenth-century intellectual history has been described so often and so well that it might be useful to strike out in a new direction, to try to get to the bottom of the Enlightenment, and perhaps even to penetrate into its underworld. Digging downward in intellectual history calls for new methods and new materials, for grubbing in archives instead of contemplating philosophical treatises. As an example of the dirt that such digging can turn up, consider the following titles taken from a

* This essay, which first appeared in *Past and Present*, 51 (May, 1971), 81–115, was the first chosen by ASECS for its annual award to the best scholarly article of the year in eighteenth-century studies. Prize-winning essays will be reprinted regularly in the Society's Proceedings. Ed.

manuscript catalogue that circulated secretly in France around 1780 and that were offered for sale under the heading "philosophical books":[1] *Venus in the Cloister, or The Nun in a Nightgown; The Woman of Pleasure; The Pastime of Antoinette* (a reference to the Queen); *Authentic Memoirs of Mme. la Comtesse Du Barry; Monastic News, or The Diverting Adventures of Brother Maurice; Medley by a Citizen of Geneva and Republican Advice dedicated to the Americans; Works of La Mettrie; System of Nature.* Here is a definition of the "philosophical" by a publisher who made it his business to know what eighteenth-century Frenchmen wanted to read. If one measures it against the view of the philosophic movement that has been passed on piously from textbook to textbook, one cannot avoid feeling uncomfortable: most of those titles are completely unfamiliar, and they suggest that a lot of trash somehow got mixed up in the eighteenth-century idea of "philosophy." Perhaps the Enlightenment was a more down-to-earth affair than the rarefied climate of opinion described by textbook writers, and we should question the overly highbrow, overly metaphysical view of intellectual life in the eighteenth century. One way to bring the Enlightenment down to earth is to see it from the viewpoint of eighteenth-century authors. After all, they were men of flesh and blood, who wanted to fill their bellies, house their families, and make their way in the world. Of course the study of authors does not solve all the problems connected with the study of ideas, but it does suggest the nature of their social context, and it can draw enough from conventional literary history for one to hazard a few hypotheses.[2]

A favourite hypothesis in histories of literature is the rise in the writer's status throughout the eighteenth century. By the time of the High Enlightenment, during the last twenty-five years of the Old Régime, the prestige of French authors had risen to such an extent that a visiting Englishman described them exactly as Voltaire had described English men of letters during the early Enlightenment: "Authors have a kind of nobility."[3] Voltaire's own career testifies to the transformation of values among the upper orders of French society. The same milieux who had applauded the drubbing administered to him by Rohan's toughs in 1726 cheered him like a god during his triumphal tour of Paris in 1778. Voltaire himself used his apotheosis to advance the cause of his "class"—the "men of letters" united by common values, interests, and enemies into a new career group or "estate." The last twenty years of his correspondence read like a continuous campaign to proselytize for his "church," as he called it, and to protect the "brothers" and the "faithful" composing it. How many youths in the late eighteenth century must have dreamt of joining the initiates, of lecturing monarchs, rescuing outraged innocence, and ruling the republic of letters from the Académie Française or a château like Ferney. To become a Voltaire or d'Alembert, that was the sort of glory to tempt young men on the make. But how did one "make it" as a *philosophe*?

Consider the career of Jean-Baptiste-Antoine Suard, a leading candidate for a representative *philosophe* of the High Enlightenment. Others—Marmontel, Morellet, La Harpe, Thomas, Arnaud, Delille, Chamfort, Roucher, Garat, Target, Maury, Dorat, Cubières, Rulhière, Cailhava—might do just as well. The advantage of Suard's case is that it was written up by his wife. A *philosophe's* rise to the top is indeed revealing when seen from his wife's viewpoint, and especially when, as in the case of Mme. Suard, the wife had an eye for domestic detail and the importance of balancing the family accounts.[4]

Suard left the provinces at the age of twenty and arrived in Paris just in time to participate in the excitement over the *Encyclopédie* in the 1750's. He had three assets: good looks, good manners, and a Parisian uncle, as well as letters of introduction to friends of friends. His contacts kept him going for a few months while he learned enough English to support himself as a translator. Then he met and captivated the Abbé Raynal, who functioned as a sort of recruiting agent for the socio-cultural élite known as *le monde*.[5] Raynal got Suard jobs tutoring the well-born, encouraged him to write little essays on the heroes of the day—Voltaire, Montesquieu, Buffon—and guided him through the salons. Suard competed for the essay prizes offered by provincial academies. He published literary snippets in the *Mercure*; and having passed at Mme. Geoffrin's, he began to make frequent appearances in *le monde*—a

85

phrase that recurs with the regularity of a leitmotif in all descriptions of Suard.[6] With doors opening for him in the salons of d'Holbach, Mme. d'Houdetot, Mlle. de Lespinasse, Mme. Necker, and Mme. Saurin, Suard walked into a job at the *Gazette de France*: lodging, heating, lighting, and 2,500 livres a year for putting polish on the materials provided every week by the ministry of foreign affairs.

At this point Suard took his first unorthodox step: he got married. *Philosophes* did not generally marry. The great figures of the early Enlightenment—Fontenelle, Duclos, Voltaire, d'Alembert—remained bachelors; or, if they fell into matrimony, as in the case of Diderot and Rousseau, it was with someone of their own station —shop girls and servants.[7] But the elevated status of the *philosophe* in Suard's time made marriage conceivable. Suard picked a girl of good bourgeois stock like himself; overcame the objections of her brother, the publisher Panckoucke, and of Mme. Geoffrin, who held old-fashioned ideas about the incompatibility of professional writing and family life; and set up house in the apartment that went with his job on the *Gazette de France*. Mme. Suard trimmed her wardrobe to fit their tight budget. Friends like the Prince de Beauvau and the Marquis de Chastellux sent them game from the hunts every week. And princely patrons like Mme. de Marchais sent carriages to carry the couple off to dinners, where the bride marvelled at "the rank and the merit of the guests."[8] This was something new: Madame Philosophe had not accompanied her husband on his forays into *le monde* before. Mme. Suard followed her husband everywhere and even began to form a salon of her own, at first a modest supper for literary friends. The friends and patrons responded so enthusiastically that something of a cult grew up around the "petit ménage" as it was known from a poem celebrating it by Saurin. Formerly a fringe character picked up for amusement by the salons and readily turned out into the street for drubbings, begging, and *embastillement*, the *philosophe* was becoming respectable, domesticated, and assimilated into that most conservative of institutions, the family.

Having made it into *le monde*, Suard began to make money. By taking over the entire administration of the *Gazette de France*, he and his collaborator the Abbé Arnaud boosted their income from

2,500 to 10,000 livres apiece. They succeeded by appealing over the head of a bureaucrat in the ministry of foreign affairs, who was "astonished that men of letters shouldn't consider themselves rich enough with 2,500 livres of revenue,"[9] to the foreign minister, the Duc de Choiseul, whose sister, the Duchesse de Grammont, was an intimate of the Princesse de Beauvau, who was a friend of the Suards and of Mme. de Tessé, who was the protector of Arnaud. Such obliging *noblesse* was vulnerable to the vagaries of court politics, however, and when d'Aiguillon replaced Choiseul, the Suards were turned out of their *Gazette* apartment. Once again *le monde* rallied to the defence of its *petit ménage*. Suard received a compensatory pension of 2,500 livres from d'Aiguillon, who was persuaded by Mme. de Maurepas, who was moved by the Duc de Nivernais, who was touched by the sight of Mme. Suard weeping in the Académie Française and by the prodding of d'Alembert and La Harpe. Then a gift of 800 livres in *rentes perpétuelles* arrived from the Neckers. The Suards rented a house in the rue Louis-le-Grand. Suard managed to get the lucrative post of literary correspondent to the Margrave of Bayreuth. His friends arranged a pension for him of 1,200 livres on the income from the *Almanach Royal*. He sold his collection of English books to the Duc de Coigny for 12,000 livres and bought a country house. He became a royal censor. Election to the Académie Française came next, bringing an income of up to 900 livres in *jetons* (doubled in 1786) and far more in indirect benefits, such as a position as censor of all plays and spectacles, worth 2,400 livres and later 3,700 livres a year. When the *Journal de Paris* was suspended for printing an irreverent verse about a foreign princess, the keeper of the seals called in Suard, who agreed to purge all future copy and to share the profits: another 1,200 livres. "He took a cabriolet, which transported him after he fulfilled the duties of his posts, to the lovely house he had given to me,"[10] Mme. Suard reminisced. They had reached the top, enjoying an income of ten, perhaps over twenty thousand livres a year and all the delights of the Old Régime in its last days. The Suards had arrived.

The most striking aspect of the Suard success story is its dependence on "protection"—not the old court variety of patronage, but a new kind, which involved knowing the right people, pulling the right strings, and "cultivating," as it was known in the eighteenth century. Older, established writers, wealthy bourgeois, and nobles all participated in this process of co-opting young men with the right style, the perfect pitch of *bon ton*, into the salons, academies, privileged journals, and honorific posts. The missing element was the market: Suard lived on sinecures and pensions, not on sales of books. In fact, he wrote little and had little to say—nothing, it need hardly be added, that would offend the régime. He toed the party line of the *philosophes* and collected his reward.

But how many rewards of that kind were there, and how typical was Suard's *cas typique*? Part of the answer to those questions lies in a box in the Archives Nationales containing a list of 147 "Men of Letters Who Request Pensions" and ten dossiers crammed with material on writers and their sources of support.[11] The list reads like a "Who's Who" of the literary world drawn up by officials in the *Contrôle général* to guide Calonne, who had decided in 1785 to increase and systematize the award of literary pensions, *gratifications*, and *traitements*. Calonne was also guided by a committee composed of Lenoir, the former lieutenant general of police, Vidaud de Latour, the director of the book trade, and two courtier-academicians, the Maréchal de Beauvau and the Duc de Nivernais. Hardly a revolutionary group. The pension list, with the recommendations of Calonne's officials and his own notes scrawled in the margins, gives a corresponding impression. It shows a strong bias in favour of established writers, especially academicians. Here Morellet appears with his 6,000 livres a year from the Caisse de Commerce; Marmontel with 3,000 livres as "historiographe de France" and 2,000 livres as perpetual secretary of the Académie Française; La Harpe complains of receiving a mere 600 livres from the *Mercure*, the Maréchal de Beauvau pushes to get him pensioned for 1,500, and the pension is granted, despite a subordinate official's observation that La Harpe also collects 3,000 livres for lecturing in the Lycée. And so the list goes, one figure of the High Enlightenment succeeding another: Chamfort (granted 2,000 livres in addition to 1,200 on the *maison du roi*), Saint-Lambert (requested 1,053 livres, decision delayed), Bernardin de Saint-Pierre (1,000 livres), Cailhava (1,000 livres), Keralio, Garat, Piis, Cubières, des Essarts, Aubert, and Lemierre.

Blin de Sainmore, a solid citizen in the republic of letters' lesser ranks, exemplified the qualities required for getting a pension. He was a royal censor, "historiographe de l'Ordre du Saint-Esprit," and protégé of the Princesse de Rochefort. "I will further add, Monseigneur, that I am the head of a family, that I was born without fortune, and that I have nothing for the support and education of my family except the post of historiographer of the king's orders, whose income is barely sufficient for me alone to live in a decent style."[1] Thus the pensions went for charity as well as good works. Saurin's widow applied because his death had left her destitute, since he had lived entirely from "the beneficence of the government."[13] And Mme. Saurin specified:

Pension of the Académie Française	2,000
Pension on the General Farms	3,000
As the son of a converted [Protestant] minister	800
As a censor	400
On an office of *trésorier du pavé de Paris*	2,400
Total	8,600

This "beneficence" generally went to serious, deserving writers but not to anyone unconnected with *le monde*. Academicians were first on the government's list—to such an extent that one ministerial aide jotted in a margin, "There is some danger that the title of academician might become a synonym for pensioner of the King."[14] Ducis demanded 1,000 livres a year for life on the grounds that "most of our confrères, either of the Académie Française or of the Académie des Inscriptions, have obtained pensions that have the character of a permanent grace."[15] This favoritism offended Caraccioli, who wrote testily,

I am pretentious enough to believe that you will have heard of my works, all of which have religion and sound morality as their object. I have been writing in this genre for thirty-five years; and despite the frivolity of the century, [my works] have spread everywhere and have been translated into various languages. Nevertheless, under ministers who preceded you and who made me the most beautiful promises, I never obtained anything, although living in a modest state that might well be called indigence. And I have seen *gratifications* as well as pensions pour down. . . .[16]

As Caraccioli's comments suggest, "sound" opinions were considered as a necessary qualification for a pension. In some cases the government subsidized writers who had produced propaganda for it. It looked favourably on the Abbé Soulavie, because "he has submitted some manuscripts on financial matters to M. le Contrôleur Général."[17] Conversely, the government avoided making payments to anyone whose loyalties were in doubt. It turned down J.-C.-N. Dumont de Sainte-Croix, a minor author on jurisprudence, because, according to the marginal note next to his name, "All the new systems of this genre would merit some encouragement, if they were made only to be known by the government and not by the public, which is incited to rebel against the established laws instead of becoming enlightened as to the means of making them better." Then, in another hand: "Nothing."[18] Rivarol also received nothing, but only because he already had a secret pension of 4,000 livres: "He is very clever, and an encouragement, which could be paid to him each year, if he remains faithful to sound principles, would be a way of preventing him from following his inclination toward those which are dangerous."[19]

So several considerations determined the state's patronage. As in the case of modern institutions like the French "Centre National de la Recherche Scientifique," the monarchy supported serious *savants*, perhaps even with the intention of recruiting a fresh intellectual élite.[20] It also dispensed charity. And it used its funds to encourage writing that would make the régime look good. In each instance, however, it restricted its subsidies to men with some standing in the world of letters. A few fringe characters like Delisle de Salles, Mercier, and Carra presumed to apply for the pensions; but they received nothing. Lenoir later revealed that he and his colleagues had turned down Carra, Gorsas, and Fabre d'Eglantine because "the academicians described them as the excrement of literature."[21] While the literary rabble held out its hands to the government, the government gave its handouts to writers situated safely within *le monde*.

It dispensed them on a large scale. A note by a subordinate official put the total payments at 256,300 livres, to which 83,153 livres were added in 1786. But that sum represented only the direct dole from the royal treasuries. Far more money flowed into the purses of "sound" writers from the appointments at the government's disposal. Journals, for example, provided an important source of income for the privileged few in the literal sense of the word. Royal privileges reserved certain subjects for the quasi-official periodicals like the *Mercure, Gazette de France,* and *Journal des savants,* which exploited their monopolies without worrying about competitors (the government permitted some discreet foreign journals to circulate, provided they passed the censorship and paid compensation to a privileged journal) and turned over part of the take to writers named by the government. In 1762 the *Mercure* paid out 30,400 livres to twenty subluminaries of the High Enlightenment.[22] Then there were many sinecures. Not only did the king require an official historiographer, but he subsidized "historiographes de la marine," "des bâtiments royaux," "des menus-plaisirs," and "de l'Ordre du Saint-Esprit." The branches of the royal family were loaded with readers, secretaries, and librarians—more or less honorific posts that one had to work *for* but not *at,* that one acquired by waiting in antechambers, improvising eulogies, cultivating acquaintances in salons, and knowing the right people. Of course it always helped to be a member of the Académie Française.[23]

The dozens of volumes about the history and *petite histoire* of the academy in the eighteenth century,[24] whether written in love or in hatred, reveal a dominant theme: the Enlightenment's successful campaign to win over the French élite. After the "chasse aux Pompignans" of 1760, the election of Marmontel in 1763, and d'Alembert's elevation to the perpetual secretaryship in 1772, the academy fell to the *philosophes.* It became a sort of clubhouse for them, an ideal forum for launching attacks against *l'infâme,* proclaiming the advent of reason, and co-opting new *philosophes* as fast as the old-guard academicians would die off. This last function, virtually a monopoly of the philosophic salons, assured that only party men would make it to the top. And so Voltaire's church was besieged by converts. The spectacle of a new generation taking up the torch warmed the old man's heart. When he congratulated Suard on his election, Voltaire exulted, "*Voilà,* God be thanked, a new career

91

assured. . . . At last I see the real fruits of philosophy, and I begin to believe that I shall die content."[25] Thus Suard and his circle, the high priests of the High Enlightenment, took over the summit of the literary world, while the mid-century *philosophes* declined and died. The new men included both writers like Thomas, Marmontel, Gaillard, La Harpe, Delille, Arnaud, Lemierre, Chamfort, and Rulhière, and philosophically-minded *grands*, powerful courtiers and clergymen, like the Marquis de Chastellux, the Maréchal de Duras; Boisgelin, Archbishop of Aix; and Loménie de Brienne, Archbishop of Sens.

The fusion of *gens de lettres* and *grands* had been a favourite theme of philosophic writing since the mid-century. Duclos had proclaimed it triumphantly in his *Considérations sur les moeurs de ce siècle* (1750). Writing had become a new "profession," which conferred a distinguished "estate" upon men of great talent but modest birth, he explained. Such writers became integrated into a society of courtiers and wealthy patrons, and everyone benefited from the process: the "gens du monde" gained amusement and instruction, and the "gens de lettres" acquired polish and standing. It went without saying that promotion into high society produced some commitment to the social hierarchy. Duclos had a keen eye for all the subtleties of status and rank; and although he took pride in the man of letter's ability to rise by sheer talent, he showed equal respect for what made a man of *le monde*: "One is an *homme du monde* by birth and by position."[26] Voltaire, the arch-apologist for *le mondain*, shared the same attitudes. His article entitled "Gens de lettres" in the *Encyclopédie* emphasized that in the eighteenth century "the spirit of the age made them [men of letters] for the most part as suitable for *le monde* as for the study. They were kept out of society until the time of Balzac and Voiture. Since then they have become a necessary part of it." And his article "Goût" in the *Dictionnaire philosophique* revealed the élitist bias in his conception of culture: "Taste is like philosophy. It belongs to a very small number of privileged souls. . . . It is unknown in bourgeois families, where one is constantly occupied with the care of one's fortune." Voltaire—who incessantly cultivated courtiers, tried to become one himself, and at least managed to buy his way into the nobility—thought that the Enlightenment should begin with the *grands*: once it had captured society's commanding heights, it could concern itself with the masses—but it should take care to prevent them from learning to read. D'Alembert believed in essentially the same strategy, but he did not share his "master's" taste for the court.[27] His *Essai sur les gens de lettres et les grands* (1752), published two years before his election to the Académie Française, amounted to a declaration of independence for writers and writing as a proud new profession (not in the present sociological sense of the term, but as it was used by Duclos). Yet despite some strong language advocating a "democratic" republic of letters in contrast to the humiliating practices of patronage, d'Alembert stressed that society was and ought to be hierarchical and that the *grands* belonged on top.[28] By the time he wrote his *Histoire des membres de l'Académie française* (1787), when he ruled the academy as Duclos's successor in the perpetual secretaryship, d'Alembert reformulated Duclos's theme in a conservative vein. He castigated the "horde of literary rebels [*frondeurs littéraires*]" for venting their frustrated ambitions in attacks on the academy. He defended the academy's mixture of *grands seigneurs* and writers. And he emphasized the role of courtiers, as experts in the realm of taste and language, in a very élitist Enlightenment—a process of gradual, downward diffusion of knowledge, in which the principle of social equality could play no part.

> Is a great effort of philosophy necessary to understand that in society, and especially in a large state, it is indispensable to have rank defined by clear distinctions, that if virtue and talent alone have a claim to our true homage, the superiority of birth and position commands our deference and our respect. . . ? And how could men of letters envy or misconstrue the so legitimate prerogatives of other estates?[29]

As spokesmen for the writer's new "estate" (but not for the brand of *philosophe* represented by Diderot and d'Holbach), Duclos, Voltaire, and d'Alembert urged their "brethren" to profit from the mobility available to them in order to join the élite. Rather than challenge the social order, they offered a prop to it.

But what was the meaning of this process? Was the establishment becoming enlightened or the Enlightenment established? Probably both, although it might be best to avoid the overworked term "establishment"[30] and to fall back on the eighteenth-century expression already cited, *le monde*. After fighting for their principles in the mid-century and consolidating their victories during the last years of Louis XV's reign, the great *philosophes* faced the problem that has plagued every victorious ideology: they needed to find acolytes worthy of the cause among the next generation. Admittedly, "generation" is a vague concept.[31] Perhaps there are no real generations but only demographic "classes." Still, the great *philosophes* form a fairly neat demographic unit: Montesquieu 1689–1755, Voltaire 1694–1778; and then Buffon 1707–1788, Mably 1709–1785, Rousseau 1712–1778, Diderot 1713–1784, Condillac 1715–1780, and d'Alembert 1717–1783. Contemporaries were naturally struck by the deaths, not the births, of great men. Voltaire, Rousseau, Diderot, Condillac, d'Alembert, and Mably all died between 1778 and 1785; and their deaths left important places to be filled by younger men, who were born, for the most part, in the 1720's and 1730's.

As age overcame them, the great *philosophes* made the rounds of the salons, searching for successors. They tried to find another d'Alembert—and came up with Marmontel, the champion of *Gluckisme*. They tried to persuade themselves that Thomas could thunder like Diderot and La Harpe bite like Voltaire. But it was no use. With the death of the old Bolsheviks, the Enlightenment passed into the hands of nonentities like Suard: it lost its fire and became a mere tranquil diffusion of light, a comfortable ascent toward progress. The transition from the heroic to the High Enlightenment domesticated the movement, integrating it with *le monde* and bathing it in the *douceur de vivre* of the Old Régime's dying years. As Mme. Suard remarked after reporting the receipt of their last pension, "I have no more events to recount, other than the continuation of a soft and varied life, until that horrible and disastrous epoch [the Revolution]."[32] Her husband, turned censor, refused to approve Beaumarchais' not so very revolutionary play, *Le Mariage de Figaro*. And Beaumarchais put most of his energy

94

in speculation, and ultimately in building the biggest townhouse in Paris—"a house that is talked about"—the *arriviste*'s dream.[33]

The establishment of the Enlightenment did not blunt its radical edge, however, because just as a generation gap separated the high *philosophes* from their predecessors, a generation split cut them off from the low-life of literature, from their contemporaries who failed to make it to the top and fell back into Grub Street.

Perhaps the literary world has always divided into a hierarchy whose extremes might be labeled a *monde* of mandarins on the one hand and Grub Street on the other. Such milieux existed in the seventeenth century and exist today. But the social and economic conditions of the High Enlightenment opened up an unusual gulf between the two groups during the last twenty-five years of the Old Régime, and this split, if examined in all its depth, ought to reveal something about one of the standard questions posed by the pre-revolutionary era: what was the relation between the Enlightenment and the Revolution?

At first glance, it seems that the writer's lot should have improved substantially by the reign of Louis XVI. The relevant data, flimsy as they are, all point in the same direction: a considerable expansion in demand for the printed word.[34] Literacy probably doubled in the course of the century, and the general upward swing of the economy, combined with improvements in the educational system, very likely produced a larger, wealthier, and more leisured reading public. Certainly book production soared, whether measured by demands for privileges and *permissions tacites* or indirectly by the number of censors, booksellers, and printers. But there is little evidence that writers benefited from any publishing boom. On the contrary, everything indicates that while the mandarins fattened themselves on pensions, most authors sank into a sort of literary proletariat.

Admittedly, information about the growth of Grub Street comes from anecdotal sources, not statistics. Mallet du Pan claimed that three hundred writers, including a heavy dose of hacks, applied for Calonne's pensions, and he concluded, "Paris is full of young men who take a little facility to be talent, of clerks, accountants, lawyers, soldiers, who make themselves into authors, die of hunger, even beg, and turn out pamphlets."[35] Crébillon *fils*, who reportedly gave out *permissions de police* for 40,000–50,000 verses of pamphlet poetry every year, was besieged by a "multitude of versifiers and would-be authors" who flooded into Paris from the provinces.[36] Mercier found these "famished scribblers," "these poor hacks" (*écrivailleurs affamés, ces pauvres barbouilleurs*) everywhere,[37] and Voltaire constantly hammered at the theme of the "ragged rabble" (*peuple crotté*) crowding the bottom of the literary world. He placed "the miserable species that writes for a living" —the "dregs of humanity," "the riff-raff of literature" (*lie du genre humain, canaille de la littérature*)—at a social level below prostitutes.[38] Writing in the same spirit, Rivarol and Champcenetz published a mock census of the undiscovered Voltaires and d'Alemberts crammed into the garrets and gutters of Paris. They produced articles on well over five hundred of these poor hacks, who scribbled for a while in obscurity, and then vanished like their dreams of glory, except for a few: Carra, Gorsas, Mercier, Restif de la Bretonne, Manuel, Desmoulins, Collot d'Herbois, and Fabre d'Eglantine. The names of those future revolutionaries look strange in Rivarol's roll-call of "the five or six hundred poets" lost in the legions of "la basse littérature," but Rivarol put them rightly in their place.[39]

That place was Grub Street, and its population, combustible at any time, was exploding during the last twenty-five years of the Old Régime. Of course this interpretation may be only a demographic fantasy based on subjective literary sources, but the sources seem suggestive enough to warrant giving the fantasy rein. They continually stress the theme of the provincial lad who reads some Voltaire, burns with the ambition to become a *philosophe*, and leaves home only to smoulder helplessly and expire down and out in Paris.[40] Even Duclos worried about this corollary to his formula for success.[41] And Voltaire, obsessed by the overpopulation of young writers in Paris ("Egypt of old had fewer locusts"), claimed that he attacked Grub Street in order to warn youth away from it.[42] "The number of those who are lost as a result of this passion [for the "career of letters"] is prodigious. They render themselves incapable of any useful work. . . . They live off rhymes and

96

hopes and die in destitution."[43] Voltaire's attacks wounded Mercier, who rose to the defence of the "poor devils" in opposition to the pampered, pensioned darlings of the academies and salons. Mercier protested that the "poor" of the "low literature" (*basse littérature*) in the Faubourg Saint-Germain had more talent and integrity than "the rich" in the "high literature" (*haute littérature*) of the Faubourg Saint-Honoré. But even he concluded pessimistically, "Ah! keep away from this career you who do not want to know poverty and humilation."[44] Linguet, another anti-Voltairean, devoted a whole book to the same theme. A constant target of would-be authors in search of a protector, he had reason to lament that "secondary schools have become a seedbed of child authors, who hurriedly scribble tragedies, novels, histories, and works of all sorts" and then "spend the rest of their lives in destitution and despair."[45]

The provincials flocked to Paris in search of glory, money, and the improved "estate" that seemed promised to any writer with sufficient talent. They did not necessarily share the motivations of the early *philosophes*, who were often nobles and clergymen enjoying enough leisure to write when the spirit moved them and who wrote before the time when "literature became a *métier*," as Meister distastefully observed.[46] J. J. Garnier, a writer with a highly developed sense of professionalism, noted that by 1764 many men of letters were moved by "the hope of gaining reputation, influence, wealth etc. The avenues of advancement having been closed to them because of their humble birth and modest fortunes, they observed that the career of letters, open to everyone, offered another outlet for their ambition."[47] Mercier agreed that the immigrant from the provinces could hope to shake off his humble origins and climb to the top in Paris.[48] But the top of Paris, the *tout Paris*, had little room for ambitious young men on the make, perhaps because, as sociologists claim, rising status groups tend to become exclusive; perhaps because of a literary version of the Malthusian crush; perhaps because France suffered from a common ailment of developing countries: a surplus population of over-educated and under-employed *littérateurs* and lawyers. In any case, it seems that the attractiveness of the new career celebrated by Duclos and the new "church" proclaimed by Voltaire resulted in a record crop of potential *philosophes*, far more than could be absorbed under the archaic system of protections. Of course the lack of statistics and the confusion of social categories in pre-revolutionary France (how does one define a "man of letters"?—someone with a literary reputation, someone who has published a book, or someone who lives by his pen?) makes these hypotheses unverifiable. But there is no need for a complete census of eighteenth-century writers in order to make sense of the tension between the men of Grub Street and the men of *le monde* on the eve of the Revolution. The facts of literary life at that time speak for themselves.

The most salient fact is that the market place could not support many more writers than in the days when Prévost and Le Sage proved that it was possible—barely possible—to live from the pen instead of pensions. Although publishers offered somewhat better terms than earlier in the century, authors were caught between the masters of the publishing-bookselling guilds, who paid little for manuscripts, and pirate publishers, who paid nothing at all.[49] None of the great mid-century *philosophes* relied much on sales except for Diderot, who never fully extricated himself from Grub Street. Mercier claimed that in his day only thirty hard-core "professionals" supported themselves by writing.[50] The open, "democratic" market that could feed large numbers of enterprising authors did not appear in France until well into the nineteenth century. Before the day of the steam press and the mass reading public, writers lived by scavenging along the road to riches that worked so well for Suard—or they dropped by the wayside, in the gutter.

Once he had fallen into Grub Street, the provincial youth who had dreamt of storming Parnassus never extricated himself. As Mercier put it, "He falls and weeps at the foot of an invincible barrier. . . . Forced to renounce the glory for which he so long has sighed, he stops and shudders before the door that closes the career to him."[51] The nephews and grand-nephews of Rameau really faced a double barrier, both social and economic; for after Grub Street had left its mark on them, they could not penetrate into polite society where the plums were passed around. So they cursed

98

the closed world of culture. They survived by doing the dirty work of society—spying for the police and peddling pornography; and they filled their writings with imprecations against the *monde* that humiliated and corrupted them. The pre-revolutionary works of men like Marat, Brissot, and Carra do not express some vague, "anti-Establishment" feeling; they seethe with hatred of the literary "aristocrats" who had taken over the egalitarian "republic of letters" and made it into a "despotism."[52] It was in the depths of the intellectual underworld that these men became revolutionaries and that the Jacobinical determination to wipe out "the aristocracy of the mind" was born.

To explain why Grub Street had no exit and why its prisoners felt such hatred for the *grands* at the top it is necessary to say a word about the cultural modes of production during the late eighteenth century; and that word is the term one meets everywhere in the Old Régime: privilege.[53] Books themselves bore privileges granted by the "grace" of the king. Privileged guilds, whose organization showed the hand of Colbert himself, monopolized the production and distribution of the printed word. Privileged journals exploited royally-granted monopolies. The privileged Comédie Française, Académie Royale de Musique, and Académie Royale de Peinture et de Sculpture legally monopolized the stage, opera, and the plastic arts. The Académie Française restricted literary immortality to forty privileged individuals, while privileged bodies like the Académie des Sciences and the Société Royale de Médecine dominated the world of science. And above all these "corps" rose the supremely privileged cultural élite who kept *le monde* all to themselves.

It may have been appropriate for a corporate society to organize its culture corporately, but such archaic organization constrained the expansive forces that might have opened up the cultural industries and supported more of the overpopulated underworld of letters. As it was, the bookdealers' guilds acted far more effectively than the police in suppressing unprivileged books, and underprivileged youths like Brissot were forced into destitution, not so much because their early works were radical as because the monopolies prevented them from reaching the market.[54] Writers therefore fed their families either from the pensions and sinecures reserved for the members of *le monde* or from the scraps tossed into Grub Street.

The corporate organization of culture was not simply an economic matter, for it contradicted the basic premises under which the young writers had flocked to Paris in the 1770's and 1780's. They had come with the conviction that the republic of letters really existed as it had been described in the works of the great *philosophes*—as the literary counterpart to the "atomic" individualism of Physiocratic theory, a society of independent but fraternal individuals, in which the best men won but all derived dignity, as well as a living, from service to the common cause. Experience taught them that the real world of letters functioned like everything else in the Old Régime: individuals got ahead as best they could in a labyrinth of Baroque institutions. To have an article published in the *Mercure*, to get a play accepted by the Comédie Française, to steer a book through the Direction de la Librairie, to win membership in an academy, entry in a salon, or a sinecure in the bureaucracy required resorting to the old devices of privilege and protection, not merely the demonstration of talent.

Talent certainly carried some to the top. Maury was the son of a poor cobbler in a village of the Venaissain, Marmontel of a poor tailor in the Limousin, Morellet of a small-time paper merchant of Lyons, Rivarol (who called himself a count) of an innkeeper in Languedoc; La Harpe and Thomas were orphans. All rose through skill and scholarships, and they were not the only examples of rapid upward mobility. But as de Tocqueville observed, it was the erratic opening up of mobility, not the absence of it, that produced social tensions. Nowhere was this general phenomenon more important than in the world of letters, because the attractiveness of writing as a new kind of career produced more writers than could be integrated into *le monde* or supported outside of it. To the outsiders, the whole process looked rotten, and they were not inclined to blame their failures on their own inability: on the contrary, they tended to see themselves as successors to Voltaire. They had knocked on the door of Voltaire's church, and the door remained closed. Not only did their status fail to rise as fast as their expectations; it plummeted, dragging them down to a world of opposites and contradictions, a *monde* turned upside down, where "estate" could not be defined at all, and dignity dissolved in destitution. Seen from the perspective of Grub Street, the republic of letters was a lie.

If the institutional realities of the established literary world contradicted its principles, at least from the viewpoint of those who failed to reach the top, what were the realities of life for those at the bottom? Grub Street had no principles, and it had no institutions of a formal kind. It was a world of free-floating individuals —not Lockean gentlemen abiding by the rules of some implicit game, but Hobbesian brutes struggling to survive. It was as far removed from *le monde* as was the café from the salon.[55]

Despite the democratic play of wit, the salon remained a rather formal institution. It did not allow any putting of elbows on the table or any admission to those without introductions. During the last decades of the Old Régime, the salon became increasingly a preserve for the high *philosophes*, who generally abandoned the cafés to the lower species of *littérateur*. The café functioned as the antithesis of the salon. It was open to everyone, just one step from the street, although there were degrees in its closeness to street life. While the great names gathered in the Procope or La Régence, lesser figures congregated in the notorious Caveau of the Palais-Royal, and the humblest hacks frequented the cafés of the boulevards, blending into an underworld of "swindlers, recruiting agents, spies, and pickpockets; here one finds only pimps, buggers, and *bardaches*."[56]

Grub Street may have lacked the corporate structure of the established culture, but it was not sheer anarchy. It had institutions of a sort. For example, the *musées* and *lycées* that sprang up in such numbers during the 1780's responded to the needs of obscure writers for a place to exhibit their wares, to declaim their works, and to make contacts. These clubhouses formalized the functions of the cafés. The *musées* of Court de Gébelin and P.C. de La Blancherie seem even to have served as counter-academies and anti-salons for the multitude of *philosophes* who could not get a hearing elsewhere. La Blancherie published a journal, *Les Nouvelles de la République des lettres et des arts,* which vented some of the frustrations of the *musée* members both by sniping at academicians and by reviewing works that were beneath the notice of the *Journal de Paris* and the *Mercure.*[57] But the most effective sniper and the most influential outsider of pre-revolutionary France was Simon-Henri Linguet. While respecting the crown and the church, Linguet blasted at France's most prestigious institutions, especially the Parisian bar and the Académie Française. His polemical genius made his pamphlets, judicial *mémoires,* and journals best-sellers; and his tirades against "aristocratic" and "despotic" corporateness reverberated up and down Grub Street, setting the tone for some of the anti-elitist propaganda of the Revolution.[58]

Grub Street therefore had a few organs and organizations to express itself. Perhaps it even had an inchoate stratification system of its own, for the underground contained several levels. Having cultivated an established *philosophe* or got some verses published in the *Almanach des muses,* some writers lived just below *le monde.* Mirabeau maintained a mandarin style of life even when in prison and in debt. He kept a stable of pamphleteers (who referred to him simply as "le comte") to produce the works published under his name.[59] Lesser figures put together the encyclopedias, dictionaries, digests, and anthologies that circulated in such profusion in the last half of the eighteenth century. Even cruder hack work could be relatively respectable—writing for ministers, pamphleteering for the *baissiers* fighting the *haussiers* on the Bourse, and producing *nouvelles à la main;* or it could be demeaning—manufacturing smut, peddling prohibited works, and spying for the police. Many writers lived on the fringes of the law, calling themselves lawyers or law clerks and taking on the odd jobs available in the *basoche* of the Palais de Justice. Some, at the bottom of the literary underworld, sank into criminality. Charles Thévenau de Morande, one of Grub Street's most violent and virulent pamphleteers, lived in a demi-monde of prostitutes, pimps, blackmailers, pickpockets, swindlers, and murderers. He tried his hand at more than one of these professions and gathered material for his pamphlets by skimming the scum around him. As a result, his works smeared everything, good and bad alike, with a spirit of such total depravity and alienation that Voltaire cried out in horror,

"There has just appeared one of those satanic works [Morande's *Gazetier cuirassé*] where everyone from the monarch to the last citizen is insulted with furore; where the most atrocious and most absurd calumny spreads a horrible poison on everything one respects and loves."[60]

Grub Street stifled respect and love. Its grim struggle for survival brought out baser sentiments, as is suggested by the following excerpts from reports submitted to the Parisian police by its legions of spies and secret agents, many of them underworld writers themselves with their own dossiers in the archives of the police.[61]

GORSAS: proper for all kinds of vile jobs. Run out of Versailles and put in Bicêtre [a jail for especially disreputable criminals] by personal order of the king for having corrupted children whom he had taken in as lodgers, he has withdrawn to a fifth floor on the rue Tictone. Gorsas produces *libelles*. He has an arrangement with an apprentice printer of the Imprimerie Polytype, who has been fired from other printing shops. He [Gorsas] is suspected of having printed obscene works there. He peddles prohibited books.

AUDOUIN: calls himself a lawyer, writes *nouvelles à la main*, peddler of forbidden books; he is connected with Prudhomme, Manuel, and other disreputable authors and book peddlers. He does all kinds of work; he will be a spy when one wants.

DUPORT DU TERTRE: solicits a position in the offices of the police; is a lawyer who is not often employed in the Palais, although he is not without merit. He failed to get a position in the Domaines. He lives in a modest, fourth-storey apartment; he hardly gives off an air of wealth [*il ne respire pas l'opulence*]. He is generally well spoken of; he has a good reputation in his neighbourhood.

DELACROIX: lawyer, writer, expelled from the bar. He produces [judicial] *mémoires* for shady cases; and when he has no *mémoires* to write, he writes scurrilous works.

MERCIER: lawyer, a fierce, bizarre man; he neither pleads in court nor consults. He hasn't been admitted to the bar, but he takes the title of lawyer. He has written the *Tableau de Paris*, in four volumes, and other works. Fearing the Bastille, he left the country, then returned and wants to become attached to the police.

MARAT: bold charlatan. M. Vicq d'Azir asks, in the name of the Société Royale de Médecine, that he be run out of Paris. He is from Neuchâtel in Switzerland. Many sick persons have died in his hands, but he has a doctor's degree, which was bought for him.

CHENIER: insolent and violent poet. He lives with Beauménil of the Opéra, who, in the decline of her charms, fell in love with him. He mistreats her and beats her—so much that her neighbours report that he would have killed her had they not come to her rescue. She accuses him of having taken her jewels; she describes him as a man capable of any crime and doesn't hide her regrets at having let herself be bewitched by him.

FRÉRON: who has neither the wit nor the pen of his father, is generally despised. It is not he who writes the *Année littéraire*, although he has its privilege. He hires young unemployed lawyers. He's an insolent coward, who has received his share of beatings—and doesn't boast about it—most recently from the hand of the actor Desessarts, whom he had called a "ventriloquist" in one of his issues. He is connected with Mouvel, who was expelled from the Comédie for pederasty.

PANIS: young lawyer of the Palais, protected by M. le Président d'Ormesson because of Panis' parents, who are his [d' Ormesson's] *fermiers*; is employed by Fréron on the *Année littéraire*. Panis has as a mistress a woman branded by the hand of the executioner.

Life in Grub Street was hard, and it took a psychological toll, because "the excrement of literature" had to face not merely failure but degradation, and they had to face it alone. Failure breeds loneliness, and the conditions of Grub Street were peculiarly suited to isolate its inhabitants. Ironically, the basic unit of life in *la basse littérature* was the garret (stratification went more by storey than by neighbourhood in eighteenth-century Paris). In their fourth- and fifth-floor *mansardes*, before Balzac had romanticized their lot, the undiscovered *philosophes* learned that they were what Voltaire had called them: the "canaille de la littérature." But how could they come to terms with such knowledge?

Fabre d'Eglantine is a case in point. A drifter and a *déclassé* who saw himself as the successor of Molière, he went down in the police dossiers as a "poor poet, who drags about in shame and destitution; he is despised everywhere; among men of letters he is considered an execrable subject [*poète médiocre qui traîne sa honte et sa misère; il est partout honni; il passe parmi les gens de lettres pour un exécrable sujet*]."[62] Sometime before the Revolution, Fabre wrote a play that reads like an escapist fantasy of an author trapped in Grub Street. The hero, an unappreciated twenty-eight-year-old genius from the provinces, writes his heart out in a Parisian garret, mocked and exploited by the evil élite that dominates French literature: mercenary publishers, crass journal editors, and the perfidious *beaux-esprits* who monopolize the salons. He is about to succumb to disease and poverty when, by a stroke of good fortune, a virtuous bourgeois tycoon discovers him, appreciates his talent and superior morality, and carries him off to the provinces, where he writes masterpieces happily ever after. The play breathes hatred of the cultural élite and a fierce egalitarianism, which confirms La Harpe's description of the pre-revolutionary Fabre as an embittered failure, "envenomed with hatred, like all the persons of his sort, against everyone who called himself an *homme du monde*, against everything that had a rank in society —a rank that he did not have and should not have had."[63]

Others probably sought refuge in similar fantasies. Marat dreamed of being whisked away to preside over an academy of sciences in Madrid.[64] Both he and Carra found solace in imagining that they had outstripped Newton, despite society's failure to appreciate them. But no amount of fantasy could erase the contradictions between life at the top and the bottom of the world of letters and between what those at the bottom were and what they wanted to be. The established writers enjoyed an "estate"; they derived honour and wealth from the established cultural institutions. But the literary proletariat had no social location. Its ragged pamphleteers could not call themselves "men of letters"; they were just *canaille*, condemned to gutters and garrets, working in isolation, poverty, and degradation, and therefore easy prey to the psychology of failure—a vicious combination of hatred of the system and hatred of the self.

The Grub Street mentality made itself heard with exceptional vehemence during the last years of the Old Régime. It spoke through the *libelle*, the hack writers' staff of life, their meat, their favourite genre and a genre that deserves to be rescued from the

105

neglect of historians, because it communicates the Grub Street view of the world: a spectacle of knaves and fools buying and selling one another and forever falling victim to *les grands*. The *grand monde* was the real target of the *libelles*. They slandered the court, the church, the aristocracy, the academies, the salons, everything elevated and respectable, including the monarchy itself, with a scurrility that is difficult to imagine today, although it has had a long career in underground literature. For pamphleteers had lived by libel since the time of Aretino. They had exploited all the great crises in French history, in the propaganda produced by the Catholic League during the religious wars, for example, and in the *Mazarinades* of the Fronde. But the ultimate crisis of the Old Régime gave them an unusual opportunity, and they rose to the occasion with what seems to have been their greatest barrage of anti-social smut.[65]

Although a survey of *libelles* published between 1770 and 1789 cannot be undertaken here,[66] it should be possible to capture some of their flavour by explicating one of their texts. Perhaps the most outspoken *libelle*—a pamphlet so sensational and so widely read that it became virtually a prototype of the genre—was the work that especially horrified Voltaire: *Le Gazetier cuirassé* by Charles Thévenau de Morande. Morande mixed specific calumny and general declamation in brief, punchy paragraphs, which anticipated the style of gossip columnists in the modern yellow press. He promised to reveal "behind-the-scenes secrets" (*secrets des coulisses*)[67] in the tradition of the *chronique scandaleuse*. But he provided more than scandal:

> The devout wife of a certain Maréchal de France (who suffers from an imaginary lung disease), finding a husband of that species too delicate, considers it her religious duty to spare him and so condemns herself to the crude caresses of her butler, who would still be a lackey if he hadn't proven himself so robust.[68]

This sexual sensationalism conveyed a social message: the aristocracy had degenerated to the point of being unable to reproduce itself;[69] the great nobles were either impotent or deviant;[70] their wives were forced to seek satisfaction from their servants, representatives of the more virile lower classes; and everywhere among *les grands* incest and venereal disease had extinguished the last sparks of humanity.[71] Vivid detail communicated the message more effectively than abstractions; for although the reader might at first merely be shocked by a particular incident,

> The Count of Noail——, having taken some scandalous liberties with one of his lackeys, this country bumpkin knocked over Monseigneur with a slap that kept his lordship in bed for eight days. . . . The lackey . . . is a Picard of the first order who had not yet been instructed how to serve a Spanish grandee, Knight of the Royal Orders, Lieutenant General, Governor of Vers ——, Prince of P——, Lord of Arpa——, Grand Cross of Malta, Knight of the Golden Fleece, and secular member of the Society of Jesus, etc., etc., etc., etc.[72]

he would know what to conclude after he had recovered from the shock. Morande led the reader toward general conclusions by piling up anecdotes and slanting them in the same direction—against *le monde.* He showed that the summit of society had decayed beyond the point of recovery, both morally and physically:

> The public is warned that an epidemic disease is raging among the girls of the Opera, that it has begun to reach the ladies of the court, and that it has even been communicated to their lackeys. This disease elongates the face, destroys the complexion, reduces the weight, and causes horrible ravages where it becomes situated. There are ladies without teeth, others without eyebrows, and some completely paralysed.[73]

Morande's chronicle of cuckoldry, buggery, incest, and impotence in high places therefore read as an indictment of the social order. And Morande did not merely leave the reader with a general impression of corruption. He associated the aristocracy's decadence with its inability to fulfill its functions in the army, the church, and the state.

> Of approximately two hundred colonels in the infantry, cavalry, and dragoons in France, one hundred and eighty know how to dance and to sing little songs; about the same number

wear lace and red heels; at least half can read and sign their names; and in addition not four of them know the first elements of their craft.[74]

As the king's confessor was disgraced for having been discovered flirting with some pages, there is now open competition for that position, which will go to the prelate who will be easiest on the king's conscience. The Archbishop of R—— has been proposed but rejected, because of the scandalous relations he has maintained for such a long time with one of his grand vicars. The cardinals of Gèv—— and of Luy—— were designated to serve by alternate semesters; but since the first doesn't know how to read and the second hasn't recovered from being slapped [a reference to a scandal involving homosexuality], one can't be sure of His Majesty's decision.[75]

Morande constantly stressed the connection between sexual and political corruption by news "flashes" like the following:[76] "Having a pretty wife of whom he was very jealous, the unfortunate Baron of Vaxen was sent to prison by a *lettre de cachet* in order to learn the customs of *le monde*, while the duke [La Vrillière, one of Louis XV's favourite ministers] sleeps with his wife." The monarchy had degenerated into despotism, this message stood out on every page: the ministers have hired an extra team of secretaries just to sign *lettres de cachet*; the Bastille and Vincennes are so overcrowded that tents have been set up inside their walls to house the guards; a new élite police corps, modelled in Louis XIV's dragonades, has been created to terrorize the provinces; the government is experimenting with a new machine that can hang ten men at a time; and the public executioner has resigned, not because he is worried about automation, but because the new Maupeou ministry offends his sense of justice. In case any reader could possibly miss the point, Morande stated it explicitly: "According to Chancellor Maupeou, a monarchical state is a state where the prince has the right of life and death over all his subjects, where he is proprietor of all the wealth in the kingdom, where honour and equity are founded on arbitrary principles, which must always conform with the interests of the sovereign."[77]

What was the king's place in this political system? "The chancellor and the Duke d'Aiguillon have come to dominate the king so much that they leave him only the liberty of sleeping with his mistress, petting his dogs, and signing marriage contracts."[78] Deriding the idea of a divine origin to royal sovereignty,[79] Morande reduced the king to the level of the ignorant, crapulous court. He made Louis XV look ridiculous, a trivial figure even in his despotism: "A notice has been published in the hopes of finding the sceptre of one of the greatest kings of Europe. After a very long search, it was found in the *toilette* of a pretty woman called a countess, who uses it for playing with her cat."[80] The real rulers of France and the villains of the book were the Countess DuBarry and the ministerial triumvirate of Maupeou, Terray, and d'Aiguillon. Seizing on Mme. DuBarry as a symbol of the régime, Morande dwelt on every detail about her that he could fabricate or extract from *café* gossip: her supposedly illegitimate birth to a servant girl who had been seduced by a monk, her career as a common whore, her use of the king's power to help her former colleagues by forbidding the police to set foot in brothels, her lesbianic relations with her maid, and so on. Similarly, Morande showed that the ministers used their authority to fatten their purses, procure mistresses, or simply enjoy villainy for its own sake.

Grotesque, inaccurate, and simplistic as it was, this version of political "news" should not be dismissed as merely mythical, because myth-making and unmaking proved to be powerful forces in the last years of a régime, which, though absolutist in theory, had become increasingly vulnerable in practice to the vagaries of public opinion. To be sure, the eighteenth-century French "public" did not exist in any coherent form; and insofar as it did exist, it was excluded from direct participation in politics. But its exclusion produced a political *naïveté* that made it all the more vulnerable to Morande's style of gazeteering. For instead of discussing issues, the *gazetier cuirassé* defamed individuals. He buried Maupeou's reforms—probably the régime's last chance to survive by destroying some of the vested interests that were devouring it—in a torrent of mud-slinging. That the Maupeou programme would have benefited the common people did not matter to Morande, because he and his fellow hacks had no interest in reform. They hated the system in itself; and they expressed their hatred by desanctifying its symbols, destroying the myths that gave it legitimacy in the eyes of the public, and perpetrating the counter-myth of degenerate despotism.

Far from being limited to Morande's works, these themes became increasingly important in *libelle* literature as the Old Régime approached its finale. *Le Gazetier cuirassé* merely set the tone for an outpouring of anti-government pamphlets that extended from the "Maupeouana" of the early 1770's to the "Calonniana" of the late 1780's. The most prolific producer of the latter was Jean-Louis Carra, an outcast from the closed circles of established science, who stated frankly that his efforts to damn the ministry had been provoked by the refusal of one of Calonne's pensions.[81] Morande's motives had not been nobler. He meant to make money, both by exploiting the market for sensationalism and by blackmailing the persons he libelled.

Did slander on such a scale, its crass motivation notwithstanding, amount to a call for revolution? Not really, because the *libelles* lacked a programme. They not only failed to give the reader any idea of what sort of society should replace the Old Régime; they hardly contained any abstract ideas at all. In denouncing despotism, Morande cried out for liberty; and in fulminating against aristocratic decadence, he seemed to advocate bourgeois standards of decency, if only by contrast.[82] But he did not defend any clear set of principles. He referred to himself as *"le philosophe cynique"*[83] and slandered everything, even the *philosophes*.[84] The same spirit animated most other *libelles*; it was a spirit of nihilism rather than of ideological commitment.

Yet the *libelles* showed a curious tendency to moralize, even in their pornography. The climax of one of Morande's obscene pamphlets about courtiers and courtesans came in an indignant description of Mme. DuBarry:

> . . . passing directly from the brothel to the throne, toppling the most powerful and redoubtable minister, overthrowing the constitution of the monarchy, insulting the royal family, the presumptive heir to the throne, and his august consort by her incredible luxury, by her insolent talk, [and insulting] the entire nation, which is dying of hunger, by her vainglorious extrava-

gance and by the well-known depredations of all the *roués* surrounding her, as she sees grovelling at her feet not only the *grands* of the kingdom and the ministers, but the princes of the royal blood, foreign ambassadors, and the church itself, which canonizes her scandals and her debauchery.[85]

This tone of moral outrage was typical of the *libelles* and seems to have been more than a rhetorical pose. It expressed a feeling of total contempt for a totally corrupt élite. So if the *libelles* lacked a coherent ideology, they communicated a revolutionary point of view: they showed that social rot was consuming French society, eating its way downward from the top. And their pornographic details got the point across to a public that could not assimilate the *Social Contract* and that soon would be reading *Le Père Duchesne.*

This gutter Rousseauism—a natural idiom for the "Rousseaus du ruisseau"[86]—may have been related to Rousseau's rejection of the culture and morality of France's upper classes. For the men of Grub Street saw Jean-Jacques as one of their own. In following his career, they could not only imagine the realization of their hopes but could also find consolation for their failures. *Débourgeoisé* like such typical *libellistes* as Brissot and Manuel, Rousseau had risen from their ranks into *le monde*, seen it for what it was, exposed élitist culture itself as the very agent of social corruption, and returned with his semi-literate, working-class wife to a humble existence in the neighbourhood of Grub Street, where he died pure and purged. The hacks respected him and despised Voltaire— Voltaire the "mondain," who had stigmatized Rousseau as a "poor devil" and who died in the same year, in the bosom of *le monde.*[87]

Is it surprising then that the writers whom Voltaire scorned as "la canaille dé la littérature" should have moralized in the manner of Rousseau in their politico-pornography? To them the Old Régime was obscene. In making them its spies and smut-peddlers, it had violated their moral core and desecrated their youthful visions of serving humanity honourably in Voltaire's church. So they became rank atheists and poured out their souls in blasphemies about the society that had driven them down into an underworld of criminals and deviants. The scatology of their pamphlets—their frequent references, for example, to venereal disease passed on from the Cardinal de Rohan to the queen and all the great figures of the court during the Diamond Necklace Affair—communicates a sense of total opposition to an élite so corrupt as to deserve annihilation. No wonder that the government kept secret files on the *libellistes* and consigned the *libelles* to the bottom of its graduated scale of illegality, or that the very catalogues of them circulated secretly, in handwritten notes, like the list of "philosophical books" quoted above. The *libellistes* spoke for a sub-intelligentsia that was not merely unintegrated but beyond the pale and that wanted not to reform society in some polite, liberal, Voltairean way, but to overturn it.

There is a danger of using the word "revolutionary" too liberally and of exaggerating the ideological distance between the top and the bottom of the literary world in the Old Régime. The first *philosophes* were "revolutionary" in their fashion: they articulated and propagated a value system, or an ideology, that undermined the traditional values Frenchmen inherited from their Catholic and royalist past. The men of Grub Street believed in the message of the *philosophes*; they wanted nothing more than to become *philosophes* themselves. It was their attempt to realize this ambition that made them see "philosophie" in a different light and to hold it up to the realities not only of society in general but also of the cultural world. The great *philosophes* had had a sharp eye for realities also, and their successors of the next generation may have been as realistic as the most hard-bitten hacks: nothing suggests that the view from the top is more distorted than the view from the bottom. But the difference in viewpoints was crucial—a difference of perspective not principle, of mentality not philosophy, a difference to be found less in the content of ideas than in their emotional colouring. The emotional thrust of Grub Street literature was revolutionary, although it had no coherent political programme nor even any distinctive ideas of its own. Both the *philosophes* and the *libellistes* were seditious in their own way: in becoming established, the Enlightenment undercut the élite's faith in the legitimacy of the social order; and in attacking the élite, the *libelles* spread disaffection deeper and more widely. Each of the opposing camps deserves its place among the intellectual origins of the Revolution.

Once the Revolution came, the opposition between the high and low life of literature had to be resolved. Grub Street rose, overthrew *le monde* and requisitioned the positions of power and prestige. It was a cultural revolution, which created a new élite and gave them new jobs. While Suard, Marmontel, and Morellet found themselves stripped of their income, Brissot, Carra, Gorsas, Manuel, Mercier, Desmoulins, Prudhomme, Loustalot, Louvet, Hébert, Maret, Marat, and many more of the old literary proletariat led new lives as journalists and bureaucrats.[88] The Revolution turned the cultural world upside down. It destroyed the academies, scattered the salons, retracted the pensions, abolished the privileges, and obliterated the agencies and vested interests that had strangled the book trade before 1789. Newspapers and theatres sprang up at such a rate that one could even speak of an industrial revolution within the cultural revolution.[89] And in destroying the old institutions, the new élite meted out a crude, revolutionary justice: Manuel took over the police department that had once hired him secretly for the suppression of *libelles,* and he published its archives in *libelle* form (carefully purging all references to his and Brissot's careers as police spies); Marat, a victim of academic persecution before the Revolution, led the movement that eventually destroyed the academies; and Fabre and Collot, frustrated actor-playwrights in the Old Régime, struck down the monopoly of the *comédiens du roi* and very nearly struck off their heads. In a sequel to his pre-revolutionary census, Rivarol interpreted the Revolution as the work of the status-hungry surplus population of men who failed to "make it" in the old order.[90]

Of course the cultural revolution did not fit perfectly into the pattern of Rivarol's counter-revolutionary propaganda any more than it corresponded to Taine's counter-revolutionary history. Many of the old élite, even academicians like Condorcet, Bailly, Chamfort, and La Harpe, did not oppose the destruction of the institutions in which they had prospered. The literary hacks scattered in a dozen directions, supporting different factions in different phases of the conflict. Some of them, particularly during the Girondist period and the Directory, showed that they wanted nothing more than to participate in a revival of *le monde.* And at least during the years 1789–91, the Revolution realized many of the ideas propagated by the High Enlightenment. But the Revolution at its most revolutionary expressed the anti-élitist passions of Grub Street. It would be wrong to interpret those passions merely as a hunger for employment and a hatred of mandarins. The Jacobin pamphleteers believed in their propaganda. They wanted to slough off their corrupt old selves and to become new men, newly integrated in a republic of virtue. As cultural revolutionaries, they wanted to destroy "the aristocracy of the mind" in order to create an egalitarian republic of letters in an egalitarian republic. In calling for the abolition of academies, Lanjuinais put their case perfectly: "The academies and all other literary corps must be free and not privileged; to authorize their formation under any kind of protection would be to make them into veritable guilds. Privileged academies are always seedbeds of a literary aristocracy."[91] From there it was but one step to Grégoire's injunction: "We must look for merit dwelling impoverished in basements and in seventh-storey garrets. . . . True genius is almost always *sans-culotte*."[92] Perhaps the propagandists of the garrets functioned as the ideological "carriers" who injected the crude, Jacobinical version of Rousseauism into the Parisian *sans-culotterie*.[93] Hébert certainly played that rôle—Hébert, who had rotted in obscurity before the Revolution and, at one point, had tried to persuade the Variétés to perform one of his plays only to get a job checking seat tickets in the *loges*.[94]

It would seem to be necessary, therefore, in looking for the connection between the Enlightenment and the Revolution, to examine the structure of the cultural world under the Old Régime, to descend from the heights of metaphysics and to enter Grub Street. At this low level of analysis, the High Enlightenment looks relatively tame. Voltaire's *Lettres philosophiques* may have exploded like a "bomb"[95] in 1734, but by the time of Voltaire's apotheosis in 1778, France had absorbed the shock. There was nothing shocking at all in the works of his successors, for *they* had been absorbed, fully integrated into *le monde*. Of course one must allow for exceptions like Condorcet, but the Suard generation of *philosophes* had remarkably little to say. They argued over Gluck and Piccini, dabbled in pre-Romanticism, chanted the old litanies about legal reform and *l'infâme*, and collected their tithes. And while they grew fat in Voltaire's church, the revolutionary spirit passed to the lean and hungry men of Grub Street, to the cultural pariahs who, through poverty and humiliation, produced the Jacobinical version of Rousseauism. The crude pamphleteering of Grub Street was revolutionary in feeling as well as in message. It expressed the passion of men who hated the Old Régime in their guts, who ached with the hatred of it. It was from such visceral hatred, not from the refined abstractions of the contented cultural élite, that the extreme Jacobin revolution found its authentic voice.

NOTES

1. Papers of the Société Typographique de Neuchâtel, Bibliothèque de la Ville de Neuchâtel, Switzerland, MS. 1108.
2. Among these histories, the following were found to be most useful: Maurice Pellison, *Les Hommes de lettres au XVIIIe siècle* (Paris, 1911); Jules Bertaut, *La Vie littéraire an XVIIIe siècle* (Paris, 1954); and John Lough, *An Introduction to Eighteenth Century France* (London, 1964), chaps. 7 and 8.
3. Quoted in Marcel Reinhard, "Élite et noblesse dans la seconde moitié du XVIIIe siècle," *Revue d'histoire moderne et contemporaine*, 3 (Jan.-March 1956), p. 21. For Voltaire's view, see the famous 23rd letter of his *Lettres philosophiques* (London, 1734).
4. The following is based on Mme. Suard's *Essais de mémoires sur M. Suard* (Paris, 1820), supplemented by the almost equally interesting reminiscences of D.-J. Garat, *Mémoires historiques sur la vie de M. Suard, sur ses écrits, et sur le XVIIIe siècle*, 2 vols. (Paris, 1820). Although Suard is a forgotten figure today, he was one of the most prominent writers of the High Enlightenment. He never produced a major work, but he made a reputation by journal articles, academic discourses, and translations, whose studied tastefulness may be appreciated from his *Mélanges de littérature*, 5 vols. (Paris, 1803–5).
5. Garat described Raynal as follows (*Mémoires historiques*, I, 107): "In the capital of France and of philosophy, he acted as a grand master of ceremonies, who introduced beginners with talent to talented celebrities and men of letters to manufacturers, merchants, farmers-general, and ministers."
6. Garat described Suard as the epitome of the *savoir-faire* and respect for social rank that made a man of *le monde* (see especially *ibid.*, I, 133–36), and he defined *le monde* as a milieu of "men powerful by virtue of position, wealth, literary talent and birth . . . those three or

115

four conditions that are the real sources of power in society" (*ibid.*, I, 263).

7. Of course well-born and wealthy *philosophes* like Montesquieu, d'Holbach, and Helvétius did not fit into this pattern. Humbler writers were expected to take mistresses or to marry when their fortune was made. Maupertuis, Marmontel, Piron, and Sedaine were famous and past fifty when they married.

8. Mme. Suard, *Essais de mémoires*, p. 59.

9. *Ibid.*, p. 94.

10. *Ibid.*, p. 137.

11. Archives Nationales, F[17a] 1212. Some unsigned, undated "Observations préliminaires" in the first dossier explained that the list was drawn up in order to implement an edict of 3 September 1785 which announced the government's intention of aiding men of letters more systematically than had been done before. The author of the "Observations" (probably Gojard, *premier commis* to the controller-general) evidently thought the proposed subsidies excessive: "Aside from the sums paid by the Royal Treasury to men of letters, and which amount to 256,300 livres, there are also pensions attached to journals and to the *Almanach royal*; and it is possible that they have been given to several authors who are applying today without having declared [that other income], as they should have done according to the terms of the first article of the edict." An incomplete (21 names missing) version of the master list in the Archives Nationales was sold at an auction and later published by Maurice Tourneux in *Revue d'histoire littéraire de la France*, VIII (1901), 281–311. Lacking the supplementary information, which he vainly sought in series O of the Archives, Tourneux was unable to explain the circumstances of the pension scheme and wrongly linked it with the baron de Breteuil. Much of the material in F[17a]1212 also covers the period 1786–88.

12. Blin de Sainmore to the Contrôleur général, 22 June 1788, Archives Nationales F[17a]1212, dossier 10.

13. *Ibid.*, dossier 6.

14. *Ibid.*, dossier 3.

15. Ducis to Loménie de Brienne, 27 November 1787, *ibid.*, dossier 6. See also the similar letter of A. M. Lemierre of 8 March 1788, *ibid.*, dossier 10.

16. Caraccioli to the Directeur général des finances, 13 August 1788, *ibid.*, dossier 6. See also Caraccioli's letter of 8 April 1785, *ibid.*, dossier 10: "I am the only author of my advanced age who has never had either a pension or a grant."

17. *Ibid.*, note in dossier 3.

18. *Ibid.*, dossier I.

19. *Ibid.*, dossier I.

20. The documents in the Archives Nationales would therefore tend to support the argument advanced by Marcel Reinhard in "Elite et noblesse," n. 3.

21. Lenoir papers, Bibliothèque municipale d'Orléans, MS. 1422.

22 Pellisson, *Les Hommes de lettres*, p. 59.

23. See the appointments listed after the names of the academicians in the annual issues of the *Almanach royal*.

24. The most revealing of these is Lucien Brunel, *Les Philosophes et l'Académie française au dix-huitième siècle* (Paris, 1884).

25. Printed in Garat, *Mémoires historiques*, p. 342.

26. Charles Pinot-Duclos, *Considerations sur les moeurs de ce siècle*, ed. F. C. Green (Cambridge, Eng., 1939 [1st edn. 1750]), p. 140 and, in general, chaps. 11 and 12.

27. On the strategical agreement and tactical differences between Voltaire and d'Alembert and their disagreements with the d'Holbach group (which apparently left Diderot somewhere in the middle), see John N. Pappas, *Voltaire and d'Alembert* (Indiana University Humanities Series, number 50 [Bloomington, 1962]).

28. D'Alembert, *Essai sur la société des gens de lettres et des grands, sur la réputation, sur les Mécènes, et sur les récompenses littéraires*, in *Mélanges de littérature, d'histoire et de philosophie* (Amsterdam, 1773 [1st edn. 1752]); see especially pp. 403 and 367.

29. D'Alembert, *Histoire des membres de l'Académie française morts depuis 1700 jusqu'en 1771* (Paris, 1787), I, xxiv and xxxii.

30. See Henry Fairlie, "Evolution of a Term," *The New Yorker*, 19 October 1968, pp. 173–206.

31. Although birth and death dates overlap too much to fall into clear categories, "generations" might be differentiated by the experience of events. Whether we are thirty or fifteen, a chasm of experienced time separates those of us who did not live through World War II from those who participated in it or who read about it in the newspapers while it took place. Perhaps a similar line of experience divided the men who wrote and read the great works of the Enlightenment when they appeared in the mid-century from those who read them after they had already begun to congeal into "classics." Suard (1734–1817) recalled, "I entered *le monde* at the time of that explosion of the philosophical spirit which has marked the second half of the eighteenth century. I read *L'Esprit des lois* at the age of nineteen [i.e. in 1753, five years after its publication]. I was in the provinces, and that reading delighted me. *L'Histoire naturelle* [of Buffon] and the works of Condillac appeared soon afterwards, the *Encyclopédie* in 1752, as did the *Découverte de l'irritabilité* by Haller" (quoted in Garat, *Mémoires historiques*, II, 445). For a survey of the literature on the problem of generations and periodization, see Clifton Cherpack, "The Literary Periodization of Eighteenth-century France," *Publications of the Modern Language Association of America*, LXXXIV (March 1969), pp. 321–28.

32. Mme. Suard, *Essais de mémoires*, p. 155.

33. Quoted in Louis de Loménie, *Beaumarchais et son temps* (Paris, 1856), II, 424. Suard did not object to *Le Mariage de Figaro* because he found it radical but because he considered its treatment of sex unsuitable for the stage (Mme. Suard, *Essais de mémoires*, p. 133). One could cite a

dozen contemporary references indicating the same attitude. Even Lenoir, more involved in the business of sniffing out sedition than anyone in France, reported on Beaumarchais: "Almost all the plays of that author were prevented from opening on the grounds of being offensive to morality, but he succeeded by his intrigues in forcing his way through the censorship. More than once I received an order to let pass plays of his that had been held up for a long time without receiving the necessary approbation and permission" (Bibliothèque municipale d'Orléans, MS, 1423). The "revolutionary" message of *Le Mariage de Figaro*, if it exists, went unnoticed in pre-revolutionary France. Is not the play's refrain a formula for political quietism: "Everything finishes with a song"? Beaumarchais was a wealthy, ennobled man-on-the-make like Voltaire, and he devoted much of his fortune to re-editing Voltaire's works.

34. For information on literacy, education, and book production in eighteenth-century France, see Michel Fleury and Pierre Valmary, "Les progrès de l'instruction élémentaire de Louis XIV à Napoléon III," *Population*, XII (Jan.-March 1957), 71–92; Pierre Gontard, *L'Enseignement primaire en France de la Révolution à la loi Guizot (1789–1833)*, (Lyons, 1959); Robert Estivals, *La Statistique bibliographique de la France sous la monarchie au XVIIIe siècle* (Paris and The Hague, 1965); and François Furet, "La 'librairie' du royaume de France au dix-huitième siècle," in *Livre et société dans la France du XVIIIe siècle* (Paris and The Hague, 1965), pp. 3–32. The *Almanach de la librairie* for 1781 lists 1,057 booksellers and printers, of whom about one fifth did business in Paris. No editions of the *Almanach* go back before 1778, so comparisons cannot be made with the early eighteenth century. But the *Almanach royal* for 1750 lists 79 royal censors, and the *Almanach royal* for 1789 lists 181, an increase that represents a greater output of books, not greater severity in controlling them. It will probably never be possible to make estimates of the number of authors in the eighteenth century, not only because of a lack of statistics but because of the problem of defining what an author was. Robert Escarpit made a brave but unsuccessful attempt in *La Sociologie de la littérature* (Paris, 1958).

35. *Mémoires et correspondance de Mallet du Pan pour servir à l'histoire de la Révolution française, recueillis et mis en ordre par A. Sayous* (Paris, 1851), I, 130. Lenoir estimated the number of applicants for pensions at "4,000" (probably a slip for 400): Bibliothèque municipale d'Orléans. MS. 1422.

36. L.-S. Mercier, *Tableau de Paris*, 12 vols. (1789), X, 26–27.

37. *Ibid.*, p. 29.

38. See *Le Pauvre Diable* and the articles in the *Dictionnaire philosophique* from which the quotations are taken: "Auteurs," "Charlatan," "Gueux," "Philosophe," and "Quisquis."

39. *Le Petit Almanach de nos grands hommes* (1788), quotation from p. 5. In the preface Rivarol explained that he would exclude all established writers from his survey: "I will gladly descend from these im-

posing colossi to the tiniest insects . . . to that innumerable mass of families, tribes, nations, republics, and empires hidden under a leaf of grass" (p. vi.)

40. For a particularly striking example of this theme, see the first chapters of J.-P. Brissot's *Mémoires,* ed. Claude Perroud (Paris, 1910). Mercier often remarked on the influx of provincial writers and even wrote a sort of parable about it: *Tableau de Paris,* X, 129–30. He claimed that some of them roamed the capital in bands, so that the native Parisian writer "has to combat Norman writers, who form a corps, and especially the Gascons, who go around citing Montesquieu, to whom they consider themselves as successors" (XI, 103).

41. *Considérations sur les moeurs,* p. 141.

42. Voltaire, *Le Pauvre Diable,* in *Oeuvres complètes de Voltaire* (1785, no place of publication), XIV, quotation from p. 162. Of course Voltaire used this theme to satirize his enemies, but it can be taken as social comment.

43. *Ibid.,* p. 164.

44. *Tableau de Paris,* XI, 187. See especially the chapters entitled "Auteurs," "Des demi-auteurs, quarts d'auteurs, enfin métis, quarterons," "Misère des auteurs," "La Littérature du Faubourg Saint-Germain et celle du Faubourg Saint-Honore," "Les Grands Comédiens contre les petits," and "Le Musée de Paris."

45. S.-N.-H. Linguet, *L'Aveu sincère, ou lettre à une mère sur les dangers que court la jeunesse en se livrant à un goût trop vif pour la littérature* (London, 1763), pp. v and vii. Linguet explained, p. iv, "I address myself to those ingenuous and inexperienced souls who could be deceived by the glory that they see surrounding the great writers."

46. *Correspondance littéraire, philosophique et critique par Grimm, Diderot, Raynal, Meister, etc.,* ed. Maurice Tourneux (Paris, 1880), XII, 402: "Since literature has become a job [*métier*], and, what's more, a job whose practice has been made easy and common, owing to the numerous models to emulate and the simplicity of its techniques . . ."

47. J.-J. Garnier, *L'Homme de lettres* (Paris, 1764), pp. 134–35.

48. Mercier, *Tableau de Paris,* XI, 104–5: "The man of letters from the provinces finds in Paris an equality that does not exist at all among the men of his small town: here his origins are forgotten; if he is the son of a tavern keeper, he can call himself a count; no one will dispute his claim." Mercier probably had Rivarol in mind when he wrote those lines.

49. On the financial relations between authors and publishers, see Pellisson, *Les Hommes de lettres,* chap. 3; Lough, *An Introduction to Eighteenth Century France,* chap. 7; and G. d'Avenel, *Les Revenues d'un intellectuel de 1200 à 1913* (Paris, 1922), although d'Avenel's study is flawed by an attempt to translate all financial transactions into francs of 1913. For vivid contemporary accounts of the dealings between authors and publishers, see P. J. Blondel, *Mémoires sur les vexations qu'exercent les libraires et imprimeurs de Paris,* ed. Lucien Faucou (Paris, 1879), which hits the publishers very hard, and Diderot's *Lettre sur le com-*

merce de la librairie in his *Oeuvres complètes,* ed. J. Assézat and M. Tourneux (Paris, 1876), p. xviii, which also deals some damaging blows, although Diderot was evidently writing as their paid propagandist.

50. L.-S. Mercier, *De la littérature et des littérateurs* (Yverdon, 1778), pp. 38–39.

51. *Tableau de Paris,* VIII, 59.

52. For documentation of this trend in the subculture of scientists and pseudo-scientists in pre-revolutionary Paris, see Robert Darnton, *Mesmerism and the End of the Englightenment in France* (Cambridge, Mass., 1968), chap. 3.

53. A trade war in the late seventeenth century had left the publishing industry in the grip of the Parisian *Chambre royale et syndicale de la librairie et imprimerie,* and the Parisian guild tightened its hold throughout the eighteenth century, despite the government's attempts to impose some reforms in 1777. The archaic, "Colbertist" conditions of the book trade may be appreciated from the texts of the edicts regulating it: see *Recueil général des anciennes lois françaises,* eds. F. A. Isambert, Decrusy, and A. H. Taillandier (Paris, 1822–33), XVI, 217–51 and XXV, 108–28. The transition from seventeenth- to eighteenth-century conditions is explored in the recent thesis by Henri-Jean Martin, *Livre, pouvoirs et société à Paris au XVIIe siècle* (1598–1701), 2 vols. (Geneva, 1969). On the even more monopolistic conditions in the theatre, see Jules Bonnassies, *Les Auteurs dramatiques et la Comédie française aux XVIIe et XVIIIe siècles* (Paris, 1874).

54. Robert Darnton, "The Grub Street Style of Revolution: J.-P. Brissot, Police Spy," *Journal of Modern History,* XL (Sept. 1968), 301–27.

55. Because Grub Street remains unexplored territory (I hope at least to map it in a later work), there are no secondary works on it. For an example of how it wrapped its tentacles around one future revolutionary, see Robert Darnton, "The Grub Street Style of Revolution: J.-P. Brissot, Police Spy." See also the fascinating biography by Paul Robiquet, *Thévenau de Morande: étude sur le XVIIIe siècle* (Paris, 1882). Morande acted as the dean of the *libellistes* and lived with a collection of underworld characters that makes some of the extravagant comments in *Le Neveu de Rameau* seem mild indeed.

56. Charles Thévenau de Morande, *La Gazette noire par un homme qui n'est pas blanc* (1784, "imprimé à cent lieues de la-Bastille . . ."), p. 212. The literature on salons and cafés is brought together in the works of Pellisson and Bertaut, cited above. See also the revealing remarks by Karl Mannheim in *Essays on the Sociology of Culture,* ed Ernest Manheim (London, 1956), pp. 91–170.

57. The only copy of *Les Nouvelles de la République des lettres et des arts,* 7 vols. (Paris 1777–87) that I have been able to locate is incomplete: Bibliothèque Nationale, Réserve Z 1149–54. See also La Blancherie's *Correspondance générale sur les sciences et les arts* (Paris, 1779), Rz. 3037 and 3392. There is a great deal of information on the *musées* and

lycées of the 1780's scattered through the *nouvelles à la main* published as *Mémoires secrets pour servir à l'histoire de la République des lettres en France* and commonly known as the *Mémoires secrets* of Bachaumont.

58. See especially Linguet's widely read *Annales politiques, civiles et littéraires du dix-huitième siècle*, which attacked the cultural élite with declamations like the following (VI, 386): "There was nothing in France that was not subordinate to it. The ministry, the judiciary, science, literary bodies, everything had been invaded by it: [the "faction" of the established *philosophes*] controlled everything, even reputations. It alone opened the gateway to glory and wealth. It filled every position with philosophizing *parvenus*. The academies as well as the courts were in its grip; the press, the censors, the journals were at its command."

59. See Jean Bouchary, *Les Manieurs d'argent à Paris à la fin du XVIIIe siècle* (Paris, 1939–43), I, and Jean Bénétruy, *L'Atelier de Mirabeau: quatre proscrits genevois dans la tourmente révolutionnaire* (Geneva, 1962).

60. *Dictionnaire philosophique*, article entitled "Quisquis."

61. "Extraits de divers rapports secrets faits à la police de Paris dans les années 1781 et suivantes, jusques et compris 1785, concernant des personnes de tout état et condition [ayant] donné dans la Révolution," Lenoir papers, Bibliothèque municipale d'Orléans, MS. 1423. As their gossipy tone indicates, these reports should not be taken as factually accurate, but they do suggest the general character of life at the bottom of the literary world. In a note at the end of the reports, Lenoir explained that he cut out sections that would incriminate respectable persons but that the remaining excerpts were untouched and could be verified by comparison with other police records (which have been destroyed since he wrote). In general, Lenoir's papers seem reliable. In the case of Manuel, for example, they contain several remarks about Manuel's life in the literary underworld which are corroborated by his dossier in the Archives Nationales, W 295, and by an anonymous *Vie secrète de Pierre Manuel* (n.p., 1793).

62. Bibl. Mun. d'Orléans, MS. 1423.

63. J. F. de La Harpe, *Lycée ou cours de littérature ancienne et moderne* (Paris, Year VII to Year XIII), XI, part 2, p. 488. Fabre's play, *Les Gens de lettres*, was published posthumously in *Mélanges littéraires par une société de gens de lettres* (Paris, 1827).

64. See Marat's letters to Roume de Saint Laurent in *Correspondance de Marat, recueillie et annotée par Charles Vellay* (Paris, 1908).

65. This interpretation, which maintains that the *libelles* increased in number and importance during the régime's last years, is based only on impressions from extensive reading in the pamphlet collections of the Bibliothèque Nationale and the British Museum, but it is supported by the similar impressions of Louis XVI's lieutenant general of police: see Lenoir's essay, "De l'administration de l'ancienne police concernant les libelles, les mauvaises satires et chansons, leurs auteurs coupables,

délinquants, complices on adhérents," Bibliothèque municipale d'Orléans, MS. 1422.
66. For a more detailed discussion of *libelle* literature, see Robert Darnton, "Reading, Writing, and Publishing in Eighteenth-Century France: A Case Study in the Sociology of Literature," *Daedalus* (Dec. 1970).
67. Charles Thévenau de Morande (anonymously), *Le Gazetier cuirassé: ou Anecdotes scandaleuses de la cour de France* (1771, "Imprimé à cent lieues de la Bastille, à l'enseigne de la liberté"), p. 128.
68. *Ibid.*, pp. 167–68.
69. *Ibid.*, pp. 169–70.
70. As examples of Morande's characteristic emphasis on impotence and sodomy, see *ibid.*, pp. 51–52 and 61.
71. *Ibid.*, pp. 79–80.
72. *Ibid.*, pp. 182–83.
73. *Ibid.*, pp. 131–32.
74. *Ibid.*, pp. 80–81.
75. *Ibid.*, p. 53.
76. *Ibid.*, pp. 36–37.
77. *Ibid.*, p. 80. This remark introduced the following reference (p. 80) to Maupeou's fellow minister, the Duke d'Aiguillon: "The peerage used to be in France a rank where the slightest stain was inadmissable; but today a peer [i.e. d'Aiguillon] can empoison, ruin a province and intimidate witnesses, provided he possesses the art of the courtier and can lie well."
78. *Ibid.*, p. 31.
79. *Ibid.*, p. 109: "A new book has just appeared, which challenges the kings of France to prove their divine institution by producing the treaty that the eternal father signed with them; the author of that book defies them to do so."
80. *Ibid.*, pp. 157–58.
81. See Carra's notes to his translation of John Gillies' *Histoire de l'ancienne Grèce* (Paris, 1787), I, 4 and 11; II, 387–89; V, 387; and VI, 98. Carra produced an influential "*Mémoire*" attacking Calonne just before the opening of the Assembly of Notables in 1787 (it was reprinted in Carra's *Un Petit Mot de réponse à M. de Calonne sur sa Requête au Roi* [Amsterdam, 1787]) and continued to pummel him in *libelles* like *M. de Calonne tout entier* (Brussells, 1788). He also turned on Lenoir (*L'an 1787: Précis de l'administration de la Bibliothèque du Roi sous M. Lenoir* [2nd edn., Liège, 1788]), because Lenoir had not only advised Calonne against giving Carra a pension but had also tried, with the help of some academicians, to get him dismissed from a subordinate post in the Bibliothèque du Roi, which was Carra's only feeble source of income: see the Lenoir papers, Bibliothèque municipale d'Orléans, MSS. 1421 and 1423. Not surprisingly, Carra's pre-revolutionary pamphlets fairly sizzle with hatred of the literary patricians who *did* get the pensions, sinecures, and seats in the academy and of the *grands* who dealt them out.

82. See his implicit contrast of "bourgeois" and aristocratic morality and of England and France in *Le Gazetier cuirassé*, pp. 83–86, 171, and 173.
83. *Ibid.*, p. 131.
84. His victims included Voltaire, d'Alembert, and their companions in the salon of Mme. Geoffrin: see *ibid.*, pp. 178 and 181.
85. Charles Thévenau de Morande (anonymously), *La Gazette noire par un homme qui n'est pas blanc; ou oeuvres posthumes du Gazetier cuirassé* (1784 "imprimé à cent lieues de la Bastille . . ."), pp. 194–95. See also the strikingly similar passage in *Vie privée de Louis XV, ou principaux événements, particularités et anecdotes de son règne* (London, 1781), IV, 139–40.
86. "Rousseau of the gutter," a term applied to Restif de la Bretonne in the eighteenth century and that fits many of Restif's Grub Street comrades.
87. As an example of this widespread identification with Rousseau in opposition to Voltaire, see *Le Tableau de Paris*, XI, 186.
88. For a striking account of a fortune labouriously built up by pensions and sinecures and then demolished by the Revolution, see the *Mémoires de l'abbé Morellet sur le dix-huitième siècle et sur la Révolution*, 2 vols. (Paris, 1921). Chapters 5 through 7 in volume II give a fascinating picture of an old veteran of the Enlightenment trying to communicate with young *sans-culottes*, who had no interest in the mid-century treatises he produced to prove the soundness of his principles but who wanted answers to questions like, "Why were you happy before the 10th of August and have you been sad since then"? (II, 124). Morellet could not make sense of the *sans-culottes* any more than they could understand him: a *cultural* revolution separated them.
89. After the abolition of the monopoly of the Comédie Française, 45 new theatres sprang up in Paris; 1500 new plays were produced between 1789 and 1799, 750 in the years 1792–94, in contrast to the mere handful produced annually before the Revolution. These new plays (which seem to resemble those of the recent "cultural revolution" in China) may have derived more from the popular *foire* theatre and *drames poissardes* than from the Comédie française, which catered to aristocratic audiences and even had direct access to the king, thanks to its governing board, made up of gentlemen of the king's bedchamber. Perhaps the genres of Grub Street (the *libelle* type of pamphlet and the *Père Duchesne* type of newspaper) gained ground as the Parisian populace gained power: the *lumpen* intelligentsia certainly knew how to speak the language of the common people. Most striking of all was the revolution that the Revolution wrought in journalism. Only a few dozen periodicals, none containing much news, circulated in Paris during the 1780's. At least 250 genuine *news*papers were founded in the last six months of 1789, and at least 350 circulated in 1790. On the theatre, see John Lough, *Paris Theatre Audiences in the Seventeenth and Eighteenth Centuries* (London, 1957); Jules Bonnassies, *Les Auteurs dramatiques, op. cit.*; and Beatrice Hyslop, "The Theatre During a Crisis:

The Parisian Theatre, During the Reign of Terror," *Journal of Modern History*, XVII (1945), 332–55. On the press, see Eugène Hatin, *Bibliographie historique et critique de la presse périodique française* (Paris, 1866); Eugène Hatin, *Histoire politique et littéraire de la presse en France* (Paris, 1859), esp. chaps. 2–8; and Gérard Walter, *Hébert et le Père Duchesne* (Paris, 1946).

90. A. Rivarol and L. de Champcenetz, *Petit Dictionnaire des grands hommes de la Révolution* (1790). For a typical comment, see p. vii: "It is by a perfect agreement between the rejects of the court and the rejects of fortune that we have arrived at this general impoverishment which alone testifies to our equality."

91. *Réimpression de l'ancien Moniteur* (Paris, 1861), V, 439.

92. Henri Grégoire, *Rapport et projet de décret, présenté au nom du Comité de l'instruction publique, à la séance du 8 août* (Paris, 1793). See also the *Discours du citoyen David, député de Paris, sur la nécessité de supprimer les académies* (Paris, 1793), made during the same session of the Convention; the polemics between Morellet and Chamfort (S.R.N. Chamfort, *Des académies*, Paris, 1791, and abbé André Morellet, *De l'Académie française* . . . , Paris, 1791); and the debates on the cultural implications of the Revolution in the *Moniteur*, for example, VII, 115–20 and 218–19; XVII, p. 176; XXII, 181–84 and 191–93; XXIII, 127–28 and 130–31. The classic statement of the revolutionaries' hatred for the Old Régime's cultural elitism remains Marat's *Les Charlatans modernes, ou lettres sur le charlatanisme académique* (Paris, 1791).

93. Albert Soboul touches on this theme in *Les Sans-culottes parisiens en l'an II* (Paris, 1958), pp. 670–73, and in "Classes populaires et rousseauisme," *Paysans, sans-culottes et Jacobins* (Paris, 1966), pp. 203–23.

94. Gérard Walter, *Hébert,* chaps. 1–2. See also R.-N.-D. Desgenettes (who knew Hébert as a starving hack writer before 1789), *Souvenirs de la fin du XVIIIe siècle et du commencement du XIXe siècle* (Paris, 1836), II, 237–54; and the description of the pre-revolutionary Hébert printed in a Robespierrist *libelle* attacking him, *Vie privée et politique de J.-R. Hébert* (Paris, Year II), p. 13: "Without a shirt, without shoes, he only left the tiny room he rented on the seventh floor in order to borrow some pennies from his friends or to pilfer them."

95. Gustave Lanson, *Voltaire*, trans. R. A. Wagoner (New York, 1966), p. 48.

The Melancholy and the Wild:

A Note on Macpherson's Russian Success

Glynn R. Barratt

FEW AUTHORS were translated into Russian more frequently, in the last ten years of the eighteenth century and the first five of the nineteenth, than Macpherson, the history of whose hoax is now almost a commonplace of Western literary history. Ossian's first appearance in Russia, in a passage from *Die Leiden des Jungen Werther* somewhat haphazardly translated in 1781, was relatively late. No less than twenty years before, within months of the appearance of *Fragments of Antient Poetry* . . . in Edinburgh,[1] French connoisseurs of the extreme and picturesque might peruse the curious extracts published in *Le Journal Etranger*.[2] His interest aroused by Werther's respect for a Gaelic bard of whom he had not heard, Yermil' Kostrov immediately began his monumental paraphrase, which finally appeared in 1792.[3] Thereafter versions followed thick and fast, from Karamzin's painstaking *Songs of Sel'ma* to the essays, more or less appalling in point of literal accuracy, of Ivan Zakharov, V. N. Olin', N. F. Grammatin, Gnedich, and half a dozen others. The Russian penchant for northern myth, Finnish and Nordic mixed in a carefree manner, had of course preceded the arrival of Macpherson. In Catherine's time, the myths of Scandinavia had come to prominence in Russian verse and drama; one has merely to think of Xeraskov's *Vladimir*, or Derzhavin's "The Waterfall" (1791), or the Empress' own pseudo-mediaeval sallies—*The Novgorod Bogatyr' Boeslayevich*, for example, or the fantastic *Historical Representation from the Life of Ryurik*—to see the point. But it was the appearance of two Russian translations of Ossian, by A. I. Dmitriyev and Kostrov, together with the rediscovery of their own oral tradition by educated liberal Russians during the 1780's, that brought to its highest pitch a fashionable interest in ancient Scandinavian and Gaelic literature. (In Russian eyes, the Western Isles would always lie within easy rowing distance of the Swedlish coastline.)[4]

In Petersburg *salons*, Ossian came as a revelation. The triumph was spontaneous, and Karamzin expressed it in his "Poeziya" (1787):

> Pouring sweet anguish into languid minds,
> Preparing us for sombre images;
> Afflicted was this dear and gentle soul.
> O Ossian, thou art great, inimitable![5]

To Ossian Russians turned (as a recent critic puts it) for "the sweet yet bitter recollection of departed happiness . . . for the melancholy of regret for glories that once were."[6] Suddenly, Caledonia was *à la mode*; grim mountains became noble prospects; in Ossian, cultivated Russians believed they caught a glimpse of primitive mankind, a race of stern and simple virtues, "standing outside contemporary civilization and preserving in remote wilds the freshness of early life, their own ancient language, their own picturesque costume . . . even, unimpaired by the contagion of luxury, all the valour of the race that had defeated the Romans themselves."[7] Herder spoke with Karamzin, the French with the Italians. All Europe believed that in the Highlands, if anywhere, poetry might be found. But here is a curious thing: how could Ossian be both wild *and* mournful, and his verses simultaneously unconstrained and melancholy, as Petrov and the Dmitriyev brothers claimed? For melancholy, save in its extreme and quasi-suicidal form, is generally associated with placidity and calm, not wildness. The question is an interesting one and bears directly, as I hope to show, on the matter of Russians' dependence, for their first knowledge of Ossian, on poor French paraphrases of Macpherson's massive work.

Not until 1788 had A. I. Dmitriyev's version of *Poems of the Ancient Bards* appeared.[8] Yet Turgot's extracts, it was seen, were published within months of the appearance of the first Scottish edition. It was both natural and inevitable that the Ossianic myth should reach Petersburg and Moscow in French translation. Through French paraphrases or "translations," one need hardly say, Russians of the last years of the century, as earlier, acquired what slight knowledge they had of German, Greek, English, and Italian literature. "The gentleman author, the St. Petersburg fashionable, the ennuied hussar, the civilized squire—all read Shakespear and Sterne . . . in French versions, and French versions only."[9] And so it was with Ossian.

There is no reason to reiterate the findings in connection with this question of French versions of Macpherson of Professor Paul van Tieghem, whose pioneering study *Ossian en France* (1914) contains a bibliography well suited to my purpose. Suffice it to remark here that by van Tieghem's count there were no fewer than eighteen French prose versions of Ossian by 1799, and fourteen different attempts to render him into French iambics or anapaestics.[10] It was not from Macpherson's text that Yermil' Kostrov worked—quixotic notion!—but from that of Pierre Prime Félicien Letourneur's *Ossian, poésies galliques* (Paris, 1777). As to Gnedich, he seems to have relied uncomfortably on the Marquis de Saint-Simon, whose *Témora, poème épique en huit chants . . .* had appeared in Amsterdam three years before. Both Saint-Simon's and Letourneur's attempts were readily available in Petersburg and Moscow by 1780 at the latest; for if Plavil'shchikov had them in stock, as well as the unhappy essays of Massot, Miger, and Lombard,[11] naturally Ol'khin had to have them too.

What, then, did these French paraphrasts make of Macpherson? The question is important to a just appreciation of that poet's Russian triumph, for as will be shown, French influence went some way towards blinding Russians—for a time—to those aspects of Ossian to which, in other circumstances they would have been most openly receptive. It is, needless to say, extremely rash to summarize some thirty different versions in one line. Nevertheless, one trait must be admitted to be common to the varying "translations" of Turgot, Letourneur and Saint-Simon, Miger and Lombard: a tendency always to moderate passion, to soften violence and jagged contours, to lose what is most wild and unconstrained in Macpherson's work. Simply because their versions of that work served as models for Russians, who also longed for Dunlathmon's misty tower and the roaring of Oithona, we must consider briefly how the French Ossianophiles served or abused their Scottish master. Because they were relatively popular in Petersburg at least by 1785, *Contes et poésies erses* (1772) and the texts of Turgot and Letourneur will be the bases of comparison, though others would serve no less well.

Turgot was a prolific and reputedly accurate translator of Latin, English, German, and Italian works.[12] He was responsible for the earliest French version of "the songs of the third-century bard."

Here, now, is a short extract from Macpherson's text and from that printed in *Le Journal Etranger* early in 1761:

> Autumn is dark on the mountains; grey mist rests on the hills. The whirlwind is heard on the heath. Dark rolls the river through the narrow plain. A tree stands alone on the hill, and marks the slumbering Connal. The leaves whirl round with the wind, and strew the grave of the dead. At times are seen here the ghosts of the departed, when the musing hunter alone stalks slowly over the heath.

> *La sombre automne règne sur les montagnes, les brouillards grisâtres se reposent sur les collines, les ouragans retentissent sur les bruyères. La rivière roule ses eaux bourbeuses à travers la plaine étroite. Souvent les âmes des morts se font voir dans ce lieu quand le chasseur solitaire et pensif se promène lentement sur la bruyère.*

Just as Macpherson's lowering plains and dark mountains magically change the smiling land of salmon and white sands found in the *Silva Gadelica* of Irish romance and in *The Dean of Lismore's Book*, so Turgot changes what he finds, and leads us as he led Kostrov into a private world. *Ouragans* are not hurricanes or whirlwinds, as *la brise* is no breeze; and where are "the ghosts of the departed"? Not, certainly, in the flat, gallicized *âmes des morts*! And how wide a gulf divides the Scottish "musing hunter" from *le chasseur solitaire et pensif* across the Channel! True, both Macpherson's and the French text do accurately depict the bleak and grandiose scenery of Ross and Inverness; but this is not the point. The point is that Turgot modified Macpherson's vision—and that Russians willingly accepted the mournful, melancholy Ossian that Turgot offered them. They had as little interest in the geological realities of northwest Scotland as Turgot had in Fiann mac-Cumhail of Geraldus Cambrensis' account. They saw, broadly speaking, what Turgot saw; and Turgot saw what he wished to see—a rather less violent, undisciplined Caledonia than Macpherson had in mind. And here is van Tieghem's strange summing-up of the earliest known French version: "Automne, brouillards, . . . montagnes, bruyères, arbre solitaire penché sur une tombe; tout ce qu'il y a de plus caractéristique et de plus nouveau dans le paysage ossianique se trouve ramassé comme à dessein dans ce court tableau."[13] But it is not so! No less characteristic of Macpherson's Caledonia than graves and mist is a strain of natural wildness, as in this brief passage (taken from Smart):

> It is night; I am alone, forlorn on the hill of storms. The wind is heard in the mountain. The torrent pours down the rock. Rise, moon! from behind thy clouds. Stars of the night, arise. . . . Speak to me, my friends! To Colma they give no reply. My soul is tormented with fears! They are dead! Their swords are red from the fight. . . .[14]

Small wonder that Venevitinov should choose to imitate the passage—sixty years after it was written![15]

Here, next, is a short extract from Oithona in Macpherson's text and that of *Contes et poésies erses*, in which the anonymous translator confuses Oscar and Toscar, Minona and Colma, Dunlathmon and Lathmon:[16]

> A rougher blast rushed through the oak. The dream of night departed. Gaul took his ashen spear. He stood in the rage of his soul. Often did his eyes turn to the east. He accused the lagging light. At length the morning came forth. The hero lifted up the sail. The winds came rustling from the hill. On the third day arose Tromathon, like a blue shield. . . .

129

Une bouffée de vent ébranle plus violemment la cime touffue des arbres, et Morni s'éveille. Il saisit sa lance et se lève furieux. Il tourne sans cesse ses yeux vers l' orient et maudit la lenteur du jour. Enfin l'aurore paraît. Il déploie ses voiles, et son vaisseau bondit. . . . Le troisième jour, l'île de Tromaton sort à ses yeux du sein des mers. . . .

Comment hardly seems necessary. *Ashen*, the sole concrete epithet, is lost; so, too, is the *blue shield* simile. Single words are swollen into phrases, phrases in the original discarded. So it is, too, in Letourneur's version:

> Come, thou huntress of Lutha, Malvina, call back his soul to the bard. I look forward to Lochlin of the lakes, to the dark billowy bay of U-thorno, where Fingal descends from ocean, from the roar of winds. Few are the heroes of Morven in a land unknown! Starno sent a dweller of Loda to bid Fingal to the feast; but the king remembered the past, and all his rage arose. . . .

> *Viens, ô Malvina, viens ranimer mon génie. Mes yeux s'arrêtent sur Lochlin, sur la sombre baie d'Uthorno où Fingal cherche un asile contre la fureur des flots et des vents. Les héros de Morven ne descendirent pas en grand nombre sur cette terre inconnue. Starno députa un enfant de Loda pour inviter Fingal à sa fête. Mais Fingal se souvint du passé et ne put contenir son indignation. . . .*

What can one say? Letourneur changes the short and jerky rhythm of the English quite beyond recognition. He omits, inserts, changes, edits, and transposes at will. Above all, he avoids the concrete, the particular, the colourful and wild. And this was the Ossian which Russians took to reflect the original (for few indeed could follow Karamzin's example and read the English).[17] Where are "the kings of Morven, their blue shields beneath the mountain mist upon some haunted heath, the hypnotic repetitions of vaguely meaningful epithets" of which Nabokov speaks so sonorously?[18] All is modified, tamed, improved; violence wilts before Good Taste. The damage done by French "translators" was compounded by their Russian followers, whose readers thereby found themselves at three removes from Gaelic texts which probably never existed. So, one sees, all study of Western sentimentalism and

130

pre-Romantic literature in Russia is fundamentally and necessarily the study of appearance and opinion, not reality and fact—the study, not of what Macpherson ever wrote or meant to write, but of what he was taken to mean and have in mind.

Educated Russians, then, accepted from the French—who could no more read Gaelic than themselves—a belief in the authenticity of Ossian, but as a modified, a melancholy bard. As Professor Simmons puts it, "it was the *melancholy* in the prose-poetry of Ossian that the Russians seized upon at once. The bard's *contemplative sadness* . . . brought tears to the eyes of sentimental Russian writers."[19] But melancholy, it was noted earlier, is commonly connected not with bloody battle scenes, but with the soft setting of country churchyards; and, of course, the spirit of Stoke Poges looms large in Russian verse of the 1780's and '90's. The tolling bells, ivy-grown tombs, and dirges all seemed to Karamzin's contemporaries the proper setting for that most engaging sadness that pervaded western sentimentalism. There is, perhaps, a certain inevitability in the way in which western authors of the later eighteenth century, caught by the Russians as it were in a single mood and setting, could never escape their allocated milieux: Crabbe's village, Gray's churchyard with the lichen-grown gate and tombs, Young's autumn. Would you find Genius? (cried a nameless poet in 1797): "Hearken to the spirit of the storm/ In Ossian's mournful verses, or with Young/ Pour forth tears."[20] The lines are significant. Juxtaposed are *mournful verses* and the *spirit of the storm*.

Here we come to a central point in our consideration of Macpherson's fate in Russia—seldom in eighteenth-century Russian literature is the mood of melancholy found in bleak isolation; almost invariably it is combined with elements of wildness, at first merely external but after 1790 both external and internal, physical and emotional.[21] Consider, first, the youthful experience of S. N. Glinka (1776–1847), a minor writer of the period, on reading *Night Thoughts* in 1793:

> In my youth [he remembered many years later] I would wander in remote places dreaming of Young, perhaps in deep forests.

131

> Once, dreaming under the pouring rain and composing in the vein of *The Nights*, I was aroused by a clap of thunder; returning home, I transferred my sombre reflections to paper. . . .[22]

"Deep forests," "clap of thunder"—there is something of foreboding here, something black like an approaching but still distant storm cloud. Where there is "pouring rain" and rumbling thunder, can there be no lightning? Six years earlier, in his "Poeziya," Karamzin too had hesitated between the melancholy and the wild, finally compromising and settling for both in equal measure. "Poeziya," one may recall, appeared before the earliest Russian translation of Ossian in 1788:

> Fingal grieved for his friends, heroes *in battle fallen*,
> And from the grave the bard evoked their shades.
> Just as *the roar of ocean waves* that sounds
> Through forests far from shore, and bearing sadness
> To hopeful hearts: so are the songs of Ossian. . . .[23]

Is there not an undercurrent here that one could hardly call melancholy? A suggestion, in the heroes and crashing waves, of later Russian verse—the verse of pre-Decembrist years, of Kyukhel'beker, Ryleyev, and Rayevsky?

"The eighteenth century," it is claimed, "surrendered itself completely to the strain of melancholy, to the sweet yet bitter recollection of departed happiness . . . the melancholy of regret for glories that once were."[24] But what happiness could Russians recollect in Cowper's or Macpherson's senses of the word? What glories could they regret in 1790? Russian arms had known recent victories and would soon know even greater ones! The whole premise of melancholy for lost glory and happiness, in other words, was as irrelevant to Russian circumstances as it was alluring. Russians had no *need* of "country churchyards" by the last years of the century; and, though as a fashionable literary setting it continued prominent in Russian verse at least until 1820, the mournful cemetery with sad poet and ivy-covered tomb grew ever more anachronistic, ever less consonant with actual Russian circumstances. It was the spirit of the storm that Liberals needed, the

Ossian tamed by Letourneur that radicals rejected in favour of the truer, wilder man and myth. Can one speak of German, French, or English needs in poetry? Or say that those countries' political health or emotional development *required* that a certain poet or kind of poetry be given air and light? I do not think so. But Russian Liberals, whose dangerous notions found expression only in literature, as they do now, *needed* a part of Ossian's message; and one need hardly labour the significance of the successes of Chateaubriand, Schiller, Macpherson as a new century began.

Ossian's legacy in Russia was expression of diffuse but powerful emotions—emotions softened by the French translators, but which Russians felt increasingly and in increasing numbers. After two decades of Turgot and Saint-Simon, Lombard and Letourneur, Russians saw the "real" Ossian. Matters had changed greatly between 1790, when Karamzin could translate *Carthon* on board a small ship in a storm and remark mildly, "What a holiday for my imagination, filled with Ossian!"[25] and the times of Batyushkov or Baratynsky. True, Karamzin did show a preference for wild and grandiose scenes in nature, but even the famous night storm in *Marfa posadnitsa* hardly compares with Baratynsky's "The Waterfall" or "The Storm" for barely restrained violence. By its nature, Ossianic influence is less easily perceived in given passages than in a general sense or mood. Yet few would deny that in these poems, as in *Eda*, and "Finlyandiya," and in a dozen pieces by Kozlov not written until the 1830's, Ossian's spirit rides:

> There the skalds sang war, and their fingers flew
> Across the burning strings . . .
> There sang the sound of swords, the whistle of
> Feathered arrows and the clash of shields. . . .

> Where are you hidden, midnight heroes?

> O wondrous Ossian! Dreaming of the mists,
> Of Innistor's mysterious barrows,
> I roamed the slumbering forests in winter
> Where storm and blizzard, raging, would alarm
> The hearing and, like corpses, howl in the dark glade. . . .[26]

Shrouded from Russian readers by layers of French prose, by emphases ill-chosen and by attitudes irrelevant to changing Russian needs, Ossian had long to wait until he could be seen in Petersburg in his true colours—deep red and blue.[27]

NOTES

1. *Fragments of Antient Poetry collected in the Highlands of Scotland, and Translated from the Galic of Erse Language* (Edinburgh, 1760).
2. See P. van Tieghem, *Ossian en France* (Paris, 1914; reprinted Geneva, 1967), I, 115–17; a fragment appeared in the *Journal* in September, 1760.
3. *Ossian, syn Fingalov; bard tret'yego veka.* For details of other versions, see *Ukazatel' k Opytu roissyskoy bibliografii*, compiled by V. S. Sopikov (St. Petersburg, 1908), Nos. 8,742, 11,544, 11,545.
4. See I. Zamotin, *Russkiy romantizm dvadtsatykh godov* (St. Petersburg, 1911), chaps. 4 and 5.
5. Lines 118–21.
6. E. J. Simmons, *English Literature and Culture in Russia, 1553–1840* (Cambridge, Mass., 1935), p. 180.
7. J. S. Smart, *James Macpherson* (London, 1905; reprinted 1969), p. 5.
8. *Poemy drevnikh bardov*, based on Pt. 2 of *Choix de contes et poésies erses* (Amsterdam, 1772).
9. A. Pushkin, *Eugene Onegin*, ed. V. Nabokov, 4 vols., II (New York, 1964), 158.
10. Van Tieghem, *op. cit.*, II, 482–85.
11. *Ibid.*, p. 485.
12. Dupont de Nemours is insistent on this point; see *Oeuvres de Turgot*, 9 vols., Vol. 1 (Paris, 1810), 18.
13. Van Tieghem, *op. cit.*, I, 115.
14. Smart, *op. cit.*, p. 81.
15. "Kolna Domna."
16. Included in the marquetry of this edition were "Ossian" (Pt. 2 of "Croma"), "Les malheurs d'Armin" (from the middle of *Chants de Selma*), "Lamor et Hidallan" (from the 3rd *duan* of "Cath-Loda").
17. See Karamzin's *Pis'ma russkogo puteshestvennika* (St. Petersburg, 1848), II, 139. An English edition was purchased in a Leipzig bookshop.
18. Pushkin, *op. cit.*, II, 255.
19. Simmons, *op. cit.*, p. 182.
20. "Sila Geniya," *Aonidy* (1797), no. 2, p. 125.
21. Exceptions must perhaps be made in the cases of Sumarokov's dully elegiac successors, Natrov, Ablesimov, Rzhevsky, much of whose work is certainly melancholy, *tout court*.
22. S. N. Glinka, *Zapiski* (St. Petersburg, 1895), p. 363.

23. Lines 113–17; italics are mine.
24. Simmons, *op. cit.*, p. 180.
25. *Pis'ma russkogo puteshestvennika*, II, 786.
26. K. N. Batjushkov, "Skal'd"; E. A. Baratynsky, "Finlyandiya" (early variant); I. I. Kozlov, "Poet i groza" (based on Lamartine's *Jocelyn*!).
27. See N. K. Piksanov, "Etyud o vliyanii ossianovskoy poezii v russkoy literature," *Sochineniya Pushkina* (St. Petersburg, 1907), I, 108–14; also V. I. Maslova, "K voprosu o pervykh perevodakh poem Ossiana-Makfersona," in *Sbornik Otdeleniya Russkogo Yazyka i Slovesnosti* (Leningrad, 1928), No. 3.

Limits of the Gothic:

The Scottish Example

Francis R. Hart

THE UNENDING and contentious search for the generic essence of the "Gothic novel" appears as futile as do most searches of the kind. Take the recent debate in *PMLA*: R. D. Hume in March 1969, and Hume and R. L. Platzner in March 1971. One contestant seeks to force a consensus, the other strives as mightily to establish momentous differences, and together they demonstrate the futility of such debates if little more. I do not mean here to dwell on the confusion in which such debates leave me, nor would substantive criticism of the positions of Hume and Platzner be fair without more preliminary analysis than is possible in a brief paper. But I do wish to begin by taking some issue with the basic critical intentions they share.

Although Hume tries at last to deny it, both disputants are bent on generic essentializing. And both are bent, as well, on evaluating a whole genre, on establishing that *the* Gothic novel has such-and-such artistic worth. The first objective, I think, is premature, and the second strikes me as critically dubious. Hume speaks of what the "form" had for its "prime feature" or its "key characteristic," as distinguished from mere "conventions," "devices," or "trappings," when it "came to full flower." In his "Rejoinder" (March, 1971), Platzner (though he speaks not of flowering form but of "mythopoeic tendencies") is equally insistent: *because* the "Gothic Romance is a conglomerate of literary 'kinds,' grafting character types and melodramatic devices of Jacobean drama and sentimental fiction onto a sensibility derived largely from graveyard poetry and the cult of the sublime"—because, that is, of the "synthetic

137

character of this genre" (the same is true, one supposes, of all genres)—"one is obliged to isolate what is conspicuously 'gothic' in the Gothic." Why? Because otherwise its formal achievement or mythopoeic tendency could not receive serious academic acclaim?

In an earlier essay (in *Experience in the Novel*, 1968), I wrote with such intentions myself, and in an excellent (still unpublished) dissertation on the nineteenth-century Gothic (Yale, 1970) James Maddox quite properly found my argument overstated. I mistake the tendency, says Maddox, for the achievement. But this danger is endemic in criticism of the Gothic, in part because of an understandable defensiveness in seeking academic respectability for a long-disgraced, flagrantly "popular" sub-genre, and in part because our sense of its "importance" declares itself on such a murkily subjective level of response. We academics respond nowadays to the rediscovered Gothic for some of the same scandalous reasons that our students respond to adult fantasy, elfin, demonic, or speculative. Our persistent Arnoldian bias then drives us to discover a rationale in moral seriousness for our enthusiasm, and in so doing to distinguish between essential value (whether formal or mythopoeic) and "conventional trappings," even though conventional trappings are a condition of our response to any mode of popular fantasy. What Maddox and others call the Gothic "tendency" is not to be understood by such solemn essentializing. We need a fuller cultural and historical understanding of the Gothic tendency. Only then will we be ready to do critical justice to the stranger confusions or mixtures of mode that the Gothic engendered in the novel.

We can say of the late eighteenth-century Gothic tendency in the novel that it consists of at least five major elements, however profoundly, superficially, or incoherently these elements may declare themselves in an individual work: (1) an antiquarian taste for what was taken to be the style or ornament of the late Middle Ages and Renaissance; (2) an ambiguously enlightened taste for the preternatural—a curious revival of the ghost story; (3) a fascination with the mystery of human malevolence, perversity, sadism; (4) a preference for the style or affective state called sublimity; and (5) a shift of aim away from the didactic. How these several

138

elements might be interrelated is not to be explained simply. To insist on a single essential form or hierarchy of these elements is to neglect or prejudge the variety of emphases in any generic movement. Some Gothic novels stress emotional atmosphere, some the psychology of the preternatural, some the mystery of malevolence and perversity. A definition of the tendency, taking into consideration its variousness, cannot stipulate which emphasis is essential, or which is mere "trappings."

Now, it is clear that the beginnings of a non-English tradition of the novel in which I am much interested, the Scottish, already belong to the Gothic tendency. Yet three of the formative figures in this Gothic origin of the Scottish novel are not usually considered Gothic novelists, even though their relations to the Gothic seem important and undeniable. This contradiction is the occasion for what follows. My purpose is to understand the Gothic beginnings of the Scottish novel, but in furthering this purpose I may also use my Scottish example as a way of exploring the limits of the Gothic tendency. The three novelists are Smollett, Scott, and Hogg; the limits may best be marked out with the three terms "grotesque," "historic," and "diabolic."

A Gothic novel may prove to have extraordinary and pertinent cultural or historical interest without having realized an integrity of mode, for modal integrity and cultural import have no necessary relation. Yet what makes a Gothic novel interesting culturally often seems closely akin to what makes it interesting as a mixture of modes. In his *Tobias George Smollett* (Twayne, 1968), Robert Spector quotes two modern critical judgments of *Ferdinand Count Fathom* that, taken together, make a revealing paradox. Albrecht Strauss calls the book "a curious melange of incongruous fairy tale material and conventional claptrap," and this, though biased, is accurate. Louis Martz sees, in *Fathom*, Smollett turning away from the picaresque and "seeking new inspiration" in the horror tale, fairy tale, Gothic, and fantastic narrative. And this is true, too. Moreover, the "curious melange" aspect of the book is inseparable (though not indistinguishable) from its eclectic cultural interest as an experiment.

139

The Gothic or "conventional claptrap" episodes have often been noted: the repeated visits of Renaldo to Monimia's supposed tomb; the awesome appearance of her "phantom"; and the flight of Fathom from the tempest in the dark wood to the old woman's bloody hut, which Scott praises as a "tale of natural wonder which rises into the sublime; and, though often imitated, has never been surpassed, or perhaps equalled." Spector adds to this last the episode of Celinda's seduction, finds here "the materials later exploited by Ann Radcliffe," and cites them both as examples of Smollett's satiric treatment of the Gothic:

> Smollett never simply yields to the devices of supernatural terror; indeed, he ridicules them even as he uses them. . . . Smollett presents not Gothic terror, but the natural turmoil of the mind and actual physical dangers. . . . If this is an early use of the Gothic in the English novel, it is one that takes little advantage of supernatural elements to harry the imagination. . . . In a way these two satiric attacks on Gothic illusion serve to undercut the terror in the one genuinely Gothic portion of the novel when Renaldo comes to what he believes to be the grave of Monimia. . . . It is all a language . . . to set doubts on the authenticity of the horror; and, while Smollett gets the most out of the new taste for terror, he does it clearly with the touch of the satirist.

Now, while perceptive, this is insufficient on two counts. First, it overlooks the curious, unarticulated, yet nonetheless suggestive way such episodes are related to other elements in the melange. Fathom's is the Hobbesian and mechanistic world of violent and gross physical needs, which Bruce rightly finds central to Smollett's vision. It is a world of warring animals, where the central symbol of depravity is the spectacle, at once horrible and ludicrous, of the close and violent interdependence of mind and body. It is a world where terror and horror are the strongest emotions, where man, preternaturally sensitized by extreme fear, supposes himself in Hell, responds in part with religious awe, and thus affirms the preternatural workings of conscience. In such a world, "Gothic" suppositions are no mere "claptrap" excrescences. Second, Spector misinterprets into parody what is a more complex ambivalence, a terror that is nonetheless real for its ludicrous aspect, an anti-sublimity that is true grotesque. I am not arguing that *Fathom* is a better novel than it is. I am saying that we have not gone far in interpreting its "Gothic" tendency if we prematurely restrict our terms of interpretation so as to ignore prima facie "melanges," exclude incidental and "unreal" supernaturalisms, or reject as irrelevant to the Gothic tendency the preclassical mode Smollett reintroduced into British fiction: that vision of a monstrously perverse, fallen, but animated world; that powerful conflation of the terrible, the horrible, and the ludicrous which we call the grotesque. Certainly, in the Scottish Gothic, the grotesque plays an essential role.

The grotesque in Smollett is inseparable from another modality which some (Kurt Wittig, for example) would see as distinctively Scottish, but which can as easily be identified with the later eighteenth century and its commitment to "the theatre of the mind," namely a radical and violent subjectivity of vision. One easily recalls the grotesque multiple distortions of subjectivity in the epistolary method of *Humphry Clinker*. The grotesque and the radically distortive nature of subjectivity are theoretically linked by Smollett in a revealing passage in *Fathom*, on the occasion of the seduction of Elinor, where the narrator explains: "There is an affinity and short transition betwixt all the violent passions that agitate the human mind. They are all false perspectives, which, though they magnify, yet perplex and render indistinct every object which they represent." The mixture, then, is no mere satiric undercutting of terror, but an express fascination with the violent and grotesque subjectivity of extreme emotional states. The mere description is enough to suggest a prima facie connection with the Gothic tendency.

We are familiar with how Roderick Random's outrage and despair at the gross caprice of the world cause him to see that world regularly through the double lenses of infernal horror and sadistic glee. What Sedlmayr calls the "secularization of Hell" in Goya, often a central vision in Gothic fiction, is nowhere more striking than in the infernal grotesque of Random's descents—into the cockpit, into the London ordinary:

> [I] found myself in the middle of a cook's shop, almost suffocated with the steams of boiled beef. . . . While I stood in amaze, undetermined whether to sit down or walk upwards again, Strap,

141

> in his descent missing one of the steps, tumbled headlong into
> this infernal ordinary and overturned the cook. . . . In her fall,
> she dashed the whole mess against the legs of a drummer . . .
> scalded him so miserably that he started up and danced up and
> down, uttering a volley of execrations that made my hair stand
> on end. . . . This poultice [of salt] was scarce laid on when the
> drummer . . . broke forth into such a hideous yell as made the
> whole company tremble . . . grinding his teeth at the same time
> with a most horrible grin.

And the grotesque horror of the battle scene where Random lies stapled to the poop deck, blinded with blood and scattered brains, surely yields nothing in "Gothic" intensity to the gloomier scenes of charnel rape in *The Monk*. The effect is identical with what Kayser describes in Brueghel's secularizing of the infernal in Bosch: "the experience of the estranged world . . . the hellish torments, like the phantasmagoric, the ghostly, the sadistic, the obscene, the mechanical"—in short, "the terror inspired by the unfathomable, that is, the grotesque." The revival of the grotesque is surely part of the Gothic tendency.

But it goes farther than that in Smollett. The grotesque world is grounded in man's original and mysterious perverseness. Random's vision of subjective and sadistic violence may seem in part caused by the world's brutality, but this is clearly not the case in *Peregrine Pickle*. Pickle acts from what Poe will later call

> a paradoxical something, which we may call *perverseness*. . . .
> With certain minds, under certain conditions, it becomes abso-
> lutely irresistible. I am not more certain that I breathe, than that
> the assurance of the wrong or error of any action is often the one
> unconquerable *force* which impels us, and alone impels us to its
> prosecution. . . . It is a radical, a primitive impulse—elementary.

Such is Perry's "preposterous and unaccountable passion" to "afflict and perplex" his fellow creatures, his sadistic perversity. Nor is this given perversity separable from his creative exuberance, the humorous power that makes him hero. He is a mysterious hero, to be sure, pawn of an infatuation of fancy and will, in a monstrous, potentially tragic world of "humors," of inexplicable hostilities, of "fantastic and maimed characters" such as Commodore Trunnion (V. S. Pritchett's phrase), whose fantastic maiming excites Perry to new heights of sadistic creativity. The moral mystery of cruel perverseness is, I think, far more explicitly central to *Peregrine Pickle* than the philosophical morality Goldberg describes as its thematic structure, wherein the educative hero systematically discovers the destructive consequences of unbridled imagination. Perry is not a naif but a demonic scourge. He makes his world; it is his victim.

He torments his world, to be sure, not for its sordidness but for its solemnity, its conventional orders. His indefatigable intrigues have two essential effects: to expose the ludicrous in the solemn, and to invert or destroy the ordered reality of conventional society. The first effects the book's grotesqueness, the second its saturnalian humor. More often than judge or scourge, Perry is Vice, demon, or Lord of Misrule. The example of Smollett's Perry suggests that we may well have overlooked in the Gothic tendency a revival of saturnalian fantasy. Anarchy in any revolutionary period is seldom merely a political impulse.

At any rate, here are two brief examples of the grotesque and saturnalian in *Pickle*. Nights at inns are filled with diabolical terror, ludicrous raptures and ecstasies. Gay and fantastic, ominous and sinister, the world here loses all rational shape, and humans become helpless puppets. Pallet the painter, amorously invading his Dulcinea's chamber, stumbles instead on the hiding Capuchin

> so that the painter having stript himself to the shirt, in groping about for his Dulcinea's bed, chanced to lay his hand upon the shaven crown of the father's head, which by a circular motion, the priest began to turn round in his grasp, like a ball in a socket. . . . one of his fingers happened to slip into his mouth, and was immediately secured between the Capuchin's teeth, with as firm a fixure, as if it had been screwed in a blacksmith's vice. . . . the unfortunate painter was found lying naked on the floor, in all the agony of horror and dismay.

This same unfortunate painter stalks about in female costume at a masquerade and is gazed at by the multitude "as a preternatural phaenomenon." Peregrine delights in manipulating such spectacles. His grotesque taste is a function of his perversity. But his even stronger delight is in disorder—as in the marvelous dinner episode, where the whole table is involved "in havock, ruin and confusion," and

> before Pickle could accomplish his escape, he was sauced with the syrup of the dormouse pye, which went to pieces in the general wreck; and as for the Italian count, he was overwhelmed by the sow's stomach, which bursting in the fall, discharged its contents upon his leg and thigh, and scalded him so miserably, that he shrieked with anguish, and grinned with a most ghastly and horrible aspect.

There is no sign here that the reader's attention is to be a moral concern with imaginative excess. Rather, it is a sharing of Perry's sadistic glee at monstrous disorder, and thus a peculiarly involved recognition of the "preposterous and unaccountable" fact of exuberant perverseness.

Now if the Gothic tendency in fiction of the late enlightenment is to be restricted to ghost stories or to a modal unity of sublime awe, then Smollett's grotesque may be declared irrelevant. But if it centers instead or as well on the terror and horror aroused by the mysterious possibilities of alienation—perversity, monomania, diabolic possession—and on the *power* of such alienation to create and destroy, delude and fascinate, then Pickle is pertinent indeed. He is an extraordinary connective between the triumphant amorality of the picaro and the late Gothic confidence men, the evil and ingenious blackmailers of Dickens. To say as much is not to argue for the artistic integrity or economy of a specific novel, but simply to discover something pertinent and slighted in the cultural interest of the tendency.

Although he does not use the word, Smollett's "Gothic" tendency was definitive for Scott, who stresses Smollett's sublimity, praises him as far above Fielding "in his powers of exciting terror," refers to "the wild and ferocious Pickle" whose jokes resemble "those of a fiend in glee," and implicitly likens Smollett to Byron:

He was, like a pre-eminent poet of our own day, a searcher of
dark bosoms, and loved to paint characters under the strong
agitation of fierce and stormy passions. Hence misanthropes,
gamblers, and duellists, are as common in his works, as robbers
in those of Salvator Rosa, and are drawn, in most cases, with the
same terrible truth and effect.

The same "Gothic" inclination is evident in Scott; no one has
failed to note it. But if Smollett is excluded from the Gothic for
his grotesque or anti-sublimity, Scott is segregated because he is
alleged to have assimilated such Gothic elements into a historical
realism; or, whereas the "historical element in the Gothic novel
does little more than contribute to the freedom conferred by distance in time and space," Scott's (and Jane Porter's) "are the first
novels whose *basis* is a specific historical setting" (Hume). The
word *basis* here leaves ample room for debate; and, while the distinction hinted at is no doubt accurate relative to Walpole and Radcliffe, it does not hold true for *Melmoth*, or, I would say, for Hume's
"greatest of Gothic novels" *Moby Dick*. But the point I want
briefly to question is (again) a double one. Is the distinction between the "Gothic" and the "historic" in tendency as real or significant as their kinship? Is the *basis* in specific historicity as essential to Scott as Hume suggests? If we allow for the characteristi-
cally Scottish setting or atmosphere of local history, we may find
Scott at his best more significantly related to the Gothic tendency
and thus understand the tendency less reductively.

Recent Scott criticism (and I have emphatically joined it) has
argued otherwise. We have followed Auerbach's description of the
ambience of Scott's novels as atmospheric historicism, but I wonder now if the term might (however awkwardly) be inverted:
historicistic atmospherism. Some of us thought Lukacs right in
placing Scott as proto-Marxist, for whom historical process is dra-
matized as cultural dialectic in novelistic realism. But I am increasingly impressed by earlier critics who saw Scott's historicism as dom-
inantly aesthetic, his settings patterned on a macabre picturesque
and conceived invariably, whatever the epochal surface, as timeless borderlands of romance where marvels jostle with human mo-

145

tives. It is the same in *Waverley*, where eighteenth-century enlightenment is stunned by the ambience of "romance," or in the late Renaissance of *Nigel*, which Scott saw spatially as foothills where the marvelous in incident still mixes with the subtly natural in character, or in the decaying Middle Ages of *Durward*, where romance ventures into a perilous, anarchic borderland between cynical pragmatism and ferocious quixotry. In all three, the same barbarous and the same civil interplay in chiaroscuro, and the picturesque esthetic renders historical confrontation as a haunted landscape. I may be overstating the case for emphasis, but put in terms of traditional Scott criticism my suggestion is that we learn again from those who said that Scott inclined more to use history in the service of romance than to assimilate romance to the interpretation of history.

Otherwise, to be specific, here is the critical situation we are faced with, seen in three juxtaposed critical propositions. *The Bride of Lammermoor* is perhaps Scott's best novel, certainly one of his best. *The Bride* is one of the most complete and effective syntheses of Gothic elements. *The Bride* is not really a Gothic novel. If purity is that exclusive, or if the "best" of a genre or an author must be atypical, then definition has lost its usefulness. But some will object that this "best" evidence is unfairly limited, so let me add two other novels also touted as "best" and also taken (by Maddox, for instance) as illustrative of "Gothic" derivations in Scott: *Old Mortality* and *Redgauntlet*. And please note, as I do: this is no denial that Scott is a very interesting and hugely influential interpreter of the historic in experience. It is merely to suggest, in shift of emphasis, that the archetypal recurrences are more "basic" than discriminations of temporal or cultural setting. The recurrences are centrally Gothic: the macabre-picturesque ambience (already mentioned), the definitive character relationship, the hereditary curse.

The central relationship in what is generally identified as the Gothic novel is a rapport of mutual fascination between fatalistic innocence and sublimely wilful evil. The Gothic hero-villain alone is not enough, and criticism that seeks definitive moral interest in him alone mistakes the persistent Gothic characterology. Perilous innocence and demonic power are drawn to each other. Archetypally—some would say incestuously—akin, together they express or

146

evoke the mysterious theodicy hinted at by even the most frivo-
lously rationalized Gothic. As Anthony Winner puts it in a splendid essay on Hoffmann, "No one knows how the primal trespass
comes about. . . . We are paradoxically and unaccountably inno-
cent and yet somehow guilty." We yearn in fantasy for both the
pastoral idyll and the godlike power. Thus as readers of Gothic
novels we identify not with individual characters, but with the
painful division or the grotesque bond of paradoxical infatuation
between them: Emily and Montoni, Antonia and Ambrosio, Caleb
and Falkland, Monster and Frankenstein, Immalee and Melmoth,
Cathy and Heathcliff—and some more mythic synthesists would
add Christabel and Geraldine, Emanation and Spectre.

Such a bond is central in many Waverley novels. Superficially at
least, it is articulated in terms of historical, cultural, or ideological division. The critical issue is whether the historic-cultural typol-
ogy Lukacs, Daiches—and Hart—have stressed in Scott's characterology has really *displaced* its antecedents in Gothic archetype or
simply, superficially, covered them up. The issue is not to be settled here in a few sentences. But having lengthily supported the
Lukacs-Daiches line elsewhere, let me at least briefly put the opposing case here.

The mutual fascinations in Scott are not really intercultural at
all, and not between opposing epochs. They are the same in every
age, and they are between moral and psychical poles, the meek
but brave civility of moderation and the noble energy of monomania, the enlightened pragmatic and the barbaric idealistic, Sancho
and Quixote—in every age; and in every age, says the ironic Stendhal, "the base Sancho Panza wins." At least on a conscious ideological level Scott evidently stood with Sancho and pragmatic civility. It is equally evident, as Scott sensed, that a semi-conscious polar
attraction for the charisma of the monomaniac, the demonic freedom of the anti-empirical absolutist, reveals itself. Scott's penchant
for Gothic outlaws, humorous Jacobites, fanatical Covenanters is
esthetically insulated, of course. But that such figures are historicized into representative anachronisms sometimes seems little more
than Scott's way of authenticating them—a familiarly Scottish way
—and of saying that they are more ancient, original, "given."

Thus, what they really represent is a pre-enlightened persistence, a demonic element, in the human inheritance, to be sought out, exorcised, and not superficially denied or perilously overlooked.

Some such recognition is implicit in the fateful and ambivalent quests and loyalties of Scott's protagonists, implicating them personally and irreversibly in the destinies of their demonic—that is, monomaniacal—counterparts. Henry Morton, barely known even as his legendary father's son, enters upon the destined path to his own identity, his birthright, by responding "helplessly" to the claims made in his father's name by the fanatical but compelling Burley. Morton suffers, but Burley is exorcised, dwindling at last into a mean devil at bay in a cave, a menace safely to be left behind. The tale of Wandering Willie sets a similar paradigm of exorcism for *Redgauntlet*. Steenie goes to Hell and demands back his birthright from a Satanic trickster-thief. Darsy Latimer likewise seeks his identity in a wild region dominated by his monomaniacal uncle —with, once more, the end in the exorcism, the comic diminution, of that demonic force. The exorcism in *The Bride of Lammermoor*, while tragically complex, is archetypally the same. The Master inherits a fanatical role he seeks to ignore, is fatefully attracted to a specious (because unstable, lifeless) innocence in Lucy Ashton. She is drawn for protection to his demonically divided inheritance. The final exorcism loses him in the Gothic role that simply disappears into the sands, as unreal at last as Caleb Balderstone's idolatrous illusion of a still noble house.

I am not denying such patterns of exorcism a historical dimension; I am saying simply that the "historic" is really an archetypal constant—how the civilized, the socialized, exorcises the "given," or how the conscious exorcises the pre-conscious. Thus "history" is still Gothic, and the Gothic can be historicized without, as a tendency, ceasing to be itself.

The role of the hereditary curse is similar in Scott. It is often the core of the protagonist's problem; it inheres in his disinheritance. Henry Morton lives in the ruins of his father's lost cause on the charity of his niggardly uncle. The Master has left only his name (hardly that), his ruined tower, and his quixotically fraudulent servant. Darsy Latimer has a friend, a fatalistic curiosity, and not even his own name. Superficially the cause of disinheritance is "history," but "history" simply stands in for the evil—the failure, the monomania, the inhumanity—in the past, the given or original barbarism of man's moral youth. The curse of the past in Scott's Gothic is transmitted not in historic process, but in the warped and despotic personality of the past's monomaniacal devotee, the parental figure who sacrifices humanity to a cruelly quixotic idea. Yet the necessary interdependence of innocence and monomania is powerful, fateful, and Scott's relation to the Gothic is nonetheless definitive for his Scottish preoccupation with local history.

The same might be said for our final Scottish test of the limits of the Gothic. But it raises other questions as well. Least controversially, yet most intriguingly "Gothic," Hogg's *Memoirs and Confessions of a Justified Sinner* is a complex narrative of diabolic possession, theological satire, and local preternatural legend. Hogg's local landscape could hardly be remoter from the vague medieval sublimities or inquisitorial dungeons of Walpole, Radcliffe, Maturin. Yet it is, even more than Scott's, a haunted locale, and it is haunted chiefly by the terror of the diabolical. But this, too, can have many meanings and shapes, and Hogg's diabolic principle is significantly different from the repressed, sadistic sublimity of the Miltonic or Sensibility Gothic. And in Hogg, the terror of the diabolic is at once more primitive and more explicitly theological—hence, in the mixture, definitively Scottish. Hogg's feat is to have conflated a terrible theological monomania with a grotesque folk diabolism to make a tale of diabolic possession whose current appeal seems wider, more various, more authentic than any other "Gothic" novel of the early period (1760–1830). At the same time, there is a current willingness, however misguided, to see it as the single, lonely masterpiece of Scottish fiction. It derives not just from the horror Gothic of Godwin and Lewis, but possibly from the newly imported macabre of Hoffmann as well, and bears significant likeness, in its treatment of the diabolic compact, to *Melmoth the Wanderer* and formal similarity to its other immediate predecessor *Frankenstein*. And yet, as Dorothy Bussy told André Gide, "This book is Scotch to its very marrow; no English-

149

man could possibly have written it." Assuming such a radical cultural division, had we not better expand our sense of the limits of the Gothic?

Gide's praise of the book centers on its conception of the diabolic: the devil is wholly believable in psychological terms without recourse to a simple supernaturalism; the end, which demands a more literal or naive credibility, is therefore weak—so says Gide. This is a major issue of interpretation in the book, and it is central to our conception of the Gothic as well: is the preternatural or the demonic to be consistently psychologized, naturalized, or is it to remain to some degree ontologically mysterious? In an earlier essay I took the former position. The example of Hogg forces me to a less reductive position, for the very nature and experience of diabolic possession in Hogg demand that the devil have some sort of metaphysically separate existence. And Hogg carefully verifies such separateness through the senses, however puzzled, of numerous observers.

The relation of "possession" in Hogg to the more familiar psychologized diabolism of other Gothic novels is not simple. Edwin Eigner, writing of Hogg as an antecedent to Stevenson in the "good" romance tradition, stresses the discovery of the power of darkness as another power or side of the self. For him, the discovery of one's shadowy double is essential to the moral shock that gives the Gothic its power: there was that *in me* that could love a murderer; part of *me* loved the spectacle of pain. It is easy enough to find the points at which Hogg's sinner is sure that "I have two souls, which take possession of my bodily frame by turns," and the devil confirms the doctrine. But that is the point: it is diabolic doctrine—and by no means the whole truth. In fact it is crucial to diabolic possession as Hogg presents it that possession is NOT mere "doubling"—that the self is possessed by an Other, that the story draws partly on the primitive fear of being bewitched, possessed, by the spirit or power of an Other, of being robbed of one's identity. The whole suspense of the struggle of Robert and Gil-Martin for Robert's soul hangs on the questions: Will Robert ultimately surrender his whole soul willingly to the Other and cease to be? When will human nature, as in *Melmoth*, relieve its torment by

yielding to the ultimate horror? To identify this proud and indefatigable scourge of the proud and the damned too facilely with
the German romantic doppelgänger is to ignore the more primordial fear of the metaphysically Other that robs one of oneself.

And yet Gil-Martin, whose reality is grounded throughout in
folk diabolism, is highly sophisticated in his powers. What is most
terrifying and bewildering about him (and terror and metaphysical bewilderment are inseparable in *The Sinner*) is his power of
impersonation:

> My countenance changes with my studies and sensations. . . .
> It is a natural peculiarity in me, over which I have not full con-
> trol. If I contemplate a man's features seriously, mine own grad-
> ually assume the very same appearance and character. And . . .
> by assuming his likeness I attain to the possession of his most
> secret thoughts.

Via impersonation comes possession, and possession is power over
the mind, intellectual power, a power of capturing one's ideas
and transforming them so as to damn one. The conception of the
evil power here in Hogg, as in Smollett and Scott, is distinctively
Scottish. In the English Gothic, with its concern for political and
clerical tyranny, the power is more apt to be vaguely political, even
when implicitly sexual—the devil is a tyrant over the will. In the
Scottish Gothic the conception appears to be more intellectual;
the power derives from the awful corruption of theological doctrine, from intellectual pride and sophistry. The tempter is a monomaniacal sophist whose power derives not from a sublimity of
will, but from a sublimity of idea—and suitably, the word "sublime" or "sublimity" in Hogg's *Sinner* is reserved to describe diabolic ideas:

> There is a sublimity in his ideas, with which there is to me a
> mixture of terror. . . . I was greatly revived, and felt my spirit
> rise above the sphere of vulgar conceptions and the restrained
> views of unregenerate men. . . . the ruinous tendency of the
> tenets so sublimely inculcated.

The diabolic is thus the sublime power of theological doctrine im-
personated by the devil.

But the diabolic is a reality of folk legend and folk belief as well. The story is focused and fixed in haunted locality and localism is rhetorically essential to the book's credibility. Hogg's Gothic includes the anti-cosmopolitan satiric impulse of the Blackwoodian, marking it off from the urbane cosmopolitanism of Walpole and Radcliffe and Scott alike, and pointing ahead to *Wuthering Heights* and other later Gothic regionalisms. In all his fiction Hogg associates his authority as narrator with the traditional local sources of his story. Yet he speaks as the traditionalist divided in allegiance between modern enlightenment and the truth of the archaic local storyteller. The way he uses this controlled ambivalence to give local immediacy to the preternatural is seen well in this narrative comment in *The Brownie of Bodsbeck*:

> These minute traditions are generally founded on truth; yet, though two generations have scarcely passed away since the date of this tale, tradition, in this instance, relates things impossible, else Clavers must indeed have been one of the infernals. Often has the present relator of this tale stood over the deep green marks of that courser's hoof, many of which remain on that hill, in awe and astonishment, to think that he was actually looking at the traces made by the devil's foot, or at least by a horse that once belonged to him.

Thus, in his complex rhetorical stance, as in his complex realization of the diabolic, Hogg achieves some of the ends of the Gothic and at the same time enlarges our sense of its limits.

This is a conclusion, then, in which little more can be concluded. I have suggested that three of the earliest Scottish novelists belong in their distinctive—and distinctively Scottish—ways to the Gothic tendency in fiction of the late enlightenment. If this is so, then the development of the novel in Scotland must be understood partly in terms of its Gothic beginnings, and, too, if we are to understand the cultural breadth and complexity of the Gothic tendency in the period 1760–1830, we need to keep a more open sense of its limits. I would postpone the more vexed and intimidating question so intriguing to recent disputants, the question of the relation between the Gothic and the Romantic. If we take the most philosophical view of the cultural shift in Europe between the mid-eighteenth and mid-nineteenth centuries—Mill's view, for instance, of a Germano-Coleridgean reaction, then obviously the Gothic and the Romantic both belong to it. But it seems equally obvious that the Gothic declared itself first and that it must therefore be understood first. Then, if the Gothic and the Romantic are taken to be in some degree chronologically discrete phases in the same cultural shift, it is predictable that the later phase will be both continuation of and reaction against the earlier. Inquiry might form itself around such a model. But if it is to reach a valid historical hypothesis, it will need to proceed more cautiously and empirically in historical terms, and not essentialize a literary form in neglect of historical diversity and cultural variation.

Meaning and Mode in Gothic Fiction

Frederick Garber

O UR UNDERSTANDING of Gothic fiction has too often depended on a view that this mode is merely an extension of "sensibility," a grim silliness which grew to become the dark underbelly of the later eighteenth century. But if we are to accept such a historical classification we have to extend the possibilities of sensibility to include more than melancholic lovers leaning on crumbling memorial stones: for neither the Gothic tradition nor the forms of sensibility which contributed to it can be easily encompassed by the usual views of what they contain. There is considerable variety within sensibility itself: kinds and qualities of feeling, attitudes toward feeling, that are related to each other, touch upon each other at various points, but are by no means identical or even very much alike. Richardson has to be brought in to make one kind of sense out of Sterne and another kind out of the Marquis de Sade; yet neither Sterne nor Sade, both extensions and forms of the tradition of sensibility, have much to do with each other. Richardson, of course, gave a good deal to Rousseau's hapless lovers (who in turn began their own complex traditions), and in this case Sade is quite relevant indeed: the movement from Clarissa to Julie to Justine is one of the more intricate and imaginatively compelling in eighteenth-century fiction. Clearly, the tradition of sensibility has parallel lines within it which are alike in having a concern with feeling but different in their irreconcilable attitudes toward the valuation of that feeling.

If there is such complex variety within the forms of sensibility, forms which did much to shape the Gothic mode, similar complex-

155

ities occur nearly everywhere else in Gothicism as well. The mode, it seems, collected within itself all sorts of intricate traditions, and not only those included in the varieties of sensibility. For example, the Gothic penchant for sublimity and *its* conglomerate of emotions is no closer than sensibility is to being comfortably homogeneous: the awe which expands consciousness as one stares deep into an immense valley is close kin to its exact inversion in the claustrophobic terrors of constrictive dungeons. The emotions felt at the top of a tower are both cognate and contraposed to those felt in the holes deep within it. In his essay on the sublime Burke had mentioned in passing (Part II, Section vii) that "the last extreme of littleness is in some measure sublime." In fact, such paired inversions echo as an elemental structure throughout Gothic fiction, the mode which also recognizes the implicating mirror images in the consanguinity of Richardson and Sade. Gothicism is full of these varied tricks. Clearly, then, we ought to consider the mode as a most complex amalgam, one which is in part a collective of other modes whose affinities were perceived with an astonishing subtlety by the best practitioners of Gothic fiction. And it is through this quality as a collective that the Gothic reaches out to fulfill its own radical form and statement.

One way of describing this amalgam is to call it a meeting of modes or, more accurately, a confrontation among them. The lovers out of the literature of sensibility do as they did (or wished they could do) in the fiction they dominated, and villains sired by Machiavelli out of the Jacobean stage still function darkly, though smarting somewhat from their pre-Gothic tumble onto a burning lake. Melancholy still finds its inspiration in rot, and garrulous servants, loyal to their masters but of the wrong class to swoon over sublimity, carry through with an occasional craftiness which, was made definitive in Figaro. Most studies of Gothic fiction have been occupied, Jack Horner-like, with picking out these separate plums. But the point is not only that Gothicism blended other modes so skillfully into a unique organic coherence but also that it destroyed none of their separate identities. Each mode remains distinct and separately recognizable, not only in recurrent instances of its kind but in themes—the reuniting of displaced lovers, or the exigencies of time—which appear throughout the best Gothic fiction. Of course this made for some famous anachronisms; eighteenth-century sensibility loved to don masks of all sorts, behind which it never ceased to hug closely the values which helped it to live. Every one of the traditions which the Gothic drew toward itself brings into the Gothic amalgam most of the distinctive values which had defined it and gave it form: e.g., graveyard melancholy carries along not only its paraphernalia of images but all that those images said about men, their monuments, and their vanity, while the Italianate villains still bear much of their gloomy disposition to extol the will and other forms of egoism in human relationships. Thus, Gothic fiction shows with subtle insistence how all these facets can relate to each other, and in doing so it shows that it can hold within itself as wide a range of the newly emergent consciousness as any other mode of its time. At its best its richness is unparalleled. But further, if the various aspects of that conglomerate which is Gothicism are still recognizably all that their values had made them, then the Gothic becomes the site of constant collisions, a battlefield of differing values in which, in a series of manifold ironies, the battles become multileveled shocks of cognition. And since each of these values holds something of use for the Gothic writer, who finds much to admire in many places, then his attitude *has* to be ambivalent. The diversity that has much to do with the imaginative sweep of the best Gothic guarantees a delicate balance of conflicting inclinations. Uncertainty is not least considerable of the qualities that emerge from Gothic fiction.

Whether that uncertainty is in the novelist himself or in several of his characters (most likely it will be comprehensive and indiscriminate), it is the product of the shocks of cognition which reveal, for some, a surprising consanguinity, and for others at least the possibility of malevolence in the immediate vicinity. The essential structure of the Gothic comes out of the activity producing those shocks. For the Gothic is not merely a decor or just a set of devices calculated to arouse a primary *nouveau frisson*, nor is it the *frisson* itself. The central form of Gothic is a confrontation, led to and symbolized by the meeting of modes, one element of which has just suddenly, rudely emerged. The confrontation follows immediately upon a revelation of what may be malevolence (there is often an initial uncertainty), a dark epiphany of which the Black Sabbath is the celebratory form; thus the relation of the epiphany to the level of witchcraft in fairy tale. All the emphasis upon sublimity is a result of the meeting and is not part of the meeting itself. The decor supports the action but does not define it or call it into being. And all the literary traditions that were drawn into Gothicism make up some elements of the meeting but do not affect its form as a fundamental pure confrontation. Here the Gothic is less akin to its immediate historical surroundings than to what seems to be an organizing element at the heart of the romance tradition which led into it. Eric Auerbach has argued that the ethos of the courtly romance has no earthly or practical purpose other than self-realization, and functions in a world holding nothing but adventure and moving according to the laws of fairy tale. Raised above earthly contingencies, the ethos gives a sense of community to the elect (a sense which, I would argue, leads down through numerous historical ironies past Puritanism into the apotheosis of Clarissa). Charles Muscatine has extended this recognition of courtly ethos as self-subsistent form and sees, at least in Chaucer's *Knight's Tale*, the struggle of those social codes against an image of chaos which seeks to destroy them. Romance is, in other words, the locale of a confrontation. Northrop Frye has seen the genre of romance as tending to emphasize the values of a ruling class against usurpers, a reading which is probably accurate for romance as a whole but is ultimately insufficient for Gothic fiction since, though Frye emphasizes confrontation, he says nothing about the ambivalence which makes for the magnificent Gothic uneasiness. It would seem, then, that Gothic fiction carries on a core structure which may well be endemic to romance and is certainly closer to where the Gothic plots begin than are the emphases upon emotional qualities (of whatever pitch) or even the values of an emergent consciousness. For the values themselves, older or newer, late Augustan or about-to-be Romantic, matter less, finally, than the fact that things have met in pure, spontaneous surprise. Indeed, it seems probable that the bare, elemental meeting is, at some stratum, beyond valuation and has its point primarily in the fact of its presence.

The progress of the Gothic plot develops out from this radical point along several tracks, some to Heaven and others to Hell, with the creatures of evil and those of good sometimes following the same track for a while, though at different paces. For everyone, even the malevolent, the progress is a process of emerging cognition, propelled into action by a meeting as necessary as the descent of Blake's Thel into the death-world of organic living. The cry of Mrs. Radcliffe's Vivaldi as he faces Inquisitional hellishness in *The Italian* is a lucid example of the force which increasing awareness exerts against the horizons of one representative of value, the man of sensibility in his role as a bachelor socialite:

> "Is this possible!" said Vivaldi internally, "Can this be in human nature!—Can such horrible perversion of right be permitted! Can man, who calls himself endowed with reason and immeasurably superior to every other created being, argue himself into the commission of such horrible folly, such inveterate cruelty, as exceeds all the acts of the most irrational and ferocious brute. Brutes do not deliberately slaughter their species; it remains for man only, man, proud of his prerogative of reason, and boasting of his sense of justice, to unite the most terrible extremes of folly and wickedness!"

This is more than the moan of a wounded sensibility, though it is surely that. We know that the values which Vivaldi and Ellena brought into the Gothic arena had grown out of a need to widen responses, to counter the mechanistic depravity of Hobbes' candidate for tyranny and the prostrate souls of Puritanism's expectant degenerates. But the treasure trove which was the un-Hobbesian order of self turned out to be Pandora's box. The values which molded the lovers in conventional sentimental fiction left Vivaldi and Ellena ill-equipped for Schedoni or those Mediterranean tortures which the Inquisition seemed to reserve for surrogate Englishmen. Those values could go so far, to assert the sweetness of the moral sense, and no further. Nor did the tie of Vivaldi's values into the moralism which bourgeois readers publicly avowed prepare such characters to expect, not to speak of comprehend, what was coming forth to greet them in strange welcome. Sensibility pulled them toward sweetness, and *The Spectator* toward sweet

reasonableness, but the limits of this warm practicality, with its pre-
scriptions for daily etiquette, stopped where the meeting began.
There, of course, Gothicism becomes for a moment a comedy of
manners, with the heroine more terrified at a slip into indecorous-
ness than at what waited around the next corner of the dark tun-
nel:

> Ellena meanwhile had retired to her cell, agitated by a variety
> of considerations, and contrary emotions, of which, however,
> those of joy and tenderness were long predominant. Then came
> anxiety, apprehension, pride, and doubt, to divide and torture
> her heart. It was true that Vivaldi had discovered her prison, but,
> if it were possible, that he could release her, she must consent
> to quit it with him; a step from which a mind so tremblingly
> jealous of propriety as hers, recoiled with alarm, though it would
> deliver her from captivity.

This complex situation is in part the comedy of the inappropriate
response, the reaction of those who have not yet learned all that
the new conditions could teach them. But under such pressures insufficient awareness cannot be more than momentary. (Sade, who
consciously used an ironic reversal of this same plot, gave his pal-
lid Clarissas no time for such mistakes.) The creature of light,
shone upon by the brightness in Gothic chiaroscuro, is confronted
—again like Blake's Thel—by something which threatens to draw
the creature down into itself in enforced incarceration. *Then* comes
the full shock of cognition and all the versions of Vivaldi's cry,
echoed by his kin throughout the history of Gothicism down to the
great instance in Emily Brontë's Lockwood, the finest parody of
his own kind. For these creatures the process of cognition, begun
with the first jolt of epiphany, becomes a fall out of innocence into increasing knowledge, a fall which, for emergent Romanticism,
was a tumble into self-consciousness from the comforting enclosure
of prelapsarian values. Maturin's late Gothicism purified the process by having his wanderer Melmoth discover and corrupt into
self-consciousness the sensibilities of Immalee, a sequestered island-
bound maiden descended from Byron's Haidee and everyone's
image of chastest Eve.

160

But the meeting need not be only between decorousness and malevolence, nor do the epiphanic jolts find recipients only where no evil was ever at home. The Gothic conglomerate of values is so intensely interconnected an organic structure that a shock of confrontation at one point reverberates throughout. And there are often shocks at more than one point at once, meetings in which various modes come together in extensive surprise and with complex results. To take one curious kind of example, in the early Gothicism of *The Castle of Otranto* and its genteel parody in *The Old English Baron*, the supernatural meets and simultaneously affects the forms of villainy as well as the clumsy versions of the lost prince of fairy-tale romance, and in doing so it reveals how these polarities work together in a rudimentary but expressive order of mirror images which plays cozily with themes of usurpation and disguise. The supernatural which wells up in the worlds of Walpole and Mrs. Reeve is purposive and busy, its business to enforce the laws of primogeniture and true succession, later if not sooner, but inevitably. One had hoped Heaven was democratic. But here, in beginning Gothic, a theme which comes down from the ethos of courtly romance supports aristocratic myths which bourgeois manners seemed to cherish, especially in this fictional mode which could satisfy numerous impulses at once. The supernatural draws upon its full powers of shock both to frighten and reveal, to force a meeting of other values not only with itself but of the expropriator and the lost prince with each other. In revealing itself it compels revelation elsewhere, raising hairs and restoring rights with several swoops of its mailed hands. This is a beneficent malevolence, selective in its effects and forcing results as mixed as the chiaroscuro in which it functions: the areas of light and no-light in Walpole's chiaroscuro dramatize the pied nature of the moral effects of his supernatural. That part of the Gothic plot which is a fall out of innocence for some is, for others, a fall out of evil into recompense. One of the great changes in Gothic fiction took place in this area, when epiphany moved from the purposive to the gratuitous, from the remnants of aristocratic myth to the democracy of the depths of the self; that is, with the shift in moral geography that took place between Walpole and Matthew Gregory Lewis, with Mrs. Radcliffe as a major instigator. A most discomfiting effect of the shift came with the recognition that the horrors had moved from that which is not like us, and is therefore conveniently externalized, to the warfares within someone whose likeness to us holds more horror than his difference. For horrors to come out of something strange into the world is one thing, but for them to come out of persons like ourselves is quite another.

Yet these intricacies of moral geography had bothered Gothicists from the beginning. The sublimest terrors in *Otranto* emerged from the same mold as the righting of moral disorder, while the great shift in the locale of horror from without to within had been prefigured in Walpole's villain: for, though Manfred's inner landscape contains contours as malevolent as any outside in the cosmos, his briefly drawn capacity for shame shows him to be as radically mixed as the Romantic heroes who were to succeed him, boasting of their sweeping evil but trapped within ambivalent personalities which enclose (like Byron's Corsair) "a single virtue and a thousand crimes." Manfred's ambivalence is inchoate; he is no Schedoni or Ambrosio. But Walpole's pristine Gothic did guess at complexities which were not fully faced until the great middle age of Gothicism, in themes that then developed. Nor do we need to rehearse here the familiar fascination with brooding Satanism which did not, however, preclude the likes of Ann Radcliffe from knowing what she ought rightly to feel.

The full Gothic plot moves from an initial confrontation to a fall into self-consciousness and then, in the third stage, to a phase of coping or learning to cope. In this last stage the strange, having drawn its moral antagonist down into its maw, chews on this Jonah for a while, then spews him forth—sometimes back into the bright world of social reasonableness, occasionally into moral darkness and death. As Gothicism grows older the reactions to this third stage show a remarkable overall change, shifting from the uneasy glimpses at horror taken by Clara Reeve through the transitional worlds of Beckford, Mrs. Radcliffe, and Monk Lewis, down to the late full stares of Maturin, Mary Shelley, and Emily Brontë. Nowhere are the activities of coping particularly comfortable, because the relations of the observer to what is seen are never less than ambivalent. That Gothicism which was closest to Shaftesbury and Addison, both in time and interest, could not return quite unscathed to the comfort of bourgeois moralism, though it did return. For even the earliest Gothicists saw that what was appallingly there was also genuinely there and intriguing to deal with, though that did not mean one had to accept it. Shaftesbury had imaged the self as the smallest in a series of concentric circles of harmony, all structurally alike because the order of one both proved and matched the order of the others. If there was that in any one of the circles which threatened its established harmony the other circles could not avoid being shaken up, tied as they all were into an order of reflecting wholenesses. Were the early Gothicists to bring into the order of being all that they saw, the individual orders would each have to expand to include what was new or the whole system would collapse. Shaftesbury, we remember, granted evil only the partial truth that is granted to any insufficient vision of the whole. To draw a weighty malevolence into universal equilibrium—to grant it rights of pure existence, to make the mailed hand less than selective in its effect—would seem to demand a correlative pure culture in both society and the soul. And that turn back to Hobbes would have raised a smile on Leviathan's old face. One watches early Gothic both recognizing and deflecting, finding satisfactions in palliation because anything less than displacement and closer to full recognition made demands on the establishment's ethos which could not yet be supported. Of course Clara Reeve and Ann Radcliffe had no such elaborate justifications in mind. One ought not to attribute profundities of philosophical pattern to these decorous ladies. They knew only (Mrs. Reeve quite unconsciously, Mrs. Radcliffe with a full grasp) that an image of order had to be held onto, that not all men were nice but that God's good points took care of unpleasantness, however fascinating it was in its strangeness, however attractive in its strength.

There is more skill evidenced in Clara Reeve's easing of what she sees than there is in the rest of *The Old English Baron*. Her ghosts are urbane and discreet, ambitious only to bring about the restoration of legitimacy and therefore flexing their spectral muscles with the minimum of movement, though with complete assurance. A ghost reveals himself fully only before a pair of ugly characters from the wrong end of the scale of values developed in the romance; and then he gives just a mild clank of his full armor, with all the restraint of aristocratic confidence in the subtle gesture. The spirits move ceremoniously through the hero's premonitory dreams with exactly the contained distinction they would show in the halls of their rightful castle, and with all the stiff-paced clarity of the novel itself. In an extraordinary instance of protective imagination Mrs. Reeve has instinctively muddled values. For most of its length *The Old English Baron* is a typical domestic novel, concerned for the righting of true order (Frye has seen such righting as a characteristic of romance) and for what it is proper to do in that order. With a precise intuition for the meaning of values in the Gothic confrontation, Mrs. Reeve transfers the standards of one world into those of another, palliating horror by giving those who might cause it all the manners of good society. Without their sepulchral groans her ghosts would have been at home in any choice gathering, as untrue to their actual state as they are faithful to the order out of which they died. This is not an uneasy marriage of values, but in fact no marriage at all. It is a deflection from a full stare at the radical differences among modes of being, an attempt to mitigate terror by disguising the unmannerliness of the terrifying. The attempt was made not in ignorance of what spirits ought to do—Walpole had given full evidence of their indelicacy—but with the compulsion to tame danger into decorum. (This is exactly the process of refinement that Frankenstein's monster was later to long for.) If this is evasion through transference it is also a feat of intuitive comprehension. Unfortunately it is the only remaining item of interest in this early celebration of the meeting of civility and strangeness.

Beckford's *Vathek* is quite another kind of fiction, different not only in its considerable imaginative reach but in what the imagination reaches to, though its ultimate recoil from epiphany and its conglomeration of the expected horrors show it to be, in part, characteristic early Gothic. The exoticism of the novel, and its internal parodies thereof, tie *Vathek* into mid-century ephemera. But the most basic links of Beckford's book are with contemporary Gothic and, historically, with two significant developments: that mixture of myth, irony, and sensibility which was handed on to Byron and Stendhal, and that inquiry into terrestrial depths which led to the mining fiction of Novalis and E. T. A. Hoffmann and the more encompassing themes of pained knowledge in both *Fausts* and in *Frankenstein*. Beckford's lascivious comedy, with its lip-licking delight in sensual extremes, functions on many levels and with a various purpose. In part it parodies the excesses of exotic fiction by taking them to the point beyond which they are both destructive and (because of their extremity) unwittingly self-mocking. Yet there is no questioning Beckford's fascination with the road that leads up to the edge of the abyss and with the meeting deep down within it; nor his sympathy with the Caliph's curiosity about all that the halls of Eblis hold, including the explorers' punishment. Beckford's mockery of sensual extremes blends strangely but brilliantly with his self-indulgent speculations about them. And the mockery serves as a protective device, a built-in moral check which permits him to play all the bases at once and yet find the game foolish. He cannot accept everything he sees, yet he permits his hero to absorb it and to walk willingly into Leviathan's maw, exploring the center from which emanates the power of evil. Deep down is all gold, but down there is also Augustinian Hell; and Beckford, like so many others, stands at a point of transition where the only illumination comes from the ambivalent lighting of moral chiaroscuro. None of the Gothicists who struck down into subterranean darkness seems to have forgotten the older moral geography which equates depths with evil and extends the full meaning of phrases such as "bowels of the earth" into a recognition of the hellish interior of the self. None was perfectly easy with the romance mode, which theoretically made it possible to draw characters as moral opposites but in practice made easy moralism difficult for the best Gothicists —for Beckford to a degree but principally for Radcliffe and Lewis among the earlier practitioners. Clara Reeve had little difficulty with these problems, finding romance dichotomies congenial to moral statements. But deep-grained metaphorical connections among all the kinds of journeys within (connections which most Romantics were later to make, though with varying assertions about the possibility of moral disinfection) made it difficult for sensibility's insistence on the instinctive sweetness of the unspoiled inner world to be fully accepted by the Gothicists, whose business it was to go down within. Their situations were various, depending in part on their willingness to make romance flexible, setting up some characters as moral opposites and others as deeply ambivalent. Beckford's own uncertainties were compounded by an attraction to the Caliph's excesses, so that he explored them lovingly but restlessly. Some Romantic descendants of Vathek found the depths to be of unalloyed value. But for Beckford and most Romantic descendants—and for his Gothic contemporaries in particular—the hearts which burst into flame in the halls of Eblis reveal both subterranean passion *and* celestial punishment. Thus, when Beckford, at the end of the novel, moves from the mockery of excess into moral condemnation, he tries to make Vathek a tragic figure fallen into immorality, and shifts the full brunt of evil onto the Caliph's aged mother. This puts him in a more comforting moral framework whose standards of transgression and recompense are more easily comprehensible. If those standards have no way of explaining Beckford's delights or his fascination with dark epiphany, they do draw him back to where he can stand without heat, far from the edge he had reached, at a point which is tenable, though not sufficient for his fiction or his vision.

The finest instances of sufficiency are those of Mrs. Radcliffe, who guesses at what Monk Lewis knew well, though she chose not to explore it, preferring to palliate where he opted to delve. She had a full-ranging comprehension of where Gothicism was going and what it was touching upon. What has dated are the absurdities and occasional stuffiness. What remains in the work of the Mistress of Romance is, in the two best novels, an exceptional skill in both drawing out and mitigating epiphany, the acts of an adroit imagination manipulating a moral and modal counterpoint that makes a book like *The Italian* a supreme fiction if not quite a great novel.

The most blatant of those acts is the familiar intellectualizing of terror, the teasing spoofs of earlier Gothicism and its susceptible *personae*. The purpose of this intellectualizing is clarified if we

166

understand it as a form of humanizing. It is not like the taming of the strange into civility, which Mrs. Reeve had attempted, but is a far more sweeping action which denies the existence of the terrifying outside of the human. This means, first, that the sources of supernatural operations are within the proclivities of the mind itself. This is one of the reasons for the occasional reprimands of overly busy sensibilities, in *The Italian* coming ironically, and justly, from the last words of its villain, Schedoni. But it also means that the real dangers in Ann Radcliffe's world are from other humans, from Schedoni or the Inquisition or the Marchesa in *The Italian*, primarily from Montoni in *The Mysteries of Udolpho*. If Mrs. Radcliffe civilizes the sources of fright and pain (the Inquisition's activities are part of civilization, though not civil) she also puts those sources where they hurt most, in the murky propensities of some human souls. Her world ought to terrify for more reasons than it did—and those reasons have outlasted the form. When she brought her good characters back up into the light, she organized the rest of the paraphernalia within comprehensible categories, not really because of the kind of unease that unnerved Beckford but from a view of human potential whose ironies she surely sensed: we have met the enemy and he is us. The order of things is, then, reasonably comprehensible, though if it is without genuine supernatural horror and if there is horror in the world—both are undeniable—then the conclusion has to be faced, and it is human, if not humane.

Mrs. Radcliffe guessed where she was going though she chose not to go all the way or to face it directly. Her recognition of the facts comes out in various ways, in part with the chiding of Vivaldi and the related teasing of her readers, but most significantly in her manipulation of the romance mode. The passage quoted above showing Vivaldi's shock of cognition does not go so far as to make the cognition a recognition. Though her creatures of sensibility emerge stirred and battle-scarred they emerge in purity, with blandly intact souls. Vivaldi cannot acknowledge what he sees out there as even potentially part of himself, nor does Mrs. Radcliffe require that he do so. If that potential is in man it is still not part of Vivaldi's personal order but separate, perhaps a part of others, kept carefully away in a moral dichotomy which borrows fairy-tale distinctions much like those of Mrs. Reeve. Yet this is not an uneasy compromise but a skilled one, which leaves no issues untouched and can satisfy something in all. For the exact moral opposite of the romance hero is found in the blackness of the Inquisition's agents who, as his moral mirror images, satisfactorily balance him off. But neither Schedoni nor the Marchesa is an exact moral opposite of Vivaldi, because they are creatures of a mottled morality whose inner struggles show that their antagonists are really within themselves, not out there in the young of the romance mode. Mrs. Radcliffe's fictional world enfolds all these possibilities, and more, in a tense but harmonious interplay, from dichotomies posed between separate selves to those at work in a single soul, from an acknowledgement of human mystery to passages of autotelic lyricism reminiscent of the self-conscious artifice of contemporary opera. All of the Gothicism before her found in her fiction a home and an imaginative potency unparalleled until then, and with few Gothic peers since.

At this point of culmination the Gothic began a manifest change, though the change was neither without prefiguration nor entirely certain of itself. In her novels Mrs. Radcliffe had matched her vision of moral geography with complex variations and extensions of fictional mode. After her work there was little to do in the kind which she had perfected. And between *The Mysteries of Udolpho* and *The Italian* had come *The Monk*, in which her humanizing of Gothic malevolence was not so much challenged as extended, with little of Mrs. Radcliffe's range but with far more mining of the depths. Yet here too there was palliation, though exactly inverse to what Mrs. Reeve had done. Lewis went far, but he still had to end up doing as Beckford did, that is, protecting the human against itself and not against the supernatural. Without Mrs. Radcliffe's decorum *or* her courage, Lewis backed off from attributing the full motivation for evil to Ambrosio, and made of Matilda's supple sexuality a supernatural trick from the Devil's workshop to entice the proud monk to Hell. He could not quite bring himself to locate all of dark epiphany entirely within. But even with this bit of hedging Lewis did face and sketch out the progress of Ambrosio's soul from a cathedral pulpit down to the mausoleums of rotting personalities. Though the locale of malevolence had rarely been entirely outside (we have seen its uneasy multiplicity of place already in Walpole) it was moving, under Mrs. Radcliffe's relentless prodding, more fully within than ever. An exactly parallel shift of habitation was occurring at much the same time though with slower pace, as evil's home became less the cherished property of exotica such as Montoni and more a product of the home garden. Maturin, one step away, made his evil Irish. In *Northanger Abbey* Jane Austen turned the chauvinistic paraphernalia of early English Gothic quite around, and Emily Brontë finished the job. The fair-skinned Protestant jingoism of her earliest predecessors found its final belittling when Emily Brontë gave her seasoned version of dark malevolence a female counterpart from pure English stock. Gothic fiction was permanently internationalized with "I *am* Heathcliff." With those two parallel tendencies toward a movement from outside to within, Gothicism found its fullest statement and its clearest vision of the geography of evil, though it was never without the ambivalence that unsettled the mode from the beginning. Hawthorne and Dostoyevsky moved on from this point. At its end stood Auschwitz, which has not yet found its interpreter.

Johnson's Art of Anecdote

Robert Folkenflik

MODERN CRITICISM of biography is still filled with *a priori* conceptions which would look highly questionable if applied to the novel, drama, or poetry. Samuel Johnson's biographies seem to have suffered particularly from this tendency. The greatest obstacle to the understanding and evaluation of Johnson's art of anecdote, for example, is judging it by Boswellian standards. In an article which has recently been praised as an "excellent essay dealing with the ineffectiveness of Johnson's use of anecdotes to delineate personality,"[1] the most influential critic of Johnson's biographical anecdotes, Clarence Tracy, says that "too often they seem to have been dragged in more out of respect to the paper value of minute facts than with any understanding of their biographical possibilities."[2] We soon learn that Tracy's harsh judgment of Johnson rests on a Boswellian norm:

> It is clear that, for all his theoretical emphasis on minute facts and the evanescent aspects of personality, Johnson made no more than a feeble effort himself in his various biographies to perceive the man entire and in action in the Boswellian manner.[3]

The biographies by Johnson and Boswell are very different in intention, form, and tone as well as scope. They are exemplars of separate biographical traditions: the concise prefatory biography and the amply documented life-and-times; and they are the products of totally different minds. The differences between them point to the necessity of seeing what Johnson himself was trying to do.

In Johnson's biographies there are indeed a certain number of details which do not seem to make an immediately apparent contri-

bution to the delineation of the subject. The isolation of such anecdotes is due, however, to more than a theoretical commitment to
"minute facts." Johnson's love of anecdotes fuses aesthetics and
morality.[4] The delineation of the subject was for Johnson only
one function of the anecdote in his work. His didactic intentions
are one of the sources of such isolated anecdotes. In his praise of
anecdotes and private details in *Rambler*, No. 60, Johnson emphasizes the personal usefulness to the reader of the detail as well as
its function in giving a picture of the whole man:

> There are many invisible circumstances which, whether we read
> as enquirers after natural or moral knowledge, whether we in-
> tend to enlarge our science, or increase our virtue, are more
> important than public occurrences. . . . Thus the story of Melanc-
> thon affords a striking lecture on the value of time, by inform-
> ing us, that when he made an appointment, he expected not only
> the hour, but the minute to be fixed, that the day might not run
> out in the idleness of suspense; and all the plans and enterprises
> of De Wit are now of less importance to the world, than that
> part of his personal character which represents him as "careful
> of his health, and negligent of his life."[5]

The detail thus may become separable from its context, a nugget of
knowledge whose value to the reader does not always depend on
its context in the subject's life. In fact Johnson's love of anecdotes,
and his musing that writers may in time forego all "preparation
and connexion and illustration," would seem to imply that certain
details have just such an independent value.

There is another kind of isolated anecdote which occasionally
appears in Johnson's biographies. Tracy mentions Johnson's remark that he learned of Pope's friend Cromwell only "that he used
to ride a-hunting in a tye-wig," and says, "This fact is left to speak
for itself whatever its message may be, for Johnson cannot use it
in creating a picture of the man."[6] But here Johnson's technique
is not that of the novelistic or dramatic biographer, but that of the
philosophical biographer. He presents in passing and with rueful
irony an inadequate anecdote as an indication of the evanescence
of human knowledge and human existence. In the *Life of Dryden*
Johnson presents two anecdotes that he had from eyewitnesses:

Of the only two men whom I have found to whom he was personally known, one told me that at the house which he frequented, called Will's Coffee-house, the appeal upon any literary dispute was made to him, and the other related that his armed chair, which in the winter had a settled and prescriptive place by the fire, was in the summer placed in the balcony; and that he called the two places his winter and his summer seat. This is all the intelligence which his two survivors afforded me.[7]

Boswell would have simply slipped the two accounts into appropriate places where they would have added a dash of color and authenticity. Johnson's complaint about his lack of material is thematically part of his biography. This is all that he could find out first-hand not about some wretched poetaster, but about Dryden; and the anecdotes are all the more poignant because they both refer to Dryden's literary dictatorship. Here we have a prose version of *The Vanity of Human Wishes*. Johnson uses his lack of knowledge to force the reader into a confrontation with the void. For the most part, however, his anecdotes contribute both to the picture of the man and the edification of the audience.

Johnson often generalizes his anecdotes. The anecdotes which he singles out for praise in *Rambler*, No. 60, are not located firmly in time and place, in the manner of Boswell, but refer rather to traits which remain constant and appear not once but often in a man's lifetime. His use of anecdotes is dependent on their not giving undue prominence to a minor and perhaps misleading aspect of a man's life. In discussing Swift's friendship with the great, he comments on the Dean's supposed "equality and independence" by saying: "In accounts of this kind a few single incidents are set against the general tenour of behaviour" (III, 21).

Boswell's interest is in the individual scene; he gives a picture of "the general tenour of behaviour" chiefly by accumulating different scenes which contain similar characteristics. Johnson often prefers to generalize, even when he obviously could present a single instance, in order to convey economically the endurance of certain characteristics. For example, he comments on his employer Edward Cave's "chilness of mind" in conversation by generalizing what would appear to be a unique event: "... he was watching the minutest accent of those whom he disgusted by seeming inattention; and his visitant was surprised when he came a second time, by preparations to execute the scheme which he supposed never to have been heard."[8] The *Life of Savage* contains many such generalized anecdotes:

> ... he was so much ashamed of having been reduced to appear as a player, that he always blotted out his name from the list when a copy of his tragedy was to be shown to his friends.

> His conduct with regard to his pension was very particular. No sooner had he changed the bill than he vanished from the sight of all his acquaintances, and lay for some time out of the reach of all the enquiries that friendship or curiosity could make after him; at length he appeared again pennyless as before, but never informed even those whom he seemed to regard most where he had been, nor was his retreat ever discovered.

> ... he could not easily leave off when he had once begun to mention himself or his works; nor ever read his verses without stealing his eyes from the page, to discover, in the faces of his audience, how they were affected with any favourite passage. [II, 340, 391, 432]

This method enables Johnson to maintain the concreteness of his anecdotes and at the same time to give the impression of recurrence. He believed that many things in life are important simply because they are frequent. The "far, far better thing" and the single intense moment, so admired in the nineteenth century, were not of as great importance to him as the daily happenings which impart to life its steady pleasure or pain. Often what is interesting in Johnson's generalizing anecdotes is his ability to epitomize character or social relationships as they exist in time. His account of Addison's marriage to the Countess of Warwick may seem by the standards of modern biography to lack details, but it strongly suggests the nature of their life together and closes with a sentence which has the lapidary quality of an epigram from the *Greek Anthology*:

> The marriage, if uncontradicted report can be credited, made no addition to his happiness; it neither found them nor made them

equal. She always remembered her own rank, and thought herself entitled to treat with very little ceremony the tutor of her
son. [II, 110–11]

This interest in the general tenor of life accounts also for his inclusion in several biographies (such as *Milton* and *Addison*) of
the "familiar day," the typical daily activities of the subject.

In addition to giving the sense of a life lived in time, every biographer must face the problem of biographic closure, the fact that
the end of a biography is in most cases simply the end of a man's
life. In the *Life of Smith*, really a counterbiography to William
Oldisworth's plaster-cast panegyric of the poet, Johnson presents,
largely through the addition of telling anecdotes, a lifelike account
of a talented hack, "Captain Rag." The mordantly satirical coda of
the biographical section is achieved through Johnson's combination
of an anecdote with the familiar data of death; literary form is
wrenched into being by simple factuality:

> He eat and drank till he found himself plethorick; and then, re-
> solving to ease himself by evacuation, he wrote to an apothecary
> in the neighbourhood a prescription of a purge so forcible, that
> the apothecary thought it his duty to delay it till he had given
> notice of its danger. Smith, not pleased with the contradiction
> of a shopman, and boastful of his own knowledge, treated the
> notice with rude contempt, and swallowed his own medicine,
> which, in July 1710, brought him to the grave. He was buried
> at Hartham. [II, 18]

The phrase "to swallow one's own medicine" had long been a
cliche. Johnson shocks us by putting it to grim literal use. He turns
factual narration into the literary language of understatement
which is at the heart of so much great eighteenth-century writing.

Boswell's biographical art is essentially comic, but Johnson's, as
we have already seen, is frequently satiric. We may take as both a
typical and excellent Boswellian scene the dinner at Dilly's, in
which Wilkes and Johnson, those mighty opposites, come together
in festive amity at the cost of a few jokes at Boswell's expense—a
cost he is quite willing to pay, incidentally, for a confrontation he
has brought about. Everyone is happy. Boswell as biographer does

not choose here between the moralist and the libertine, the supporter of the crown or its enemy. In this *discordia concors* Boswell himself has yoked the opposites together through all his social arts. In Johnson's *Lives* the moral judgment may be complex, but it is always present, even when delivered through the restraints and obliquities of irony. Boswell generally presents; Johnson frequently exposes.

Tracy, quoting Johnson's description of Savage's "scheme of life for the country," complains, "But how much of vividness [of Savage's speech] must have been lost in the indirect discourse."⁹ A look at one paragraph should convince us that what we have is not loss but gain:

> With these expectations he was so enchanted, that when he was once gently reproached by a friend for submitting to live upon a subscription, and advised rather by a resolute exertion of his abilities to support himself, he could not bear to debar himself from the happiness which was to be found in the calm of a cottage, or lose the opportunity of listening without intermission to the melody of the nightingale, which he believed was to be heard form every bramble, and which he did not fail to mention as a very important part of the happiness of a country life. [II, 410]

We have both Savage's words and Johnson's implicit ironic judgment upon them. The scene is the more ironic for its quietness. The friend (undoubtedly Johnson himself) reproaches Savage "gently," the cottage he will retire to is "calm," nightingales will sing "from every bramble." What Savage fails to recognize is that those brambles have thorns and that human beings, with their quotidian troubles, are not able to do anything, even listen to birdsong, "without intermission." Much of the rest of Johnson's biography is given over to a sympathetic though critical account of Savage's altercations and death in the country. And we hear of nightingales once more in the *Life*. Writing from jail to a friend (again, probably Johnson), Savage says:

> I am now more conversant with the Nine than ever; and if, instead of a Newgate-bird, I may be allowed to be a bird of the

Muses, I assure you, Sir, I sing very freely in my cage; sometimes indeed in the plaintive notes of the nightingale. . . . [II,
423]

Johnson often builds his satiric passages on a slight anecdotal
framework. Of Shenstone's improvidence he says: "In time his ex-
penses brought clamours about him that overpowered the lamb's
bleat and the linnet's song; and his groves were haunted by beings
very different from fauns and fairies" (III, 352). The actual bai-
liffs and tradesmen who hounded Shenstone remain shadowy figures, but the implication that Shenstone has lost himself in a fanci-
ful world is clear. The Leasowes, as described by Johnson, seem to
be a projection into the real world of the dangerous prevalence of
the imagination against which he was always on guard, and it
comes as no shock to find that he thinks Shenstone's care for his
garden contributed to his early death.

One more satirical anecdote should make the pattern clear.
Though Johnson recognizes the scope that imagination plays in the
creation of literary characters, he delights in contrasting the pastoral name of the heroine of Prior's lyrics and its implied innocence
with the Newgate behavior of her empirical counterpart:

His Chloe probably was sometimes ideal [i.e., imaginary]; but
the woman with whom he co-habited was a despicable drab of
the lowest species. One of his wenches, perhaps Chloe, while he
was absent from his home, stole his plate, and ran away. . . . [II,
199–200]

The last part of the second sentence sounds like an unrecorded
variant from "Tom, Tom, the Piper's Son." Johnson takes Prior's
mistress out of a genre which idealizes its characters and puts her into a highly realistic nursery rhyme. The homely monosyllables at
the end of the passage forcefully clinch his point. All three of these
satiric anecdotes criticize pastoral ideas. Johnson uses the realm
of facts in order to demythologize false notions. Within this literary setting, the "real" calls the "fictional" to account. Johnson's
view of life is highly normative, and deviations from that norm
often lead to satire.

177

I have been dealing with isolated Johnsonian anecdotes, but Johnson is also capable of great analytical skill in "preparation and connexion and illustration." The *Life of Addison,* like the lives of *Pope, Milton, Savage, Smith, Thomson,* and the *King of Prussia* —to name only a few of the more obvious examples—contains splendidly integrated anecdotes. If Johnson was unable to make anything of Henry Cromwell's tye-wig in the *Life of Pope,* he was perfectly able to place Mandeville's reference to Addison's wig in the context of both men's personalities:

> The remark of Mandeville, who, when he had passed an evening in his company, declared that he was a parson in a tye-wig, can detract little from his character; he was always reserved to strangers, and was not incited to uncommon freedom by a character like that of Mandeville. [II, 123]

This analysis in turn rests upon a number of anecdotes which show Addison's timidity and reserve. His timidity is apparent in the story of his changing Pope's prologue to *Cato* from "Britons arise, be worth like this approved" to "Britons, attend" for fear that "he should be thought a promoter of Insurrection" (II, 100). It is also apparent in the criticism he deployed to prepare the way for *Cato,* in his packing the house for the first performance of the play, and in his unwillingnes to own himself the author of *The Drummer* (II, 100).[10] Johnson uses the testimony of Addison's contemporaries to establish his reserve. He quotes Pope on the charm of Addison's familiar conversation and his stiff dignity before strangers. Johnson later uses Pope's comment as a basis for interpreting both the Mandeville anecdote and Addison's excessive drinking. The private knowledge of Addison's timidity and his high opinion of his own abilities permit the reader to understand why someone as moral as Addison should be apt to drink too much.

Johnson's skill at combining the narrative anecdote with his interpretive commentary shows the importance he placed in actual practice on "those arts by which a big book is made." An excellent example is to be found in his treatment of an anecdote of Pope which appears in none of the earlier biographies. We all know the passage in the *Life of Johnson* which Boswell, chagrined at John-

son's refusal to be manipulated into an unsolicited interview with
the Earl of Marchmont, offers as an indication of Johnson's dere-
liction of biographical duty: "If it rained knowledge I'd hold out
my hand; but I would not give myself the trouble to go in quest of
it." More significant, however, is the use to which Johnson put his
information when, his defensive pride assuaged, he finally did
meet Marchmont.

Johnson begins Marchmont's anecdote of Pope's last sickness in
a low key:

> While he was yet capable of amusement and conversation, as he
> was one day sitting in the air with Lord Bolingbroke and Lord
> Marchmont, he saw his favourite Martha Blount at the bottom
> of the terrace, and asked Lord Bolingbroke to go and hand her
> up. Bolingbroke, not liking his errand, crossed his legs and sat
> still; but Lord Marchmont, who was younger and less captious,
> waited on the Lady, who, when he came to her, asked, "What, is
> he not dead yet?" [III, 189–90]

In the context of Johnson's *Life* we are reminded of Pope's petu-
lance and his pride, like that of Swift, in being able to treat noblemen on terms of equality; and the action takes on a retrospective
irony when we see Bolingbroke, choked with emotion following
Pope's death, unable to complete a sentence eulogizing his friend.
But what we certainly do not expect in this atmosphere of petty
bickering and lordly *politesse* is Martha Blount's cruel question:
"What, is he not dead yet?" The anecdote evidently captured in
concrete form something Johnson felt deeply about the instability
of human relationships, for it leads in this biography to a masterly
short analysis of Pope's friendship with Martha Blount:

> She is said to have neglected him with shameful unkindness
> in the latter time of his decay; yet, of the little which he had to
> leave, she had a very great part. Their acquaintance began early:
> the life of each was pictured on the other's mind; their conver-
> sation, therefore, was endearing, for when they met there was
> an immediate coalition of congenial notions. Perhaps he consid-
> ered her unwillingness to approach the chamber of sickness as
> female weakness or human frailty; perhaps he was conscious to
> himself of peevishness and impatience, or, though he was of-

179

fended by her inattention, might yet consider her merit as over-
balancing her fault; and, if he had suffered his heart to be alien-
ated from her, he could have found nothing that might fill her
place: he could have only shrunk within himself; it was too late
to transfer his confidence or fondness. [III, 190]

Through what might best be called a flashback, Johnson gives a
generalized account of their long, close relationship. But this quickly fades into multiple conjectures on the effect upon Pope of her
coldness, as his sickness progressed. As each conjecture is considered, we move inexorably towards the full pathos of Pope's situation, the certainty that regardless of how Pope chose to interpret
her actions or act himself, he could only suffer. One ought also to
notice the prose which conveys this analysis. The poignancy begins
with the monosyllabic description of Pope's legacy—"of the little
which he had to leave, she had a very great part." (There is irony
here, too, for we learn later that Pope had to insult Allen in his will
in order to placate Martha Blount.) And it is completed by a judi-
cious metaphor. Had Pope given up his friendship with her, "he
could have only shrunk within himself." The horror of further
shrinkage within that already shrunken body is not dwelt upon,
but we are given in full the contraction of human scope as Pope
moves towards his death. The cruelest part of Martha Blount's remark is that she is not far from wrong.

This nearly unremarked passage surpasses a better-known biographical scene which blends death and human relationships, Lyt-
ton Strachey's celebrated *tour de force* at the end of *Queen Victoria*. There Strachey conjectures that "shadows of the past,"
images of the dominant personalities whom she knew, appeared to
the dying queen.[11] And these images—a shallow stream of consciousness if we think of the novels of the early nineteen twenties
—recapitulate the major personages and settings of the biography.
Strachey once spoke, with characteristic impishness, of the "fore-
taste of Stracheyan artistry"[12] to be found in Johnson's *Lives*, but
Johnson at his best is capable of fusing morality and art in a manner that Strachey could never reach and hardly aspired to. The tone
of Johnson's passage on Pope and Martha Blount with its blend
of sympathy and restraint is something of which Strachey would

180

be incapable. Johnson's illumination of his subjects through the use of anecdote shows an understanding of the complexity of character and humanity which needs no apology even in the light of the Boswellian aftermath and the Stracheyan revolution.

NOTES

1. Robert E. Kelley, "Studies in Eighteenth-Century Autobiography and Biography: A Selected Bibliography," in *Essays in Eighteenth-Century Biography*, ed. Phillip B. Daghlian (Bloomington, Ind., 1968), p. 108.
2. C. R. Tracy, "Johnson and the Art of Anecdote," *University of Toronto Quarterly*, XV (1945), 90.
3. Tracy, pp. 92–93.
4. Johnson defines "anecdote" in his *Dictionary* (1755) as "something yet unpublished; secret history" and in his fourth edition (1773) adds, "a minute passage of private life." Historically, we can distinguish different kinds of anecdotes, but my intentions take another direction in this paper. For such distinctions see Elizabeth Hazelton Haight, *The Roman Use of Anecdotes* (New York, 1940).
5. *The Rambler* (Yale Edition), III, ed. W. J. Bate (New Haven, 1969), 321–22.
6. Tracy, p. 90.
7. *Lives of the English Poets*, ed. George Birkbeck Hill (Oxford, 1905), I, 408–9. All references to this work hereafter will be by volume and page in the text.
8. "Life of Cave," in *The Works of Samuel Johnson, LL.D.*, ed. [F. P. Walesby] (Oxford, 1825), VI, 434–35.
9. Tracy, p. 91. Tracy, as Savage's best modern biographer, has more right to this complaint than another critic might have.
10. For a fuller account see James L. Battersby, "Patterns of Significant Action in the 'Life of Addison,'" *Genre*, II (1969), 28–41.
11. (New York, 1921), p. 423.
12. Quoted from a letter in his possession by Frederick W. Hilles, "The Making of *The Life of Pope*," in *New Light on Dr. Johnson*, ed. Frederick W. Hilles (New Haven, 1959), p. 266. André Maurois also is "struck by the Stracheyesque touch" he finds in the *Lives of the Poets*. With an Olympian disregard of chronology he adds, "In fact, one has but to entitle one half of the work *Eminent Jacobeans* and the other *Eminent Augustans* to make it a wholly modern book" (*Aspects of Biography* [New York, 1966], trans. S. C. Roberts, p. 69).

Hervey's Memoirs as Autobiography[*]

Robert Halsband

APPLIED TO A LITERARY GENRE, "memoirs" is a fairly ambiguous term; its meaning ranges from (at one extreme) a first-
person diary or journal to (at the other extreme) an impersonal
historical chronicle or even an ordinary biography written in the
third person. It need not even be a factual account; the memoirs
popular in France at the end of the seventeenth century are sometimes a mixture of fact and fiction—the best-known are the memoirs
of Comte de Gramont by his brother-in-law Anthony Hamilton,
published in 1713. Hervey's memoirs, the subject of this paper, fall
under one definition of the term current since 1659—"a record of
events, a history treating of matters from the personal knowledge
of the writer or with reference to particular sources of information" (OED). By separating the three main elements in Hervey—
the historical, the biographical, and the autobiographical—we can
see more clearly their limits and interrelation.

Hervey modestly entitled his work *not* memoirs but *Some Mate-*
rials Towards Memoirs of the Reign of King George II. Why did
he bother to compile these "materials"? In 1730, when he was an
M.P. supporting Sir Robert Walpole's ministry, he was appointed
Vice-Chamberlain of the King's Household. This court post, even
though its duties were shared by the Lord Chamberlain, was no
sinecure. He (or the Lord Chamberlain) had to be in residence
all year round to supervise such functions as receptions for ambassadors and royal visitors, celebrations of birthdays and anniversa-

---

[*] Several passages of this essay have been extracted from my biography
Lord Hervey: Eighteenth-Century Courtier, to be published in 1973.

ries, balls, concerts, Drawing-Room assemblies (held twice a week during the London season), and Royal marriages and funerals. He also had the duty of assigning, repairing, and furnishing lodgings at Court. When the Court moved, as it frequently did, between the palaces at St. James's, Kensington, Windsor, Richmond, Hampton, and Kew, he had to assign servants, transportation, and lodgings; and if disputes arose among attendants and servants as to their duties or perquisites he had to arbitrate. Although the Lord Chamberlain's secretary and two clerks no doubt took on the routine tasks, the work was still continuous and confining, as Hervey often complained to his friends and family. While he occupied the post for ten years (giving it up when he was advanced to the far more elevated and profitable one of Lord Privy Seal) he was in the most favored position to gather "materials" for his memoirs. He was in close and frequent contact with the Royal family, and he had access to the King and Queen in what he calls "their private and leisure hours." He had no need to look through a keyhole, someone has said, because he was inside the room itself.

He did not begin to write his memoirs at this time, but three or four years later—in 1733 or 1734. What was the reason? In the spring of 1733 he was called up to the House of Lords because the King wished to reward him for his loyalty, and Walpole wished to strengthen his supporters among the Lords, several of whom (notably Chesterfield) had defected to the Opposition because of the Excise Bill. Hervey confesses (in the memoirs) that his "pride and vanity were fed with the air of being called out of the whole House of Commons upon this occasion." It must have seemed the portentously dazzling moment for him to gather his "materials." Or it is possible that the publication in February 1734 of the second volume of Bishop Burnet's *History of His Own Time*, a work which Hervey discusses, stimulated him to begin his own, or spurred him on if he had already begun.

Quite logically he begins his memoirs by explaining why he is well qualified to undertake such a work: "Boasting of intelligence and professing impartiality are such worn-out prefaces to writings of this kind, that I shall not trouble my readers nor myself with any very long exordium upon these topics." Very briefly he then points out that his residence at Court most of the year, enabling him to observe its inhabitants in their public and private lives, has made accessible to him a rich source of information; and since his memoirs will not be published during his lifetime he can be frank and impartial. He is determined to report everything just as he sees it; and he warns the reader that

> those who have a curiosity to see courts and courtiers dissected must bear with the dirt they find in laying open such minds with as little nicety and as much patience as in a dissection of their bodies, if they wanted to see that operation, they must submit to the stench.

Although, as I have said, he began to compile his memoirs in 1733 or 1734, he opened his narrative with the accession of George II in 1727 and the state of the Whig and Tory parties at the time. He treated the early years of the reign in broad, summary outline compared to the detailed narrative and dialogue for the years after 1733, when he could depend on written notes, memoranda, journals, and (for the final weeks of the Queen's illness) a diary. Sometimes he set down a conversation immediately after hearing it, or he telescoped into one episode conversations that were intermittent over a long period. He seems to have had a Boswellian gift of total recall: not shorthand (in the famous quip) but a long head. When he needed them he also relied on documents, speeches, and letters, which he copied into the memoirs.

He was well aware of other memoirists, two of whom he mentions: the Cardinal de Retz in France (whose memoirs were published in 1717) and Bishop Burnet in England. He had read the first volume of Burnet's *History* (published in 1724), and quotes from it in his own memoirs. "I think like you of Burnet's history," he wrote to a friend after reading the second volume (ten years later), "'tis the Common Chit-chat of a talkative, credulous old fellow that frequents coffee houses and reads newspapers." In his own he condemns de Retz and Burnet, these two "ecclesiastical heroes of their own romances" who "aim at that useless imaginary glory of being thought to influence every considerable event they relate." He would steer clear of such "disagreeable egotisms," he promises his readers, by referring to himself in the third person; like the chorus in Greek drama, he says, he will only comment on the events he observed.

This, at any rate, was his intention. But when he reaches the summer of 1734 in the memoirs, he digresses to apologize for so frequently mentioning himself, and expresses a more charitable view of other memoirists. He now realized that since they generally related events in which they were concerned, they could not avoid egotisms: what he had imputed to vanity he now finds from experience was owing to necessity. He also apologizes for the "loose, unmethodized, and often incoherent manner" in which his memoirs are put together: he had too little leisure for writing and revising. Instead he tells of "things only just as they occur" in his memory, he says (when he reached the year 1737), "and as I happen to have leisure to set them down" without the trouble or time to go back and interweave them in their proper places. As for his being too particular in "relating little circumstances": since he has no guide to tell him what will please other people, he has allowed himself to be guided by what pleases himself best. But it was more than self-indulgence that made him write with such particularity; he looked on "these papers rather as fragments that might be wove into a history, than a history in themselves," and hence he put in the little details that few historians could discover for themselves.

The knowledge that what he heard and saw at Court would find a place in his memoirs undoubtedly sharpened his ears and his eyes there; and during the next four years he was both involved actor and witty commentator, important actor and Greek chorus, in the mixed human drama enacted on the various stages where his Court duties placed him.

At the end of 1737, soon after recording in anguished detail the death of his beloved Queen, Hervey terminated the memoirs. Sections of them are written in a fair copy; others still show passages revised or struck out. He does not tell why he stopped so abruptly. Perhaps the shock of the Queen's death dispirited him, and he no longer had the heart to describe the Court whose principal ornament she had been. (Sometimes his memoirs seem to be materials for the reign of Queen Caroline.) Perhaps the uncertainty of his position at Court also made him unwilling to chart its future

course. As a legacy to his descendents the memoirs were appreciated by his grandson the first Marquis of Bristol to the extent that
he destroyed a two-year segment (which probably cast an unflat-
tering light on the Prince of Wales). What remained was first
published in 1848, edited in the Victorian mode by John Wilson
Croker; and a more complete version was edited by Romney Sedgwick in 1931. Yet incomplete as they are the memoirs remain un-
dimmed as a brilliant historical and literary legacy to posterity, and
as Hervey's most enduring monument.

As a historical document they are unique. No other chronicler
of his time can match Hervey's intimate and incisive depiction of
the Royal family in their private and political life. Although several
other prominent political figures of the time were reputed to be
writing the history of George II's reign—Carteret, Bolingbroke,
and Chesterfield—their memoirs (if written) have never come to
light.

In style the memoirs are easily in the same class as Horace Walpole's, his only other eighteenth-century rival as memoirist. His
turn for wit, his love of antithesis—not so exaggerated and inept
as in his verse—and his sensitivity to the intricacy and nuance of
prose style make the memoirs a triumph. His love of paradox scat-
ters throughout his pages a wry wisdom similar to La Rochefou-
cauld's; and his pen portraits, especially of those he despised,
crackle with an *esprit* that is closer to La Bruyère than to any English model. The speeches and official papers that he copied into the
memoirs as well as the long disquisitions on foreign policy may
strike the modern reader as dull compared to the passages in which
people move and speak and come alive. His skill in building the
dramatic confrontations of his characters glows, at its best, with
genius. What memoirs can match the almost incredibly tragicomic
deathbed scene of Queen Caroline, as she consoles her blubbering
husband with the solace of mistresses and a new wife? The memoirs are so important a historical document and so accomplished a
literary one that they justify the years Hervey spent at the court of
George II.

There is another memoirist of the same period, James 2nd Earl
Waldegrave, who is comparable to Hervey in that he served for
four years, from 1754 to 1758, as governor to the Prince of Wales,

the future George III. He found himself painfully involved in court intrigue—the complicated tug-of-war between George II and the Dowager Princess of Wales over the Prince's upbringing. The memoirs that he wrote to tell the story of these years and their chief actors are frequently drawn on by political historians, never by literary ones, and with good reason. What a contrast they are to Hervey's! Waldegrave's are very brief; as uninspired as a shopkeeper's inventory, and with as little that is personal and self-revealing. He makes the customary disclaimer at the beginning: "I will advance no facts which are not strictly true, and do not mean to misrepresent any man; but will make no professions of impartiality, because I take it for granted that it is not in my power to be quite unprejudiced." And what he says at the end of these memoirs also echoes Hervey's situation:

> The constant anxiety, and frequent mortifications, which accompany ministerial employments, are tolerably well understood; but the world is totally unacquainted with the situation of those whom fortune has selected to be the constant attendants and companions of royalty, who partake of its domestic amusements, and social happiness.
>
> But I must not lift up the veil; and shall only add, that no man can have a clear conception how great personages pass their leisure hours, who has not been a prince's governor, or a king's favorite.

"But I must not lift up the veil," Waldegrave says. The phrase is apt: Hervey did lift up the veil to reveal a human drama of the most compelling interest, in which he himself played an important part.

We may assess his memoirs from three points of view: as history, as biography (of the Royal Family), and as autobiography.

How reliable are the memoirs as a historical document? In brief, Basil Williams and Romney Sedgwick have testified as to their factual reliability, and a student of the great Hanoverian historian, Wolfgang Michael, has devoted a doctoral dissertation to answering that very question. Much of the memoirs can be paralleled in the Egmont diary, those pious and conscientious daily entries made by the Irish peer who sat in the Commons during the same years;

and Hervey's personal letters to his intimate friends, particularly Stephen and Henry Fox, also corroborate the memoirs at many points.

Similarly his portraits of the King, the Queen, and Frederick, Prince of Wales, find corroboration in other witnesses, including Lady Mary Wortley Montagu, Chesterfield, and Horace Walpole. Hervey admits his bias in favor of the Queen and against the Prince, yet when all due allowance is made his judgments have remained unchallenged.

And now for the third element: how much autobiography did Hervey put into his court memoirs? The most striking episodes are those about his friendships with the Honorable Anne Vane, the Prince of Wales, and the Queen. All of these relationships are connected and all have political significance or overtones. Miss Vane, a Maid of Honor, had been Hervey's mistress when she was elevated (so to speak) to become the Prince's; but this triangular friendship was shattered because of political rather than sexual jealousy. Then, when she found her hold on the Prince weakening, Miss Vane resumed her friendship—and her affair—with Hervey; and together they conspired to exact a generous settlement from the Prince, Hervey for the pleasure of vexing his former friend, Miss Vane for the sake of living in luxury the rest of her life. We can see that Hervey shaped this episode around its political contours, for as soon as Miss Vane's final settlement is gained she is bundled offstage in one sentence that tells us she finished her life at Bath (Hervey writes) after *two* months. Actually she survived for *three* months; Hervey had lost interest in her both as a woman and as a political pawn.

Hervey's friendship with the Queen is one of the main themes of the memoirs; this of course has a political importance—was he not (in Walter Bagehot's phrase) "Walpole's Queen-watcher"? —but he often goes beyond politics to sketch an intriguingly complex relationship. For the hatred between the Queen and her elder son was exactly paralleled by that between Hervey's mother, Lady Bristol, and himself. This is made explicit more than once in the memoirs. During one of the conversations between Hervey and the Queen he remarked, "Supposing I had had the honour to be born

189

Your Majesty's son"—when she impulsively interrupted him with —"I wish to God you had." On another occasion, after he had praised his father's character he observed the Queen weeping, for a reason that she then revealed. "He is a happy as well as a good man to have as well as to deserve such a son; and your mother is a brute that deserves just such a beast as my son. I hope *I* do not"—she continued, before revealing the most astonishing part of her confession—"and [I] wish with all my soul we could change, that they who are so alike might go together, and that you and I might belong to one another." If the Queen was Hervey's maternal surrogate, so he was her filial one. The political implication of this design is negligible compared to its psychological bearing on Hervey's autobiography.

If Hervey put into his memoirs some sections that might be more clearly labeled autobiography, what—we may wonder—did he omit? During these years he was engaged in satiric warfare with Pope and in love affairs with first Stephen Fox and then Francesco Algarotti, the Italian writer on a visit to England. In the memoirs Pope is mentioned only once, and for a political reason—that Lady Suffolk's disgrace in the King's eyes was partly due to her friendship with Pope, whose satire (Harvey writes) had "more than obliquely sneered" at the Royal Family. Stephen Fox comes into the memoirs very briefly in a political context, and Algarotti not at all.

When we compare the autobiographical element in Hervey's memoirs with Bishop Burnet's or with Horace Walpole's (in his memoirs of George II and of George III), we are struck by the prominent and intimate nature of Hervey's. His memoirs may in a sense be regarded as a hybrid form of autobiography crossed with memoirs. Not only did he dramatize an engrossing story of court life and intrigue but, one may suspect, he took some extra satisfaction in seeing himself play such an important role in the drama as he set it down on paper. In reversion, so to speak, was his posthumous satisfaction, when his memoirs would be read by his descendants and other readers yet unborn.

Ana-Books and Intellectual Biography in the Eighteenth Century

Paul J. Korshin

I

INTELLECTUAL BIOGRAPHY is unquestionably familiar to most educated readers today, but it is not identified as an individual genre in the writing of literary history. The term, when it is used at all, appears as an occasional subtitle, as in Barbara Shapiro's recent life of John Wilkins, the scientific bishop.[1] As a distinguishing name for a particular kind of study, it is employed rather haphazardly. It is uncertain whether a modern work so described differs appreciably in point of view and methodology from books whose authors do not employ this distinction. After all, since psychological analysis and attention to the history of ideas have become standard tools for the twentieth-century biographer, are not most serious biographies to some extent intellectual portraits, studies of a subject's thought, ideas, and mental processes? Thus intellectual biography today seems to be mainly a matter of authorial attitude or methodology as exercised in portions of a general study of a subject's life. At its best, it is something approaching a style, less a *kind* of biography than a *mode*, elements of which are found in certain works.

Even as a mode, intellectual biography enjoys very little status within the broader genre. Students of eighteenth-century biography and autobiography say very little about it. And how seldom do we encounter it in early autobiography: the author may discuss

191

his studies, ideas, and even theoretical conceptions, but seldom says anything about his mental processes or how he arrived at them.[2] The most exhaustive examination of eighteenth-century biography, that of Donald A. Stauffer, anatomizes the subject down to its smallest categories, yet ignores the development of intellectual biography completely.[3] James L. Clifford, in a discussion of the "types" of biography, does not mention it either, though two of his types, the "scholarly-historical" and the "artistic-scholarly," embrace many works, including his own, which study a given subject's intellect.[4] It is hard to conceive of intellectual biography as ever being more than a mode or a style, introduced by an author for special but temporary reasons in a larger work. For if an entire volume were given over to a subject's intellect, the result would probably not be biography; it would tend to become a critical study, an interpretation, or a commentary on somebody's writings. And the intellectual portrait, one for instance by Sainte-Beuve, is just that—a brief critique limited to aspects of the subject's mind rather than the story of an entire life narrated in rich detail and at length.

Let me propose, then, in a preliminary attempt at a working definition, that the term intellectual biography describes a certain kind of inquiry or mode of biographical analysis. The intellectual biographer is like the intellectual historian, but he focuses on the history of a single person's mind, thoughts, and ideas as a means toward illuminating the subject's life, personality, and character. Sometimes he is a prosopographer as well, applying the comparative method of group biography to set off particular characteristics of his subject.[5] But the earliest collections of biographies, as we shall see, are not prosopography in the modern historical sense; they are Plutarch- or Suetonius-like gatherings of worthies' lives, revealing no effort to ascertain group affinities. Works like Foxe's *Acts and Monuments of the Church* (1563) and the early volumes of hagiographies will often stress common themes—piety, devotion, suffering—but discussion of a martyr's or saint's intellectual qualities is non-existent.

Tracing the nature of intellectual biography, elusive and difficult to define though it may be, can be undertaken; it can be treated as an exercise in the literary history of a genre or a methodology. It emerged, as I hope to show, in the eighteenth century, the age in which modern biography, and especially large-scale biographical collections, began. The collections include numerous ambitions ventures like Bayle's *Dictionnaire historique et critique*, translated and substantially enlarged by Thomas Birch and others as *A General Dictionary Historical and Critical* (10 vols., 1734–41), and the two editions of the English *Biographia Britannica* (1747–66 and 1778–93). Several scholarly Continental undertakings, like Gesner's academic biographies or Ménage's lives of the philosophers, will also be relevant.[6]

II

The beginnings of intellectual biography are very modest and unpromising, seldom more than a few lines in an entire work, far too little to qualify as a genre. Aubrey's *Brief Lives*, usually cherished for their modish scandal and colorful portraits, and which furnished material for a play in the West End a few years ago, would seem an unlikely place to look for the intellectual biography. But Aubrey does not wholly disappoint; traces of the genre can be found, mainly in his longest "brief" life (82 pages in the Clarendon edition), that of Hobbes. In the manner of lives of the learned, Aubrey concentrates on Hobbes's studies and participation in controversies (this was standard Renaissance practice), but we see a foreshadowing of later practice when he talks about Hobbes's intellectual habits. For example, "He thought much and with excellent method and stedinesse, which made him seldome make a false step."[7] This is promising, though it does not go beyond a one-sentence *aperçu*. Elsewhere, Aubrey adds miscellaneous notes (the entire sketch is nothing more than marginalia) on Hobbes's reading habits, methods of composition, and circle of friends and acquaintances. There is an amorphous and incomplete attempt to place Hobbes in a setting, though hardly what literary critics today would call an intellectual milieu; the introduction of the milieu concept is a big step in biography, one which does not mature until the later eighteenth century. The bulk of Aubrey's brief lives,

193

as we might expect, reveal nothing about the thoughts of his subjects.

The eighteenth century in England is a period of great biographical collecting, from compilations of lives of poets, clergymen, naval heroes, and titled names to more universal efforts like Birch's ten folio volumes of Bayle and the two separate editions of the *Biographia Britannica*.[8] But whereas Aubrey and some of his contemporaries had moved in the direction of personal reminiscences and the recovery of intimate details, the eighteenth-century compilers were goaded by antiquarian zeal, a desire to discover and print documents, and an overriding concern with the subject's tangible accomplishments or *acta*. The new lives which Birch and his assistants added to Bayle, even those of philosophers, literary men, and scholars, are concerned almost exclusively with "indisputable matters of fact."[9] One can read dozens of lives in the *Biographia Britannica* without uncovering a single notion as to what somebody thought, how he composed, or whom he knew. The authors might mention a subject's learning or scholarship, as in the life of Sir Thomas Browne, but without depth or analytical vision.[10] The author of the life of Oliver Cromwell saw the need for "indisputable evidence" in order to rebut the influence of flattery, prejudice, and superstition, but his concern with Cromwell's thought is relatively shallow. "There is a natural curiosity to enter, as it were, into the privacies of extraordinary persons, which is a kind of slipping behind the scenes, and taking a more nice and certain view of their conduct, by getting on the wrong side of the theatre."[11] This is less intellectual inquiry than it is conventional "secret history." The fixation with documentary evidence, which Birch and his successors printed as long footnotes and appendices, steered the biographical enterprise toward solid evidentiary foundations. There was less speculation and more scholarship than there had been in the previous century.

The character sketch is not entirely absent, for the compilers sometimes describe personality and behavioral traits. Like contemporary memoirists, they cherish the pejorative whenever possible. It would be tedious to cite many examples, and there are hundreds of them. But one of my favorites is the observation about the poetical abilities of Margaret Cavendish, Duchess of Newcastle, and her husband: "Of all the riders of Pegasus, . . . there have not been a more fantastic couple than his Grace and his faithful Duchess, who was never off her pillion."[12] When we learn that the Duchess' poetical efforts filled a dozen folios, ten of them still in print in the late 1770's, we sense that the point has been adequately made. Much similar ironic wit appears in numerous lives in both editions of the *Biographia*. Although this huge compilation, whether in Birch's seven volumes or in Andrew Kippis' six, is a valuable source for studying the evolution of eighteenth-century biographical techniques, it has received comparatively little attention from scholars. But when we see anything in the *Biographia Britannica* about a subject's mind, it is usually through the old-fashioned and somewhat limited perspective of traditional character writing.

There are other specialized collections before Johnson's *Lives of the Poets*, such as Thomas Mortimer's *British Plutarch* (6 vols., 1762), Cibber's and Shiels' *Lives of the Poets* (5 vols., 1753), and Cibber's *Lives of the Actors* (1753), but they are completely undistinguished. The lives in these collections are often derived from an earlier biography, with occasional interpolations, as we have recently seen to be the case with eighteenth-century accounts of Shakespeare's life.[13] Even generally reliable commentators like Johnson, Chalmers, and Robert Anderson often rely on earlier works, sometimes printing long extracts from them. Intellectual biography, which is critical and interpretative almost by definition, obviously could not flourish when biography was conceived of mainly as an account of a person's actions and works.

This was clearly the case, in England and on the Continent, for most of the eighteenth century, whether we look at individual lives or collections. For example, there are two eighteenth-century biographies of Sir Walter Raleigh, by William Oldys (1740) and Thomas Birch (1751). Both, especially that of Oldys, are excellent narratives, with many details drawn from documents now lost, and are generally meticulous with regard to fact. Neither is in the least interpretative or intellectual. Birch barely notices the productions of Raleigh's intellect; Oldys mentions some of the poetry and *The History of the World* only as historical or antiquarian artifacts, not as aspects of the man's genius.[14] Other lives of individuals are similar, immersed in an unrelenting tide of detail, insensitive to all but the most obvious interpretative possibilities.[15]

Consider an immense and, for some time, authoritative work like John Jortin's *Life of Erasmus*. Jortin spends much time settling controversies and repeating historical circumstances he had found in earlier works. We hear a lot about Erasmus' physical side, as, "We have observed in many places that Erasmus could not endure even the smell of fish, and had a most Lutheran stomach."[16] Erasmus' stomach can be summoned to help decide a doctrinal point, but we hear nothing about his mind, presumably a somewhat better witness. Nor do his mental powers come off any better in Jortin's "Remarks" on Erasmus' works, consisting almost wholly of extracts from other writers (II, 1–120). In the second half of the century, it became usual for the more ambitious biographies to include a "character" of the subject, but even in the most elaborate works, these are usually confined to discussions of personality traits or the listing of literary accomplishments. Seldom do we find analyses of intellectual qualities. Two of the best, Ruffhead's *Life of Alexander Pope* (1769) and Malone's life of Dryden (1800), prefer to list facts and quote the opinions of others.[17] An occasional Continental compilation looks promising, but such works as Bayle's *Dictionnaire*, Johann Gesner's *Biographia Academica Gottingensis* (1768–69), or Gottlieb Harless' *De Vitis Philologorum* (1767–72) are in the tradition of *acta*, and favor lengthy extracts dealing with dead controversies. There is not much satisfactory evidence, then, in the standard biographical sources of the eighteenth century, especially in England, for an evolving genre of intellectual biography.

III

Genre change is gradual and is seldom self-generated. Johnson's interest in the quality of intellectual biography, evident from the elaborate "characters" in his longer *Lives of the Poets*, is not without certain antecedents. The surprisingly neglected life of Johnson by Robert Anderson (1795), who was usually just a journeyman practitioner, contains some remarkable attempts at an interpretative style. Neither Johnson's nor Anderson's techniques are wholly new. We find very few such forerunners of this methodology in the standard biography-oriented literary histories of the eighteenth century.[18] Yet there is a plausible source for late eighteenth-century attempts at intellectual biography. It is a body of literature which today may seem trivial and second-rate and which has been ignored, so far as I know, by most students of the eighteenth century.

These are the books which at the time were called *ana*, from the final three letters of the title. They must be distinguished from our use of "ana" in literary studies in the twentieth century. We speak today of Swiftiana, Popiana, Johnsoniana, and so on; in doing so, we refer to materials peripheral to but in some way concerned with the writings or life of a literary or historical figure. So a Johnson autograph letter would not qualify; it would be an important, central document. But some miscellaneous anecdotes by an acquaintance which mention Johnson once or twice could be construed as Johnsoniana. "Ana," according to the *NED*, is a suffix appended to proper names, denoting "notable sayings of a person, literary trifles, society verses, items of gossip, etc." This is helpful, but it is a modern definition. In the eighteenth century, "books in *ana*" were collections of the memorable sayings of the learned. The fashion began in the Renaissance, when the first books in *ana* were of classical authors: Virgiliana, Horatiana, Maniliana, Appiana, and so on. (At first, they were little more than choice quotations from classical authors; the genre continues with such twentieth-century reincarnations as *Quotations from Chairman Mao Tse-tung* or the parodic *Quotations from Chairman LBJ*.) In the Renaissance, such books were serious, and usually were arranged alphabetically by subject, so that a reader could easily locate an author's thoughts on numerous topics. In the late sixteenth and seventeenth centuries, first in France and later in the Low Countries and Germany, books in *ana* begin to appear for famous statesmen, religious thinkers, and scholars. Before 1600 there were collections of the sayings of Luther, Calvin, and Melancthon.

Originally, they were principally collections of pithy sayings and *pensées diverses*, but as the genre developed, the books in *ana* became embryonic intellectual biographies, significant efforts at recording the intellectual history of a single person.

This development is quite dramatic. The early books in *ana* are virtually all *excerpta ex ore*. *Perroniana*, for Cardinal Jacques du Perron (Geneva, 1669), *Thuana*, for Jacques Auguste de Thou (Paris? 1669), and the two collections relating to Scaliger, *Scaligeriana* (Hague, 1666) and *Prima Scaligerana* (Utrecht, 1670), consist mainly of extracts from the conversations and writings of these notables. They are somewhat like the modern anthology or chrestomathy. Although they contain almost no commentary on or interpretation of the various subjects' thoughts and mental processes, they have the virtue of assembling specimens of a man's ideas on various topics, arranged systematically. There are more than a score of similar seventeenth-century compilations, most of them French.[19]

Far more relevant to the emergence of intellectual biography is the historian Jean Le Clerc's collection of extracts on his own thought and opinions, the *Parrhasiana* (1699–1701). *Parrhasiana* is an ambitious work, in two volumes, consisting of mini-essays from various parts of Le Clerc's extensive *opera*, all translated into French. The materials gathered together are substantial enough to give us a very good idea of what he thought, in depth, on many topics.[20] Perhaps the *Parrhasiana* should not be counted as a proper book in *ana*, since Le Clerc compiled it himself under the pseudonym of Theodore Parrhase. Le Clerc was a controversial figure, so there is an element of apology in his work, but it is significant because it presents a full-length picture of a major scholar's mind and intellectual processes. Similar to the *Parrhasiana* is Johann Christopher Wolf's *Casauboniana* (1710). It is another collection of extracts from the diverse editions and controversial writings of the important Continental scholar-humanist Isaac Casaubon (1559–1614). Casaubon had been a center of controversy in a way that Scaliger and Le Clerc had not, so Wolf found it necessary to make a further advance on previous books in *ana* by including a lengthy preface wherein he could display Casaubon's wisdom to the greatest advantage against his Catholic adversaries.[21] Books in *ana* had come to be regarded as a distinct biographical genre; at least Wolf's preface contains a bibliography (the most detailed one undertaken to that time) of all previous works of this type.[22] Since Wolf's announced intention is to give the reader a good impression of all that Casaubon said and thought on numerous topics, and since the preface emphasizes major points in the development of his ideas, it is clear that *Casauboniana* may be considered a proto-intellectual biography.

Even more suggestive is Jacques l'Enfant's work on Bracciolini Poggio (1380–1459). *Poggiana, ou la Vie, le Caractère, les Sentences, et les Bon Mots de Pogge Florentin* (1720) is still technically a book in *ana*, but the genre has matured considerably. Poggio is little studied today, but in the eighteenth century he was widely acknowledged the foremost Renaissance restorer of ancient letters and an early historian of Florence.[23] He was extremely attractive as well because of his great success as a controversialist: his sharp tongue, savage satiric style, and nasty disposition were legendary. Such qualities would naturally be appealing in a century which thrived on intellectual controversy of all kinds. Appropriately, then, *Poggiana* is very much a life-and-ideas intellectual biography of Poggio. L'Enfant's "Vie de Pogge" includes remarks on his contemporaries, in a rudimentary attempt at prosopography. The life of Poggio is not the usual apology focusing on the subject's deeds and writings. In fact, it concludes with a long and extremely critical character evaluation.[24] L'Enfant does not extenuate Poggio's faults, and even professes to be shocked at his bad temper and harsh polemic style. But he interprets these characteristics in light of what was prevalent at the time: such qualities, when seen in the perspective of fifteenth-century Florentine academic disputes, are not unusual. It seems clear that l'Enfant's intellectual character of Poggio, which is strongly suggestive of some of those Johnson would later write for his *Lives of the Poets*, is meant as a step toward writing the history "d'un esprit fort libre."[25]

The high point in the *ana* tradition is reached in the 1720's with Pierre Daniel Huet's *Huetiana* (1722). Huet prepared this collection of his thoughts on numerous subjects, scholarly, critical, theological, and general, before his death; it was published post-humously with an "Eloge historique de l'auteur" by an unnamed friend.[26] The "Eloge," though brief, touches upon central intellectual themes like Huet's early studies and reading during his formative years, his early scholarly friendships, and the books which influenced his later development. We learn, for example, that Samuel Bochart's inspired etymological interpretation of Scripture, *Geographia Sacra* (1647), made a strong impression on the youthful Huet.[27] Thus we get some hint of its influence in forming his theories of exegesis as expressed in his first work, *De Interpretatione* (1661), and in his early editing of Origen. The book's 140 articles contain his latest observations on subjects as diverse as St. Augustine, Hesychius, the Ancients-Moderns controversy, classical literature, ancient architecture and gardens, and the court of Louis XIV. Some of the essays appear to deal with Huet's own intellectual experiences, such as "Des obstacles de l'érudition" and "Difference des grands & des mediocres esprits."[28] Hence *Huetiana* is a kind of intellectual autobiography, carefully arranged to present not only an overview of the author's thought but also a picture of the growth of many of his opinions.

This is the most satisfactory of the books in *ana*, so far as intellectual biography is concerned, but the genre continues to flourish on into the early nineteenth century, mainly in France. After the first third of the eighteenth century, however, these compilations tend toward the trivial, the jocular, and the commonplace. Some are mere jest books, others collections of witty sayings and polite conversation. Ultimately, they become collections of *bons mots* and anecdotes, and cease to have substantial biographical value. One author, Charles Yves Cousin (1769–1840), surely the most prolific of *ana*ists, compiled nearly twenty books in *ana* between 1801 and 1820. These included *Bonapartiana* (1801), *Diderotiana* (1810), *Staëliana* (1820), *Voltairiana* (1801), and—suggestive of the limits of the genre—*Grimmiana* (1813). There was also an *Encyclopédiana* (Paris, 1791), an universal dictionary of *ana*, which points toward the twentieth-century encyclopedic dictionary (like the *Columbia Encyclopedia*).

IV

It is impossible precisely to ascertain the influence of the *ana*-tradition on later eighteenth-century biography.[29] The books were published as cheap duodecimos, which turn up widely in English and Continental libraries throughout the century. Certainly they influenced such English collections as Isaac Disraeli's *Curiosities of Literature* (1791) and Spence's *Anecdotes* (1820), both of which are similar to the early *ana*-books except that they deal with many literary figures rather than with one author.[30] The tradition was undoubtedly known to Johnson, whose longer *Lives* resemble several of the more ambitious intellectual-history books in *ana*. While we cannot be certain whether Johnson recognized the efforts of the Continental books in *ana* to present a kind of intellectual biography, there can be no doubt that he was sensitive to the implications of intellectual history, for he was probably the first person ever to use the term in anything like its modern sense.[31] Boswell did not try to write an intellectual biography of Johnson, but he, too, was aware of the tradition; in the next century, Robert Southey would describe *The Life of Johnson* as "the *Ana* of all *Anas*."[32] Robert Anderson, whose *Life of Samuel Johnson* (1795; 3rd ed. 1815) may be the first genuine intellectual biography by an English author, includes a 100-page critique of Johnson's intellect and actually explains some of Johnson's infirmities "by referring to the history of his mind."[33] And when the scholar-clergyman Samuel Parr proposed to write *his* life of Johnson (which he not only never finished but never even started), he described it in such a way that it is clear that he intended to make it an intellectual biography, and included a number of the most important books in *ana* on his working list of valuable materials.[34]

This essay is a sketch rather than a labored analysis. I have tried to suggest that the point of view of the intellectual biographer, as expressed in a distinctive quality or mode of inquiry into a subject's thought—the history of his or her mind—is an eighteenth-century development. We see it emerge as a noticeable methodology late in the century in a few works such as Johnson's *Lives of the*

Poets, to a lesser extent in Boswell, and most emphatically in Anderson's neglected *Life of Johnson*. And the intellectual biographer's mode must include among its predecessors the long-ignored, mainly Continental, tradition of the *ana*-book. Books in *ana* flourished in the late Renaissance and throughout the eighteenth century, ultimately establishing paradigms which successfully combine intellectual history and biography. Evidently very popular with learned and general readers alike, they bequeathed to late eighteenth-century and nineteenth-century biographers a mode of inquiry to which, at some distance, modern students continue to be indebted. Perhaps the continued relevance of these old collected sayings of the wise will suggest the value of other "neglected" genres and modes in interpreting eighteenth-century literature.

NOTES

1. See her *John Wilkins, 1614–1672: An Intellectual Biography* (Berkeley and Los Angeles: Univ. of California Press, 1969), p. 11, for the suggestion that intellectual biography simply combines biography and intellectual history.
2. On autobiography, see Donald Greene, "The Uses of Autobiography in the Eighteenth Century," in *Essays in Eighteenth-Century Biography*, ed. Philip P. Daghlian (Bloomington, Ind.: Indiana Univ. Press, 1968), pp. 43–66; Greene suggests that the genre gives us "authentic reports of subjective states" (p. 45), but does not go into intellectual analysis in detail. Paul Delany, *British Autobiography in the Seventeenth Century* (New York: Columbia Univ. Press, 1969), pp. 172–73, mentions the scarcity of secular intellectual autobiography, partly because "seventeenth-century intellectuals had little sense of what we now call the sociology of knowledge" (p. 173).
3. See *The Art of Biography in Eighteenth-Century England* (Princeton: Princeton Univ. Press, 1941), pp. 257–307; Stauffer traces fashions in describing spiritual and mental torment, but is silent about analytical qualities.
4. *From Puzzles to Portraits: Problems of a Literary Biographer* (Chapel Hill: Univ. of North Carolina Press, 1970), pp. 83–98, esp. p. 85.
5. On group biography as a kind of intellectual history, see Lawrence Stone, "Prosopography," *Dædalus*, 100 (1971), 46–79.
6. I refer to Johann Matthias Gesner, *Biographia Academica Gottingensis*, 3 vols. (Halle and Göttingen, 1768–69) and Gilles Ménage, *Historia Mulierum Philosopharum* (Leyden, 1690).
7. *"Brief Lives," chiefly of Contemporaries, set down by John Aubrey,*

between the Years 1669 and 1696, ed. Andrew Clark, 2 vols. (Oxford: Clarendon Press, 1898), I, 349.

8. For a comprehensive list of eighteenth-century biographical dictionaries and collections, see the *New CBEL*, II, 1797–1808.

9. See *A General Dictionary Historical and Critical*, I, 373 (on Sir Francis Bacon; cf. I, 369–412); the accounts of Dryden (IV, 676–87), Samuel Parker (VIII, 142–48), and scores of other intellectuals are equally circumstantial.

10. *Biographia Britannica*, 2nd ed. (London, 1778–93), II, 998–99.

11. *Ibid.*, III, 1537–38, 1577.

12. *Ibid.*, III, 338.

13. See S. Schoenbaum, *Shakespeare's Lives* (Oxford: Clarendon Press, 1970); see pp. 126–43, the best study of the derivative qualities of many early lives of Shakespeare.

14. See Oldys, *The Life of Sir Walter Raleigh* (London, 1740), pp. 110–14.

15. For a full list of Birch's biographical writings, see the *New CBEL*, II, 1702–4. His usual method is to discuss his subject's public career and literary works with great circumstantial detail, and to conclude with brief observations on such matters as conversation, wit, and style. See, for an example, his "Life of John Tillotson," in *The Works of the Most Reverend Dr. John Tillotson*, 3 vols. (London, 1752), I, xcvi–xcvii.

16. *The Life of Erasmus*, 2 vols. (London, 1758–60), I, 581.

17. Ruffhead, *The Life of Alexander Pope* (London, 1769), pp. 428–64, has a loosely constructed section on Pope's "genius" which occasionally (pp. 461–64) shows analytic skill. Malone's "Life," in *The Critical and Miscellaneous Prose Works of John Dryden*, 3 vols. in 4 (London, 1800), I, i, 469–78, 511–13, and 518–20, lists rather than analyzes Dryden's personal and mental qualities.

18. See René Wellek, *The Rise of English Literary History* (Chapel Hill: Univ. of North Carolina Press, 1941), pp. 136–43. Lawrence Lipking, *The Ordering of the Arts in Eighteenth-Century England* (Princeton: Princeton Univ. Press, 1970), pp. 415–22, discusses some of the "precedents" for Johnson's *Lives*, but does not mention the books in *ana* as a possibility.

19. F. P. Wilson, "Table Talk," *HLQ*, 4 (1940), 27–46, discusses a number of books in *ana*, principally of the later period; the only early book to receive attention is the very popular *Menagiana* (1693), on the scholar Gilles Ménage, which had eight editions.

20. LeClerc's full title is *Parrhasiana, ou Pensées diverses sur des matières d'histoire, de morale, et de politique*, 2 vols. (Amsterdam, 1699–1701); there was a second edition of both volumes in 1701.

21. *Casauboniana, sive Isaaci Casauboni Varia de Scriptoribus . . .*, ed. Jo. Christopher Wolf (Hamburg, 1710), Sig.)(5ʳ⁻ᵛ.

22. *Ibid.*, pp. 8–42. The most exhaustive list of *ana*-books ever attempted is P. Namur, *Bibliographie des ouvrages publiés sous le nom d'ana* (Brussels, 1839).

23. See John Edwin Sandys, *A History of Classical Scholarship*, 3 vols. (Cambridge, 1908), II, 25–34, and Georg Voigt, *Die Wiederbelebung des classischen Alterthums, oder das erste Jahrhundert des Humanismus*, 3rd ed., 2 vols. (Berlin, 1893), I, 235–51, 257–60.
24. See *Poggiana*, 2 vols. (Amsterdam, 1720), I, 81–110.
25. *Poggiana*, I, 89.
26. See *Huetiana, ou Pensées diverses de M. Huet, Evesque d'Avranches* (Paris, 1722), p. xviii. The "Eloge" fills pp. iii–xxiv.
27. *Ibid.*, pp. v–vi.
28. See No. LXXIX, pp. 195–98, and No. CXXIV, pp. 350–52.
29. Stauffer, *The Art of Biography in Eighteenth-Century England*, pp. 491–93, deals only with the late eighteenth-century books in *ana* like *Walpoliana* (1799), *Addisoniana* (1803), and *Swiftiana* (1803); these are simply collections of anecdotes rather than attempts at intellectual biography. The influence of the Continental tradition has not hitherto been studied
30. Spence's *Anecdotes*, although not published until 1820, were compiled before his death in 1768. See *Observations, Anecdotes, and Characters of Books and Men*, ed. James M. Osborn, 2 vols. (Oxford: Clarendon Press, 1966), I, xvii–xxi, for a discussion of "Ana and Anecdotes as Literary Genre." Osborn mentions several of the Continental books in *ana* without elaboration. John Nichols, the publisher and antiquarian, is the compiler of *ana* books perhaps most frequently referred to; see *Minor Lives: A Collection of Biographies by John Nichols*, ed. Edward L. Hart (Cambridge, Mass.: Harvard Univ. Press, 1971), pp. xv–xviii.
31. See the "Preface" to the *Dictionary of the English Language*, 2 vols. (London, 1755), I, Sig. Cl^r; cf. Felix Gilbert, "Intellectual History," *Dædalus*, 100 (1971), 80–97, for various modern definitions.
32. See *NED*, x. v. "Ana," B1, quots.
33. See Anderson, *The Life of Samuel Johnson, LL.D.*, 3rd ed. (Edinburgh, 1815), pp. 468–583, esp. pp. 488–89. See also my essay "Robert Anderson's *Life of Johnson* and Early Interpretative Biography," *HLQ*, 37 (1973).
34. For a description of Parr's projected work, see Rev. William Field, *Memoirs of the Life, Writings, and Opinions of the Rev. Samuel Parr, LL.D.*, 2 vols. (London, 1828), I, 164–65; cf. the catalogue of Parr's library, *Bibliotheca Parriana* (London, 1827), pp. 706–8.

Opera and Incipient Romantic Aesthetics in Germany

M. G. Flaherty

ROMANTICISM HAS LONG BEEN a subject of study and debate. Ever since the 1790's, poets, writers, philosophers, and scholars have sought to analyze the phenomenon, determine its antecedents, and explain its implications. Their collective efforts have succeeded in showing that the Romantic movement in Germany was the culmination and consolidation of certain ideas and intellectual tendencies that had been steadily evolving since the Renaissance. Among the most important of these tendencies was empirical philosophy, with its emphasis on particulars rather than universals. Another was the organic concept of history, with its affirmation of cultural differences. And closely related to it was the reverence for the past, which stimulated reevaluation and careful study of the Middle Ages and the sixteenth century as well as of classical antiquity. Yet another was the concern about the primitive, the folkloristic, and the unity of certain societies. Increasing interest in human psychology was also important, for it led to closer scrutiny of imagination, intuition, pleasure, and dreams.

Time and time again students of Romanticism have pointed out that new artistic attitudes, sensibilities, and habits developed as these tendencies increased in strength and began to converge. The English garden, the bourgeois tragedy, the sentimental novel, the Gothic novel, the graveyard poem, the ancient folk poem, the criminal story, the fairy tale, the poetic descriptions of primordial nature, and the poetic adoration of ruins are some of the forms regularly considered symptomatic of the changes in premises of taste. The coining of the word aesthetics by A. G. Baumgarten, the affirmation of the wondrous by J. J. Bodmer and J. J. Breitinger, the rejection of predetermined rules by G. E. Lessing, and the demand for creative freedom by the Storm and Stress writers are always mentioned as significant indications of the changes that were taking place in literary criticism and aesthetics.

One of the best indicators of the changes in German aesthetic premises and critical attitudes is never, or hardly ever, mentioned in works discussing the evolution of the Romantic movement. And that is opera: the art form which the German Romantics themselves considered the ultimate artistic possibility. Opera had originated during Renaissance experimentations with the dramatic forms of Greek antiquity. Because of the experimental attitudes out of which it developed, it soon lost all resemblance to the forms it was intended to restore and became a thoroughly independent form of theater that continued to spawn new variants as well as influence old ones. While dilettantes and practising playwrights were producing such musical dramatic works before live audiences, scholars and critics were discussing the theoretical writings of the ancients and comparing them with actual theatrical practices. Many wanted to revise such practices according to their own interpretations of ancient theory, but others tried to suit their theories to the new practices. From its very inception—and throughout most of its early history—opera was closely associated with the rediscovery of ancient dramatic theories and with the development of modern aesthetic thought, not to mention the emergence of modern theater.

Germany's earliest operatic experimentations were made at the beginning of the seventeenth century by Martin Opitz.[1] In addition to outlining his intentions and his approach, he explained that he had deviated from accepted convention in order to make his works more acceptable and pleasing to modern audiences.[2] As the new form of entertainment became increasingly popular, many German poets and playwrights followed Opitz' precedent in creating libretti and in explaining their creations.[3] While some claimed to be reviving what they considered the long-lost ancient art of synthesizing word, action, and music, others claimed to be perfecting something brand new in the history of theater. They maintained that historical and cultural changes had nurtured different tastes and consequently necessitated the invention of different theatrical forms. A few of them, like Christian Heinrich Postel, even took colleagues to task, contending that those who strove to copy the Greeks failed to understand not only antiquity and its dramatic forms but also their own era and its artistic prerequisites.[4] Observance of preestablished rules or imitation of past masters could not, in their opinion, be of any importance when the ultimate aim was effectiveness in modern living theater. In such theoretical discussions, the newly invented forms, whether theatrical poems, *Dantzspiele*, *Singspiele*, musical plays, musical dramas, musical comedies, musical tragedies, or musical tragicomedies, were often described with the German word for work or with its equivalent from Italian, the word *opera*. Late seventeenth-century German theorists, like Daniel Georg Morhof, obviously chose to use it because it subsumed all the new forms and thus served to distinguish them from the more conventional spoken dramatic forms.[5] None of these writers questioned their own or anyone else's right to experiment and to create such unconventional works.

This attitude changed, however, when more and more Germans began taking notice of French Neoclassicism, which was quickly crystallizing into a fixed set of dogmas. By the early decades of the eighteenth century, German Neoclassicists were roundly criticizing opera's failure to imitate nature, observe the unities, and teach a moral lesson.[6] They claimed that its magical machines, marvelous, music, and stunning splendor dangerously distracted the mind while tantalizing the eye and seducing the ear. Furthermore, its total lack of generic purity prevented their finding a category for it within their systems of legitimate arts. For Neoclassicists like J. C. Gottsched and J. H. Zedler, opera was comparable to Gothic architecture, mediaeval doggerel, chivalric romances, Chinese plays, harlequinades, and assorted varieties of Baroque exotica: it represented to them either the return of the barbarous irrationality of past ages or the advent of alarmingly relativistic attitudes.[7] Consequently they felt they had no choice but to condemn it.

Strong opposition to such condemnations manifested itself immediately in writings affirming opera's right to exist as a musical theatrical art form. Instead of merely making counterassertions, their authors generally began by scrutinizing and then eventually rejecting Neoclassical assumptions and critical methods. The first and most frequently mentioned objection was that opera's opponents were theorizing about something of which they had little firsthand knowledge; they did not attend performances, and even if they did, they were too concerned about their rulebooks to relax and enjoy the full effect of what they were experiencing. A second objection was that the Neoclassicists did not observe all the facts of the matter very carefully; opera's overwhelming popularity at major courts and in important capitals should have indicated to them that it could not be quite as tasteless or barbaric as they asserted. A third objection to the Neoclassicists had to do with their failure to view opera within the historical context for which it was created. They ignored its musical, architectural, and painterly components, opera's defenders believed, and judged it by irrelevant, outdated dramatic standards because they lacked the common sense to accept it as a new type of theater, one which was still developing because of changing modern needs.

Preferring what was empirically proven to what was theoretically speculated, opera's earliest defenders established the primacy of the individual work. Since many of them were practising playwrights, they selected and made their own only those ideas whose validity could be tested in the theater and substantiated by live audiences. Consequently they observed actual audience reactions and, taking such reactions into consideration, concluded that no one went to the theater solely for moral edification. This then led to discussions of theater's attraction and analyses of pleasure and its sources. While some early eighteenth-century librettists contended that opera soothed the tired spirit and prepared it for serious duties, others maintained that it satisfied an innate human need for variety and change. Still others, like Hinrich Hinsch, claimed that opera provided a pleasurable poetic experience precisely because it titillated the senses of its audiences without addressing their reason or understanding.[8] According to one writer in the 1720's, opera enchanted the rational faculties of its spectators and, appealing directly to their imagination (*die sanfte Einbildung*), so totally absorbed their attention that they felt transported into some other world.[9] If the first generation of critics justified pleasure only as a means of conveying a moral lesson, then the next generation emphasized the necessity of pleasure, and the generation following that considered the possibility of just providing pleasure for its own sake.

In addition to analyzing the sources and effects of theatrical pleasures, opera's defenders concentrated on the imitation of nature and investigated its validity as an artistic principle. They sought its origins in earlier dramatic writings and considered its implications for modern theater. One conclusion which they then drew was that there had been general disagreement even among those writers revered as reputable authorities by the Neoclassicists. Another conclusion, even more important in light of subsequent developments, was that opera was a man-made poetic fabrication, no less real than other forms of art and consequently no more harmful or deceptive. Some critics maintained that operatic reality was something created by artists who, without aiming to duplicate nature, selected certain essential features from nature and, using a particular medium, presented them in a meaningfully different order. Others, like Barthold Feind, went on to explain that all the arts had to be make-believe because they depended on media which were artficial to begin with. According to him, some media certainly were more naturalistic than others and allowed for closer simulation or approximation of nature, but variation in the degree of simulation did not change the fact that all art is artificial. Considering opera nothing more than an intangible silhouette (*Schattenspiel*) formed out of poetic fictions, he argued that the order it presented had to be based on an artificial or at least a different kind of logic.[10] Views such as these challenged the Neoclassical arbiters of taste and gradually forced them to admit certain exceptions into their artistic systems. The steadily increasing number of exceptions which the self-styled authorities were forced to incorporate served first to expand, but then to weaken and eventually destroy all such systems. As this happened, opera developed into a major symbol for those critics who opposed the rigidity of Neoclassical aesthetics.

It also became symbolic for a third group of early eighteenth-century writers who were dissatisfied with both of the other points of view. For them, opera was not a unique, new theatrical form, but rather an aberrant version of one the Ancients had perfected and the Moderns had not yet successfully revived. Johann Ulrich König, for example, did not want to reject opera and what it represented, yet he was unable to accept it unquestioningly because of his Neoclassical predilections.[11] Unable to condone opera's contemporary form without reservation, writers like König concentrated on its artistic potentialities and suggested reforms designed to realize such potentialities. Their suggestions for reform indicated that they were reevaluating the intentions of opera's Renaissance originators, and that they were beginning to wonder just how the Greeks had achieved noble simplicity in their syntheses of so many seemingly divergent components. Such writers refused to relinquish the idea of mimesis, but as their concept of nature began to change, so too did their theories of its imitation.

Although several earlier German critics had explained opera as an imitation of either pastoral, heroic, fantastic, or wondrous nature, this became the crux of the interpretation advocated by Georg Friedrich Meier[12] and other mid-eighteenth-century Germans who subscribed to Charles Batteux's theories. For them the imitation of nature was the common denominator of all the arts and the logical basis for classifying and distinguishing them. In order to include several arts that did not imitate any conceivable aspect of actual nature, they adjusted their concept of probability to allow for the imitation of various types of nature. They considered probable any kind of art that imitated the particular kind of nature which suited its form, medium, and character; if it ignored or exceeded its basic generic limitations, it lost *vraisemblance* and became improbable. According to such reasoning, opera could only be probable if its music, decorations, machines, and stage effects were used to present the actions of gods, demigods, and other superhuman or supernatural creatures who required marvelous artifacts and exalted means of communication. These critics accomplished what earlier critics of Neoclassical persuasion had been unable to do; they secured for opera a legitimate place within a unified artistic system, and they did so, ironically enough, by classifying it as the dramatic imitation of wondrous nature.

Other mid-eighteenth-century Germans objected to having opera confined to the realm of the wondrous or to any other predetermined realm. Johann Adolph Schlegel, father of the Romantics, and Johann Elias Schlegel, their uncle, compared opera to other forms of art and concluded that all artistic media, whether music, singing, verse, paint, or plaster, were merely the formal conventions used for communication and not necessarily the factors determining the choice of subject.[13] Although they submitted that super-human characters performing marvels increased the probability of opera's media, they believed that verisimilitude had to be achieved through internal structure or the relationship of individual parts. Agreeing with earlier operatic writers who had broached the subject of imitation, they maintained that the artist used the medium of his choice to create another possible world, an artificial but equally true world that was governed according to its own intrinsic laws. Several of them went a step further and contended that this operatic world was a creation of the artist's imagination rather than a product of any kind of imitation. According to Justus Möser, for example, opera brought to life in the real world something the librettist and his collaborators had imagined and, through their artistry, had made seem probable.[14] When they borrowed from the tangible world of facts and figures, or when they imitated it in some other naturalistic way, they merely revealed the limitations and weaknesses of their own imagination. Nothing great, beautiful, original, or awe-inspiring could therefore, in Möser's opinion, ever result from imitation or from observance of *a priori* rules.

Those who defended opera in the 1750's and 1760's viewed rules such as the unities as dramatic conventions whose applicability depended solely on the individual artist's intentions. The genuine artist, they held, could go beyond the established limitations of his art and, because of his self-regulating ability, would do so without abusing his freedom. The other reason these critics gave for rejecting the immutability of the rules was a more sophisticated version of one that had repeatedly been used to defend opera in the past. They argued that the rules pertained only to the theatrical forms of the particular age that had formulated them. And since each age developed its own forms to satisfy its own needs, no one corpus of rules could possibly account for the new and different theatrical forms which human ingenuity and talent were constantly devising. Justus Möser spoke of such continuing artistic development in terms of Germanic law by precedent, whereas Johann Adolph Schlegel compared it to the burgeoning of trees and to the discovery of new continents.[15] They rejected Batteux's rationally compartmentalized artistic system on the same three grounds as earlier defenders of opera had rejected other such systems: first, it failed to allow for artistic progress; second, it overlooked the all-important fact that the arts were neither methodical nor predictable; and third, it ignored man's aesthetic reaction. For critical theorists such as this, opera was more than a genre of rationally explicable wonders; it was one of the clearest indications of the unlimited possibilities of the creative imagination.

Like opera's first defenders, these mid-eighteenth-century writers also observed and studied what they considered its overwhelming power to please. The spectator, they generally began, knows that opera is senseless and absurd if compared with reality; however, he enjoys it when he experiences it in a theater. Since his pleasure obviously does not come from any such comparisons, he must enjoy opera by submitting to the artificial order it presents on the stage and by using his imagination to pretend along with the performers. The question of how opera brought about this reaction then arose, and it was answered in various ways. Christian Gottfried Krause attributed the response to the concentrated emotional impact which resulted from opera's synthesizing the effects of several arts for the sake of serving one grand, ultimate purpose.[16] Justus Möser contended that total participation in any artificial creation, whether opera or a harlequinade, was pleasing because it satisfied man's urgent need for recreation.[17] Johann Adam Hiller explained it as appealing to certain mysterious human inclinations towards the unknown and the ineffable. It was, in his opinion, a riddle that reason could not possibly solve because it was posed magically, as if in a dream.[18]

The persistence of such attitudes into the late eighteenth century stimulated more and more Germans to investigate the subject of opera. They studied its origins, its history, its relationship to ancient drama, and also the critical opinions it had engendered in the past. When they observed the contemporary theatrical scene, however, they were disappointed to find that opera's vast artistic potentialities were not being realized. Gotthold Ephraim Lessing, for one, complained that contemporary opera emphasized either the music or the words; it failed to coalesce and blend into an indivisible unity arts that appealed simultaneously to different senses. He stated that librettists and composers did not understand the limitations of their respective arts well enough to bring them into a grand union as the Greek tragedians had succeeded in doing. Lessing then set out to analyze the limitations of the arts and to find the means for recapturing the spirit of the ancient classics.[19]

Christoph Martin Wieland's ideas on opera were yet another indication of the decisive turning away from the French version of classicism towards the original Greek. He considered the operatic form a potential heir to Euripidean tragedy and, like so many before him, not only experimented with it but also tried to explain its probability, its media, and its aesthetic appeal. According to his explanation, all operatic productions were based on a tacit agreement between collaborators, performers, and spectators to suspend the laws of causality for the sake of pleasure.[20] This and the other points he made show that he recognized the viable critical ideas of the past and attempted to apply them meaningfully to the present.

Such ideas also captivated the critical as well as artistic imagination of Johann Gottfried Herder. In his opinion, operas provided unsurpassed pleasure because they instantaneously transported their spectators from the conceptual world into a magical, dreamlike world; that is, they appealed directly to the imagination and enchanted it with new and different verities. Because of this, Herder firmly believed that opera contained the seeds of an art form as sublime as Greek tragedy. His complaint, however, was that these seeds were not being cultivated and harvested because librettists, composers, designers, and performers competed with each other and worked at cross purposes. Consequently he longed for the appearance of a universal genius who would be able to fuse poetry, music, action, and decoration into one lyrically unified new entity.[21]

The last decades of the eighteenth century saw opera receiving still greater attention from German writers. In addition to studying its accomplishments and contemplating its aesthetic potentialities, they experimented with its various forms, wrote libretti, worked as producers, and occasionally even borrowed operatic techniques for their spoken dramas. Their views served to reinforce the ideas of their innumerable predecessors and to establish opera as a symbol for all art. Goethe used opera to exemplify the work of art as a carefully circumscribed, artificial little world (*eine kleine Kunstwelt*) and to explain the aesthetic experience as participation in that world.[22] According to his theory, the creator of opera, like any artist, integrated his chosen components into such an indivisible unity that his audience had no opportunity to analyze them or to think of deception. As Goethe explained, the audience derived its pleasure from being elevated up to the artist's lofty level and from being allowed for a short while at least to share in the process of creation.

Schiller also viewed opera as an example of artistic creativity and freedom. He believed that even mediocre operas revealed certain artistic potentialities whose cultivation could lead to the development of an ideal theatrical form. One of these potentialities was the theatrical probability it could create without servilely imitating nature. Another was the mysterious way its music and its technical marvels had of obviating even blatant dramatic deficiencies. Yet another was its ability to unify divergent elements and thereby transcend its own limitations. As Greek tragedy had developed out of the Dionysian chorus, so too, Schiller hoped, would a new, ideal, art form develop out of opera.[23]

By the time the first generation of German Romantics reached maturity, the ideas reflected in operatic writings had permeated all branches of criticism and aesthetic theory. It was left to them to refine these ideas still further, articulate them more clearly, and make them programmatic. The Romantics then brought to a successful conclusion that revolt against Neoclassicism which had originated in Germany with opera. Like the generations of theorists before them they tried to find the aesthetic secrets of the ancients and, in so doing, discovered heretofore unknown ones.

NOTES

1. As early as 1618 operas had been given in Italian at the Salzburg court of Archbishop Marx Sittich von Hohenems. See Willi Flemming, "Einführung," *Die Oper, Barockdrama*, V, Deutsche Literatur: Sammlung literarischer Kunst- und Kulturdenkmäler, in Entwicklungsreihen (2nd rev. ed. Hildesheim, 1965), p. 65. What is generally accepted as the first opera in the German language, however, was the result of a collaborative effort by the poet Martin Opitz and the composer Heinrich Schütz. Their adaptation of Ottavio Rinnuccini's *Daphne* was successfully performed in 1627 at the castle of Hartenfels near Torgau. Opitz also prepared a heroic opera from the *Judith* of Andreas Salvadori, but it was not printed until 1635.
2. *Dafne*, in *Martini Opitii Weltliche Poemata* (Pt. 1, 4th rev. ed. 1644), *Deutsche Neudrucke: Barock*, ed. Erich Trunz (Tübingen, 1967), p. 104. See also, *Judith/ auffs neu außgefertiget; worzu das vördere Theil der Historie sampt den Melodeyen auf iewedes Chor beygefüget*, ed. Andreas Tscherning (Rostock, 1646), sig. Aiii–iv^v.
3. Andreas Gryphius, Caspar Stieler, Johann Rist, Georg Philipp Harsdörffer, Johann Ludwig Faber, Christoph Adam Negelein, Christian Reuter, Simon Dach, and Jacob Schwiger wrote original libretti; others like Anselm von Ziegler, Hofmann von Hofmannswaldau, and Johan Christian Hallmann translated texts into German.
4. *Der Geliebte Adonis, in einem Singe-Spiel* ([Hamburg], 1697), sig.)(2^r-)( )(2^v.
5. *Unterricht Von der Teutschen Sprache und Poesie/ deren Uhrsprung/ Fortgang und Lehrsätzen* (Kiel, 1682), pp. 737–38. Compare also, Heinrich Elmenhorst's *Dramatologia Antiquo-Hodierna, Das ist: Bericht von denen Oper-Spielen* (Hamburg, 1688), p. 99. According to Elmenhorst's research, "Opern ist ein aus dem Lateinischen herfliessendes Wort/ zu teutsch heissets: Wercke; verstehe/ wie die nachgehende Beschreibung weiter lehret/ nicht alle und jede der Menschen Wercke/ sondern Poetische und Musicalische/ welche in sonderbarem Gebrauch dieses Wörtleins/ *Operen*, oder Oper-Spiele benahmet werden. Hierbey lasse ich jeden/ der es will/ gedencken/ dass solche Wercke nach Italiänischer Art werden Operen genennet; Wiewol denen der Italiänischen Sprache und Umstände Kündigen gnug bekant ist/ dass selbige Nation ihre Sing-Spiele nicht eben mit dem Namen Operen bezeichnet/ sondern heissets *Melodrama, Drama per Musica.*"
6. Christian Wernicke's satire "Helden-Gedichte Hans Sachs genannt" (1702) was directed against the Hamburg opera and its leading librettists; see *Christian Wernickes Epigramme*, ed. Rudolf Pechel, *Palaestra*, LXXI (Berlin, 1909), pp. 543–66. Johann Burckhard Mencke assailed opera in "Ausführliche Vertheidigung Satyrischer Schriften," which was included in his *Schertzhaffte Gedichte* (1706); see Bruno Markwardt, *Geschichte der deutschen Poetik*, Vol. 1: *Barock und Frühaufklärung* (3rd ed. Berlin, 1964), pp. 330–31. Gottlieb Stolle's

views on opera are to be found in *Anleitung zur Historie der Gelahr-heit* (3rd ed. Jena, 1727), pp. 195–97.

7. Gottsched, *Beyträge zur Critischen Historie*, III, No. 12 (1735), 614. Zedler, *Grosses vollständiges Universal-Lexikon aller Wissenschaften und Künste* (64 vols., Halle, 1732–50; 4 suppl. vols., Leipzig, 1751–54), XXXVII, *s.v.* "Singspiel," cols. 1661–62.

8. *Die verdammte Staat-Sucht/ Oder Der verführte Claudius, In einem Singspiel* (Hamburg, 1703), sig. a4ᵛ.

9. *Der Patriot,* ed. Michael Richey, I, No. 25 (Hamburg, 22 June 1724), 246. This is an anonymous report by a young man who supposedly wanted to compare his own reactions to Hamburg opera performances with his uncle's rationalistically oriented views.

10. "Gedancken von der Opera," *Deutsche Gedichte* (Stade, 1708), pp. 77–78.

11. "Vorrede," *Theatralische, geistliche/ vermischte und galante Gedichte* (Hamburg and Leipzig, 1713), sig. *4ᵛ and sig. **ʳ.

12. *Beurtheilung der Gottschedischen Dichtkunst* (Halle, 1747–48), pp. 359–60.

13. *Johann Elias Schlegels Aesthetische und Dramaturgische Schriften*, ed. Johann von Antoniewicz, Deutsche Litteraturdenkmale des 18. und 19. Jahrhunderts, XXVI (Heilbronn, 1887), pp. 163–64. See p. 313 of J. A. Schlegel's essay "Von der Eintheilung der Poesie," which was appended to *Einschränkung der schönen Künste auf Einen einzigen Grundsatz* (Leipzig, 1751), his translation of Batteux's *Les Beaux Arts réduits à un même principe* (Paris, 1746).

14. M. G. Flaherty, "Justus Möser: Pre-Romantic Literary Historian, Critic, and Theorist," in *Traditions and Transitions: Studies in Honor of Harold Jantz*, ed. L. E. Kurth, W. H. McClain, and H. Homann (Bad Windsheim, 1972), pp. 95–96.

15. J. A. Schlegel, *Einschränkung*, pp. 307–8.

16. *Von der Musikalischen Poesie* (Berlin, 1752), pp. 446–47.

17. Flaherty, "Justus Möser," p. 97.

18. "Abhandlung von der Nachahmung der Natur in der Musik," *Neue Erweiterungen der Erkenntnis und des Vergnügens*, III, No. 14 (1754), 140–68. It was later reprinted in Friedrich Wilhelm Marpurg's *Historisch-Kritische Beyträge*, I, No. 6 (1755), pp. 515–43. The section to which I refer can be found in Marpurg's reprint, p. 534.

19. M. G. Flaherty, "Lessing and Opera: A Re-Evaluation," *The Germanic Review*, XLIV, No. 2 (March 1969), pp. 95–109.

20. "Versuch über das deutsche Singspiel und einige dahin einschlagende Gegenstände" (1775), *Wielands Werke*, ed. William Kurrelmeyer, XIV, (Berlin, 1928), 81–82.

21. *Adrastea* (1801), in *Herders Sämmtliche Werke*, ed. Bernhard Suphan, XXIII (Berlin, 1885), 336.

22. "Über Wahrheit und Wahrscheinlichkeit der Kunstwerke" (1798), *Goethes Sämtliche Werke: Jubiläums Ausgabe*, XXXIII (Stuttgart and Berlin, 1903), 91.

23. *Der Briefwechsel zwischen Schiller und Goethe*, eds. Hans Gerhard Gräf and Albert Leitzmann, I (3rd ed., Leipzig, 1955), No. 394, 459–60.

The Application of the Aesthetics of Music in the Philosophy of the Sturm und Drang:
Gerstenberg, Hamann, and Herder

Paul F. Marks

THE DEVELOPMENT of both the Viennese Classic and the Romantic periods in music is generally accepted as being chronologically and culturally consecutive, and thus as originating at different periods. There is evidence, however, of their simultaneous growth, particularly in the interreaction of their forms. The leaders of the dynamic changes taking place in music, literature, aesthetics, and philosophy after the middle of the eighteenth century believed that they were reviving archaic and forgotten forms. In music, this amounted to a revitalization of Baroque principles: fugue, canonic fugue, strict canon, and the textural and formal structure of the *sonata da chiesa*: indeed, what we have come to call the Viennese Classic period (as well, for that matter, as the pre- or proto-Classic period) was out of phase with other art forms. Swift and Pope were both dead before J. S. Bach, and Johnson died before the mature works of Mozart were written. In any case, the essentially classic principles in the music of any period are realized fully during only a fraction of the swing of the historical pendulum. Much of the High Classic phase was Rococo on the surface, and had as well innovative, forward-looking elements of Romanticism.

The interreaction of the Baroque fugal ideal and the spun-out melodic style with the sonata-allegro process was very important for the refinement of the emotional *Geniebewegung* then emerg-

219

ing; of equal importance, however, at least in the self-image of the last half of the eighteenth century, were its grammatical and rhetorical principles, what Arnold Schering called *das redende Prinzip*.[1]

Hand in hand with the change from the Baroque doctrine of the "affections" to the Classic/Romantic ideal of the *Gefühlsbegriff* went an alteration in the relationship between word and music. Many of the early concepts of nineteenth-century Romanticism had their source in this new word-tone relation. There is interesting evidence on the application of aesthetic theory in the artistic associations between Heinrich Wilhelm von Gerstenberg (1737–1823) and Carl Philip Emanuel Bach (1714–88), between Johann Georg Hamann (1730–88) and Johann Reichardt (1752–1814), and between Johann Gottfried Herder (1744–1803) and Johann Christoph Friedrich Bach (1732–95).

It was Carl Philip Emanuel Bach who set the tone for most of the second half of the eighteenth century. Particularly after Bach's move from Berlin to Hamburg in 1768 and his establishment as a respectable *burgher* of international reputation, he was very often in correspondence with the leading German poets and aesthetic philosophers of the period, and was quite familiar with the theories and experiments in the application of dramatic, rhetorical, and grammatical principles to music. Bach was a musician at the court of Frederick the Great from 1740 to 1768, at a period when artistic circles in Berlin—though not necessarily at Sans Souci—shared greatly the current interest, French and German in origin, in folk-nationalistic ideals and their influence on both instrumental and vocal music.

C. P. E. Bach's innovative, daring—and often chaotic—harmonic language, formal structure, and technique of word setting, typical as they were of the often simple, yet dramatic, qualities of certain aspects of the musical *Sturm und Drang*, were known to Gerstenberg and his contemporaries. Bach combined in his music some of the tenets of the so-called First Berlin *Liederschule* (c. 1750–70), though he could not be considered an adherent of its doctrine of ultra-simplicity for its own sake. Led by Christian Gottfried Krause (1717–70), the Liederschule made use of the ideas on comparative aesthetic analysis of musical expression and the application of symbolism to music current with the members of the prestigious Thursday Club. That German Parnassus the *Berliner Kreis* provided Bach with a foil against which to direct his own ideas on musical expression, as did fleeting but problematical experiments with word and tone by Friedrich Klopstock, Matthius Claudius, J. H. Voss, and Gerstenberg. As members of the Thursday Club, Bach and Gotthold Ephraim Lessing (1729–81), the latter a corresponding member, often exchanged ideas in letters during Bach's tenure at Berlin. As a dramatist, essayist, and translator of Shakespeare, Lessing was not antagonistic to Romantic elements, but he was still "rationalist" enough to hold with the Baroque ideal of the unity and singleness of effect dependent upon rhetoric and symmetrical verse form, though Bach had already applied lyrical and emotional articulation to his instrumental music. Bach anticipated the work of Reichardt, Johann Abraham Peter Schulz (1747–1800), and Friederich Zelter (1758–1832), the leaders of the Second Berlin *Liederschule*, in their concern with a song style simple and *Ossian*-like, yet with a highly expressive accompaniment. It was only natural, then, that Bach's vocal and keyboard works should have had some effect on the literati of his day.

Of special interest is the connection between Bach and Heinrich Wihelm von Gerstenberg. Gerstenberg had an above-average interest in music for a typical eighteenth-century philosopher. His experiments with text parody, made in his home in Copenhagen in collaboration with Klopstock, were a pastime that involved most of the German literary school at some time or another. The term "parody," musically defined, does not have the pejorative meaning that it does in other arts. At the end of the eighteenth century and the beginning of the nineteenth, parody was considered to be a legitimate means of perfecting vocal music. Gerstenberg and Klopstock had a wide selection of music to "play" with. The two poets extracted melodies from large works at will, to which they added words, changed original texts, or combined wordless tunes with words from another melody.

In a letter to Friedrich Nicolai in Berlin, Gerstenberg wrote from Copenhagen on December 5, 1767:

> . . . I must tell you that I am making a musical experiment in which you might be interested. First, I hold that music without words can only express general ideas, but can be made to express its full content with added words. Second, the experiment is involved with only those instrumental works where the expressiveness is very clear and grammatical. On this basis I have added a manner of text to a keyboard work of Bach, which of course was not at all intended for voice, and Klopstock and Jedermann have assured me that the result is the most expressive vocal music that one could hear. I have put Hamlet's monologue with the *Phantasie* of the sixth sonata. . . .[2]

The *Phantasie* to which Gerstenberg refers is the final movement of the last of the six three-movement didactic sonatas which Bach appended to his *Versuch über die wahre Art das Clavier zu spielen*[3] (Wotquenne 63/6). Thirty years after the *Phantasie* was originally published in 1753, C. F. Cramer wrote about the origins of Gerstenberg's parody in his *Magazin der Musik* (1783),[4] and in the same year Cramer received permission from Gerstenberg for the parody to be published, with both the Hamlet text and another that Gerstenberg added (not mentioned in his letter to Nicolai quoted above), his own version of Socrates' last words on drinking the hemlock. Both texts were printed in one score by Nicolai;[5] however, it is obvious from the intent of the parodies and the music that each was meant to stand alone.

There seems to be no definite evidence to indicate whether or not Gerstenberg made his own translation of the monologue from *Hamlet*. It seems to me that several statements by Gerstenberg would point to the strong possibility that he provided his own German version. Another letter to Nicolai, dated April 27, 1768,[6] reminds Nicolai of the parody again and goes into much more detail in describing Gerstenberg's design for the parody. It is important enough to quote several passages in their entirety:

> Sie verlangen dass ich Ihnen meinen Text für Bachische Phantasie schicken soll? Ich will es wagen aber ich sage Ihnen vorher, dass ich diesen Text nur dem Freunde, der meine Amüsemens mit Nachsicht beurtheilt, nicht dem strenger Kunstrichter, mitheile. Hier ist er. Die römische Zahl bedeudet das Noten system, die deutsche den Takt. Sie werden von selbst er-

rathen, dass einige Stellen die unisono mit dem Bass gehen wür-
den, eine etwas veränderte Modulation für die Singstimme
haben müssen. Doch eben besinne ich mich, dass die Phantasie
eine freye ohne genaue Taktabmessung in den beiden Allegros
ist. Wie soll ich Ihnen nun das Unterlegen meines Textes ohne
Noten verständlich machen? Am besten, ich überlasse das Ihrem
eigenen Geschmack, und sage Ihnen bloss, dass das erste Wort
sich am Ende des ersten Systems anhebt, so namlich.

Hamlet

I. Seyn!
II. oder nichtseyn!
II. Das ist die grosse Frage!
II. Das ist die grosse Frage!
III. Tode! Schlaf!
IV. Schlaf! und Traum!
IV. Schwarzer Traum!
V. Todesträum!
VI. Ihn träumen, ha! den Todesträum
VI. Ins Lebem schaun!
VII. ins Tränenthal!
VII. wo Tücke lauscht!
VII. Du Bosheit lacht!
VII. Die Unschuld weint!
VIII. O, nein! O, nein!
IX. ins nichtseyn—hinab—zuschlummern!

Largo

Eine Stimme aus den Gräbern
Ins Licht zum seyn erwachen!
Zur Wonn hinaufwarts Schaun!
So Seele!
die Unschuld Sehn,
die Dulderinn
Wie sie empor ins Leben blüht
Die Ewigkeit!
Die alle sehn die wir geliebt,
nicht mehr von uns beweint!
Hoch tönts, hoch tönts im Ärm der Zärtlichkeit.
Das war widersehen!
Dann struzt (2 achtel Pausen)
Ach! vom Entzücken heiss,

Ach! vom Entzücken heiss,
die Himmelsthräne hin

(Cembalo solo für die zwei letzte Takt)

Allegro Moderato: Hamlet

I. Wo ist den Dolch?
II. ein Schwert?
II. ins Grab des Seyns
II. hinabzufliehen!
II. zu sterben, ach!
III. den edlen Tod.
III. des hohen Seyns.
III. Wo ist ein Dolch?
III. ein Schwert?
IV. vom Thal des Fluchs
IV. des Fluchs!
IV. ins Grab des Seyns hinab
IV. zum Leben zu entschlafen.

Noch ein paar Worte vom Text zu sagen, liesse sich aus dem Anblicke desselben vermuthen, dass ich den musikalischen Rhythmus nicht beobachtet habe. Aber ich glaube diesem Rhythmus so sorgfältig als möglich nochgegangen zu seyn.

The important points in the letter are the references to "my text," and the explanation that the meter of the words had not been constructed in connection with the instrumental *Phantasie*. The first point may be merely a figure of speech, but the second seems a stronger indication that Gerstenberg provided his own translation.

It would seem, though, the monologue is not the work of Wieland. Gerstenberg, in more than one instance in his letters to Nicolai and in his *Briefe über Merkwürdigkeiten der Literatur* (1770), admits to a dislike for Wieland's translations of Shakespeare. In Gerstenberg's letter to Nicolai of December 5, 1767, he mentions admiration for the translations of Shakespeare into Danish by Christoph Felix Weisse. These Danish translations were the basis for Gerstenberg's work.

In the second volume of his *Briefe über Merkwürdigkeiten der Literatur*, Gerstenberg systematically arranged his ideas on the relation between language and music. Gerstenberg, in five main points, proposed the technique of combining the spoken word with musical accompaniment, at a time when neither the textual-dramatic reforms of Gluck nor Jean-Jacques Rousseau's ideas on the combination of words and music, which led to his melodrama *Pygmalion* (1770), were known in northern Europe.[7] Before the publication of the *Merkwürdigkeiten der Literatur,* however, Lessing knew of Gerstenberg's works in this area, and refers to them in his *Studien der Dramaturgie* (1767–70).[8]

It seems likely that Gerstenberg conveyed his concepts to C. P. E. Bach in the summer of 1773, as Bach's answer is dated October 21st of that year. As a keyboard performer C. P. E. Bach agreed with Gerstenberg's ideas on expression, especially Gerstenberg's points concerning the printing of appropriate expression marks in music; however, when it came to Gerstenberg's ideas on appending literary quotes to sonatas, Bach felt that "words are words, and are meant to be spoken—we need go no further."[9] Previously, C. P. E. Bach had mentioned his misgivings about programmatic instrumental music in general and its lack of success.

Despite the playful, experimental nature of Gerstenberg's parodies (Goethe's parodies were meant to be accepted in a considerably more serious manner) and the sometimes chaotic and incoherent structure of C. P. E. Bach's declamatory instrumental fantasies, the synthesis of verse form, language, and instrumental music (in particular the developing dramatic qualities inherent in the structure of the sonata-allegro process) was of seminal importance for both the Viennese Classic period and the nineteenth century.

It was Johann Georg Hamann who was the true prophet of the change to the type of vocal music that was to be considered most anti-rational. The basis for the understanding of music, for both Hamann and Herder, was Hamann's ideas on language and speech. His ideal was a "ringing language," the lexical and semantic properties of which are integrated with the aesthetically perceived tones of the words. Hamann outlined these ideas mainly in his "Aesthetica in Nuce" (1762).[10]

> Not a lyre—but a simple thing—a winnowing shovel for my
> muse to empty the threshing floor of holy literature.— Hail the

guardian Archangel over the relics of the language of Canaan. Poetry is the mother tongue of the human race; in the form of a garden, older than the soil: painting: as the written word; song: as declamation; imitation:—as the key: exchange: as transaction. The quietude of our original ship's draft was a deeper sleep; and its movement a giddy dance. Seven days of silence— we sat in thought or astonishment—and when the mouth was opened—there was prosaic judgment.

It is upon these mystic and symbolic lines that Herder seems to have based much of his musical aesthetics, particularly in his work with folk song and in his *Auszug aus einem Briefwechsel über Ossian und die Lieder alter Völker* (1773).[11] It was Hamann who provided the basis for the principle that poetic language, based on the rhythmic-musical qualities of ancient, uncontaminated tongues, was the *Ursprache* of the human race. This was the main connection between music and language for Hamann. The question whether the speculative quality of this theory could be applied in actuality to music was taken up not only by Herder but by the song composers of the Second Berlin *Liederschule*, in particular by Reichardt and Zelter.

Modern linguistics, allied with ethnomusicological techniques, has imparted respectability to certain aspects of Hamann's theories, especially through the current use of linguistic transformational model analysis to define inherent "endomusical" and "exomusical" elements in folk song. In modern terms, then, analogies between music and language continue to be sought. However, in both music and language there are two types of content, and as William Bright has pointed out in a paper read at the seventh conference of the Society for Ethnomusicology at Philadelphia in 1961,[12] it has become necessary to distinguish between them in more scientifically precise terms than were possible in the eighteenth century:

> The content of a sentence is in part derived from its associations outside of language, from the objects, actions and relationships to which the sentence refers. But at the same time it also derives content from its linguistic structure—from the phonological and grammatical relationships between the parts, and be-

tween it and other sections. The former type of content has been referred to as *exolinguistic*, and the latter as *endolinguistic*. . . . We may thus refer to the similar content structures found in music and in language with the term endosemantic. . . .

In more recent investigations of structural affinities between language and music, the methodological technique of working with transformational models has been applied. Linguistic forms used with music will show the same deviations from normal speech as does poetry. Single models can be made of normal speech, poetry, and song text by the application of model transformation. Basically, this begins with enough knowledge of the language to supply a generative model for the infinite number of grammatically acceptable structures. The method accounts for two components: *deep structure*, the mechanics underlying the entire language, and *surface structure*, the physical sound generated by the deep structure. If the deep structure has been correctly stated, the proper grammatical structures will be manifest on the surface.

Music, without the aid of lexical meaning, can be viewed as a similar kind of code, with *endomusical* and *exomusical* components. Within almost every musical system, sounds are "coded" to have deep and surface meanings. Information theory indicates that all codes, to be effective, must have a fairly high level of redundancy. This is the concept of entropy, the concept that identical items shall reappear regularly for identical or similar purposes. It is the inherent redundancy in language and music which enables the users to reapply the same sets of constraints any number of times in producing a structure. It is redundancy that makes analysis possible.

At the end of "Aesthetica in Nuce" Hamann gives the first suggestion as to his own solution to these problems. Homer's unified meter and strophic form should be the model for the spontaneous musical creations of "sense-perceptive" peoples. In 1775, at the period when Herder was applying Hamann's ideals to *Ossian*, Herder began his collections of folk song. The work of Hamann and Herder in this field was well known; Reichardt, in his biography, mentions songs that the two philosophers had overlooked.[18] It is not sure how many of the songs mentioned by Herder were actually heard by him. The texts and the German translations of the original Latvian and Lettish songs in Herder's collection were arranged and edited by Alexander Wegner.[14] The music of the collected songs have two points in common, both among themselves and with the "art" songs of the German composers: the music is merely a mutation of the words into pitch-tone and rhythm, and the music does not seem to have any real independent existence. Reichardt, his disciple Heinrich Wilhelm Wackenroder (1773–98), and his pupil E. T. A. Hofmann carried this characteristic, as an ideal, forward into the early nineteenth century.

Johann Reichardt was another member of the court musical establishment at Berlin under Frederick the Great, as well as under Frederick's successor Frederick William II. Reichardt was one of the most cosmopolitan musicians at the court, and most likely the most highly educated and widely read. At the age of 23 he became *Kapellmeister* at Berlin and remained there, composing, conducting, and writing numerous books and articles, until, because of his sympathetic attitude toward the French Revolution, he lost favor and was dismissed by Frederick William II in 1794. A good deal of the period between 1767–94 was spent on leave in any case, in particular at Paris, where he attempted to get his operas produced. Reichardt had little opportunity of getting them performed at Berlin, as Frederick the Great had taken an almost immediate dislike to his opportunistic flattery. Reichardt ended his days as an inspector of salt mines, after spending a short time as *Kapellmeister* for Jerome Bonaparte at Kassel.

Reichardt's song and *Singspiel* style was in opposition to the rationalistic Rococo manner of word-setting. The aesthetic basis of the First Berlin *Liederschule* lay in an extremely simplistic setting of the words. With the Second *Liederschule* at the Prussian capital speech rhythm and the inherently musicial quality of poetic language (and language as poetry) became the prime factors. There was a conscious effort on Reichardt's part to avoid increasing the importance of the music by musical-technical devices, whether by imitation, fast harmonic rhythm, or idiomatic instrumental writing as in the manner of the intentionally artistic *Lied*. There seems to have developed a twofold style for the *Lied* prior to Schubert: the

Romantic ideal of the folk idiom, in a simple strophic setting (which meant the primacy of the words), and on the other hand the consciously artistic, and therefore primarily musical, setting. One can safely say that Reichardt, Schulz, and Zelter all wanted merely to illustrate the words rather than write "music." Poets such as Goethe, who felt their words enhanced by the simplest of musical settings, disliked the genius of Schubert because he created something entirely apart from either the folk song or the long, artistic, narrative *Lied*; Schubert managed to submerge the words into a whole with the music and to negate the ego of the poet.

Strangely, however, Reichardt still adhered in the main to Lessing's dictum that a musical entity could only encompass one emotional stance, and derided those works that used materials of contradictory emotional moods. This makes Reichardt of an extremely conservative stamp for his date; the last half of the eighteenth century had been moving inexorably toward the primacy of the dramatic contrast, the foundation for the structure of the sonata process and, as the contrast became more marked, for the Romantic movement. And yet, despite his reactionary tendencies, Reichardt remained highly aware of new developments.

Another important difference between the two Berlin *Liederschulen* was in the literary capability of Reichardt, Schulz, and Zelter. They all three were personal acquaintances of Goethe, Herder, and Hamann—Reichardt was a school mate of Hamann's in Königsberg, and Reichardt's father taught Hamann the lute. Besides being highly conscious of the qualities of poetry, they themselves were able to produce literary works of at least momentary importance.

The composers of the Viennese Classic school, such as Haydn, Mozart, and Beethoven, were in the main just as well read, but they were not interested in producing literature. The word as the source of inspiration is, of course, one of the prime factors in the Romantic musical spirit. Gerald Abraham puts it quite precisely when he states that the Romantic composers were romantic because they were literary, and not the other way round.[15]

Hamann's and Herder's influence in this direction was of tremendous importance in crystallizing trends. By placing importance on a spontaneous, primitive *Ursprache*—relating this ideal particularly to ancient Greek and Hebrew—far above that of any vernacular, Hamann helped to make rhetoric one of the elements of Romanticism in music.

There was an essential difference between Hamann and Herder, however. For Hamann language was, in the final analysis, a God-given element and therefore not completely understandable. For Herder, language was man-made, with a natural, organic growth, an historically relative perspective. Herder's attitude had the same foundations as Kant's, but with the added element, from Hamann, of giving a lesser value to logic and a greater to intuition. It was the conception of instinctual feeling in the Hellenistic renaissance in Germany that appealed to Herder, not rationalistic thought. Music was not to be set apart from current philosophical theories (neither teleological nor phenomenological), but was at the root of the historical process. Music was aesthetic not in itself, but in direct relation to the formation of historical structures.

The concept of the inseparability of heightened speech and language depended on an irrational element in speech. Hamann had given Herder the idea of the lyric aspect in natural speech tone. He also taught Herder that primitive man was poet, musician, thinker, historian, and priest at the same time (yet, Herder realized that "modern" man is not at all under the necessity of combining art forms). In the main, however, Herder derived his conceptions of the primitive union of the arts from Dr. John Brown's *Dissertation on the Rise, Union, and Power, the Progressions, Separations and Corruptions of Poetry and Music*,[16] translated by J. J. Eschenberg in 1769. While Herder agreed with Brown's basic premises on the effectiveness of the unity of music, poetry, and dance, he could not pardon Brown for omitting all discussion of primitive language, which for Herder had become identical with primitive poetry. Herder was less concerned with practical aesthetics than with the overall role of the *Gesamtkunstwerk* within culture.

In 1771 Herder began a five-year stay at the court of the militant Count Wilhelm zu Lippe in the Palatinate town of Bückeburg, where he became involved at several levels in the production of music. The *Konzertmeister* was Johann Christoph Friederich

Bach. During the course of his stay, Herder wrote the texts for several cantatas, which Bach set to music: *Kindheit Jesu* (1772), *Pfingskantate* (1773), *Auferweckung Lazarus* (1773), and the *Michaelskantate* (1775).

During this period, in 1773, Herder began work on his important *Auszug aus einem Briefwechsel über Ossian und die Lieder alter Völker*. Herder's reaction to the Ossianic forgeries of Macpherson arose from his experiences with the Bible as poetry and from his admiration for Homer, Shakespeare, and folk song. Herder regarded the poems of Ossian as inseparable from melody and dance. Ossian's songs are "songs of the people, songs of an uncultivated, sensuous [sense-perceptive] people."[17] Herder was one of the prime forces in the development of the nationalistic view of song in the nineteenth century, despite his relativistic viewpoint; it was he who coined the term *Volkslied*.

It was with melodrama, however, that Herder became most intrigued during the first half of the 1770's while at Bückeburg. Herder used the form as invented by Rousseau for *Pygmalion* as the basis for the unification of speech, music, and dance. Herder became a sharp critic of what he considered to be a misunderstanding of the role of words and music in French opera.[18] Herder's several libretti for melodramas, two written at Bückeburg, show a reaction to the stylized unities of the French theater. For Herder all should be readily comprehensible: even a deaf person should be able to comprehend! *Brutus* (1774) was written in close imitation of Plutarch and Shakespeare, and *Sokrates* (1774) and *Der Tod der Naemi* (1793–96) are both even more realistic in their human situations. Herder consciously tried to reverse the aspects of what he considered to be French triviality of text, formal superficiality of music, and the compression of the texts into independent, artificial musical forms. These points come very close to the reforms outlined by Gluck in the preface to *Alceste*. His final work in the medium of melodrama, *Ariadne-Libera* (1802), is not a poem spoken to a musical accompaniment; rather, its designation as melodrama now stands for opera. Herder's governing concern was the combination of poetry and music into a whole which was more than the sum of its parts.

In *Brutus* Herder sought to squeeze a music drama out of the spirit of *Sturm und Drang*. *Brutus* was the only one of the lyric texts which was set to music. J. C. F. Bach wrote the score, which was performed twice, on February 27 and March 3, 1774. Robert T. Clark, in the definitive book on Herder in English, mistakenly states that Herder first sent the libretto to Gluck.[18] Georg Schünemann, in the *Bach-Jahrbuch* for 1914,[19] and F. E. Kirby, in the *Journal of the American Musicological Society* for 1948,[20] are nearer the truth in leaving Gluck out of the picture until a bit later.

Common to all Herder's libretti is the typical *Sturm und Drang* theme of man versus fate. The insistence on an ethical theme is by no means typical of an eighteenth-century librettist. Many conventional elements are eliminated in such a work: the sub-plots, the *confidants*, and the scenes of spectacle. There is nothing to mitigate the intensity of the situation; in *Brutus*, for instance, all attention is drawn to the main character. Another unusual characteristic is the absence of real action. There is only a series of static tableaux. In *Der Tod der Naemi* almost nothing of the Jephthah legend takes place on stage; it is simply reported by the entering and exiting characters. Similar to Gerstenberg's drama *Ugolino* (1767) and Goethe's *Götz von Berlichingen*, Herder's work is more of an elegy than a drama, musical or otherwise, even though designated as a *musikalisches Drama*.

A most important document, expressive of Herder's views at the time and explaining his intentions in writing *Brutus*, is his letter to Gluck of November 5, 1774, quoted in several sources.[21]

> The great quarrel between poetry and music, which indeed has greatly increased the distance between the two arts, is the question: which is to serve? which is to rule? The musician desires his art to rule: the same is true of the poet; and thus they often stand in each other's way. . . . It could be, then, that the musician should give way and follow the poet—and this is the view you have expressed in your writings on music. Or should it be that the poet should give way, that he should provide only a sketch, a loose outline, and that the otherwise undetermined sensations are left to the music—and this effort, *Brutus*, is directed to this end. It is intended to be what the inscription on a picture or statue is, the explanation, the guide, for the musical

stream, by words inserted in between. . . . It is not to be read, it is to be heard. The words are only to enliven the stirring of the music . . . following the spirit of the poet and the outline provided by him.

Considering the influence of Herder, it is not surprising that J. C. F. Bach felt antipathy toward programmatic music without words. This Bach had received a letter from Gerstenberg similar to the one the latter had written to C. P. E. Bach. J. C. F. Bach answered Gerstenberg on April 1, 1773. Bach objected to a suggestion from Gerstenberg for a keyboard work inspired by the story of Cleopatra. First, Bach wrote, the performers would have to know the details of the story, and how many keyboard artists had that background? Then, there would be no leeway for ability (i.e., improvisation), no adequate instruments, nor any possible correct form for the work. J. C. F. Bach went on to ask Gerstenberg if he knew of C. P. E. Bach's sonata for two violins and bass (1769, Wotquenne 161/1), subtitled a "Discourse Between Sanguinity and Melancholia"; J. C. F. Bach felt that in spite of all the efforts that his brother put into the work it did not succeed, nor could it without words—and that "Cleopatra" would have the same fate.[22] J. C. F. was most likely just repeating his brother's disappointment with his attempt at programmatic instrumental music.

(The fact is that neither theorist, aesthetician, nor composer felt ready, by the 1770's, to concede real importance to purely instrumental music; though there was some recognition of the influence of rhetorical principles, verse-equivalent thematic fragmentation and phrase symmetry, and a growing acceptance of the dramatic element in the sonata-allegro procedure, instrumental music was still felt to be a mere tickling of the ear.)

By 1774, as we have seen, Herder had decided to emphasize the music over the text; but over the long run he became opposed to the melodrama. By 1803 he felt that the poetry in a musico-dramatic work should be sung, not spoken.[23] Herder had two distinct sides to his musical aesthetics. On the one hand, when Herder wrote of wholeness and truthfulness in music he meant intuition. Music was to express the subconscious, the sensual, the vibrant body energy, sentiment, manifestations of the spirit—all of personal experience. On the other hand, Herder could be quite explicit in outlining the serious purpose of music. The composer had three choices for the future: 1) an historical approach, with a purposeful interreaction of forms and models, though even this might lead to thoughtless artificialities (that is, to instrumental music); 2) a complete reversal toward Baroque forms, restricted to church music; or 3) an acceptance of the aesthetics of folk music: nationalism, Gothic moods, sense perception, language and speech rhythm.[24]

The last half of the eighteenth century, then, saw an especially dynamic association of ideas among composers and aesthetic philosophers, an association of principles that affected most of the next century.

NOTES

1. Arnold Schering, "Carl Philip Emanuel Bach und das 'redende Prinzip' in der Musik," *Jahrbuch der Bibliothek Peters für 1938* (Leipzig: Peters, 1939) pp. 13–29.
2. R. M. Werner, "Gerstenbergs Briefe an Nicolai nebst einer Antwort Nicolais," *Zeitschrift für deutsche Philologie*, herausgegeben von Hugo Garing und Oskar Erdmann, XXIII (Halle, 1891) 61. Quoted in Ernst Fritz Schmid, *Carl Philip Emanuel Bach und seine Kammermusik* (Kassel: Barenreiter, 1931) pp. 52–53.
3. Carl Philip Emanuel Bach, *Versuch über die wahre Art der Clavier zu spielen, Mit Examplen und achtzehn Probe-Stücken in Sechs Sonaten* (Berlin: Georg Ludwig Winter, 1753/59) = ed. Walter Niemann (Leipzig: C. F. Kahnt, 1906), 220 pp. Translated into English by William J. Mitchell (New York: Norton, 1948) 349 pp.
4. C. F. Cramer, *Magazin der Musik* (Hamburg: Cramer, 1783), I, 1252–54.
5. C. F. Cramer, *Flora*, Erste Sammlung. A collection of songs by Gräven, Gluck, Bach, Adolph Kunzen, F. L. Ae. Kunzen, Reichardt, Schwanenberger. Edited by C. F. Cramer (Kiel: Cramer and Hofmannischen Buchhandlung, 1787), pp. xii–xiv.
6. R. M. Werner, "Gerstenbergs Briefe," pp. 64–66.
7. Heinrich Wilhelm von Gertsenberg, *Briefe über Merkwüdigkeiten der Literatur* (Schleswig and Leipzig: Joachim Friedrich Hanend, 1766/67). Included in *Sturm und Drang: Kritische Schriften* 3, ed. Erich Loewenthal (Heidelberg: Lambert Schneider, 1963), p. 37–59. Quoted also in Friederich Chrysander, "Eine Klavier-Phantasie von Karl Philip Emanuel Bach mit nachträglich von Gerstenbergs eingefügten Ge-

sangmelodien zu zwei verschiedenen Texten," *Vierteljahrschrift für Musikwissenschaft*, VIII (1891), 24.

8. Gotthold Ephraim Lessing, *Studien der Dramaturgie (Hamburgische Dramaturgie*, May 26, 1767) = *Lessings Werke in Einem Band*, ed. G. Stenzel (Salzburg: Bergland, no date) pp. 693–94.

9. E. F. Schmid, *Carl Philip Emanuel Bach*, p. 48.

10. Johann Georg Hamann, "Aesthetica in Nuce," *Kreuzzüge des Philologen* (Königsberg: Kanter, 1762) p. 1. Also in *Sturm und Drang: Kritische Schriften* 3, p. 121.

11. Johann Gottfried Herder, *Auszug aus einem Briefwechsel über Ossian und die Lieder alter Völker* (Hamburg: Bode, 1773) = in *Von deutscher Art und Kunst*.

12. William Bright, "Language and Music." Paper read at the Seventh Conference of the Society for Ethnomusicology, Philadelphia, 1961.

13. Hans Michael Schletterer, *J. F. Reichardt: Sein Leben und sein Werk* (Augsburg, 1865). Volume 1 contains Reichardt's autobiography.

14. Josef Müller-Blattau, *Hamann und Herder in ihren Beziehungen zur Musik* (Königsberg: Grafe und Unzer, 1931) = *Schriften der Königlichen Deutschen Gesellschaft zu Königsberg, Pr.*, Heft 6, p. 22.

15. Gerald Abraham, *100 Years of Music* (Chicago: Aldine Publishing Co., 1964), p. 21.

16. Dr. John Brown, *A Dissertation on the Rise, Union, and Power, the Progressions, Separations, and Corruptions of Poetry and Music. To which is Prefixed the Cure of Saul, A Sacred Ode* (London: L. Davis and C. Rymers, 1763), 244 pp.

17. Johann Gottfried Herder, *Auszug*, p. 6.

18. Robert T. Clark, *Herder: His Life and Thought* (Berkeley, California: University of California Press, 1955, 1969) p. 156.

19. Georg Schünemann, "Johann Christoph Friedrich Bach," *Bach-Jahrbuch*, XI (1914), 97–98.

20. F. E. Kirby, "Herder and Opera," *Journal of the American Musicological Society*, XV (1962), 320.

21. The translation given here is by F. E. Kirby. The original appears in Schünemann's article on J. C. F. Bach.

22. E. F. Schmid, *C. P. E. Bach und sein Kammermusik*, p. 58. See also Hans Mersmann, "Ein Program-trio K. P. E. Bachs," *Bach-Jahrbuch*, XIII (1917).

23. Johann Gottfried Herder, *Adreasta (Vignette)* (Leipzig: Hatknoch, 1801–4), Book V, Part 1 (1803–4).

24. Johann Gottfried Herder, *Die Beitrachtungen über die Wissenschaft und Kunst des Schönes. Kritische Wälder. Viertes Waldschen über Riedels Theorie des Schönen Kunst.* To have been published by: Riga: J. F. Hartknoch, 1769. This reference to Herder's aesthetic precepts, and all the previous ones, except where otherwise indicated, come from the fourth of the *Kritische Wälder*. The fourth of the *Critical Groves* was never published as such. Herder held it back from the bookseller, though it was already bound in its first printing, in order to outmaneu-

ver his rival essayist Klotz, who had already written a review of the unpublished *Grove*. As well, Herder was beginning to have second thoughts about his own abilities.

BIBLIOGRAPHY

Abraham, Gerald. *100 Years of Music*. Chicago: Aldine Publishing Co., 1938, 1949, 1964, 1966, 1967. 320 pp.

Bach, Carl Philip Emanuel. *Versuch über die wahre Art der Clavier zu spielen. Mit Examplen und achtzehen Probe-Stücken in sechs Sonaten*. Berlin: Georg Ludwig Winter, 1753/1759 = edited by Walter Nieman. Leipzig: C. F. Kahnt, 1906. 220 pp. Translated into English by William J. Mitchell. New York: Norton, 1948. 349 pp.

Bright William. "Language and Music." Paper read at the Seventh Conference of the Society for Ethnomusicology. Philadelphia. 1961.

Brown, Dr. John. *A Dissertation on the Rise, Union and Power, the Progressions, Separations, and Corruptions of Poetry and Music. To Which is Prefixed the Cure of Saul, A Sacred Ode*. London: L. Davis and C. Rymers, 1763. 244 pp.

Chrysander, Friederich. "Eine Klavier-Phantasie von Karl Philip Emanuel Bach mit nachträglich von Gerstenberg eingefügten Gesangmelodien zu zwei verschiedenen Texten." *Vierteljahrschrift für Musikwissenschaft*, VII (1891), 1–25.

Clark, Robert T. *Herder: His Life and Thought*. Berkeley: University of California Press, 1955 and 1969. 457 pp.

Cramer, C. F. *Flora. Erste Sammlung*. A Collection of Songs, edited by C. F. Cramer. Kiel: Cramer and Hofmannischen Buchhandlung, 1787. xxii + 76 pp.

———— *Magazin der Musik*, Vol. I. Hamburg, 1783.

Gerstenberg, Heinrich Wilhelm von. *Briefe über Merkwürdigkeiten der Literatur*. Schleswig und Leipzig: Joachim Friedrich Hanend, 1766/67 = *Sturm und Drang*, Vol. III: *Kritische Schriften*, edited by Erich Loewenthal. Heidelberg: Lambert Schneider, 1963. Pp. 37–59.

Hamann, Johann Georg. "Aesthetica in Nuce." *Kreuzzüge der Philologen*. Königsberg: Kanter 1762 = *Sturm und Drang*,

Vol. III: *Kritische Schriften*. Edited by Erich Loewenthal. Heidelberg: Lambert Schneider, 1963. Pp. 121–43.

Herder, Johann Gottfried. *Adreasta* (*Vignette*). Leipzig: Hartknoch, 1801–4. 5 Volumes. = *Herders Sämtliche Werke*. Edited by Bernhard Suphan. Berlin: Wiedmannsche Buchhandlung, 1879–1913. XXIII, 177–320.

——— *Auszug aus einem Briefwechsel über Ossian und die Lieder alter Völker*. Hamburg: Bode, 1773 = in the volume *Von Deutscher Art und Kunst = Herders Sämtliche Werke*. Edited by Bernhard Suphan. Berlin: Wiedmannsche Buchhandlung, 1879–1913. V, 155–96.

——— *Der Beitrachtungen über die Wissenschaft und Kunst des Schönes. Kritische Wälder. Viertes Waldschen über Riedels Theorie des Schönen Kunst*. Riga: Joseph Friedrich Hartknoch, 1769 = *Herders Sämtliche Werke*. Edited by Bernhard Suphan. Berlin: Wiedmannsche Buchhandlung, 1879–1913. IV, 3–220.

Kirby, F. E. "Herder and Opera." *Journal of the American Musicological Society*. XV (1962), 316–29.

Lessing, Gotthold Ephraim. *Studien der Dramaturgie = Hamburgische Dramaturgie*, May 26, 1767 = *Lessings Werke in Einem Band*. Edited by G. Stenzel. Salzburg: Bergland, no date. 1027 pp.

Mersmann, Hans. "Ein Program-Trio K. P. E. Bachs." *Bach-Jahrbuch*, XIII (1917), 1–18.

Müller-Blattau, Josef. *Hamann und Herder in ihren Beziehungen zur Musik*. Königsberg: Grafe und Unzer, 1931. 55 pp. = Schriften der Königlichen Deutschen Gesellschaft zu Königsberg, Pr. Heft 6.

Schering, Arnold. "Carl Philip Emanuel Bach und das 'redende Prinzip' in der Musik." *Jahrbuch der Bibliothek Peters für 1938*. Leipzig: Peters, 1939. Pp. 13–29.

Schletterer, H. M. *Johann Friedrich Reichardt: Sein Leben und Sein Werke*. Augsburg, 1865. Volume I only. Contains the edited compilation of Reichardt's autobiographical material originally scattered in various periodicals and volumes.

Schmid, Ernst Fritz. *Carl Philip Emanuel Bach und sein Kammermusik.* Kassel: Barenriter, 1931. x + 189 pp. Music supplement 71 pp.

Schünemann, Georg. "Johann Christoph Friedrich Bach." *Bach-Jahrbuch* XI (1914), 45–165.

Werner, R. M. "Gerstenbergs Briefe an Nicolai nebst einer Antwort Nicolais." *Zeitschrift für deutsche Philologie.* Edited by Hugo Gering and Oskar Erdmann. XXIII (Halle, 1891), 43–67.

Symposium: Racism in the Eighteenth Century

Introduction

A T THE SECOND ANNUAL meeting of the American Society
for Eighteenth-Century Studies, three members gave brief presen-
tations on eighteenth-century racial views. Professor Harry M.
Bracken spoke on Bishop Berkeley's racism, Professor David Fate
Norton spoke on Hume's view about non-whites, and Professor
Leonora Cohen Rosenfield spoke on some eighteenth-century attitudes about American Indians. The points raised generated such
interest that it was decided to devote the meeting of Section E in
1972 to the subject of racism in the eighteenth century, as well
as to have a symposium on the matter. At the third annual meeting, during the discussion of some of the first papers to have been
presented, the question was raised as to whether racism really
existed at that time, and whether various authors discussed were
properly being classified as racists. Some suggestions were made
that twentieth-century standards were being applied anachronisti-
cally to an earlier situation that was quite different. In the discussion following the symposium the following exchange occurred
in an effort to clarify what was meant by "racism" and how this differs from "ethnocentrism." Professors Magnes Mörner and Winthrop Jordan were discussants at the symposium, and Professor Herbert Marcuse was the chairman of the session. Professor Richard
Popkin was one of the speakers and the presiding officer.

Magnes Mörner: . . . If I disagree somewhat with the term racism
here, speaking about the eighteenth century, I do so on the
basis of the experience of my work with Spanish American social history and because I would like to replace the term with
"social racial prejudice and discrimination". . .

Winthrop B. Jordan: . . . I think I agree with Professor Mörner,
sharing a certain unhappiness about the use of the term rac-

ism. Some of us have sat here since 9:00 listening to papers coming from various angles on the problem of racism in the eighteenth century, and I am really troubled by the fact that we have not, that I have heard, had a definition of what is meant by racism. I think that one of the unfortunate results has been a tendancy on the part of some of those giving papers to try to decide whether individual writers were racist or not. This seems to be unprofitable when one is talking about pervasive cultural attitudes. Take for instance the Abbé Grégoire; he was interested in freeing slaves. In some senses he was a real equalitarian, and yet when he set out to prove that Negroes were not inferior, what did he do? He gathered together a collection of writings by Negro writers and he published these as evidence that, here indeed, Negroes can perform intellectually. And he also wrote about the fact that there were important empires and cities in Africa, but if one examines that, it needed to be done at the time; fair enough, but is that racist, or is it not racist? I guess it is not a terribly profitable question, because one could argue that in making the proposition that he was making, he was asking Africans and the descendents of Africans in the New World to perform like Europeans, and it was not possible for him then, or, I suspect, for anyone then, to accept the possibility that there were different attributes of African culture which were valuable which the European culture lacked. I suspect that many of the people who have been talking today (and I'm a bit raising a question rather than trying to make a point at this juncture, because I hope many people will ask questions when I am through), I suspect that many people would say that racism is an ideology which grew up as a way of rationalizing the overseas exploration of Europe, and the exploitation of less technologically advanced peoples, which the Europeans undertook . . .

From the floor: I have a question: Have we really defined racism yet? Where does ethnocentrism end and racism begin? I want that cleared up—are they the same, do they go hand in hand?

Professor Jordan: One of the reasons I don't use the term racism (I managed to write a long book without ever using it once) is that I think that it is terribly hard to define. I think that it is much easier to talk about racial attitudes, that is to say, the attitudes of one racial group toward another. Of course, how a racial group is defined is a matter of where the society is at a particular point in time. Ethnocentrism seems to me to be somewhat different from racism in that it applies internally to a group which is looking at itself, is essentially centered upon itself. If there are no objects to which that ethnocentrism becomes strongly attached, you can have an ethnocentric people without there being a racist one. If such an ethnocenric group, particularly one like the sixteenth-century English, who came into contact with a different-seeming people they were exploiting, there, I think, you would get a situation which is extremely likely to lead to racism. Putting together a good definition of racism right on the spot is not easy, and I don't think I've done it.

From the floor: Somebody once mentioned that racism didn't really come about until the eighteen forties. Philip Curtin, in his book on Africa, says that you have racism only when you have some systematized body of scientific knowledge, and try to use scientific facts to do something. It makes it seem like it was a matter of position.

Professor Popkin: On that definition you would have to say that it existed in the eighteenth century: the people had a systematic body of justification.

From the floor: There is a very good set of distinctions between ethnocentricity and ethnic attitudes as opposed to racial and racist attitudes that at least I have found useful, in Pierre Van den Berghe's *Race and Racism*. He draws a number of distinctions based not only on a tendency (as Professor Jordan was saying), of a group to see itself as a group, but on the ways in which a group, for instance an ethnic group, will have retained over a long period its sense of identity, its language, its set of social institutions and so on. Such a group may have no great problem of understanding other ethnic groups in the society. I think the trouble is, though, that each generation has a different set of prejudices on ethnic groups, races, or whatever, and it is terribly hard for a historian to take these into consideration. But the distinction between ethnocentricity and racism ought to be made because otherwise you get to the point of saying that of every ethnic group that regards itself as different from other groups, or that regards any other group as inferior at all, that it is racist. Ethnocentricity may be present in any group, of any size, in the world.

Herbert Marcuse: May I suggest a very simplistic definition? I would say that racism is any "theory" which assumes that a race other than the *dominant* white race is, by this very fact, naturally inferior. It seems to me that there is a very important implication which has not been brought out. The group discriminated against cannot be equal in power to the dominant white group. If that would be the case, it would be very difficult to apply a racist theory. For example, it seems to me that to the degree China is becoming a world power, the inferiority traditionally attributed to the Chinese is losing its hold.

From the floor: Isn't the definition you gave also an ethnocentric definition?

Marcuse: I don't think so, because it does not contain the element of naturally inferior.

From the floor: What about the traditional Chinese attitude regarding those not Chinese, not Oriental, is it the same?

Marcuse: Well, then it is racism. There is absolutely no necessity that racism be a privilege of the white people.

From the floor: Those are the terms in which your definition is made.

Marcuse: Yes, it is the predominant form, I would say. Historically.

Professor Popkin: I would like to suggest that maybe one could define it from Von Humboldt's claim that no group is more noble than another; anyone holding the contrary, no matter what diversity he finds in groups, is holding that one group is more noble and then this view becomes the racist theory again. Von Humboldt was offering his thesis to counter the

242

claims of the leading American ethnologist of the time, Dr. Samuel Morton, that because there were differences in cranial capacity between racial groups, therefore some were superior to others.

The Philosophical Basis of Eighteenth-Century Racism*

Richard H. Popkin

HISTORIANS OF PHILOSOPHY are just beginning to become aware that many of the philosophical heroes of the Enlightenment, such as Locke, Berkeley, Hume, Voltaire, Franklin, Jefferson, and Kant, expressed views that sound shockingly racist today. When I have given lectures on modern racism, and have quoted the following note which Hume added to his essay "Of National Characters," philosophers, for whom Hume is the major intellectual hero before Russell and Wittgenstein, have been shocked and dismayed:

> I am apt to suspect the negroes and in general all the other species of men (for there are four or five different kinds) to be naturally inferior to the whites. There never was a civilized nation of any other complexion than white, nor even any individual eminent either in action or speculation. No ingenious manufactures amongst them, no arts, no sciences. On the other hand, the most rude and barbarous of the whites, such as the ancient GERMANS, the present TARTARS, have still something eminent about them, in their valour, form of government, or some other particular. Such a uniform and constant difference could not happen in so many countries and ages, if nature had not made an original distinction betwixt these breeds of men. Not to mention our colonies, there are NEGROE slaves dispersed all over EUROPE, of which none ever discovered any symptoms of inge-

* I should like to thank Professors Harry M. Bracken and David F. Norton of McGill University for their helpful suggestions in the many conversations we have had on the problem of racism. I should also like to thank the Guggenheim Foundation for their support while I was doing some of the research for this study.

245

> nuity, tho' low people, without education, will start up amongst
> us, and distinguish themselves in every profession. In JAMAICA
> indeed they talk of one negroe as a man of parts and learning;
> but 'tis likely he is admired for very slender accomplishments
> like a parrot, who speaks a few words plainly.[1]

The immediate tendency has been to assume that this quotation represents an aberrant prejudice, and has nothing to do with Hume's philosophy in general. People remember that Hume also made prejudicial remarks about the Irish, about Catholics, about religious people in general, and they conclude that he was just being human when he expressed his anti-colored view. But when one investigates Hume's position in the totality of his essay, and in his philosophy in general, including his role as Under-Secretary of State (wherein he dealt in part with colonial affairs), and the influence of his essay "Of National Characters," his view about non-whites cannot be dismissed as a fleeting observation. It is intimately related to his thought, and to one of the problems of eighteenth-century thought—the justification of European superiority over the rest of mankind.

Historians of philosophy are, I believe, obliged to rethink and reevaluate the development of theories about the nature of man in the eighteenth century. As soon as one is willing to look into this, and compare the theories with the data concerning what prominent intellectuals of the Enlightenment said about non-whites, Jews, Irish, etc., one is faced with a paradox. The dominant theories about the nature of man in modern times, from Montaigne onward, including those of Descartes, Hobbes, Spinoza, Malebranche, Locke, Leibniz, Bayle, Berkeley, Hume, and Kant, are all universalistic. They all define man in terms of mental and psychological characteristics. Size, skin color, religious beliefs, etc. do not enter into the question of whether a given individual is to be considered human, and whether he is to be treated in certain ways which differentiate him from animals or machines. However, the same people in the Enlightenment who could develop these theories of human nature could also provide the bases for theories claiming that some individuals, in fact millions of them, were less than men because they were dark, or accepted the wrong religion. How can one explain this phenomenon?

246

It seems to me that the theories outlining what Hume called the science of man were transformed to meet eighteenth-century conditions. (This duplicates to some extent a similar transformation that occurred in the sixteenth century to justify giving the American Indians an inferior status.) Four major views were offered during the Enlightenment. The first was that the mental life of non-whites, especially Indians and Africans, is significantly different from that of whites (Hume, Linnaeus, etc.). The second was that being non-white is a sign of sickness or degeneracy: the normal, natural condition of man is that of whiteness, but due to unfortunate environmental factors, some people have lost their whiteness and with this, part of their human nature (Buffon, Blumenbach, etc.). A third theory was that some beings that look human are really not so, but are lower on the great chain of being and represent a link between man and apes (Edward Long). And the fourth theory was that there were separate creations of mankind, the Caucasian being the best; the others, the pre-Adamitic creations, never contained the stuff of genuine men.[2] For the purposes of this study, I will ignore racist theories based on the Bible, since for Enlightenment thinkers such religiously based views played a small role.

I think that one could show that the root theory in each of these cases was universalistic, benign, and neutral, but that each went through a transformation during the eighteenth century so that it became a basis for a racist ideology. In the first case, it was argued that Indians and Africans could have no abstract ideas, could not engage in prudential reasoning, or, in the worst claims, could not understand or appreciate true religion. Their lack of adequate mental life justified the way they were treated.

Bartolomé de las Casas had attacked this view by insisting,

> All the people of the world are men . . . all have understanding and volition, all have the five exterior senses and the four interior senses, and are moved by the objects of these, all take satisfaction in goodness and feel pleasure with happy and delicious things, all regret and abhor evil.[3]

Pope Paul III agreed with him, and in the Bull "Sublimus Deus" declared, "We . . . consider, however, that the Indians are truly

247

men and that they are not only capable of understanding the Catholic faith, but, according to our information, they desire exceedingly to receive it."[4] Las Casas believed that Indians, if properly instructed by Spaniards (the right ones), would show their potentiality to be better Europeans than Europeans.

The opposition was trying to prove that the Indians were the people Aristotle had described as being by nature slaves, and that therefore, God bless them, they ought to be enslaved.[5] Sixteenth-century Spanish and Portuguese literature by advocates of the enslavement of the Indians is full of claims that the Indians do not meet Aristotle's definition of man—a rational animal. In a complete reversal of Christian history, in which the pagans and infidels could participate in Christian society by understanding or accepting the Revelation, some were claiming they now had found "people" incapable of sufficient rationality for such participation.[6] As Winthrop Jordan has shown, the same point was made in seventeenth- and eighteenth-century America.[7]

During the Enlightenment, the lack of proper intellectual equipment among non-whites became a major basis for judging them inferior in terms of their "philosophy" and "way of life." Linnaeus' classification of kinds of man clearly indicates this.

1. HOMO
   Diurnal; varying by education and situation.
2. Four-footed, mute, hairy.   *Wild Man*
3. Copper-coloured, choleric, erect.   *American*
   Hair black, straight, thick; *nostrils* wide, *face* harsh; *beard* scanty; *obstinate*, content free. *Paints* himself with fine red lines. *Regulated* by customs.
4. Fair, sanguine, brawny.   *European*
   Hair, yellow brown, flowing; *eyes* blue; *gentle*, acute, inventive. *Covered* with close vestments. *Governed* by laws.
5. Sooty, melancholy, rigid.   *Asiatic*
   Hair black; *eyes* dark; *severe*, haughty, covetous. *Covered* with loose garments. *Governed* by opinions.
6. Black, phlegmatic, relaxed.   *African*
   Hair black, frizzled; *skin* silky; *nose* flat; *lips* tumid; *crafty*, indolent, negligent. *Anoints* himself with grease. *Governed* by caprice.[8]

The studies of languages in the eighteenth century often deal with the inadequacy of the structure and content of Indian and African languages, among others, to express crucial intellectual notions.[9]

Hume's blanket claim, which Edward Long took as established,[10] that no non-whites had contributed to civilization, to the arts and sciences, confirmed that in terms of mental factors, the dumbest white was closer to the philosophical definition of man than the "wisest" black, red, swarthy, or sooty individual. The articles "Americans," "Complexion," and "Negroes" in the first American edition of the *Encyclopedia Britannica* are in this vein; the article on "Negroes" begins:

> NEGRO, *Homo pelli nigra*, a name given to a variety of the human species, who are entirely black, and are found in the Torrid zone, especially in that part of Africa which lies within the tropics. In the complexion of negroes we meet with various shades; but they likewise differ far from other men in all the features of their face. Round cheeks, high cheek-bones, a forehead somewhat elevated, a short, broad, flat nose, thick lips, small ears, ugliness, and irregularity of shape, characterize their external appearance. The negro women have the loins greatly depressed, and very large buttocks, which give the back the shape of a saddle. Vices the most notorious seem to be the portion of this unhappy race: idleness, treachery, revenge, cruelty, impudence, stealing, lying, profanity, debauchery, nastiness and intemperance, are said to have extinguished the principles of natural law, and to have silenced the reproofs of conscience. They are strangers to every sentiment of compassion, and are an awful example of the corruption of man when left to himself.[11]

Though man was defined universalistically, in terms of his mental properties, blacks, Indians, etc. were said to lack these properties. If so, then the revolutionary ideas of the philosophers from Montaigne to Kant as to how men should be treated did not have to apply to people who might meet Buffon's criterion for belonging to the human species; that is, that they could copulate with other members of the species and produce fertile offspring. This view as to the lack of mental equipment or ability allowed a kind of transformation from universalism to racism, or it was itself the basis of one form of racism.

249

Part of the burden of the abbé Henri Grégoire's counterattack against eighteenth-century racism was the argument first that Jews had the proper mental equipment and had made contributions to "civilization," and later, in his *De la littérature des Nègres,* that there actually were black writers, scientists, professors, etc. The Jewish case, on this level, was easy, with everyone from Philo and Maimonides to Moses Mendelssohn to throw into the argument.[12] The gist of many Enlightenment theories was not that Jews were by nature stupid, but that their religious tradition and practices had deadened their minds and kept them from knowing the achievements of modern thought.

It is interesting that Mendelssohn, whose role in European thought was enormous, was regarded as both a freak case and as a proof that the Jews, no matter how bad they might be, had the potentiality to be fully human intellectually. It is instructive in this regard that as soon as Mendelssohn made his mark in the intellectual world as a serious contributor to philosophical discussion, he was asked why, if he was so bright, he did not become a Christian.[13] The same thing happened to Hume's one Jewish friend, Isaac de Pinto, the chairman of the Board of Directors of the Amsterdam Synagogue (Hume referred to him as a good man "tho a Jew"),[14] who was one of the first to advance the economic theory of modern capitalism. A decade before Mendelssohn's startling success, de Pinto tangled with Voltaire over whether the Jews were *Untermenschen,* and de Pinto pointed to all of the glorious achievements of the Spanish and Portuguese Jews as contributors to culture and to the intellectual world. Voltaire then asked de Pinto why, if he was so bright, he did not give up Judaism and become a *philosophe.* De Pinto's reply was to the effect that he was *un philosophe juif,* which to Voltaire was like a square circle.[15] To many Enlightenment theoreticians, like Jefferson, *un philosophe noir,* or *un philosophe indien* would have been even more incredible or impossible: the people of color just did not have the right things going on in their heads to qualify as men in the philosophical sense.

Count Buffon, in his analysis of the human scene, could show the state of affairs and offer an elaborate explanation of it. People were once all equal (and white), but owing to unfortunate factors, like climate, diet, and culture, they had become sick and degenerated. The present condition of the less-than-white could be accounted for, and maybe overcome, if they could be moved to better climates, fed French food, and given a European education.[16] Lord Kames, Oliver Goldsmith, and J. F. Blumenbach elaborated on Buffon's theory.[17] They might all agree that people were once equal mentally and morally, but that something terrible had happened. Most people had degenerated, so that, as Buffon declared, the true idea of humanity could only be gained from those who live in a belt from the Caucasus mountains to Paris.

> The most temperate climate lies between the 40th and 50th degree of latitude, and it produces the most handsome and beautiful men. It is from this climate that the ideas of the genuine colour of mankind, and of the various degrees of beauty, ought to be derived. The two extremes are equally remote from truth and from beauty. The civilized countries, situated under this zone, are Georgia, Circassia, the Ukraine, Turkey in Europe, Hungary, the south of Germany, Italy, Switzerland, France, and the northern part of Spain. The natives of these territories are the most handsome and most beautiful people in the world.[18]

Thus, the universalistic idea of human nature could be reconciled with the diversity of human types. And, the types could then be classified so that some (in fact, the non-whites) could be regarded as less than human in mental life.

This is one transformation that became a basis for modern racism; perhaps a more startling one is the development of the pre-Adamite theory. In the attempt to explain the origins of the American Indians, all sorts of proposals were offered—that they were the Lost Tribes of Israel, they were Arabs, Phoenicians, Asians, Norwegians, etc.[19] In the midst of these conjectures, the modern pre-Adamite theory was proposed, first by Paracelsus, that the Indians did not have a source in common with the other peoples of the world. Paracelsus' theory, stated in 1520, might be called racist. He classified the Indians with mermaids, griffins, nymphs, sirens, and salamanders, all as beings without souls.[20]

251

The crucial statement of the pre-Adamite theory was that of Isaac La Peyrère (1596–1676), a most benign view. La Peyrère held that Adam was the first Jew, but not the first man. In La Peyrère's version of the polygenetic theory, all people except Jews were pre-Adamites, including Europeans, Eskimos, American Indians, Africans, and Asians.[21] But, as he insisted, everyone, Adamite and pre-Adamite, was made of the same biological matter, the same blood and the same flesh.[22] Even more important, everyone— pre-Adamite, Adamite, and post-Adamite, would share in the world to come and would be saved *no matter who they were or what they believed*.[23] The only racist aspect of La Peyrère's view is his claim that Adamite (that is, Jewish) bodies will resurrect better than non-Adamite (that is, Gentile) bodies.[24]

La Peyrère's theory was based on a Messianic vision of what was supposed to happen to the Adamites in the seventeenth century, namely, the Recall of the Jews.[25] His pre-Adamite theory was rejected by almost everybody at the time.[26] The theory slowly got revived during the eighteenth century, and flowered in the nineteenth. The revival involved a radical and racist transformation. The virtue of the theory, seen through Enlightenment eyes, was that it explained the evidence of the diversity of mankind *and* allowed for an evaluation of the diversity.[27]

All through the eighteenth century, owing to the discoveries in geology, the work on fossils, and archeological and anthropological findings, the pre-Adamite theory kept being revived. The antiquity of Mexico, China, Peru, Mount Vesuvius, the Indian scriptures, pre-historic axes, etc., kept pointing to a mankind older than 4004 B.C.[28] Every time somebody realized this, they rediscovered La Peyrère and his pre-Adamite theory. The theory has had amazing explanatory force in that, if one is willing to sacrifice the Biblical story, it can account for the empirical evidence about man, animals, and nature. In the eighteenth century, thinkers began to realize the racist value of the theory. The separate origins of different groups of mankind allowed for the possibility that some groups were, from their creation, inferior to others. The theory of the diverse origins of mankind began to emerge in the late eighteenth century as a better basis for making normative judgments about presently existing mankind. Lord Kames could see that if the American Indians and the Europeans had different origins, then the superiority of the Europeans could be assured.[29] Edward Long could claim that it was so obvious "that none but the blind can doubt it" that Negroes and whites were separate species.[30] The revival and development of pre-Adamism in nineteenth-century America clearly showed how the theory could provide the basis for racism and slavery. The work of Dr. Samuel Morton and his disciples, and the articles on La Peyrère in the early anthropological journals are adequate testimony to what had happened.[31] The opponents of racism had to fight for the unity of the human species, while pre-Adamism continued up to Alexander Winchell's *Pre-adamites* in 1880, with photographs,[32] to be a fertile source of justification of the inferiority of men of color compared to the Caucasians.

La Peyrère's Messianic humanism had been transformed into scientific racism and a basic justification of slavery. The pre-Adamite racists were amused that their source was an off-beat theologian, and they ignored his humanistic theology while making him the Galileo of anthropology,[33] the man who dared to state the original diversity of the races and suffered accordingly.

If these two examples, the fate of the view that man is a rational animal, and the fate of the pre-Adamite theory, indicate that what happened intellectually was not that various eminent thinkers had aberrational racist views, but that they were transforming the basic explanations of human diversity from neutral to normative ones, then I hope that historians of philosophy will follow in detail how these transformations took place. I personally am working on the history of the pre-Adamite theory from its beginning to its end in the early twentieth century. Studies of what happened to each of the other explanations may reveal to us the intellectual events that have led to our present racist ideologies.

But, one wonders why this all happened. Why the explanations of human diversity did not remain neutral, without evaluations of the diversities? I suspect that the abbé Grégoire was essentially right when he diagnosed the situation in his *De la littérature des Nègres*. People had given up Biblical humanism, and with it the conviction that everyone, no matter what he looked like, was an image of God. Secondly, naturalistic explanations of human nature allowed for normative evaluations. And, thirdly, and most important, there was an economic need to justify African slavery and the rape of America.[34] The last factor, no doubt, played the greatest role in the theorizing that went on. And, to nobody's surprise, the theorizers from Locke to Blumenbach managed to find that people with "wrong," or "inferior" mental properties just happened to have the wrong skin color, or the wrong religious beliefs and practices. In finding this out, the philosophers and natural philosophers were not being aberrational; they were acting as the theoreticians for a major stream of thought that was transforming the universalistic conception of man into a view of the gradations of mankind, a transformation that could justify what was occurring.[35]

While considering how this happened, I believe we also have to study the counter-movement, to see what alternative theories of man were offered to oppose the growing racism of the Enlightenment, and to propose a view of man without invidious gradations and evaluations. The two major figures who need restudy are, I think, the abbé Grégoire and Alexander von Humboldt. Professor Necheles has set us on the way to realizing Grégoire's importance as the great egalitarian of the era.[36] His conception of man, born of a Biblical humanism and Messianism (partly fueled by La Peyrère), made him insist on the potential equality of all mankind, no matter what their present conditions might be. Von Humboldt, especially after his encounter with the American racists, Dr. Morton and his disciples, insisted not only on the unity of the human species, but more important, on the view that no matter how human beings differed in civilization, culture, or achievement, no nations are "in themselves nobler than others."[37] Grégoire's egalitarianism and von Humboldt's total cultural relativism may provide a viable theory of man for our present era.

NOTES

1. David Hume, "Of National Characters," in *The Philosophical Works*, ed. by T. H. Green and T. H. Grose (London, 1882), III, 252 *n.*

The Philosophical Basis of Racism

2. Philip D. Curtin, in his *The Image of Africa, British Ideas and Action, 1780–1850* (Madison, 1964), indicates that though polygenesis was a minority position in the eighteenth century, it "was extremely attractive to the eighteenth-century *philosophes.*" Cf. pp. 41–42. My researches suggest that until the end of the eighteenth century very few significant thinkers were willing to advocate a polygenetic theory, either of pre-Adamism, co-Adamism, or double Adamism. From the time of La Peyrère's publication of the theory in 1655 it was constantly being refuted and ridiculed. Diderot, in his article in the *Encyclopédie* "Pré-adamite" treats the theory as having been demolished by the refutation of Samuel Desmarets in 1656. Cf. Denis Diderot, *Oeuvres complètes* (Paris 1876), XVI, 387–89. On the other hand, Spinoza seemed sympathetic, and borrowed many of La Peyrère's ideas, as did Charles Blount. Voltaire accepted pre-Adamism, and Lord Kames offered a form of double Adamism. The theory became really forceful in the first half of the nineteenth century.

3. Cited in Lewis Hanke, *The Spanish Struggle for Justice in the Conquest of America* (Philadelphia, 1949), p. 125. Hanke, in this work and in his *Aristotle and the American Indians* (Chicago, 1959), examines the debate in the sixteenth century over whether the Indians had rational souls and deserved to be called men.

4. Cited in Hanke, *The Spanish Struggle for Justice*, p. 73. The Bull is dated June 9, 1537. There is a separate study of it by Hanke, "Pope Paul III and the American Indians," *Harvard Theological Review*, XXX (1937), 65–102.

5. Cf. Hanke, *Aristotle and the American Indians*, chaps. 2–5. As late as 1844, Alexander von Humboldt noted in *Cosmos* that "The very cheerless, and in recent times too often discussed, doctrine of the unequal rights of men to freedom, and of slavery as an institution in conformity with nature, is unhappily found in Aristotle's *Politica*, i.3, 5, 6." *Cosmos: A Sketch of a Physical Description of the Universe* (London, 1888), I, 368 *n.*

6. This view was opposed by Las Casas in his *The Only Method of Attracting All People to the Truth Faith*, and by Pope Paul III in "Sublimus Deus." The Pope said, "By virtue of our apostolic authority, we declare . . . that the said Indians and other peoples should be converted to the faith of Jesus Christ by preaching the word of God and by the example of good and having living." Cf. Hanke, *The Spanish Struggle for Justice*, pp. 72–77. The citation from the Pope is on p. 73.

7. Cf. Winthrop Jordan, *White over Black: American Attitudes Toward the Negro, 1550–1812* (Chapel Hill, 1968), chap. 5 on "The Souls of Men, The Negro's Spiritual Nature." Cotton Mather declared, "Indeed their [the Negroes'] *Stupidity* is a *Discouragement*. It may seem, unto as little purpose, to *Teach*, as to *wash an Æthiopian.*" However, Mather saw this as a challenge, while a lot of his contemporaries claimed it was not possible to instruct the Negro slaves to become Christians. Jordan, pp. 186–87. Hanke, in the last chapter of *Aristotle and the*

255

American Indians, gives some interesting citations of English and American views from the late sixteenth century onward of the less than human state of Indians and Polynesians. Cf. pp. 99–101.

8. Linnaeus (Karl von Linné), *A General System of Nature through the Three Grand Kingdoms of Animals, Vegetable, and Minerals* (London, 1806), Vol. I, section "Mammalia. Order I. Primates." Linnaeus is generally credited with being the first to classify man with the animals. In his classification he added a catch-all final group, "*Monstrosus*. Varying by climate or art," "1. Small, active timid.—*Mountaineer*; 2. Large, indolent.—*Patagonian*; 3. Less fertile.—*Hottentot*." (this is given in the version cited in Jordan, *op. cit.* as "single-testicled, so less fertile," p. 221); 4. Beardless.—*American*; 5. Head Conic.—*Chinese*; 6. Head flattened.—*Canadian*." Jordan's version also includes "Rush-like girls with narrowed stomach: in Europe," but omits 4.

9. For instance, see James Harris, *Hermes: or a Philosophical Inquiry concerning Language and Universal Grammar* (London, 1751), pp. 407–26. Harris claimed that "the *wisest* Nations, having the *most* and the *best Ideas*, will consequently have the *best* and *most copious Languages*," p. 408.

James Burnet, Lord Monboddo, in his *Of the Origin and Progress of Language*, Vol. I (London, 1773), in accounting for the inferiority of the languages of barbarous nations, said "for, as it is well known, savages are very indolent, at least with respect to any exercise of the mind, and are hardly excited to action by any curiousity, or desire of learning" (p. 182).

Johann Gottfried von Herder, after explaining the wonderful features of the languages of the Greeks, Romans, Germans, and Gauls, then turned to that of the Africans, and announced "the slothful African stammers brokenly and droopingly." *Herders sämtliche Werke*, ed. Bernhard Suphan (Berlin, 1877–1913), I, 1–2.

I am most grateful to Mr. James Groves of California State University, San Diego for pointing out these citations to me. He is preparing a dissertation on late eighteenth-century language theories.

10. At least as regards Africans. Cf. Edward Long, *The History of Jamaica* (London, 1774), Vol. II, Book III, chap. I, "Negroes," pp. 351–76. Long was willing to credit the Chinese, Mexicans, and North American Indians with some intellectual ability, but the Negroes with none. Speaking of the black slaves in America, he said, "We find them marked with the same bestial manners, stupidity, and vices, which debase their brethren on the continent, who seem to be distinguished from the rest of mankind, not in person only, but in possessing, in abstract, every species of inherent turpitude, that is to be found dispersed at large among the rest of of the human creation, with scarce a single virtue to extenuate this shade of character, differing in this particular from all other men; for, in other countries, the most abandoned villain we ever heard of has rarely, if ever, been known unportioned with some good quality at least in his composition. It is astonishing, that

although they have been acquainted with Europeans, and their manufactures, for so many hundred years, they have, in all this series of time, manifested so little taste for arts, or a genius either inventive or imitative. Among so great a number of provinces on this extensive continent, and among so many millions of people, we have heard but of one or two insignificant tribes, who comprehend any thing of mechanic arts, or manufacture; and even these, for the most part, are said to perform their work in a very bungling and slovenly manner, perhaps not better than an *oranoutang* might, with little pains, be brought to do" (pp. 354–55). In discussing Hume's claim, Long refined it to be just a condemnation of Africans: "Mr. *Hume* presumes, from his observations upon the native Africans, to conclude, that they are inferior to the rest of the species, and utterly incapable of all the higher attainments of the human mind" (p. 376). James Beattie's answer to Hume is dismissed because he mixes cases of Mexican Indians and Negroes together.

11. *Encyclopedia Britannica*, 3rd editon (Philadelphia, 1798), XII, 794. *The Encyclopedia Britannica* continued expounding this sort of view into the twentieth century. In the 9th edition (New York 1884), Vol. XVII, *s.v.* "Negro," Prof. A. H. Keane of University College, London, explained that the cranial sutures of Negroes close much earlier than in other races. "To this premature ossification of the skull, preventing all further development of the brain, many pathologists have attributed the inherent mental inferiority of the blacks, an inferiority which is even more marked than their physical differences. Nearly all observers admit that the Negro child is on the whole quite as intelligent as those of other human varieties, but that on arriving at puberty all further progress seems to be arrested" (p. 317). "It is more correct to say of the Negro that he is non-moral than immoral" (p. 317). "No full-blood Negro has ever been distinguished as a man of science, a poet or an artist, and the fundamental equality claimed for him by ignorant philanthropists is belied by the whole history of the race throughout the historic period" (p. 318 [New York, 1911]).

In the famous 11th edition of the *Britannica* the article "Negro" by Thomas Athol Joyce repeats the same theory about the skull development of Negroes, taking it from the same source, Filippo Manetta's *La razza negra nel suo stato selvaggio* (Turin, 1864). The article then says, "This explanation is reasonable and even probable as a contributing cause [of the mental inferiority of Negroes to whites]; but evidence is lacking on the subject and the arrest or even deterioration in mental development is no doubt very largely due to the fact that after puberty sexual matters take the first place in the negro's life and thought. . . . But though the mental inferiority of the negro to the white or yellow races is a fact, it has often been exaggerated: the negro is largely the creature of his environment" (XIX, 344).

The 15th edition gives a neutral account of how Negroes differ from other races, and then in the section on "Negro, American," discusses

Negroes who made a significant impression on American life, from Phyllis Wheatley to the present.

12. Henri Grégoire, *Essai sur la régénération physique, morale et politique des juifs* (Metz, 1789; photoreproduced Paris, 1968), esp. chaps. 15 and 16. Grégoire announced "Certainement une nation qui s'honore d'avoir possédé Mendelssohn en est au moins a l'aurore de la raison" (p. 106). *De la littérature des Nègres, ou Recherches sur leurs facultés intellectuelles, leur qualités morales et leur littérature; suivies de notices sur la vie et les ouvrages des Nègres qui se sont distingués dans les sciences, les lettres et les arts* (Paris, 1808). The English translation by D. B. Warden, *An Enquiry concerning the Intellectual and Moral Faculties, and Literature of Negroes; with an Account of the Life and Works of 15 Negores and Mullatoes, distinguished in Science, Literature and the Arts*, appeared in Brooklyn in 1810. The American racist Josiah C. Nott, in his *Two Lectures on the Connection Between the Biblical and Physical History of Man* (1849, photoreproduced New York, 1969), said "H. Gregoire, the Bishop of Blois, has written a very stupid and often quoted book, on the intellect and literature of negroes, in which the distinction between the pure and mixed breeds is entirely overlooked" (p. 35).

13. The Swiss physiognomist and theologian Johann Casper Lavater challenged Mendelssohn in 1769 either to demonstrate the falsity of Christianity or convert to it. The French translator of Mendelssohn's *Phädon*, Junker, was so impressed by Mendelssohn, "Un genie si extraordinaire né & élevé dans le sein d'une Nation [the Jews] qui croupit dans une crasse ignorance," that he also translated his answer to Lavater. Cf. Moses Mendelssohn, *Phédon, ou Entretiens sur la spiritualité et l'immortalité de l'ame* (Paris and Bayeux, 1772), Avertissment. It is interesting that Herder supported Mendelssohn in the dispute.

14. David Hume, letter to Thomas Rous, August 28, 1767, unpublished, India Office, Miscellaneous Letters Received, E/1/49, fol. 66. Hume wrote "Allow me to recommend to your patronage, M. Pinto, whom I venture to call my Friend, tho' a Jew." The English ambassador in the Hague, Sir Joseph Yorke, used the same phrase in his letter introducing de Pinto to Yorke's brother, the Earl of Hardwicke (British Museum Ms. 35368, Hardwicke Papers XX, fol. 207v, letter of June 23, 1767). In a forthcoming article on Hume and de Pinto, I will publish several manuscript letters of Hume, plus other hitherto unpublished materials. On Hume's relations to de Pinto, see R. H. Popkin, "Hume and Isaac de Pinto," *Texas Studies in Literature and Language*, XII (1970), 417–30.

15. De Pinto's answer to Voltaire is his *Réflexions critiques sur le premier chapitre du VIIe tome des Oeuvres de monsieur de Voltaire, au sujet des Juifs* (Paris, 1762). On the controversy, see J. S. Wijler, *Isaac de Pinto, sa vie et ses oeuvres* (Apeldoorn, 1923), esp. Deuxième Partie; and Arthur Hertzberg, *The French Enlightenment and the Jews* (New York, 1968), pp. 284, 287, 291, and 361. Voltaire in

his answer had said that de Pinto should be as he pleased, even be a Jew, but be a *philosophe*. Voltaire's various analyses of Judaism indicate he really could not see how a Jew could be a *philosophe*.

16. George Louis Leclerc, Comte de Buffon, *Natural History, General and Particular*, trans. by William Smellie, 2nd ed. (London, 1785), Vol. III, *The Natural History of Man*, sec. IX, "Of the Varieties of the Human Species," pp. 57–207. On p. 207, Buffon stated that the present sad situation could be remedied if the causes that generated them, climate, food, mode of living, epidemic diseases, and the mixture of dissimilar individuals ceased to operate.

17. Henry Home, Lord Kames, *Sketches of the History of Man*, 3 vols. (Glasgow, 1819), II, Sketch 12; Oliver Goldsmith, *A History of the Earth and Animated Nature* (Glasgow, Edinburgh, and London, 1857), I, 209–18, "Of the Varieties in the Human Race"; and Johann Friedrich Blumenbach, *On the Natural Varieties of Mankind* (New York, 1969), a reprint of the 1865 English translation.

18. Buffon, *op. cit.*, p. 205. Buffon may be the source of the term "Caucasian" for "white," because of his admiration for the beauty of the women in the Caucasus region.

19. Cf. Lee Eldridge Huddleston, *The Origin of the American Indians: European Concepts, 1492–1729* (Austin and London, 1967).

20. Paracelsus (Theophrast von Hohenheim), *Astronomia magna*, and *Weiteres zur Astronomia magna*, in *Sämtliche Werke*, ed. K. Sudhoff and W. Matteissen (Munich, 1922–33), Abt. I, Band 12, pp. 35–36 and 469–70. Portions of these texts and other related ones are translated in J. S. Slotkin, *Readings in Early Anthropology* (Chicago, 1965) pp. 42–43. See also Paracelsus' *De quator homines non animatis / De Nymphis, sylphis, pymaeis et salamandris /*, in *Sämtliche Werke*, Abt. I, Band 14. Paracelsus' version of the pre-Adamite theory is discussed in my forthcoming study "The Pre-Adamite Theory in the Renaissance," to appear in the Festschrift for Paul Oskar Kristeller.

21. On La Peyrère, see Don Cameron Allen, *The Legend of Noah* (Urbana, 1963), pp. 86–90 and 130–37; David R. McKee, "Isaac de la Peyrère, a Precursor of the 18th Century English Critical Deists," *Publications of the Modern Languages Association*, LIX (1944), 456–85; René Pintard, *Le Libertinage érudit* (Paris, 1943), pp. 355–61, 379, 399, 420–24 and 430; R. H. Popkin, introduction to the photoreproduction edition of La Peyrère's *Men Before Adam*, forthcoming; Hans Joachim Schoeps, *Philosemitismus im Barok* (Tubingen, 1952), pp. 3–18, and *Baroke Juden Christen Juden-Christen*, (Bern and Munich, 1965), pp. 15–24; and Leo Strauss, *Spinoza's Critique of Religion*, trans. E. M. Sinclair (New York, 1965), chap. 3. I am preparing a book-length study on La Peyrère and his influence.

22. Isaac La Peyrère, *Men Before Adam* (London, 1656), in *A Systeme of Divinity*, p. 59. "For they [the Jews] were made up of the same flesh and blood as the Gentiles, and were temper'd with the same clay of which other men were fram'd." The original text is in *Systema The-*

ologicum ex PraeAdamitarum Hypothesi (n.p., 1655), Lib. II, cap. 1, p. 49.

23. La Peyrère, *Systema Theologicum*, Lib. V, especially cap. 9.

24. Isaac La Peyrère, *Du Rappel des Juifs* ([Paris], 1643), Livre II, p. 65; "les Corps des Juifs sont capables de plus de Grace & de plus de Gloire que les corps des Gentils" when they are resurrected and made immortal.

25. La Peyrère's pre-Adamite theory was originally the prologue to *Du Rappel des Juifs*. Richelieu forbade the publication of the work on pre-Adamism, and a revised version was published twelve years later in 1655. After this, the work was condemned, and La Peyrère was forced to recant. He spent his last years trying to redraft his *Rappel des Juifs* and to publish a new version; he could not get permission. La Peyrère's Messianism will be dealt with in a paper I have in preparation, "The Marrano Theology of Isaac La Peyrère."

26. The theory was condemned by both Catholics and Protestants. La Peyrère complained that all the rabbis also rejected his view. Refutations were written by many theologians in England, France, Holland, and Germany at the time, and the theory kept being refuted through the eighteenth century. The only contemporaries who admitted accepting it were Claude Saumaise and Juan de Prado. Spinoza, who borrowed much from La Peyrère, seems to tacitly accept it.

27. Charles Blount, in *The Oracles of Reason* (London, 1693), advanced the theory. Voltaire introduced it occasionally in the *Dictionnaire philosophique*. Edward Long, in his *History of Jamaica*, Book II, chap. 13, pp. 336–37, advocated it and reported that "A certain philosopher [unnamed] of the present age confidently avers that 'none but the blind can doubt it' " (p. 337). Long was, of course, trying to establish that white and Negroes were of different species.

28. See for instance P. Brydone, *A Tour through Sicily and Malta, in a Series of Letters to William Beckford* (London, 1773), I, 131–32, where Brydone discussed the evidence that Mount Vesuvius had been erupting for at least 14,000 years. "Recupero [his guide] tells me he is exceedingly embarrassed, by these discoveries, in writing the history of the mountain. —That Moses hangs like a dead weight upon him, and blunts his zeal for inquiry; for that really he has not the conscience to make his mountain so young, as that prophet makes the world" (p. 132). Francois Xavier Burtin tried to account for fossil evidence by claiming there were non-human rational creatures before Adam. The *Monthly Review*, III (1790), in its discussion of his *Réponse à la Question physique proposée par la Societé de Teyler sur les Revolutions generales, qu'a subies la surface de la Terre, et sur l'ancienneté de notre globe* (Haarlem, 1789), said that "provided he excepts the human species, he may believe rational animals to have existed on the earth before Adam, without being guilty of this terrible heresy, for which, about the middle of the last century, poor Isaac de la Pereira was so roughly handled by the Inquisition" (p. 543). On the next page the *Monthly Review* dealt with a Dr. Van Marum who had found an

unidentifiable jawbone: "Hence we have some suspicion of its having been a Pre-Adamite, perhaps the owner, if not the maker, of the wonderful hatchet discovered near Brussels" (p. 544).

The first translator of the Hindu scriptures, Nathaniel Brassey Halhed, was overwhelmed by the claims of Hindu chronology, going back 7,205,000 years. The evidence seemed convincing to him that the Hindu scriptures predated the Biblical world. Halhed finally insisted it had to be a matter of faith, based on Divine Revelation, that the Mosaic account is accurate, since it cannot be reconciled with the Indian materials. See his preface to *A Code of Gentoo Laws, or Ordinations of the Pundits, from a Persian Translation, made from the Original, written in the Shanscrit Language,* (London, 1776), esp. pp. xxxvii–xliv.

29. Henry Home, Lord Kames, *Sketches of the History of Man,* Vol. I, "Preliminary Discourse concerning the Origin of Men and Languages," esp. pp. 27 and 40–42, and Vol. II, Sketch 12, "Origin and Progress of American Nations," esp. pp. 235–40. "If we admit more than one act of creation, even the appearance of difficulty from reiteration of acts, totally vanisheth." ". . . every rational conjecture leans to a separate creation" (p. 240).

30. Edward Long, *History of Jamaica,* II, 337. In his racist analysis in Book III, chap. I, "Negroes," Long asked, "When we reflect on the nature of these men, and their dissimilarity to the rest of mankind, must we not conclude that they are a different species of the same genus?" (p. 356). Then, instead of the polygenetic explanation he had favored earlier, he advocated the view that Negroes were lower on the great chain of being than the rest of mankind, and were closer to orangutangs than to other men.

31. Two recent studies deal in detail with the work of Dr. Samuel Morton and his disciples; George M. Fredrickson, *The Black Image in the White Mind* (New York, 1971), chap. 3; and William Stanton, *The Leopard's Spots* (Chicago and London, 1960). The *Anthropological Review,* II (1864), has an article by Philalethes entitled, "Peyrerius and Theological Criticism," pp. 109–16. La Peyrère was discussed in many of the articles in the early anthropological journals in England, France, and America. A student of mine at McGill University, Mr. Norbert Hornstein, has written an interesting paper that I hope will be published, arguing that if one judged solely on the basis of evidence in the argument between the polygenecists and the monogenecists before Darwin, the polygenecists had the better scientific case.

32. Alexander Winchell, *Preadamites; or a Demonstration of the Existence of Man before Adam* (Chicago, 1880). The photographs are of a Dravidian, a Mongoloid, a Negro, an Eskimo, a Hottentot, a Papuan, and an Australian aborigine. Winchell was professor of geology and paleontology at the University of Michigan.

33. Henry S. Patterson, "Memoir of the Life and Scientific Labors of Samuel George Morton," in Josiah C. Nott and George R. Gliddon, *Types of Mankind, or Ethnological Researches based upon the Ancient Monuments, Paintings, Sculptures and Crania of Races, and upon their Nat-*

ural, Geographical, Philological and Biblical History (Philadelphia, 1854), pp. xliii–xliv: "The celebrated book of Peyrerius on the pre-Adamites was written to solve certain difficulties in biblical exegesis . . . for the writer was a mere scholastic theologian. He met the fate of all who ventured to defy the hierarchy; . . . at a day when they had the civil power at their back . . . they had their fagots in the Place de Grève, and as they could not catch Peyrerius, the Sorbonne ordered his book publicly burned by the common hangman."

Alexander White, *A History of the Warfare of Science with Theology in Christendom* (New York, 1960) (the first edition was in 1896), I, 255: "In some parts of Europe a man holding new views on chronology was by no means safe from bodily harm. As an example of the extreme pressure exerted by the old theological system at times on honest scholars, we may take the case of La Peyrère. . . . He was taken in hand at once: great theologians rushed forward to attack him from all parts of Europe . . . , the Parliament of Paris burned the book, and the Grand Vicar of the Archdiocese of Mechlin threw him into prison, and kept him there until he was forced, not only to retract his statements, but to adjure his Protestantism."

Most histories of anthropology give La Peyrère an honorific and heroic place in the early development of the subject.

34. Henri Grégoire, *Enquiry concerning the Intellectual and Moral Faculties and Literature of Negroes*, p. 39.

35. It must be recognized that many of those developing the theory of different grades of mankind opposed slavery. Their theories were used by the proslavery advocates nonetheless. For example, Buffon, in his "Of the Varieties of the Human Species," strongly attacked the dreadful treatment of slaves (see pp. 152–53). However, Buffon's views on why many people were non-white were taken, in whole or part, by the racists to justify slavery.

36. Ruth F. Necheles, *The Abbe Grégoire, 1787–1831: The Odyssey of an Egalitarian* (Westport, 1971).

37. Alexander von Humboldt, *Cosmos*, I, 368: "Whilst we maintain the unity of the human species, we at the same time repel the depressing assumption and inferior races of men. There are nations more susceptible of cultivation, more highly civilized—but none in themselves nobler than others."

Patterson's "Memoir of Samuel George Morton" pointed out that when von Humboldt was writing *Cosmos* he sent Dr. Morton a letter praising the latter's researches on crania, (pp. xxxiv–xxxv). When the racist implications of Morton's polygenetic views became apparent, von Humboldt rejected them. Morton and his disciples insisted they were just being scientific, and that moral evaluation should not enter into scientific research (pp. li–liii). The dispute between von Humboldt and Morton much resembles the present argument over the claim by Stokely, Herrenstein, and others that there is a genetic basis for black intellectual inferiority.

Feijoo and the Problem of Ethiopian Color

A. Owen Aldridge

SOMETIMES IN THE HISTORY of ideas, certain authors are associated with major concepts even though these concepts may not be original with them or even particularly significant to the totality of their literary work. A good example is the theory of the influence of climate upon human character, which has been universally associated with Montesquieu; yet it was not originated by the author of *L'Esprit des lois*, he did not develop it in any significant manner, and he actually referred to it only briefly and casually in his great treatise on government. The concept played a much greater role in the work of the learned Spanish ecclesiastic Benito Gerónimo Feijoo (1676–1764). Indeed he was in his *Mapa intelectual y cotejo de naciones* the very first of all the many authors who discussed this question to distinguish between theory and fact in regard to climate.[1] As a result Feijoo rejected the theory that climate has the power of influencing human character. Most of the psychological, biological, and metaphysical concepts treated by the French *philosophes* in the first half of the eighteenth century are also discussed or touched upon in Feijoo's *Teatro crítico*, which could just as appropriately have been entitled, like one of the works of Voltaire, a *Dictionnaire philosophique*.

I have chosen Feijoo as the focus of my discussion not because of his preeminence as a writer or thinker, but on the contrary because he is relatively obscure. Even though he may possibly be classed as the foremost author of eighteenth-century Spain, he was of minimum consequence in the European Enlightenment as a whole. He serves as a better medium for illustrating the history

263

of an idea than such luminaries as Montesquieu, Voltaire, or Goldsmith, however, for they are *sui generis*, less than representative, and their brilliance tends to dazzle the reader or obscure the issue. A further advantage in using Feijoo is that he wrote a self-contained essay, *Color etiópico*, entirely devoted to the problem of skin color, whereas most of the other writers concerned with the problem considered it as subsidiary to some other topic of inquiry.[2]

The question of skin color had been raised by a number of thinkers, including the members of Montesquieu's Academy of Bordeaux.[3] In the year 1741 the Academy offered a prize for the best essay on the subject, and one of the contestants quoted extensively from the 1739 edition of Feijoo's *Teatro crítico*.[4] In his essay *Color etiópico*, which appears in this collection, Feijoo attempted to decide whether blackness is a result of biological structure or climatic conditions—in other words, whether it is caused purely by heredity or by the cumulative effects of environment. This problem is closely related to a number of other questions debated in the eighteenth century at large and in Feijoo's works in particular— whether the world is in a state of gradual decay; whether American Indians are a separate race or descendants of Europeans; whether biological species, including plants, animals, and human beings, degenerate when transported from Europe to America; and whether procreation takes place through the continual communication of fully-formed individuals all formerly contained in the sperm of the first father, Adam, or whether the male sperm and female egg together contribute to form entirely new beings.

Feijoo's *Color etiópico* represents an original approach to a subject of international significance, and it is by no means the product of a provincial mind working in isolation. In the following discussion I shall try to reveal both the development of Feijoo's thought on skin color and the relationship of his ideas to those of his contemporaries in other literatures.

Following his usual practice, Feijoo divided his arguments between those based on accepted Catholic doctrine and those based on natural reason. At first glance it would seem that there would be no danger to orthodox doctrine in affirming either that the black color of the Ethiopians is "congénito a aquella raza de hombres,

que por ningún accidente puede alterarse ni en ellos ni en sus suce-
sores," or that it is a characteristic acquired through the operation
of nature. From a twentieth-century perspective, it would seem
that of the two, the congenital theory would be closer to orthodoxy
since it could be interpreted as supporting the doctrine of special
creation. Feijoo saw in this theory, however, a resemblance to a
theological error he had already confuted, the so-called pre-Adamite heresy, that God had created other generations before Adam
and Eve. In order to expose this heresy as implicit in the doctrine
of separate biological races, Feijoo cited a French, deistically mo-
tivated, imaginary voyage, the title of which he gave as *La Relación
sus nuevos viajes por la América Septentrional*, by the Baron de Lahontan, apparently without realizing that it was fictitious although
suspecting that it was tainted with impiety.[5] In this imaginary voyage, a Portuguese physician maintains that the black color is absolutely inherent in Ethiopians; that it is not lost when they change
their diet or move to other geographical areas, and that it is passed
on invariably from generation to generation. From this evidence,
the physician concludes that Adam was not the first parent of non-
whites, or if he was, he must have been black and therefore whites
could not have descended from him. In similar fashion he argues
that the natives of America could not be descended from the same
stock as Europeans because of the impossibility of the movements
of people across the ocean prior to the means of navigation discovered in modern times. Feijoo had already disposed of these arguments in his *Solución del gran problema histórico sobre la población de la América, y revoluciones del orbe terráqueo* in such a
manner as to vindicate the doctrine of Adam as the first parent of
all mankind.[6] Since he had already thus declared himself as an op-
ponent of the view that black color is an invariable physical characteristic, it is not surprising that he should find reasons to support
the contrary opinion, that it is caused by natural forces.

Many Biblical scholars, following Josephus, St. Jerome, and
Eusebius, had previously affirmed that the black race stemmed
from Cush, son of Cain and grandson of Noah, according to the
genealogy in the tenth chapter of Genesis. Feijoo pointed out that
the Scriptures do not specifically affirm that Cush and his descen-

dants were black; moreover, even if Cush were black, Feijoo reasoned, the problem remains to explain how Cush sprang from white parents. A German scholar in 1677 had published a treatise in which he maintained that blackness had settled on Cush and his descendants through a miracle, the result of a malediction uttered by Noah against the father of Cush for exposing Noah's nakedness.[7] This scholar maintained as well that such natural causes combined to produce their blackness as excessive heat, climate, the contexture of the complexion (*cutis*), and the force of imagination. Feijoo replied that the theory of a malediction is just as arbitrary as the simple attribution of blackness to the sons of Cush and, therefore, not an authoritative interpretation of the Scriptures. Feijoo took a more tolerant view, however, as we shall see, of the contributing natural causes suggested by this author, adopting some of them for his own purpose as primary causes.

Feijoo consulted a third theological source, an article in the French Jesuit periodical *Mémoires de Trévoux*, concerning the theories of a member of the order, Père Auguste.[8] The latter carried the quest for the original Negro back to Cain, maintaining that blackness was the curse which God placed upon the slayer of Abel and his descendants; furthermore, the French Jesuit claimed that the American Indians came from Lamech, and the rest of mankind from the three sons of Noah, Shem, Ham, and Japhet. Feijoo rejected this hypothesis as being both arbitrary and contradicted by other parts of Scripture, particularly the declaration that the Flood covered the entire universe and destroyed the entire human race with the exception of the family of Noah.[9] Some time after Feijoo had written his *Color etiópico*, he received a subsequent issue of the *Mémoires de Trevoux*, containing an independent refutation of the theory of Père Auguste from the pen of Père Tournemine, a learned Jesuit now famous as one of the mentors of Voltaire during his early days in the Lycée. Tournemine and Feijoo agreed in substance in their objections to the theory of blackness as a result of a malediction, but Feijoo learned for the first time that the first author to express it had been William Whiston, an English theologian and propounder of many paradoxes. As Feijoo expressed it, not only was he a protestant and therefore a heretic, but he was considered a heretic by other heretics.[10]

In turning to arguments based on natural reason rather than Scripture, Feijoo cited the opinion characterized as *recibidisima del vulgo* that the black color is caused by the heat of the sun, an opinion found in such ancients as Pliny and Ovid. It was moreover accepted and propagated after Feijoo by Buffon in his highly influential *Histoire naturelle*.[11] Feijoo rejected this argument in simple terms; Negroes live in temperate areas of northern Africa as well as at the Cape of Good Hope, and the natives of some very hot areas in Europe and South America are not Negroes. Voltaire somewhat later, in his *Essai sur les moeurs*, used similar arguments to prove that skin color could in no way be caused by climate: "des Nègres et des Nègresses, transportés dans les pays les plus froids, y produisent toujours des animaux de leur espèce, et que le mulâtres ne sont qu'une race bâtarde d'un noir et d'une blanche, ou d'un blanc et d'une noire."[12] Although on this particular point, Feijoo and Voltaire thought alike, on the related question of whether whites and blacks belong to the same or to distinct species, they parted company. Feijoo maintained that they are of the same species because to affirm the contrary would be to deny that Adam was the parent of all of humanity. Voltaire maintained that they are of distinct species because basic anatomical differences separate them.

A further natural cause which some authors assigned for blackness was the imagination of pregnant mothers, an explanation which Feijoo had not seen presented with complete clarity in any author, but which he nevertheless knew well enough to cite. As he presented the argument, the imagination of the mother of the first Ethiopian had been struck forcibly during pregnancy by some black object and thus negritude had become fixed and extended to succeeding generations. Feijoo admitted that many stories circulate concerning the effect of imagination during conception or pregnancy, but he was personally inclined to doubt that the mind could be strong enough to produce such a physical result. Also this phenomenon could not very easily be reconciled with the theory of procreation, which Feijoo had proclaimed in another article and which he considered to be the most modern, the so-called Chinese box theory, that in each egg of every human ovary are already fully formed from the beginning of the world all the subsequent individuals of all future generations.[13] Feijoo admitted that St. Thomas discussed the theory of imagination in pregnancy, but added that he did so in such an ambiguous manner that he came closer to a denial than an affirmation of its possibility. Feijoo also cited one of the most famous tales from antiquity, "Theoganes and Chariclea" or the "Ethiopian History," by Heliodorus, which many eighteenth-century critics considered as a forerunner of the modern novel. In the story, Chariclea, the offspring of Negro parents, was born white because her mother had been impressed at the time of generation by a painting of Andromeda. Quintilian, moreover, in one of his orations described a white woman who from inspecting the portrait of an Ethiopian gave birth to a black infant. Feijoo in summarizing these and similar tales remarked that they were feigned or fictitious, designed to advance the literary aims of their authors.

Yet Feijoo would not take it upon himself to deny categorically the force of the imagination in this connection. He pointed out, however, that one could believe that the imagination could possibly change the color of an individual foetus without believing that this process had anything to do with the Ethiopian race. His chief objection to applying the theory to an entire race is that for it to be tenable all mothers in a particular area must have experienced the same impression upon their imagination. Also Feijoo suggested that some Negro men or women in slavery have experienced a vehement passion for a white individual; this passion has exercised a violent effect on their imaginations, but nevertheless white offspring have never been produced.

A variant of the imagination theory may be found in the works of Malebranche, one of Feijoo's favorite sources for philosophical concepts. Malebranche stated confidently that "women who during pregnancy see persons with marks on certain parts of their faces will imprint these marks on the corresponding parts of their children's bodies."[14] Another of Feijoo's sources, Leibniz, in speaking of animals, affirmed that "it is possible for a female to produce an animal belonging to a species different from her own, a fact caused solely by the imagination of the mother."[15] More important, one of Feijoo's contemporaries, a French Jesuit, Lafitau, had applied the imagination theory to the black and red races three years before the essay on *Color etiópico*. In his *Moeurs des sauvages américains comparées aux moeurs des premiers temps*, Lafitau expressed a theory concerning the populating of the western hemisphere very much like that of Feijoo's *Solución del gran problema histórico sobre la población de la América, y revoluciones del globo terráqueo*.[16] According to Lafitau, the Americans had not been created by God as a separate race, but they had descended from the ancient Greeks. The black color of the black race had come from some women in the distant past seeing the bodies of their husbands painted in black and their imagination being so stricken that their successive progeny took on the color. The red of the Caribbean races similarly had come about through women seeing their husbands painted in red. As proof of this theory, Lafitau cited the stratagem of Jacob in Chapter 30 of Genesis in breeding lambs of whatever color he pleased. Somewhat later Voltaire scornfully rejected Lafitau's entire system, both the main theory of populating America and the subordinate one of imagination. "Le jésuite devait savoir," he taunted, "que tout ce qui arrivait du temps de Jacob n'arrive plus aujourd'hui." "Si l'on avait demandé au gendre de Laban pourquoi ses brébis, voyant toujours de l'herbe, ne faisaient pas des agneaux verts, il aurait été bien embarrassé."[17]

Another opinion advanced to account for skin color was that of an English physician of the seventeenth century, Thomas Browne, whose prose work exposing vulgar errors, *Pseudodoxia Epidemica*, 1646, has many parallels to Feijoo's *Teatro crítico*. From the periodical *Actorum Eruditorum*, Feijoo reported Browne's theory that the blackness of the Ethiopians derives from "los efluvios fuliginosos y vitriólicos que despiden sus cuerpos hacia la superficie; y que estos efluvios proceden de las aguas y alimentos de que usan." This opinion is based on the testimony of Pliny concerning two fountains in Greece; one of which produces white characteristics and the other black in those who drink from it, "no sólo a los ganados, mas también a los hombres." Feijoo pointed out, however, that Pliny himself never actually saw such a fountain, nor has any traveler in modern times. Feijoo doubted the entire hypothesis because of "la grande inverisimilitud de que en muchas grandes provincias, cuyos habitadores todos son negros, todas las fuentes tengan esta rara propiedad." After dismissing all of the preceding theories, Feijoo unequivocally stated his own, "que la causa verdadera y única del color de los etíopes es el influjo del clima o país que habitan." Lest his readers be confused by the apparent inconsistency between this opinion and his previous rejection of the heat of the sun as well as food and water as causes, he hastened to explain that the climatic qualities which he believed to be instrumental are "los jugos, hábitos o efluvios de la tierra." The major cause, in other words, is the atmosphere. "Y los vapores, exhalaciones o corpúsculos de la atmósfera, ¿qué son sino efluvios de la tierra? Luego éstos o los cuerpos de donde se exhalan se deben reconocer (regularmente hablando) por causa de las particulares cualidades buenas o malas del país."

Feijoo provided no clue to his source for this concept, but a parallel exists in one of the most important treatises on society and art of the century, *Réflexions critiques sur la poésie et la peinture*, by abbé Jean Baptiste Du Bos, published originally in 1719, fourteen years prior to Feijoo's essay. According to Du Bos,

> "Les qualités de l'air dependent elles mêmes de la qualité des émanations de la terre que l'air enveloppe. Suivant que la terre est composée, l'air qui l'enserre, est différent. Or les émanations de la terre qui est un corps mixte dans lequel il se fait des fermentations continuelles, ne sçauroient être toujours précisément de la même nature dans une certaine contrée.[18]

The theory of the particular effect of air goes all the way back to Hippocrates, *De aere, aquis et locis*, and an extensive and influential treatment on the subject, by Dr. John Arbuthnot. *Essay concerning the Effects of Air on Human Bodies*, was printed in England in the same year that Feijoo's discussion appeared.

Whether or not Feijoo was aware of Du Bos's treatise, his extensive consideration of the theory of air is an independent and highly original contribution. He presented evidence from various countries of Europe to illustrate the influence of soil and air. In Russia, the inhabitants of Georgia possess a rose color, and in the

Crimea the women are extremely beautiful. The English have a complexion whiter than that not only of Mediterranean peoples, but also of other peoples of the same northern latitude; therefore this quality cannot be attributed to the cold. Feijoo based another positive proof of his climatic theory upon the analogy with plants and vegetables, which vary drastically according to the soil. Turning to the argument that color comes from inheritance alone (the view of which Voltaire was to become a vocal defender later in the century), Feijoo replied that no unbroken racial lines exist among human beings, the mixture of races having taken place in all nations.

The strongest objection to the theory of climate was based on the circumstance that descendants of Negroes who move to other climates do not change their color. Feijoo again used the method of analogy. The metal gold is also produced by many years in the earth and is not changed when moved to another location. "Puede el clima etiópico producir la negrura, sin ser necesario para conservarla." His principal answer, however, consisted in labelling as false the assumption that Negroes do not change color in different environments. He cited the *Dictionnaire de Trévoux* and various ecclesiastics as authority for the principle that "etíopes trasplantados a Europa, a segunda o tercera generación van blanqueando." According to Feijoo, these authorities are more credible than the Baron de Lahontan, who, in his opinion, may be suspected of impiety or charlatanism. Abbé Du Bos supports Feijoo on this principle, citing the descendants of original Portuguese settlers who had lived in African colonies over three centuries and as a result had acquired all the physical characteristics of Negroes.[19] Voltaire, however, insisted firmly that in whatever regions white, red, yellow, or black races are transported, they do not change at all as long as they do not mix with the natives of the country.[20]

One of the arguments of the Baron de Lahontan to support separate races was based on the allegation that descendants of natives of Brazil transported to Portugal continued to have no beards even after living more than a century in Europe. The lack of beards among the natives of North and South America was one of the main arguments used in an effort to prove that biological species in the New World degenerated from the Old, a beard being considered a sign of virility.[21] Feijoo, first of all, doubted the truth of the allegation that American Indians lack beards, citing the insufficiency of the available testimony on that subject. Even if the allegation were true, he objected, it may have taken centuries for the people of America to lose their beards and it might require many more to get them back. Also the process of losing and gaining beards may be very slow, but that of changing color may be relatively fast. Feijoo reported his own observation of two inhabitants of Oviedo, born in Mexico of Spanish parents, who both began life with a color between white and olive, that appropriate for Mexico. One of them, a bishop, left America as an adult and kept his dark color for the rest of his life; the other left at the age of seven and had become appreciably lighter by the age of nineteen, and, according to Feijoo, the lightening process continued noticeably every day. Returning to the subject of beards, Feijoo remarked that even if the Brazilians in Portugal never grow beards, one ought not to conclude that their ancestors never had them. It is not necessary that beards should return to a race which has lost them. Once again relying on analogy, he remarked that wine may turn to vinegar, but the reverse process never takes place. Finally Feijoo affirmed that the beardlessness of American Indians is no proof that the population of the New World did not come from Europe, another reference to the theory which he held in common with Lafitau that the Indians had descended from Europeans. According to Feijoo, it would not be possible for any Indians whatsoever to possess beards if the theory of two separate and unconnected races were true, but travelers had reported seeing Indians with beards in Darien.

Feijoo concluded his essay with some particulars concerning Negroes which he thought might interest his readers. To compare these particulars with similar statements in other eighteenth-century authors may be of equal interest. Relying on the *Mémoires de l'Académie Royale des Sciences*, he reported that the Ethiopians are white at birth. A North American clergyman of the seventeenth century, Roger Williams, solemnly affirmed that the Indians acquired their red skin "by the Sunne and their annoyntings," but they were actually "borne white."[22] Williams by the way was the

272

only author I cite who had actually known the culture of either Indians or Negroes at first hand. Although he had lived and slept with Indians in order to learn their language, he still believed, like Feijoo, that they were born white.

Feijoo also reported, from the *Académie Royale des Sciences*, that the blackness of the Ethiopians resides only in the skin; that their sperm, as many believed, is not black; that both their blood and seminal fluids are the same as those of Europeans; that human skin is composed of three layers, the difference in skin color residing in the intermediate or second layer, the reticular membrane. Finally, Feijoo reported the experiments of Littré to prove that no glutinous black fluid is contained in this membrane, but the texture itself causes the blackness. Voltaire cited an experiment by the celebrated Ruysch in Amsterdam, who was the first by dissection to isolate this mucous membrane, "which resembled a black gauze."[23] But Voltaire used this evidence to prove a point contrary to Feijoo's, namely, that the Negro race is as different from the white as is a spaniel from a greyhound. The *Encyclopédie* of Diderot and d'Alembert in the article "Nègres" offered two different explanations for black skin color: (1) the presence of a black subcutaneous tissue, and (2) an excess of black bile. The article in the *Encyclopédie* on American Indians, "Canadiens," affirmed that they are born white like Europeans, but acquire their red tint from the paint and grease which they regularly apply to their bodies and which the sun burns into their skin.

The Swedish naturalist Linnaeus agreed with orthodox theologians that all men have sprung from a common parent, but he adopted the unusual opinion that this common parent was black. The English novelist, essayist, and poet Goldsmith agreed with Linnaeus and Feijoo on a common parent, but disagreed on his being black. By observing that black parents more often have white children than the reverse, he came to the conclusion that blackness is a recessive characteristic.[24] Feijoo, as we have seen, believed that since all men have descended from Adam, the diversity of races was caused by the forces of climate. Voltaire, however, declared that providence dispersed the various races over the globe, using the term "providence" in an ambiguous manner to indicate natural causes, but particularly rejecting climate as a natural cause of skin color.[25] Goldsmith repudiated the view that man was propagated from several sources in different parts of the globe, in other words, that man is "indigenous, or sprung from the soil," but instead of basing his opinion like Feijoo on the Book of Genesis, he brought his private logic to bear. Since in his opinion the inhabitants of the southern hemisphere are more barbarous than the people of the northern, but the natural beauty of the southern hemisphere is superior to that of the northern, he concluded that man first developed in the north but had not yet crossed the equator in sufficient numbers to balance the population of the two hemispheres.[26]

On the question of whether Negroes are a separate race, most of the authors of the century outside Spain lined up with Voltaire against Feijoo, insisting on the separateness of the races. An English author, Edward Long, introduced the concept of the Great Chain of Being into the argument, affirming that Negroes are not even human beings but rise "progressively in the scale of intellect the further they mount above the orang-outan and brute creation."[27] Montesquieu similarly maintained that Negroes are not subject to natural law because they are of a different species. "One could not imagine," he wrote, probably with a degree of irony, "that God, who is a very wise being, would have placed a soul, especially a good soul, in a body entirely black."[28]

Maupertuis, President of the Berlin Academy of Sciences, proposed a few years after Feijoo's essay a biological explanation of procreation which would explain black skin color without relying on the theory of climate. Sketching a system of conception and generation very much like the modern one in which characteristics are inherited from both male and female, Maupertuis hazarded as a conjecture "que le blanc est la couleur des premiers hommes, & que ce n'est que par quelque accident que le noir est devenu une couleur héréditaire aux grandes familles qui peuplent la zone." Maupertuis felt such an explanation, bordering on the twentieth-century theory of mutations, would eliminate the difficulty of an apparent contradiction between a hereditary explanation of negritude and the account of Genesis, "qui nous apprend que toutes les peuples de la Terre sont sortis d'un seul père & d'une seule mère."[29]

There seems to be little doubt that the need to consider Adam as the single ancestor of all mankind had a great influence, perhaps the decisive one, on Feijoo's adopting the opinion that skin color is caused by climate.

In his *Mapa intelectual y cotejo de naciones*, as we have already seen, Feijoo came to the conclusion that climate does not play a decisive role in determining the intelligence or philosophical acuity of entire nations or peoples; he arrived at this opinion on the evidence of the achievements of actual individuals of particular countries.[30] There may seem to be a paradox in his thought, therefore, that he would reject the influence of climate in regard to intellectual or psychological characteristics, but accept it in regard to physical. He does not in his *Mapa intelectual* actually deny, however, that climate may have a strong influence upon intellectual characteristics, but merely refutes some of the traditional opinions held concerning this influence upon particular nations. The main difference between the two essays is that he relies more on theory than on fact in his *Color etiópico*, but more on fact than theory in his *Mapa intelectual*.

Both essays, however, are remarkable examples of a modern scientific spirit in eighteenth-century Spain. Not only was Feijoo more cautious than Montesquieu in attributing human psychological characteristics to climate, but he followed the most informed medical opinion of his day in attributing physical changes to the particular influence of air.[31] More important, the original evidence he adduced in support of this scientific theory shows him to be with one or two exceptions a respectable representative of his times.

NOTES

1. See Roger Mercier, "La théorie des climats des *Réflexions critiques* à *L'esprit des lois*," *Revue d'histoire littéraire de la France*, LIII (1953), 36.
2. *Teatro crítico*, Vol. VII (1736), Discurso III.
3. No previous study has been devoted to Feijoo's essay, and relatively little attention has been even given to the history of the discussion of Negro color, a very important subject in the history of ideas. It has been touched upon by David Brion Davis in *The Problem of Slavery in Western Culture* (Ithaca, 1966), pp. 450–54. Davis mentions Strabo among the Greeks and summarizes traditions based upon the Koran and

the Talmud. From modern times, he treats English authors primarily, including Purchas' *Pilgrimes*, 1617, and Thomas Browne's *Pseudodoxia Epidemica*, the latter a work known to Feijoo.

4. P. Barrière, *L'Académie de Bordeaux, centre de culture internationale au XVIIIe siècle* (Bordeaux, 1951), pp. 203–5.

5. Louis Armand de Lorn D'Arce, Baron de Lahontan, *Nouveaux voyages de Mr. le Baron de Lahontan* (La Hague, 1703).

6. Feijoo does not in this essay, however, undertake to solve another intriguing problem—where Noah obtained all the animals from the American continent and how these animals returned to America after the flood. This question was raised by Feijoo's French contemporary the Marquise du Châtelet, Voltaire's mistress and collaborator. See Ira O. Wade, *Voltaire* (Princeton, 1969), p. 524.

7. *Curiosum scrutinium nigredinis posterorum Cham id est Æthiopum Aut. Io. Lud. Hanneman* (Kiloni, 1677). Feijoo apparently did not see this treatise in the original, but relied on extracts in *Journal des Sçavans*. [24 juillet 1679, pp. 111–12.] He failed to mention in his own essay that the French periodical cited a "beau traité" by the learned Pecklinius, *De habitu & colore Æthiopum*, which rejects all natural explanations except the principle of generation. Pecklinius is probably the source of the title of Feijoo's essay.

8. "Mémoire sur l'origine des nègres & des américains," novembre 1733. The *Mémoires de Trévoux* was one of Feijoo's major literary and scientific sources, and his enemies accused him of plagiarizing from it. See P. Ramon Ceñal, S.L., "Fuentes jesuíticas francesas de la erudición filosófica de Feijoo," *El P. Feijoo y su siglo* (Oviedo, 1966), II, 285–314. P. Ceñal does not treat the essay *Color etiópico*.

9. The author of the article expresses a theory almost identical with that of Feijoo concerning the population of America, which refutes both the pre-Adamite theory and the theory that Noah's deluge was less than universal. According to this writer, America and Asia were perhaps joined in the past, and possibly even at the time of writing.

10. "Remarques du père Tournemine Jésuite, sur le mémoire touchant l'origine des Nègres. . . ," avril 1734. According to Tournemine, all theories tracing Negroes to punishment by the alteration of inherited racial characteristics are refuted by remarks in Scripture concerning the beauty of the daughters of Cain and Lamech.

11. III (1749), 482–83. Another well-known treatment was that of the German Romanticist Herder, who in his *Ideen zur Philosophie der Geschichte der Menschheit* affirmed that the intense sun of the tropics brings out an oil from the body which produces the thick, soft velvet skin of the Negro, which everybody could have merely by living under the same conditions. The curly hair of the Negro, Herder explained by an abundance of oil in the head (*Sämmtliche Werke*, hg. Bernhard Suphan [1877–1913], 13 Bd., 234). La Condamine, in his *Relation abrégée*, 1745, of his famous expedition to Peru, came to the conclusion that the skin color of Indians is due entirely to climate; Pierre Bou-

guer, a member of the expedition, reached the same conclusion. *Mémoires de l'Académie des Sciences*, 1744, pp. 273–74.
12. *Œuvres*, Moland ed., XI, 16.
13. "Consectario a la materia del discurso antecedente, contra los filósofos modernos."
14. *Recherche de la verité*, II, 7.
15. *Nouveaux essais* (Paris, Flammarion, 1966), p. 262.
16. Feijoo makes no reference whatsoever to Lafitau in *Color etiópico*, but he had discussed his work in some detail in his previous *Mapa intelectual y cotejo de naciones*, Sec. VI.
17. *Œuvres*, Moland ed., XI, 24.
18. Seconde Partie, Sect. 14, 6e ed. (Paris, 1760), p. 230. Du Bos is not mentioned as a source of Feijoo in G. Delpy, *L'Espagne et l'esprit européen*, "Sources étrangères de Feijoo."
19. *Op. cit.*, Seconde Partie. Sec. 14.
20. *Œuvres*, Moland ed., XII, 380.
21. For a discussion of this polemic see the splendid work by Antonello Gerbi, *La disputa del Nuevo Mundo, 1750–1900*, (Milan, 1955).
22. *Key into the Language of America*, Williams, *Writings* (Providence, R.I., 1866), I, 80.
23. *Œuvres*, Moland ed., XII, 357.
24. *History of the Earth and Animated Nature* (1774).
25. *Œuvres*, Moland ed., XI, 7.
26. Arthur Friedman ed., *Collected Works* (Oxford, 1966), III, 74.
27. Quoted by John C. Greene, "The American Debate on the Negro's Place in Nature, 1780–1815," *JHI*, XV (1954), 384–96.
28. *Esprit des lois*, Livre XV, chap. V.
29. *Vénus physique*, Seconde partie, chapitre VI *Œuvres* (Lyon), II, 128.
30. Although Feijoo said nothing concerning Negroes in this essay, his remarks have reference to a famous remark of Fontenelle, "On ne sait . . . si l'on peut espérer de voir jamais de grande auteurs lapons ou nègres" (*Digression sur les anciens et les modernes*). Voltaire later reacted in the manner of Feijoo to this remark by citing the American poetess Phyllis Wheatley.
31. The separation between scientific and literary treatments of the theory of climate on human anatomy was almost total in the eighteenth century. In 1775 J. F. Blumenbach presented at Göttingen a medical thesis on the subject crammed with bibliographical citations. Of the sources which I have mentioned in this article, however, the only ones which Blumenbach cites are the *Mémoires de Trévoux* and Linnaeus. Joann. Frider. Blumenbach, *De Generis Humani Varietate Nativa* (Göttingen, no date on title page). Pages 101–12 concern climate and color. An expanded treatment of the subject appears in a third edition (Göttingen, 1795), pp. 210–22.

Racism in the Old Province of Quebec

Hilda Neatby

No ONE CONTEMPLATING today what is often called the French fact in Canada can be blamed for assuming that the roots of the dangerous and occasionally even violent French-English racial-nationalist confrontation in the modern province of Quebec must have taken hold in the period immediately after the Conquest. Superficial evidence supports this assumption, but recent research is showing the actual situation as more complex than has been supposed and the issues as far from fitting neatly into a racial-nationalist pattern.

It was in the years 1759–60 that a British naval force and British troops operating from bases in the British-American colonies completed the military occupation of the French province on the St. Lawrence and prepared for the events that resulted in surrender of the whole French empire on the mainland in North America to Britain in the peace treaty of 1763. This for Britain was a great but almost embarrassing victory. It necessarily involved London, at a time of great political instability, in a major reorganization of vast territories formerly ruled or claimed by France, territories in which almost every colony along the Atlantic seaboard had its claims and interests, at a period when there was considerable friction among the colonies themselves and a good deal between them and Great Britain.

The necessary reorganization eventually helped to precipitate American armed resistance to Britain in 1775, the American Declaration of Independence in 1776, and the ensuing war which ended in 1783 with recognition of the United States of America.

Meanwhile, Great Britain had in 1763 created on the St. Lawrence a new province destined to be the nucleus of the later Dominion of Canada, the province of Quebec. This province was, roughly, a parallelogram extending along both sides of the St. Lawrence River from a little above the prosperous fur-trading town of Montreal to a little below the older, more dignified, government and military centre of Quebec, an area roughly 700 miles in length and something over 200 in breadth, a considerable extent but trifling compared with the other tremendous continental spaces now ruled by Britain. The province included most of the Canadian settlements which were clustered along the banks of the St. Lawrence and Richelieu Rivers, as well as very considerable tracts of vacant land.

The Royal Proclamation of October 7, 1763, which had created this province, had also, and indeed as its primary purpose, established the tremendous area south of the Lakes, north of the Ohio, and east of the Mississippi, known generally as the Ohio country, as a large Indian reserve. Restless Americans and any others who wanted to settle there were strictly prohibited from entering; they were instead invited to occupy the vacant lands made available in the new province of Quebec and were promised, should they respond to the invitation, "the enjoyment of the benefit" of English law, and an elected assembly as soon as one could be summoned. This historic document, the basis of the first Canadian constitution under British rule, saw the beginning of a problem which has always looked large to Canadians, and has often not been much noticed by Americans—the problem of Canadian-American relations.

Not many frontiersmen or would-be farmer settlers responded to the invitation of the Proclamation, but some hundreds of others did. These were the traders and merchants from Boston, New York, and other American towns, and from London and elsewhere in Britain, all of them eager to supply the army and to take over the fur trade in which, as was well known, merchants on the St. Lawrence had important natural advantages. Some of them no doubt also were interested in buying up seigneuries which might be made available by Canadians who, by treaty, were allowed to sell their property and return to France. On their arrival these new settlers found detachments of British troops at Quebec, Montreal, and elsewhere, troops which had been in occupation since 1760 and had administered the colony until the Proclamation made possible a return to civil law. These troops were also responsible for supplying the network of forts and posts maintained on the Great Lakes and in the Ohio country. The newcomers also found an English Governor, or rather a Scottish one, General James Murray, and a few English-speaking officials. Apart from these their neighbours were the "new subjects," some 65,000–75,000 Canadians, the name then and for several generations later applying only to the ancient settlers, the French-speaking inhabitants of the former colony of New France.

This was the first contact, as fellow-citizens or fellow-subjects, of the French and English, who for a century and a half had been neighbors, and often bitter foes, in eastern North America. There were of course misunderstandings and tensions which were very obvious and which were given sufficient prominence at the time to make it natural for historians to adopt a simple French-English pattern as the theme of Canadian history from 1760 onward.

Canadians, so goes the story, first met the conquering army from Britain and found it surprisingly humane, benevolent, and tolerant of all their ways—their language, their laws and their relgion. The later introduction of civil government in 1764, though vexatious in some ways, left them still with the humane soldier—Governor Murray. Meanwhile, however, they witnessed an influx of English and American merchants, who (no doubt unthinkingly) treated Quebec as an English province and demanded that Murray establish English law courts, summon an elected assembly, presumably English-speaking and Protestant, and recognize more fully the place of the Church of England as the established Church. Murray, generous defender of Canadian claims, resisted and with his officials headed what came to be called the "French party" to oppose these English demands.

According to this version of history Murray's successor, Guy Carleton, continued to support and indeed to invigorate the French party, and secured that key piece of legislation the Quebec Act of

1774 as a "French Canadian charter." The Quebec Act was indeed a remarkably tolerant piece of legislation in its concessions to a conquered people: it recognized Canadian civil law; it recognized the generous concessions already made in practice to the Roman Catholic worship and discipline; it instituted a special oath of office which would give Roman Catholics the civil equality not to be enjoyed by their co-religionists in England or Ireland until 1829; and it conceded that an assembly would be for the present "inexpedient." A concession to English merchants was the redrawing of the boundary of this formerly restricted province to include the enormous area of the Ohio country and the area surrounding the Great Lakes as far as the height of land which divided them from the Hudson Bay. The colonies to the south were outraged by the Act, and particularly by this provision, but that is another story. The English and Americans in Quebec protested at the provisions as an infringement of the rights promised them in the Proclamation of 1763 and, in practice, as injurious to commerce in its substitution of Canadian for English civil law.

For the next fifteen years the English demanded modifications, particularly the granting of an elected assembly and of at least some English commercial law. The "French Party" resisted successfully for about ten years, until the end of the American Revolutionary War and the arrival in the province of thousands of displaced loyalists made it essential to consider some changes. As a result, after due consideration, the province, already greatly reduced by the concession of the Ohio country to the new United States of America, was divided, each part receiving an assembly. Surprisingly, the Canadians, who had supposedly been rejecting everything English in favour of their traditional institutions, took to the English ways as ducks to water and were soon dominating the assembly of the new province of Lower Canada, to the confusion of English merchants and English governors.

It has long been recognized that this French-English pattern, with English officials sponsoring the helpless French majority against the assimilating energies of the English, does not completely fit the facts. It was based on the official correspondence and legal documents most readily available to historians and these suited the nineteenth-century political national approach well enough. Even this interpretation, however, does not offer much suggestion of racial nationalism. There was, indeed, no tradition of race in New France as such. The Indians were referred to as *sauvages* but "*sauvages*" is a gentle enough word, and it was hoped that they would be converted to Christianity. The English were "heretics," but English children captured in Indian raids were rescued by the French, treated well, and converted in many instances. Racism appears, as one would expect, in relation to slaves. It is indeed something of a shock to find a Canadian merchant, charitable, kind, affectionate, and upright, bemoaning the love affairs carried on by his Negro servant in the attic, and regretting that the law forbade the surgical operation which was to him the only obvious remedy; or trying to sell his little *panise*—too attractive for the peace of mind of the Negro—to some trader of the West Indies. "Anybody would be glad to have her as she is so pretty."[1] There were, however, only a few thousand slaves in the whole history of New France. A recent historian sets the French-English pattern aside altogether. This perhaps goes too far, but it is important to bear in mind that New France and its successor the old province of Quebec was an eighteenth-century colony, an integral part of a Western civilization not yet subjected to the violent national and racial patterns of the nineteenth and twentieth centuries.

What struck the soldier-governors, apart from the fact that the Canadians were a likeable people needing protection from the representatives of a conquering nation, was that this was a society ordered and decent, apt to fight but willing to obey, delightfully unlike the turbulent American colonies, who generally would neither fight nor obey. These saw in New France a kind of Roman colony, a placid but potent mass of habitants ranged in orderly obedience under priests and seigneurs. And one of them, Guy Carleton, who partly planned and chiefly implemented the Quebec Act, seems to have decided that this was a better kind of colony than Britain had ever devised. It was not merely that Carleton was willing and anxious to protect conquered Canadians against English bullying; he was moved at least equally by an admiration for the kind of government and society that he thought he saw in Quebec, and he wanted to preserve and maintain it as good for Canadians, good for English, and good for the British empire in North America.

Unfortunately for Carleton's conclusions, he and the historians who have concentrated on his early dispatches overlooked a very important group of people. Canadians were not confined to priests, seigneurs, and habitants. There was a small but very significant class of Canadian townsmen: merchants, traders, and a few professionals. They were not powerful economically. Within a few years, for example, although their numbers were fewer, the English had decidedly the larger investment in the fur trade, a development to be expected since the richer Canadian merchants, indeed all Canadians who could afford it, had returned to France.[2]

The Canadians who remained, however, were culturally and politically significant. They were not merely literate; they had positive intellectual tastes and political interests. When the Loyalists arrived in the country after the American Revolution, they spoke much of the illiteracy of the Canadians in contrast to the English, who maintained the Protestant tradition of literacy as a religious and moral duty. Yet the increasingly numerous Canadian merchants and professional men who could read generally made a serious business of it. In the 1770's one young merchant, ambitious and very busy, wrote to France to order the works of Voltaire, Rousseau, "and other good writers"; another accepted with gratitude a French edition of Blackstone from the English Lieutenant-Governor; a third, apparently after very little formal schooling, in letters written throughout his long life made frequent references to more or less serious reading and showed the fruits of it in his reflections and also in his increasingly mature and effective style of writing.[3]

Some of these Canadian townsmen owned seigneuries, or intermarried with seigneurial families. They might share in some measure the seigneurial outlook, and they did not necessarily like or trust the English entirely. When certain of the English merchants in 1764 had launched a rather bitter attack on Murray and his policy through a Grand Jury presentment, a Canadian merchant, alarmed at an apparent hostility to Roman Catholic rights and the Canadian law, wrote, "If we are not careful they will destroy our nation." At the same time, while joining in petitions for concessions to Canadians, these men were very far from supporting the seigneurial demands for a "national charter," "sacred and inviolable," which should forever preserve the mummified structure of New France.[4]

As early as 1765 a Canadian writer to the Quebec *Gazette* asked to be instructed in the true nature of the English liberties and rights of which he had heard so much and which as a British subject he now hoped to enjoy. Although there is a faint suggestion that this particular letter may have been written with tongue in cheek, it may have been genuine; and there is no doubt that the *Gazette*, a bilingual publication, offered a steady diet of articles on English rights and liberties to its Canadian readers.[5] Moreover, in Montreal in 1766 there was a serious protest of Canadian and English merchants against an informal "assembly" that had gathered there to discuss Canadian problems; the merchants protested that it was composed of seigneurs only, and yet professed to speak for "the nation." On this occasion the merchants, Canadians and English, demonstrated together and tried to gain access to the meeting. When this was forbidden, forty-one of them, fifteen English and twenty-six Canadians, literally registered, in notarial instruments, two protests, one English and the other French, asserting the bad effect of a so-called representative meeting which did not include both Canadians and English, merchants and seigneurs.[6]

It was not the Canadian merchants alone, however, but a legal pundit (who was also a small seigneur) who, when the Quebec Act was under consideration, organized some of his fellow seigneurs and some Canadian merchants to prepare a petition for an assembly which would secure to them, as they said, the rights of British subjects and enable them to protect their own laws and customs to an extent that under an appointed council they might not be able to do. The leading seigneurs, however, held aloof, and the English merchants, also asking for an assembly, refused to be as explicit as the Canadians felt it necessary to be in dictating the form of it. Therefore, in spite of interest at both Quebec and Montreal, and of efforts at co-operation, Canadians and English failed to agree, and the formal Canadian petitions which were presented made no mention of an assembly.[7]

As a result the Quebec Act in 1774, representing ostensibly the desires of the Canadians, decreed as has been said that an assembly at the moment was inexpedient. This is not surprising and need not be attributed to current trouble with assemblies along the Atlantic coast, although the authorities were not unaware of these troubles. It would have been difficult, even had the neighbouring colonies been at perfect peace, to turn the colony over to a representative assembly composed chiefly of Canadians, yet an assembly which did not do so would, of course, have been a mockery of Parliament comparable to the one in Ireland: and the English probably thought that one Ireland was enough.

It seems quite certain, however, that in 1774 the Canadians were not united in the rejection of an assembly, and there is good evidence that some at least among the Canadian merchants were dismayed at a government which, professing to meet the wishes of Canadians, gave control to a partnership of the official "French" party and the leading seigneurs. Chief Justice Hey, who had been on leave in England, arrived in the province just after the Act came into force in May, 1775. He wrote a number of letters home during the summer and fall, giving his impression of the Canadian reception of the Act. He noted that, contrary to Governor Carleton's expectations, the Canadians had not, in their gratitude, taken up arms to repulse the invading Americans. As he said, in complete astonishment, he must attribute the fact partly to pure ignorance preyed on by "malignant minds"—no doubt American ones. In addition, he saw clearly, and apparently for the first time, that the seigneurs as a class were neither liked nor trusted by the habitants. He reported that the Canadians had noted that Canadian members of the newly appointed council were all seigneurs, that these men were boasting foolishly and without cause of the great power now restored to them, and that they "have carried themselves in a manner very offensive both to their own people and to the English."[8]

Fortunately there is also evidence on this matter from Canadians. The strongest comment comes from a Canadian merchant in Quebec, the same one who employed his winter leisure in reading Voltaire, Rousseau, and other good works. He wrote to his business correspondent in Montreal that, largely owing to the activities of the "monsters"—presumably the seigneurs—in Montreal, Canadians would be sorry that they had asked for a change in government; to which his Montreal friend agreed, congratulating him on being a bachelor and free to leave the country if he chose. Another merchant remarked that Canadians might soon find that they had changed "King Log" for "King Stork."[9]

The conclusion must be, I think, that even before the American Revolution, Canadians, although aware of dangers to their language, customs, and religion, were almost, if not quite, as much interested in a social-economic resistance to their own seigneurs as in a cultural-national resistance to the English. Some indeed were beginning to see that the English had very good ideas about liberty and self-government which, with English help, might well be turned to French-Canadian advantage.

The American war, breaking out in 1775 immediately after the coming into force of the Quebec Act, put an end to effective political agitation for the time, but the diligent distribution of American propaganda undoubtedly enlarged Canadian ideas of English liberty, even though Canadians gave no very material assistance to the American invaders. Immediately after the war there is fragmentary but important evidence of political activity splitting the whole Canadian community and allying one section of it more or less with the English against the Governor's "French party." A small but significant incident occurred when the council was debating a piece of legislation long sought by the English but resisted by the official French party: a precise definition of the right of habeas corpus. The French party, in a delaying action, insisted that there must be a clause exempting religious communities from this dangerous privilege. Thereupon from the nuns of the Ursuline convent, cloistered but obviously well briefed on political events, came a message deploring the inclusion of any such unwanted exception. And the Bishop, when applied to, supported the nuns. Meanwhile six English and five Canadian merchants had been jointly but vainly petitioning for admission to the council chambers, that they might hear the debates on this important matter.[10]

Even while this debate was going on in the council, a group of Canadian merchants, privately supported by leaders of the Church but not by the seigneurs, were sending a deputation to England to ask for permission to invite French priests to Quebec to fill the many vacancies in seminaries and parishes. Britain was naturally hostile to any such idea, being convinced that the French priest would always be also a political emissary. What is interesting is the supporting argument offered by the deputation, almost certainly inspired by American teaching and example, and surely not approved by the Canadian clerics, that religious freedom, "a natural right" promised them at the time of the Conquest, must necessarily include the right to choose their own priests.[11]

The failure in this primary demand led directly to another, a renewed petition for an assembly; "our only hope," said one of the disappointed delegates in London, "is in this change."[12] By the fall of 1784, English and Canadian committees were hard at work together on renewed petitions which were presented to the Lieutenant-Governor for transmission to Britain early in 1785. These were followed by counter-petitions against any such measures, which had been diligently circulated by the seigneurial party. Their opponents accused the seigneurs of having claimed as one of their manorial rights the privilege of transcribing to these counter-petitions the names of a number of their reluctant *censitaires*.[13]

The Canadian petitions for an assembly did secure a formidable number of signatures, but their seigneurial opponents presented almost twice as many against the measure. Hugh Finlay, the provincial postmaster who knew the province well, believed that the majority of literate English and literate Canadians wanted an assembly; the habitants he thought were too ignorant to think much of anything except escaping taxes.[14]

Government by assembly was granted in 1791. The province was divided into Lower Canada, which included Quebec, Montreal, and the old established seigneuries, and Upper Canada, composed of the new settlements of the Loyalists. The concession is generally attributed to Loyalist demands and to the penury of Great Britain, bent on local representative institutions because only through them could she now legitimately tax her colonies. During the five or six years preceding this grant, however, the political situation in the colony was involved, and was very far from conforming to an English-French pattern. Canadians were all somewhat resentful of the Loyalist assumption of moral and intellectual superiority, and of their often unconcealed contempt for the Canadian way of life,[15] but the division between Canadian merchants and seigneurs had not been healed by this apparent English threat. On the contrary, fed by all sorts of propaganda from revolutionary France, Canadians were writing to the radical Montreal *Gazette*, pouring contempt on the idle and ignorant seigneurs and even on their priests.[16] Now at last the national theme was beginning to emerge, but less as an attack on the English than as an assertion of the claim of the radical merchant and professional group that they, and not the seigneurs, truly represented *le corps de la nation*. Political and, still more, racial nationalism in Canada attained self-awareness not through the English Conquest, but through the liberal and radical ideas disseminated first by the American and later by the French revolutionaries. These ideas, rejected by the seigneurs as damaging to their social pretensions and economic hopes, were eagerly received by the bourgeoisie and even by some of the clergy.[17]

Meanwhile national distinctions were being reinforced by economic and social factors. The Treaty of Paris (1783) surrendered to the United States the area of the Ohio country, hitherto the preserve of the Quebec fur merchants, both Canadian and English. Henceforth the fur trade became, far more than it had been, a big business requiring extensive partnerships which could command large sums of risk capital. Such enterprises were alien to Canadians, who were generally devoted to the small, secure family business. As a result, the closing years of the eighteenth century and the beginning of the nineteenth century saw great prosperity for Quebec, but for English Quebec alone, since the English now controlled not only the fur trade but also the rapidly growing commerce in timber and wheat. Canadians tended to move into the retail trade, into the professions, and especially into politics. Far from rejecting the assembly, said by the "French party" to be alien to their customs, they swarmed in, took possession, and dominated it with considerable skill and determination, eagerly claiming full parliamentary privileges from the English Governor and from the now predominantly English council. At first linked with some English radicals, they spoke as before in the name of liberty; but, as the eighteenth century moved into the nineteenth and as greater prosperity and closer communications brought them nearer to the intellectual currents of Europe, they began, by a very easy and natural transition, to speak more and more in the name of the Canadian nation.

It is not accurate, then, to see Canadian nationalism as emerging immediately after the Conquest in a homogeneous Canadian society. Canadians in the eighteenth century, like other peoples, were more excited by the new political ideas of liberty and equality than they were by the romantic ideas of nationalism. They were stirred by revolutionary thought before, during, and after the American Revolution. They were greatly stimulated by the French Revolution and by the experience of the English institutions which were given them at the very moment that similar institutions were being introduced into France. By the early nineteenth century a chiefly bourgeois group, which a decade or so before had associated political liberty with the right to import priests from France, was beginning to be touched with anticlericalism and was launching into a true racial-nationalist campaign against the Church, which had heretofore been benevolent, though naturally standing somewhat aside.

The generation after the Conquest has, I believe, been misread. What happened was not a solid confrontation, French against English, with the French "chartered" by the Quebec Act, but a social-political conflict in which the dynamic Canadians joined the English in protesting against the Quebec Act, not because they were not potentially nationalist but because to them the Quebec Act was an instrument of class domination which denied them the one valuable fruit of the English Conquest, political liberty. It was their cooperation in seeking the assembly and in learning to use it for their political purposes, and their increasing awareness of current European thought that led them on to a sense of community and to a possible national fulfillment.

NOTES

1. Public Archives of Canada, Baby Collection, Letters, pp. 2812, 2833, 2860, 2952. (Hereafter cited as PAC Baby Letters.)
2. PAC, CO 42, Vol. XXVII, p. 140, (microfilm of original in Public Records Office); Quebec, Internal Correspondence (S. series) IX, 34;

"Fur Trade Returns, 1767," *Canadian Historical Review*, III (1922), 35; see also Roquebrune, "L'exode des Canadiens aprés 1760," *La Nouvelle Revue Canadienne*, September-October 1953; Neatby, *Quebec: The Revolutionary Age*, p. 22 ff.

3. PAC Baby Letters, pp. 3022, 3300, 5021, 6519, and various other letters of Pierre Guy in this series.

4. PAC, Minutes of the Legislative Council, Vol. E, pp. 171, 178, 204.

5. *Quebec Gazette*, September 26, 1765. Quoted by Pierre Tousignant, "La Genèse et L'Avènement de la Constitution, 1791." Ph.D. Thesis Université de Montréal (unpublished), p. 23 ff. Mr. Tousignant accepts this letter literally, and my own doubt may be without foundation. I am much indebted to this valuable work for a vast amount of new material and new insights into the operation of Canadians who opposed "the French Party" and who did not regard the Quebec Act as a "sacred and inviolable charter."

6. PAC Minutes of the Legislative Council, pp. 128–32; CO 42 Vol. XXVI, p. 22; Archives de L'Archevêché de Québec; Gouvernement, V, 25.

7. PAC Baby Collection, Political Papers, Vol. XL, letter to *Quebec Gazette*, July 21, 1773, Address to His Majesty, July 24, 1773 (p. 30,938); Baby Letters, pp. 3222, 3619; A. Shortt and A. G. Doughty, *Documents Relating to the Constitutional History of Canada*, pp. 504, 507, henceforth cited as S.D. Tousignant, *op. cit.*, p. 132 ff., discusses the Canadian movement in detail.

8. Hey to Dartmouth, July 20, 1775, Dartmouth Papers, Original documents, Vol. III, Part II. An English seigneur confirmed this, writing that the Quebec Act was agreeable only to a dozen of the seigneurs "and, which the Canadians dreaded in bringing them back to that state of apprehension they formerly laboured under in the French government." (H. Caldwell to Barré, September 17, 1775, *ibid.*). See also, Hey to Dartmouth, Aug. 28, 1775, printed in S.D., p. 668.

9. PAC Baby Letters, pp. 3832, 3904, 3906.

10. PAC Minutes of the Legislative Council. Vol. B. p. 159 ff.

11. Archives de L'Archevêché de Québec, Copies des Lettres, IV, 589; Gouvernement, V, 44, 46; PAC M.G. 17.7, Montreal, St. Sulpice, Vol. IV, "1783, Mémoire etablissant le besoin de prêtres Français."

12. Archives de L'Archevêché de Québec Gouvernment, I, 34.

13. See PAC, Baby Letters, pp. 6024–25, for example. This letter refers to an incident of a later seigneurial campaign (1788) against an assembly.

14. PAC, CO 42, Vol. XVIII pp. 101 ff., 160, XL, 311, XXVII, 179 ff., XLVIII, 217, 219, XLLX, 28 ff.; Monk Papers, II 137; Baby Letters, pp. 5234, 5252–53, 5256, 5429, 5521. For a detailed discussion and a list of signatures to the Canadian petition see Tousignant, *op. cit.*, Chap. VI, 3, p. 447 ff. Mr. Tousignant believes that the Canadian petition (1436 signatures) represented a very significant section of the population.

15. PAC, *Quebec Herald*, I, 129 (February 23, 1789).
16. *Montreal Gazette*, July 1, 8, and 29, 1790.
17. *Ibid.*, December 3, 1790, July 7, 1791; *Quebec Herald* II, 376 (October 14, 1790). For clerical radicalism see Neatby, *op. cit.*, p. 242 ff.

The Idea of Racial Degeneracy in Buffon's Histoire Naturelle*

Phillip R. Sloan

I

IN THE HISTORY of eighteenth-century racial speculation, Buffon's *Histoire naturelle, générale et particulière* occupies a position of paradoxical ambiguity. Supplying the Enlightenment with the first fully articulated analysis of man as a natural and primarily zoological phenomenon, a world-wide species whose "natural history" was to be studied in the same terms and categories as that of any other species of animal,[1] Buffon offered a model of a naturalistic and empirical science of man which would leave its deep imprint on scientific anthropology of the succeeding two centuries.[2]

In insisting, as an integral part of this empirical science, that theory be grounded on concrete empirical evidence, Buffon departed from the previous, largely speculative, approach to the question of racial origin and diversity. Against the polygenetic theory deriving from the writings of Paracelsus, Giordano Bruno, and Isaac de la Peyrère, which had provided the backbone of much of the speculation on the origin of the races in the early Enlightenment,[3] Buffon unequivocally asserts that an empirical test, fertile interbreeding, is to stand as the sole criterion of specific identity, taking precedence over all distinctions made on the basis of mor-

* Revised from a paper delivered at the American Society for Eighteenth-Century Studies, annual meeting, March 24, 1972. The author wishes to acknowledge partial support for this research from the University of Washington Graduate School Research Fund, 11-1984. The author also wishes to express his appreciation to Dr. Paul L. Farber for useful comments on an earlier version of the paper.

phology, culture, intellectual achievement, and technological advance:

> Les hommes différent du blanc au noir par la couleur, du double au simple par la hauteur de la taille, la grosseur, la légèreté, la force, &c., & du tout au rien pour l'esprit; . . . mais ces différences de couleur & de dimension dans la taille n'empêchent pas que le Nègre & le Blanc, le Lappon & le Patagon, le géant & le nain, ne produisent ensemble des individus qui peuvent eux-mêmes se reproduire, & que par conséquent ces hommes, si différens en apparence, ne soient tous d'une seule & même espèce. . . .
> Si le Nègre & le Blanc ne pouvoient produire ensemble, si même leur production demeuroit inféconde, si le Mulâtre étoit un vrai mulet, il y auroit alors deux espèces bien distinctes; . . . mais cette supposition même est démentie par le fait, & puisque tous les hommes peuvent communiquer & produire ensemble, tous les hommes viennent de la même souche & sont de la même famille.[4]

But to emphasize only Buffon's strict monogenism, his occasional eloquent outcries against human slavery,[5] and his glimmerings of egalitarianism[6] would be to call attention to only part of the picture. For even though Buffon supplied, in its historically most influential form, the empirical criterion that was seen by many of his contemporaries to break the back of the polygenecist theory,[7] he also used arguments that are cited by later polygenecists in support of their thesis.[8] And if he hints in several places at the fundamental unity of mankind and the basic natural equality of men, explicit statements suggesting his intellectual, physical, and moral inequality could readily be culled by Buffon's contemporaries and successors from the fifteen volumes and supplements of the *Histoire naturelle*.

To discern some intelligible unification of Buffon's thought in the face of the overt ambivalence which a catalog of his statements on the race issue would disclose, Buffon must be read not so much against the background of the main currents of prior racial speculation, from which he departs in significant respects, but rather in terms of his claimed resolution of seemingly remote problems in early eighteenth-century biological science concerned with the generation of organisms. Through the underlying biological theory that stems from Buffon's confrontation with this issue, his speculations on the race question are given a curious unity with far-reaching consequences.

In this paper, I will first summarize in brief the general background of the eighteenth-century problem of generation and its implications for the problem of the historical origin of the races of man. I will then discuss Buffon's theoretical resolution of the question, and the framework which this resolution supplies for a restatement and reinterpretation of traditional theories of racial origin. I will conclude by discussing the evolution in Buffon's thought on certain of these issues, and its connection with his thesis of historical and geographical degeneration of the races.

II

The crisis over the phenomenon of organic generation that arose in scientific circles in the latter half of the seventeenth century took its origin from the failure of the "mechanical" philosophy, in its initial formulations, to supply a satisfactory explanation of the teleological character of biological phenomena, and in particular those presented by the generation and formation of living creatures.[9]

The radical extirpation from nature of all vital faculties and directing substantial forms, which had provided intrinsic efficient and formal causes of the generation of organisms for their Renaissance predecessors, committed the early mechanists, both methodologically and metaphysically, to accounts of generation solely in terms of the twin categories of matter and motion. In their attempts to supply such mechanical accounts of bisexual generation, the early mechanists treating this issue—Kenelm Digby, Henricius Regius, Gassendi, Nathaniel Highmore, and (posthumously) Descartes—had offered accounts which explained the orderly formation and differentiation of the embryo in terms of such material efficient causes as the degree of heat in the uterus of the mother, chemical fermentation reactions, and the transferral of specific amounts of motion in the semen.[10]

These early mechanistic accounts were, however, confronted with difficulties of a theological and empirical nature which served, in effect, to create significant conceptual lacunae within seventeenth-century mechanism over the generation of organisms. On the theological plane, such mechanistic accounts threatened to give to the material world the ability to create by mechanical laws all living things, with man forming no exception. Such a threat to a theistic and providential view of the world was only reinforced by Descartes' banishment of the appeal to final causation from science.

With the empirical refutation by William Harvey in his *Exercitationes de Generatione Animalium* of 1651 of the central material assumption of all these early mechanistic accounts of bisexual generation—the existence of the male and female *semina*, and their combination as the material substrate from which the foetus took its origin—a critical difficulty for the mechanical account of generation was created on the empirical level.[11]

This combination of theological and empirical opposition set the stage in the latter half of the seventeenth century for the one solution to the problem of generation which seemed capable of resolving all the various difficulties while still remaining within the general confines of mechanism, the theory of the preexistence of the embryo. This singular theory, understood either in the panspermist version of the French physician Claude Perrault,[12] or in the famous *emboîtment* version of the Dutch physician Jan Swammerdam and the French philosopher Nicholas Malebranche,[13] resolved the problem of generation simply by denying all actual generation of one creature by another. All generation was instead pushed back to the initial creation of the world, positing that all creatures and all their historical progeny had been created at the moment of the foundation of the world and either dispersed in minute seeds throughout nature, as the panspermists held, or else in its more popular form, encased in the sexual organs of their archetypal parents.

Supported by a complex blend of theological and metaphysical assumptions and seemingly verified by, or at least consistent with, the empirical observations of Harvey, Marcello Malpighi, Niels

Stensen, William Croone, Theodore Kerckring and Anton van Leeuwenhoek, the preexistence theory, in its various forms, was able to achieve a majority, if not a unanimous, endorsement by physicians and biologists of the Continent and England from the 1680's through most of the eighteenth century.[14]

By resolving the problem of the generation of organisms in terms of the preexistence theory, however, the mechanistic biologists and physicians had, in effect, removed man and all other creatures from one central dimension of historical process. In their presumption that all organisms had been created contemporaneously, complete in their fundamental features, the generation of the offspring by its parents in historical time was only an appearance, actually involving nothing more than the stimulation of the growth and unfolding of an already existent embryo. In such a conceptual framework, varieties in food, environment, climate, and geography could at most act only in immediate and superficial ways on each generation, and would be unable to affect in any substantial and permanent way the hereditary characteristics of each natural kind.[15]

As regards the bearing of the above matters on the problem of racial origin and diversity in the context of early Enlightenment thought, the preexistence theory implied conclusions which, if reflected upon at all, could be seen to lead to a position in fundamental opposition to common non-theological accounts of the origin of the races.[16] The ancient environmentalist theory, given influential Renaissance restatement by Jean Bodin,[17] and endorsed by such figures as the Abbé Dubos[18] and John Arbuthnot[19] in the early eighteenth century, presumed a common historical origin of man, with a subsequent diversification into races under the action of climate and migration. In light of the preexistence theory, however, such an account gave no satisfactory explanation of how such factors could produce their presumed permanent hereditary effect on men whose creation and embryonic organization dated from the foundation of the world.[20] The polygenetic theory endorsed, as we have seen above, by numerous intellectuals of the period explained the origin of the races by presuming multiple origins of mankind. This account was, however, incompatible with the preexistence theory once it was combined with the interbreeding criterion of specific identity, as was done by several biologists of the period. The interbreeding criterion, stating that fertile interbreeding takes precedence over morphological or behavioral distinctions in defining the unity of a natural species of organisms, was in rising ascendancy in scientific circles in the early eighteenth century, and had been applied specifically to the question of the unity of the human species by John Ray in 1674.[21] And while the interbreeding criterion could in no sense be considered to be an implication of the preexistence theory, it was fully consistent with it.[22] For the strict preformationists, the question of the origin of the races became, like the question of the origin of the creature itself, one which was ultimately to be resolved by appeal to divine design, forming simply one more ingredient in the providential world view of theocentric mechanism.[23]

To reinsert man into history in a way in which time and circumstance could effect a permanent and cumulative change on his anatomy and physique sufficient to account for the origin of the races was an issue which, at least in scientific circles of the early Enlightenment, hinged on more than simple assertion. With claims in support of a quite literal version of the theory of *emboîtment* continuing to be made by some of the most competent microscopists of the period,[24] a breakthrough in reigning concepts of how man came into being was a critical precondition for the scientific acceptability of a historical and naturalistic theory of the origin of the races by natural process.

As several commentators have pointed out, the controversy that broke out in the early 1740's over the discovery of the phenomenon of regeneration, centering particularly around Abraham Trembley's discovery in 1740 of the regenerative powers of the green hydra, involved much more than an isolated biological observation.[25] With increasing clarity it was perceived by many scientists and intellectuals that to account for these new empirical facts required either a drastic alteration or complete abandonment of the preexistence theory. Coupled with the other difficulties which were by 1740 overburdening the theory—the problem of the origin of monsters, with its attendant theological questions, the difficulty in explaining hereditary resemblance, the issue created by the sterility of hybrids, and certain amounts of simple implausibility—the effect was to send at least a limited number of scientific thinkers in search of an epigenetic theory which could accord with the total body of accumulated empirical observations, and also give at least a nominally mechanistic alternative to the encasement theory.[26] Not accidentally, the two figures to make the primary public rupture with the preexistence theory, Pierre de Maupertuis and his friend and intellectual successor Buffon, were to draw explicit connections between their claimed resolution of the problem of generation in epigenetic terms and the historical origin of the races.

Maupertuis' own brief speculations on the problem of generation, stimulated by his own early experimental work in biology, his reflections on the general difficulties in the preexistence theory, his careful observations on the hereditary transmission of polydactyly in the Ruhe family during his residence in Berlin from 1741–45, and his interest in the possible explanation of the widely-discussed exhibit of negro albinism in Paris in 1744, forms the direct background of Buffon's subsequent theoretical resolution.[27]

Returning for his theory of generation to the Atomist-Hippocratic theory of pangenesis and the doctrine of the male and female *semina*,[28] and summoning now the action of Newtonian attractive forces between analogous particles as the all-important efficient and formal causes of the orderly and sequential formation of the embryo,[29] Maupertuis offers a mechanistic epigenetic theory to replace preexistence, allegedly at least in accord with all relevant empirical data.

With such a theory, and the particulate theory of inheritance that it embodies,[30] Maupertuis assembles the conceptual ingredients for finally integrating a theory of environmental determinism, operating at a reductive level, with an epigenetic theory of development in which man and other organisms are asserted actually to have been created and organized in historical time.

Turning to the question of the origin of the races in the second dissertation of the *Vénus physique* of 1745, Maupertuis suggests that the action of climate and food, acting on the particulate determinants of skin color, might possibly become hereditary through the direct incorporation of these same particles in the male and female semen, and thence into the historical formation of the embryo. With his epigenetic theory, which allows for the impact of historical circumstance into the ancestor-descendant lineage, Maupertuis hints that the gradual but cumulative influence of the environment, operating on the hereditary material transmitted from one generation to another, is a possible explanation of the origin of the races from a common historical root.

The key ingredients of Maupertuis' loose synthesis, combining a return to a mechanistically conceived epigenetic theory of development, a particulate theory of inheritance, the reliance on semi-Newtonian concepts of force and attraction, and the new twist given to classic environmentalism in explaining racial origin, all can be seen to reappear, with significant modification, in Buffon's lengthy analysis of the two questions of generation and the origin of the races in the second and third volumes of his *Histoire naturelle* of 1749.[31] Furthermore, with Buffon we are given an analysis of the issues which in scope, explanatory power, empirical detail, and alleged experimental support reaches far beyond the chatty and popularized discussion of Maupertuis, an analysis progressively integrating the generation of organisms and the origin of the races of man into a general naturalistic cosmological theory.

In his lengthy analysis of the problem of generation, which logically and chronologically precedes his "Histoire naturelle des hommes," Buffon presents a lengthy attack on the preexistence theory, giving both a history of the problem and a discussion of the difficulties the theory was confronting by the late 1740's. In offering his own resolution of the question, a resolution which was admittedly formulated prior to any experimental work, through reflection on the difficulties facing the doctrine of preexistence, Buffon suggests his famous hypothesis that all living creatures are composed of a basically homogenous but particulate *matière vivante*, the so-called *molécules organiques*, constant in total quantity and simply recycled throughout animated nature by assimilation through food and return by excretion and death.[32] As his resolution of the classic problem facing all mechanistic and materialistic epigenetic theories, the explanation of the form and organization

300

of the embryo simply from material particles in motion, Buffon, like Maupertuis before him, summons the activity of Newtonian-type penetrating forces between the organic molecules. Differing significantly from Maupertius' suggestions, however, Buffon's conception of the operation of these attractive forces, setting up veritable type-specific fields of force, provides his theoretical resolution of the problem with a concept of implicit substantial forms, the *moules intérieures*, serving as the ultimate efficient and formal causes of biological phenomena and also as immanent archetypes explaining the existence and permanence of discrete species.[33]

With this set of explanatory entities, relying on an indestructible, recycling, living matter, and the form and organization-giving activity of the internal molds, Buffon claims to be able to render a coherent theoretical explanation of the main phenomena of organic life. Growth and nutrition, on his assumptions, take place through a species-specific sorting and assimilation of appropriate particles from the food through the action of the internal mold. Reproduction is now explained by the assumption that out of the excess of these same *molécules organiques* are formed the male and female *semina*, the particles in these pairing in specific configurations, upon intercourse, through the action of the maternal internal mold, and creating in turn a replicate internal mold to govern the growth and development of the embryo.[34] With suitable modifications, Buffon claims, the theory can explain reproduction in parthenogenetic insects as described earlier by Bonnet and Réaumur and the self-regeneration of Trembley's polyp. Other anomalous empirical phenomena facing the preexistence theory—hereditary transmission and biparental resemblance, the explanation of monsters, the empirical evidence which at least since the observations of Harvey had suggested a serial and epigenetic formation of the embryo, and the problem of the sterility of hybrids[35]—are all, at least implicitly, resolved to Buffon's satisfaction by his theoretical principles.

With the claimed empirical verification of the main predictive consequences of his theory of generation—the existence of a particulate male and female semen, and the presumed demonstration of similar particles in macerations of various organic materials—

through experiments carried out in the spring of 1748 in the company of the microscopist Father John Turbeville Needham and three other competent naturalists,[36] Buffon was provided at the beginning of the writing of the *Histoire naturelle* with a fundamental set of empirical certitudes and an enduring theoretical framework upon which his subsequent speculations on the race issue would subsequently be developed.[37]

III

When Buffon turns to the specific treatment of the origin of the races of man, at greatest length in the "Variétés dans l'espèce humaine" of the third volume, and to a limited extent throughout various articles of the succeeding eighteen years, he offers the progressive development of a highly significant synthesis of ideas, integrating a rather traditional thesis of monogenetic origin and a historical diversification of the races under environmental influence with the underlying reductive materialism of Buffon's biological theory, a theory by then allegedly supported in its main features by concrete empirical evidence.

This synthesis only develops gradually, however, and is at best only implicitly discerned in the discussion of the "Variétés" where one might readily expect it. Here we find Buffon's analysis to be rather traditional in form, making no mention of the role of the *moule intérieure* and the *molécules organiques,* and relying on direct climatic influence as the primary cause of differences in skin color,[38] with unspecified effects of differences in food, rigors of life, and form of social organization to account for the remaining hereditary differences between the races.[39]

The underlying structure of Buffon's biological theory has, however, provided a route by which direct environmentalism, with all its attendant empirical difficulties, could be deemphasized in favor of a more subtle influence of climate, geography, and food, via slight variations in the organic molecules, and hence on the internal mold itself.

The express development of this idea takes place not specifically in the context of the discussion of the races of man, but rather as part of the explanation of the geographical variability within the species of domestic and wild animals, a matter that increasingly occupies Buffon's attention during the course of the *Histoire naturelle*. By defining conspecificity solely in terms of reproductive compatibility, Buffon was forced to confront the general question of geographical variation in a way which had not been appreciated by the preceeding biological tradition. And to do this required some account of variation which reconciled with the implicit essentialism and form-conserving activity of the *moule intérieure*.

The problem is raised immediately with the treatment of the domestic animals opening the *Histoire naturelle des quadrupèdes*, commencing in 1753. In the lengthy article on the horse, Buffon asserts that the first horse has served as the external and internal archetype for all horses past, present, and to come. But he concludes that this archetypal form does not perpetuate itself perfectly unchanged:

> . . . Ce modèle, dont nous ne connoissons que les copies, a pû s'altérer ou se perfectionner en communiquant sa forme & se multipliant; l'empreinte originaire subsiste en son entier dans chaque individu; mais quoiqu'il y en ait des millions, aucun de ces individus n'est cependant semblable en tout à un autre individu, ni par conséquent au modèle dont il porte l'empreinte.[40]

Furthermore, the variation Buffon conceives is not simply individual and random, but is also directional and determinate in direct response to factors related to geography and climate having an indirect influence via the food on the internal mold itself:

> On fait par expérience que des animaux ou des végétaux transplantés d'un climat lointain, souvent dégénèrent & quelquefois se perfectionnent en peu de temps, c'est-à-dire, en un très-petit nombre de générations: il est aisé de concevoir que ce qui produit cet effet est la différence du climat & de la nourriture: . . . le développement de la forme, qui dépend en partie de la nourriture & de la qualité des humeurs, doit donc changer aussi dans les générations: ce changement est à la verité presque insensible à la première génération, . . . mais le jeune animal essuyera, dans un âge tendre & foible les influences du climat, elles lui feront plus d'impression qu'elles n'en ont pû fair sur le père & la mère,

celles de la nourriture seront aussi bien plus grandes & pour-
ront agir sur les parties organiques dans le temps de l'accroisse-
ment, en altérer un peu la forme originaire, & y produire des
germes de défectousités qui se manifesteront ensuite d'une
manière très-sensible.[41]

Although Buffon continues to assert in this and other articles of
this period the operation of "moral" causes as also instrumental in
producing this geographical variation—causes which he sees as
particularly important in the case of man, whose technology and society serve to isolate him from environmental circumstances in
many instances—when he turns to the discussion of the wild animals in Volume Six, it is primarily physical causes that he envisions as operating, creating most importantly a geographical specif-
icity in the organic molecules themselves, and thereby transmitting
its effect through the entire food chain, with effects reaching beyond
the purely anatomical level to that of temperaments as well:

> Et comme tout est soûmis aux loix physiques, que les êtres même
> les plus libres y sont assujétis, & que les animaux éprouvent,
> comme l'homme, les influences du ciel & de la terre; il semble
> que les mêmes causes qui ont adouci, civilisé l'espèce humaine
> dans nos climats, ont produit de pareils effets sur toutes les
> autres espèces: le loup, qui dans cette zone tempérée est peut-
> être de tous les animaux le plus féroce, n'est pas à beaucoup
> près aussi terrible, aussi cruel que le tigre, la panthère, le lion de
> la zone torride, ou l'ours blanc . . . de la zone glacée. Et non
> seulement cette différence se trouve en général, comme si la Na-
> ture, pour mettre plus de rapport & d'harmonie dans ses pro-
> ductions, êut fait le climat pour les espèces, ou les espèces pour
> le climat, mais même on trouve dans chaque espèce en particu-
> lier le climat fait pour les moeurs, & les moeurs pour le cli-
> mat. . . .

> Les végétaux qui couvrent cette terre, & qui y sont encore at-
> tachés de plus près que l'animal qui broute, participent aussi
> plus que lui à la nature du climat; chaque pays, chaque degré de
> temperature a ses plantes particulières; . . . des climats excessifs
> . . . l'on tire les drogues, les parfums, les poisons, & toutes les
> plantes dont les qualités sont excessives: le climat tempéré ne
> produit au contraire que des choses tempérées: les herbes les
> plus douces, les légumes les plus sains, les fruits les plus suaves,

les animaux les plus tranquilles, les hommes les plus polis sont l'apanage de cet heureux climat. Ainsi la terre fait les plantes, la terre & les plantes font les animaux, la terre, les plantes & les animaux font l'homme; car les qualites des végétaux viennent immédiatement de la terre & de l'air; le tempérament & les autres qualités relatives des animaux qui paissent l'herbe, tiennent de près à celles des plantes dont ils se nourrissent; enfin les qualitiés physiques de l'homme & des animaux qui vivent sur les autres animaux autant que sur les plantes, dépendent, quoique de plus loin, de ces mêmes causes, dont l'influence s'éntend jusque sur leur naturel & sur leurs moeurs. . . . Ces changemens ne se font que lentement, imperceptiblement; le grand ouvrier de la Nature est le Temps: comme il marche toûjours d'un pas égal, uniforme & réglé, il ne fait rien par sauts . . . ; & ces changemens, d'abord imperceptibles, deviennent peu à peu sensibles, & se marquent enfin par des résultats auxquels on ne peut se méprendre.[42]

In the article on the stag deer of the same volume, Buffon explains in more detail how this influence of food is conceived:

Ce qu'il y a de plus constant, de plus inaltérable dans la Nature c'est l'empreinte ou le moule de chaque espèce, tant dans les animaux que dans les végétaux. . . . La matière, en général, paroit être indifférente à recevoir telle ou telle forme, & capable de porter toutes les empreintes possibles: les molécules organiques, c'est-à-dire les parties vivantes de cette matiére, passent des végétaux aux animaux, sans destruction, sans altération, & forment également la substance vivante de l'herbe, du bois, de la chair & des os. Il paroit donc à cette première vûe, que la matière ne peut jamais dominer sur la forme. . . . Cependant, en observant la Nature plus particulièrement, on s'apercevra que quelquefois ces molécules organiques ne s'assimilent pas parfaitement au moule intérieur, & que souvent la matière ne laisse pas d'influer sur la forme d'une manière assez sensible: la grandeur, par exemple, qui est un des attributs de la forme, varie dans chaque espèce suivant les differens climats: la qualité, la quantité de la chair, qui sont d'autres attributs de la forme, varient suivant les différentes nourritures. Cette matière organique que l'animal assimile . . . n'est donc pas absolument indifférente a recevoir telle ou telle modification: . . . elle agit donc elle-même par sa propre forme sur celle du corps organisé qu'elle nourrit; & quoique cette action soit presque insensible, . . . il doit en résulter avec le temps des effets très-sensibles.[43]

305

With man in his aboriginal condition more closely analogous (in Buffon's view) to the wild animals than to the domestic, geographically confined, and more directly dependent on endemic and unrefined foodstuffs, his early isolation from the effects of geographical determinism is at best partial.[44]

Armed with such a thesis, we see how Buffon's strict monogenism can become a monogenism with a vengeance. The unity of mankind, given its empirical guarantee by the interbreeding criterion, is still a unity permitting significant and progressive populational divergence within the absolute limits imposed by the *moule intérieure*, creating geographically delimited hereditary lineages within the human species. Furthermore, for Buffon the changes produced by this geographical speciation are always conceived in distinctly valuational terms. Progressive change away from the primitive type is for Buffon primarily, although not exclusively, what it has been for the preceeding tradition—a literal degeneration, imperfection and decline.[45]

The consequences of this developing train of thought are revealed with increasing force as Buffon proceeds towards an integration of his theory of geographical variability and historical degeneration with his developing cosmological theory. In the important articles of the 1760's, wherein he begins to put together the various dimensions of his speculative theories, culminating in the great synthesis of historical geological process, biological development, and cosmology of the *Des époques de la nature* of 1778, Buffon relies on an increasingly naturalistic account of the origin of the organic molecules, now attributing their source to the simple action of light and heat on an original *matière brute*:

> Les molécules vivantes répandues dans tous les corps organisés sont relatives, & pour l'action & pour le nombre, aux molécules de la lumière qui frappent toute matière & la pénètrent de leur chaleur; par-tout où les rayons du Soleil peuvent échauffer la terre, sa surface se vivifie, se couvre de verdure & se peuple d'animaux.[46]

Given such a hypothesis, the abundance, and more importantly, the degree of inherent vitality of the organic molecules becomes a function of temperature and the degree of solar irradiation, variables directly related to the tilt of the earth on its axis, the elevation of the land, and such variables as the degree of cloud cover:

> L'inclinaison de l'axe de la Terre produisant, dans son mouvement annuel autour du Soleil, des alternatives durables de chaleur & de froid, que nous avons appelées *des saisons*. . . . La constitution particulière des animaux & des plantes est relative à la température générale du globe de la Terre, & cette température dépend de sa situation, c'est-à-dire de la distance à laquelle il se trouve de celui du Soleil: à une distance plus grande, nos animaux, nos plantes ne pourroient ne vivre ni végéter; . . . à une distance moindre, elles s'évanouiroient & se dissiperoient en vapeurs: la glace & le feu sont les élémens de la mort; la chaleur tempérée est le premier germe de la vie.[47]

The valuational connotation that Buffon has, from his earliest articles, given to the concept of geographical variation is now interpreted in terms of natural differences in the degree of fertility and vitality of various geographical regions, in direct dependence on cosmological conditions outside any human control. With the influence of such conditions reaching to the very foundation of all organic life, transmitting to the entire food chain a corresponding vitality and vigour, or weakness and degeneracy, Buffon's theoretical principles had supplied a foundation upon which he could subsequently argue for a natural hierarchy of races and human groups as the product of the impersonal forces of nature. As Buffon's later thought reveals, such determining environmental factors do not simply affect the physical level of organisms, but that of temperament and, in man, the level of intellectual achievement and the capacity for cultural advance.

With the temperate climatic conditions of northern Europe and to some extent those of Asia the locus, conveniently enough, of Nature's optimal generative power, at least as far as the human species is concerned, and with this region being, as he will argue in the *Des époques de la nature*, the all-important site of the origin of man,[48] Buffon develops the empirical evidence for a geographical degeneration of man as he has moved from his place of origin into different regions, paralleled in some but, significantly, not all cases by a corresponding degeneration of the other quadrupeds.[49] The most apparent applicability of this theme to the races of man can be seen in the discussion of the degenerate nature of the New World. Here in the East-West direction as well, Nature's creative power is weak and imperfect. It is reflected in the absence of animals of the magnitude of the great cats, rhinos, and elephants in the New World, and in the smaller size of the bison, for example, which Buffon interprets as common to both continents, and is particularly apparent in the degenerate nature of the American aborigine:

> Il y a donc dans la combinaison des élémens & des autres causes physiques, quelque chose de contraire à l'agrandissement de la Nature vivante dans ce nouveau monde; il y a des obstacles au développment & peut-être à la formation des grandes germes; ceux mêmes qui, par les douces influences d'un autre climat, ont recû leur forme plénière & leur extension toute entière, se resserrent, se rapetissent, sous ce ciel avare & dans cette terre vuide, où l'homme en petit nombre étoit épars, errant; où loin d'user en maître de ce territoire comme son domaine, il n'avoit nul empire; . . . & n'existoit pour la Nature que comme un être sans conséquence, un espèce d'automate impuissant, incapable de la réformer ou de la seconder. . . . Car quoique le Sauvage du nouveau monde soit à peu près de même stature que l'homme de notre monde, cela ne suffit pas pour qu'il puisse faire une exception au fait général du rapetissement de la Nature vivante dans tout ce continent: le Sauvage est foible & petit par les organes de la génération; il n'a ni poil, ni barbe, ni nulle ardeur pour la femelle; . . . il est aussi bien moins sensible, & cependant plus craintif y plus lâche; il n'a nulle vivacité, nulle activité dans l'ame; . . . il demeurera stupidement en repos sur ses jambes ou couché pendant des jours entiers. Il ne faut pas aller chercher plus loin la cause de la vie dispersee des Sauvages & de leur éloignement pour la société: la plus précieuse étincelle du feu de la Nature leur a été refusée.[50]

This geographical degeneracy which Buffon sees the human species to exhibit in any direction away from Europe, is, through its explanation in terms of his reductive categories, cumulative, historically progressive, and irremedial in any short duration of time.

To effect a restoration of the degenerate races to the purity and vigor of the original type, Buffon argues that a veritable transplantation of these peoples to the temperate zones, a change of diet, and a long expanse of time would be required.[51] And, with the possibility raised in the "Nomenclature des signes" of 1766 that the orang-outang might simply be the most degenerate of men, one step beyond the Hottentot[52]—a possibility which is, to be sure, rejected on the basis of Buffon's residual Cartesian dualism[53] and the empirical guarantee of the interbreeding criterion[54]—an indication may be drawn as to the gap which Buffon sees to have arisen between the European and African races through the degenerative process, in spite of their biological conspecificity.

If Buffon does not openly condone human slavery, it is, I would conclude, for reasons inconsistent with the logical consequences of his theoretical principles, and such reasons, if they are to be found at all, must be sought in those dimensions of his thought which prevent him from drawing a completely materialistic interpretation of man.[55] The weak and vitiated savage peoples have neither the power to improve themselves, nor, because of their degenerate condition, can they bring about the technological domination of nature that Buffon sees as imperative if European man is to escape similar geographical determinism as he migrates to the tropics and the New World.[56] Such peoples are but excess baggage on the earth, contributing nothing to its control, and by implication at least, would either have to be eliminated or else made instruments of labour in the immediate technological advance of man.[57]

Even granted a strict monogenetic origin of mankind, such conclusions are latent in Buffon's thought. And with the weakening at his own hands, in the latter volumes of the *Histoire naturelle*, of the keystone of his monogenism, the universal validity of the interbreeding criterion, Buffon effectively removes the one thing separating him unequivocally from the polygenecists. Buffon, by suggesting in the "Dégénération des animaux" of Volume XIV— an article which ostensibly opens with a proclamation of the biological unity of the human species—that perhaps the interbreeding criterion is not universally valid,[58] and by then arguing in the

"Nomenclature des signes" of the same volume that fertile crosses of Negroes and apes have taken place and entered both lineages,[59] creates an overt ambiguity that will quite understandably provide an opening for his data to be used to advantage by polygenecists,[60] and that will supply scientific support for a return by some scientists to a morphological criterion of species, with its latent polygenecist consequences.

More significant than any support his later writings may have given to a revitalization of polygenecism was, however, that he had really rendered polygenecism and Biblical curses unnecessary as rationalizations for racial domination. Through his break with the ahistorical assumptions of the preexistence theory, Buffon had suggested within a scientifically respectable context the means by which a naturalistic view of man, a scientific materialism, and a secular philosophy of history could be synthesized with traditional ideas of geographical determinism and historical degeneration, with the action of general physical and historical causes deemed a sufficient explanation of the origin of a presumed invidious hierarchy of races and peoples. Similar combinations of the same intellectual ingredients, if not the specifics of Buffon's biological theory, reappear in the anthropological treatises of Kant,[61] John Hunter,[62] Blumenbach,[63] and Lacépède,[64] with Buffon's influence apparent on each of these works.

Perhaps of primary importance, however, in assessing Buffon's significance in the spectrum of racial speculation of the eighteenth and early nineteenth centuries is a more general dimension of his thought. Notable about the anthropological treatises from the 1770's onward, whether the author be a monogenecist or polygenecist, physiologist or anatomist, pro- or antislavery, is the presumption that the central issues in the race question are empirical issues, questions in which anatomical data, physiology, zoogeographical analysis, and tests on the interbreeding criterion are presumed to be decisive, taking precedence over all philosophical, ethical, and theological tenets.[65] And it seems to have been Buffon's analysis and empirical approach to the question, posing problems which animal breeders, zoogeographers, natural historians, and anatomists could presumably solve, presenting these in a work rivalling the *Encyclopédie* in general dissemination,[66] which was able to produce most significantly this transition to an empirical level of argument.

With such assumptions guiding the anthropological writings of the succeeding decades, not surprisingly the answers the empirical data could supply were totally ambiguous, lending support to any conclusions the various scientists wished to read into them.

NOTES

1. As Buffon summarizes the approach to characterize his natural history: "L'histoire d'un animal doit être non pas l'histoire de l'individu, mais celle de l'espèce entière de ces animaux; elle doit comprendre leur génération, le temps de la pregnation, celui de l'accouchement, le nombre des petits, les soins des pères & des mères, leur espèce d'éducation, leur instinct, les lieux de leur habitation, leur nourriture, la manière dont ils se la procurent, leurs moeurs, leurs ruses [et] leur chasse. . . . *"Histoire naturelle, générale et particulière, avec la Description du Cabinet du Roi* (Paris: Imprimerie Royale, 1749–67), (1st series) "Premier discours" I, 30. All references will be made to this edition, now generally available in the *Landmarks of Science* microprint series (New York: Readex Microprint). Most of Buffon's references can also be found in: *Oeuvres philosophiques de Buffon,* ed. J. Piveteau (Paris: Presses universitaires de France, 1954).
2. As Pierre Flourens writes in 1847: "Anthropology sprung from a great thought of Buffon. Up to his time man had never been studied, except as an individual; Buffon was the first who studied the species." P. Flourens, "Life of Blumenbach," in: J. F. Blumenbach, *The Anthropological Treatises,* trans. T. Bendysche (London: Longman & Green, 1865), p. 55. Compare to similar assements in Cuvier's *Histoire des sciences naturelles* (Paris: Fortin, Masson et Cie, 1845), IV, 173.
3. On the origins of the polygenetic theory, see R. H. Popkin, "The Pre-Adamite Theory in the Renaissance," (in press, Paul O. Kristeller *Festschrift,* 1973). I wish to thank Professor Popkin for allowing me to see a manuscript of this paper. See also M. T. Hodgen, *Early Anthropology in the Sixteenth and Seventeenth Centuries* (Philadelphia: Univ. of Pennsylvania Press, 1964), pp. 272–76. Endorsements of variants of the polygenecist theory can be seen in Hume, "Of National Characters" (1748), n. 4, reprinted in: D. F. Norton and R. H. Popkin (eds.), *David Hume : Philosophical Historian* (Indianapolis: Bobbs-Merrill, 1965), p. 47; Voltaire, *Traité de métaphysique* (1734), chap. 2, in *Oeuvres complètes* (nouvelle ed.) (Paris: Garnier Frères, 1879), XXII, 191–93; Guillaume Rei, *Dissertation sur l'origine des negres* (Lyons: 1744), cited by W. Scheidt, "Der Begriff der Rasse in

der Anthropologie," *Archiv fur Rassen- und Gesellschaftsbiologie* XV (1924), trans. (in part) in E. W. Count, *This Is Race* (New York: H. Schuman, 1950), p. 378; Benoît de Maillet, *Telliamed* (1748), trans. anon., (London: Osborne, 1750), p. 255.

4. "De l'asne," H.N., IV (1753), 387–89. See also "Le Chèvre," H.N., V (1755), 60. The earliest statement of the criterion in Buffon's writings is at the beginning of the "Histoire générale des animaux," H.N., II (1749), 10–11. A lengthy passage from "De l'asne," without specific citation of the passage relating to man, forms the substance of the article "Espèce: histoire naturelle" of Diderot's *Encyclopédie* (V [1755], 956–57). See also article "Humaine espèce," *Encyclopédie* VIII (1765), 348.

5. See "Variétés dans l'espèce humaine," H.N. III (1749), 469.

6. *Ibid.*, pp. 492–93.

7. Buffon's arguments in favor of a unitary origin of man, with the races conceived as originating by subsequent diversification under differing environmental conditions, were regarded as conclusive by many of his contemporaries. See review of *Histoire naturelle* in M. Freron, *Lettres sur quelques écrits de ce tems*, nouv. ed. (London: Duchesne, 1752), IV, 98–99. See also "Humaine espèce," *Encyclopédie*, VIII (1765), 348.

8. See note 60, below.

9. For a full account of the issues summarized here, the reader is referred to the profound study of Professor Jacques Roger, *Les Sciences de la vie dans la pensée française du XVIIIe siècle: la génération des animaux de Descartes a l'Encyclopédie*, 2nd ed. (Paris: Colin, 1971). Aspects of these problems are also treated in depth in H. B. Adelmann, *Marcello Malpighi and the Evolution of Embryology* (Ithaca, N.Y.: Cornell University Press, 1966), esp. vol. II; and E. Gasking, *Investigations into Generation: 1651–1828* (Baltimore: Johns Hopkins Press, 1967).

10. K. Digby, *Two treatises, in the one of which the Nature of Bodies, in the other the Nature of Mans Soule is looked into* (Paris: Blaizot, 1644); H. Regius, *Fundamenta physices* (Amsterdam: Elzevir, 1646); N. Highmore, *The History of Generation* (London: J. Martin, 1651); Descartes, *De la formation du foetus*, appended to the second (French) edition of the *Traité de l'homme*, ed. Clerselier (Paris: Girard, 1664). On each of these accounts, see Roger, *op. cit.*

11. The theory of the formation of the foetus from two analogous seeds, drawn from the body and collected in the testes of the male and the *testes foeminae* (ovaries) of the female, is presumed in the ancient accounts of generation offered by Hippocrates, Democritus, Lucretius, and in a modified form by Galen. These stood in opposition to the Aristotelian theory of sexual generation, which assumed the formation of the embryo to take rise solely from material supplied by the female, with the male contributing only the immaterial substantial form. Harvey regarded his observations to have refuted both theories. On Har-

vey's refutation, see Gasking, *op. cit.,* chap. 2. Harvey's observations were frequently cited by opponents of the mechanical theories of generation. See, for example, John Ray, *The Wisdom of God Manifested in the Works of the Creation,* 2nd ed. (London: Innys, 1692), p. 32.

12. Perrault, *Essais de physique* (1680). See Roger, *op. cit.,* pp. 334–44.
13. Swammerdam, *Historia insectorum generalis* (Utrecht, 1669); Malebranche, *Recherche de la vérité* (1674), Bk. I, chap, 2. For a recent analysis of the origins of the preexistence theory, see P. J. Bowler, "Preformation and Pre-existence in the Seventeenth Century; A Brief Analysis," *J. Hist. Biol.* IV (1970), 221–44.
14. Although the concept of the literal preexistence of a fully-formed miniature organism was modified by many scientists by the 1740's (Roger, *op. cit.,* pp. 318–22), endorsements of highly literal versions of the theory can be encountered at mid-century and beyond. See, for example, Henry Baker, "The Discovery of a Perfect Plant *in Semine,*" *Phil. Trans. Roy. Soc. Lond.* XLI (1739), 448–55. See also Richard Mead, *Medical Precepts and Cautions,* trans. T. Stack (London: Brindley, 1751). As Mead writes: "The animalcula which by the help of microscopes we discover swiming [sic] in the *semen masculinum,* are really little men; which being received into the womb, are there cherished as in a nest, and grow in due time to a proper size for exclusion" (pp. 10–11).
15. As Roger remarks: "Dans la theorie de la préexistence . . . touts les êtres vivants, morts, présents ou à naître, sont en réalité tous contemporains de la Création, tous indépendants les uns des autres. . . . La préexistence exclut le temps, exclut tout idée d'une histoire de la vie." Roger, *op. cit.,* p. 389.
16. This is not to deny the presence of certain important counterinstances to this assertion. Leibniz, as a notable example, gave his endorsement to a highly literal version of the pre-existence theory at the same time that he expounded elsewhere a rather traditional theory of racial origin by climatic influence. See his "New System of Nature and of the Communication of Substances" (1695), trans. in Leibniz, *Selections,* ed. P. P. Wiener (New York: Scribners, 1951), pp. 109–10, and compare with "Lettre à M. Sparvenfeld," *Otium Hanoverano* (1696) in *Opera Omnia* (Geneva: De Tournes, 1768), V, 545.
17. On Bodin's environmentalism with reference to anthropology, see Hodgen, *op. cit.,* chap. 7.
18. J. B. Dubos, *Réflexions critiques sur la poésie et sur la peinture* (1719), as summarized by Hodgen, *op. cit.,* p. 486, and H. Vyverberg, *Historical Pessimism in the French Enlightenment* (Cambridge, Mass.: Harvard Univ. Press, 1958), chaps. 14, 17.
19. J. Arbuthnot, *An Essay Concerning the Effects of Air on Human Bodies* (London: J. Tonson, 1733), pp. 146–48. I wish to acknowledge my debt to remarks of Professor A. O. Aldridge in his paper "Father Feijóo and the Question of Race in the Eighteenth Century," delivered at the annual meeting of the *American Society for Eigh-*

teenth-Century Studies, 24 March 1972, for leading me to this reference.

20. Significant empirical arguments against the environmentalist theory had also been raised with the demonstration by Sanctorius, Malpighi, and other anatomists of the anatomical basis of Negro skin color. In Barrère's treatise on the subject in 1741 (*Dissertation sur la cause physique de la couleur des Nègres* [Paris: Simon, 1741] as summarized in the unsigned review in the *Journal des Sçavans*, CXXXII [May, 1742], 23–45), this is considered a decisive refutation of the environmentalist theory, and Barrère asserts that ". . . c'est l'opinion généralement reçue que dans le germe des corps des animaux se trouvent comme concentrées toutes les parties qui les composent avec leur figure & leur couleur determinées." (Barrère, as quoted in review, p. 39.) More general empirical arguments against environmentalism as a cause of the origin of the races are raised by Robert Boyle (*The Experimental History of Colours Begun* in *Works*, ed. T. Birch [London: Mill, 1744], II, 34–47), and in an unsigned article sometimes attributed to Francois Bernier ("Nouvelle division de la terre, par les differentes espèces ou races d'hommes . . . ," *Journal des Scavans* XII [April, 1687], 150) in terms of the hereditary permanence of racial characteristics in different climates.

21. John Ray, "A Discourse on the Specific Differences of Plants," read to the Royal Society in 1674 and published in T. Birch, *The History of the Royal Society* (London: Millar, 1756), II, 171. The interbreeding criterion can be traced in an elliptical form to Aristotle (*Generation of Animals*, 746a 30, and *History of Animals*, 491a 1–5). The interbreeding criterion, although without specific reference to the race question, is also stated by Ray in his influential *The Wisdom of God*, p. 7, and by the preformationist Réné Réaumur (*Memoires pour servir à l'histoire des Insectes* [Paris: Imprimerie royale, 1736], II, xl), and is implicitly endorsed by Linnaeus in his early writings (see his *Critica botanica* [1737], trans. A. Hort [London: Ray Society, 1938], aphs. 270–71, p. 150). Although, following his discovery of *Peloria* in 1741, Linnaeus came to accept the production of new species by genuine interspecific hybridization, he refused to extend this conclusion, with its polygenecist consequences, to the origins of the human races, a possibility readily suggested by his inclusion of the Orang-outang in his genus *Homo* (see his *Metamorphoses Plantarum* [1755], quoted in E. Callot, *La Philosophie de la vie au XVIIIe siècle* [Paris: Rivière, 1965], p. 428). Buffon stands as unique within this tradition, however, in insisting upon the interbreeding criterion as the *sole* criterion of specific identity and distinction.

22. Preexistence theory, by itself, does not, to be sure, necessarily imply a monogenetic conclusion, and Voltaire, for example, could endorse both polygenecism and the preexistence theory (see Roger, *op. cit.*, p. 733). Carried to its extreme conclusion, the preexistence theory could not only suggest that the races of men comprised distinct species, but even

that each individual is a separate species. (See, for example, Charles Bonnet, *Contemplation de la Nature* [1764] in *Oeuvres d'Histoire naturelle et de philosophie* [Neuchatel: Fauche, 1774] IV, 131.) Bonnet, writing after Buffon's statement of the interbreeding criterion, immediately clarifies his suggestion, however, so as to be taken as implying only that there are infinite *varieties* within the human species as defined by the interbreeding criterion (*ibid.*, p. 130 n; see also p. 287).

23. As Maupertuis summarizes the consequences of the preexistence theory for the race question in 1745: "If all men began by being formed from one egg inside another, there must have been in the first mother eggs of different colors. These must have contained an innumerable series of the same kinds of eggs, to hatch only in their proper order of development, after a number of generations and at the time Providence had intended for the origin of the peoples so contained. . . . Were we to accept the system of animalcules and say that all men had been originally contained inside the animals swimming in the first man's semen, we would have to repeat about animacules what we have said about eggs." Maupertuis, *The Earthly Venus*, trans. S. B. Boas (New York: Johnson Reprint, 1966), pp. 69–70. See also Roger, *op. cit.*, pp. 215–16.

24. For example, Henry Baker; see n. 12, above.

25. See C. W. Bodemer, "Regeneration and the Decline of Preformationism in Eighteenth Century Embryology, "*Bull. Hist. Med.* XXXVIII (1964), 20–31. See also A. Vartanian, "Trembley's Polyp, La Mettrie and Eighteenth Century Materialism," *J. Hist. Ideas* XI (1950), 259–86; and *idem, Descartes and Diderot: A Study of Scientific Naturalism in the Enlightenment* (Princeton: Princeton Univ. Press, 1953), chap. 4.

26. The major embryologists of the mid-eighteenth century—Haller, Bonnet, Trembley, Réaumur, and Spallanzani—opted for a modification of the preformation theory. See Bodemer, *op. cit.*, and Gasking, *op. cit.*

27. Maupertuis' theory is proposed in his two pseudonymous, partially identical treatises, the *Dissertation physique à l'occasion du nègre blanc* (Leyden, 1744) and its expanded version, the *Vénus physique* (The Hague, 1745). In spite of its title, the first treatise has neither a discussion of albinism nor of the origin of the races, which are only taken up in the second section of the *Vénus*. On Maupertuis' theory of epigenesis and generation, see Roger, *op. cit.*, pp. 468–87; B. Glass, "Maupertuis, Pioneer of Genetics and Evolution," in *Forerunners of Darwin: 1745–1859*, ed. B. Glass, O. Temkin, and W. L. Strauss (Baltimore: Johns Hopkins, 1959), chap. 3; E. Callot, *La Philosophie de la vie au XVIIIe siècle* (Paris: Rivière, 1965), chap. 4; and Gasking, *op. cit.*, chap. 6.

28. See note 11, above. Harvey's refutation of the "two seeds" theory had lost much of its force with the discovery of the microscopic size of male spermatozoa. See Maupertuis, *op. cit.*

29. For brief remarks on the use of Newtonian attraction in eighteenth-

century embryology, with direct reference to Maupertuis and Buffon, see A. E. Gaissinovich, 'Le Rôle du Newtonianisme dans la renaissance des idées épigénétique en embryologie du XVIIIe siècle," *Actes XIe Cong. Int. Hist. Sci.* V (1968), 105–10.

30. The particulate theory of inheritance assumes that hereditary characters are governed by the transmission of determinate material particles, transmitted from one generation to the next. See remarks in Glass, *op. cit.*

31. On the testimony of Buffon's collaborator in his famous experiments, Father John Turbeville Needham, Buffon had frequently discussed the question of generation with Maupertuis (Needham, "A Summary of some late Observations upon the Generation, Composition, and Decomposition of Animal and Vegetable Substances," *Phil. Trans. Roy. Soc. London* XLV [1750], [633]).

32. I am avoiding here discussion of certain complexities in Buffon's initial statements on the *molécules organiques* in which Buffon seems to hold to a theory of species-specific and structure-specific molecules for each kind of animal (see Roger, *op. cit.*, pp. 544–45). By 1753, however, Buffon had largely abandoned this possibility in favor of a generally homogeneous conception of the organic molecules, with the internal mold responsible for all form and structure. See "Le Boeuf," H.N IV (1753), 437 and "Le Cerf," H.N. VI (1756), 87.

33. For a detailed analysis of the concept of the internal mold, and its relation to both the problem of generation and Buffon's concept of species, see Paul L. Farber, "Buffon's Concept of Species," (unpublished dissertation, Indiana University, 1970), chaps. 5–6, and my own dissertation, "The History of the Concept of the Biological Species in the Seventeenth and Eighteenth Centuries, and the Origin of the Species Problem" (unpublished dissertation, University of California, San Diego, 1970), chap. 6.

34. "Histoire générale des animaux," H.N. II (1749), 341.

35. In light of the importance of this issue for the preformationists (see Roger, *op. cit.*, pp. 386–90), it is somewhat surprising that Buffon never makes fully explicit the connection between hybrid sterility and his concept of the *moule intérieure*, although this connection is certainly implicit in the discussions in "De l'asne." It would follow, as a direct consequence of Buffon's analysis of the *moule intérieure*, that the failure of interspecific crosses, or the sterility of hybrids when crosses are successful, would have an almost mechanical explanation in terms of Buffon's theory. In such a case, the pairing of analogous particules shed from the various parts of the body would either not take place in proper order, through variations in their respective forces of attraction, or else the hybrid internal mold of the mule would be incapable of self-perpetuation. In his later explanations of hybrid sterility, however, Buffon offers only more routine anatomical and physiological explanations (see "De la dégénération des animaux," H.N. XIV [1766] 336 ff.).

36. Buffon's assistants on the experiments, in addition to Needham, included the anatomist and subsequent collaborator on the *Histoire naturelle*, Louis Daubenton, the naturalist Gueneau de Montbeillard and the botanist Thomas Dalibard.

37. As Buffon expresses his conviction at the conclusion of the experiments: "Il est clair pour quiconque entendra bien le système que nous avons établi . . . & que nous avons prouvé par des expériences, . . . que la reproduction se fait par la réunion de molécules organiques renvoyées de chaque partie du corps de l'animal ou du végétal; . . . que les mêmes molécules qui servent à la nutrition & au dévéloppement du corps, servent ensuite à la reproduction; que l'une & l'autre s'opèrent par la même matière & par les mêmes loix. Il me semble que j'ai prouvé cette vérité par tant de raisons & de faits, qu'il n'est guère possible d'en douter. . . . ("Histoire générale des animaux," H.N. II [1749], 332). Buffon's adherence to the fundamental tenets of his theory from this point onward will prove to be one of the most enduring aspects of his biological thought.

38. "Variétés dans l'espèce humaine," H.N. III (1749), 526 ff. Buffon attempts to circumvent the empirical difficulties raised by Barrère, Boyle, and Bernier (see n. 20, above) against simple environmentalism by claiming that the uniformity of climate throughout the New World is the explanation of the uniformity of color of the aborigines of the New World.

39. *Ibid.*, pp. 447–48. Buffon's admission of mode of life and type of social organization as important factors in creating a hereditary diversity among human groups bears some resemblance to Hume's discussion in "Of National Characters," of the preceeding year, and Buffon's awareness of current English thought allows one to suspect familiarity with Hume's essay. However, Buffon is clearly at odds with Hume in arguing against the attribution of "national characters" to peoples and races produced by language and culture, and is inclined to explain even the effects of culture and society in terms of the indirect effect of physical conditions, with the level of social organization simply providing a means by which man is isolated in varying degree from this environmental determinism.

40. "Le Cheval," H.N. IV (1753), 216.

41. *Ibid.*, pp. 217–19.

42. "Les Animaux sauvages," H.N. VI (1756), 58–60.

43. "Le Cerf," H.N. VI (1756), 86–88. A decade later, Buffon expresses this same idea with direct reference to human races: ". . . Il faut admettre pour ces altérations [of the races] . . . quelques autres causes réunies avec celle du climat: la plus générale & la plus directe est la qualité de la nourriture; c'est principalement par les alimens que l'homme reçoit l'influence de la terre qu'il habite, celle de l'air & du ciel agit plus superficiellement: & tandis qu'elle altère la surface la plus extérieure en changeant la couleur de la peau, la nourriture agit sur la forme intérieure par ses propriétés qui sont constamment relatives à

celles de la terre qui la produit." "De la dégénération des animaux," H.N. XIV (1766), 315.

44. "Variétés dans l'espèce humaine," H.N. III (1749), 447. See also "Les Animaux domestiques," H.N. IV (1753), 171–72.

45. For an analysis of the concept of degeneration in writings prior to Buffon, see especially Hodgen, *op. cit.*, chap. 7. Remarks on Buffon's relationship to the general question of historical pessimism in the Enlightenment can be found in Vyverberg, *op. cit.*, chap. 13. Whereas Professor Vyverberg sees Buffon as primarily ambiguous on the progress-decline issue, I would interpret Buffon as endorsing progressive regeneration and advancement of man and other organisms under their species-specific optimal conditions of temperature and nutrition (e.g. temperate northern latitudes for man), with historical degeneration and decay occurring under excesses of cold or heat. See *Des époques*, "VIIe Epoque," and "La Chèvre," H.N. V (1755), 60.

46. "De la Nature, Seconde vue," H.N. XIII (1765), vi–vii. See also "De la Nature, Premièr vue," H.N. XII (1764), ix. Compare with "Le Boeuf," H.N. IV (1753), where he simply speaks of God as organizing the organic molecules into the primeval archetypes of each kind, without explaining their origin.

47. "Seconde vue," H.N. XIII (1765), vi. See also similar statements in the later *Des époques de la nature* (supplement to H.N. V, 1778) in the recent critical edition of Jacques Roger (*Memoires du Museum national d'histoire naturelle*, N.S., serie C, X (1962), "VIIe Epoque," p. 216. As Roger's careful study has shown, however, the *Epoques* adds to the concept of solar irradiation the idea of a residual heat in the earth, gradually diminishing in time and thereby affecting life independently of extraterrestial conditions.

48. *Ibid.*, p. 206–7. Buffon places the probable origin of "le premier peuple digne de porter ce nom" in central Asia between 40–55 degrees of latitude, with the rise of China as the presumed first great civilization a result of this originally optimal climatic state. With Buffon in the *Epoques* presuming a gradual historical progression in response to the gradual cooling of the earth, resulting in the extinction of the large quadrupeds whose remains are found in the ice of Siberia, the southward shift of the optimal conditions of temperature are, by implication, the cause of the technological, intellectual, and cultural achievements and the presumed superiority of the European peoples (*ibid.*, "VIe Epoque," pp. 195 ff, and "VIIe Epoque," pp. 210–11), with Asia now inhabited by rude and degenerate barbarians. See also "Variétés dans l'espèce humaine," H.N. III (1749), 528.

49. This parallelism is mainly asserted as holding between man and the domestic animals, however, both having spread far from their places of origin. As he writes in the article on the cat in Volume Six: "On a vû que les différentes races de ces animaux domestiques suivent dans les différens climats le même ordre à peu près que les races humaines; qu'ils sont, comme les hommes, plus forts, plus grands & plus cou-

rageux dans les pays froids, plus civilisés, plus doux dans le climat tempéré, plus lâches, plus foibles & plus laids dans les climats trop chauds" ("Le Chat," H.N. VI [1756], 16. See also "Le Chien," H.N. V [1755], 202–3). The wild animals, less susceptible to geographic transposition, and thus to the forces of degeneration, presumably do not, in most cases, exhibit a geographical degeneration, exhibiting instead more of a valuationally-neutral geographical endemism (see quote above, p. 14 and "Dégénération des animaux," H.N. XIV [1766], 322). The conveniently *ad hoc* quality of Buffon's position is apparent, however, in his conclusions on the parallel degeneration of man and the wild animals under the same natural causes in the case of the New World.

50. "Animaux communs aux deux continens," H.N. IX (1761), 103–4.
51. "De la Dégénération des animaux," H.N. XIV (1766), 314. See also "Variétés dans l'espèce humaine," H.N. III (1749), 523–24.
52. "Nomenclature des signes," H.N. XIV (1766), 31–32. See also "Les Animaux carnassiers," H.N. VII (1758), 27–29. Thus in opposition to Rousseau's speculations in the *Discours sur l'inegalité*, to which Buffon refers directly in the last article, Buffon does not consider the orang-outang to be a possible historical ancestor of man, but if anything the terminus of human degeneration. For useful remarks on Buffon's intellectual relationship to Rousseau see especially Otis Fellows, "Buffon and Rousseau: Aspects of a Relationship," reprinted in *idem, From Voltaire to La Nouvelle Critique* (Geneva: Droz, 1970), pp. 33–53.
53. "Nomenclature des signes," H.N. XIV (1766), 32. Throughout the *Histoire naturelle*, Buffon repeatedly appeals to the Cartesian criterion of rational discourse as the sign that man is comprised of both a material body and an immaterial mind, thus insuring his radical distinctness from the animals and the impossibility of his evolutionary origin from the apes (see "De la nature de l'homme," H.N. II [1749], 439–40, and "Les animaux carnassiers, H.N. VII [1758], 29). For remarks on Buffon's relationship to eighteenth-century French Cartesianism see Roger, *Des époques*, "Introduction," p. lxxix. See also Vartanian, *Descartes and Diderot*, pp. 262–72.
54. But see below, nn. 58, 60.
55. For example, in the Cartesian dualism that persists in his thought. See above, n. 53.
56. The need for man to dominate and subdue nature by his technology, a theme through numerous articles of the *Histoire naturelle*, takes on absolute urgency in the *Des époques de la nature* with the prospects of a gradually cooling and dying earth. See "VIIe Epoque," Roger ed., p. 213. See also "De la Nature, Première vue," H.N. XII (1764), esp. xiv–xv.
57. As he writes in *Des époques*: "Comparez en effet la Nature brute à la Nature cultivée; comparez les petites nations sauvages de l'Amerique avec nos grands peuples civilisés; comparex même celles de l'Afrique . . . ; voyez en même temps l'état des terres que ces nations habitent,

vous jugerez aisément du peu de valeur de ces hommes par le peu d'impression que leurs mains ont faites sur leur sol; soit stupidité, soit paresse, ces hommes à demi-brutes, ces nations non policées, grandes ou petites, ne font que peser sur le globe sans soulager la Terre, l'affamer sans la féconder, détruire sans édifier, tout user sans rien renouveler" (Des époques, "VIIe Epoque," Roger ed., pp. 211–12). See also "De la nature, Première vue" H.N. XII (1764), xii–xiii.

58. H.N. XIV (1766), 336 ff. The relevant section of this article was also reprinted under the title "Sur la dégénération des animaux par le melange des espèces," in Collection académique VIII (1770) "Appendix," 25–30. The growing strain upon the empirical validity of the interbreeding criterion can be observed in Volume Eleven of 1764, where Buffon is forced into arguing that the one and two-humped camels are conspecific because of fertile interbreeding, even though their specific distinctness has been recognized "beyond all memory," "Le Chameau et le dromadaire," H.N. XI (1764).

59. H.N. XIV (1766), 31.

60. As Lord Kames writes in justification of his polygenetic theory with direct reference to Buffon and the interbreeding criterion: "Has [Buffon] proved this to be a law of nature? On the contrary, he more than once mentions several exceptions. . . . Though in distinguishing a horse from an ass, he affirms the mule they generate to be barren, yet afterward, entirely forgetting his rule, he admits the direct contrary." Henry Home, Six Sketches on the History of Man (Philadelphia: R. Bell, 1776; first published London, 1774), I, 7–8. Kames' assertion is, of course, strengthened considerably by Buffon's further weakening of the interbreeding criterion in the "Des mulets" of 1776 (supplement to H.N. III), in which Buffon now cites empirical evidence for the fertility of hybrids and claims that hybrid sterility is simply a matter of degree. The apparent inconsistency of Buffon's position is only enhanced by the rearrangement of the articles in some later editions of the Histoire naturelle. The English translation by William Smellie (2nd ed.), for example, places in a single volume Buffon's articles on the horse, the ass, the "Degeneration of Animals," and the dissertation on mules.

61. Kant, "Von den verschiedenen Racen der Menschen," (1775), trans. in Count, op. cit., pp. 16–24.

62. J. Hunter, Disputatio Inauguralis Quaedam de Hominum Varietatibus (1775) trans. in J. Blumenbach, The Anthropological Treatises of Johann Friedrich Blumenbach, trans. and ed. by T. Bendysche (London: Longman & Green, 1865), p. 360 ff.

63. Blumenbach, "On the Natural Variety of Mankind," (1795), in Anthropological Treatises. Blumenbach acknowledges, however, the difficulties raised by Buffon and others against the interbreeding criterion, and is inclined to accept a morphological criterion of species (p. 73) without going so far as to embrace polygenism. He acknowledges later in the treatise, however, that interbreeding is usually a valid sign of conspecificity.

64. B. G. E. Lacépède, *Les Ages de la nature et histoire de l'espèce humaine* (Paris: Levrault, 1830), I, 233 ff. Lacépède was Buffon's understudy and generally regarded as the continuator of the *Histoire naturelle* following Buffon's death (*Histoire naturelle des quadrupèdes ovipares*, 1788–89; *Histoire naturelle des poissons*, 1798–1803; *Histoire naturelle des cétacés*, 1804).

65. Samuel Stanhope Smith argues, for example, with evident consternation, that the whole force of the eighteenth-century appeal to a universal human nature and a moral sense as a foundation of ethics depends purely on the unity of the human species, a unity which he feels rests solely on the debatable empirical validity of Buffon's interbreeding criterion. *An Essay on the Causes of the Variety of Complexion and Figure in the Human Species*, ed. W. D. Jordan (Cambridge, Mass.: Belknap Press, 1965) (reprint of 2nd ed., 1810), pp. 8–10.

66. For an indication of Buffon's popularity, at least as reflected in the holdings of private libraries of Enlightenment France, see D. Mornet, "Les Enseignements des Bibliothèques privées (1750–80)," *Revue d'Histoire litteraire de la France* XVII (1910), 460. In order of frequency of holdings, the *Histoire naturelle* ranks third, preceeded only by Baylés' *Dictionnaire* and the works of Marot. Diderot's *Encyclopédie*, by comparison, ranks in twenty-first position.

Racism Without Race:

Ethnic Group Relations in Late Colonial Peru

Leon G. Campbell

IN 1912, Lord James Bryce, the British Ambassador to the United States, returned from Spanish America and proclaimed the region an excellent laboratory for the study of race relations.[1] No doubt his view was the result of Spanish America's unique population. Miscegenation had taken place there since the sixteenth century, at an unparalleled rate, so that the idea of race as it applied to Latin America referred to a peculiarly complex reality. Despite Bryce's implicit advice to social scientists, the subject of Spanish American race relations is still virtually untouched,[2] and so is the related subject of racism.

Racism has been defined as "the assumption that psychocultural traits and capacities are determined by biological race and that races differ decisively from one another which is usually coupled with a belief in the inherent superiority of a particular race and its right to domination over the others."[3] As a phenomenon in Spanish America, it is usually associated with the turn of the nineteenth century. Buffeted by the harsh winds of international economics and internal strife, Latins rejected their indigenous past and sought their future among waves of European immigrants, whom they felt would infuse the region with a dynamism that was biologically inspired. The "scientifically" based ideas of European intellectuals such as Gobineau, Huxley, and Spencer that a racial hierarchy with whites, or Aryans, constituting the upper stratum formed the proper basis for world society seemed little more than belated recognition of what had been a reality in Latin America for three centuries.

323

The purpose of this paper is to explore the colonial antecedents of this phenomenon. By reviewing briefly the social structure and racial composition of late colonial Peru, Spanish racial attitudes, and ethnic group relations, it may be possible to determine whether Spanish American racism can be said to have existed prior to the nineteenth century, and perhaps more importantly, if so, on what bases it was predicated. Peru, as the seat of the former Inca empire, produced a variety of racial strains and thus offers an opportunity for an interesting case study of ethnic group relations. Hopefully, this study will aid in the more precise analysis of a universal phenomenon that is of concern to all thinking persons.

Following the conquest of America, social rank or status was based largely upon phenotype, i.e. color and physiognomy, with a whitish skin indicating *limpieza de sangre*, or purity of the blood from Moorish or Jewish ancestry, a virtue prized since the days of the Reconquest. Yet although Spanish law regarded each racially-definable group as a separate social stratum, with attendant rights and obligations, by the eighteenth century, and probably well before, miscegenation, or race mixture, had caused racial lines in Peru and elsewhere to become hopelessly blurred. Definition for the purposes of maintaining social stratification on the basis of race alone became virtually impossible, so that the Spaniards perforce adopted sociocultural indices to maintain intact the social system.

As early as 1560 the social pyramid in Peru consisted of a small upper stratum of Spaniards, numbering between 5,000 and 10,000 persons, who by this date had been matched in number by *Mestizos*, the issue of their liasons with Indian women. Negroes, both free and slave, brought from Africa, ranked directly below them. The base of this social pyramid consisted of a large number of Indians who formed a separate culture from the above.[4] There is considerable disagreement among scholars as to the exact configurations of this social structure, with one authority viewing it in terms of multiple hierarchies rather than a single pyramid;[5] the point for our purposes, however, is simply that "racial" identification by the mid-sixteenth century was becoming difficult. A 1796 census in Peru indicated a population of 1,115,207 persons. Of this number 56.5 percent were classified as Indians, 26.5 percent as Mestizos, 4 percent as Negroes, both slave and free, and 13 percent as *Españoles*, or whites.[6] This population was ranked by the Spanish authorities according to at least twenty-one "racial" categories, fourteen of which applied to mixed-bloods alone.[7]

Because of the distinct minority position of the whites in Peru, and the omnipresent fear which they harbored of native rebellion, society was necessarily predicated upon the concept of racial separation rather than integration. This was facilitated by the fact that ethnic groups tended to reside in different geographic regions. A majority of Peruvian Indians tended to reside at the higher elevations which had been the centers of the Inca empire, while most Mestizos lived in or around the Spanish towns where they had been born. Whites lived in the major urban areas, notably the capital of Lima, located on the coast, which by the eighteenth century had an estimated population of nearly 60,000 persons. Most Negroes also resided on the coast, either as laborers on the great landed estates or as tradesmen and mechanics in the towns.

This geographic and residential separatism was reinforced by the Laws of the Indies, which constituted an attempt to apply the corporate, hierarchical society of estates existing in late medieval Castile to the multiracial situation developing in Spanish America.[8] Laws ordered Indians to remain in their own towns, which were placed under Spanish governance. Similarly, laws covering dress, admission into trade guilds, militia units, universities, hospitals, as well as those on intermarriage, taxation, and the bearing of arms, were all predicated upon the existence of a racially-definable social system. Peruvian viceroys received their subjects in three separate rooms: those for whites, Indians, and *Castas*, or mixed-bloods. The Church retained separate parish registers on the same basis, while military units were organized along similar lines.[9]

Certain features of this Spanish quest for separatism should be noted as a basis for understanding ethnic group relations in Peru. First, it was probably never strictly enforced. Owing to extensive miscegenation, it became impossible to distinguish light mestizos from darker Creoles or American-born whites or, for that matter, from Indians who spoke and dressed as Mestizos. Secondly, the demands for free labor, especially in the urban centers, facilitated some limited upward social mobility. Finally, the rivalry between Peninsular Spaniards and Creoles for appointive office in the Spanish imperial bureaucracy provided some limited opportunities for men of talent, regardless of birth, to ascend to positions of responsibility normally closed to them. It is probable, however, that the number of lower-class individuals appointed by the Spaniards in preference to the Creoles was small, because of the pernicious effect it might have on the hierarchical social system.

There are numerous examples in late colonial Peru of mixed-bloods serving in the trade guilds, the military, and the Church, attending the university, and even participating at the lower echelons of the imperial bureaucracy, regardless of the provisions of the Laws of the Indies.[10] To a much lesser degree, the same was true for Negroes of talent and Indians, especially those of noble birth, who were used as minor provincial administrators. Moreover, the Crown allowed wealthy *Castas* to purchase *cédulas de gracias al sacar*, or "certificates of whiteness" which theoretically entitled them to admission into the fringes of the colonial elite. Similarly, the Church might, for a fee, register an infant into a higher social category in the baptismal records to achieve the same results.

The foregoing should not be construed as examples of Spanish racial toleration. By and large, Spaniards in Peru viewed Indians as being sensual, fatalistic, alcoholic, stupid, and lazy. Although the Crown had taken several measures to assure their protection during the sixteenth century by relegating them to the status of perpetual minors under the care and protection of the Church, the need for a servile labor force in the silver mines, which were an economic mainstay of the empire, dictated their ultimate decimation and brutalization during most of the colonial period.[11] By the eighteenth century, Spanish commentators exhibited little concern for the plight of the once-noble savage unless he demonstrated a willingness to renounce his cultural heritage and accept Mestizo status in the Spanish-speaking world. Even then there was never any hint that the Indian could ever become the equal of the white in any sense.[12]

By and large, the Spaniards considered Negroes, especially freedmen, to be sensualists and troublemakers, and, if anything, less adaptable than the Indian to the ways of Spanish civilization.[13] Because of the aridity of coastal Peru, no extensive system of plantation agriculture developed there as it did in other parts of Latin America, notably Cuba and Brazil. Although the number of Negro slaves rose dramatically during the last years of the colonial period, blacks never constituted more than four percent of the total population. While it may have been true that the Spaniards regarded slavery as more a matter of military misfortune or social class than of race, there is no body of convincing evidence that these attitudes caused Peruvian, or Latin American, slavery to be less oppressive than elsewhere.[14]

Over half of all Negroes in Peru were freedmen, employed in the interstitial trades and professions.[15] Although there were vocational opportunities as middlemen available to blacks that were often not available to Indians, it would be incorrect to assume that this indicated any significant degree of racial toleration towards them. Using the military as a case study, I have found numerous examples of socioracial discrimination in promotion, pay scales, and judicial sentences against Negroes in both the regular and militia components of the Army. Royal attempts to tax free blacks on the same basis as Indians, which placed them in the category of subject peoples, were strenuously resisted.[16]

Because of the stigma of illegitimacy which attached to mixed bloods and their marginal position in Peruvian society, fully accepted neither by whites nor native peoples, discrimination was especially pronounced against these groups. One category of Mulattos were known collectively as *salto atrás*, literally, "a jump backwards" from the white ideal. Perhaps employing a play on words, Alonso Carrió de la Vandera, an eighteenth-century social critic, likened the mulatto to a mule, because both pretended to be gentle in order to kick their masters when they so desired.[17] In 1742, the Spanish naval lieutenants Jorge Juan and Antonio de Ulloa, who were visiting Peru on a secret mission for the King, noticed that Mestizos there disdained manual labor and preferred to live dissolute lives, oftentimes outside of the law.[18] After 1780, owing primarily to the massive rebellion against royal authority launched by the Mestizo Túpac Amaru, additional restrictions were placed upon Mestizos in an effort to limit their revolutionary potential.[19]

By the eighteenth century in Peru, Spanish attempts to impose a caste system had failed as the direct result of race mixture. As it became impossible to distinguish ethnic groups on the bases of color and ancestry alone, cultural and behavioral patterns were employed in their places as primary status determinants. Language, dress, the wearing or non-wearing of shoes, diet, and sleeping arrangements gradually had replaced color and physiognomy as definitions of a person's "racial" category. As historian Woodrow Borah has noted for Mexico, "the family which wears peasant dress, goes barefoot or in sandals, eats corn tortillas to the exclusion of wheat bread, and sleeps on the ground may be classified as Indian."[20] Conversely, those who chose to speak Spanish and wear Spanish dress became Mestizos. Thus it was not rare or impossible for Indians to "pass" into the Mestizo category, and talented mixed-bloods might also ascend into the fringes of the colonial elite groups. The hectic pursuit of higher "racial" classifications by the lower social groups in Peru indicates that white superiority was institutionalized and that most groups subscribed to white values as a means of self-improvement.

Besides the labor force and revenues which accrued to the Crown, this policy of limited social mobility performed another important function. By absorbing small numbers of talented, and potentially hostile, leaders of the masses into higher social categories, the system of social stratification based on white dominance was preserved with minimal changes, since these entrants were forced, as terms of admission, to accept elite standards and values in place of those of the groups from which they came.[21] In order to combat a potentially threatening racial situation, the white Spanish minority in Peru had thus substituted for an unworkable caste system a pragmatic and rather flexible system of cooptation, in which limited social and vocational mobility was afforded talented individuals, who thus became valuable adjuncts of the colonial elites. Denied leadership, the masses rarely could rise in successful opposition to the Crown. For example, during the massive revolt of 1780 led by Túpac Amaru, practically no Mestizo or Indian leaders defected to the rebel standard, a fact that insured the eventual defeat of the insurgents.[22]

Although most Peruvian Indians remained segregated in their own towns, separated both residentially and occupationally from whites, and though Negroes and mixed-bloods in urban centers were similarly restricted to areas which were ghettos in all but name, one observes significant differences between these Spanish racial policies and modern South African *apartheid*. The intent behind Spanish separatism was to protect the Indian from the vicious mixed-bloods, rather than to protect whites from the people of color—as is at least nominally the case in South Africa. Yet at the same time, it is notable that no mixed-bloods in Spanish Peru, much less Negroes or Indians, ever achieved membership on the town councils or in the high courts; nor were they promoted to senior rank in the ecclesiastical, military, or imperial bureaucracies. The distrust of Mestizos and Indians prompted by the revolt of Túpac Amaru tended to restrict their passage, both occupationally and socially, into the colonial elite groups. Creoles thus preserved their status as an establishment during and after independence in Peru, with only minimal concessions granted to the lower social groups.[23]

There is evidence that in Peru the efforts made by the late Bourbon reformers to undercut the power of this entrenched Creole elite by permitting mixed-bloods to assume positions of responsibility, especially in the Church and the military, prompted no small number of racist remarks against these groups. This leading conclusion has prompted the assertion that socioracial prejudice was on the increase in Spanish America by the late eighteenth century.[24] However, the fact that these racial remarks were widely reported by European travellers may reflect less an increase in socioracial prejudice than an increase in publication of ideas regarding race which had been held for centuries.[25] Nor is the increase, both in number and intensity, of mass rebellion in late colonial Peru any clearcut indication of increasing dissatisfaction on the part of lower social groups with the racial policies of the Crown. Although it is not certain that the insurgents did not feel themselves to be the objects of socioracial prejudice, the list of grievances set out by them indicate that factors other than racism were prevailing causes behind the revolts.[26]

Because the white Creole elites assumed control over the masses during the Wars for Independence in Peru, no basic changes took place to alter the relationships between ethnic groups during the early nineteenth century. Aside from a few military men who climbed the social ladder as *caudillos*, or political bosses, the basic structure of Peruvian society continued to resemble closely that of colonial times, and the policy of cooptation of talented mass leaders remained in force. While the legal and administrative usage of ethnic classifications, save that of Indian, or *indígena*, was officially abolished in 1825 in Peru, these had long been useless as status determinants, which were culturally derived; needless to say, the edict did nothing to reduce socioracial discrimination. Not until 1854 was Negro slavery abolished and the Indian freed from the payment of tribute.

During the nineteenth century, a declining economic situation and a disastrous loss to Chile in the War of the Pacific (1879–83) combined to increase the mood of racial pessimism in Peru. At about the same time, the mass emancipation of Negroes after 1854 assured their entrance into society at the lowest economic levels and thereby increased socioracial prejudice over what it had been earlier, when Negro freedmen constituted an important part of the economic system.[27] As late as 1911, Lord Bryce noted that the Peruvian Indian was still a citizen for military, but not for political, purposes, in the sense that he could neither vote nor hold office, because of a variety of unofficial restrictions.[28] As a direct result, ideas rationalizing the socioracial inferiority of darker social groups in Peru were widely accepted as explanations for the situation in which the nation found itself.[29]

In conclusion, the heritage of the colonial period to the future of ethnic group relations in Peru was in providing a social structure and a domestic tradition which remained virtually intact after independence and was largely congruent with European racist viewpoints. Ever since Spanish times, Peruvians have tended to accept socioracial factors as influencing and determining the potential of the diverse ethnic groups which comprise their population. Today, these beliefs still affect the relationships between various ethnic groups and pose a serious obstacle to Peruvian nation-building.[30]

NOTES

1. Lord James Bryce, who served as British Ambassador to the United States, 1907–13, visited South America in 1911–12. His book, *South America: Observations and Impressions* (New York, 1912), is still a valuable assessment of the region. For his analysis of the contemporary racial situation there, see pp. 454 ff.
2. The best work has been done by the Swedish historian Magnus Mörner, whose works include (ed.), *Race and Class in Latin America* (New York and London, 1970)—a book of readings on the subject—and *Race Mixture in the History of Latin America* (Boston, 1967). For an historiographical overview, see his article "The History of Race Relations in Latin America: Some Comments on the State of Research," *Latin American Research Review*, I:3 (1966), 17–44.
3. *Webster's Third New International Dictionary, Unabridged* (Springfield, Mass., 1961). For a general overview of this phenomenon, see the works of Philip Mason, especially *Patterns of Dominance* (London, 1970) and *Prospero's Magic* (London, 1962).
4. James Lockhart, *Spanish Peru, 1532–1560: A Colonial Society* (Madison, Wisc., 1968), p. 231.
5. L. N. McAlister, "Social Structure and Social Change in New Spain," *The Hispanic American Historical Review*, XLIII (August, 1963), 369–70. The "multiple hierarchies" model of the Peruvian social structure is offered by Karen Spalding, "The Colonial Indian," *Latin American Research Review*, VII:1 (Spring, 1972), 66.
6. A 1796 Peruvian census is reproduced in John Fisher, *Government and Society in Colonial Peru. The Intendant System, 1784–1814* (London, 1970), pp. 250–53.
7. Carlos Deustua Pimentel, "Un Testimonio sobre la conciencia del Perú en el siglo XVIII," in *La Causa de la Emancipación del Perú* (Lima, 1960), pp. 293–94; Mörner, *Race Mixture*, pp. 58–59. For a discussion of *mestizaje* in nineteenth century Peru, see the essay by Mario Vásquez in Mörner, *Race and Class*, pp. 73–95, as well as in Mörner, *Race Mixture*, pp. 1–3, 58–60, 68–70.
8. L. N. McAlister, "Social Structure and Social Change," 349–70.
9. Mörner, *Race Mixture*, pp. 45–48, 59–60, 62.
10. Fernando Romero, "José Manuel Valdés, Great Peruvian Mulatto," *Phylon*, III:3 (1942), 297–319; Guillermo Feliú Cruz, "Un mulato ilustre: José Romero," *Boletín de la Academia Chilena de la Historia*,

IX:21 (1942), 548–60; Roberto MacLean y Estenós, "Negroes en el Perú," *Letras*, XII:1 (1947), 13–15.

11. For a history of Spanish efforts to protect the Indian, see the works of Lewis Hanke, especially *The Spanish Struggle for Justice in the Conquest of America* (Philadelphia, 1959).

12. See the remarks of Alonso Carrió de la Vandera (Concolorcorvo), a Spanish bureaucrat and astute social critic in colonial Peru, in *El Lazarillo: A Guide for Inexperienced Travellers Between Buenos Aires and Lima, 1773*. Translated by Walter D. Kline (Bloomington, Indiana, 1965), pp. 21–22, 232–34, 237, 245, 248, 250. A similar view of the Indian in eighteenth-century Mexico is reproduced in Stanley J. and Barbara H. Stein, *The Colonial Heritage of Latin America* (New York, 1970), pp. 56–57.

13. Concolorcorvo, *El Lazarillo*, pp. 230, 237, 247, 254. After 1780, the revolt of Túpac Amaru shattered the myth of Indian passivity and adaptability.

14. Emilio Harth-terre, "El esclavo Negro en la sociedad indoperuana," *Journal of Inter-American Studies*, III:3 (July, 1961), 297–340. This field has been only superficially examined. Frederick Bowser's forthcoming book, *Peru and the African, 1529-1570*, should clear the subject of Peruvian slavery up considerably. For other details on the African in Peru, see Lockhart, *Spanish Peru*, pp. 192–98; Mörner, *Race Mixture*, pp. 41–42, 63. For a discussion of work completed in the field of comparative slavery, see Laura Foner and Eugene Genovese (eds.), *Slavery in the New World: A Reader in Comparative History* (Englewood Cliffs, N.J., 1969), pp. 238–55.

15. Fernando Romero, "The Slave Trade and the Negro in South America," *The Hispanic American Historical Review*, XXIV:3 (August, 1944), pp. 373–86.

16. Leon G. Campbell, "The Military Reform in the Viceroyalty of Peru, 1762–1800," unpublished doctoral dissertation, University of Florida, 1970. For example, units were segregated by "race" and officered by whites. Negroes were punished more severely for their crimes by military courts than their white counterparts. Royalist authorities often refused to use Negro militiamen in the highlands to combat the Indian rebellions out of a belief that blacks could not function efficiently in higher altitudes. Although field commanders rejected these biological stereotypes, many are still uncritically accepted even today. For a case study of black rebellion, see my "Black Power in Colonial Peru: The 1779 Tax Rebellion in Lambayeque," *Phylon: The Atlanta University Journal of Race and Culture*, XXX:2 (Summer, 1972), 140–52. Although the revolt was economically based, it had racial overtones as well.

17. Concolorcorvo, *El Lazarillo*, p. 257. Jean Descola, *Daily Life in Colonial Peru* (London, 1968), p. 34. For a legalistic view of the Mestizo in colonial Peru, see Richard Konetzke, "Noticias documentales acerca de la importancia política y social de los mestizos peruanos a fines del siglo XVIII," *Revista Histórica*, XXVIII (Lima, 1965), 221–27.

18. Jorge Juan and Antonio de Ulloa, *Noticias secretas de América*, 2 vols. (London, 1826), I, 164.
19. Leon G. Campbell, "Military Reform," 207–65.
20. Woodrow Borah, "Race and Class in Mexico," *Pacific Historical Review*, XXIII:4 (November, 1954), 332; Mörner, *Race Mixture*, pp. 53–70 *passim*.
21. This conclusion has been reached by Stanley J. and Barbara H. Stein, *The Colonial Heritage of Latin America*, pp. 117–18, and by Frederick P. Bowser, "The African in Colonial Spanish America: Reflections on Research Achievements and Priorities," *Latin American Research Review*, VII:1 (Spring, 1972), 86.
22. Oscar Cornblit, "Levantimientos de masas en Perú y Bolivia durante el siglo dieciocho," *Revista Latinoamericana de Sociología*, VI:1 (March, 1970), 100–43.
23. Leon G. Campbell, "A Colonial Establishment: Creole Domination of the Audiencia of Lima During the Later Eighteenth Century," *The Hispanic American Historical Review*, LII:1 (February, 1972), 1–26.
24. Mörner, *Race Mixture*, 57.
25. Frederick Bowser, "The African in Spanish America," pp. 93–94, note 66. Mörner himself has called for a critical analysis of the background and attitudes of travellers in evaluating their observations on Latin American race relations (*Race and Class*, p. 207).
26. See Boleslao Lewin, *La rebelión de Túpac Amaru y los orígenes de la emancipación americana* (Buenos Aires, 1957), and Carlos Daniel Valcárcel, *La rebelión de Tupac Amaru*, 2nd ed. (Mexico, 1965), which document Tupac Amaru's desire to free "Americans" of all races from Spanish domination. Both my article "Black Power in Colonial Peru" and Juan Bromley's account of a Negro revolt in Lima in 1775, in *Virreyes, Cabildantes y Oidores* (Lima, 1944), pp. 85–93, indicate that Peruvian Negroes considered themselves discriminated against on the basis of race. Only recently have sociologists such as Roberto MacLean begun to analyze the incidence of alcoholism, suicide, and mental illness among Peruvian Negroes in calculating the adverse effects of this discrimination (*Racismo* [Lima, 1945]).
27. Bowser, "The African," p. 87.
28. Bryce, *South America*, p. 469.
29. See especially the works of Francisco García Calderón (1883–1953) and of José Santos Chocano (1875–1934). The brilliant Marxist intellectual José Carlos Mariategui, in his *Seven Interpretive Essays on Peruvian Reality*, translated by Marjory Urquidi (Austin, 1971), synthesizes this legacy of socioracial discrimination.
30. Frederick B. Pike, *The Modern History of Peru* (London, 1967), p. 5. See also Phillip Mason, "Gradualism in Peru: Some Impressions on the Future of Ethnic Group Relations," *Race*, VIII:1 (July, 1966), 43–62.

Free Colored West Indians:

A Racial Dilemma

David Lowenthal

SLAVERY WAS SCARCELY a racial issue in the eighteenth-century West Indies; it was a racial fact. Seventeenth-century European entrepreneurs established tropical plantations in the Caribbean with African slave labor; their successors universally presumed all slaves to be black and all whites to be free. West Indian whites never seriously questioned the virtues of slavery as an institution until Europe forced emancipation on them in the nineteenth century.

West Indian contrasts with the North American colonies are striking. During the eighteenth century, more and more Americans considered slavery morally repugnant and socially dangerous. By the time of the American Revolution, most of the northern colonies had abolished slavery, and many southerners, themselves reluctant slaveholders, sought to limit its scope and to abolish the slave trade so as to promote eventual emancipation. Most Americans viewed the "peculiar institution" as a source of unmitigated evil.[1] But in the West Indies, slavery was not a peculiar institution, it was a universal one. There were ten slaves to every non-slave, and few free men of any complexion regarded Negro slavery as immoral or unjust.

Notwithstanding the ubiquitous character of West Indian Negro slavery, two kinds of people constituted categories outside the system: whites who were not free, and non-whites who were free. Emigration soon eliminated the first: a hundred thousand white indentured servants, made redundant by African slavery on the sugar estates, streamed out of the Caribbean to the Atlantic seaboard of North America and elsewhere. The few thousand poor whites who remained endured general contempt for ways of life little distinguishable from those of slaves; indeed, many called them "white Negroes."

West Indians who were free but not white were a more serious and pervasive anomaly. These were of two kinds. Some were slaves who had fled plantation servitude to the mountainous and wooded hinterlands, whence they sporadically raided towns and estates while avoiding recapture. Two substantial groups of runaways and rebels, the Maroons of Jamaica and the Bush Negro tribes of Surinam and French Guiana, resisted all efforts to subdue them; colonial regimes and European empires had to treat with them as self-governing black enclaves, which have maintained their autonomy up to the present time. Rebel slaves in French St. Domingue went much further: they brought down the plantocracy and expelled the whites. Even in the smaller islands, some runaway slave hideouts survived for generations, a remote but ominous presence of which slaveowners always had to take notice.

Rebel and runaway slaves remained essentially outside the West Indian social order, however, when they did not entirely overwhelm it; they constituted a force to be reckoned with, not one that invited intimate commingling. The opposite was true of the free colored—those set free or born free, often the offspring of planters and slaves. Free colored West Indians were an integral part of the social order, and they accepted its regulations and internalized its values, even the perspectives that denigrated them. The free colored population grew slowly until the middle of the eighteenth century and thereafter became increasingly numerous. By the time of emancipation they outnumbered whites everywhere but Jamaica, Barbados, and the Leeward Islands.

This essay discusses the conflicts between racial theory and practice engendered by West Indian acceptance of this free colored element, ambiguously positioned between black and white. I shall refer primarily to British, French, and Dutch colonies in and around the Caribbean, where large-scale plantations and African slavery were generally more pervasive and came earlier than in Latin America and mainland North America. But this framework is at once too narrow and too sweeping. The non-Hispanic West Indies, which included most of the islands and Guiana in South America, developed patterns of culture and society that set them off from Latin America.[2] But in contrast with the slave states of North America the condition of the free colored in Cuba, Puerto Rico, Brazil, and the Spanish American mainland in many ways resembled that in the West Indies.[3] At the same time, the free colored situation in each West Indian territory was in some respects unique. Conditions differed from island to island, from town to countryside, from community to community, and from period to period, varying with local economy, demography, topography, society, and the impact of external pressures; even dependencies of the same imperial power displayed quite dissimilar racial patterns and prejudices.[4] This paper focuses not on these territorial differences, however, but on the mutual implications and common consequences of this middle group, neither slave nor free, in West Indian plantation societies.

Not only did West Indians, unlike North Americans, recognize an intermediate free colored category; they elaborated subdivisions in a graded series ranging from almost black to nearly white. French St. Domingue, for example, recognized Sacatra, Griffe, Marabou, Mulâtre, Quarteron, Métif, Mamelouc, Quarteronné, and Sang-mêlé. Moreau de St. Méry devotes sixteen pages of his description of that island to mathematical calculations of the 128 parts of white and black blood produced in seven generations of miscegenation; he notes that a mixed descendant of thirteen consecutive white unions would be only 1/8191th black, an invisibly small fraction of pigmentation.[5]

These theoretical gradations in fact played little part in everyday life and almost none in law; given the small size of the whole mixed population, many of the categories could have had no actual exemplars. The significant point is that West Indian whites engendered and encouraged a mixed racial order that was itself stratified by color. Such a racial hierarchy harmonized with the idea of the Great Chain of Being, approvingly alluded to even by the Jamaican Edward Long, who believed that black and white were separate species whose offspring would fail to reproduce. Between the Great Chain of Being and the hybrid infertility of mulattoes Long saw no contradiction whatever, for colored variations constantly arose out of unions involving pure whites or pure blacks.[6]

The notion of hybrid infertility achieved great popularity *not* in the West Indies, indeed, but in the United States, where belief in polygenesis reinforced hopes that miscegenation would prove to be a biological failure. Such views were attractive to a majority white society that had little place for free people of color and regarded their very existence as an enormity.[7] In the West Indies, by contrast, racial miscegenation was so widespread, so generally recognized, and so socially permissible that such matters as polygenesis and mulatto sterility were only of academic interest.

Free colored West Indians were distinguishable from slaves not only by freedom but by color, for many of them owed their freedom to white paternity. To be sure, some free persons were black and some slaves were "colored"—indeed, half or more of all persons of mixed ancestry were slaves. But the preponderance of mixed ancestry—mulatto, quadroon, octoroon—among free nonwhites, and of unmixed African descent among slaves,[8] shaped a tendency to designate free persons as "colored" and slaves as "black."

West Indian whites, unlike Americans, held the free colored superior not only to slaves but also to free blacks. Status and fortune depended on closeness to European features; "the souls of the free colored are elevated," declared a French Antillean white, "in proportion as their skin color lightens."[9] A Jamaican proprietor suggested that whites advance the free colored as allies against the growing number of free blacks,[10] and a Barbadian Assemblyman sought to extend the legal right to testify to "the enlightened class of the free people of colour" as opposed to "the vulgar class."[11] West Indian whites frequently exploited the consequent rivalry between black and brown. In the United States, by contrast, colored men had no social identity separate from that of blacks.

One crucial difference lay in the relative proportions of white and black. Greatly outnumbered by slaves, West Indian whites thought of free colored people as allies against slave insurrection;

French Antillean whites termed the free colored the "safeguard of the colonies," whose strength had staved off Maroon insurrection like that in Jamaica.[12] Opposing a bill to prevent colored freedmen from acquiring slaves, land, and houses, a Barbadian white thought it "politic to allow them to possess property; it . . . will keep up that jealousy which seems naturally to exist between the free colored people and the slaves." He warned his fellow legislators that "if we are to reduce the free colored people to a level with the slaves, they must unite with them and will take every occasion of promoting and encouraging a revolt."[13]

Certain Caribbean slaves were on occasion freed and armed in time of war. Thus in 1763 Martiniquans were so eager for free-colored assistance against a threatened English attack that they evaded strict laws against large-scale manumission by pretending to sell slaves into other islands and having them return as free men.[14] By contrast, American whites saw free colored men more as leaders of slave revolt than as buffers against rebellion; free colored employment was bitterly opposed by competing white laborers; and state after state required freedmen to depart or face re-enslavement.[15] In the West Indies, the scarcity and exorbitant cost of white artisans encouraged free colored men to take up skilled occupations; Edward Long himself urged Jamaica to encourage free colored artisans, who "would oblige the white artificers to work at more moderate rates."[16]

Most important, white West Indians were essentially *Europeans*, who took a socially stratified order for granted and viewed the separate identity and special privileges of the free colored as a means of consolidating their own status and power. By contrast, the American egalitarian mystique made free colored people an embarrassment even to whites who detested slavery; there was no room for color gradations in a social order where all free *white* men were equal.

In the West Indies, interracial sexual liaisons were openly countenanced, especially where white women were few, as was generally the case. Whites customarily had colored mistresses, and white fathers commonly placed their colored daughters as concubines; a visitor to Barbados was told that "many colored parents educated their children for this special purpose."[17] So few colored girls were exempt from this system that brown men were said to have "no other recourse than black women."[18] The practice was heavily criticized; visitors and local luminaries both deplored its evil consequences. But they inveighed in vain against a well-nigh universal custom, perpetuated in a moral climate that discouraged European women from taking up residence in the West Indies. When a candidate for Lieutenant Governor of Jamaica was called unsuitable because "he frequently Lyes with Black Women," his supporters rejoined that "the same could be said of virtually every planter on the Island."[19] An equivalent system of *plaçage* spread from French St. Domingue to Creole New Orleans and to Charleston, but elsewhere in the South enduring relationships between white men and colored women were usually clandestine and socially reprobated.

Well-to-do West Indian whites not only recognized their colored offspring, but often had them educated in Europe and left them large inheritances. Some colored families came to rival whites in wealth and style of life. Prominent men of color could sometimes exempt themselves from the usual disabilities. The Jamaican legislature passed hundreds of bills granting well-educated and well-to-do colored individuals the perquisites of whites. And in the French Antilles, highly placed men of color and whites married to colored women bought birth certificates "proving" Carib Indian ancestry so as to disavow African.[20] Passing for white was important for such West Indians, but the mechanism and social significance were unlike the North American. In the United States, a person who sought to pass would move to a remote milieu where his background was unknown. In the West Indies, the small size of the society and the limited number of white families, most with well-known genealogies, made such a procedure impossible. West Indian "passing" was not the achievement of the stranger whose African ancestry no one could know; it was accomplished by the prominent figure who was legally accepted as white despite what everyone surmised of his ancestry.[21]

The lot of most West Indian free colored and free black people was far less agreeably "white," however. The great majority of them in every territory were reputed to be poor or destitute. They were barred from many types of employment, their residence, travel, dress, and diet were restricted, and they suffered indignities from whites of all classes. White paupers got more money than colored ones. Colored men were always subordinate to whites in the militia and other organizations. Every joint function was hierarchically organized. Religion also reinforced color distinctions. Church bells tolled longer for whites than for colored folk in Jamaica; in Antigua a smaller bell announced a colored demise.[22] More severe sentences were meted out to colored than to white for similar offenses. A lone instance of equality shows rare common sense: in 1785 the Dominica Assembly extended the fine for "those who shall wilfuly gallop any horse, mare, or mule in any of the streets" from the colored to all free inhabitants, "as the lives of His Majesty's Subjects are equally endangered by any Person galloping through the Streets, the committee recommend that the like punishment be extended to Whites."[23]

Free black and colored people were moreover constantly at the risk of reenslavement. Slave escapes or rebellion led to a general hue and cry in which non-whites had to prove their free status by written certificate. And no document was adequate defense against unscrupulous whites. "They live in constant alarm for their liberty," observed one former slave, "and even this is but nominal, for they are continually insulted and plundered without the possibility of redress." Those in bondage might well "prefer even the misery of slavery to such a mockery of freedom."[24]

Growing free colored numbers and the affluence of some further strained their relations with whites. During and after the French Revolution they were suspected of republican sympathies and harassed by countless onerous rules. In St. Domingue white–colored rivalry became so fierce that the embattled groups ignored portents of the slave revolt that overwhelmed them both. The Haitian debacle fed post-Revolutionary reaction, and free colored people came under stricter surveillance throughout the Caribbean. White–colored conflict in the French Antilles engendered lasting bitterness; even after France abolished legal distinctions, white Creoles excluded people of color from the suffrage through high property requirements. In the British and Dutch territories, Surinam excepted, barriers between white and colored also remained high; for color distinctions were considered crucial to the stability of the social order and the maintenance of slavery. Up to the eve of emancipation, law as well as custom discriminated against the free colored, and when the legal disabilities of color were terminated, the free colored remained, like the slaves, an inferior social order. The small white minority exercised absolute power over social institutions that everywhere discriminated against non-whites, slave and free.

Like men in all societies, colonial West Indians thought in one set of ways, behaved in another, and sought to ignore or to gloss over the disparities between deeds and beliefs. I have described how the local social structures incorporated, not without stress, growing numbers of free colored persons intermediate in status between white and black.

Conflict between personal and group identity illumines white attitudes and behavior toward the free colored. As a *group*, West Indian whites continually sought to prevent or to curtail the freeing of slaves, voiced fears about growing free colored influence, and passed legislation or promulgated orders to keep them from infringing on white prerogatives. Almost without exception these laws became dead letters or were constantly circumvented, because their very authors were *individually* the lovers and fathers of colored women and children whose welfare they wished to promote. Thus the *Code Noir* debarred French Antillean slaveowners from freeing concubines and their offspring; yet such manumissions never ceased. Many territories limited colored inheritance from white fathers, but deeds and gifts commonly broke the intent of the law.[25]

White devotion to the well-being of colored dependents was woven into the fabric of West Indian life, though critics warned of the consequences. "How many *Negresses*," complained a St. Domingue colonist, "have . . . appropriated the entire fortune of their masters, brutalized by libertinage and incapable of resisting their power over reduced and feeble souls."[26] And in Jamaica Edward Long limned a similar portrait of the African mis-

342

tress with "all her kindred, and most commonly her very para-mours, . . . fastened upon her keeper like so many leeches."[27] But the benefits were by no means one-sided. "It is to the affection of their concubines," remarked a white Creole on St. Domingue, "that whites have owed the discovery of several conspiracies."[28] Illegitimate colored offspring served as convenient and reliable personnel in many white Creole enterprises. The family ramifications of colored liaisons were often advantageous to the white partner, too. In one instance a white proprietor in Clarendon, Jamaica, summarily killed a slave for stealing coffee, and was brought to trial. But "his mistress was the coroner's natural daughter, and the coroner himself was similarly connected with the custos [governor] of Clarendon. In consequence of this family compact, no inquest was held, no enquiry was made; the whole business was allowed to be slurred over."[29]

But such familial intimacy betokened no white willingness to accept colored people as equals. A case in point comes from Berbice, British Guiana. The prosperous, well-educated, free colored community, most of them the children or grandchildren of leading whites, petitioned in 1822 against a court decision reserving certain estate positions to whites. The Council reversed the ruling and made free coloreds eligible for certain other positions hitherto "exclusively admitted to whites." But when the Governor proclaimed this decision and appointed a few colored men to the militia, white public opinion was outraged. He was shocked. "I . . . never could have anticipated a future objection on their part," he wrote, "more particularly so when I considered (as the fact is) that every member of the Council has a large family of coloured children himself. . . . Really I thought they would feel these appointments a compliment to themselves and their connections." But what the whites most resented, in fact, was the Governor's reference to colored people as "brethren." Colored people were *not* whites, and to put them in positions of power and trust would deny "an order of things coeval with European superiority." Their own children perhaps excepted, whites would not accord equality to free colored persons but "little emerged from ignorance above the slave population."[30]

West Indian whites saw nothing amiss in relationships of the greatest intimacy which would forever remain asymmetrical in power and status. What could be more agreeable, after all, than to become the father of numerous devoted offspring who could never threaten your own position, never push you out of the way? The white West Indian patriarch's position was in some respects uniquely enviable.

Nor did white West Indians see anything incompatible in *personal* behavior that violated decrees they themselves had urged. And they showed a keen awareness of what was circumstantially appropriate as opposed to technically legal. Hence the common form in Jamaican wills, bequeathing property to various free colored mistresses and offspring "according to the manners and customs of this country,"[31] a clear recognition that it was not according to English law.

How was it that whites horrified by free colored pretensions in general could give their own colored offspring every benefit of education and inheritance? What could these children do with their schooling and their money in a society that barred them from the ruling elite? Each white parent making such arrangements must have hoped or believed that *his* children might escape these constraints. In places like Jamaica, where more than five hundred colored became white by legislative fiat in the last decades of the eighteenth century, this was a real prospect. And money and education might buy them places as whites in England or in France if not in the West Indies. Finally, few West Indians reasoned from the particular to the general. Although they saw most other whites doing as they did, they never drew the conclusion that their own actions helped to enlarge and enrich the free colored group which must, with the diminution of the proportion of pure whites, continually erode claims to racial exclusivity.

The free colored were accepted elements in eighteenth-century West Indian social systems only so long as they could be regarded primarily as *individuals* allied by family loyalty to whites. Whenever, in the eyes of the whites, they became a *group* they constituted a threat to the social order. Group identity implied corporate self-regard, pressures, and demands for relaxing and ultimately erasing distinctions of color.

Free colored persons were only acceptable, therefore, when they were considerably less numerous than the whites, endured without question their subordinate rank in society, and were divided among themselves by distinctions of shade. Until the late eighteenth century or afterward, these conditions characterized most West Indian colonies. Free colored numbers grew slowly during the first half of the century and began to increase more rapidly only after about 1760. In the 1790s they were still less numerous than whites everywhere except Trinidad, Curaçao, and Dominica but were almost three-fourths the number of whites in St. Domingue and Surinam and about half in Jamaica and Martinique.[32] As the free colored began to achieve numerical equivalance, whites became increasingly alarmed about their role.

The absolute decline of white populations made more difficult the denial of free colored participation in civil affairs. Jamaica enfranchised the Jews to increase the number of whites competent to take part in government.[33] Fear of free colored demands led English whites in Dominica, on the other hand, to refuse extending the suffrage to local French Catholic whites. Were they to acknowledge "that among the white population . . . it is impossible to select a sufficient number of persons properly qualified to sit in the House of Assembly, the Free Coloured (whose clamourous pretensions already menace the Peace of the Colony) would have another pretext for urging their claims."[34] Only the Dutch in Surinam did not hinder free colored advance; many of them held high administrative posts during the half century before the end of slavery in 1863.[35]

But even where the free colored were most numerous, for a long time they accepted their subordinate position without demur. To complain at all was to risk being regarded as troublemakers, to arouse white wrath, and to jeopardize existing prerogatives. "To such restrictions as have already been laid, we have always submitted, not only without murmuring or repining, but with cheerful rejoicing that it has been our lot to live under so free and happy a constitution," averred a group of Barbadian freedmen, asking the Assembly not to *rescind* their privileges. They were "sensible that in a country like this where slavery exists, there must necessarily be a distinction between the white and free coloured inhabitants, and that there are privileges which the latter do not expect to enjoy."[36] The Trinidad free colored population remained entirely passive in the face of threatened loss of privileges; "they made no petitions, advanced no claims, claimed no rights."[37] A memorial signed by 236 of them in 1810 merely sought to ensure against retrogression, disclaiming any new pretensions as "highly unbecoming."[38] A similar petition from the free colored of Dominica noted that they "have been always foremost to oppose rather than to promote innovations."[39] And the free colored of St. Domingue were emboldened in 1790 to ask for political representation only as a "Third Estate," inferior to the presumed nobility of the island whites.[40] Free colored people not only failed to combine to demand privileges or to deplore iniquities; they seldom banded together at all. The wealthiest and best positioned of them were either in Europe or leagued with individual whites, precluding any common free colored social organization.

The discrepancy between the sexes was also incompatible with a sense of community: white preemption of almost all the lighter-skinned women left brown men without partners or prospects of establishing durable positions through family connections. The separation of free colored women, as mistresses of whites, from free colored men, who had to seek black partners, suited the whites not only for sexual reasons, but also because it tended to preclude the formation of a durable free colored class remote from both white and black progenitors. Long's theory of mulatto infertility was less a justification of polygenesis than a support for the hope that the free colored would never become a permanent class, which could only develop by procreation within the group. Mixtures of free colored with black slaves, on the one hand, sank insensibly into the black mass; offspring of white and colored, on the other hand, were disarmed by fealty to whites, by the hope of upward mobility, and by color shade prejudice.

Finally, the prospect of upward mobility and the white bias of all segments of the population was inimical to free colored solidarity. The lighter distanced themselves from the darker; those who held properties and slaves drew close to the whites and shunned the free colored townsfolk, artisans, pilots, shopkeepers, and indigents. The free colored, having internalized the unfavorable white stereotype of their group, tried only to exempt themselves from it as individuals. Thus one Jamaican white in 1782 sought legislative concessions for his illegitimate children on the ground that he intended "to bestow on them such fortunes as to raise them above the common level of people of color." A colored petitioner in 1797 asked special privileges for herself and her sister on the ground that they had "conducted themselves in a more decent and creditable manner than persons of their complexion in general."[41] In Curaçao and Surinam the free colored of Jewish descent, better off and more "respectable" than the rest, lived apart in separate quarters.[42]

But there were inconsistencies in all this, and especially in white stereotypes, which ultimately destroyed the existing racial balance and altered the role of the free colored. If the free colored were to remain divided, they needed faith in the prospect of upward mobility for individuals, including recruitment into white society for those who were most European in appearance and ancestry. Many free colored efforts were bent toward just this end. The plight of the free colored majority, visibly mulatto or darker, is seldom recorded; what dominates the records are the pleas of the almost white who would be regarded as white, or the reputed white who forged documentary evidence of racial purity. Since a hierarchy of class as well as of color thoroughly imbued colonial West Indians, it is no surprise to find the free colored leadership of St. Domingue, on the very eve of revolution, bending every effort to gain a measure of political participation for those who were quadroon or lighter, well educated, rich, and of attested good character—a combination of traits that, they themselves agreed, characterized less than one-tenth of the free colored population.[43] It was to enhance divisiveness that white West Indians urged privileges for those closest to white, and in some cases even their incorporation into white society.

But this ameliorative strategy was doomed because it was unworkable in everyday practice. It became patently unrealistic with the growth of an urban free colored proletariat, including some runaway slaves, who were not intimately linked by family and favor with whites and who could not hope to achieve whiteness. Amelioration also flew in the face of another white requirement, racial purity. Many whites feared that a settled policy of racial amalgamation would endanger the whole social structure. The occasional light-skinned individual might pass, manufacturing an accredited Carib Indian ancestor when necessary; but only a few could be accommodated in this fashion if white endogamy were to be preserved—a matter essential not merely for racial purity *qua* purity, but for the reputed whiteness on which supposed slave respect depended.

Free colored equality with whites would destroy "the ascendancy which the white population holds over the blacks," was a typical expression of this view. "The Dominion which we hold over the Blacks, arises from an acknowledged Superiority of the Whites. . . . Destroy this opinion by a degrading association with an inferior class (whom they despise, and are jealous of) and you break down the only barrier between us and insurrection."[44] Hence the local white opposition to a militia commission for a St. Domingue Creole whose white descent had, some years before, been unsuccessfully challenged; the mere fact that his color had ever been called into question corroded respect for the racial hierarchy.[45] Undermine the general faith in elite whiteness, and the slaves would cease to hold their masters in awe.

Slave subordination in West Indian society was felt to require both racial stratification and segregation, but these two principles were mutually incompatible. When the whites lumped all free colored together and closed off avenues for individual advance, they impelled the free colored to unite, to regard themselves as a *group*, not just as individuals seeking to eschew group identity, and inspired them toward egalitarian, if not revolutionary, credos.

At the same time, familial ties between whites and free colored West Indians were frayed, and as white sex ratios became more balanced and a stricter code of sexual morality came into being, white-colored liaisons were less openly avowed, illegitimate offspring less freely accepted. And free colored demands for equality —demands the more intensely expressed lest emancipation leave them not only racially segregated but reduced in status to the mass of the blacks—were rejected by increasingly beleaguered whites. Tactical reasons, not any diminution of racism, persuaded them to accede to free colored citizenship on the eve of emancipation.

In summary, West Indian whites continually emphasized the need for a free colored group intermediate between themselves and the blacks. The distinction of color at each end of the free colored spectrum was crucial. The racial structure of slave society required the free colored to be *colored*—neither black nor white. If there were many free blacks, the mass of slaves would come to resent their own servitude; the spectacle of free Negroes was said to be dangerous to slave discipline. But to place the free colored on a par with whites or to let too many infiltrate the white elite would jeopardize slave respect for the *absence* of African blood among whites. (Although there were many free colored slaveholders, it was a white stereotype that slaves respected only *white* masters.)

Thus the criterion of color was the essential distinction between whites and free colored, and whites resisted any blurring of the line as inimical to the social order. In this they read the future rightly; for once the free colored gained equal civil (but not social) status, racial distinctions in post-emancipation society no longer rested on a legal foundation. Bereft of the whole racial code, whites erected elaborate social and economic barriers against black and colored people but had to do so on the basis of class, not of color.

Notwithstanding the discontinuance of legal discrimination, the former free colored continued to dominate the non-white hierarchy, and to this day their descendants constitute the bulk of the elite and middle class. Advantages of wealth, education, and status gave them a head start over the former slave population. Lighter skinned than most of the emancipated slaves, they were, moreover, the beneficiaries of white preference and of the internalization of a white bias at all levels of society.

Yet the West Indian colored middle classes today evince little if any sense of corporate identity or group consciousness. Like their free colored forebears, they remain conspicuously individualistic and socially conservative. This resemblance is a joint consequence of structural similarities between the West Indies of the past and of the present day, and of the inculcation and retention of traits among colored middle-class West Indians that underscore their own distance from the mass of the people but also emphasize their differences from one another.

NOTES

1. William W. Freehling, "The Founding Fathers and Slavery," *American Historical Review*, LXXVII (1972), 81–93; David Brion Davis, "Anti-Slavery Ideology: Problems of Liberty and Authority," paper delivered at symposium on Racism in the Eighteenth Century, Third Annual Meeting of the American Society for Eighteenth-Century Studies, Los Angeles, California, March 24, 1972.
2. The differences are explored in David Lowenthal, *West Indian Societies* (London and New York: Oxford University Press, for the Institute of Race Relations, 1972).
3. Recent comparative overviews are David W. Cohen and Jack P. Greene, eds., *Neither Slave nor Free: The Freedmen of African Descent in the Slave Societies of the New World* (Baltimore and London: Johns Hopkins University Press, 1972); and Carl N. Degler, *Neither Black nor White: Slavery and Race Relations in Brazil and the United States* (New York: Macmillan, 1971).
4. See, for example, H. Hoetink, "Surinam and Curacao," in Cohen and Greene, *op. cit.*, pp. 59–83.
5. Médéric-Louis-Élie Moreau de Saint-Méry, *Description topographique, physique, civile politique et historique de la partie française de l'isle Saint-Domingue* [1797], 3 vols. (Paris: Société de l'Histoire des Colonies Françaises et Librairie Larose, 1958), I, 86–102.
6. Edward Long, *The History of Jamaica, or General Survey of the Antient and Modern State of That Island*, 3 vols. (London: T. Lowndes, 1754), II, 333–37, 351–58, 484–85.
7. For polygenesis and preadamism, see J. S. Slotkin, ed., *Readings in Early Anthropology*, Viking Fund Publications in Anthropology No. 40 (Chicago: Aldine, 1965), pp. 81 ff., 96–97, 208–11 (on Long). For North American views and attitudes, see Winthrop D. Jordan, *White over Black: American Attitudes toward the Negro, 1550–1812* (Chapel Hill: University of North Carolina Press, 1968), pp. 167–78, 402–26, 469–75, 491–94 (on Long), 542–51; and George M. Fredrickson, *The Black Image in the White Mind: The Debate on Afro-American Character and Destiny,1817–1914* (New York: Harper & Row, 1971), pp. 161–64, 172–73, 277–78.
8. The free non-white people of Surinam in 1830, for example, included

350

3,947 colored and 1,904 black; the slaves numbered 3,033 colored and 45,751 black (Hoetink, *op. cit.*, p. 62).

9. Yvan Debbasch, *Couleur et liberté: le jeu du critère ethnique dans un ordre juridique esclavagiste.* Vol. I: *L'Affranchi dans les possessions françaises de la Caraïbe (1653–1833)* (Paris: Dalloz, 1967), p. 114.

10. Douglas Hall, "Jamaica," in Cohen and Greene, *op. cit.*, pp. 193–213, ref. p. 203.

11. Journal of the Assembly of Barbados, October 8, 1816, C.O. 31/47, quoted in Jerome S. Handler and Arnold A. Sio, "Barbados," in Cohen and Greene, *op. cit.*, pp. 214–57, ref. p. 253. See also Hoetink, *op. cit.*, pp. 63, 70.

12. Debbasch, *op. cit.*, p. 113.

13. John Beckles, in Minutes of the Barbados Privy Council, November 1, 1803, quoted in Handler and Sio, *op. cit.*, p. 233.

14. *Code le la Martinique*, II, 557, n. 389, cited in E. Hayot, "Les Gens de couleur libres du Fort-Royal, 1679–1823," *Revue Française d'Histoire d'Outre-Mer*, LVI, No. 203 (1969), 13.

15. Eugene D. Genovese, "The Slave States of North America," in Cohen and Greene, *op. cit.*, pp. 258–77, ref. pp. 266, 274–76; Letitia Woods Brown, *Free Negroes in the District of Columbia, 1790–1846* (New York: Oxford, 1972), pp. 60–63. The Federal capital was the principal exception to American intransigeance against the free colored. For the free colored lot in general, see Jordan, *op. cit.*, pp. 167–70; Lowenthal, *op. cit.*, p. 47, n. 1.

16. Long, *op. cit.*, II, 334.

17. [B. Browne], *The Yarn of a Yankee Privateer*, quoted in Handler and Sio, *op. cit.*, p. 251.

18. M. G. Lewis, *Journal of a West India Proprietor, 1815–17* (Boston: Houghton Mifflin, 1929), p. 144. See also J. Stewart, *A View of the Past and Present State of the Island of Jamaica* (Edinburgh: Oliver and Boyd, 1823), p. 328; and Hoetink, *op. cit.*, p. 79.

19. Quoted in George Metcalf, *Royal Government and Political Conflict in Jamaica, 1723–1783* (London: Longmans, for the Royal Commonwealth Society, 1965), p. 100.

20. Sheila J. Duncker, "The Free Coloured and Their Fight for Civil Rights in Jamaica, 1800–1830," M. A. thesis, University of London, 1961, pp. 39–48; Hayot, *op. cit.*, p. 127. Frederick P. Bowser, "Colonial Spanish America," in Cohen and Greene, *op. cit.*, pp. 19–58, ref. p. 46, discusses similar Latin American certificates. In the Caribbean the American Indian was romanticized because he was a "noble savage" and also virtually extinct (Lowenthal, *op. cit.*, pp. 184–85).

21. The situation was similar to that in Brazil, where an early nineteenth-century visitor asked a mulatto if the local *capitão-mór* was a mulatto and was told, "He was, but is not any more" (Joao Maurício Rugendas, *Viagem pitoresca através do Brasil*, quoted in A. J. R. Russell-Wood, "Brazil," in Cohen and Greene, *op. cit.*, pp. 84–133, ref. p. 113). See also Franklin W. Knight, "Cuba," in *ibid.*, p. 290.

22. Duncker, *op. cit.*, 117–20, 126; Debbasch, *op. cit.*; C. L. R. James, *The Black Jacobins* (New York: Vintage Books, 1963); and Charles H. Wesley, "The Free Colored Population in the British Empire," *Journal of Negro History*, XIX (1934), 137–70, provide summary sketches of free colored conditions.

23. To Lord Bathurst, August 1, 1822, C.O. 71/59, Public Records Office, London.

24. Olaudah Equiano, *Equiano's Travels* [1789], ed. Paul Edwards (London: Heinemann, 1967), pp. 83–84. In Curaçao free colored conditions were often worse than those of slaves (Hoetink, *op. cit.*, p. 67). For the plight of free colored persons, see also Elsa Goveia, *Slave Society in the British Leeward Islands at the End of the Eighteenth Century* (New Haven: Yale University Press, 1965), pp. 181, 221–22.

25. Debbasch, *op. cit.*, pp. 72, 85, 102–3; Handler and Sio, *op. cit.*, pp. 227, 231–32; Léo Elisabeth, "The French Antilles," in Cohen and Greene, *op. cit.*, pp. 134–71, ref. p. 161.

26. Hilliard d'Auberteuil, *Considerations sur l'état présent de la colonie française de St. Domingue*, 2 vols. (Paris: 1776–77), II, 80–81, quoted in Gwendolyn Midlo Hall, "Saint Domingue," in Cohen and Greene, *op. cit.*, pp. 172–92, ref. p. 186.

27. Long, *op. cit.*, II, 331.

28. Emilien Petit, *Traité sur le gouvernement des esclaves*, 2 vols. (Paris: Knapen, 1777), II, 72–75, quoted in G. M. Hall, *op. cit.*, p. 186.

29. Lewis, *op. cit.*, p. 335.

30. Beard to Lord Bathurst, November 22 and December 18, 1822, C.O. 111/94–95, quoted in Rawle Farley, "The Shadow and the Substance —A Study of the Relations between White Planters and Free Coloured in a Slave Society in British Guiana," *Caribbean Quarterly*, IV, No. 2 (December, 1955), 132–51, ref. pp. 145–48.

31. Will of George Girton Saunders, December 28, 1815, quoted in Duncker, *op. cit.*, pp. 59–60. "Surinam marriages" involved similar provisions (Hoetink, *op. cit.*, pp. 186, 188).

32. See population tables in Cohen and Green, *op. cit.*, pp. 335–39.

33. Duncker, *op. cit.*, p. 233.

34. Alex Robinson, in despatch of March 11, 1824, C.O. 71/61, Public Records Office, London.

35. Hoetink, *op. cit.*, p. 64.

36. Minutes of the Barbados Privy Council, November 1, 1803, and letter to the Honorable John Beckles, Speaker of the House of Assembly and the Rest of the Honorable and Worshipful Members, March 4, 1817, C.O. 28/86, in Handler and Sio, *op. cit.*, pp. 233–36.

37. James Millette, *The Genesis of Crown Colony Government: Trinidad 1783–1810* (Curepe, Trinidad: Moko Enterprises, 1970), p. 112.

38. Petition to Governor Hislop, May 7, 1810, in C.O. 295/23, quoted in *ibid.*, p. 261.

39. Humble Petition and Memorial of the Colored Inhabitants of His Majesty's Island of Dominica, January 10, 1822, in Richard Wilson to Lord Bathurst, February 21, 1822, Misc. C.O. 71/59.

40. Debbasch, *op. cit.*, p. 313, n. 5.
41. Journal of the Assembly of Jamaica, VII, 537 of 18 December 1782, and IX, 169 of 4 December 1792, quoted in Edward Brathwaite, *The Development of Creole Society in Jamaica 1770–1820* (Oxford: Clarendon Press, 1971), pp. 171, 172.
42. Hoetink, *op. cit.*, pp. 64, 69.
43. Debbasch, *op. cit.*, pp. 123–24.
44. "Report of the Meeting of Planters Merchants and Others interested in the Island of Dominica held at the City of London, 4 February 1822," in J. Colquhon to R. Wilmot, February 22, 1822; and Alex Robinson to John Blackburn, December 15, 1822, C.O. 71/59, Public Records Office, London.
45. The "Affaire Chapuizet," in Debbasch, *op. cit.*, pp. 66–69.

Grégoire and the Egalitarian Movement

Ruth F. Necheles

IN 1787, at the outset of Henri-Baptiste Grégoire's political career, the word "equality" had little practical meaning because pre-
revolutionary European society consisted of numerous classes,
each possessing its separate rights, privileges, and disadvantages.
But some groups—Jews, Africans, and American Indians, for example—were less equal than others. Justifying discrimination on
cultural grounds, eighteenth-century men defined their civilization in religious rather than strictly ethnic terms, claiming that
pure Christianity surpassed any other moral system. Such people
as Jews, who later would be discriminated against on racial
grounds, were granted the same status as their Christian counterparts if they were willing to join the dominant faith. Prejudice
based on the Jews' supposed racial characteristics developed only
in those regions where a significant number converted to Christianity.

Europeans who ventured outside their continent confronted an
entirely new problem, and they responded by developing racist
attitudes. Although Negro and Indian cultural inferiority appeared obvious, the colonists were uncertain about the mixed offspring produced by intercourse with African slaves. The several
European nations assigned different roles to the mulattoes; King
Louis XIV's *Code Noir*, for example, treated them as native Frenchmen. But the planters in the colonies steadfastly refused their children the same opportunity to assimilate that was offered to the
Jews at home, and throughout the eighteenth century placed increasing restrictions on the mulattoes.

Without the Revolution, discrimination against Jews and mulattoes might have remained unquestioned for several more decades.[1] But the opening of the Estates General in May 1789 made their status a national issue because, of all native-born Frenchmen, only Jews and mulattoes were denied representation in the assembly.

On the surface, the mulatto and Jewish questions seemed dissimilar. In the one case discrimination rested on ancient religious antipathies, reinforced by the unpopular economic role played by the northeastern Jews. In the other, discrimination against mulattoes appeared essential in order to preserve a racially defined caste system. But the connection between the two cases was obvious to the spokesman for France's egalitarian movement, the radical Abbé Grégoire.

As an eighteenth-century cleric, Grégoire had been trained in Enlightenment as well as in Roman Catholic ideology. Combining the two traditions, he hoped to pave the way for a universal society of men, all of whom would believe in a reformed, revitalized Christianity, share the same rights and duties, and be divided for convenience's sake into self-contained national states. Realizing that this goal was utopian, he worked to create in France the foundations upon which this social order might eventually spread to other nations. As far as he was concerned, the Revolution had to reform the Roman Catholic church and enact a code of civil and social rights that would apply to all residents of the French empire.[2]

Racial equality was never more than one aspect of Grégoire's program, and at first he discarded arguments concerning racial inequality as outmoded. "I swear," he wrote in December 1789, "that I am a bit ashamed to fight such an objection at the end of the eighteenth century."[3] Although he refrained from discussing anti-Semitism as a racial issue, the religious and political assumptions underlying his early arguments for Jewish emancipation served as a foundation for his subsequent anti-racist campaign, and they merit some attention here.

God, according to Grégoire, created all men free and equal.[4] Even if the Jewish people[5] had earned God's disfavor for the crime of deicide, vengeance belonged to God alone; He had not delegated its exercise to secular rulers.[6] Indeed, Grégoire assumed that God eventually intended to save the Jews by permitting them to become Christians.[7]

Grégoire believed that the Jews in northeastern France were not yet ready to accept Christianity because the conditions under which most of them lived during the eighteenth century rendered them incapable of making any reasonable decisions. Probably they would accept Roman Catholicism only in order to escape the tyrannical laws that condemned them to a life of poverty. Once Jews were freely admitted into French society, given a rational education, and permitted to attain a decent standard of living, Grégoire assumed they would readily recognize the truths embodied in Christianity.[8]

Grégoire had secular as well as religious reasons for wishing to free the Jews. According to the economic ideas of his day, the northeastern Jews' concentration on money-lending and peddling caused serious hardships to their Christian countrymen. Ignoring the numerous restrictions which so channeled the Jews' activities, anti-Semitic writers accused them of deliberately impoverishing the peasants. Grégoire blamed the Christians, however. "Look at our work," he admonished his readers. "In [the Jews'] place we would have been the same—perhaps worse,"[9] and he advised the anti-Semites, "let he who among you is without sin cast the first stone."[10]

Jews were not innately wicked, Grégoire asserted. Relegating that concept "to the class of absurd and desolating hypotheses," he believed that man's character was "in large part" formed by circumstances.[11] With typical Enlightenment optimism, he insisted that such people as Jews, who displayed antisocial qualities, might be redeemed by changing their environment. "Virtue and talents," he claimed, "are the normal fruit of liberty."[12] Thus integration was the best solution to the Jewish problem, and he urged their immediate dispersal throughout the French countryside.

Grégoire's prerevolutionary recommendations for Jewish reform required rigorous supervision over their daily lives. Along with other revolutionaries, he thought that people might have to be forced to be free. But, he cautioned, "national character cannot be changed like a military uniform."[13] As the Revolution progressed, he became less interested in imposing reforms on the Jews and instead asserted their right to develop their own institutions. He encouraged his Jewish friends to modify their ritual so that they might mingle with Christians, and he wholeheartedly approved the assimilationist program devised by the 1806 sanhedrin.[14]

Just as Grégoire at first had failed to recommend complete liberation for the Jews, so for several years he hesitated to advocate black emancipation. As late as 1791 he reportedly said that immediate abolition would have the same effect as "kicking a pregnant woman to make her give birth sooner."[15] Since the Negro slaves had been excluded from the civilizing influence of French Christian culture, they would not know what to do with their freedom, and they would have to undergo a transitional period of improved treatment and education before slavery could be abolished.

Yet Grégoire could see no such practical reasons for denying freedom to West Indian mulattoes. Since the planters justified disenfranchising their children on racial grounds, their anti-mulatto polemics forced Grégoire to recognize racism as a current issue. Nonetheless, he refused to regard it as a universal phenomenon, and throughout the Revolution he casually dismissed it as the product of pride and greed.[16] "Justice, good sense, and policy,"[17] he insisted, required mulatto enfranchisement because, he added, "national security is based on justice, the striving of all spirits toward the same goal, and the unity of [all] interests."[18]

Failing to respond systematically to the planters' arguments, during the first years of the Revolution Grégoire discussed only incidental aspects of racism. For example, he denied that racial mixture produced an inferior population and favored intermarriage because he thought it would create a stronger nation. Regarding the mulattoes as a stabilizing element in colonial society, he urged the planters to marry their black concubines.[19] He certainly did not believe that the mulattoes would necessarily ally with their African relatives against their white fathers.

In part at least as a result of Grégoire's propaganda and political maneuvers, mulattoes achieved civil equality in 1791. Although he steadfastly denied that slavery could be justified on racial grounds, he paid little attention to the blacks until 1793, when he suddenly denounced "the nobility of the skin" and asked the National Convention to apply "the principles of equality to our brothers in the colonies, who do not differ from us in any way besides color." Still, he neglected to explain how the intervening two years had prepared the blacks for liberation.[20]

When the National Convention formally abolished slavery in February 1794, Grégoire's egalitarian activities took on a new form. Now for the first time he seriously confronted the problems involved in creating an egalitarian colonial society. His ideas concerning economics were—to be charitable—anachronistic, and he wisely avoided such questions. Instead, he helped to found the Société des Amis des Noirs et des Colonies. But he took only a minor part in this society's proceedings because he realized that its goal—to investigate the economic, medical, and scientific problems peculiar to the colonies—lay beyond his talents.[21]

Moral and educational questions were Grégoire's forte, and he hoped to reconstruct West Indian religious and academic institutions shattered by five years of civil war. Convinced that political reforms were useless unless Christianity helped to mold a virtuous citizenry, he was particularly anxious to create a revolutionary or so-called Constitutional church for the colonies.

Grégoire expected a revitalized church to play a significant role in all aspects of colonial life. According to him, republican priests would carry out the plans devised by the Société des Amis des Noirs. They would establish schools for illiterate blacks, where they would teach the rights and obligations of French citizens as well as the traditional subjects.[22] He also assumed that his priests would provide the colonies with medical care and charity.

Grégoire could not send a sufficient number of priests to the West Indies because many French parishes had fallen vacant during the preceding five years, and the metropolitan church could spare only a few clerics. Nonetheless, he developed a long range plan for providing the colonies with a ministry by creating a Constitutional hierarchy for the Caribbean.[23]

According to Grégoire, Constitutional bishops would perform several functions, the most important of which would be to prepare and ordain a black and mulatto ministry. In Grégoire's mind, nothing would so strikingly demonstrate the equality of all men before God as black priests performing the sacraments.[24] Ultimately, he assumed, this black ministry would become autonomous, and he dreamed of the day when a bishop of African descent would preside over the West Indian church.

Grégoire sent only one bishop and a few missionaries to Saint-Domingue before Napoleon reimposed slavery in 1802. Thus his ambitious religious program came no closer to realization than did the various schemes for economic reform devised by the Société des Amis des Noirs. But although military conditions and governmental apathy prevented him from implementing his plans, Grégoire did recognize and try to resolve problems that most eighteenth-century egalitarians ignored.[25]

Excluded from political influence by Napoleon's increasingly authoritarian government, Grégoire turned to a serious examination of Negro problems. Still confused about the causes of racism, after 1802 he at least recognized their significance.[26] Some of his other attitudes had also been modified by his revolutionary experiences. For example, he reassessed the relationship between innate talents and environment, attributing to genetics a larger role than he had previously. Still, he thought that inherited characteristics would only emerge under favorable circumstances, and he compared the environment to a block of steel against which the flintstone strikes, releasing the spark of genius.[27]

Genius was the subject of one of Grégoire's most influential books, his *Littérature des Nègres*, which he published in 1808. Taking as his theme the assertion that Negroes were as capable as whites of producing civilized works, he asked why they had failed to do so. He approached this question in several ways, but his theoretical argument is the most interesting.

By 1808 Grégoire had sufficient leisure to read a considerable amount of pseudo-scientific racial literature, but the biologists' definition of and criteria for racial distinctions did not convince him. "How can they agree wth regard to the consequences when they disagree concerning the anatomical facts which ought to serve as their basis?" he queried.[28]

Still Grégoire confused race, species, and nation. He accepted the vague concept "national character," which he defined as "those diversities hereditarily transmitted, . . . which are the effect of climate, of education, of dietetic regimes, or of habit. . . ."[29] According to him, nature (in the eighteenth-century sense of a vague, impersonal force) had created a continuum of characteristics which led to infinite variations rather than to two or three clearly distinct racial patterns. Indeed, he insisted, all but one contemporary scientist found "in the human race, the unity of the primitive type."[30] Thus, he concluded, "notwithstanding the different shades of the colour of the skin . . . the organization is the same; [and the various races] constitute under a different coloured skin, our identical species."[31]

Since Africans and Europeans shared the same physiological features, racial differences could not explain their divergent cultures. Grégoire had always believed the physical and social environment to be the determining factor for developing civilization, which he defined as the ability to create mechanical arts and crafts as well as complex political structures and fine arts. Using travelers' reports, he proved to his own satisfaction that interior Africa had cities, organized governments, sophisticated diplomatic relations, moral religions, and so forth. That the Africans had not progressed further could be attributed to an overly favorable climate which made survival too simple and did not stimulate them to invent advanced technology. "Nature," he commented, "is there prodigal of her riches."[32]

By the eighteenth century, numerous Africans had been transported to the more challenging environment of the new world, where, willingly or not, they were encouraged by example and forced by hardship to adopt European culture and technology. Slavery, which placed the black "in the scale of beings between man and the brute,"[33] hindered rather than assisted assimilation, and Grégoire could find no justification for continuing this immoral institution. Indeed, at the end of his *Littérature des Nègres* he predicted that technological developments soon would make slavery obsolete.[34]

The assumption upon which Grégoire's work rested—that men could be improved through proper educational, social, and religious institutions—was essentially optimistic. But by 1808 he took an increasingly pessimistic view of European society. Once he had served as spokesman for French revolutionary nationalism; but now that France had submitted to an emperor, he could no longer believe in her destiny to reform the world. Regarding France as too corrupt to govern colonies, and recognizing that various nationalities had the right to develop their own culture and institutions,[35] he expected the new world to create a way of life that would correct the ills of the old.

Grégoire searched among the several candidates for the utopia of the Western Hemisphere. He was most interested in Haiti, where blacks not only had succeeded in gaining their freedom, but in 1804 had won independence from European domination.[36] Although they still had many readjustments to make, Grégoire thought that "a good education, good laws, a free regime, and above all, religious principles" would make of the former slaves "men whom perhaps the masters would be unworthy of serving."[37] "The Haitian republic," he wrote, "by the mere fact of its existence, perhaps will have a great influence on the destiny of Africans in the New World."[38] If blacks were to prove their abilities anywhere, this would be the place.

Between the declaration of Haitian independence and the collapse of the Napoleonic empire in 1814, Grégoire could do nothing for Haiti. When peace finally came, the island again faced the serious tasks of rebuilding its economic, educational, and political institutions, even while it fended off the French landowners' attempts to reconquer the lost colony.[39] Although concerned about the planters' influence under the restored monarchy, Grégoire regarded racial prejudice as the greater threat to Haitian independence.

Believing that a viable state in Haiti would best refute racist arguments, Grégoire advised the government on various religious, moral, and social problems.[40] The several epistles he wrote between 1816 and 1827 demonstrate his willingness to be flexible and his attempts to understand the difficulties of a former slave society. He knew far too little about West Indian conditions, however, and he proposed creating an anachronistic utopia made up of independent yeoman farmers.

Toward the end of his life, Grégoire became as disillusioned with the Western Hemisphere as he was with Europe. Although the new republics had abolished the traditional aristocracy of parchments, they all, including Haiti, had retained a racial aristocracy in one guise or another.

Haiti's caste system based on color forced Grégoire to recognize racism as a universal phenomenon, and in his last work on egalitarian questions, his *Noblesse de la peau*, he tried to discover the causes of and cure for this prejudice. No longer believing in man's essential goodness, he finally realized that racism could be traced to man's most destructive impulses. But once again he failed to pursue his more interesting points and instead indulged in a moralistic tirade against those who sought to degrade entire classes of men for their own egotistical purposes. Thus, he glossed over the role played by sexual passions, and, although he noted the connection between racism and material greed, he dismissed economic motivation as unimportant—"as if such calculations could balance justice and deflect the rigor of principles . . . ,"[41] he scoffed. He was pessimistic about the future, because, according to him, "to extirpate vanity grafted on avarice is an enterprise that far exceeds human forces."[42] Only religious values could combat such ingrained evils, and so far the Roman Catholic church had failed to take a stand against racism.

Grégoire's *Noblesse de la peau* shows several valuable flashes of insight, which his unsystematic mind could not fully develop. Increasing ill-health as well as disillusionment with nineteenth-century society discouraged him from further pursuing his anti-racist campaign. Nonetheless, this book, along with his earlier *Littérature des Nègres*, raises issues that are current today.

In 1831, when Grégoire died, the major racist controversies still lay in the future. His career had spanned three eras in the history of the egalitarian movement. In his early days, although prejudice founded on religious differences had largely declined in importance, it still played a role in the revolutionary debates on enfranchising Protestants and Jews.

More important to the Revolution and the nineteenth century were the rising claims of xenophobic cultural nationalism. Not only Jews, but other ethnic groups suffered from the revolutionaries' attempts to impose a uniform culture within the nation's boundaries. Although Grégoire remained a fervent missionary for French culture through 1802,[43] he thought that men should first be admitted into society and then gradually be encouraged to adopt its mores. He no more believed in using violence to spread language and culture than he had advocated coercive religious proselytization.

Grégoire did not regard the third form of inequality—racism— as significant until after his revolutionary career had ended. Eventually he recognized that it was potentially more dangerous because one could never become white as one could convert to Christianity or to Francophonism.

Moving through three eras as he did, Grégoire managed to escape many of the prejudices and assumptions shared by his contemporaries. But his egalitarianism was not perfect, as indeed no one's can be. Tolerant as he was in comparison with his colleagues, he nonetheless wanted to make Jews and West Indian mulattoes resemble as closely as possible Christian Frechmen. With all his sympathy for the sufferings of Jews and blacks, he thought himself better able than they to judge which traditional religious and social institutions they should retain and which they should modify. Although he finally recognized the Jews' right to devise their own reform ritual, his cultural imperialism antagonized his friends in Haiti and contributed to his abrupt break in relations with the island in 1827.[44]

Grégoire's unconscious acceptance of some of the assumptions upon which racism rested was even more important than his cultural imperialism. Thus he failed to develop a clear definition of the word "race," confused the concept of "race" and "nation," and proclaimed the virtue of "racial mixture" in his writings on both Jews and mulattoes. Resting on such vague terminology, his pamphlets could not refute the equally vague and specious statements made by later biological racists.

But Grégoire was writing for a late eighteenth-, early nineteenth-century audience, and his pride and ignorance as a Christian European were shared by his readers. Christian-based reasoning, as shown by the nineteenth-century American abolition controversy, was the most powerful weapon available to him. If his writings found only a small audience, the fault lies with the course of revolutionary and Restoration politics. Save for the first two years of the Revolution, Grégoire had no organized body behind him, and when he embarked on the most constructive phase of his program— his attempt to create a Constitutional church in the West Indies —he was a "tainted outsider" to whom neither the orthodox Roman Catholic church nor the fervently anti-Catholic officials under the Directory would listen.[45] Lacking the kind of support provided by the successive English abolition societies, Grégoire was one voice in a wilderness of apathy, serving as a conscience for enlightened Europe, commanding the admiration and respect of many, but, unfortunately, followed by only a very few.

NOTES

1. Zosa Szajkowski asserts that "had the Revolution of 1789 not come Jewish emancipation might not have been realized till a much, much later date" (*Jews and the French Revolutions of 1789, 1830 and 1848* [New York: Ktav Publishing House, 1970], p. xviii).
2. For details on and references to Grégoire's career, see Ruth F. Necheles, *The Abbé Grégoire, 1787–1831: The Odyssey of an Egalitarian* (Westport, Conn.: Greenwood Publishing Co., [1971]).
3. Grégoire, *Mémoire en faveur des gens de couleur ou sang-mêlés de St.-Domingue, & des autres Iles françoises de l'Amérique, adressé à l'Assemblée Nationale,* in *La Révolution française et l'abolition de l'esclavage,* I (Paris: ERHIS, [1968]), 2.
4. Grégoire, *Essai sur la régénération physique, morale et politique des juifs,* in *La Révolution française et l'émancipation des juifs,* III (Paris: EDHIS, 1968), 194; Grégoire, *Motion en faveur des juifs, Par M. Grégoire, Curé d'Embermenil [sic], Député de Nancy, précédé d'une Notice historique, sur les persécutions qu'ils viennent d'essuyer en divers lieux, notamment en Alsace, & sur l'admission de leurs Députés à la Barre de l'Assemblée Nationale,* in *La Révolution française et l'émancipation des juifs,* VII (Paris: EDHIS, 1968), 45–46.
5. Here Grégoire uses the words "race" and "nation" interchangeably (*Essai,* pp. 15–16).
6. *Essai,* p. 193.
7. *Essai,* pp. 130–31. He thought that the conversion of the Jews might require miraculous intervention by God (letter to Scipione d'Ricci, 18 August 1808, Florence state archives).
8. *Essai,* p. 132.
9. *Essai,* p. 71. This same sentence, variously worded, also appears on pp. 37, 43–44, 194, and 230 n.

10. [Grégoire], *Observations nouvelles sur les Juifs, et spécialement sur ceux d'Allemagne* (n.p., [1806]), pp. 1–2.
11. *Essai*, pp. 108, 109.
12. *Observations* [1806], p. 47.
13. *Essai*, p. 98, repeated in *Motion*, p. 30.
14. Letters to Joel Barlow, 26 October 1807 and 1 September 1808, Harvard AM 1648 (606) and (603); Grégoire, *Observations nouvelles sur les Juifs, et spécialement sur ceux d'Amsterdam, et de Francfort; par M. Grégoire, ancien évêque de Blois, Sénateur, etc.* (n.p., [1807]), p. 4.
15. Thomas Millet to Grégoire, open letter in *Annales politiques et littéraires*, 13 May 1791, p. 399.
16. Grégoire, *Lettre aux philanthropes, Sur les malheurs, les droits et les réclamations des Gens de couleur de Saint-Domingue, et des autres îles françoises de l'Amérique*, in *La Révolution française et l'abolition de l'esclavage*, IV (Paris: EDHIS, [1968]), 1.
17. *Moniteur*, réimpression, 12 May 1791, p. 366.
18. *Moniteur*, réimpression, 16 May 1791, p. 400.
19. *Mémoire*, pp. 38–39, and *Essai*, pp. 165, 154. Judeo-Christian intermarriage was one of the few points on which Napoleon and Grégoire agreed, although for different reasons. Napoleon believed that after a few generations "Jewish blood would cease to have a particular character" (memorandum for Champagny, 29 November 1806, in *Correspondance de Napoléon Ier publiée par ordre de l'Empereur Napoléon III*, XIII [Paris: Henri Plon, 1963], 584). See also *Archives parlementaires de 1787 à 1860. Recueil complet des débats législatifs et politiques des chambres françaises*, XXVI (Paris: Imprimerie et Librairie Administratives et Chemins de Fer, 1887), 70 (hereafter, AP), and Grégoire, *De la noblesse de la peau ou du préjugé des blancs contre la couleur des Africains et celle de leurs descendans noirs et sangs-mêlés* (Paris: Baudouin Frères, 1826), p. 46.
20. AP, LXVI, 57.
21. *Journal du citoyen*, 1 prairial 6 (20 May 1798), pp. 481–82, for example. Their papers are in the Bibliothèque de Port-Royal, carton TUVWXYZ (hereafter BPR).
22. *Annales de la religion*, XI (1800), 428, and XIV (1801), 79–80.
23. Jean-Antoine Maudru, Constitutional bishop of Saint-Dié, wanted to establish a seminary for the eastern departments, but his efforts failed; see Grappin to Grégoire, 12 thermidor 6 (30 July 1798), BPR, CD.
24. Grégoire, *Compte rendu par le citoyen Grégoire au Concile national, des travaux des évêques réunis à Paris* (Paris: Imprimerie-Librairie Chrétienne, 1797), p. 37; *Epître des évêques réunis à Paris aux pasteurs et aux fidèles des colonies françaises* (Paris: Imprimerie-Librairie Chrétienne, 1799); *Annales de la religion*, IX (1799), 55–56 and XI (1800), 428–29.
25. Winthrop Jordan discusses the failure of Anglo-American abolitionists to devise post-emancipation programs for the blacks: *White over*

Black: American Attitudes Towards the Negro, 1550–1812 (Baltimore: Penguin Books, [1969]), pp. 353–62.

26. Grégoire, *Lettre aux citoyens de couleur et nègres libres de Saint-Domingue, et des autres iles françoises de l'Amérique*, in *La Révolution française et l'abolition de l'esclavage*, IV (Paris: EDHIS [1968], 10; *Mémoires de Grégoire, ancien évêque de Blois*, ed. H. Carnot, (Paris: Ambrose Dupont, 1838), I, 306.

27. Grégoire, *An Enquiry Concerning the Intellectual & Moral Faculties, & Literature of Negroes; with an Account of the Life & Works of 15 Negroes & Mulattoes, Distinguished in Science, Literature & the Arts*, trans. David Bailie Warden (1810; repr. College Park, Maryland: McGrath Publishing Co., 1967), p. 164 and *Essai*, p. 109.

28. *An Enquiry*, p. 26.

29. *An Enquiry*, p. 35.

30. *An Enquiry*, p. 41.

31. *An Enquiry*, p. 72.

32. *An Enquiry*, p. 47.

33. *An Enquiry*, p. 71; See also, *Motion*, p. 12.

34. *An Enquiry*, p. 251.

35. [Grégoire], *De la traite de l'esclavage des noirs et des blancs; par un ami des hommes de toutes les couleurs* (Paris: Adrien Egron, 1815), p. 77; Grégoire, letter to Mustoxidi, 14 April 1820, in M. Lascaris, *L'Abbé Grégoire et la Grèce* (Paris: A. Maretheux & L. Pactat, 1932), pp. 14–15; Grégoire, letter to Trongnon, 11 January 1829, Archives Départmentales, Loir-et-Cher, F 529, fo. 87; Grégoire, *Observations* [1807], p. 3; Grégoire, *Histoire des sectes religieuses qui, depuis le commencement du siècle dernier jusquá 'l'époque actuelle, sont nées, se sont modifiées, se sont éteintes dans les quatre parties du monde* (Paris: Potey, 1810), II, 351.

36. *Noblesse*, pp. 23–24 and incomplete manuscript in BPR: Concile 1811.

37. *Observations* [1807], pp. 2–3.

38. *Noblesse*, p. 44.

39. See Earl Leslie Griggs and Clifford H. Prator, eds., *Henry Christophe, Thomas Clarkson: A Correspondence* (Berkeley: University of California Press, 1952), p. 225, for threats to Haitian independence.

40. See Grégoire's letters to President Boyer in Alexis Beaubrun-Ardouin, *Etudes sur l'histoire d'Haiti, suivies de la vie du Général J. M. Borgella* (Paris: Dezobry & E. Magdeleine, 1853–55), and Necheles, *The Abbé Grégoire*, chap. 12.

41. *Noblesse*, p. 8.

42. *Noblesse*, pp. 19, 37.

43. See Ferdinand Brunot, *Histoire de la langue française des origines à nos jours* (repr. 1905–53: Paris: Librairie Armand Colin, 1967), IX, pt. 2.

44. Letters to Barlow, 26 October 1807 and 1 September 1808, Harvard AM 1648 (606) and (603), and Grégoire, *Epître aux Haitiens* (Port-au-Prince: Imprimerie du Gouvernement, 1827).

45. Henri Brunschwig, "The Origins of the New French Empire," from *Mythes et réalités de l'impérialisme colonial français, 1871–1914* (Paris: Armand Colin, 1960), trans. E. D. and G. H. Nadel, in George H. Nadel and Perry Curtis, eds., *Imperialism and Colonialism* (New York: Macmillan, 1964), p. 115.

Le Cat and the Physiology of Negroes

G. S. Rousseau

T HE ORIGIN of *Negroes*," Ephraim Chambers wrote in the
1728 *Cyclopaedia*, "and the cause of that remarkable difference in
complexion from the rest of mankind, has much perplexed the naturalists; nor has anything satisfactory been yet offered on that
hand." A generation later, in the 1750's, this was still true, although
Claude Nicolas Le Cat was to influence considerably the picture.
It is hard to know if Chambers, no scientist or medical man, would
have been at all impressed by Le Cat's theories. But if he had heard
or read them, he might have modified somewhat his statement in
the *Cyclopaedia*.

From the vantage of the history of science, Le Cat's entire career,
quite unsurveyed, incidentally, is as exciting as that part of it represented by his contribution to the age-old debate about the color
of negro skin, its origins and history, from the beginning of man
to the eighteenth century. Born in 1700 and dead by 1768, Le Cat
was the chief physician and surgeon of the Hôtel-Dieu, the leading
hospital in Rouen, a member of many French and foreign scientific societies, and the author of over a dozen medical treatises. In
1762 he retired from his hospital post, and during his remaining
seven years wrote most of the books that utilize his researches, observations, and reading of over fifty years.[1]

His scientific contribution to the race argument has either been
neglected or thought so insignificant until now that one looks in
vain for his name in most modern reference books in the history of
science and medicine as well as in encyclopaedias and dictionaries
of biography. And yet, careful scrutiny of his works reveals that

369

he played a role in advancing biological understanding of skin color. He himself was apparently aware of this role, and he accordingly devoted his greatest scientific energies to what we today must regard as his most significant medical work, *Traité de la couleur de la peau humaine en général & de celle des Nègres en particulier*, published in Amsterdam in 1765.[2]

Le Cat's treatise contradicts previous theories maintaining that bile is responsible for the color of human skin; this argument had been advanced as indisputable scientific fact in the earliest writings of Egyptian medicine, later appeared in Homer, Strabo, Ovid, and Pliny, and was advanced throughout the Renaissance and for much of the eighteenth century. The *Teatro Crítico* of Father Feijoo is typical of the impressionistic manner in which the bile argument was set forward: succinctly, without experimental support, and as an *ipse dixit* argument.[3] Other eighteenth-century naturalists, including Raymond de Vieussens, Buffon, La Mettrie, D'Holbach, and numerous travel writers, also repeated the argument as if it were gospel truer than truth.

In Italy Albinus and Sanctorini supported a bile theory (although these men recanted and at several junctures even displayed skepticism about the belief), and in France, where it seems to have been extremely popular, it attracted numerous advocates, and none more vocal than Pierre Barrère, a Perpignanese physician and medical author who strenuously championed it in 1741 in a dissertation on the cause of skin color, *Dissertation sur la cause physique de la couleur, des Nègres, de la qualité de leurs cheveux, & de la génération de l'un & de l'autre*. Germans, Scandinavians, and Englishmen also gave the belief their stamp and seal, and it is accurate to say that by 1750 the belief was prevalent—truly as popular as the "monster-mongering" sport, to use the phrase of Professor Jordan in his edition of Samuel Stanhope Smith's *Essay on the Causes of Complexion*[4]—that blacks were another species of man, *sans* the ordinary human organs, tissues, and heart, and (of course) *sans* soul.[5] Le Cat's theory, in contrast, introduces a black substance, "ethiops" (in other words, melanin and its cell the melanocyte), which, he maintained, is present to some extent in all creatures, white and dark, but to a greater degree in blacks; and it is this that distinguishes them. This theory had been Malpighi's,[6] and as I shall show in the paragraphs below, Le Cat, who had read and studied Malpighi's works, developed it. Establishment of the precise connection between the theories of the two men is important because one cannot understand the significance or implications of Le Cat's theory of ethiops without first understanding Malpighi's.

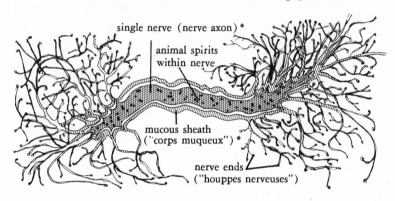

single nerve (nerve axon) *

animal spirits within nerve

mucous sheath ("corps muqueux") *

nerve ends ("houppes nerveuses")

Figure 1. Nerves in the dermis and epidermis (one dimensional view)

* According to Le Cat, neither the nerve axon nor the mucous sheath contains melanin (i.e., ethiops).

Both Malpighi and Le Cat believed that ethiops is contained in the nerve tips, where it permanently resides. But whereas this idea is merely suggested, without detailed development, in Malpighi's writings, Le Cat made it the central focus of his argument. Furthermore, he tried to show that ethiops is not governed by the liver, pancreas, or gall bladder, but is indigenous to the membrane surrounding the tips of nerve cells. Le Cat based this assumption on microscopic experiments he had done with frogs and other animals. In the frog, for example, "ethiops" (i.e. melanin) *is* in fact present anatomically in nerve cells, but not in human beings. In our anatomy, pigment is exclusively located in epidermal tissue, which is apart from the nerve cells. Le Cat could not have known this; microscopes in the 1730's and 40's were not powerful enough to distinguish sharply within human dermal tissue. Nerve tips, under weak microscopes of the type Le Cat is likely to have used, would appear to extend as far up as the epidermis, whereas, in fact, they do not; they are subdermal. It was not until the nineteenth century that microscopy enabled medical men to see that an epidermal-subdermal barrier (basement membrane) exists and that nerve cells do not penetrate this barrier.

Le Cat, who was logical and reasonable in his inference that human anatomy is almost identical with animal anatomy (frogs, chameleons), was so much convinced of the presence of ethiops in nerve cells that he directed his energies to other questions about the physiological nature of ethiops. For example, he asked how blacks originally acquire this ethiops—a question we might think would have interested Malpighi but which apparently never did. Le Cat tried to formulate an answer, but it was not as clear as we would hope: ethiops, he maintained, comes not from the sun, climate, or torrid zones alone, but from these climatic conditions in conjunction with the peculiar physiological traits Negroes developed over long periods of time. Not a perfectly clear formulation, to be sure, but in 1765 there was no Darwinian evolutionary theory of selection. Yet Le Cat's staunch belief that ethiops is somehow indigenous to blacks reveals a color argument scientifically more sophisticated than the theories of his contemporaries or near-contemporaries Malpighi, Feijoo, Sanctorini, and Barrère.

Like all scientific hypotheses, Le Cat's must be judged for its ultimate accuracy. In this regard it fails, as I shall show in detail below. But it ought also to be viewed in the context of his basic assumptions concerning physiology and the common assumptions of his age. In this regard, Le Cat's theory shows up rather well on several counts, not merely one. First, he believed that the nervous system controls the organism—not a revolutionary assumption in the 1760's, but one that was in constant need of focusing and that required application to the racist debates in medicine. In assuming this view, he was in line with the most progressive mainstream of current European medicine and physiology. It was a view demonstrating that he had read and understood Willis' brain theory and Haller's radical but nevertheless accurate thesis about nervous action in relation to muscular contraction. Second, he was right to assume that ethiops is somehow controlled in its action by the nervous system. We today know that the pituitary, an integral part of the nervous system, regulates many of the functions of melanin; Le Cat could not have known this, but was not very far from the truth in assuming that nerve tips extending into the epidermis regulate pigment cells.

If his conception of the nervous system is lacking in certain areas, we ought to be tolerant within reasonable limits. For example, Le

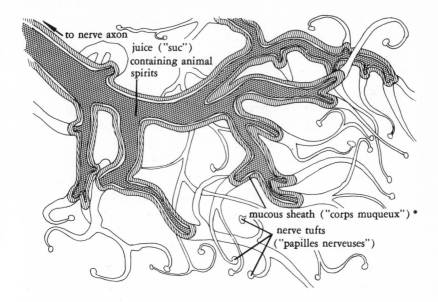

Figure 2. Enlarged section of nerve ends according to Le Cat

* It is important to note that according to Le Cat animal spirits do not flow in the mucous sheath ("corps muqueux").

Cat believed that the animal spirits, not subject to the laws of physics and chemistry, pervade the hollow tubes of the nerves. This is untrue, but most scientists—good scientists—of his epoch also believed it. Moreover, Le Cat held that a mucous sheath (*corps muqueux*) wraps the entire nerve cell.[7] Although this idea is not entirely true, it is closer to the truth than the notion of many of his contemporaries, and it is certainly a more advanced concept of the anatomy of this part of the nervous system than Malpighi's. Controversies about the precise physiological structure of the "outsides" of nerve cells had vigorously been carried on throughout the eighteenth century in England, where the question was debated in the Royal College of Physicians and in the Royal Society, as it was too on the Continent by Boerhaave, Hoffman, and lesser-known figures. It is true that Le Cat could not add substantially to these debates or radically change the theories of these men. But he did spend more time than they examining ganglions, the ends of nerves, under the microscope, and eventually he developed a fairly sophisticated conception of nerve tufts (*papilles nerveuses*) which he likened to the nipple-like structures of the tongue. Furthermore, he demonstrated that they expand and contract mechanistically, especially when regenerating themselves.

Considering the assumptions of physiologists in his age, therefore, Le Cat did not fare badly. In fact, he did exceptionally well, erring only in the points described above and, importantly, in his mistaken idea that the nervous system of humans is exactly, or almost exactly, the same as in frogs. To summarize his anatomical reasoning, he built his theory on some of the best physiology of his day and buttressed his assumptions with microscopic observations of several decades.

But even so, he was unsatisfied about the precise nature, histologically, of ethiops. And as a result of his dissatisfaction he reconsidered the matter, he says in his *Traité*, many times before satisfying himself. The most puzzling question, he believed, related to the *origin* of ethiops. He had seen this substance expand and contract under the microscope, so there could be no question of its physical nature: it could not be non-material, as were animal spirits. He was also certain, although it is hard for us to know why, of its presence at birth in blacks, and that there was no possibility of its being acquired after maturation. It was transmitted from generation to generation by the sun's rays, he thought, but these rays alone could not *produce* the substance. Heat could expand it, he believed, in the same way that heat causes other types of physical expansion.

Since Le Cat's experiments with various animals played an important role in his theory in the *Traité*, something, however brief, must be said about these, as well as about the significance of these experiments for modern medicine. Le Cat was convinced of the necessity of microscopic investigation, unlike many of his contemporaries, rationalists at heart who placed little faith in the microscope. He had seen ethiops in many animals and fish, but especially in the cuttlefish or squid (*sèche*). For two decades (1740–60) he observed their large black cells under various kinds of microscopes and deduced that human skin tissue must be similar. What he actually saw under the lens were melanocytes, microscopically quite prominent and very large in squid; but he was ultimately incorrect to assume that melanocytes in black men were structured similarly to those he observed in cuttlefish. Such reasoning by analogy was far from outlandish (scientists today, for example, experiment on mice and then extrapolate all their findings to humans); nor was his thoroughly logical assumption that Negroes have some sort of greater melanocyte production than do whites. Time has proved him correct, although his reasons were different from ours. But he had no conception of the melanocyte cell itself, its nature, anatomical structure, boundaries within the basal layer, accumulation at the base of the epidermis, chemical composition, and evolution throughout the life of a normal human being.[8]

If Le Cat's theory is "translated" into modern medical terminology (and extreme caution must be employed in such a translation), these approximate statements obtain. Melanocytes are scattered throughout the epidermis but do not appear, whether in whites or blacks, in the basement membrane or dermis. These two layers, dermis and epidermis, are separated by a boundary (the basement membrane) through which nerve tissue does not penetrate. Therefore, it is quite impossible, by the standards of modern anatomy, to imagine melanocytes in the dermis, or, conversely, nerve cells in the epidermis. Moreover, these melanocytes do not differ significantly, if at all, in chemical composition in whites and blacks, although their number does. Blacks are known to have many more melanocytes per epidermal area than whites, but present-day knowledge of the hormonal activity of melanocytes is not sufficient to indicate if this disparity influences bodily functions. But it does influence skin pigmentation, thereby accounting in part for the difference between fair and dark peoples. There are of course other factors, mostly genetic, that influence this coloration, but they need not be explained in detail here.

To turn now to Le Cat within this brief "translation": as I have already indicated, Le Cat was wrong on several counts, especially in his notion that nerve cells penetrate through the basement membrane. But he must be given credit for his intuitive leap in suspecting that bile cannot influence pigment, and thus for changing the whole course of physiological theory about skin. He must, it seems to me, also be given credit for his suspicion that the nerves play a more extensive role in the body than was thought at this time. Haller, Whytt, and other neurologists demonstrated in his own age that the brain required further examination, but it was Le Cat who suggested, however primitively, that the blood channel and nervous system were connected more intimately than most medical men thought.[9] Le Cat, viewed in this light, clearly emerges as a more important physiologist than Malpighi, especially if his contribution to the racist debates is the yardstick of measurement.

Malpighi, who died in 1694 (only six years before Le Cat was born), believed in an altogether different theory, one much less

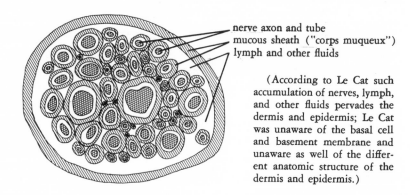

nerve axon and tube
mucous sheath ("corps muqueux")
lymph and other fluids

(According to Le Cat such accumulation of nerves, lymph, and other fluids pervades the dermis and epidermis; Le Cat was unaware of the basal cell and basement membrane and unaware as well of the different anatomic structure of the dermis and epidermis.)

Figure 3. Accumulation of the cross-sections of nerves, lymph, and other fluids

scientific and sophisticated: that all men were originally white, but that sinners among them had degenerated into black. In putting forward this remote divine cause of black skin, Malpighi impeded rather than advanced arguments regarding race among scientific men. It is true that he later abandoned his divine cause and substituted a proximate physiological cause: namely, a mucous sheath separating the dermis from the epidermis, recognition of which solved the physiological riddle puzzling anatomists for centuries. But he was wrong here, as wrong as Le Cat, although in a different way: the basement membrane, Malpighi's mucous sheath, does not contain melanin. Malpighi also theorized about a "mucous liquor" determining skin color, but he never stated where this liquor is located or how it operates, and Le Cat sensed this gap early in his researches. He dedicated his experiments, in part, to a refinement of this theory, but never could convince himself that ethiops was confined to a single sheath within the dermis. In other words, Le Cat argued for more area within skin tissue, for the whole basal cell and its surroundings as a zone wherein ethiops was contained. Malpighi, on the other hand, was persuaded that a localized substance must necessarily be the cause of differences in skin color.[10] Having established to his own satisfaction that the cutis as well as cuticle of blacks is white, he reasoned that blacks differ anatomically only in this mucous liquor. In this regard he was certainly more advanced than all his seventeenth-century colleagues, but not so advanced as Le Cat, who consciously tried to *show* the connections between the "mucous liquor" and the nervous system—a connection that we are now just beginning to learn does exist.[11] Le Cat, in his own way, was saying that the nervous system (brain, nerves, etc.) has some control of pigment activity (we know that the pituitary controls the hormonal activity of melanocytes). No one would wish to argue that this discovery in anatomy should bear Le Cat's name, but he was closer to the truth than his colleagues in France, and certainly those in England. And it is precisely in the bold imaginative leap of this connection, however primitively made, that Le Cat demonstrated his sound scientific intuition.

His contemporaries failed to understand him. Most never deemed his ideas worthy of the labor of serious comprehension: they continued the racial debate, usually asserting once again all the inadequate previous theories—but no one veered from the age-old lure of the bile theory. Riolan, Littre, and Morgagni, for example, were perplexed by the origin of black skin, and hypothesized that since most Negro skin had white patches, black men must originally have been white: a curious argument possessing little anatomic veracity. Later on, the sun turned their bile black (so the argument continued) and also their skin. For these scientists the relation of sun and bile was cause and effect: too much sun caused bile to blacken, and bile determined skin color. QED. Albinus, an eighteenth-century Italian scientist (whose name, incidentally, has no connection to "albino") proved to his own satisfaction that Negro bile, both hepatic and cystic, was black.[12] Sanctorini concurred with Albinus in considering bile the *only* substance in the body capable of influencing skin color.[13] These men, oppressed by the tyranny of the ancient theory of bile, with centuries of weight behind it, had either not read Malpighi or did not comprehend him. (It is naturally possible that they read and rejected him, but this seems unlikely in view of the zeal with which Sanctorini and Albinus approached the theories of others; one wonders, moreover, why they would not have refuted him in print if they had renounced his theories.) Elsewhere than in Italy, the situation was not different. Winslow in Denmark was undecided,[14] and Grossard, a Le Cat student who later became a professor at the medical school in Montpellier and who also happened to have undertaken important research into the lymph system, impressionistically speculated that *lymph* was more important than bile in determining color; but he was surprised to discover in autopsies that Negro lymph is every bit as white as the white man's.[15]

Then in 1741, a momentous episode in the eighteenth-century history of this medical debate occurred. Barrère, in France, published experiments asserting that Negro bile is black, and that it alone causes the black pigment in Negro skin.[16] Not the theory but the experiments won him attention. The bile theory was centuries old; but Barrère now endowed it with an authority it had never had. His book stated that his conclusions were based entirely on laboratory studies, thus creating the impression that black bile and its effects, long suspected but never seen, were as verifiable as the second law of motion. But the careful reader would have found that Barrère gave himself away. Blacks acquired black bile, he postulated, by dwelling in hot jungles. He himself had not, of course, seen black bile in Negroes, nor could he account for the fact that generations of white men living in Africa never turned black. He somehow took black bile on "faith," having viewed something abnormal resembling it, perhaps, in a few diseased bodies.

It is therefore greatly to Le Cat's credit that, only twenty years after Barrère's theory won universal acclaim, especially in France, he intuited and then demonstrated that it was specious. Historians of science may in the future show that certain French and English medical men anticipated Le Cat in this regard, but even so, some credit, however little, must go to him; at least, he must be rescued from the total oblivion in which he has until now remained. This is all the truer when it is remembered that towns like Rouen were somewhat isolated. If Le Cat had done his experiments in Paris, with the aid of many exceptional colleagues, we might feel more wary of granting him much honor; but he swam against the tide alone, in a small northern French city that had never been a medical center. An idea of his courage in rejecting the dominant belief in bile as the single and sole determinant of skin color is glimpsed by examining reviews of Barrère's theory in comparison to those of Le Cat. If Barrère was recognized and praised, Le Cat was disparaged as a shallow rationalist, even by English scientists who ought to have known better. Monsieur Eloy, author of the four-volume *Dictionnaire historique de la médecine*, published in 1778, commented favorably upon Barrère's bile theory but criticized Le Cat's nerve-ethiops theory as a wild hypothesis: "Il explique ensuite le sentiment qu'il a adopté, mais comme il n'est fondé, ni sur l'observation, ni sur l'expérience, on est en droit de le renvoyer dans la classe des hypotheses qui sont plus ingénieuses que concluantes."[17]

Two years after Le Cat's systematic demolition of the bile theory in the *Traité*, the Abbé Demanet published a *Dissertation physique et historique sur l'origine des Nègres et la cause de leur couleur* (1767),[18] wherein he repeated the old bile arguments without mentioning Le Cat. Such an omission in itself is insignificant, but it reveals the typical neglect of Le Cat before the beginning

379

of the nineteenth century. While it is true that his research on skin was occasionally mentioned during the last quarter of the eighteenth century—for example, in Jean Paul Marat's *Philosophical Essay on Man* (London, 1773)—his theory, however inchoate, of the interactions of ethiops and the nerve system was either too advanced or physiologically too radical, or appeared too clouded by physiological details, to admit of acceptance or recognition in his own time. Or it may have been left unregarded altogether, though this possibility is hard to understand in view of Le Cat's reputation. This was the man, after all, who had won the esteemed Berlin prize in physiology and about whom the editors of the *Gentleman's Magazine* said in 1753 he "ought to be universally read."

Throughout the last quarter of the eighteenth century, the scientific-medical community debated questions regarding the origin of Negroes and their black skin. As revolution approached and man's thoughts were deflected, it abated; but until then the question consumed them, though it seemed to arrive nowhere. Although some writers pointed out the loopholes inherent in the hot sun-black bile argument, none gave quite such specific reasons as Le Cat. Samuel Stanhope Smith professed to have read much literature before turning up any tangible conclusions in his *Essay on the Causes of Complexion* . . ., and ultimately admitted that not much new could be said on the subject. Essentially a synthesizer, he was satisfied to relegate Le Cat to a single mention in a voluminous footnote in which the Rouen surgeon is, of course, lost.[19] Whether Smith actually read Le Cat is doubtful, but his estimate cannot be misconstrued under any circumstances. (He had at least heard of Le Cat and his theories, which is more than can be said for other writers; most authors simply disregarded Le Cat altogether, and I have already suggested that this is not likely to have been prompted by his obscurity.) In 1768, three years after Le Cat's *Traité* was published, the first edition of the *Encyclopaedia Britannica* appeared. In the article entitled "Negroes," the anonymous author commented: "Dr. Barrère alleges that the gall of Negroes is black, and being mixed with their blood is deposited between their skin and scarf-skin." But no mention appears of Le Cat, or of his magistral, though cautious, challenge to the theory of bile as the cause of color. Though this anonymous author took notice of "Dr. Mitchell of Virginia" (John Mitchell, author of "an Essay upon the Causes of the Different Colours of People in Different Climates"), he apparently had never heard of Le Cat, or if he had, could not see the difference between the sophistication of Le Cat's theory and the primitiveness (as well as repetitiveness) of Barrère's.[20] Like Barrère, he confused himself in this article by citing bizarre cases of color change; yet he never paused to ask what the physiological basis of skin color was.

Le Cat himself took time out to study such fantastic cases of blacks turning white, or whites turning black, but in each instance he attributed the change to severe illness, body change during pregnancy, or wild growth of the "ethiops." That is, he perceived these were exceptional cases, and drew no paradigms from them. His balance of induction and deduction was intelligently managed, and one observes few cases in the *Traité* of his going out on a limb or forcing a conclusion from an isolated example. But when it was time to generalize, he surrendered prejudice and tradition to his empirical findings. He ruled out climate as a primary cause: a Norwegian clan migrating to the Sudan could never become black, at least not in the course of a few centuries. He thereby discarded adaptive conditions and concentrated on physiological processes. If he could have known the approximate age of the world, he might have been able to anticipate Charles Darwin in *The Descent of Man and Selection in Relation to Sex*, and might also have reasoned that there must have been selection for lightly pigmented individuals in higher latitudes since they could better utilize sunshine. But the chronology of the world in 1765 was still in doubt, and so it remained until the nineteenth century; the age of man, indeed, is still to be determined. And Le Cat, who really cannot be criticized for this lack of knowledge, demonstrated his abilities as a model-maker by refuting the bile theory and turning to the nervous system's interaction with other systems.[21]

The significance of this essay for a symposium on racism in the eighteenth century is not easily grasped. For the men it treats, Le Cat, Malpighi, and to a lesser extent Albinus, Sanctorini, and Grossard, were never involved in the debates about race. Philosophers like Voltaire and Diderot held their personal opinions about the real status of black men, and especially about their physiological similarity or dissimilarity to white men. But Voltaire and Diderot never engaged, to my knowledge, in medical experiments, as did Le Cat; besides, they allowed other concerns—nationalistic, economic, religious, philosophic—to influence their final decision about the species to which black men belonged.[22]

Le Cat, so far as I know, had no such complicated concerns. He was not a "philosophical" scientist in the way his English colleague Dr. Robert Whytt was; he was content to experiment and report his observations. This is not to imply that his scientific assumptions were simple or lacking in any way, but Le Cat, unlike the French *philosophes* discussed elsewhere in this volume, had less ambitious plans for himself. He desired, understandably, to rise as high as possible in medical research, and for this aspiration he was respected in his own age. Yet he remained content to leave it to others to comment on the social implications of his discoveries.

Perhaps, then, the significance of Le Cat's work is that there is no significance. I am personally persuaded that thinkers who debate a topic like racism without understanding something about the physiological bases of skin color cannot be sophisticated thinkers. They may have a great deal that is important to say about other topics, e.g. the nature of man, God, the life processes, the human condition, and so forth. But this is a different matter from making a significant statement, one worthy of recording in the annals of history, about racism. Too many examples of my point abound in this volume for me to provide detail; and no one is going to think less of a Montesquieu or a Voltaire because either thought blacks were a different species of man, without taking the trouble to read contemporary scientists like Le Cat. But we may be certain that if more people in the eighteenth century had read scientists like Le Cat, the nature of the debates discussed today would be different. Laymen cannot be expected in any age to comprehend the technical writings of medical men, but the ideas of a Le Cat, for example, were explained in popular magazines like the *Gentleman's*, and were epitomized in everyday language for the common man.

If I may conclude on a modern note, it seems to me that the situation today is not altogether different from that in Le Cat's age.

Thinkers from the common man to professional philosophers have their personal views about the black man, his capabilities, limitations, potential.[23] Yet not very many of these thinkers have taken the trouble to read the recent radical theories of Dr. Jensen and his team.[24] The content of these theories is not in question: they may be right, they may be wildly wrong. But they have been put forward by scientists of a very high caliber, with credentials beyond question, who hopefully have scientific truth as their first concern. Who knows if historians of science two centuries in the future will prove Jensen and company correct? Who knows what changes in the social structure of American life will be effected by Jensen's theories, if they are accurate? Or has a monumental change occurred, and do we now live in an age when certain theories are simply too dangerous to be put forward regardless of veracity? These are big questions, but must be left for another occasion.

NOTES

1. There is no biography. Information, and precious little exists, is scattered: see N. F. Eloy, *Dictionnaire historique de la médecine ancienne et moderne*, 4 vols. (Paris, 1778), I, 565–71, for the only brief sketch. Nothing at all is said about Le Cat in the standard histories of medicine by Arturo Castiglione, Fielding H. Garrison, Sir William Osler, Theodor Puschmann, Henry E. Sigerist, Charles J. Singer, René Taton, and E. A. Underwood. René Taton's *Enseignement et diffusion des sciences en France au xviii*e *siècle* (Paris, 1964), briefly discusses Le Cat's anatomy courses at the Hôtel-Dieu in Rouen. Robert Darnton, *Mesmerism and the Enlightenment* (Cambridge, Mass., 1967), mentions Le Cat in relation to hypnotism. Le Cat's private papers survive and are available in the Archives of the City, Rouen, France. On January 31, 1739, Le Cat was elected a foreign member of the Royal Society, London (Thomas Thomson, *The History of the Royal Society* [London, 1912], Appendix, xli). After this time his anatomical works were regularly translated into English and reviewed in English journals. His interactions with Dr. James Parsons, F.R.S., are described by John Nichols, *Literary Anecdotes of the Eighteenth Century*, 6 vols. (London, 1812), V, 475–76. By 1753 Le Cat, many of whose communications were now published in the *Philosophical Transactions of the Royal Society of London*, was sufficiently well known to be referred to by a columnist in the *Gentleman's Magazine*, XXIII (1753), 403 as "the ingenious writer . . . who ought to be universally read." In 1765 Le Cat won the prize of the Berlin Academy by answering their set of physiological questions on the structure of nerves. Offered by the Acad-

emy since 1753 but without a candidate, the prize answers were published as Le Cat's *Dissertation sur l'existence & la nature du fluide des nerfs & son action* (Berlin, 1765). The actual questions and an account of Le Cat's achievement in answering them are found in A. von Harnack, *Geschichte der Königlich Preussischen Akademie der Wissenschaften zu Berlin* (Berlin, 1901), I, 400. Le Cat was congratulated by the acclaimed scientist Haller for his attainment.

2. Extending to almost two hundred pages, it was not translated into English or reviewed in English periodicals as almost all Le Cat's other works had been. The reasons are not clear: perhaps the subject matter was too controversial for the more sedate reviews and too conservative for others.

3. Benito Feijoo, *Teatro Crítico Universal* (Madrid, 1736). VIII, Third Discourse, pp. 69–94.

4. Published in the John Harvard Library Series (Cambridge, Mass., 1965), p. viii.

5. A long list of comments and works could be compiled for the period 1700–80. Without making a search, I have found no fewer than two dozen comments in travel books alone. See, for example, Edward Long, "Negroes," in *The History of Jamaica* (London, 1774), chap. I, the third book. Some of these works appear in Winthrop Jordan's "Guide to Smith's References," in Smith, *Essay*, pp. 253–68.

6. See *Opera Omnia* (London, 1686), II, 221.

7. *Traité de la couleur*, p. 30 ff.

8. This concept arose in the mid-nineteenth century and required at least Schwann's theory of the cell. See Bobbie Williams, "Human Pigmentation," *General Anthropology* (forthcoming, 1973), pp. 487–523, the best scientific treatment of skin color I have seen. I am grateful to Professor Williams, Department of Anthropology, University of California, Los Angeles, for making this unpublished material available to me.

9. This is a chapter of the history of science not yet surveyed.

10. *Opera Omnia*, II, 215–38. This notion was transmitted to the eighteenth century as is made clear by dictionaries and encyclopedias. See, for example, Abraham Rees' article "Complexion" in *The Cyclopaedia; or, Universal Dictionary* (Philadelphia, 1810–24), IX, no pages.

11. I.e., the pituitary regulating functions of melanocytes. Precisely why this is the case is unknown as yet, as most histology textbooks explain. In general, little is known about the influence of the nervous system on hormonal activity. As an example of another area in which the influence of the nervous system is not well understood there is the glyal cell, separating the blood system and the brain. Before the 1920's it was not known that medicines could pass through this barrier, i.e., penetrate from the blood into the brain, and consequently affect the nervous system.

12. See Bernardus Albinus, *De Sede et Causa Coloris Aethiopum* (Leiden, 1737), pp. 267–78.

13. *De Statica Medicina* (The Hague, 1664), p. 221. Sanctorius, an influential writer of aphorisms, never developed his theory.

14. Jacob Winslow, *An Anatomical Exposition of the Structure of the Human Body*, trans. G. Douglas, 2 vols. (London, 1733), and *A Description of the Integuments of the Vessels* (London, 1784).
15. Grossard never published books, but his ideas and writings were circulated in France among interested doctors. He consulted frequently with Le Cat in Rouen and at scholarly meetings.
16. *Dissertation sur la cause physique de la couleur des Nègres, de la qualité de leurs cheveux, & de la génération de l'un & de l'autre* (Paris, 1741). A brief survey of Barrère's life appears in Elroy's *Dictionnaire historique de la médecine*, I, 265. Although Barrère's books never attained the same importance in England as Le Cat's, his name and theory (i.e., as champion of the bile theory) carried great weight there. Nothing in France contributed more to the prestige of Barrère's theory than the extensive review and serious treatment he received in the *Journal des Sçavants* (February 1742), pp. 97–107. See, for example, Edward Long's discussion of the scientific origins of Negro skin in his important treatise *A History of Jamaica*, 3 vols. (1774), II, 351–52, which reckons with Barrère but has never heard of Le Cat: "Anatomists say, that this *reticular membrane*, which is found between the *Epidermis* and the skin, being soaked in water for a long time, does not change its colour. Monsieure Barrère, who appears to have examined this circumstance with particular attention, as well as Mr. Winslow, says, that the *Epidermis* itself is black, and that if it has appeared white to some that have examined it, it is owing to its extreme fineness and transparency; but that it is really as dark as a piece of blackhorn, reduced to the same gracility [sic]. That this color of the *Epidermis*, and of the skin, is caused by the bile, which in Negroes is not yellow, but always as black as ink. The bile in white men tinges their yellow skin; and if their bile was black, it would doubtless communicate the same black tint. Mr. Barrère affirms, that the Negroe bile naturally secrets itself upon the *Epidermis* in a quantity sufficient to impregnate it with the dark colour for which it is so remarkable. These observations naturally lead to the further question, 'why the bile in Negroes is black?' " The tone and weight of Long's prose in this passage makes it clear that Barrère's authority is beyond question and that he represents the most valid school of thought. Only Buffon receives an equal amount of esteem in Long's chapter.
17. I, 571. An earlier version of the dictionary appeared in 1755.
18. Published in Paris. I have found no biographical information about Demanet of any note.
19. *Essay*, p. 53.
20. The author throughout refers to Barrère as an authority. The truly amazing thing, from my vantage at least, is the attention Barrère's treatise received and the almost complete neglect of Le Cat's.
21. A study in depth of Le Cat's scientific writings would, of course, have to explain why Le Cat was able to posit connection. His books on the physiology of the nervous system made him eminently qualified. See, especially, his prize-winning volume, *Dissertation sur l'existence & la*

nature du fluide des nerfs (Berlin, 1765), in many ways one of the genuinely radical theories of the age. Also of help were his medical treatises on the anatomy of the passions, such as *Traité des sensations & des passions en général* (Paris, 1767).

22. Much "history" can of course be accumulated documenting virtually every aspect of the racism debates of the eighteenth century. But every age adheres, whether it knows it or not, to primitive assumptions about what constitutes "scientific belief"; and we cannot penetrate to the core of racism in the Enlightenment unless we know precisely what it believed about the scientific bases of the skin question.

23. This is an important point as many of my colleagues in this volume are aware even if they do not say so explicitly. What a vast sense of the monumental changes of belief and emphasis, as well as theories of cause and effect, one derives by approaching the problem vertically rather than horizontally, starting, let us say, with Robert Boyle's analysis in *The Works of the Hon. Robert Boyle*, ed. Peter Shaw (London, 1772; first ed., 1699), I, 714–19, "Of Colours: Experiment XI." A brief reading list after 1780 might include: E. G. Bosé, *De Mutato per morbum colore corporis humani* (Leipzig, 1785); Robert Know (ethnologist), *The Races of Man* (London, 1850–62) and *Man: His Structure and Physiology* (London, 1857); Franz Pruner-Bey, "Notions preliminaires sur la coloration de la peau chez l'homme," *Bulletins de la Société d'Anthropologie*, V (1864), 65–135; C. H. G. Pouchet, *Des colorations de l'épiderme* (Paris, 1864); L. Dunbar, *Ueber Pigmenterungen der Haut* (Berlin, 1884); Ashley Montagu, *Man's Most Dangerous Myth: The Fallacy of Race* (New York, 1952, 3rd ed. rev.); Richard Bernheimer, *Wild Men in the Middle Ages* (Cambridge, Mass., 1952); J. S. Slotkin, "Eighteenth Century Social Anthropology," in *Readings in Early Anthropology* (London, 1965), pp. 244–356; John S. Haller, *Outcasts from Evolution: Scientific Attitudes of Racial Inferiority, 1859–1900* (Urbana, 1971).

24. Arthur R. Jensen has argued that genetic rather than environmental factors account for differences in IQ for the most part. He further claims that those environmental factors that do operate are likely to be nutritional, dating to the prenatal period: "How Much Can We Boost IQ and Scholastic Achievement?" *Harvard Educational Review*, XXXIX (Winter, 1969), 1–123. Those who replied to Jensen in the next issue of the journal seem more bent on airing their own views than in considering his: "Discussion," *HER*, XXXIX (Spring, 1969), 273–356.

THE AMERICAN SOCIETY FOR
EIGHTEENTH-CENTURY STUDIES

PROGRAM
OF THE THIRD ANNUAL MEETING

March 23–25, 1972
University of California at Los Angeles

Thursday, March 23

Morning Session

THE STATE OF SCHOLARSHIP AND INSTRUCTION IN
EIGHTEENTH-CENTURY STUDIES

Presiding: Donald Greene, secretary of the Society

Musicology: "Hadyn, Mozart, and Beethoven? Problems in Teaching Music of the Classical Period"
  Malcolm S. Cole (University of California, Los Angeles)
English Literature: "The Whig Interpretation of Literary History"
  Henry Knight Miller (Princeton University)
British History: "Whigs and Tories: Namier and After"
  John B. Owen (University of Calgary)
Luncheon Address: " 'Racism' in the Old Province of Quebec"
  Hilda Neatby (Queen's University)

Afternoon Session

Presiding: G. S. Rousseau (University of California, Los Angeles)

"Liberty and Libertinism: Form and Content in Picaresque Fiction"
  Maximillian E. Novak (University of California, Los Angeles)
"Pigault Lebrun: A Late Eighteenth-Century Prescursor of the Popular Novel"
  Gregory Ludlow (New York University)

387

"Greek Architectural Forms in the Eighteenth Century"
Beata Panagopoulos (San Jose State College)
"The Application of the Aesthetics of Music in the Philosophy of
the *Sturm und Drang*: Gerstenberg, Hamann, and Herder"
Paul F. Marks (McGill University)

Evening Session
Business Meeting of the Society

Friday, March 24
Morning Session
Section Meetings
Section A: *English and American Literatures*

THE GOTHIC

Chairman: Howard Anderson (Michigan State University)
"Gothic and Pastoral in the Beginning of the Scottish Novel"
Francis R. Hart (University of Virginia)
"Washington Allston and American Gothic"
Stuart McDougal (Michigan State University)
"Meaning and Mode in Gothic Fiction"
Frederick Garber (State University of New York, Binghamton)

Section B: *Other Modern Languages and Literatures*
Chairman: Alison C. Scott (University of Alberta)
"Benjamin Constant and the Enlightenment"
Beatrice C. Fink (University of Maryland)
"Sade: Between the Enlightenment and the *Mal de Siècle*"
Paul Dobson (University of Houston)

Section B-1: *Slavic Literatures*
Chairman: Marvin Kantor (Northwestern University)
"The Uses of History in Eighteenth-Century Russian Literature"
Harold B. Segel (Columbia University)

"The Melancholy and the Wild: A Note on Macpherson's Russian Success"
 Glynn R. Barratt (Carleton University)
"Fonvizin and Catherine's *The Companion of Lovers of the Russian Word*"
 Marvin Kantor (Northwestern University)
"Recasting a Seventeenth-Century Tale: A Note on 'Frol Skobeev' and Novikov's 'Christmas Evening' "
 Richard S. White (Northwestern University)

Section C: *Classics, Comparative Literature, Linguistics, Speech, and Drama*

Chairman: A. O. Aldridge (University of Illinois)
"Pope's *Eloisa* and the *Heroides* of Ovid"
 Hoyt Trowbridge (University of New Mexico)
"The Sufficient Moment in Eighteenth-Century Literature"
 Peter Salm (Case Western Reserve University)
"The Image of German Literature Abroad, 1700–1770"
 Peter Boerner (Indiana University)
"Opera and Incipient Romantic Aesthetics in Germany"
 M. G. Flaherty (Bryn Mawr College)
"Diderot, Wordsworth, and the Creative Process"
 Theodore E. D. Braun (University of Delaware)

Section D: *History, Economics, Political Science*

Chairman: W. Reynolds McLeod (West Virginia University)
Commentaries on Thursday's papers by Hilda Neatby and John B. Owen, with replies and discussion

Section E: *Philosophy, History of Ideas, Religion*

Chairman: Richard H. Popkin (City University of New York, Lehman College)

RACISM IN THE EIGHTEENTH CENTURY

Chairman: Harry M. Bracken (McGill University)

"Father Feijoo and the Question of Race in the Eighteenth Century"
A. O. Aldridge (University of Illinois)
"Dr. Claude-Nicolas Le Cat and the Physiology of Negroes"
G. S. Rousseau (University of California, Los Angeles)
Chairman: Franz Nauen (University of California, San Diego)
"All Men Are Created Equal, but Women?"
Leonora Cohen Rosenfield (University of Maryland)
"Racism in Eighteenth-Century Peru"
Leon G. Campbell (University of California, Riverside)
Chairman: Virgil Topazio (Rice University)
"Buffon and the Science of Man"
Phillip Sloan (University of Washington)
"The Abbé Grégoire and the Egalitarian Movement During the French Revolution"
Ruth F. Necheles (Long Island University)

Section F: *The Fine Arts*

Co-Chairmen: Barry S. Brook (City University of New York)
Frederick J. Cummings (Detroit Institute of Art)

Section G: *Science, Medicine, Technology*

Chairman: Arthur L. Quinn (University of California, Berkeley)

"Conceptual Conflicts in Early Eighteenth-Century Medicine"
Lester S. King, M.D. (American Medical Association and the University of Chicago)
"Science in the Scottish Enlightenment"
Arthur Donovan (University of Illinois, Chicago Circle)

Section H: *Ancillary Disciplines: Bibliography, Biography, History of the Book*

Chairman: W. J. Cameron (University of Western Ontario)

Afternoon Session

Presiding: Herbert Marcuse (University of California, San Diego)

SYMPOSIUM: RACISM IN THE EIGHTEENTH CENTURY

Moderator: Richard H. Popkin (City University of New York, Lehman College)

"Anti-Slavery Ideology: Problems of Liberty and Authority"
David Brion Davis (Yale University)
"The Problem of Race in the West Indies"
David Lowenthal (American Geographical Society)
"The Philosophical Basis of Eighteenth-Century Racism"
Richard H. Popkin (City University of New York, Lehman College)

Panel Discussion led by:
Winthrop B. Jordan (University of California, Berkeley)
Magnes Mörner (Institute of Latin American Studies, Stockholm; visiting professor, University of Texas)

Evening Banquet

Master of Ceremonies: G. S. Rousseau (University of California, Los Angeles)

Remarks: Philip J. Levine (University of California, Los Angeles)
Louis Gottschalk, president of the Society

Address: James L. Clifford (professor emeritus, Columbia University)

A Program of Baroque Court and Theatrical Dances of the Eighteenth Century
The Wendy Hilton Dance Troupe

Saturday, March 25

Option A

A tour of the Henry E. Huntington Library and Art Gallery, with an informal lecture guide
Robert R. Wark (Huntington Library and Art Gallery)

A tour of the Claremont Colleges

Option B

Visit to the William Andrews Clark Memorial Library, UCLA

SYMPOSIUM: THE DANCE IN EARLY EIGHTEENTH-CENTURY EUROPE

Presiding: Pia Gilbert (University of California, Los Angeles)

Commentator: Karl Geiringer (University of California, Santa Barbara)

"A Personal Discovery of Baroque Dance"
  Wendy Hilton, dancer

"Images of Early Eighteenth-Century Dance"
  Shirley Wynne (Ohio State University)

Executive Board
July 1, 1972 to June 30, 1973

President: James L. Clifford, *Columbia University*
Past Presidents: Lester G. Crocker, *University of Virginia*
 Louis Gottschalk, *University of Illinois, Chicago Circle*
First Vice-President: Roy M. Wiles, *McMaster University*
Second Vice-President: Georges May, *Yale University*
Secretary: Donald Greene, *University of Southern California*
Treasurer: Peter J. Stanlis, *Rockford College*
 A. Owen Aldridge, *University of Illinois, Urbana*
 William J. Cameron, *University of Western Ontario*
 Adrienne D. Hytier, *Vassar College*
 Gwin J. Kolb, *University of Chicago*
 Richard H. Popkin, *University of California, San Diego*
 Charles R. Ritcheson, *University of Southern California*

393

American Society for Eighteenth-Century Studies List of Members

INSTITUTIONAL MEMBERS

Alfred University
Bryn Mawr College
Butler University
University of California, Berkeley
University of California, Davis
University of California, Irvine
University of California, Los Angeles
University of California, Riverside
Case Western Reserve University
University of Cincinnati
City College of the City University of
    New York
Claremont Graduate School
Cleveland State University
University of Colorado, Denver
University of Connecticut
University of Delaware
Detroit Institute of the Arts, Founders'
    Society
Fordham University
Georgia State University
University of Illinois, Chicago Circle
University of Illinois, Urbana
University of Iowa
Kent State University
University of Kentucky
Lehigh University
Lehman College of the City University
    of New York
The Lewis Walpole Library
University of Maryland
University of Massachusetts, Boston
McMaster University/Association for
    18th-Century Studies

The Paul Mellon Center for British Art
    and British Studies
Michigan State University
Middle Tennessee State University
University of Minnesota
State University of New York, Fredonia
State University of New York, Oswego
University of North Carolina, Chapel
    Hill
Northern Illinois University
North Georgia College
Northwestern University
Ohio State University
University of Pennsylvania
University of Pittsburgh
Portland State University
Princeton University
Purdue University
Rice University
Rockford College
University of South Carolina
University of Southern California
Stanford University
Swarthmore College
Sweet Briar College
Temple University
Tulane University
University of Virginia
Washington and Lee University
Wayne State University
West Chester State College, Pennsylvania
University of Western Ontario
The Henry Francis du Pont Winterthur
    Museum
Yale University

INDIVIDUAL MEMBERS

C— Charter member (joined before April 17, 1970)
Sp—Sponsoring member
S— Student member
Members not so indicated are regular members

ABDELLA, Christina
Comparative and foreign literature
 (assistant professor)
Rutgers University
314 Glenn Avenue
Trenton, N. J. 08638

ACOMB, Frances D.   C
History (associate professor)
Duke University
Box 6777 College Station
Durham, N. C. 27708
*Political and social ideas, esp. Mallet du
 Pan*

ADAMS, Geoffrey   C
History (associate professor)
Loyola College
7141 Sherbrooke St. W.
Montreal 262, Quebec
*Relation between French protestants
 and philosophes*

ADAMS, Leonard   C
French (lecturer)
University of Guelph
Guelph, Ontario
Eighteenth century in France

ADAMS, Margaret E.   Sp
Modern languages (associate professor)
State College at Boston
Woods End Road
Lincoln, Mass. 01773
*Development of liberal thought; early
 encyclopedists*

ADAMS, Percy G.
English (professor)
University of Tennessee
Knoxville, Tenn. 37916
*Travel literature; novel; Franco-British
 relations*

ADAMS, Thomas M.
History
University of Kansas
Lawrence, Kansas 66044
The "dépots de mendicité,"   ᴜ4-1789

ADLER, Jacob H.   C
English (professor)
Purdue University
Lafayette, Indiana 47907
Pope; literary criticism

AGNIERAY, Gérard   C
Romance languages (lecturer)
University of Arizona
Tucson, Arizona 85721
Pierre Bayle

ALDRIDGE, A. Owen   C
Comparative literature (professor)
University of Illinois
Urbana, Illinois 61801
Ibero-American enlightenment

ALKON, Paul K.   C
English (associate professor)
University of Minnesota
Minneapolis, Minn. 55455
English literature, esp. Samuel Johnson

ALLAIN, Mathé   C
Foreign languages (instructor)
University of Southwestern Louisiana
Box 1542
Lafayette, Louisiana 70501
Voltaire; colonial Louisiana

ALLEGO, Donna M.   C
English (instructor)
Western Illinois University
Macomb, Illinois 61455
*Burke; Swift; Johnson; American
 political writing*

List of Members

ALLEN, Robert R.
English (assistant professor)
University of Southern California
Los Angeles, California 90007
Bibliography; printing; Samuel Johnson

ALLENTUCK, Marcia   C
English (associate professor)
City College, CUNY
5 West 86th St. Apt. 12B
New York, N. Y. 10024
Aesthetics and criticism; British and American literature

ALLISON, Daniel Brian   S
English (teaching assistant)
University of Southern California
2077 Chestnut Ave.
Long Beach, California 90806
English literature

ALLISON, Henry E.
Philosophy (associate professor)
University of Florida
Gainesville, Florida 32601
Philosophy; theology

ALVERSON, J. Stewart   S
History
Case Western Reserve University
315 Wyandot Place
Huron, Ohio 44839
French revolution; intellectual history

AMETER, Brenda   S
English
Indiana University
1303 North Allen Street
Robinson, Illinois 62454
Fiction: Richardson, Gothic

AMMERLAHN, Hellmut
Germanic languages and literature
  (assistant professor)
University of Washington
Seattle, Washington 98105
Goethe; philosophy; music

ANDERSON, David L.   C
French (assistant professor)
Pennsylvania State University
S-408 Burrowes

University Park, Pa. 16802
French literature

ANDERSON, George L.   C
English (professor)
University of Hawaii
Honolulu, Hawaii 96822
Queen Anne period; criticism; literature and politics

ANDERSON, Howard   C
English (professor)
Michigan State University
East Lansing, Michigan, 48823
Novel, esp. gothic novel; Laurence Sterne

ANDERSON, Rodney E.   S
History
Southern Illinois University
Rural Route No. 1
Eldorado, Illinois 62930
French and German history

ANDERSON, William L.   C
History (assistant professor)
Western Carolina University
Box 888
Cullowhee, North Carolina 28723
European history (1700-1815)

ANDREWS, Norwood, Jr.
Classical and Romance languages
  (professor)
Texas Tech University
Lubbock, Texas 79409

ARNASON, H. Harvard   C
Art History
1075 Park Ave., Apt. 14D
New York, N. Y. 10028
French sculpture; Jean-Antoine Houdon

ASKEW, Pamela
Art (professor)
Vassar College
Poughkeepsie, New York 12601
Art history

ASTMAN, Joseph G.
Foreign languages (professor)
Dean, College of Liberal Arts and
  Sciences

397

Hofstra University
2 Border Lane
Levittown, New York 11756
*German literature; influence of Greek
tragedians on dramas of Kleist*

ATKINS, G. Douglas   C
English (assistant professor)
University of Kansas
Lawrence, Kansas 66044
*Restoration and eighteenth-century
English literature*

ATTERIDGE, Thomas
English (lecturer)
Syracuse University
203 Hall of Languages
Syracuse, New York 13210
Swift

AUBERY, Pierre
French (professor)
State University of New York at Buffalo
Buffalo, New York 14214

BACKSCHEIDER, Paula   S
English
Purdue University
1515 Marilyn Avenue
W. Lafayette, Indiana 47906
Defoe, Swift, Wycherley

BADIR, Magdy Gabriel
Romance languages (lecturer)
University of Alberta
Edmonton, Alberta
Voltaire and Islam

BADURA-SKODA, Eva   C
Music (professor)
University of Wisconsin
1D University Houses
Madison, Wisconsin 53705
History of music in Vienna

BAER, Joel H.   C
English (instructor)
Macalester College
St. Paul, Minn. 55101
Switf; Defoe; Johnson; Scottish folksong

BAHR, Ehrhard
Germanic languages (associate
professor)
University of California
Los Angeles, California 90024
Goethe; Lessing; irony

BAIRD, John D.   C
English (assistant professor)
Victoria College, University of Toronto
Toronto 5, Ontario
*William Cowper; later eighteenth-
century literature*

BAIRD, Thomas R.
History (assistant professor)
St. Francis College
159 West 12th Street
New York, New York 10011
*Social origins of notables born after
1750*

BAKER, Van R.   C
English (associate professor)
York College
York, Pennsylvania 17403
English literature; Pennsylvania history

BALKAN, Katherine S.
Art history (graduate student)
University of California, Los Angeles
10554 Lauriston Avenue
Los Angeles, California 90064
Art history (England)

BALL, David   C
French (lecturer)
Smith College
Northampton, Mass. 01060
Swift, Voltaire

BAMFORD, Paul W.
History (professor)
University of Minnesota
Minneapolis, Minnesota 55455
*France, social history,
maritime history (Old Regime)*

BANERJEE, Chinmoy
English (assistant professor)
Simon Fraser University
Burnaby 2, British Columbia
Novel in English

BANNON, Peter   C
English (professor)
Memphis State University
340 South Prescott St.
Memphis, Tennessee 38111
*Eighteenth-century poetry: Pope and
   Blake*

BAREIKIS, Robert P.
German (associate professor)
Indiana University
Bloomington, Indiana 47401
*Drama; lyric; Johann C. Gottsched;
   Benjamin Neukirch; Lessing*

BARKER, David E.
Modern foreign languages (instructor)
Saginaw Valley College
2250 Pierce Road
University Center, Michigan 48710
*Voltaire et "l'infâme";
   histoire des idées*

BARKER, Gerard A.   C
English (assistant professor)
Queens College, CUNY
Flushing, New York 11367
Novel; history of ideas

BARKER, John C.
History (associate professor)
Trent University
Peterborough, Ontario
*History of ideas; history of science;
   intellectual contacts between England
   and France*

BARKER, Rosalind   C
English (lecturer)
Victoria College
University of Toronto
Toronto 5, Ontario
Drama; literary criticism

BARLOW, Walter L.   S
French (graduate student)
Rice University
Houston, Texas 77001
Rousseau

BARNES, Clifford R.   C
Music (associate professor)

Brigham Young University
HFAC E454
Provo, Utah 84601
Opéra-Comique

BARNES, Donald Grove   C
History (professor emeritus)
Case Western Reserve University
2300 Overlook Road
Cleveland, Ohio 44106
British history

BARR, Mary-Margaret H.   C
French
P.O. Box 716
Portland, Indiana 47371
Voltaire; Franco-American relations

BARTON, H. Arnold   C
History
Southern Illinois University
Carbondale, Illinois 62901

BASNEY, Lionel
English (assistant professor)
Houghton College
Box 25
Houghton, New York 14744
Johnson; development of aesthetics

BATTEN, Charles L., Jr.   C
English (assistant professor)
University of California
Los Angeles, California 90024
Non-fiction travel literature

BATTERSBY, James L.
English (associate professor)
Ohio State University
Denney Hall
164 West 17th Avenue
Columbus, Ohio 43210
Samuel Johnson; critical theory

BATTESTIN, Martin C.   C
English (professor)
University of Virginia
Charlottesville, Virginia 22901
*Fielding and the novel; the period
   1660-1750*

399

BAUKE, Joseph   C
German (professor)
Columbia University
423 W. 120th Street
New York, N. Y. 10027
*Enlightenment and classicism in
Germany*

BAXTER, Charles Langtry, Jr.
317 West 11th Street
New York, New York 10014
Richardson; Swift; history of ideas

BEALE, Georgia Robison   C
History (professor)
University of Kentucky
Lexington, Kentucky 40506
Directory; L.-A.-G. Bosc

BEATTIE, J. M.   C
History (associate professor)
University of Toronto
Toronto 5, Ontario
*Social history; crime and the
administration of justice*

BEAUMONT, Charles
English (professor)
University of Georgia
Athens, Georgia 30601
British literature; satire in general

BECK, Lewis White
Philosophy (professor)
University of Rochester
Rochester, New York 14627
Philosophy; history of ideas

BEDFORD, Emmett G.   C
English (assistant professor)
University of Wisconsin-Parkside
Kenosha, Wisconsin 53140
Alexander Pope; religious symbolism

BEHRENS, Laurence   S
English (graduate student)
University of California
3283 Sepulveda Boulevard
Apt. 3
Los Angeles, California 90034
Novel

BEIK, Paul H.   C
History (professor)
Swarthmore College
Swarthmore, Pa. 19081
French revolution

BELCHER, William F.   C
English (professor)
North Texas State University
Denton, Texas 76203
Pope; Swift; the novel

BENHAMOU, Paul
Modern languages (assistant professor)
Purdue University
Lafayette, Indiana 47907
*French periodicals—l'Encyclopédie,
les antiphilosophes*

BENNETT, Fordyce
English (professor)
Pasadena College
Howard at Bresee
Pasadena, California 91104
Johnson; Prior; Cowper

BENNETT, Pamela J.   S
English (graduate student)
Indiana University
Bloomington, Indiana 47401

BENTON, Rita
Music (associate professor)
University of Iowa
School of Music Library
Iowa City, Iowa 52240
France

BERGMANN, Frederick L.   C
English (professor)
DePauw University
Greencastle, Indiana 46135
Drama; David Garrick

BERKVAM, Michael L.
French and Italian (lecturer)
Indiana University
Bloomington, Indiana 47401
*Society and Literature in 18th-Century
France; Pierre-Michel Hennin*

BETTS, Marilyn J.   S
University of Florida
3722 S.W. 19th Street
Gainesville, Florida 32601

BEVILACQUA, Vincent M.   C
Speech (associate professor)
University of Massachusetts
367 Bartlett Hall
Amherst, Mass. 01002
*Rhetorical literature; aesthetics and art
    theory*

BEYER, Charles J.   C
French (professor)
State University of New York
Buffalo, New York 14214
Montesquieu

BILL, Shirley A.
History (professor)
University of Illinois at Chicago Circle
1907 University Hall
Chicago, Illinois 60680
*U.S. constitutional and early national
    history; U.S. Revolution*

BILLINGS, Elizabeth
Modern languages (instructor)
Dickinson College
Route 944, R.D. 2
Carlisle, Pa. 17013
French and German literature; music

BINGHAM, Alfred J.   C
French (professor)
University of Maryland
College Park, Maryland 20742
Voltaire; philosophical controversies

BIRN, Raymond   C
History (associate professor)
University of Oregon
Eugene, Oregon 97403
France; the press and the book trade

BJORNSTAD, William B.   C
English (professor)
Drake University
Des Moines, Iowa 50311
*Swift, Pope, French-English intercultural
    relations*

BLACKALL, Eric A.
German (professor)
186 Goldwin Smith Hall
Cornell University
Ithaca, New York 14850

BLANCO, Richard L.
History (professor)
SUNY at Brockport
Brockport, New York 14420
Military and medical history

BLAYDES, Sophia B.
English (associate professor)
West Virginia University
Morgantown, West Virginia 26505
Christopher Smart

BLEWETT, D. L.   C
English (lecturer)
McMaster University
Hamilton, Ontario
Fiction

BLYTHE, Harold R., Jr.
English (assistant professor)
Adrian College
Adrian, Michigan 49221
Eighteenth-century novel; Smollett

BOERNER, Peter   C
Comparative literature (professor)
Indiana University
1213 East First Street
Bloomington, Indiana 47401
Prose fiction; autobiography; Goethe

BOGORARD, Samuel N.   C
English (professor)
University of Vermont
Burlington, Vermont 05401
Drama; satire; Swift

BOHNE, Frederick J.   C
English (professor)
Edenboro State College
R.D. 3
Edinboro, Pa. 16412
Literature; esp. Swift, Pope

BOND, Richmond P.   C
English (professor)

401

University of North Carolina
101 Pine Lane
Chapel Hill, N. C. 27514
Periodicals

BONGIE, Laurence L. C
French (professor)
University of British Columbia
Vancouver 8, British Columbia
David Hume; French history of ideas

BONNEVILLE, Douglas A.
Romance languages (associate professor)
University of Florida
Box 415 GSIS
Gainesville, Florida 32601
Voltaire's romans; Diderot's early works; Eighteenth-century French novel

BORDEN, Gavin
English
Garland Press, Inc.
24 West 45th Street
New York, New York 10036
Novel and criticism

BOSSE, Malcolm J. C
English (lecturer)
City College, CUNY
91 Charles Street
New York, N. Y. 10014
Late eighteenth-century fiction

BOULBY, Mark C
German (professor)
University of British Columbia
Vancouver 8, British Columbia
Pietism and mysticism in German literature

BOULLE, Pierre H. C
History (assistant professor)
McGill University
Montreal 110, Quebec
History of France; colonies

BOWEN, Vincent
French (associate professor)
University of Illinois
Urbana, Illinois 61801
French fiction, esp. Diderot

BOWERS, Bro. Francis R., FSC C
English (associate professor)
Manhattan College
Bronx, New York 10471
George Crabbe; drama

BOWRON, Edgar Peters
The Minneapolis Institute of Arts
201 E. 24th Street
Minneapolis, Minnesota 55404

BOYCE, Benjamin C
English (professor emeritus)
Duke University
1200 Dewire Place
Durham, North Carolina 27706
English and French prose fiction

BOYER, Bruce H.
Dramatic Arts
Amherst College
Amherst, Massachusetts 01002
Plays and play publication (printing history), 1700-1750

BOYER, G. Bruce
English (instructor)
Allentown College
Center Valley, Pennsylvania 18034

BOYER, Mildred
Spanish and Portuguese (professor)
University of Texas
902 Lund Street
Austin, Texas 78704
Spanish literature; drama

BRACK, O M, Jr. C
English (associate professor)
Arizona State University
Tempe, Arizona 85281
History of printing; prose fiction

BRACKEN, Harry M.
Philosophy (professor)
McGill University
Montreal 110, Quebec
Bayle; Berkeley; Scottish philosophy

BRADBURY, Miles L.
History (assistant professor)
University of Maryland

List of Members

College Park, Md. 20740
Political theory; education; religion

BRADHAM, Jo Allen
English (assistant professor)
Agnes Scott College
Box 923
Decatur, Georgia 30030
Pope, Swift

BRADSHER, Greg   S
History (graduate student)
University of Massachusetts
21 Prince House
Amherst, Massachusetts 01002
American intellectual-religious history

BRADY, Patrick
French and Italian (professor)
Rice University
Houston, Texas 77001
Rococo style; the novel form

BRADY, Valentini Papadopoulou
c/o Patrick Brady
Department of French and Italian
Rice University
Houston, Texas 77001
Marivaux

BRANAM, George C.   C
English (professor; vice chancellor)
Office of Academic Affairs
Louisiana State University
New Orleans, Louisiana 70122
Theater and literary criticism

BRAUDY, Leo   C
English (assistant professor)
Columbia University
416 Hamilton Hall
New York, N. Y. 10027
Novel; history; satire

BRAUER, George C., Jr.   C
English (professor)
University of South Carolina
17-G Cornell Arms Apartments
Columbia, South Carolina 29201
*Classical influences; Swift; Pope;
    Johnson; novel*

BRAUN, Theodore E. D.   C
Languages and literature (professor)
University of Delaware
Newark, Delaware 19711
*French literature; poetry; theater;
    Voltaire*

BRENNER, Rosamond Drooker   C
Music history
726 North Park Boulevard
Glen Ellyn, Illinois 60137
*German baroque opera (Reinhard
    Keiser)*

BREWER, Gwen W.
English (associate professor)
California State University
Northridge, California 91324
Restoration drama; novel; folklore

BRICKE, John J.   C
Philosophy (assistant professor)
University of Kansas
Lawrence, Kansas 66044
*British empiricist philosopher, esp.
    David Hume*

BRIDGMAN, Richard
English (associate professor)
University of California
Berkeley, California 94720

BRISLANE, Daniel V.
English (assistant professor)
Saint Bonaventure University
Saint Bonaventure, New York 14778

BROFSKY, Howard   C
Music (professor)
Queens College, CUNY
Flushing, New York 11367
*Musicology: Italian and French
    instrumental music*

BRONSON, B. H.   C
English (professor emeritus)
University of California, Berkeley
927 Oxford St.
Berkeley, California 94707
*Arts and literature (esp. music and
    poetry)*

BROOK, Barry S.   C
Musicology (professor)
City University of New York
505 West End Ave.
New York, N. Y. 10024

BROOKS, Douglas
English (lecturer)
University of Manchester
11 Agnes Road
Blundellsands
Liverpool L23 6ST, England
Literature; music; art/architecture

BROOKS, Richard A.   C
Humanities (professor)
Richmond College, CUNY
Staten Island, N. Y. 10301
Voltaire; French Enlightenment;
  bibliography

BROWN, Jack R.   C
English (professor)
Marshall University
Huntington, West Virginia 25701
Fielding; drama

BROWN, Lorraine A.
English (assistant professor)
George Mason College of the University
  of Virginia
4400 University Drive
Fairfax, Virginia 22030

BROWN, Richard G.   C
English (assistant professor)
Ball State University
Muncie, Indiana 47306

BROWNE, Dennis J. M.   S
English (graduate student)
University of California
Hershey Hall
805 Hilgard Avenue
Los Angeles, California 90024
Augustan literature; political thought

BROWNELL, Morris R.
English (assistant professor)
Cornell University
Ithaca, New York 14850

BROYLES, Michael E.   C
Music history (assistant professor)
University of Maryland, Baltimore
  County
5401 Wilkens Avenue
Baltimore, Maryland 21228

BRÜCKMANN, Patricia
English (associate professor)
Trinity College, University of Toronto
Toronto 5, Ontario
Pope; Scriblerus Club

BRYAN, Paul R.   C
Music (associate professor)
Duke University
Box 6695 College Station
Durham, N. C. 27708
Music: Mozart and Haydn milieu

BUCHANAN, Michelle
French and Italian (assistant professor)
University of Southern California
Los Angeles, California 90007
Novel; memoirs; theater

BUCSELA, John   C
Russian (associate professor)
Emory University
Atlanta, Georgia 30322
Russian language and literature

BUFORD, Lenore V.   C
Foreign languages (head)
Cuyahoga Community College
13800 Terrace Road, Apt. 717
East Cleveland, Ohio 44112
Voltaire, Diderot, theater

BURLINGAME, Leslie J.
History (assistant professor)
Mount Holyoke College
South Hadley, Mass. 01075
French biological ideas, esp. evolutionary
  speculations (Lamarck)

BURNETTE, Rand   C
History (assistant professor)
MacMurray College
Jacksonville, Illinois 62650
American colonial history and English
  history

404

BURROUGHS, Sara
Languages (associate professor)
Northwestern State University of
Louisiana
Natchitoches, Louisiana 71457
*Biography; Gentleman's Magazine;
Johnson*

BUSCH, Gudrun   C
Music (assistant professor)
D 4050 Mönchengladbach
Roemonder Str. 58
Germany
*History of eighteenth-century German
Lied*

BYRNES, Joseph A.   C
English (assistant professor)
New York University
P.O. Box 283
Elizabeth, New Jersey 07207
Dramatic literature; theater history

CALDWELL, Gilbert L., Jr.   C
English (teaching fellow)
Bowling Green State University
Bowling Green, Ohio 43403
Drama

CALLAHAN, Anne M.   C
French (assistant professor)
Chestnut Hill College
2100 Walnut Street
Philadelphia, Pa. 19103
French literature of Enlightenment

CAMERON, William J.
Library and information science (dean)
University of Western Ontario
1510 Western Road
London 72, Ontario

CANAVAN, Francis, S.J.   C
Political science (associate professor)
Fordham University
Loyola Hall
Bronx, New York 10458
Edmund Burke; political philosophy

CANE, Edric   S
Romance languages
University of Michigan

2307 Fernwood
Ann Arbor, Michigan 48104
Influence of John Locke

CANEPA, Andrew M.   S
History
University of California
Los Angeles, California 90024
*Italian and French intellectual history;
travel accounts*

CANFIELD, J. Douglas   C
English (assistant professor)
University of California
Los Angeles, California 90024
Restoration drama

CAPRIO, Anthony Salvatore
French (instructor)
Lehman College, CUNY
P.O. Box 765
Poughquag, N. Y. 12570

CARDY, M. J.
Romance Studies (associate professor)
Brock University
St. Catharines, Ontario
J. F. Marmontel; Diderot; literary theory

CARELS, Peter Edgerton
German and Russian (instructor)
Miami University
214 West Collins Street
Oxford, Ohio 45056
Satire; decorative arts

CARMODY, Terence F.
English (assistant professor)
Fairleigh Dickinson University
Rutherford, New Jersey 07070
The Age of Johnson

CARNIE, Robert Hay
English (professor)
University of Calgary
Calgary 44, Alberta
*Bibliography; Scottish literature;
Johnson group*

CARNOCHAN, W. B.   Sp
English (associate professor)
Stanford University

405

Stanford, California 94305
Swift; satire; the "Augustans"

CARR, Thomas M., Jr.
Modern Languages
University of Nebraska
Lincoln, Nebraska 68508

CARRITHERS, David W.
History (assistant professor)
University of Tennessee at Chattanooga
Chattanooga, Tennessee 37401
French enlightenment; Montesquieu

CARROLL, Charles M.
Music (professor)
St. Petersburg Junior College
1701 80th Street North
St. Petersburg, Florida 33710
*French opéra comique, 1750-1800; chess
and chess-players, 1750-1800*

CARTWRIGHT, Michael T.   C
French (assistant professor)
Peterson Hall
McGill University
Montreal, Quebec
Diderot; aesthetics and art criticism

CASH, Arthur H.   C
English (professor)
State University of New York
New Paltz, New York 12568
Novel, esp. Laurence Sterne

CASSIDY, Hélène Monod-
French (associate professor)
Van Hise Hall
University of Wisconsin
Madison, Wisconsin 53711
Novel; theater; history of science

CASTELLANI, Joseph   C
English (instructor)
Ball State University
14 Duane Road
Muncie, Indiana 47304

CAVANAUGH, Gerald J.   C
History (assistant professor)
University of California
Berkeley, California 94720

*Old regime France; European
Enlightenment*

CAVE, Michael
Romance and classical languages
(lecturer)
University of Connecticut
19 Little Bay Lane
Short Beach, Connecticut 06405
*Spanish literature; baroque; the
Comedia*

CHAPDU, Robert E.   C
English (instructor)
University of Illinois
507 Westlawn
Champaign, Illinois 61820
*Johnson; Boswell; printing house
practice*

CHAPIN, Chester F.   C
English (professor)
3506 N.R.
University of Michigan
Ann Arbor, Michigan 48104
Johnson; history of ideas

CHERPACK, Clifton   C
Romance languages (professor)
University of Pennsylvania
Philadelphia, Pennsylvania 19104
French fiction

CHRISTIAN, William
Economics and political science
(assistant professor)
Mount Allison University
P.O. Box 1233
Sackville, New Brunswick

CHRISTIANSON, Eric Howard   S
History (graduate student)
University of Southern California
Los Angeles, Calif. 90007
*Science; cultural, social, and intellectual
history*

CHUBB, Charles Stuart   S
English (graduate student)
Queen's University
King Pitt Road
Kingston, Ontario
Augustan journalism; personal literature

CHURGIN, Bathia   C
Music (professor)
Bar-Ilan University
Ramat Gan, Israel
Music (eighteenth-century symphony)

CLARK, Anthony Morris   Sp
Art history
Director, The Minneapolis Institute of
  Arts
201 East 24th Street
Minneapolis, Minn. 55404
*18th-c. Roman painting, other arts,
  social history*

CLARK, E. Roger   C
French (assistant professor)
Memorial University of Newfoundland
St. John's, Newfoundland
Utopian novel in French

CLARK, Evalyn A.   C
History (professor emeritus)
Vassar College
Poughkeepsie, New York 12601
*French Enlightenment and French
  Revolution*

CLARK, John R.   C
English (associate professor)
New York University
30 Woodcliff Drive
Madison, New Jersey 07940
Swift; Pope; English literature; satire

CLEMENTS, Frances M.   C
English (assistant professor)
University of Wisconsin
Green Bay, Wisconsin 54305
Novel and social history

CLEVER, Glenn
English (assistant professor)
University of Ottawa
Ottawa 2, Ontario
Novel; narrative poetry; diaries

CLIFFORD, James L.   C
English (professor emeritus)
Columbia University
25 Claremont Avenue
New York, N. Y. 10027

*English literature; Samuel Johnson and
  his circle*

COBURN, William Leon
English (assistant professor)
University of Nevada
Las Vegas, Nevada 89109
The novel; Henry Fielding; criticism

COGEN, Jill R.   C
Music (librarian)
University of California, Los Angeles
5072 Gaviota Ave.
Encino, California 91316
*Cultural history of French Revolution;
  English political history, 1750-1800*

COHEN, Murray   C
English (assistant professor)
University of California
Berkeley, California 94720
Novel; intellectual history

COHEN, Ralph   C
English (professor)
University of Virginia
Wilson Hall
Charlottesville, Va. 22901

COHEN, Richard   C
English (professor)
Illinois Benedictine College
Lisle, Illinois 60532
The novel

COLE, Malcolm S.   C
Music (assistant professor)
University of California
Schoenberg Hall
Los Angeles, California 90024
*Haydn; Mozart; Beethoven; instrumental
  rondo*

COLEMAN, Philip C.
English
Charles Scribner's Sons
597 Fifth Avenue
New York, N. Y. 10017
English belles lettres

COLTON, Judith
Visual Arts

407

Bennington College
525 West End Avenue, Apt. 14G
New York, New York 10024
*Eighteenth-century French and British
art: social and intellectual background*

COLUMBUS, Thomas M.   C
English (instructor)
University of Dayton
Dayton, Ohio 45409
English literature; Augustan age

COMER, David B., III   C
English (professor)
Georgia Institute of Technology
Atlanta, Georgia 30332

COMMAGER, Henry Steele   Sp
History (professor)
Amherst College
405 S. Pleasant St.
Amherst, Mass. 01002
*European relations; American
  Enlightenment*

COMPEAN, Richard   S
English (graduate student)
University of California
Davis, Calif. 95616
Religion; wit; humor; satire; Swift

CONLON, Pierre M.   C
French (professor)
McMaster University
Hamilton, Ontario
Voltaire

CONNORS, Joseph B.   C
English (professor)
College of St. Thomas
St. Paul, Minnesota 55101
Johnson circle; 18th-century London

COOK, Cynthia M.   S
French (graduate student)
University of Texas
208 Lee Hall
Austin, Texas 78712
French literature; Voltaire

COOK, Marlinda Bruno   S
French

University of Pittsburgh
1617 C. L.
Pittsburgh, Pennsylvania 15213
Les Mémoires secrets de Bachaumont

COPELAND, Thomas W.
English (professor)
University of Massachusetts
251 Sunset Avenue
Amherst, Mass. 01002
Edmund Burke

CORMICK, Jean A.
Literature (graduate student)
University of California, San Diego
718 Sycamore Avenue, No. 31
Vista, California 92083

CONSENTINI, John W.   C
French (professor)
St. John's University
Jamaica, New York 11432
The Dialogue

COUGHLIN, Donald J.
English (assistant professor)
Loyola University
6525 N. Sheridan
Chicago, Illinois 60626
Samuel Johnson; Jonathan Swift; genre

COUGHLIN, Edward
Romance languages (assistant
  professor)
University of Cincinnati
Cincinnati, Ohio 45221
Spanish literature

COUGHLIN, Howard James, Jr.
P.O. Box 9
South Windham, Connecticut 06266
*Gibbon; La Blèterie; other historians and
  biographers*

COUMONT, Eileen   S
English
Rice University
Houston, Texas 77001
*English and classical literature;
  imitations of Greek and Latin
  poetry; epic*

408

COURTNEY, Alice K.　　　　C
Romance languages (instructor)
Ohio Wesleyan University
Delaware, Ohio 43016
French literature, esp. the novel

COWLER, Rosemary E.　　　C
English (professor)
Lake Forest College
Lake Forest, Ill. 60045
Pope; Richardson

COX, R. Merritt
Modern Languages
College of William and Mary
Williamsburg, Virginia 23185
Spain: critical theory, poetry

CRAGG, Olga B.
French (assistant professor)
University of British Columbia
Vancouver 8, B. C.
Novel; Mme Riccoboni

CRANDALL, Joan　　　　　S
Interdisciplinary (graduate student)
Michigan State University
863 N. Kentview Drive, NE
Grand Rapids, Michigan 49505
History; art; literature

CRAWFORD, Frederic M., Jr.　　C
History (assistant professor)
Middle Tennessee State University
Box 142
Murfreesboro, Tenn. 37130
*Communication of ideas; intellectual
　history*

CREIGHTON, Douglas G.
French (associate professor)
University of Western Ontario
London 72, Ontario
French literature and thought; Diderot

CROCKER, Lester G.　　　　C
French (professor)
University of Virginia
Charlottesville, Virginia 22903
French literature; European thought

CRONIN, Grover, Jr.　　　　C
English (professor)
Fordham University
Bronx, N. Y. 10458
Eighteenth-century England

CROUT, Robert Rhodes　　　S
History Department
University of Georgia
Athens, Georgia 30601
French imperialism

CUMMINGS, Frederick J.　　C
Art history
Assistant director, Detroit Institute of
　Arts
5200 Woodward Ave.
Detroit, Michigan 48202

CUNNINGHAM, William F., Jr.　C
English (professor)
Le Moyne College
Syracuse, New York 13214

CURLEY, Thomas M.
English (assistant professor)
Fordham University
294 Bronxville Road, Apt. 4-A
Bronxville, New York 10708
*English literature; Samuel Johnson;
　prose fiction*

DAGHLIAN, Philip B.　　　C
English (professor)
Indiana University
Bloomington, Indiana 47401
Johnson; Boswell; Horace Walpole

DALSANT, John B.
English (assistant professor)
Humboldt State College
Arcata, California 95521
Pope; Hogarth and graphic art; novel

DARNTON, Robert
History (associate professor
Dickinson Hall
Princeton University
Princeton, New Jersey 08540
*Grub Street literature in France,
　publishing, and J. P. Brissot*

DASH, Irene   S
English (graduate student)
Columbia University
161 West 16th Street
New York, N. Y. 10011
*Shakespeare's plays in eighteenth
century*

DAUTERMAN, Carl C.   C
Art history (curator)
The Metropolitan Museum of Art
New York, N. Y. 10028
Western European arts

DAUTERMAN, (Mrs.) Carl C.
1326 Madison Avenue
New York, N. Y. 10028

DAVIDSON, Hugh M.   C
Romance languages (professor)
Ohio State University
3838 Chiselhurst Place
Columbus, Ohio 43220
*Rhetoric and "philosophie";
Montesquieu; Rousseau*

DAVIE, Donald   C
English (professor)
Stanford University
989 Cottrell Way
Stanford, California 94305
*Poetry; scientific vocabulary; Jefferson
and John Adams*

DAVIES, Richard A.
English (assistant professor)
Box 168
Acadia University
Wolfville, Nova Scotia
Laurence Sterne

DAVIS, Bertram H.
English (general secretary AAUP)
3009 Daniel Lane N. W.
Washington, D. C. 20015
*Sir John Hawkins; Samuel Johnson;
music*

DAVIS, Charles George
English
Boise State College
Boise, Idaho 83704
Novel; satire; Henry Fielding

DAVIS, James Herbert, Jr.   C
Romance languages (associate
professor)
University of Georgia
Athens, Georgia 30601
Eighteenth-century French theater

DAVY, Francis X.
English (professor)
Box 1031
Eastern Kentucky University
Richmond, Kentucky 40475
Jonathan Swift; the rise of the novel

DAY, Robert Adams   C
English (professor)
Queens College, CUNY
Flushing, New York 11367
English fiction, poetry, bibliography

DE ARMAS, Frederick A.
Foreign Languages (assistant professor)
Louisiana State University
Baton Rouge, Louisiana 70803
Spanish literature

DE BUSSY, Carvel
Foreign Languages (associate professor)
District of Columbia Teachers College
1100 Harvard Street, N.W.
Washington, D. C. 20009
*Rousseau: the impact of the Social
Contract in Europe and America*

DESAUTELS, Alfred R., S.J.   C
Modern languages (professor)
Holy Cross College
Worcester, Mass. 01610
Intellectual history of the philosophes

DESCHÊNES, Martin O.   C
French (assistant professor)
Tennessee State University
411 North Wilson Blvd.
Nashville, Tenn. 37205
Voltaire

DE SOLE, Gloria M.   C
English (assistant professor)
Skidmore College
29 South Manning Boulevard
Albany, New York 12203
The Scriblerians

410

DESROCHES, Richard H.   C
Romance languages (associate
    professor)
University of Oregon
Eugene, Oregon 97403
French literature, esp. novel

DEWEES, Charles W., Jr.   C
English (associate professor)
Philadelphia College of Textiles and
    Science
Schoolhouse Lane & Henry Ave.
Philadelphia, Pa. 19144
Fiction

DICKEY, William   C
English (associate professor)
California State University
San Francisco, Caiif. 94132
*Augustan poetry; Swift; eighteenth-
    century novel*

DIRCKS, P. T.   C
English (assistant professor)
C. W. Post College of Long Island
    University
72 Halstead Ave.
Yonkers, N. Y. 10704
Eighteenth-century drama

DIRCKS, Richard J.   C
English (professor)
St. John's University
72 Halstead Ave.
Yonkers, New York 10704
*Henry Fielding; eighteenth-century
    drama and novel*

DOBSON, Paul   C
History (assistant professor)
University of Houston
Cullen Boulevard
Houston, Texas 77004
*Historiography; dissemination of ideas
    of philosophes*

DOCK, Terry Smiley   S
French (graduate student)
Vanderbilt University
Box 1651, Station B
Nashville, Tennessee 37203

DOLMETSCH, Carl R.
English (professor)
College of William and Mary
Williamsburg, Virginia 23185
American literature

DOLMETSCH, Joan
Art history
Department of Collections
Colonial Williamsburg
Williamsburg, Virginia 23185

DONNELLY, Jerome
English (assistant professor)
Florida Technological University
Box 25000
Orlando, Florida 32816

DONOVAN, Arthur
History (assistant professor)
University of Illinois, Chicago Circle
Chicago, Illinois 60680
*History of science and technology;
    Scottish Enlightenment*

DORRIS, George   C
English (assistant professor)
York College, CUNY
Bayside, New York 11363
Augustan poetry, tragedy, opera

DOWLING, John
Romance languages (professor)
University of Georgia
Athens, Georgia 30601
Drama

DOWNEY, James   C
English (associate professor)
Carleton University
Ottawa 1, Ontario
*Church history, esp. homiletics; Laurence
    Sterne*

DOYLE, Charles Clay   C
English (assistant professor)
University of Southern California
Los Angeles, Calif. 90007
Interregnum and Restoration verse

DRUESEDOW, John E., Jr.   C
Music (instructor)

411

Miami University
Oxford, Ohio 45056
Music in Spain and Latin America

DUBRO, James R.
English (teaching fellow)
Victoria College, University of Toronto
51 Grosvenor St., Apt. 206A
Toronto 5, Ontario
*Johnson; Lord Hervey; Lady Mary
Wortley Montagu*

DUCHOVNAY, Gerald C.   C
English
JU Box 27
Jacksonville University Station
Jacksonville, Florida 32211
Prose fiction; literature and the arts

DUIKER, Yvonne V.   S
French (graduate student)
Pennsylvania State University
430 Sylvan Drive
State College, Pa. 16801
Eighteenth-century French novel

DU PONT, Bernard L.   S
Romance languages (teaching assistant)
University of Washington
Seattle, Washington 98105
*Eighteenth-century novel; Anglo-French
relations*

DURER, Christopher S.
English (assistant professor)
University of Wyoming
Box 3353, University Station
Laramie, Wyoming 82070

DUSSINGER, John A.   C
English (associate professor)
University of Illinois
1612 Chevy Chase Drive
Champaign, Illinois 61820
*Fiction; history of ideas; Johnson and
his circle*

EBERWEIN, Robert   C
English (assistant professor)
Oakland University
379 West Frank
Birmingham, Michigan 48009
Criticism

EDINGER, William Carter
English (assistant professor)
University of California
3657 Sawtelle Boulvard
Los Angeles, California 90066
Literary criticism, esp. Johnson's

EHRENPREIS, Irvin
English (professor)
University of Virginia
1830 Fendall Avenue
Charlottesville, Virginia 22903
Jonathan Swift

EINBOND, Bernard L.   C
English (assistant professor)
Lehman College, CUNY
Bronx, New York 10468
Samuel Johnson; poetry and poetics

EISEN, Donald G.   C
English (associate professor)
Indiana University of Pennsylvania
Indiana, Pennsylvania 15701

EISENSTEIN, Elizabeth L.   C
History (adjunct professor)
American University
82 Kalorama Circle, N. W.
Washington, D. C. 20008
Enlightenment and French Revolution

ELDER, A. T.   C
English (professor)
University of Alberta
Edmonton 7, Alberta
Johnson, periodicals

ELIOSEFF, Lee Andrew   C
English (associate professor)
University of Kentucky
Lexington, Ky. 40506
Literature: intellectual history

ELLIOTT, Robert C.   C
Literature (professor)
University of California, San Diego
La Jolla, Calif., 92037
Literary satire; Swift

ELLIS, William D., Jr.   C
English (professor)

412

List of Members

St. Peter's College
Jersey City, N. J. 07306
Theory of genres

EMERSON, Roger   C
History (associate professor)
University of Western Ontario
London, Ontario

ENGLAND, R. Dickinson   S
English (graduate student)
University of Wisconsin
308 North Bassett
Madison, Wisconsin 53703
Smollett; Vanbrugh

ENGLISH, John C.   C,
History (professor)
Baker University
P.O. Box 537
Baldwin, Kansas 66006
*Empiricism, Platonism, and
   Augustinianism; John Wesley*

ENOMOTO, Ryukichi
Senshu University
3-52-5 Hayamiya
Nerima-Ku
Tokyo 176, Japan
English novel

EPSTEIN, William H.
English (instructor)
Purdue University
Heavilon Hall
Lafayette, Indiana 47907
British literature; English novel

ESSICK, Robert N.
English (assistant professor)
California State University, Northridge
100 South Chester Avenue, Apt. 9
Pasadena, California 91106
*William Blake and the relationship
   between the pictorial and literary arts
   in the 18th century*

EVANS, David L.   C
English
University of British Columbia
Vancouver 8, B. C.

EVANS, Howard V.   C
History (associate professor)
Central Michigan University
30 Cedar Drive
Hiawatha Hills
Mt. Pleasant, Michigan 48858
*European Enlightenment; French
   Revolution*

EVANS, James E.
English (assistant professor)
University of North Carolina
   at Greensboro
Greensboro, North Carolina 27412
English novel; Swift

EVANS, John Maurice   C
English (associate professor)
Washington and Lee University
Lexington, Virginia 24450
Augustan satirists

EVERSOLE, Richard   C
English (assistant professor)
University of Kansas
Lawrence, Kansas 66044
Eighteenth-century poetry

FALK, Joyce Duncan   C
History
1231 Harvard, Apt. O
Santa Monica, Calif. 90404
*French political and social thought;
   European history*

FALLE, George   C
English (professor)
Trinity College, University of Toronto
Toronto 5, Ontario
Dryden; Restoration drama; Swift

FARBER, Paul   C
History of science
Oregon State University
1658 N.W. Harrison Blvd.
Corvallis, Oregon 97330
History of science; Buffon

FAULKNER, Thomas C.
English (assistant professor)
Washington State University
Pullman, Washington 99163

413

*Political literature; late
18th-century poetry*

FEDER, Lillian C
English (professor)
Queens College, CUNY
80 Central Park West
New York, N. Y. 10023
Classical background; satire

FEILER, Seymour C
Modern languages (professor)
University of Oklahoma
Norman, Oklahoma 73069
French literature

FELD, Patricia L. (Mrs.) S
Drama (graduate student)
Tufts University
46 Coolidge Hill Road
Watertown, Massachusetts 02172
*Drama on the English and
American stages*

FENNER, A. F.
English (professor)
University of Detroit
Detroit, Michigan 48221
Pope; satire; music

FERGUSON, Oliver W. C
English (professor)
Duke University
Durham, North Carolina 27706
Swift; Goldsmith

FERLING, John E.
History (assistant professor)
West Georgia College
Carrollton, Georgia 30117
*The American Revolution; loyalism in
American Revolution; political theory*

FIFER, Charles N. C
English (professor)
Stanford University
Stanford, California 94305
*Johnson and Boswell; biography
and autobiography*

FINK, Beatrice C. C
French and Italian (assistant professor)

University of Maryland
6111 Madawaska Rd.
Washington, D. C. 20016
*Eighteenth-century French literature,
esp. Diderot, Rousseau, Sade*

FINNELL, Robert
English (assistant instructor)
University of Texas
Austin, Texas 78712
Pope; architecture

FITZGERALD, Robert P. C
English (associate professor)
Pennsylvania State University
33 South Burrows Building
University Park, Pa. 16802
Swift; pre-Romantic poetry

FITZSIMONS, James M., Jr. C
English (assistant professor)
University of Detroit
4001 W. McNichols Rd.
Detroit, Michigan 48077
*Swift; Fielding; parodic shapes and
strategies*

FLAGG, James C
Romance languages (lecturer)
Boston College
148 Oak Crest Drive
Framingham, Mass. 01701
Early 18th-century French literature

FLAHERTY, M. G. C
German (assistant professor)
Bryn Mawr College
Bryn Mawr, Pa. 19010
Literary criticism; aesthetics; opera

FLEISCHAUER, Charles C
French (associate professor)
Carleton University
Ottawa 1, Ontario
*Voltaire; Diderot; French art;
rationalism*

FOLKENFLIK, Robert C
English (assistant professor)
University of Rochester
Rochester, New York 14627
*Biography, criticism, novel, Johnson,
Fielding*

414

FONTAINE, Ligeia Z.　　　　S
English (graduate student)
University of Pennsylvania
4605 Cedar Avenue
Philadelphia, Pa. 19143

FORD, Alvin E.　　　　C
Foreign languages (lecturer)
California State University
Northridge, Calif. 91324

FOREMAN, Kenneth J., Jr.
Executive Director, Historical Foundation of the Presbyterian and
　Reformed Churches
Box 847
Montreat, North Carolina 28757
*Presbyterian and Reformed Church
　history*

FORNO, Lawrence J.
European languages (assistant
　professor)
University of Hawaii
Honolulu, Hawaii 96822
French enlightenment; French novel

FORTUNA, James Louis, Jr.　　　　S
English (graduate student)
University of Florida
1009 SW 6th Avenue
Gainesville, Florida 32601
Richardson; Fielding; Smollett

FOWLER, W. Robert　　　　C
History (teaching assistant)
American University
17 Webster St.
Lynn, Mass. 01904
British intellectual and social history

FRANK, Charles E.
English (professor)
Illinois College
Jacksonville, Illinois 62650
Poetry; novel; Edward Young

FRAUTSCHI, Richard L.　　　　C
Romance languages (professor)
Pennsylvania State University
602C Parkway Plaza
State College, Pennsylvania 16801
Prose fiction; quantative stylistics

FREASE, Cynthia R.
English (associate professor)
University of Northern Colorado
1901 21st Ave. Court
Greeley, Colorado 80631
Biography, letters, drama

FREEMAN, Robert N.　　　　S
Music
University of California, Los Angeles
505 Hillgreen Drive
Beverly Hills, Calif. 90212
History of musicology

FREEMAN, Sara Angeline　　　　S
English (graduate student)
Bloomsburg State College
317½ West Street
Bloomsburg, Pennsylvania 17815
Satire, esp. Swift

FREEMAN, William
Speech communications (assistant
　professor)
California State University
Northridge, California 91324
*American public address; history;
　religion*

FREIBERG, Pearlee
Fine arts (instructor)
Colgate University
Hamilton, New York 13346
British painting

FRENCH, David P.　　　　C
English (professor)
University of Oklahoma
Norman, Oklahoma 73069
English literature

FRICKE, Donna G.
English (assistant professor)
Bowling Green State University
Bowling Green, Ohio 43403
Swift; novel

FRIEDLAND, Bea　　　　S
Music (graduate student)
City University of New York
155 W. 20th Street
New York, N. Y. 10011
Haydn; Sturm and Drang in music

415

FRIEDMAN, Glenn S.   S
French (graduate student)
Pennsylvania State University
413 South Burrowes
University Park, Pa. 16802

FRIGUGLIETTI, James   C
History (assistant professor)
Case Western Reserve University
Cleveland, Ohio 44106
*Reign of Louis XVI, origins of
Revolution*

FRITZ, Paul S.
History
McMaster University
Hamilton, Ontario

FRUSHELL, Richard C.   C
English (assistant professor)
Indiana State University
Terre Haute, Indiana 47809
Drama

FUCHS, Jacob   S
English and comparative literature
University of California, Irvine
335 Lakeview Ave.
Long Beach, Calif. 90803

FULLARD, Joyce
Comparative literature (graduate
  student)
101 N. Busey Avenue, Apt. 4
Urbana, Illinois 61801
*Comparative literature; literature and
  science; literature and visual arts*

FULLER, David R.   C
Music (associate professor)
State University of New York
Buffalo, New York 14214
French keyboard music

GAGLIARDO, John G.   C
History (associate professor)
Boston University
Boston, Mass. 02215
*German history; history of absolute
  monarchy*

GALLANAR, Joseph M.   C
History (associate professor)
Claremont Graduate School
Claremont, California 91711
*Intellectual history, 1760-1800;
  historiography*

GALLIANI, Renato   C
French (assistant professor)
Carleton University
Ottawa 1, Ontario
Mably and history

GANNON, Susan R.   C
English (instructor)
Pace College, Westchester
861 Bedford Road
Pleasantville, N. Y. 10570
English literature

GARBER, Frederick
Comparative literature
  (associate professor)
SUNY, Binghamton
Binghamton, New York 13901
*Comparative literature; literature
  of sensibility; fiction: sentimental
  and Gothic*

GARDNER, Paula R.
French
Boston University
5 Purchase Street
Salem, Massachusetts 01970
*Montesquieu; crisis between 17th and
  18th centuries*

GAROSI, Frank J.   C
History (associate professor)
California State College
Sacramento, California 95819
History of Italy, France, Central Europe

GARRARD, John G.   C
Slavic languages and literatures
  (associate professor)
University of Virginia
Charlottesville, Va. 22903
*Cultural relations between Russia and
  Western Europe*

416

GARSON, Helen S.
English (professor)
George Mason College of the University
of Virginia
4400 University Drive
Fairfax, Virginia 22030
English novel

GAYLORD, Susan Delaronde   S
English (teaching assistant)
Michigan State University
970 Hogsback Road
Mason, Michigan 48854
English novel; Samuel Richardson

GEIRINGER, Karl   C
Music (professor)
University of California, Santa Barbara
1823 Mira Vista Avenue
Santa Barbara, California 93103
Music

GAUNT, John L.
English (assistant professor)
West Chester State College
West Chester, Pennsylvania 19380
Fiction; popular literature

GENDZIER, Stephen J.   C
Romance languages and comparative
literature (associate professor)
Brandeis University
36 Hayes Avenue
Lexington, Mass. 02173
French and English novel; Encyclopédie

GERSHOY, Leo   C
History (professor emeritus)
New York University
29 Washington Square
New York, N. Y. 10011

GERSON, Frederick   C
French (assistant professor)
New College, University of Toronto
Toronto 5, Ontario
Les philosophes

GIANTURCO, Elio   C
Italian and comparative literature
(professor)
Hunter College

2025 Huidekoper Place, N.W.
Washington, D. C. 20007
Anglo-Italian literary relations; Vico

GIBBS, Thomas, Jr.   C
Music (graduate student)
University of Texas
1217 Greensboro Road
Birmingham, Alabama 35208
Musical classicism; Haydn; Mozart

GILBERT, Bennett Bruce   S
History and philosophy (student)
Yale College
1042 Yale Station
New Haven, Connecticut 06520

GILBERT, Vedder M.   C
English (professor)
University of Montana
Missoula, Montana 59801
*Thomas Edwards; dramatists and
    novelists*

GILLIARD, Fred, Jr.   C
English (teaching assistant)
University of Utah
315 South 7th Avenue
Pocatello, Idaho 83201
Drama

GINSBERG, Elaine K.
English (instructor)
West Virginia University
Morgantown, W. Va. 26506
American literature

GINSBERG, Robert   C
Philosophy (assistant professor)
Pennsylvania State University
Delaware County Campus
25 Yearsley Mill Road
Media, Pennsylvania 19063
*Theories of war, peace, and revolution;
    aesthetics*

GLENN, Jerry
German (associate professor)
University of Cincinnati
Cincinnati, Ohio 45221
*Influence of Latin literature on German;
    G. E. Lessing*

417

GLEESON, Larry A.
Art (associate professor)
North Texas State University
Denton, Texas 76203
Art history

GLOCK, Waldo S.
English (assistant professor)
New Mexico State University
Las Cruces, New Mexico 88001
Fielding; the novel

GOARD, Robert R.   C
Romance languages (instructor)
Ohio Wesleyan University
Delaware, Ohio 43105
French novel, esp. 1750-89

GOETZ, Walter L.   S
English (associate)
University of California, Irvine
Irvine, California 92664
*Literary and aesthetic theory from
  1660-1798*

GOITEIN, Denise
Tel Aviv University
P.O. Box 3725
Jerusalem, Israel

GOLDEN, Herbert H.   C
Romance languages and literatures
  (professor)
Boston University
Boston, Mass. 02215
French literature; history of ideas

GOLDEN, Morris   C
English (professor)
University of Massachusetts
Amherst, Mass. 01002
English literature

GOLDSTEIN, Harvey D.   C
English (associate professor)
University of Southern California
Los Angeles, Calif. 90007
Criticism; aesthetics

GOLDSTEIN, Morton Ellis   C
History (assistant professor)
Callison College, University of the
  Pacific

Stockton, California 95204
Spain, France

GOOD, Stephen H.   C
English (assistant professor)
Mount Saint Mary's College
Emmitsburg, Maryland 21727

GOODREAU, David A.
Art history
Carleton University
Ottawa 1, Ontario
Eighteenth-century English art

GOSSMAN, Lionel   C
French (professor)
Johns Hopkins University
Baltimore, Maryland 21218

GOTTERBARN, Donald
Philosophy (assistant professor)
Wichita State University
Wichita, Kansas 62708
British philosophy

GOTTSCHALK, Louis   C
History (professor)
University of Illinois, Chicago Circle
5551 University Avenue
Chicago, Illinois 60637

GOTWALS, Vernon   C
Music (professor)
Smith College
Sage Hall
Northampton, Mass. 01060
Bach; Handel; Haydn; Mozart

GOUREVITCH, Victor
Philosophy (professor)
Wesleyan University
Wesleyan Station
Middletown, Conn. 06457
Rousseau

GRANNIS, Harvey Newell, Jr.
R. R. 2
Ewing, Ky. 41039
History of 18th-century France

GRAY, James   C
English (professor)

418

Dalhousie University
Halifax, Nova Scotia
Johnson circle; religion, theater,
biography in later 18th century

GREASON, A. LeRoy, Jr.
English (professor)
Bowdoin College
256 Maine Street
Brunswick, Maine 04011
English literature

GREEN, Mary Elizabeth   C
English (assistant professor)
Arizona State University
Tempe, Arizona 85281
Augustan satires on learning

GREENBAUM, Louis S.   C
History (professor)
University of Massachusetts
Herter Hall 636
Amherst, Mass. 01002
French church and social history;
Lavoisier

GREENBERG, Bernard L.
English (professor)
Director of Admissions
Gallaudet College
Washington, D. C. 20002
Sterne; novel; history of ideas

GREENBERG, Irwin L.
Romance languages (assistant
professor)
University of Cincinnati
Cincinnati, Ohio 45221
Diderot; French novel

GREENE, Donald J.   C
English (professor)
University of Southern California
Los Angeles, California 90007
Johnson; English intellectual and
cultural history

GREENE, Mildred S.   C
English (assistant professor)
Arizona State University
Tempe, Arizona 85281
17th-, 18th-century English and French
novel

GREENWAY, John L.   C
English (assistant professor)
University of Kentucky
Honors Program
233 Office Tower
Lexington, Kentucky 40506
Scandinavian literature; German
literature; mythology

GREENWOOD, David C.
English (assistant professor)
University of Maryland
College Park, Maryland 20742
Neo-Latin; history of England

GRIFFIN, William D.   C
History (assistant professor)
St. John's University
Grand Central & Utopia Parkways
Jamaica, New York 11432
Ireland in era of Grattan's Parliament
(1782-1800)

GRIFFITH, Philip Mahone   C
English (professor)
University of Tulsa
600 South College
Tulsa, Oklahoma 74104
Novel; Samuel Johnson and his circle;
periodical

GRIMALDI, Alfonsina Albini   C
French and Italian (teacher)
Hoboken High School
204 5th Street
Hoboken, New Jersey 07030
Giambattista Vico

GRINDELL, Robert M.   C
English (assistant professor)
State University College
Geneseo, New York 14454
English novel

GROLLMAN, Marilyn   C
Romance languages
Douglass College
New Brunswick, N. J. 08901
The Jew in 18th-century French
literature

419

GROSS, Doris Koren   S
French
Boston University
45 Verndale Street
Brookline, Mass. 02146
French literature

GROSS, Jeffrey T.
English (assistant professor)
St. Andrews Presbyterian College
Laurinburg, North Carolina 28352
*Pope, Johnson, music in the
    early 18th-century*

GROSSMAN, Walter
History (professor)
Director of Libraries
University of Massachusetts
Boston, Massachusetts 02116

GRUDER, Vivian R.   C
History (assistant professor)
Queens College, CUNY
890 West End Avenue
New York, N. Y. 10025
France; Ancien Régime and revolution

GRUSHOW, Ira
English (associate professor)
Franklin and Marshall College
Lancaster, Pennsylvania 17604
English literature; bookbinding

GUÉDON, Jean-Claude
Natural Science (lecturer)
York University
Glendon College
2275 Bayview Avenue
Toronto 317, Ontario, Canada
*History of chemistry and related sciences
    in the 18th century*

GUILHAMET, Leon M.   C
English (assistant professor)
City College, CUNY
New York, N. Y. 10031
English literature

GUY, Basil   C
French (professor)
University of California
4125 Dwinelle

Berkeley, Calif. 94820
Voltaire; novel; cosmopolitanism

HAAC, Oscar A.   C
Romance languages (professor)
SUNY, Stony Brook
Stony Brook, N. Y. 11790
Marivaux; Voltaire

HACKEL, Roberta
Modern languages
50 Center Street
Rutland, Vermont 05701

HAFTER, Monroe Z
Romance languages (professor)
University of Michigan
Ann Arbor, Michigan 48104
Spanish literature

HAGSTRUM, Jean H.   C
English (professor)
Northwestern University
819 Michigan Avenue
Evanston, Illinois 60202
Visual arts; Johnson; Blake

HAHN, H. G.
English (assistant professor)
Towson State College
Linthicum Hall
Baltimore, Maryland 21204
English novel; literary biography

HAHN, Roger   C
History (associate professor)
University of California
Berkeley, California 94720
*Science and technology; institutional
    history; history of ideas*

HAIG, Robert   C
English (professor)
University of North Carolina
Chapel Hill, N. C. 27514

HALL, Inez Jean   C
English (instructor)
Ball State University
North Annex 217
Muncie, Indiana 47306
Major English writers, esp. Swift

420

HALL, Thadd E.   C
History (assistant professor)
State University of New York
Binghamton, New York 13901
Eighteenth-century France

HALSBAND, Robert   C
English (professor)
University of California
Riverside, California 92502
Literary and social history, 1700-1750

HAMBRIDGE, Roger A.   S
English (student)
University of California, Los Angeles
1520 S. Purdue Ave. No. 4
West Los Angeles, Calif. 90025
Alexander Pope

HAMILTON, James F.
Romance languages (assistant
   professor)
University of Cincinnati
Cincinnati, Ohio 45221
Rousseau

HAMMOND, Antony
English (assistant professor)
McMaster University
Hamilton, Ontario
Theater; drama; biography (Langbaine, Oldys)

HANDLER, Pearl P.
English (lecturer)
University of California, Los Angles
2931 Club Drive
Los Angeles, California 90064
Mandeville; Johnson; science and medicine

HANKINS, Richard   C
English (assistant professor)
Baldwin-Wallace College
559 Prospect Rd.
Berea, Ohio 44017
Biography as a genre

HANKINS, Thomas L.
History (associate professor)
University of Washington
315 Smith Hall

Seattle, Washington 98015
History of science; Jean d'Alembert

HANNA, Blake T.   C
French, modern languages (professor)
Université de Montréal
21 Rue Echenay
Lorraine, Quebec
Denis Diderot

HANSELL, Sven H.   C
Music (assistant professor)
University of California
Davis, California 95616

HANSEN, David A.   C
English (assistant professor)
University of California
Riverside, Calif. 92502
Theories of prose style

HANSON, Blair   C
Modern languages (professor)
Allegheny College
Meadville, Pennsylvania 16335
French eighteenth century

HARBERT, Earl H.
English (associate professor)
Tulane University
New Orleans, Louisiana 70118
American literature; autobiography; biography

HARDESTY, Kay
Modern languages (instructor)
Clayton Junior College
Morrow, Georgia 30260
Encyclopédie and its supplement; American-French relations

HARDIE, Graham   S
Music (graduate student)
University of Michigan
Ann Arbor, Michigan 48105
Early eighteenth-century Italian opera

HARE, Robert R.
English (associate professor)
Youngstown State University
3805 Sampson Road
Youngstown, Ohio 44505

The later period 1750-1800,
  English, French, American;
  St. John de Crèvecoeur

HARRIS, Jane Gary
University of Pittsburgh
5412 Howe Street
Pittsburgh, Pennsylvania
Poetry and poetics—Russian

HARRIS, Svetlana Kluge   C
History (graduate student)
Columbia University
55 Park Avenue
New York, N.Y. 10016
France; Russia; international relations

HARROLD, Frances   C
History (associate professor)
Georgia State University
33 Gilmer St. S.E.
Atlanta, Georgia 30303
18th-century constitutional and legal
  ideas, esp. Jefferson

HART, Edward L.   C
English (professor)
Brigham Young University
Provo, Utah 84601
English literature (age of Johnson)

HARTH, Phillip   C
English (professor)
University of Wisconsin
352 Bascom Hall
Madison, Wisconsin 53706
Dryden; Swift; intellectual history

HARVEY, A. Mosby
Romance languages and literatures
  (assistant professor)
Dartmouth College
RFD 331
Norwich, Vermont 05055
French law; French literature

HASSLER, Donald M.   C
English (associate professor)
Kent State University
Kent Ohio 44242
Late 18th-century poetry; science;
  Erasmus Darwin

HATCH, Ronald B.
English (assistant professor)
University of British Columbia
Vancouver 8, British Columbia
George Crabbe; social reform

HATZFELD, Helmut A.   C
Romance languages (professor
  emeritus)
Catholic University of America
2401 Calvert St. N.W.
Washington, D. C. 20008
Rococo

HAVENS, George R.   C
Romance languages (professor
  emeritus)
Ohio State University
415 Glen Echo Circle
Columbus, Ohio 43202
France, esp. Voltaire, Rousseau

HAWES, Lloyd E., M.D.   C
Art history
Harvard Medical School
690 Beacon Street
Boston, Mass. 02215
Ceramics

HEARTZ, Daniel   C
Music (professor)
University of California
Berkeley, California 94720
Italian opera; French theater; Mozart

HECHLER, Sandra S.   C
French (assistant professor)
Cleveland State University
922 Dresden Road
East Cleveland, Ohio 44112
Diderot; women in 18th century

HEHR, Milton G.   C
Music (associate professor)
University of Missouri, Kansas City
4420 Warwick Blvd.
Kansas City, Missouri 64111
Music

HEIN, Rebecca F.   C
Romance languages
University of Michigan

List of Members

1215 Three Mile Drive
Grosse Pointe, Michigan 84230
French-American intellectual relations

HEITNER, Robert R.   C
German (professor)
University of Illinois at Chicago Circle
Chicago, Illinois 60680
*Drama (German): Lessing, Schiller,
  Goethe*

HELSING, Lyse D.   S
Romance languages (graduate student)
Johns Hopkins University
2730 Wisconsin Avenue N.W.
Washington, D. C. 20007

HENRY, Rolanne   C
English (instructor)
Rutgers University
10 Pine Tree Terrace
Madison, New Jersey 07940
Thomas Birch; biographical dictionaries

HERBY, Valdo
French (instructor)
California State College
Sacramento, Calif. 95819

HERRING, Maben D.
English (graduate student)
University of Notre Dame
1139 Helman Drive
South Bend, Indiana 46615
*English literature; Afro-American
  literature*

HERRMANN, Rolf-Dieter
Philosophy (associate professor)
University of Tennessee
Knoxville, Tennessee 37916
*Philosophy (Baumgarten, Kant,
  Rousseau)*

HESSE, Alfred W.   C
English
U. S. Department of Defense
86 Eldrid Drive
Silver Spring, Maryland 20904
*Nicholas Rowe; early 18th-century
  English drama*

HESTER, Robert F.   C
Interior design (professor)
Virginia Commonwealth University
901 West Franklin Street
Richmond, Virginia 23220
Art and architecture

HEUSTON, Edward F.   C
English (associate professor)
Plattsburgh State Univ. College, SUNY
Plattsburgh, N. Y. 12901
Augustan satire

HICKS, Thomas William   C
English (assistant professor)
Georgia State University
33 Gilmer Street, S.E.
Atlanta, Georgia 30033
*Restoration drama; influence of science
  on English literature*

HIGUCHI, Kinzo
Literature (assistant professor)
Osaka City University
3-2-8-409 Shinkanaoka-cho
Sakai City
Osaka, Japan
The English novel

HILL, Emita B.
Romance languages (associate professor
  and chairman)
Herbert H. Lehman College, CUNY
Bronx, New York 10468
Diderot; 18th-century novel in France

HILL, George R.
Fine arts (associate librarian)
University of California, Irvine
3800 Parkview Lane, Apt. 13-B
Irvine, California 92664
*18th-century symphony; musical
  performance and practice*

HILL, John   C
Music (graduate student)
Harvard University
4519 Larchwood Avenue
Philadelphia, Pennsylvania 19143
Eighteenth-century music

423

HILLES, Frederick W.   C
English (professor emeritus)
Yale University
P.O. Box 525
Old Lyme, Connecticut 06371
*Johnson's Lives of the Poets; Boswell's
Letters*

HINNANT, Charles H.   C
English (assistant professor)
University of Missouri
231 Arts and Sciences
Columbia, Missouri 65201
Dryden; Swift

HNATKO, Eugene
English (professor)
State University of New York
Cortland, New York 13045
Laurence Sterne; drama; prose style

HODGSON, Judith F.   S
English (graduate student)
University of Pennsylvania
4513 Pine Street
Philadelphia, Pennsylvania 19143

HOFFMAN, Arthur W.   C
English (professor)
Syracuse University
203 Hall of Languages
Syracuse, New York 13210
Dryden; Congreve; Pope; Fielding

HOLLY, Grant Innes
English (instructor)
Hobart and William Smith Colleges
Geneva, New York 14456
Novel

HONICK, Lois
6736 Wilmont Drive
Baltimore, Maryland 21207
Biography; history of ideas

HOPKINS, Robert H.   C
English (associate professor)
University of California
Davis, California 95616
The Johnson circle; Swift; Pope

HOTCH, Douglas R.   C
English (assistant professor)
University of Illinois
100 English Building
Urbana, Illinois 61801
Swift; Sterne

HUANG, Roderick   C
English (professor)
University of Windsor
Windsor, Ontario
Pope; late Augustan poets

HUEBNER, Wayne V.   C
English (associate professor)
California State College at Fullerton
930 Barbara Avenue
Placentia, Calif. 92670
Augustan satire

HUGHES, Peter M.   C
English (associate professor)
Victoria College, University of Toronto
17 Elm Avenue, Rosedale
Toronto 5, Ontario
*English literature; comparative literature
(English and French); intellectual
history*

HUME, Robert D.   C
English (assistant professor)
Cornell University
Ithaca, New York 14850
*Literary aesthetics and criticism; English
drama*

HUNT, Russell A.   C
English (assistant professor)
Saint Thomas University
Fredericton, New Brunswick
*Politics in literature; development of
drama*

HUNTER, J. Paul   C
English (professor)
Emory University
Atlanta, Georgia 30322
Satire and the novel

HUNTER, Kathryn Montgomery   C
English (assistant professor)
Morehouse College

Atlanta, Georgia 30314
Satire; Dryden; the Restoration

HUTCHENS, Eleanor N.   C
English (professor)
University of Alabama
300 Williams Ave., S.E.
Huntsville, Alabama 35801
Fielding

HYDE, Mrs. Donald F.   C
English
Four Oaks Farm, RFD #3
Somerville, New Jersey 08876
Johnson; Boswell; Mrs. Thrale

HYTIER, Adrienne D.   C
French (professor)
Vassar College
Poughkeepsie, N. Y. 12601
Philosophes and enlightened despotism;
  Jacobites

ILIE, Paul
Romance languages (professor)
University of Michigan
Ann Arbor, Michigan 48104
Spanish intellectual history, 1701-1759;
  aesthetics

IMMERWAHR, Raymond
German (professor)
University of Western Ontario
London 72, Ontario
Concepts of the romantic, sublime and
  beautiful and their associations;
  Schlegel; Tieck; Novalis; Schiller

ISHERWOOD, Robert M.   C
History (assistant professor)
Vanderbilt University
Box 1667
Nashville, Tenn. 37203
Musical ideas and influence of the
  philosophes

IVKER, Barry   C
English (assistant professor)
Dillard University
New Orleans, La. 70122
Libertinism; fiction; history of ideas

JACOB, Margaret
History (assistant professor)
Baruch College, CUNY
17 Lexington Avenue
New York, New York 10010
Newtonism; free thinkers; republic of
  letters

JACOBSON, David Y.   S
History (graduate student)
Brown University
228-20 Stronghurst Avenue
Queen's Village, New York 11427
French history; criminal law reform in
  late 18th-century France

JAMISON, Suzanne
French and Italian (instructor)
University of Texas
Austin, Texas 78712
French eighteenth century

JANES, Regina Mary   C
English (teaching fellow)
Harvard University
Eliot House N-43d
Cambridge, Mass. 02138
English literature

JARRETT, H. Marshall   C
History (associate professor)
Washington & Lee University
Lexington, Virginia 24450
D'Alembert; Encyclopédie; social,
  political theory

JEFREY, David K.   C
English
Haley Center
Auburn University
Auburn, Alabama 36830
Smollett

JEFFRIES, Theodore
History of science (associate professor)
Lorain County Community College
North Abbe Road
Elyria, Ohio 44035
Science and technology

JENKINS, Annibel   C
English (associate professor)

425

Georgia Institute of Technology
Atlanta, Georgia 30332
*Early 18th-century drama; periodicals;
N. Rowe*

JENKINS, Clauston
English (assistant professor)
North Carolina State University
201 Holliday Hall
Raleigh, North Carolina 27607
Textual criticism; Swift

JENNINGS, Edward M.   C
English (assistant professor)
State University of New York
441 Loudonville Road
Loudonville, New York 12211
Narrative (English); "time"

JENSEN, H. James   C
English (assistant professor)
Indiana University
Ballantine Hall
Bloomington, Indiana 47401
*Dryden; 18th-century criticism and
aesthetics*

JOHNSON, Clifford Ross
English (assistant professor)
University of Pittsburgh
Pittsburgh, Pennsylvania 15213
Swift; Defoe; diary literature, esp. Pepys

JOHNSON, James LeRoy
939 West College Street, Apt. 201
Los Angeles, California 90012
*History and transmission of classical and
medieval texts; translation*

JOHNSON, Lathrop P.   C
German (instructor)
University of Illinois
Urbana, Illinois 61801
German lyric

JOHNSON, Maurice
English (professor)
University of Pennsylvania
Philadelphia, Pennsylvania 19104
English literature; satire

JOHNSON, Neal R.
Languages (assistant professor)
University of Guelph
Guelph, Ontario
Public opinion in 18th-century France

JOHNSTON, Shirley W.   C
English (assistant professor)
University of Colorado, Denver Center
2311 S. High St.
Denver, Colorado 80210
Samuel Johnson

JOLY, Raymond   C
French (associate professor)
Faculté des Lettres
Université Laval
Quebec 10, Quebec
Eighteenth-century French literature

JONES, B. W.   C
English (associate professor)
Carleton University
Ottawa, Ontario
Collins; symbolic theory; Blake

JONES, Joseph Stephen L.
English (assistant professor)
Arizona State University
Tempe, Arizona 85281

JONES, William Powell   C
English (professor emeritus)
Case Western Reserve University
Berkshire Rd.
Gates Mills, Ohio 44040
Gray; relations of science and literature

JORDAN, Daniel P.
History
Virginia Commonwealth University
9405 University Boulevard
Richmond, Virginia 23229

JOSEPHS, Herbert   C
Romance languages (associate
    professor)
Michigan State University
East Lansing, Michigan 48823
Diderot; 18-century novel

JOSEPHSON, David   C
Music (lecturer)
Columbia University
43 Stephen Hopkins Court
Providence, Rhode Island 02904
Music (Canadian history)

JOST, François
French and comparative literature
  (professor)
University of Illinois
244 Lincoln Hall
Urbana, Illinois 61801
Novel; history of ideas (French,
German, English)

JOVICEVICH, Alexander
French (professor)
126 Oakview Ave.
Maplewood, N. J. 07040
French literature: Voltaire, La Harpe,
  and general

JOY, Neill R.   C
English (assistant professor)
Colgate University
Hamilton, New York 13346
Burke; Gibbon; satire; Richardson

JULIARD, Pierre   C
History (assistant professor)
Lehigh University
Bethlehem, Pa. 18015
French social and intellectual history

KAFKER, Frank A.   C
History (associate professor)
University of Cincinnati
McMicken Hall
Cincinnati, Ohio 45242
Encyclopedists; French Revolution

KAILIN, Susan A.   S
French (graduate student)
University of Chicago
4900 Marine Drive
Chicago, Illinois 60640
Eighteenth-century French novel and
  philosophes

KALLICH, Martin
English (professor)

Northern Illinois University
DeKalb, Illinois 60115

KALMAN, Harold D.   C
Art history (assistant professor)
University of British Columbia
Vancouver 8, B. C.
Eighteenth-century British architecture;
  art history generally

KALMEY, Robert P.
English (associate professor)
Shippensburg State College
320 E. Burd Street
Shippensburg, Pa. 17257

KANTOR, Marvin   C
Slavic languages (assistant professor)
Northwestern University
Evanston, Illinois 60201
Russian language and literature of
  18th-century

KAPLAN, Steven Laurence
History (assistant professor)
Cornell University
West Sibley Hall
Ithaca, New York 14850
Comparative history and literature;
  social and economic history; material
  culture (emphasis France)

KARAFIOL, Emile
History (assistant professor)
University of Chicago
5811 South Ellis Avenue
Chicago, Illinois 60637
Administration, political theory, esp.
  German-speaking Central Europe

KARLE, Joan   S
History (graduate student)
Columbia University
5 Tudor City Place
New York, N. Y. 10017
German intellectual history

KASINEC, Edward   S
History (graduate student)
Columbia University
438 East 75 Street
New York, N. Y. 10021
Russian history; bibliography

427

KATZ, Eve   C
French (assistant professor)
New York University
4 Washington Square Village 5P
New York, N. Y. 10012

KATZ, Wallace B.
History
c/o SPO
University of the South
Sewanee, Tennessee 37375
Intellectual history;
    "Democracy in Theory and Practice:
    the Uses of Rousseau 1755-1794"

KAUFMAN, Paul   C
Library science (consultant in
    bibliography)
University of Washington Library
Seattle, Washington 98105
Popular libraries as social forces

KEARNEY, Flora
English (associate professor)
Ball State University
419 Tyrone Drive
Muncie, Indiana 47304
Age of Johnson; bibliography

KEEN, Sandra H.   S
History (student)
New York University
112-12 72nd Avenue
Forest Hills, New York 11375
French enlightenment; Diderot; poor
    relief; utopias

KEENAN, Joseph J., Jr.   C
English (assistant professor)
Duquesne University
Pittsburgh, Pa. 15219
Late 18-century drama, esp. comedy

KEIG, Judith   C
English (assistant professor)
University of Pennsylvania
One Sherman Square, Apt. 5L
New York, N. Y. 10023
Ideas of cultural history; biography

KELLER, Theodore D.   C
English (associate professor)

East Stroudsburg State College
Box 431
East Stroudsburg, Pa. 18301
Swift; satire

KENNEDY, Joyce H. Deveau   C
English (assistant professor)
University of Alberta
Edmonton, Alberta
Daniel Defoe

KENNELLY, Laura (Mrs. Kevin J.)
English
North Texas State University
2205 W. Oak
Denton, Texas 76201

KENNY, Shirley Strum
English (associate professor)
University of Maryland
College Park, Maryland 20742
Drama; bibliography; satire

KERN, Jean B.   C
English (associate professor)
Coe College
1639 Ridge Road
Iowa City, Iowa 52240
Drama; satire; novel

KIDD, Ronald R.   C
Music (assistant professor)
Purdue University
Stanley Coulter Hall
Lafayette, Indiana 47907
English instrumental music; sociology of
    music

KIM, Hwal   S
English
Soodo Women's Teachers College
Sungdong-Ku
Seoul, Korea
English literature

KING, James
English
McMaster University
Hamilton, Ontario, Canada
Alexander Pope; The Sister Arts;
    William Blake; William Cowper

428

KING, Lester S., M.D.
American Medical Association
4204 N. Greenview Avenue
Chicago, Illinois 60613
History of medicine; history of ideas

KINSLEY, William   C
English (assistant professor)
Université de Montréal
Montreal 101, Quebec
*Pope, esp. "Dunciad"; satire; media
    study*

KINZER, Ilona Ricardo
French (lecturer)
Massachusetts Institute of Technology
168 Winthrop Road
Brookline, Massachusetts 02146
French novel

KIRBY, John P.   C
English (professor)
Randolph-Macon Women's College
Lynchburg, Virginia 24504
Boswell; Horace Walpole; novel

KIRK, Gerald A.   C
English (associate professor)
North Texas State University
Denton, Texas 76203
Novel; drama

KIRKENDALE, Warren   C
Musicology (associate professor)
Duke University
2422 Tyron Road
Durham, North Carolina 27705
Austrian chamber music; Austrian mass

KLEIN, Milton M.   C
History (professor)
University of Tennessee
Knoxville, Tenn. 37916

KLEIN, Suzanne M. L.   C
French (assistant professor)
Pitzer College
18644 Galatina Street
Rowland Heights, California 91745
*Novel, esp. Robert Chasles to Marquis
    de Sade*

KLINE, Richard B.   C
English (associate professor)
SUNY, Fredonia
Fredona, New York 14063
Prior; satire, Queen Anne period

KLINGER, Uwe Roland
German (teaching intern)
Wesleyan University
Fisk Hall
Middletown, Conn. 06457
German literature

KNAPP, Mary E.   C
English (professor)
Albertus Magnus College
120 Dwight Street
New Haven, Connecticut 06511
Garrick

KNAPP, Richard Gilbert   C
Languages (assistant professor)
102 Furman Ave., No. 7
Asheville, N. C. 28801
French and English literature

KNODEL, Arthur J.   C
French (professor)
University of Southern California
Los Angeles, California 90007

KOCH, Philip
French and Italian (professor)
University of Pittsburgh
620 LIS
Pittsburgh, Pennsylvania 15213
*Galiani; Diderot; Marivaux;
    Italo-French literary relations*

KOLB, Gwin J.   C
English (professor)
University of Chicago
1050 E. 59th St.
Chicago, Illinois 60637
Johnson and his circle

KOLODNY, Annette
English (assistant professor)
University of British Columbia
Vancouver 8, British Columbia
*Development of an "American" national
    consciousness*

KOON, Helene
English (assistant professor)
California State College
5500 State College Parkway
San Bernardino, California 92407
Drama 1700-1735

KORS, Alan Charles
History (assistant professor)
University of Pennsylvania
Philadelphia, Pa. 19104
French Enlightenment

KORSHIN, Paul J.   C
English (associate professor)
University of Pennsylvania
Philadelphia, Pa. 19104
Poetics; religion and literature

KRA, Pauline   C
French (assistant professor)
Yeshiva University
109-14 Ascan Avenue
Forest Hills, New York 11375
French literature

KRANTZ, Charles K.
Humanities (associate professor)
Newark College of Engineering
Newark, New Jersey 07102
History of free-thought

KRENIS, Lee B.
English (graduate student)
University of Denver
2390 South High Street
Denver, Colorado 80210
*Literary criticism, esp. Scottish
   historical critics*

KRITZER, Hildreth   C
English (associate professor)
Long Island University
Brooklyn, New York 11201
Critical theory; novel

KRIZSAN, Emery I.
French (assistant professor)
Davis and Elkins College
Elkins, W. Va.
French language and literature

KROITOR, Harry P.   C
English (professor)
Texas A. & M. University
College Station, Texas 77843
Johnson; Pope

KROPF, Carl R.   C
English (assistant professor)
Georgia State University
33 Gilmer Street, S.E.
Atlanta, Georgia 30303
*Religious backgrounds of British
   literature*

KUPERSMITH, William   C
English (assistant professor)
University of Iowa
Iowa City, Iowa 52240
English satire

LABORDE, Alice M.   C
French (assistant professor)
University of California
Irvine, Calif. 92664
Aesthetics; novel

LACOMBE, Anne
French (assistant professor)
University of Kansas
Lawrence, Kansas 66044
French novel; theater

LAFARGE, Catherine
French (assistant professor)
Byrn Mawr College
Bryn Mawr, Pennsylvania 19010
*Robert Challe; the myth of Paris
   in eighteenth-century literature*

LAGARDE, Marie L.   C
French (professor)
Louisiana State University
New Orleans, Louisiana 70122
French literature

LAIDLAW, G. Norman
French and Italian (professor)
SUNY, Stony Brook
48 William Penn Drive
Stony Brook, New York 11790
*Diderot; encyclopédie; science; prose
   technique*

430

LAMPE, David R.   S
English (graduate student)
University of Iowa
618 N. Dodge Street
Apt. 3-E
Iowa City, Iowa 52240

LANDA, Louis A.   C
English (professor emeritus)
Princeton University
Princeton, New Jersey 08540
*Queen Anne period; intellectual and
   social background*

LANE, James Martin   S
History (student)
St. Francis College
28-35 34th Street
Astoria, New York 11103
Colonial and European history; Burke

LANG, Louise S.   S
French (graduate student)
9211 S.W. 36th Ave.
Portland, Oregon 97219
French literature

LANGE, Victor
German literature (professor)
Princeton University
230 E. Pyne Building
Princeton, New Jersey 08740
*Enlightenment; neoclassicism; literary
   theory literature and the arts*

LAPREVOTTE, Guy   C
French (assistant professor)
University of Illinois
Foreign Language Building
Urbana, Ill. 61801
French and English science and poetry

LAROCH, Philippe   C
Romance languages (instructor)
Banff School of Fine Arts
Banff, Alberta
*Libertine novels, Crébillon fils to Laclos;
   Stanislas de Boufflers*

LATTINVILLE, Ronald E.
English (associate professor)
Jacksonville State University

Jacksonville, Alabama 36265
Drama

LAUDON, Robert T.   C
Music (associate professor)
University of Minnesota
Minneapolis, Minn. 55455
French opera and aesthetics

LAWRY, Jon S.   C
English (professor)
Laurentian University
Sudbury, Ontario
Swift; Prior

LAWTON, Joseph   S
English (teaching fellow)
University of Oregon
Eugene, Oregon 97401

LEBRUN, Richard   C
History (associate professor)
University of Manitoba
Winnipeg 19, Manitoba
French political thought (de Maistre)

LECLERC, Paul O.
Modern languages (associate professor)
Union College
Schenectady, N. Y. 12308
Voltaire; Morellet

LEDER, Lawrence H.   C
History (professor)
Lehigh University
Bethlehem, Pennsylvania 18015
*American-English politics and political
   thought*

LEE, Douglas A.
Music (associate professor)
Wichita State University
Wichita, Kansas 67208
*Instrumental music—German;
   pamphletizing*

LEE, Jae Num   C
English (assistant professor)
Portland State University
Portland, Oregon 97207
Swift; Pope

431

LEE, J. Patrick   C
Romance languages (assistant
  professor)
University of Georgia
Athens, Georgia 30601
Voltaire's philosophical sermons;
  Matthew Maty

LEE, Vera G.   C
Romance languages (associate
  professor)
Boston College
Chestnut Hill, Mass. 02167

LEED, Jacob   C
English (associate professor)
Kent State University
Kent, Ohio 44240
Samuel Johnson

LEITH, James A.   C
History (professor)
Queen's University
Kingston, Ontario
Educational thought; aesthetics and the
  visual arts

LEMAY, J. A. Leo   C
English (assistant professor)
University of California
Los Angeles, California 90024
American literature; Benjamin Franklin

LENFEST, David S.   C
English (assistant professor)
Loyola University of Chicago
6525 N. Sheridan Road
Chicago, Illinois 60626
Swift; Pope; eighteenth-century poetry
  and painting

LENNENBERG, Hans H.   C
Musicology (associate professor)
Library/Department of Music
University of Chicago
7458 S. Constance
Chicago, Ill. 60649
Eighteenth-century theory, music

LePAGE, Peter V.
English (associate professor)
University of Cincinnati

3535 Mooney Avenue
Cincinnati, Ohio 45208
The novel; satire; music and
  poetic texts

LETZRING, Monica
English (assistant professor)
Temple University
Philadelphia, Pa. 19122

LEVENTHAL, Herbert   C
History (graduate student)
Graduate Center, CUNY
New York, N. Y. 10036
Colonial American history

LEVIN, Colette G.   S
French and Italian (student)
University of Pittsburgh
820 Evergreen Drive
Washington, Pennsylvania 15301

LEVINE, George R.   C
English (associate professor)
SUNY, Buffalo
Annex B
Buffalo, New York 14214
Interdisciplinary studies; novel

LEVINE, J. A.   C
English (professor)
University of Illinois at Chicago Circle
Chicago, Ill. 60680
English literature

LEVINE, Philip
English (assistant professor)
Tulane University
New Orleans, Lousiana 70118
Johnson, Boswell

LEVY, Darline Gay
History (assistant professor)
Rutgers University, Newark
100 Bleecker St. Apt. 18D
New York, N. Y. 10012
France, social history of ideas

LEVY, Robert H.
English (assistant professor)
Brown University
Providence, R. I. 02912

English literature; Enlightenment
philosophy

LEWIS, Wilmarth S.
English
The Lewis Walpole Library (Yale
University)
Main Street
Farmington, Connecticut 06032
Horace Walpole and his times

LIEBEL, Helen   C
History (associate professor)
University of Alebrta
Edmonton, Alberta
German-Austrian political and economic
thought

LIND, Kermit   C
History (instructor)
Cleveland State University
4300 Euclid Avenue
Cleveland, Ohio 44115
Intellectual history

LINDBERG, John D.
Foreign languages (professor)
University of Nevada, Las Vegas
4505 Maryland Parkway
Las Vegas, Nevada 89109
German literature of the 18th century

LINDSTROM, David H.
English (assistant professor)
Colorado State University
Fort Collins, Colorado 80521
Swift, periodical literature, Henry Hills,
satire

LINKER, Anita K.   S
Art history (graduate student)
Pennsylvania State University
636 Sunset Road
State College, Pa. 16801
British social history; 18th century art,
esp. painting

LINKER, Ronald W.   C
History (associate professor)
Pennsylvania State University
University Park, Pa. 16802
English landed families, particularly
Roman Catholics

LOCKE, Miriam   C
English (professor)
University of Alabama
Box 1484
University, Alabama 35486
Fielding; Swift

LODGE, Martin E.
History (assistant professor)
State University College
New Paltz, New York 12561
British colonies

LOKKEN, Roy N.   C
History (associate professor)
East Carolina University
P.O. Box 2744
Greenville, North Carolina 27834
Colonial and revolutionary American
history

LONGYEAR, R. M.
Music (professor)
University of Kentucky
Lexington, Ky. 40506
Music; German literature
(Empfindsamkeit, Sturm und Drang)

LOPEZ, Cecilia L.
Language arts (instructor)
Chabot College
25555 Hesperian Boulevard
Hayward, California 94545
Alexander Pope

LOUIS, Frances D.
English (instructor)
Queens College, CUNY
190-11 Nero Avenue
Holliswood, New York 11423

LOY, J. Robert   C
Modern languages (professor)
City University of New York, Brooklyn
312 Hicks Street
Brooklyn, New York 11201
French literature and thought

LUDLOW, Gregory   C
French (instructor)
New York University
3 Washington Square Village Apt. 2E

New York, N. Y. 10012
*Comparative study of English and
French 18th-century novel*

LUNN, Alice Coyle   C
English (assistant professor)
University of Michigan
2607 Haven Hall
Ann Arbor, Michigan 48104
English literature; Alexander Pope

LUSTIG, Irma S.   C
English (lecturer)
Bryn Mawr College
2023 Boxwood Drive
Broomall, Pa. 19008
Boswell; Johnson; biography

LYLES, Albert M.
English (professor)
Virginia Commonwealth University
Richmond, Virginia 23220
*Congreve, Richardson, Boswell, and
Johnson*

McALLISTER, Harold Stanwood
206 San Lorenzo, N.W.
Albuquerque, New Mexico 87107
Samuel Richardson; gothic novelists

MacANDREW, Elizabeth
English (assistant professor)
Cleveland State University
2804 East 130th Street
Cleveland, Ohio 44120

McCALL, Raymond G.   C
English (professor)
The College of Wooster
Wooster, Ohio 44691

McCARTHY, John A.
German (assistant professor)
University of Pennsylvania
Philadelphia, Pennsylvania 19104
Ch.M. Wieland; Lessing; Goethe

McCORMICK, Thomas J.   C
Art (professor)
Wheaton College
Box 426
Norton, Mass. 02766
Architecture, esp. Neoclassicism

McCOY, Kathleen   C
English (assistant professor)
Seton Hall University
South Orange, N. J. 07079
Novel; aesthetics

McCRACKEN, David
English (assistant professor)
University of Washington
439 - 36th Avenue
Seattle, Washington 98122
Later 18th-century English literature

MACCUBBIN, Robert P.
English (assistant professor)
College of William and Mary
Williamsburg, Virginia 23185
Satire; music

McCUE, Daniel L., Jr.
English (assistant professor)
Boston College
458 Carney Center
Chestnut Hill, Massachusetts 02167
*Interaction of literature and science;
   newspapers and periodicals;
   England and French Revolution*

McDERMOTT, John Francis
Adjunct Research Professor
Southern Illinois University at
   Edwardsville
6345 Westminster Place
St. Louis, Missouri 63130
The French in the Mississippi Valley

McDONALD, Robert H.
History (lecturer)
California State College
Hayward, California 94542
*Intellectual and cultural history, esp.
   Voltaire*

MacDONALD, Russell C.   C
English (associate professor)
West Virginia University
Morgantown, W. Va. 26506
Novel

McDONALD, W. Wesley   S
Political science (graduate research
   assistant)

434

State University of New York
352 State Street, Apt. 3
Albany, New York 12210
Edmund Burke; political thought

McDOUGAL, Stuart Y.
3009 Geddes Avenue
Ann Arbor, Michigan 48104

McGHEE, Dorothy M. C
Modern languages (professor emeritus)
Hamline University
St. Paul, Minnesota 55101
*The philosophic tale and moral tale;
  narrative devices and plans*

McGILL, William J.
History (associate professor)
217 N. Wade Avenue
Washington, Pennsylvania 15301
Hapsburgs, diplomatic and social history

McGUINNESS, Arthur E. C
English (associate professor)
University of California
Davis, California 95616
*Eighteenth-century English literature
  and criticism*

McHENRY, Lawrence C., Jr., M.D.
Department of Neurology
Bowman Gray School of Medicine
Winston-Salem, North Carolina 27103
*Samuel Johnson; eighteenth-century
  medicine*

McHENRY, Robert
English (assistant professor)
University of Hawaii
1733 Donaghho Road
Honolulu, Hawaii 96822
History of ideas; Pope

MacINTOSH, Fred H. C
English (professor)
University of North Carolina
Chapel Hill, N. C. 27515
Pope; Swift; literary criticism

McINTOSH, R. Carey C
English (assistant professor)
University of Rochester

Rochester, New York 14627
Johnson; Augustan genres

MacINTYRE, Jean
English (associate professor)
University of Alberta
Edmonton 7, Alberta
*English literature, mostly
  Pope and Johnson*

MacKEITH, Ronald, M.D. C
Guy's Hospital
35 Bloomfield Terrace
London, SW1, England
Samuel Johnson

McKENTY, David E. C
English (professor)
West Chester State College
West Chester, Pa. 19380
Restoration drama, history

McKENZIE, Alan T. C
English (assistant professor)
Purdue University
Lafayette, Indiana 47907
*English literature; Johnson, Baretti,
  Pope, Swift*

McKILLOP, David E. S
History (graduate student)
Case Western Reserve University
615 Ivan Drive, Apt. 7
Grove City, Pennsylvania 16127
Russo-European diplomatic history

McLAUGHLIN, Blandine L.
French (associate professor)
University of Alabama, Birmingham
900 42nd Street, South
Birmingham, Alabama 35222
Diderot (ethics and aesthetics); Rousseau

McLEOD, W. Reynolds C
History (assistant professor)
West Virginia University
Morgantown, W. Va. 26506
*Great Britain; nobility in reign of
  George I*

McMILLAN, Cynthia Anne C
History

Tufts University
Medford, Massachusetts 02155
History of science; intellectual history (European)

McNEIL, Gordon H.
History (professor)
University of Arkansas
Fayetteville, Arkansas 72701
Rousseau and French revolution

McTIGUE, Joan E.   S
English (assistant instructor)
Indiana University
213 North Grant Street
Bloomington, Indiana 47401

MACARY, Jean L.
Romance languages (assistant
  professor)
Princeton University
Princeton, New Jersey 08540

MACEY, Samuel L.
English (assistant professor)
University of Victoria
Victoria, British Columbia
*Satire; German literature; influence of
  science and technology*

MACK, Maynard   C
English (professor)
Yale University
1314 Yale Station
New Haven, Connecticut 06520

MADSEN, Roy
Modern languages and literatures
  (instructor)
Oakland University
2899 Edna Jane
Pontiac, Michigan 48057
Abbé Prévost; novel; theater

MAGNUSON, Paul A.
English (assistant professor)
University of Pennsylvania
Philadelphia, Pennsylvania 19104
Wordsworth; Coleridge

MAHAFFEY, Kathleen
English

c/o Mrs. Dixie Smith
430 South Lahoma Avenue
Norman, Oklahoma 73069
*Writers of the Augustan period, esp.
  Pope*

MALCOLMSON, Robert W.   C
History (lecturer)
Queen's University
Kingston, Ontario
English social history

MALEK, James S.
English (associate professor)
University of Idaho
Moscow, Idaho 83843
British aesthetics; British drama

MALUEG, Sara Ellen
Modern languages (associate professor)
Oregon State University
Corvallis, Oregon 97331
*Diderot; Encyclopédie; Franco-American
  relations*

MANCUSO, Joseph Charles
English (instructor)
University of North Carolina
Chapel Hill, N. C. 27514
Poetry of Christopher Smart

MANDLE, Earl Roger
Art history (assistant director)
Minneapolis Institute of Arts
201 East 24th Street
Minneapolis, Minn. 55404
Eighteenth-century Dutch painting

MANN, David D.
English (assistant professor)
Miami University
Oxford, Ohio 45056
Congreve; Gay; drama

MANTOVANI, Juanita Marie   S
English (teaching assistant)
University of Southern California
Los Angeles, Calif. 90007

MARKIEWICZ, Susanna   C
French and Italian (instructor)
Miami University

436

22 North College
Oxford, Ohio 45056
Denis Diderot

MARKS, Paul F.   C
Music (graduate student)
University of Washington
330 Marlatt St.
St. Laurent 378, Quebec
*Musical Sturm und Drang; Viennese
classic style*

MARSAK, Leonard M.   C
History (professor)
University of California
Santa Barbara, Calif. 93106
Social history of science

MARSHALL, Donald G.   C
English (assistant professor)
University of California
Los Angeles, California 90024

MARSHALL, Geoffrey   C
English (assistant professor)
University of Oklahoma
760 Van Vleet Oval
Norman, Oklahoma 73069
*Restoration, eighteenth-century drama;
Dryden*

MARSHALL, Robert L.   C
Music (assistant professor)
Princeton University
Princeton, N. J. 08540
Music of J. S. Bach

MARTIN, Donald L.
English (teaching fellow)
Kent State University
Kent, Ohio 44242

MARTIN, Jean-Claude   C
French (assistant professor)
City University of New York
420 East 72nd St.
New York, N. Y. 10021
French literature and art

MARTIN, Peter E.   C
English (assistant professor)
Florida Atlantic University

Boca Raton, Florida 33432
*Pope; eighteenth-century gardening;
John Gay*

MARTINS, Heitor   C
Spanish and Portuguese (professor)
Indiana University
Bloomington, Indiana 47401
*Portuguese and Brazilian literature and
history*

MAST, Daniel D.   C
English (instructor)
Eastern New Mexico University
Portales, New Mexico 88130
Samuel Johnson

MATHIEU, Elizabeth   S
French (student)
Vassar College
255 Waterman Street
Providence, R. I. 02906

MATLACK, Cynthia
English
University of Pittsburgh
1140 Wrightman Street
Pittsburgh, Pennsylvania 15217

MAY, Georges
French (professor)
Yale University
New Haven, Connecticut 06520
French literature; the novel

MAY, Gita   C
French (professor)
Columbia University
404 West 116th Street
New York, N. Y. 10027
*French Enlightenment and Revolution;
preromanticism; aesthetics*

MAYFIELD, P. M.   C
History (professor)
Ball State University
Muncie, Indiana 47306
British naval and administrative history

MAYO, Robert D.
English (professor)
Northwestern University

Evanston, Illinois 60201
English fiction, periodicals

MAZZEO, Guido E.
Romance languages (professor)
George Washington University
6902 Highland Street
Springfield, Virginia 22150
Spanish Jesuits in exile

MEIER, Peter P.   S
Romance languages (graduate student)
175 East 151 Street
Bronx, N. Y. 10451

MELL, Donald C., Jr.   C
English (assistant professor)
University of Delaware
Newark, Delaware 19711
Early eighteenth century; age of
Johnson; elegy

MENGEL, Elias F., Jr.   C
English (associate professor)
Georgetown University
1340 29th St., N. W.
Washington, D. C. 20007

MESSENGER, Ann P.   C
English (assistant professor)
Simon Fraser University
Burnaby 2, British Columbia
Drama; Restoration period

METGER, Helen Kendall
French (teacher)
Warrensburg Central School
220 Ash Street
Corinth, New York 12822
French literature

MEYER, Eve R.   C
Music (associate professor)
Temple University
Philadelphia, Pa. 19122
Music

MEYER, Horst E.
English (research assistant)
Ruhr-Universität Bochum
4505 Bad Iburg
Sophienstrasse 30

West Germany
Shaftesbury; Sterne; Young

MEYER, Paul H.   C
Romance languages (professor)
University of Connecticut
Storrs, Conn. 06268
French philosophes; comparative
literature

MICHAEL, Colette Verger
University of Wisconsin
806-A Eagle Heights
Madison, Wisconsin 53705

MICHAELS, Brian   S
English (teaching assistant)
University of Florida
P.O. Box 1336
Gainesville, Florida 32601
Swift

MIDDENDORF, John H.   C
English (professor)
Columbia University
610 Philosophy Hall
New York, N. Y. 10027
Samuel Johnson; economics and
literature

MILIC, Louis T.   C
English (professor)
Cleveland State University
Euclid Ave. at 22nd St.
Cleveland, Ohio 44115
Swift and prose style

MILLER, Arnold   C
French and Italian (associate professor)
University of Wisconsin
Madison, Wisconsin 53706
French Enlightenment and its influence
in 19th-century Russia; Diderot

MILLER, B. J.   C
English (assistant professor)
Bloomsburg State College
44 West Third Street
Bloomsburg, Pa. 17815
British literature

438

MILLER, Henry Knight   C
English (professor)
Princeton University
22 McCosh Hall
Princeton, N. J. 08540
Henry Fielding and the Augustan age

MILLNER, Stuart A.
English (assistant professor)
Suffolk University
390 Weld Street
West Roxbury, Massachusetts 02132
Thomas Gray

MILNE, Victor J.   S
English
26 Charlotte Crescent
Kitchener, Ontario
Aesthetics; Samuel Johnson

MINDAK, M.
French (teaching associate)
University of Texas
2301 West 11th
Austin, Texas 78703
French literature

MINER, Earl   C
English (professor)
Princeton University
Princeton, N. J. 08540
Dryden; Restoration poetry and criticism

MISENHEIMER, James B., Jr.   C
English (professor)
Indiana State University
Terre Haute, Indiana 47809
Age of Johnson; novel; satire

MITCHELL, Daniel T.   C
English (associate professor)
Loyola University of Los Angeles
4133 Locust Avenue
Long Beach, California 90807
Oliver Goldsmith

MITTMAN, Barbara G.
French (assistant professor)
University of Illinois, Chicago Circle
640 Judson
Evanston, Illinois 60202
Diderot's theatre

MOGGIO, Anna-Maria   C
History
P.O. Box 227
Fort Lee, New Jersey 07024
French Revolution

MOLNAR, Géza von
German (associate professor)
Northwestern University
Evanston, Illinois 60201

MOMMSEN, Katharina
German (professor)
Carleton University
Ottawa K1S 5B6 Ontario
German literature (Goethe; Herder; Schiller)

MONAHAN, Patrick J., Jr.
Modern languages (instructor)
Gonzaga University
Box 56
Spokane, Washington 99202
Diderot, Voltaire

MONTGOMERY, Lyna Lee
English (assistant professor)
University of Arkansas
Fayetteville, Arkansas 72701
Drama

MONTY, Jeanne R.   C
French (associate professor)
Tulane University
New Orleans, La. 70118
French literature

MOORE, Elizabeth L.   C
French (professor emeritus)
Western College for Women
1325 Market Street
Parkersburg, W. Va. 26101
Ethnology and French literature of the eighteenth century

MOORE, James W.
Political science (assistant professor)
Loyola College
7141 Sherbrooke Street West
Montreal 262, Quebec
Eighteenth-century political thought

439

MOORE, Josephine K.
English (instructor)
Foreign languages and literature
National Taiwan University
Taipei, Taiwan, China
English literature, esp. Swift

MOORE, Judith K.   S
English (graduate student)
Cornell University
137 Judd Falls Road
Ithaca, New York 14850
*Relation of literature to economic,
   social, political thought*

MOORE, Nancy   C
English (professor)
Butler University
Indianapolis, Indiana 46208
Johnson; Swift

MOORE, Nathan
English (associate professor)
Walla Walla College
College Place, Washington 99324
English literature; enthusiasm

MOORE, Robert E.
English (professor)
University of Minnesota
Minneapolis, Minnesota 55455
*English literature; music and the visual
   arts*

MOORE, William M.   S
French and Romance philology
   (graduate student)
Columbia University
1572 Massachusetts Avenue, Apt. 6
Cambridge, Massachusetts 02138
Diderot; Eighteenth-century novel

MORBY, John E.
History (assistant professor)
California State College
Hayward, California 94542
*History; French musical institutions,
   esp. at court of Versailles*

MORIN, H. S.
French (associate professor)
Secretariat of State

400 Stewart Street
Apt. 1605
Ottawa 2, Ontario
Sensibility (Marmontel, Rousseau)

MORRISROE, Michael, Jr.
English (assistant professor)
University of Illinois at Chicago Circle
1126 West Granville Avenue
Chicago, Illinois 60660
David Hume and the Enlightenment

MORRISSEY, L. J.
English (associate professor)
University of Saskatchewan
Saskatoon, Saskatchewan
Drama

MORSE, Donald E.
English (associate professor)
Oakland University
Rochester, Michigan 48063
Satire

MOSS, Harold Gene   C
English (assistant professor)
University of Florida
Gainesville, Fla. 32601
Drama

MOSS, Jean D.   C
English and history (instructor)
West Virginia University
Morgantown, W. Va. 26506
Tudor England
Drama

MOTSCH, Markus F.
Germanic languages and literatures
Vanderbilt University
Nashville, Tennessee 37235
*Eighteenth-century German literary
   criticism*

MOUNT, Elizabeth F.   S
French (graduate student)
Tulane University
The Pembroke
2077 Center Avenue
Fort Lee, New Jersey 07024
Diderot

440

MULVANEY, Robert J.
Philosophy (associate professor)
University of South Carolina
Columbia, South Carolina 29208
*Leibniz and early 18th-century
philosophy*

MURPHY, Orville T.
History (professor)
State University of New York
Buffalo, New York 14214
*Old régime France; diplomacy;
education*

MURPHY, Patricia   C
Modern languages (assistant professor)
University of New Mexico
Albuquerque, New Mexico 87106
French literature (novel)

MURPHY, Richard J.
English (assistant professor)
Providence College
Providence, Rhode Island 02918
Jonathan Swift; the novel

MYERS, Mitzi
c/o Dennis Hengeveld
Department of English
California State University
Fullerton, California 92631
Eighteenth-century fiction

MYERS, Robert Manson   C
English (professor)
University of Maryland
2101 Connecticut Avneue, N.W.
Washington, D. C. 20008
*Handel; music criticism; music and
literature in eighteenth century*

MYERS, Sylvia H.   C
English
1575 La Vereda Road
Berkeley, Calif. 94708
*Novel; life and letters of Mrs. Piozzi;
women writers*

NABARRA, Alain Marie
French
Lakehead University
Thunder Bay "P", Ontario

*French literature (novel; literature and
society)*

NATHAN, George J.
Philosophy (assistant professor)
Brock University
St. Catharines, Ontario
*British empiricism, esp. Berkeley and
Hume*

NAUEN, Franz
History
University of California at San Diego
4437 30th Street
San Diego, California 92116

NAUGLE, Helen H.   C
English (assistant professor)
Georgia Institute of Technology
Atlanta, Georgia 30332
Periodical literature

NEATBY, Hilda   C
History (professor)
Queen's University
Kingston, Ontario
Canadian history

NEBEL, Henry M., Jr.   C
Russian (associate professor)
Northwestern University
Evanston, Illinois 60201
Russian literature of eighteenth century

NEBEL, Sylvia Sue   C
German (assistant professor)
Loyola University of Chicago
6525 N. Sheridan
Chicago, Illinois 60626
German literature of eighteenth century

NECHELES, Ruth F.   C
History (associate professor)
Long Island University
191 Willoughby Street, 14A
Brooklyn, New York 11201
French Revolution (history)

NEEDHAM, Gwendolyn B.   C
English (professor)
University of California
Davis, California 95616
Novel; social milieu; arts and crafts

441

NELSON, Jeffrey M.   S
History (graduate student)
Harvard University
77 Prescott Street, Apt. 6
Cambridge, Mass. 02138
*English political thought; Hume, Burke,
   American Revolution*

NELSON, John Walter   C
English
Eastern Kentucky University
Richmond, Kentucky 40475
William Blake

NELSON, Malcolm A.   C
English (associate professor)
State University College
Fredonia, New York 14063
Catches and glees; popular culture

NELSON, Nicholas H.
English (assistant professor)
Indiana University at Kokomo
2300 South Washington Street
Kokomo, Indiana 46901
English literature, esp. satire

NELSON, Ronald R.   C
History (professor)
Western Carolina University
Cullowhee, N. C. 28723
Eighteenth-century British

NESBITT, John D.   S
English (student)
University of California, Davis
P.O. Box 642
Davis, California 95616
English literature

NEUBAUER, John   C
German (associate professor)
Case Western Reserve University
Cleveland, Ohio 44106
Aesthetics; science; Romantic poetry

NEUFELD, Evelyn   C
Foreign languages (assistant professor)
State University of New York
McAllister Road, R.D. 1
Fredonia, New York 14063
*Novel (Spain, France, Germany,
   England)*

NEW, Melvyn   C
English (assistant professor)
University of Florida
Gainesville, Florida 32601
Laurence Sterne; novel; satire

NEWELL, Julia   C
French (professor)
Dawson College
386 Roslyn Avenue
Westmount 215, Quebec
French literature

NEWMAN, Edgar Leon
History (assistant professor)
New Mexico State University
Box 3-H
Las Cruces, New Mexico 88001
*Bourbon Restoration 1814-30; French
   Louisiana*

NEWMAN, Robert   C
English (assistant professor)
SUNY, Buffalo
Annex B
Buffalo, New York 14214
Criticism, drama

NICHOLLS, James C.   C
Romance languages (associate
   professor)
Colgate University
Hamilton, New York 13346
Anglo-French literary relations

NIEMAN, Lawrence J.   C
English (assistant professor)
Canisius College
2001 Main Street
Buffalo, N. Y. 14208
Eighteenth-century English literature

NIERENBERG, Edwin   C
English (associate professor)
San Francisco State University
1600 Holloway Avenue
San Francisco, Calif. 94132
Pope; Swift; Scriblerus group; satire

NOETHER, Emiliana P.   C
History (professor)
University of Connecticut
Storrs, Connecticut 06268
Italian intellectual history

NOLTE, Edgar V.
Moravian Music Foundation, Inc.
Drawer Z
Winston-Salem, N. C. 27108

NORMAN, Sister Marion, IBVM   C
English (associate professor)
University of Alberta
Edmonton 7, Alberta
*Thomas Sprat; influence of science on
    literature*

NORTON, David Fate
Philosophy
McGill University
215 Carlyle Avenue
Town of Mount Royal, Quebec
Philosophy; Scottish Enlightenment

NOVAK, Maximillian E.   C
English (professor)
University of California
405 Hilgard Avenue
Los Angeles, California 90024
Defoe; Dryden; Congreve; novel; drama

NOWINSKI, Judith   C
French (assistant professor)
Hostos Community College, CUNY
90 La Salle Street
New York, New York 10027
French Enlightenment

NUSSBAUM, Felicity
English (assistant professor)
Indiana University at South Bend
South Bend, Indiana 46615

O'BRIEN, Charles H.
History (assistant professor)
Wittenberg University
Springfield, Ohio 45501
*Enlightened absolutism; religious
    toleration; Austria: history and
    culture*

ODEN, Richard L.
English (assistant professor)
Texas Tech University
Lubbock, Texas 79409
Dryden; Fielding

O'DONNELL, Rev. Terrence F. X.   C
Church history
Church of St. Barnabas
409 E. 241st Street
Bronx, New York 10470
Roman Catholic, esp. Papal history

O'GORMAN, Donal   C
French (professor)
St. Michael's College
University of Toronto
Toronto 5, Ontario
Diderot; Rousseau; satire

O'LEARY, Kenneth   C
English (assistant professor)
Seton Hall University
South Orange, New Jersey 07079
English literature

OLIVER, Louis A.   C
Romance languages (senior instructor)
University of Oregon
Eugene, Oregon 97403

OLSEN, Donald J.   C
History (associate professor)
Vassar College
Poughkeepsie, N. Y. 12601
*English history; urban development and
    estate management*

OLSEN, Leslie A.   C
English (assistant professor)
University of Michigan
College of Engineering
Ann Arbor, Michigan 48104
Poetry; stylistics; computer techniques

OLSHIN, Toby A.   C
English (assistant professor)
Temple University
Philadelphia, Pa. 19122
Novelists; Laurence Sterne

O'MEARA, Jean Marie
Humanities (lecturer)
University of Michigan, Dearborn
4901 Evergreen Road
Dearborn, Michigan 48195
*English literature; age of Johnson;
    Thomas Percy*

OPPER, Jacob
Music (assistant professor)
Frostburg State College
Frostburg, Maryland 21532
Musical classicism; cosmology; science

OSBORN, James M.   C
English (research associate)
Yale University
1603 A. Yale Station
New Haven, Conn. 06520

OWEN, John B.
History (professor)
University of Calgary
Calgary 45, Alberta
English history

PAGLIARO, Harold E.   C
English (professor)
Swarthmore College
Swarthmore, Pa. 19081
*Structural and rhetorical patterns in
   poetry and prose*

PALMER, Joe L.
Romance languages (assistant professor)
University of Georgia
Athens, Georgia 30601
Spanish 18th Century

PALMER, R. R.   C
History (professor)
Yale University
46 Cliff Street
New Haven, Conn. 06511

PANAGOPOULOS, Beata
Tutorials (assistant professor)
San Jose State College
San Jose, California 95114
Art history

PANAGOPOULOS, Epaminondas P. C
History (professor)
San Jose State College
San Jose, Calif. 95114
*American constitutional and intellectual
   history*

PANNELL, Anne G.   C
History (professor)

President, Sweet Briar College
Sweet Briar, Virginia 24595
*Anti-slavery agitation; the Society of
   Friends*

PAOLINI, Gilberto   C
Spanish and Portuguese (associate
   professor)
Tulane University
New Orleans, La. 70118
Spanish and Italian literature

PAPPAS, John N.   C
Romance languages (professor)
Fordham University
Bronx, New York 10458
*D'Alembert's role in the French
   Enlightenment*

PARK, William   C
English
Sarah Lawrence College
Bronxville, New York 10708
English novel

PARKER, James   C
Art history (curator)
Metropolitan Museum of Art
Fifth Ave. at 82nd Street
New York, N. Y. 10028
European decorative arts

PARKIN, Rebecca P.   C
English (professor)
California State College
Sacramento, Calif. 95819
Eighteenth-century verse

PASSLER, Susan M.
English (associate professor)
Georgia State University
1418 E. Rock Spring Road, Apt. 4
Atlanta, Georgia 30306
Novel (Fielding); Johnson

PATTERSON, Emily H.
English (assistant professor)
San Diego State College
San Diego, California 92115
Swift, Pope

444

PATTERSON, Frank M.　　　　C
English (associate professor)
Central Missouri State College
Warrensburg, Mo. 64093
Drama

PATTERSON, Sylvia W.
English (assistant professor)
University of Southwestern Louisiana
Lafayette, Louisiana 70501
Johnson and Boswell

PEACOCK, Valerie S.　　　　S
Literature (graduate student)
University of California, San Diego
354 N. Sierra
Solana Beach, California 92075
*Jonathan Swift; history of science and
　technology; status of women; the
　dance*

PELLI, Moshe
Modern Hebrew literature (senior
　lecturer)
Negev University
P.O.B. 2053
Beersheva, Israel
*Hebrew Haskalah (enlightenment);
　deism; Jewish intellectual history*

PERKINS, Jean A.　　　　C
French (associate professor)
Swarthmore College
Swarthmore, Pennsylvania 19081
*French 18th-century literature and
　philosophy*

PERRY, Thomas W.　　　　C
History (associate professor)
Boston College
Chestnut Hill, Mass. 02167
British history

PETERSON, R. G.　　　　C
English (associate professor)
St. Olaf College
Northfield, Minnesota 55057
*Dryden and Restoration; Pope; early
　18th-century Neoclassicism*

PETERSON, Spiro　　　　C
English (professor)

Miami University of Ohio
115 N. University Ave.
Oxford, Ohio 45056
Defoe; novel; satire

PETIT, Bernard
French (instructor)
SUNY, Brockport
8223 Ridge Road
Brockport, N. Y. 14420
Prose fiction; journals

PETTIT, Henry　　　　C
English (professor)
University of Colorado
Boulder, Colorado 80302
Mid-eighteenth-century poetry

PHELPS, Leland R.
German (professor)
Duke University
Durham, North Carolina 27706
*Goethe; Herder; German-English
　Literary Relations*

PHILLIPS, Steven R.
English (assistant professor)
Alfred University
Alfred, New York 14802

PHILLIPSON, John S.　　　　C
English (associate proessor)
University of Akron
Akron, Ohio 44325
Novel

PICKEN, Robert A.　　　　C
Romance languages
Queens College, CUNY
Flushing, New York 11367
French literature of the 18th century

PIERSON, 'Harry H.
3026 Harcross Road
Redwood City, California 94062
Johnson and Boswell and their circle

PIPER, William Bowman　　　　C
English (professor)
Rice University
Houston, Texas 77001
*The literature of conversation and
　common sense*

PISANO, Brother Anthony, F.S.C.   S
Brownson Hall
University of Notre Dame
Notre Dame, Indiana 46556

PITOU, Spire   C
Language and literature (professor)
University of Delaware
Newark, Delaware 19711
Comedy; tragedy; repertory

POCOCK, J. G. A.   C
History (professor)
Washington University
St. Louis, Mo. 63130
Political and historical thought

POLT, John H. R.
Spanish and Portuguese (professor)
University of California
Berkeley, California 94720
Spanish literature

POMERLAU, Cynthia S.   S
English (graduate student)
University of Pennsylvania
158 W. Durham Street
Philadelphia, Pennsylvania 19119

POPIKA, Wanda
6810 N. 72nd Place
Scottsdale, Arizona 85253
Diderot

POPKIN, Richard H.   C
Philosophy (professor)
Washington University
St. Louis, Missiouri 63130
*History of philosophy; history of
Judaism*

PORTER, Charles A.
French (associate professor)
Yale University
188 Bishop Street
New Haven, Connecticut 06511
Restif de la Bretonne; L'Encyclopédie

POSNER, Donald
Art history (professor)
Institute of Fine Arts
New York University

1 East 78th Street
New York, N. Y. 10021
French and Italian art

POWER, Mina Waterman
French
Finch College
169 East 78th Street
New York, N. Y. 10021
*Voltaire, Pascal, Diderot, ethics,
aesthetics*

PRESTON, Robert E.
Music (professor)
Newcomb College of Tulane University
New Orleans, Louisiana 70118
*Musicology; 18th-century French music;
violin sonatas; performance practice*

PRESTON, Thomas R.   C
English (associate professor)
University of Tennessee
Chattanooga, Tenn. 37403

PRIMER, Irwin   C
English (associate professor)
Rutgers University
Newark, New Jersey 07102
Mandeville

PROWN, Jules D.   C
Art history (director)
The Paul Mellon Center for British
Art and British Studies
Box 2120 Yale Station
New Haven, Connecticut 06520
*Eighteenth-century American and
English art*

QUAINTANCE, Richard E., Jr.   C
English (associate professor)
Douglass College
New Brunswick, N. J. 08903
Satire and erotic poetry; novel

QUINTANA, Ricardo   C
English (professor emeritus)
University of Wisconsin
2100 Commonwealth Ave.
Madison, Wis. 53705
Swift; Oliver Goldsmith

RACEVSKIS, Karlis
Foreign Languages (assistant professor)
Antioch College
604 Phillips Street
Yellow Springs, Ohio 45387
*The French Academy and the
philosophes*

RADER, Ralph W.
English (professor)
University of California
Berkeley, California 94720
*The novel; Boswell and Johnson;
prose literature*

RADFORD, James Elliot   S
English
1452 East Rock Springs Road, N.E.
Apt. 4
Atlanta, Georgia 30306
Literature and the visual arts

RADNER, John B.   C
English (assistant professor)
Harvard University
Warren House 9
Cambridge, Mass. 02138
Criticism; satire; moral philosophy

RAGUSA, Olga
Italian (professor)
Columbia University
601 Casa Italiana
New York, N. Y. 10027
Franco-Italian relations

RAINBOLT, John C.
History (associate professor)
University of Missouri
153 Arts and Science
Columbia, Missouri 65201
*American colonial and Revolutionary
history*

RAITIERE, Anna   C
Humanities (assistant professor)
York College, CUNY
401 West 118th Street
New York, N. Y. 10027
Theater and novel in French literature

RAMSEY, Clifford Earl   C
English (assistant professor)
Bryn Mawr College
Bryn Mawr, Pa. 19010
*Pope; Restoration drama; pastoral and
landscape literature*

RANUM, Orest
History (professor)
Johns Hopkins University
208 Ridgewood Road
Baltimore, Maryland 21210
French history, history of ideas

RAPPAPORT, Rhoda   C
History (assistant professor)
Vassar College
Poughkeepsie, N.Y. 12601
History of science (France)

RASMUSSEN, Kirk G.   S
English (teaching assistant)
Salem College
Salem, W. Va. 26426
Studies in the novel

RASSIAS, John A.
Romance languages (professor)
Dartmouth College
Hanover, New Hampshire 03755
Diderot; theater (in general)

RAWSON, C. J.   C
English (professor)
University of Warwick
Coventry, Warwickshire
England
Fielding; Swift; Thomas Parnell; satire

RAYNAUD, Jean-Michel
French (professor)
University of Ottawa
130 Somerset West
Ottawa 4, Ontario
Voltaire

REARDON, Ruth C.   C
French (assistant professor)
New York University
New York, N. Y. 10003
*French literature of the 18th century;
philosophes*

REEDY, Rev. Gerald, S.J.
English (student)
University of Pennsylvania
4520 Chester Ave.
Philadelphia, Pennsylvania 19143

REGAN, John   S
English (graduate student)
University of California, Davis
13-C Solano Park
Davis, California 95616
Poetry of Alexander Pope

REISH, Joseph G.
Modern and classical languages
Western Michigan University
Kalamazoo, Michigan 49001
French literature; linguistics

REITAN, Earl A.   C
History (professor)
Illinois State University
Normal, Illinois 61761
*British constitutional and political
history, 1689-1832*

RENZ, Joan K.
English (instructor)
Northern Michigan University
1420 W. Center Street
Marquette, Michigan 49855

RETZLEFF, Garry V.
English (assistant professor)
Bishop's University
Lennoxville, Quebec
*Aesthetic theory; landscape literature,
the picturesque*

REUTINGER, Martin   S
English (graduate student)
University of California, Berkeley
P.O. Box 126
Stinson Beach, Calif. 94970
English literature; Swift

REVITT, Paul J.   C
Music (professor)
University of Missouri at Kansas City
4420 Warwick Blvd.
Kansas City, Missouri 64111
Music

REYNOLDS, John F.
German (assistant professor)
University of Virginia
Charlottesville, Virginia 22903
German literature; C. F. Gellert

REYNOLDS, Richard
English (assistant professor)
University of Connecticut
Hillyndale Road
Storrs, Conn. 06268
Johnson; Pope

REZLER, Marta   C
Romance languages (assistant
  professor)
Hunter College, CUNY
695 Park Avenue
New York, New York 10021
History of ideas; D'Alembert; Voltaire

RICCIARDELLI, M.   C
Italian (professor)
State University of New York
221 Crosby Hall
Buffalo, New York 14214
Italian history, art, literature

RICE, Scott B.
English (assistant professor)
San Jose State College
125 South 7th Street
San Jose, California 95114
Travel literatue; Smollett

RICHARDSON, Robert D., Jr.   C
English (associate professor)
University of Denver
Denver, Colorado 80210
*Mythology and mythography; American
  romanticism*

RICHARDSON, Sharon B.   S
Comparative literature (graduate
  student)
University of North Carolina
13708 Superior Road
Cleveland, Ohio 44112
Letters

RICHESON, Edward, Jr.
English (associate professor)

448

List of Members

University of Texas at El Paso
Box 128, UTEP
El Paso, Texas 79902
Pope and the Augustan Age

RICHTMAN, Jack
French (associate professor)
SUNY at Albany
151a Commercial Street
Provincetown, Massachusetts 02657
*French theater; actors and their
condition; acting styles*

RIDGWAY, R. S.   C
French and Spanish (professor)
University of Saskatchewan
Saskatoon, Saskatchewan
Voltaire; theater; sensibility

RIELY, John C.   C
English (teaching fellow)
University of Pennsylvania
409 Whitney Avenue
New Haven, Connecticut 06511
Johnson, Boswell, and their circle

RIGAULT, Mme. Claude
Etudes françaises (adjunct professor)
Université de Sherbrooke
Sherbrooke, Quebec
*Marivaux; meaning and development of
le burlesque*

RIPPEY, Arthur G.
English
2525 E. Exposition Avenue
Denver, Colorado 80223
*Johnson; Boswell (early editions;
collector)*

RIPPY, Frances M.   C
English (professor)
Ball State University
4417 W. Jackson
Muncie, Indiana 47304
*Restoration and eighteenth-century
British poetry*

RITCHESON, Charles R.
History (professor)
University of Southern California
Los Angeles, California 90007

*Late eighteenth- and early nineteenth-
century British and American*

ROBBINS, Caroline
History (professor)
Bryn Mawr College
815 The Chetwynd
Rosemont, Pennsylvania 19010
History of ideas

ROBERTS, David D.   C
English (assistant professor)
University of Wyoming
Laramie, Wyoming 82070
English literature

ROBERTS, Edgar V., Jr.   C
English (associate professor)
Herbert H. Lehman College, CUNY
Bronx, N. Y. 10468
Plays of Henry Fielding

ROBINSON, Lucius S.
German (associate professor)
California Western Campus
United States International University
3928 Milan Street
San Diego, Calif. 92106
*German and French literature; U. S.
cultural history*

ROCHE, John F.   C
History (associate professor)
Fordham University
New York, N. Y. 10023
*History of American revolution;
American architecture*

RODES, David Stuart   C
English (assistant professor)
University of California
405 Hilgard Avenue
Los Angeles, Calif. 90024
*Theater; French-English relations;
Dutch influences*

RODEWALD, Albert F.
Music (assistant professor)
University of Virginia
113 Old Cabell Hall
Charlottesville, Virginia 22903
Opera; theatre

449

RODGERS, Gary B.
Foreign languages
Louisiana State University
Baton Rouge, Louisiana 70803
Diderot; 18th-century French press

ROGAL, Samuel J.   C
English (associate professor)
State University College
Oswego, N. Y. 13126
*Hymnody; emphasis on Isaac Watts and
the Wesleys*

ROGERS, Adrienne
French (associate professor)
Russell Sage College
Troy, New York 12180
*Censorship in France; Voltaire;
Rousseau*

ROGERS, William B.
Literature (assistant professor)
Rensselaer Polytechnic Institute
Troy, New York 12181
The novel

ROSBOTTOM, Ronald C.   C
Romance languages (assistant
  professor)
University of Pennsylvania
1015 S. 48th Street
Philadelphia, Pennsylvania 19143
French literature, art, history

ROSCH, Hopewell Selby
English (assistant professor)
University of Illinois, Chicago Circle
Chicago, Illinois 60680
Swift; Restoration drama

ROSEN, George
History of science and medicine
  (professor)
Yale University
1480 Ridge Road
North Haven, Connecticut 06473
Medicine, science, literature, culture

ROSEN, Richard L.
History of science (assistant professor)
Drexel University
Philadelphia, Pennsylvania 19104
History of science, esp. Italy

ROSENBERG, Aubrey   C
French (lecturer)
Victoria College
University of Toronto
Toronto 5, Ontario
Voyages imaginaires and utopias

ROSENFIELD, Leonora Cohen
French and Italian (professor)
University of Maryland
3749 Chesapeake Street, N.W.
Washington, D. C. 20016
*History of ideas (France); French
  Enlightenment and its relations with
  other countries*

ROSENHEIM, E. W., Jr.
English (professor)
University of Chicago
Chicago, Illinois 60637
Satire

ROSOWSKI, Susan   S
English (graduate student)
University of Arizona
1810 So. 25th
Lincoln, Nebraska 68502
Laurence Sterne

ROSS, David A.
Foreign languages (assistant professor)
California State University
Fresno, California 93710
Anglo-French relations

ROSS, Ian   C
English (associate professor)
University of British Columbia
3845 W. 37th Avenue
Vancouver 13, British Columbia
Hume circle; Scottish vernacular poetry

ROTHMAN, Irving N.
English
University of Houston
Houston, Texas 77004

ROTHMAN, Lynne Karen   S
French (graduate student)
Vassar College
Noyes House
Poughkeepsie, New York 12601

Music; French literature; English literature; Diderot; Richardson

ROTHSCHILD, Harriet Dorothy
French (associate professor)
University of Rhode Island
Kingston, Rhode Island 02881
Benoît de Maillet

ROTHSTEIN, Eric
English (professor)
University of Wisconsin
7195 White Hall
Madison, Wisconsin 53706
Drama; fiction; Anglo-French literary relationships

ROUSSEAU, George S.   C
English (associate professor)
University of California
Los Angeles, California 90024
Literature and science; medicine 1660-1800; Pope

ROWE, Constance
French (associate professor)
Southeast Missouri State College
318 North Sprigg Street
Cape Girardeau, Missouri 63701
Voltaire

ROWSOME, Beverly   C
History
100 West Street
Geneva, New York 14456
Colonial American legal tradition

RUDOLPH, Valerie C.   C
English (instructor)
Purdue University
Lafayette, Indiana 47907
Drama; satire; Fielding

RUFF, Lawrence Albert   C
English (associate professor)
University of Dayton
Dayton, Ohio 45409
Novel

RUGGLES, Rebecca D.   C
English
Brooklyn College, CUNY

606 West 116th St. Apt. 23
New York, N. Y. 10027

RUHE, E. L.   C
English (professor)
University of Kansas
Lawrence, Kansas 66044
Johnson; Milton tradition; Edmund Curll

RULE, John C.   C
History (professor)
Ohio State University
216 N. Oval Drive
Columbus, Ohio 43210
European history; age of Louis XIV, French diplomacy

RUNTE, Roseann   S
French and Italian (graduate student)
University of Kansas
Box 76
Shrub Oak, New York 10588
La Fontaine's reputation and influence in 18th-century France

RUPPRECHT, Oliver C.
English and fine arts (professor)
Concordia College
1108 Kavanaugh Place
Milwaukee, Wisconsin 53213
Literature, music, art

RYLEY, Robert M.   C
English (assistant professor)
York College, CUNY
Jamaica, N. Y. 11432
Criticism

RYNES, Theodore J.
English (assistant professor)
University of Santa Clara
Faculty Residence
Santa Clara, Calif. 95053
English literature; visual arts; religion

SACKS, Sheldon   C
English (professor)
University of Chicago
Chicago, Illinois 60637
Prose fiction; Henry Fielding

SAETA, Maurice   C
English
2373 Silver Ridge Avenue
Los Angeles, California 90039
Boswell; Johnson

SAINE, Thomas P.
Germanic languages and literature
  (assistant professor)
Yale University
307 W. L. Harkness Hall
New Haven, Conn. 06520
*German literature; intellectual history;
  aesthetics*

SAINE, Ute M.
Romance languages and literatures
  (post-doctoral teaching fellow)
Wesleyan University
211 Highland Street
New Haven, Connecticut 06511
*Utopian narrative; political and social
  theory; aesthetics; encyclopédie;
  Rousseau*

SAISSELIN, Rémy B.   C
Comparative literature (professor)
University of Rochester
Rochester, New York 14627
Aesthetics theory; art; pre-romanticism

SALM, Peter   C
Comparative literature (professor)
Case Western Reserve University
Division of Modern Languages
Maher Memorial Building
Cleveland, Ohio 44106
*Literature and philosophy; relationship
  between science and literature*

SAMPSON, H. Grant   C
Drama (director)
Department of English
Queen's University
Kingston, Ontario
Drama

SAREIL, Jean   C
French (professor)
Columbia University
New York, N. Y. 10027
Literature; history

SARICK, Hyman
English (lecturer)
Queen's University
Kingston, Ontario
Swift; Johnson

SARICKS, Ambrose   C
History (professor)
Wichita State University
Dean, Graduate School
Wichita, Kansas 67207
*Economic and religious thought;
  French Revolution*

SASLOW, Edward L.
English (assistant professor)
University of California, Riverside
1805-I Loma Vista
Riverside, California 92507
Dryden

SAVELLE, Max   C
History (professor)
University of Illinois, Chicago Circle
Chicago, Illinois 60680
*Anglo-American intellectual history;
  the Enlightenment and America*

SCHAKEL, Peter J.   C
English
Hope College
Holland, Michigan 49423
Jonathan Swift

SCHELLE, Hansjörg
German (assistant professor)
University of Michigan
1221 Island Drive, Apt. 202
Ann Arbor, Michigan 48105
Wieland and his relations

SCHENCK, Peter E.
English (instructor)
University of Dubuque
1051 McCormick Street
Dubuque, Iowa 52001
English literature

SCHICK, Edgar B.
German
Vice-President for Academic Affairs
St. John Fisher College

3690 East Avenue
Rochester, New York 14618
Age of Goethe; German literature;
intellectual history and influence on
20th century

SCHLEGEL, Dorothy B.   C
English (professor)
Norfolk State College
476 Linkhorn Drive
Virginia Beach, Virginia 23351
Rosicrucian and Masonic symbolism;
Shaftesbury (3rd Earl)

SCHLERETH, Thomas J.
American studies (professor)
University of Notre Dame
Notre Dame, Indiana 46556
Scottish and American Enlightenments

SCHNITZER, Shirley   C
English (graduate student)
City University of New York
430 East 86th Street
New York, N. Y. 10028
Pope; Swift

SCHNORRENBERG, Barbara B.   C
History (lecturer)
University of North Carolina
Chapel Hill, N. C. 27514
English and German history,
especially diplomatic

SCHOFIELD, Robert E.   C
History of science (professor)
Case Western Reserve University
Crawford Hall
Cleveland, Ohio 44106
Natural philosophy, esp. British;
Joseph Priestley

SCHRADER, William C., III   C
History (assistant professor)
Tennessee Technological University
Cookeville, Tenn. 38501
Habsburgs; cultural parallels

SCHUTZ, Herbert
German (associate professor)
Brock University
St. Catharines, Ontario

German enlightenment; German middle
class; pedagogical theories

SCHUTZ, John A.   C
History (professor)
University of Southern California
Los Angeles, Calif. 90007
Massachusetts politics; American Tories

SCHWANDT, Pamela Poynter
English
811 Greenvale
Northfield, Minnesota 55057
Pope; translation; Homeric criticism

SCHWARTZ, Judith L.   C
Music (instructor)
University of California
Riverside, Calif. 92502
Classical music and musical theory

SCHWARTZ, Leon   C
Foreign languages (professor)
California State University at Los Angeles
1032 So. El Molino
Alhambra, Calif. 91801
French literature

SCHWARTZ, Richard B.   C
English (associate professor)
University of Wisconsin
Madison, Wisconsin 53706
Literature and science; Samuel Johnson

SCHWARTZ, Robert G., Jr.   C
English (assistant professor)
Central Missouri State College
Warrensburg, Missouri 64093
English literature

SCHWARZ, Herbert J., Jr.   C
History
435 East 57th Street
New York, N. Y. 10022
History (evolution of the souvenir
industry)

SCHWARZBACH, Bertram E.
French (assistant professor)
Elmira College
1304 Brooklyn Avenue
Brooklyn, New York 11203

*Voltaire, Bible criticism, history
of science*

SCOTT, Alison   C
Germanic languages (professor)
University of Alberta
Edmonton 7, Alberta
*German literature, especially Lessing;
Anglo-German and Franco-German*

SCOUTEN, Arthur H.
English (professor)
University of Pennsylvania
Philadelphia, Pennsylvania 19104
Restoration drama; Swift

SCRUGGS, Charles   C
English (assistant professor)
University of Arizona
Tucson, Arizona 85721
Swift

SEBBA, Gregor
Liberal arts (professor)
Graduate Institute of Liberal Arts
Emory University
Atlanta, Georgia 30322
Rousseau, Goethe, history of ideas

SEBOLD, Rusell P.
Spanish (professor)
University of Pennsylvania
Philadelphia, Pa. 19104
*Spanish literature; novel, pre-
romanticism (European literatures);
aesthetics*

SEGAL, Lester A.   C
History (assistant professor)
University of Massachusetts
Boston, Mass. 02116
*French intellectual history;
religious skepticism*

SEGEL, Harold B.   C
Slavic languages (professor)
Columbia University
213 Lewisohn Hall
New York, N. Y. 10027
*Russian and Polish 18th-century
literature*

SELLS, Larry F.   C
English (instructor)
Westminster College
4 Beechwood Drive
New Wilmington, Pa. 16142
English novel, esp. Fielding

SELSS, Steven L.   C
History (student)
Queens College, CUNY
192-24B 64th Circle
Flushing, New York 11365
*Military, Jewish, music, N. Y.
city history*

SENA, John F.
English (assistant professor)
Ohio State University
Columbus, Ohio 43210
Samuel Garth; literature and medicine

SHAW, Edward P.
Romance languages (professor)
State University of New York, Albany
1400 Washington Avenue
Albany, New York 12203
French literature

SHEA, John S.   C
English (assistant professor)
Loyola University of Chicago
6525 N. Sheridan Road
Chicago, Ill. 60626
Dryden; Gay; the fable

SHEPS, Arthur   C
History (lecturer)
Scarborough College, University of
Toronto
West Hill, Ontario
*Political philosophy; Anglo-American
intellectual history; American
Revolution*

SHERBO, Arthur   C
English (professor)
Michigan State University
East Lansing, Michigan 48823
English literature in all its aspects

SHERMAN, Carol
Romance languages (instructor)

University of North Carolina
Chapel Hill, N. C. 27514
Diderot and the philosophic dialogue

SHERWOOD, Irma Z.
English (assistant professor)
University of Oregon
Eugene, Oregon 97403
Samuel Johnson

SHERWOOD, John C.
English (professor)
University of Oregon
Eugene, Oregon 97403
Dryden

SHIMIZU, Kazuyoshi
English (assistant professor)
Aichi University
116-68, Ippongi, Ueda-cho
Toyohashi 440, Japan
*Authors, publishers and readers of
    18th-century England*

SHIPLEY, John B.   C
English (professor)
University of Illinois at Chicago Circle
Box 4348
Chicago, Illinois 60680
*Novel; Johnson circle; aesthetics;
    the newspapers*

SHOWALTER, English, Jr.   C
Romance languages (assistant professor)
Princeton University
Princeton, New Jersey 08540
French literature, esp. fiction

SHULIM, Joseph I.   C
History (professor)
City University of New York
2601 Glenwood Road
Brooklyn, New York 11210
*Old Régime (France); French
    Revolution; Napoleon*

SIEBERT, Donald T., Jr.
English
University of South Carolina
Columbia, South Carolina 29208
English literature

SIEGEL, June Sigler   C
French, English
6 Carol Lane
New Rochelle, New York 10804
French-English, esp. novel

SIEVERT, William   C
English (assistant professor)
Pace College
41 Park Row
New York, N. Y. 10038
Satire

SIGWORTH, Oliver F.   C
English (professor)
University of Arizona
Tucson, Arizona 85721
Poetry, criticism

SILBAJORIS, Frank R.   C
Slavic studies (professor)
Ohio State University
1841 Millikin Road
Columbus, Ohio 43210
*Russian 18th-century poetics,
    drama, and prose*

SILBER, C. Anderson   C
English (lecturer)
Victoria College, University of Toronto
43 Hambly Avenue
Toronto 260, Ontario
English literature, esp. poetry

SILBER, Gordon R.   C
French (professor)
SUNY, Buffalo
124 Brookedge Drive
Williamsville, N. Y. 14221
*French literature; Franco-American
    cultural relations*

SILBER, Mrs. Gordon R.
124 Brookedge Drive
Williamsville, New York 14221

SILVERBLATT, Bette G.   C
French
4169 Oak Hill Avenue
Palo Alto, California 94306
*Charles Pinot Duclos; French
    literature and thought*

455

SIMMONS, Sarah
Romance languages (assistant professor)
Colorado College
Colorado Springs, Colorado 80903
Eighteenth-century French novel

SIMONEAU, Joseph R.   S
French (student)
Pennsylvania State University
519 West College Ave.
State College, Pa. 16801
Diderot and L'Encyclopédie

SJOGREN, Christine
Modern languages (professor)
Oregon State University
Corvallis, Oregon 97331
Enlightenment

SKINNER, Mary-Lynn   C
English (assistant professor)
Virginia Commonwealth University
Richmond, Virginia 23220
*Novel; Restoration and eighteenth-
    century drama*

SKUBLY, Jacqueline de L.
Foreign languages (assistant professor)
Housatonic Community College
555 Clinton Avenue
Bridgeport, Conn. 06605
Marivaux

SLATTERY, William C.
English (professor)
Southern Illinois University
Edwardsville, Illinois 62025
Richardson, the Dutch novel

SLAVIN, Morris   C
History (associate professor)
Youngstown State University
262 Outlook Ave.
Youngstown, Ohio 44504
French Revolution

SLOAN, Sheldon   S
English (graduate assistant)
University of Maryland
3417 Toledo Terrace, H4
Hyattsville, Maryland 20782

SMITH, Beverlee A.
English (assistant professor)
Purdue University
4608 W. 175th Place
Country Club Hills, Illinois 60477
Defoe; non-fiction relating to the poor

SMITH, D. I. B.   C
English (associate professor)
University College, University of
    Toronto
Toronto, Ontario
Editing; history of ideas; poetry

SMITH, D. W.   C
French (associate professor)
Victoria College, University of Toronto
Toronto 5, Ontario
Helvétius

SMITH, David E.   C
American studies (professor)
Hampshire College
Merrill House
Amherst, Mass. 01002
American 18th-century studies

SMITH, Frederik N.   C
English (assistant professor)
Case Western Reserve University
Cleveland, Ohio 44106
Swift; 17th-18th-century prose style

SMITH, Joan Van Rensselaer
Art (associate professor)
Michigan State University
East Lansing, Michigan 48823
Art and architecture

SMITH, Lyle E.
English (assistant professor)
California State College
1000 East Victoria Street
Dominguez Hills, California 90747
English literature

SMITH, Peter L.   S
French and Italian (teaching assistant)
University of Wisconsin
909 Hamlin Street
Evanston, Illinois 60201
Correspondence of Pierre-Michel Hennin

SMITTEN, Jeffrey
English (assistant professor)
Texas Tech University
Lubbock, Texas 79409
English literature; philosophy

SPACKS, Patricia Meyer   C
English (professor)
Wellesley College
16 Abbott Street
Wellesley, Mass. 02181
Pope; poetry

SPEAKMAN, James S.
English (associate [in Subject A])
University of California, Davis
2821 17th St.
Sacramento, California 95818
*Comic theory; theory and practice
   of the novel*

SPEAR, Frederick A.   C
French (professor)
Skidmore College
Saratoga Springs, New York 12866
*Voltaire bibliography; Diderot
   bibliography*

SPEAR, Richard E.   C
Art history (associate professor)
Oberlin College
Oberlin, Ohio 44074
The rococo

SPECTOR, Robert D.   C
English (professor)
Long Island University
1761 East 26th Street
Brooklyn, New York 11229
Novel; periodicals

SPENCER, David G.   C
English (professor)
California State College
212 Haggin
Bakersfield, Calif. 93309
*Restoration and 18th-century theater;
   political satire*

SPENCER, Jeffry B. (Mrs. David G.) C
English (adjunct associate professor)
California State College

212 Haggin
Bakersfield, California 93309
Literature and the visual arts; poetry

SPIKER, Sina K.   C
English (associate professor—retired)
Southern Illinois University
209 Brook Lane
Carbondale, Illinois 62901
Restoration literature

SPURLIN, Paul M.
French (professor emeritus)
University of Michigan
505 N. Seventh Street
Ann Arbor, Michigan 48103

SRABIAN de FABRY, Anne
French (assistant professor)
King's College
117 Rollingwood
London 72, Ontario
J. J. Rousseau

STANLIS, Peter J.   C
English (professor)
Rockford College
Rockford, Illinois 61101
Burke and his times

STARKEY, Margaret M.   C
English (associate professor emeritus)
Brooklyn College, CUNY
Box 383
Williamsburg, Virginia 23185
*Age of Pope, dominant ideas
   in the poetry of the age*

STARNES, Thomas C.   C
German (assistant professor)
Tulane University
New Orleans, La. 70118
C. M. Wieland

STEDMOND, John   C
English (professor)
Queen's University
Kingston, Ontario
Prose fiction; Laurence Sterne

STEELE, Elizabeth   C
English (assistant professor)

457

University of Toledo
3219 Cheltenham Rd.
Toledo, Ohio 43606
Horace Walpole

STEENSMA, Robert C.   C
English (associate professor)
Uniiversity of Utah
Salt Lake City, Utah 84112
Jonathan Swift; Sir William Temple;
naval history

STEESE, Peter   C
English (associate professor)
State University of New York
Fredonia, N. Y. 14063
Biography; verse paraphrases of the
Bible

STEFANSON, Donald H.   S
English (doctoral candidate)
University of Iowa
3416 Davis
Sioux City, Iowa 51106
History of printing; prose fiction

STEINER, Thomas R.
English (assistant professor)
University of California at Santa Barbara
Santa Barbara, California 93106
English literature, esp. poetry; literature
and society; the classical tradition

STEPP, Nancy T.   C
3894 Healy Road
Memphis, Tennessee 38111
Dryden; novel; satire; satirical allegory

STERN, Monique   S
Graduate student
University of Maryland
12 Furber Lane
Newton Centre, Mass. 02159

STEVENSON, Julie
French (assistant professor)
University of Nevada, Las Vegas
311 S. 10th Street
Las Vegas, Nevada 89101
French thought and its expression in the
literary genres, esp. the novel

STEWART, Gordon M.
German (assistant professor)
University of Virginia
1607 Greenleaf Lane
Charlottesville, Virginia 22903
German enlightenment; Anglo-German
literary relations

STEWART, Keith   C
English (associate professor)
University of Cincinnati
Cincinnati, Ohio 45221
Literary theory—mid- and later
eighteenth-century

STEWART, Maaja A.   C
English (assistant professor)
Newcomb College
New Orleans, La. 70118
Fiction; novel and history, biography,
journal

STEWART, Mary Margaret   C
English (professor)
Gettysburg College
Gettysburg, Pennsylvania 17325
William Collins; Henry Fielding; James
Boswell

STEWART, Philip   C
Romance languages
Duke University
Durham, North Carolina 27706
French literature, especially novel

STOCK, Robert D.
English (associate professor)
University of Nebraska
304 Andrews Hall
Lincoln, Nebraska 68502
Johnson; Burke; history of ideas

STOCKTON, Constant Noble
History and philosophy (associate
     professor)
Wisconsin State University
River Falls, Wisconsin 54022
Intellectual history, philosophy,
historiography, law

STOCKWELL, Joseph E.
English (assistant professor)

Mississippi State University
Box 5242
State College, Miss. 39762
Samuel Johnson's criticism

STOEFFLER, F. Ernest
Religion (professor)
Temple University
Philadelphia, Pennsylvania 19122
*German criticism and German
Enlightenment*

STOLLERY, C. William   C
R.R. 2
Aurora, Ontario
Johnsonian letters

STRAKA, Gerald M.
History (associate professor)
University of Delaware
Newark, Delaware 19711
Political theory

STRAULMAN, Ann T.
English (assistant professor)
University of Western Ontario
London 72, Ontario
English novel and drama

STRAUSS, Albrecht B.   C
English (associate professor)
University of North Carolina
2 Dogwood Acres Drive
Chapel Hill, N. C. 27514
English novel; prose style; Johnson

STRICKLEN, Charles G., Jr.   C
History (assistant professor)
University of North Carolina
Chapel Hill, N. C. 27514
*Social and political thought
(1770-1789)*

STRONG, Philip
English (assistant professor)
Northern Arizona University
Flagstaff, Arizona 86001
*Christopher Smart; mid-century English
periodicals*

STUMPF, Thomas A.
English (assistant professor)

University of North Carolina
104 Bennington Drive
Chapel Hill, North Carolina 27514
1660-1740; Pope

STURGILL, Claude C.   C
History (associate professor)
University of Florida
630 N.E. 10th Ave.
Gainesville, Florida 32601
French military history

STURM, Norbert A.   C
English (associate professor)
University of Dayton
3849 Germantown Street
Dayton, Ohio 45418

SULLIVAN, Maureen   C
English
University of Pennsylvania
119 Bennett Hall
Philadelphia, Pa. 19104
Restoration, 18th-century drama; novel

SUNGOLOWSKY, Joseph
Romance languages (associate
professor)
Queens College, CUNY
Flushing, New York 11367
*Romanticism and 18th century in
France; theater; Beaumarchais*

SUTTON, Betty S.   C
English (associate professor)
Ohio State University
138 Arden Road
Columbus, Ohio 43214

SUZUKI, Zenzo
English literature (associate professor)
Tohoku University
Sendai, Japan
*Pope; oriental impact on 18th-century
English literature*

SWEDENBERG, H. T.   C
English (professor)
University of California
Los Angeles, Calif. 90024
Dryden; poetry

SWITZER, Richard   C
Humanities (dean)
California State College
San Bernardino, Calif. 92407
Theater; pre-romanticism

TARAS, A. F.
Foreign languages (professor)
Ithaca College
1137 Warren Road
Ithaca, New York 14850
Lesage; Voltaire; Rousseau

TARBET, David W.   C
English (assistant professor)
State University of New York
Buffalo, New York 14214
Johnson; philosophy

TASCH, Peter A.   C
English (instructor)
Temple University
5430 Wayne Avenue
Philadelphia, Pa. 19144
Drama; Scriblerus Club

TATE, Robert S., Jr.   C
French and Italian (assistant professor)
University of Iowa
141 Grand Avenue Court
Iowa City, Iowa 52240
French literature; Bachaumont; Lesage

TAYLOR, Charlene M.   C
English (assistant professor)
University of Arizona
8120 Calle Potrero
Tucson, Arizona 85715
Restoration and 18th-century drama

TAYLOR, Myron L.
English
Box 112
Barnett, Missouri 65011
Oldham; restoration and 18th-century

TAYLOR, Robert E.
French
University of Massachusetts
Amherst, Massachusetts 01002

TEMMER, Mark J.   C
French and Italian (professor)
University of California
Santa Barbara, Calif. 93106
J. J. Rousseau

THACKRAY, Arnold
History of science (associate professor)
University of Pennsylvania
117 E. F. Smith Chemistry Laboratory
Philadelphia, Pa. 19104
*Science, technology, the Industrial
   Revolution*

THELANDER, Dorothy R.   C
French (associate professor)
University of Illinois at Chicago Circle
Box 4348
Chicago, Ill. 60680
Epistolary fiction; satire

THERRIEN, Madeleine B.   C
French (associate professor)
Emory University
Atlanta, Georgia 30322
French novel; Laclos

THIELEMANN, Leland J.
French and Italian (professor)
University of Texas
206 Robert E. Lee Hall
Austin, Texas 78712

THOMASSON, Brenda Faith
French (graduate student)
University of Kentucky
Cooperstown F-312
Lexington, Kentucky 40506
Diderot; materialists

THOMPSON, Nancy M.   C
French and Spanish (assistant
   professor)
University of Saskatchewan
Saskatoon, Saskatchewan
Voltaire

THOMPSON, Paul V.   C
English (professor)
University of Colorado
325 16th Street
Boulder, Colorado 80302
Swift

THORNE, Charles Greenwood, Jr.   C
Cultural history
Box 427
Ephrata, Pa. 17522
*Cultural and intellectual history; silver;
  architecture*

THORSON, James L.   C
English (assistant professor)
University of New Mexico
Albuquerque, New Mexico 87106
Satire; Jonathan Swift; Hogarth

THRO, Michael   S
English (graduate student)
University of Southern California
Los Angeles, California 90007
The novel—Defoe, Sterne

TOBORG, Alfred   C
History (associate professor)
Lyndon State College
Lyndonville, Vermont 15851
Prussian history, esp. Frederick the Great

TODD, Dennis   C
English
Wayne State University
Detroit, Michigan 48202
Pope; Gay

TONELLI, Giorgio
Philosophy (professor)
State University of New York
Binghamton, N. Y. 13901
*18th-century German, French, English
  philosophy*

TOPAZIO, Virgil W.   C
French (professor)
Rice University
236 Rayzor Hall
Houston, Texas 77001
Voltaire; Rousseau; D'Holbach

TORCHIANA, Donald T.
English (professor)
Northwestern University
Evanston, Illinois 60201

TORIGIAN, Janine
French and Italian (assistant instructor)

University of Texas
2712 Maria Anna Road
Austin, Texas 78746
Political theory of the dispersion

TOTTEN, Charles F.   S
English (graduate assistant)
Wayne State University
Detroit, Michigan 48202
English drama, criticism

TOTTEN, Darla R.   S
Art history (graduate student)
Wayne State University
Detroit, Michigan 48202

TRACY, Clarence   C
English (professor)
Acadia University
Wolfville, Nova Scotia
Johnson

TRACY, Nicholas
c/o Dr. C. Tracy
Box 117
Wolfville, Nova Scotia
Naval, diplomatic, imperial history

TRAPNELL, William H.   C
French (assistant professor)
Indiana University
Ballantine Hall
Bloomington, Indiana 47401
Marivaux, Voltaire

TROTT, David A.   C
French (lecturer)
Erindale College, University of Toronto
Toronto, Ontario
French drama; Marivaux

TROUT, Paul A.
English
Montana State University
Bozeman, Montana 59715
Swift, satire

TROWBRIDGE, Hoyt
English (professor)
University of New Mexico
Albuquerque, New Mexico 87106
*Dryden, Swift, Pope, Johnson, literary
  criticism*

461

TUMINS, Valerie A.   C
Russian (associate professor)
University of California
Davis, Calif. 95616
Russian literature and culture

TURNER, Maxine T.
English
Georgia Institute of Technology
Atlanta, Georgia 30332

TURNER, Richard C.
English
5306 N. Capitol
Indianapolis, Indiana 46208
Augustan poetry and drama

TYNE, Rev. James L., S.J.   C
English (associate professor)
Fordham University
Bronx, New York 10458
Jonathan Swift

TYSON, Gerald P.
English (assistant professor)
University of Maryland
College Park, Md. 20740
Scottish writers and Scots nationalism

UPHAUS, Robert W.   C
English (assistant professor)
School of English
University of Leeds
Leeds 2, England
Poetry and aesthetics

VALES, Robert L.   C
English (assistant professor)
Gannon College
Erie, Pa. 16501
Late eighteenth-century studies

VALLIER, Robert   C
English
University of Tennessee
Chattanooga, Tennessee 37403
Swift's rhetorical satire

VAN ALSTYNE, Richard W.
History (professor)
Callison College, University of the
  Pacific

Stockton, California 95204
*American revolution; American
nationalism; comparative history
(Britain, France, America)*

VAN DUSEN, R.   C
German (associate professor)
McMaster University
Hamilton, Ontario
*German: popular philosophie,
comparative literature*

VAN EERDE, John A.   C
Romance languages (professor)
Lehigh University
Bethlehem, Pa. 18015
Theater

VAN MARTER, Shirley   C
English and comparative literature
  (assistant professor)
University of California
Irvine, California 92664
Literature

VAN TREESE, Glenn J.   C
Modern languages (assistant professor)
Sweet Briar College
P.O. Box 18
Sweet Briar, Virginia 24595
D'Alembert; Frederick the Great

VARNELL, O. Paul   C
English (instructor)
North Illinois University
835 Edgebrook, Apt. 3
De Kalb, Illinois 60115
Swift; political and social philosophy

VARTANIAN, Aram   C
Romance languages (professor)
New York University
19 University Place
New York, N. Y. 10003

VÁZQUEZ-RAMPA, Washington   C
Spanish and Portuguese (assistant
  professor)
Miami University
Oxford, Ohio 45056
*Spanish and Portuguese literature; esp.
satire and fable*

VERDURMEN, J. Peter
English (assistant professor)
University of Cincinnati
727 Red Bud Avenue
Cincinnati, Ohio 45229
*Restoration drama; later
18th-century drama*

VIETH, David M.   C
English (professor)
Southern Illinois University
Carbondale, Illinois 62901
*John Wilmot; Restoration literature;
Swift and Pope*

VINCENT, Howard   C
English (professor)
Kent State University
Kent, Ohio 44240

VINCENT, Thomas B.   C
English (lecturer)
Royal Military College of Canada
Kingston, Ontario
*English novel; aesthetic theory and
literary criticism*

VOIGT, Milton
English (professor)
University of Utah
Salt Lake City, Utah 84112
Swift

VOITLE, Robert   C
English (professor)
University of North Carolina
Chapel Hill, N. C. 27514
Johnson; 3 Earl of Shaftesbury; deism

VOS, Marie Ann Heiberg   C
Music (assistant professor)
McHenry County College
207 North Main St., Apt. 203
Crystal Lake, Ill. 60014
*J. C. Bach; 18-century Italian church
music*

WACHS, Morris   C
French (professor)
Vanderbilt University
Nashville, Tenn. 37235
D'Alembert; Diderot; Voltaire

WADAS, Walter E.
3738 Miller St.
Baden, Pa. 15005
Art history

WAINGROW, Marshall   C
English (professor)
Claremont Graduate School
Claremont, Calif. 91711
*Johnson and Boswell; eighteenth-century
novel*

WALDINGER, Renée   C
French (professor)
City College, CUNY
Convent Avenue at 138th Street
New York, N. Y. 10031
French literature

WALKER, Rev. John M., Jr.
Church history
First Presbyterian Church
16 East 5th St.
Roanoke Rapids, N. C. 27870
Theology; church history; art; Johnson

WALKER, Robert Gary   S
English (graduate student)
University of Florida
P.O. Box 13189, University Station
Gainesville, Florida 32601
Johnson; English poetry

WALLACE, J. O.
Library science (librarian)
San Antonio College
1001 Howard Street
San Antonio, Texas 78284

WALLS, Aileen S.
English (associate professor)
George Mason College
Fairfax, Virginia 22030
*Charles Brockden Brown; Phillip
Freneau; William Byrd II*

WALTON, Craig
Philosophy (associate professor)
University of Nevada
Las Vegas, Nevada 89109
*Logic; ethical and political theories;
philosophy of history; history of
philosophy; historiography*

463

WANLASS, Dorothy C.   C
English (professor)
California State University, San Diego
4646 Norma Drive
San Diego, Calif. 92115
Architecture; painting; Neoclassicism

WARK, Robert R.   C
Art history (curator)
The Henry E. Huntington Library and
  Art Gallery
San Marino, Calif. 91108

WARREN, Joseph A., III
American studies (chairman)
Lansing Community College
419 N. Capitol Avenue
Lansing, Michigan 48914

WARSHAW, Dan
History (assistant professor)
Fairleigh Dickinson University
Teaneck, New Jersey 07666
Though and opinion; social stratification

WASSERMAN, George R.
English
Russell Sage College
Box 572
Newtonville, New York 12128

WATSON, Richard A.
Philosophy (associate professor)
Washington University
Philosophy 1073
St. Louis, Missouri 63130
Metaphysics; epistemology

WATT, Ian   C
English (professor)
Stanford University
Stanford, Calif. 94305
*Novel; Augustan poetry; social
  background*

WATZLAWICK, Helmut
22, Chemin de l'esplanade
CH-1214 VERNIER (Geneva)
Switzerland
*Anonyma and pseudonym literature;
  literary production of adventure
  writers: Casanova, Goudar,
  Zannowich, d'Afflisio*

WEBB, Donald P.
French (assistant professor)
University of Wisconsin, Green Bay
Green Bay, Wisconsin 54302

WEBSTER, T. S.   C
History (professor)
Queen's University
Kingston, Ontario
France-North America, 1763-1815

WEGMAN, Nola J.   C
English (associate professor)
Valparaiso University
Valparaiso, Indiana 46383
*Swift; Pope; satire; theological-literary
  relations*

WEIGAND, Ann K.
Modern languages (instructor)
Rosemont College
118 West Rittenhouse St.
Philadelphia, Pa. 19144
Novel

WEINBROT, Howard D.   C
English (associate professor)
University of Wisconsin
Madison, Wisconsin 53706
Pope; Johnson; imitation; satire

WEINSTEIN, Minna F.   C
History (associate professor)
LaSalle College
Philadelphia, Pa. 19141
English Enlightenment

WEISBERGER, R. William
Social science (instructor)
Butler County Community College
Apt. 3D, Green Acres
204 Litman Road
Butler, Pennsylvania 16001
Intellectual history

WEITZMAN, Arthur J.   C
English (associate professor)
Northeastern University
Boston, Mass. 02115
Oriental tale; satire

WENNER, Evelyn W.   C
English (professor)
Western Maryland College
158 Pennsylvania Avenue
Westminster, Maryland 21157
Life and works of George Steevens

WERNER, Stephen   C
French (assistant professor)
University of California
Los Angeles, Calif. 90024
Diderot; Rousseau

WEST, Elsie L.   C
English (associate professor)
Johnson State College
Box 164
Johnson, Vermont 05656
American and English literature

WEYANT, Robert G.
Psychology (professor)
University of Calgary
Calgary, Alberta
*Psychological and related philosophical
and social thought; history of ideas*

WEYGANT, Peter S.   C
English (graduate student)
University of Pennsylvania
324 Chester Avenue
Moorestown, N. J. 08057
Restoration poetry

WHEELOCK, James T. S.   C
Italian (instructor)
University of Colorado
1607-6th Street
Boulder, Colorado 80302
*Anglo-Italian literary relations in
eighteenth century*

WHITE, Douglas H.   C
English (assistant professor)
Loyola University, Chicago
6525 Sheridan Rd.
Chicago, Ill. 60611
Pope; Swift; intellectual history

WHITE, Fred H.
English (assistant professor)
Westhampton College

University of Richmond
Box 32
Richmond, Virginia 23173
Pope and his circle

WHITE, John Charles   C
History (assistant professor)
University of Alabama
Huntsville, Alabama 35807
*Humanitarian reform; French naval
administration*

WHITE, Maurice L.   C
Music (honors choir director)
Detroit Schools
36408 Rayburn
Livonia, Michigan 48154
*Musicology; composers (1775-1825);
Cherubini*

WHITE, Richard S.   C
Russian (instructor)
Dept. of Slavic Languages and
Literatures
Northwestern University
Evanston, Illinois 60201
Russian fiction in 18th century

WHITE, Robert B., Jr.   C
English (associate professor)
North Carolina State University
Raleigh, N. C. 27607
Periodicals; early satire

WHITWORTH, Kernan B., Jr.   C
French (professor)
University of Missouri
27 A and S
Columbia, Missouri 65201
French novel; Voltaire; Diderot

WICHE, Glen Norman   S
History (student)
Allegheny College
655 Thornwood Drive
Napierville, Illinois 60540
*Cultural life of Virginia (dramatic,
musical, bibliographical aspects)*

WIDMAYER, Jayne A.
English (instructor)
The College of Idaho

465

Caldwell, Idaho 83605
*The picturesque; late 18th-century
    poetry*

WIESENFARTH, Joseph   C
English (associate professor)
241 Langdon St.
Madison, Wisconsin 53703
Novel, esp. Fielding and Sterne

WILES, R. M.   C
English (professor emeritus)
McMaster University
Hamilton, Ontario
Johnson; provincial press

WILKINS, Kay S.   C
French
Montclair State College
Upper Montclair, New Jersey 07043
*Jesuit influence in France; occult in
    literature*

WILLCOX, William B.   C
History (professor)
Yale University
1603 A. Yale Station
New Haven, Conn. 06520
*Franklin; War of American
    Independence*

WILLEY, Edward P.
English (assistant professor)
Clemson University
Clemson, S. C. 29631
Periodicals

WILLIAMS, David   C
Romance languages (associate
    professor)
McMaster University
Hamilton, Ontario
Voltaire, aesthetics

WILLIAMS, Kathleen   C
English (professor)
University of California
Riverside, Calif. 92502
Swift; Pope

WILSON, Arthur M.   C
Biography and government (professor
    emeritus)

Dartmouth College
1 Brookside
Norwich, Vermont 05055
*Encyclopédie; Diderot; the
    Enlightenment*

WILSON, Diana G.
Art history (graduate student)
University of California, Los Angeles
20907 Via Verde
Covina, California 91724

WILSON, James R.   C
English (professor)
University of Alaska
6913 Madelynne Way
Anchorage, Alaska 99504
Swift; drama; Pope

WILSON, JoAnn H.   S
English (graduate student)
University of Oregon
2683 Hilyard
Eugene, Oregon 97405

WILSON, Lester N.   C
History (associate professor)
Long Island University
Zeckendorf Campus
Brooklyn, N. Y. 11201
Diplomacy

WIMSATT, W. K.   C
English (professor)
Yale University
1882 Yale Station
Pope, Johnson

WINESANKER, Michael   C
Musicology (professor)
Texas Christian University
Fort Worth, Texas 76129
*English musical drama (comic opera)
    of the eighteenth century*

WINSLOW, Donald J.   C
English (professor)
Boston University
236 Bay State Road
Boston, Mass. 02215
Biography

466

WINTON, Calhoun   C
English (professor)
University of South Carolina
Columbia, S. C. 29208
*English and American non-fictional
   prose*

WOLFF, C. Griffin   C
English (assistant professor)
Manhattanville College
415 West 115th St. Apt. 51
New York, N. Y. 10025
Novel

WOLFF, Christoph
Music (associate professor)
Columbia University
New York, New York 10027
Music

WOLPER, Roy S.   C
English (associate professor)
Temple University
Philadelphia, Pa. 19122
*Satire of Restoration; drama; Pope,
   Swift, and group*

WOMACK, William R.
Modern and classical languages
   (assistant professor)
University of Wyoming
Hoyt Hall
Laramie, Wyoming 82070
French literature; Guillaume Rayanal

WOOLF, Harry
Office of the Provost
The Johns Hopkins University
34th and Charles Streets
Baltimore, Maryland 21218
History of science

WOOLLEY, James David   S
English (graduate student)
Marquette University
Milwaukee, Wisconsin 53233
Satiric verse; Swift; literature and society

WORDEN, John L., Jr.   C
English (assistant professor)
California State University
Chico, Calif. 95926
Johnson

WORTHINGTON, Anne   S
Graduate student
University of Maryland
12309 Stonehaven Lane
Bowie, Maryland 20715

WRAGE, William   C
Modern languages (associate professor)
Ohio University
Athens, Ohio 45701
French literature

WRIGHT, Andrew   C
English (professor)
University of California, San Diego
P.O. Box 109
La Jolla, Calif. 92037

WRIGHT, H. Bunker   C
English (professor)
Miami University
Oxford, Ohio 45056
*English literature and history;
   Matthew Prior*

WRIGHT, John W.
English (associate professor)
University of Michigan
Ann Arbor, Michigan 48104
*British and German philosophy;
   Johnson; Blake*

WRIGHT, William E.   C
History (associate professor)
Associate dean, international programs
University of Minnesota
201 Nolte, West
Minneapolis, Minn. 55455
*History; Austria, central Europe,
   Enlightenment*

WUNDER, Richard P.
Art history (senior research fellow)
Smithsonian Institution
National Collection of Fine Arts
Brookside, Orwell
Vermont 05760

YASHINSKY, Jack   C
French (lecturer)
Erindale College
University of Toronto

467

Toronto 5, Ontario
Voltaire's theater

YOUNG, Donald L.   C
English (professor)
Dean of the College
Eastern Nazarene College
Wollaston Park
Quincy, Mass. 02170

ZANTS, Emily   C
French and Italian (assistant professor)
University of California, Davis
708 N Street
Davis, California 95616
French novel

ZIMANSKY, Curt A.   C
English (professor)
University of Iowa
Iowa City, Iowa 52240

ZIRKER, Malvin R., Jr.   C
Indiana University

Bloomington, Indiana 47401
Novel

ZOLTOWSKA, Maria Evelina   C
French (assistant professor)
Université de Moncton
Moncton, New Brunswick
The novel; Jean Potocki

ZUCKERMAN, Arnold
History (professor)
Northeast Missouri State College
Social Science Division
P.O. Box 11
Kirksville, Missouri 63501
History of medicine

ZYLAWY, Roman
Foreign languages (instructor)
University of Montana
Missoula, Montana 59801
*Marivaux, Prévost, and the
    feminist problem*